Personal Data Protection and Legal Developments in the European Union

Maria Tzanou
Keele University, UK

A volume in the Advances in Information Security, Privacy, and Ethics (AISPE) Book Series

Published in the United States of America by
 IGI Global
 Information Science Reference (an imprint of IGI Global)
 701 E. Chocolate Avenue
 Hershey PA, USA 17033
 Tel: 717-533-8845
 Fax: 717-533-8661
 E-mail: cust@igi-global.com
 Web site: http://www.igi-global.com

Library of Congress Cataloging-in-Publication Data

Names: Tzanou, Maria, editor.
Title: Personal data protection and legal developments in the European
 Union / Maria Tzanou, editor.
Description: Hershey PA : Information Science Reference, 2019. | Summary:
 "This book analyzes the latest advancements and developments in personal
 data protection in the European Union"-- Provided by publisher.
Identifiers: LCCN 2019002541 | ISBN 9781522594895 (hardcover) | ISBN
 9781522594918 (ebook) | ISBN 9781522594901 (softcover)
Subjects: LCSH: Data protection--Law and legislation--European Union
 countries.
Classification: LCC KJE6071 .P44 2019 | DDC 343.2409/99--dc23
LC record available at https://lccn.loc.gov/2019002541

This book is published in the IGI Global book series Advances in Information Security, Privacy, and Ethics (AISPE) (ISSN: 1948-9730; eISSN: 1948-9749)

British Cataloguing in Publication Data
A Cataloguing in Publication record for this book is available from the British Library.

For electronic access to this publication, please contact: eresources@igi-global.com.

Advances in Information Security, Privacy, and Ethics (AISPE) Book Series

Manish Gupta
State University of New York, USA

ISSN:1948-9730
EISSN:1948-9749

MISSION

As digital technologies become more pervasive in everyday life and the Internet is utilized in ever increasing ways by both private and public entities, concern over digital threats becomes more prevalent.

The **Advances in Information Security, Privacy, & Ethics (AISPE) Book Series** provides cutting-edge research on the protection and misuse of information and technology across various industries and settings. Comprised of scholarly research on topics such as identity management, cryptography, system security, authentication, and data protection, this book series is ideal for reference by IT professionals, academicians, and upper-level students.

COVERAGE

- Privacy-Enhancing Technologies
- Global Privacy Concerns
- Network Security Services
- Technoethics
- Information Security Standards
- CIA Triad of Information Security
- Computer ethics
- Electronic Mail Security
- Telecommunications Regulations
- Cyberethics

IGI Global is currently accepting manuscripts for publication within this series. To submit a proposal for a volume in this series, please contact our Acquisition Editors at Acquisitions@igi-global.com or visit: http://www.igi-global.com/publish/.

Titles in this Series

For a list of additional titles in this series, please visit:
http://www.igi-global.com/book-series/advances-information-security-privacy-ethics/37157

Privacy Concerns Surrounding Personal Information Sharing on Health and Fitness Mbile Apps
Devjani Sen (Independent Researcher, Canada) and Rukhsana Ahmed (University at Albany, SUNY, USA)
Information Science Reference • © 2020 • 300pp • H/C (ISBN: 9781799834878) • US $215.00

Safety and Security Issues in Technical Infrastructures
David Rehak (VSB – Technical University of Ostrava, Czech Republic) Ales Bernatik (VSB – Technical University
of Ostrava, Czech Republic) Zdenek Dvorak (University of Zilina, Slovakia) and Martin Hromada (Tomas Bata
University in Zlin, Czech Republic)
Information Science Reference • © 2020 • 499pp • H/C (ISBN: 9781799830597) • US $195.00

Cybersecurity Incident Planning and Preparation for Organizations
Akashdeep Bhardwaj (University of Petroleum and Energy Studies, Dehradun, India) and Varun Sapra (University
of Petroleum and Energy Studies, India)
Information Science Reference • © 2020 • 300pp • H/C (ISBN: 9781799834915) • US $215.00

Blockchain Applications in IoT Security
Harshita Patel (KLEF, Vaddeswaram, Guntur, Andhra Pradesh, India) and Ghanshyam Singh Thakur (MANIT,
Bhopal, Madhya Pradesh, India)
Information Science Reference • © 2020 • 300pp • H/C (ISBN: 9781799824145) • US $215.00

Modern Theories and Practices for Cyber Ethics and Security Compliance
Winfred Yaokumah (University of Ghana, Ghana) Muttukrishnan Rajarajan (City University of London, UK)
Jamal-Deen Abdulai (University of Ghana, Ghana) Isaac Wiafe (University of Ghana, Ghana) and Ferdinand
Apietu Katsriku (University of Ghana, Ghana)
Information Science Reference • © 2020 • 302pp • H/C (ISBN: 9781799831495) • US $200.00

Handbook of Research on Multimedia Cyber Security
Brij B. Gupta (National Institute of Technology, Kurukshetra, India) and Deepak Gupta (LoginRadius Inc., Canada)
Information Science Reference • © 2020 • 372pp • H/C (ISBN: 9781799827016) • US $265.00

Security and Privacy Applications for Smart City Development
Sharvari C. Tamane (MGM's Jawaharlal Nehru Engineering College, India)
Information Science Reference • © 2020 • 300pp • H/C (ISBN: 9781799824985) • US $215.00

701 East Chocolate Avenue, Hershey, PA 17033, USA
Tel: 717-533-8845 x100 • Fax: 717-533-8661
E-Mail: cust@igi-global.com • www.igi-global.com

Table of Contents

Section 1
GDPR: The Foundational Questions

Section 2
A Closer Look at the GDPR: Basic Definitions, Purposes, New Technologies,
Implementation, and Its Relationship With Other Instruments

Section 5
Jurisprudential Developments on the Right to Be Forgotten

Detailed Table of Contents

Section 1
GDPR: The Foundational Questions

This section considers the foundational questions regarding privacy and data protection examined within the context of the main data protection legislative instrument in the EU, the GDPR.

Chapter 1
Protection of Personal Data Regulation and Public Liberties: A Polyhedron With Unexpected
Effects 1
> *Ana Neves, School of Law, University of Lisbon, Portugal*

The Regulation (EU) 2016/679 on the protection of natural persons with regard to the processing of personal data and on the free movement of such data is much more than a personal data regulation. It has a wide range of impacts, of different nature: substantive, procedural, and organisational ones. In each of these dimensions, it is the personal autonomy and the equilibrium of the relationship of individuals with those processing their data that are at stake, hence, the centrality that individual rights over their own data shall have. Nonetheless, the access, the flow, and the free movement of information, including personal data, are the essential foundations of a free and democratic society in which the freedoms and rights of individuals are guaranteed. Despite having the necessary premises to guarantee it, the GDPR carries the risk of being used by public authorities to condition the space for public freedoms.

Chapter 2
Revisiting the Basics of EU Data Protection Law: On the Material and Territorial Scope of the
GDPR 19
> *Dimosthenis Lentzis, Aristotle University of Thessaloniki, Greece*

It is often said that the EU General Data Protection Regulation (GDPR) has a much broader material and territorial scope than the EU Data Protection Directive it has recently replaced. This chapter tries to find out if (and, if so, to what extent) this assumption is correct. To this end, it analyzes, in the light of the existing case-law of the Court of Justice of the EU, the relevant provisions of the GDPR, namely Articles 2 and 3. It comes out that the GDPR has a slightly different (but not necessarily broader) material scope and a broader (but not as broad as one would expect) territorial scope than the old EU Data Protection Directive.

Chapter 3
Selling Personal Data: The Legal Framework and Nature of Personal Data Selling Transactions
Konstantina Samara, University of Macedonia, Greece & Democritus University of Thrace,
Greece

The prevalent and currently unanimous European legal system regarding personal data comprises a set of protective rules, enshrining, amongst others, the prerequisites for lawful processing. The venture of the ensuing aims to examine, under the scope of both constitutional rules and the ius cogens provisions of the Regulation (EU) 2016/679, the validity of a transaction pertaining to the processing of personal data. The objective of the herein argumentation specifically focuses on the juridical act of selling personal data, in accordance with the principle of contractual freedom and its compatibility with the core of constitutional provisions, which safeguard human value. The correlations examined below are referred to the contractual interaction between the subject of the personal data and the data controller under the scope of a double facet approach of GDPR, as a legal system both personal and property oriented.

Section 2
A Closer Look at the GDPR: Basic Definitions, Purposes, New Technologies,
Implementation, and Its Relationship With Other Instruments

This section focuses on a plethora of complex questions that arise when considering the GDPR. These concern the uncertainties regarding basic definitions, such as 'controllers' and 'processors', the challenges that new technologies such as AI and profiling present, the purposes of EU data privacy law, the problems of its implementation at the national level, and its relationship with other instruments.

Chapter 4
Data Controller, Processor, or Joint Controller: Towards Reaching GDPR Compliance in a Data-
Yordanka Ivanova, Sofia University, St. Kliment Ohridski, Bulgaria & Vrije Universiteit
Brussel, Belgium

This chapter aims to examine critically the existing legal provisions on the concepts of controller, processor, and joint controller, as interpreted by the relevant non-binding guidelines and case law, and to propose a new "value chain" method for allocating responsibilities among joint controllers that is more effective and appropriate for the technology- and data-driven world. It also examines the corresponding data protection responsibilities of different data processing actors, in particular through the prism of the new accountability principle, which arguably includes not only obligations for means but also result-oriented obligations for compliance in terms of data subjects' effective and complete protection.

Chapter 5
GDPR in Between Profiles and Decision-Making: How the General Data Protection Principles
Elena Georgiou, University College London, UK

The creation and application of profiles may affect individuals and their lives. The lack of transparency and accuracy that may result from these profiles can cause asymmetries of knowledge and unbalanced distribution of powers between business entities and individual subjects. As such, profiling challenges the protection of individuals and generates concerns over the individuals' privacy and data protection. In using profiling practices, every business entity must comply with data protection legislation. The purpose of the chapter is to examine the effectiveness of the GDPR to ensure protection for individuals within the context of profiling. It identifies and analyses, from a profiling point of view, a number of strengths and weaknesses associated with the general data protection principles as adopted under the Article 5 GDPR. The author argues that profiling contradicts the transparent nature of data protection principles, and thus of the GDPR. In practice, the law is ineffective to ensure fair, lawful, and transparent profiling activities to safeguard individuals and their rights.

Chapter 6

Arletta Gorecka, University of Strathclyde, UK

The relationship between competition law and privacy is still seen as problematic with academics and professionals trying to adequately assess the impact of privacy on the competition law sphere. The chapter looks at the legal development of the EU merger proceedings to conclude that EU competition law is based on the prevailing approach and assesses decisions involving data through the spectrum of keeping a competitive equilibrium in hypothetical markets. Secondly, it considers the legal developments in the EU Member States' practice, which acknowledges the apparent intersection between the phenomena of competition law and privacy. This chapter attempts to propose that privacy concerns appear to hold a multidimensional approach on competition legal regime; nevertheless, it does not result in the need of legal changes within the remits of competition law, as the privacy concerns are already protected by the data protection and consumer protection law.

Chapter 7

Graça Canto Moniz, Lusofona University, Portugal & Nova School of Law, Portugal

The entry into force of the General Data Protection Regulation (GDPR) was expected to cause difficulties to data controllers and data processors mostly due to the practical consequences of the accountability principle and the role of risk. However, in Portugal, there were supplementary problems triggered by two events: the long legislative process of the national law implementing the GDPR and the decision of the national supervisory authority to disapply nine provisions of it. In August 2019, the Portuguese Parliament adopted the law implementing the GDPR, Law 58/2019, and one month later, the Portuguese supervisory authority, Comissão Nacional de Proteção de Dados, decided that nine articles of the recently adopted national law were incompatible with European Union Law. This chapter aims to address this chain of events, to understand the reasoning behind the decision of the Portuguese authority, and to tackle its practical consequences to day-to-day data-processing activities of data controllers and data processors. Overall, it also aims to evaluate what is left of the national piece of legislation after this decision.

Chapter 8

Athena Christofi, KU Leuven, Belgium
Pierre Dewitte, KU Leuven, Belgium
Charlotte Ducuing, KU Leuven, Belgium
Peggy Valcke, KU Leuven, Belgium

This chapter examines the interplay between the GDPR and parallel private regulation in the form of privacy-related standards adopted by the International Organisation for Standardisation (ISO). Focusing on the understanding of 'risks' in the GDPR and ISO respective ecosystems, it compares the GDPR requirement for Data Protection Impact Assessments (DPIAs) with ISO/IEC 29134:2017, a private standard on Privacy Impact Assessment explicitly referred to by EU Data Protection Authorities as relevant in the context of DPIA methods. The resulting gap analysis identifies and maps misalignments, critically reflecting on whether the parallel form of ISO regulation, in the context of DPIAs, could support or rather blurs GDPR's objective to protect fundamental rights by embracing a risks-based approach.

Section 3
Data Privacy at and Beyond the EU's Borders

The EU has established over the years digital, 'smart' borders through the operation of large databases that store the personal—including the biometric—data of TCNs. While the GDPR has strengthened data protection standards, the latter protections do not apply to TCNs. Beyond the EU's borders, it is worth noting that many countries are adopting their own data protection laws and it is important to also pay attention to these developments as well.

Chapter 9

Sarah Progin-Theuerkauf, Fribourg University, Switzerland
Margarite Zoeteweij, Fribourg University, Switzerland
Ozan Turhan, Swiss Refugee Council, Switzerland

In May 2019, the elections to the European Parliament and the political consequences of the new composition of the Parliament, as well as the never-ending Brexit debate, in which there seems to be a new dramatic turn every week, received a lot of media attention. So, it is perhaps not surprising that two regulations adopted by the Council on 20 May 2019 have so far gone almost unnoticed. However, this is completely unjustified, as they will have far-reaching consequences. Specifically, the chapter concerns regulations 2019/817 and 2019/818, establishing a framework for the interoperability (i.e. linkage) between EU information systems in the field of borders and visa and in the area of freedom, security, and justice. The regulations are part of the EU's idea to create smart borders (i.e., borders that can be better and more easily controlled by using new digital systems). This chapter critically analyses the establishment of the individual databases and their interoperability, with a particular focus on data protection issues that result from them.

Chapter 10

Simone Casiraghi, Vrije Universiteit Brussel, Belgium
Alessandra Calvi, Vrije Universiteit Brussel, Belgium

Biometrics technologies have been spreading cross-sector in the public and private domains. Their potential intrusiveness, in particular regarding privacy and data protection, has called the European legislators, in the recent EU data protection reform, to introduce a definition of "biometric data," and to grant biometric data specific protection, as a "special category of data." Despite the reformed framework, in the field of border management, the use of biometric data is expected to increase steadily because it is seen as a more efficient and reliable solution. This chapter will look into the reformed data protection and border management legal frameworks to highlight discrepancies between the two, and ultimately assess to what extent the new data protection reformed regime for biometric data is satisfactory.

Chapter 11

Maria Casoria, Royal University for Women, Bahrain
Eman Mahmood AlSarraf, Al Zayani Investments, Bahrain

The chapter discusses the influence of the General Data Protection Regulation (GDPR) on legal systems extra-EU and particularly the Kingdom of Bahrain, country member to a regional organisation located in the Arabian Gulf denominated Gulf Cooperation Council (GCC), which is exclusive to six states (i.e., Saudi Arabia, United Arab Emirates, Oman, Qatar, and Kuwait in addition to Bahrain). Amongst these countries, Bahrain is the only one that has recently enacted its own separate Personal Data Protection Law (PDPL) mostly resembling the GDPR due to the ever-increasing commercial relationship with business undertakings in Europe. Moreover, the adoption of the data protection law counts as a huge leap forward taken by the kingdom in reforming its legal framework, since it is the state's striving strategy to grow into a midpoint for data centre, just on time for the launch of data centres opening in Bahrain that are endorsed by Amazon Web Services.

Section 4
Studying Data Privacy Under Different Lenses

This section focuses on studying data protection beyond the boundaries of a traditional legal analysis.

Chapter 12

Ine van Zeeland, imec-SMIT, Vrije Universiteit Brussel, Belgium
Jo Pierson, imec-SMIT, Vrije Universiteit Brussel, Belgium

The aim of this chapter is to take readers beyond the prescriptions of the law to present them with a practical perspective on what happens when organizations try to protect personal data. This is based on the acknowledgement that different sectors of society will have different concerns when it comes to the protection of personal data and privacy. The various conceptions of privacy connect a wide variety of academic disciplines, from anthropology to urban planning. We need to understand that there are many different perspectives on what privacy signifies, and hence, that there are many different considerations regarding what to do to protect it.

Chapter 13

Tomáš Pikulík, Faculty of Management, Comenius University in Bratislava, Slovakia
Peter Štarchoň, Faculty of Management, Comenius University in Bratislava, Slovakia

Implementation of the GDPR changed the way how personal data of EU customers are processed. The purpose of this chapter is to explore the links between the rights of customers as a data subject and related aspects of customer satisfaction. Entities in modern economy (encompassing not only goods and services but also intellectual property) generate and process huge quantities of customer data. Information and communication technology (ICT) infrastructure became a basis for the digital economy and society in the EU (settled by Eurostat as ISOC) that definitely replaced the previous era of the information economy that was based on the effective acquisition, dissemination, and use of information. Data-driven marketing puts data at the center of additional value creation and brings new insights and perspectives, included in the results of this research. The impact of GDPR on customer-centric ICT, stronger consumer awareness of data protection rights, creates new pathways to customer centricity and the legal and technical aspects of data processing within the digital economy ecosystem.

Section 5
Jurisprudential Developments on the Right to Be Forgotten

This section focuses on case law developments regarding the right to be forgotten by taking a closer look both at the EU and the Member States' levels.

Chapter 14

The right to be forgotten as established in the CJEU's decision in Google Spain is the first online data privacy right recognized in the EU legal order. This contribution explores two currently underdeveloped in the literature aspects of the right to be forgotten: its unexpected consequences on search engines and the difficulties of its implementation in practice by the latter. It argues that the horizontal application of EU privacy rights on private parties, such as internet search engines—as undertaken by the CJEU—is fraught with conceptual gaps, dilemmas, and uncertainties that create confusions about the enforceability of the right to be forgotten and the role of search engines. In this respect, it puts forward a comprehensive legal framework for the implementation of this right, which aims to ensure a legally certain and proportionate balance of the competing interests online in the light of the EU's General Data Protection Regulation (GDPR).

Chapter 15

The right to be forgotten has come to the forefront of the academic debate as a reaction to Court of Justice's decision in case C-507/17 Google LLC c. CNIL concerning the issue of geographical extension of the delisting obligation. Along with the development of CJEU jurisprudence, national courts have developed their own caselaw interpreting and adapting the right to be forgotten, now included in art 17 of the General Data Protection Regulation, to the pre-existing legal framework. Italian courts, and in particular the Italian Supreme Court, have addressed in several occasions the features and facets of the right to be forgotten, and the recent decision of the Grand Chamber (n. 19681, 22 July 2019) is the last though not the least. Starting form this decision, the chapter will analyse how the Supreme Court has attempted to systematise the right to be forgotten distinguishing what is called the traditional application of the right from the ones emerging in the digital context.

Increased recognition of the pervasiveness of information collected and accessed has led to concern as to its impact on privacy. The ability to impact people's lives with the easy availability of information that in other eras would have remained hidden or "forgotten" is highlighted by the use of the internet for instant recall. Such information, which organizations often hold for commercial benefit, is increasingly made available through search results or from online archives. This chapter will focus on the impact of the Google Spain case, which was believed to have created a new right to be forgotten, leading to the finalization of Article 17 of the General Data Protection Regulation. The author will then examine more recent cases where the new right has been applied and their impact on defining its scope. In particular, the author will focus on the UK joined cases of NT1 and NT2.

Preface

It seems that data protection law in the European Union (EU) is living its golden age. Data protection has been recognised as a fundamental right alongside the right to privacy (Tzanou, 2017); data privacy regulation has been modernised to face the 'information technology-driven challenges' of the 21st century through the adoption of the General Data Protection Regulation (GDPR); and, the Court of Justice of the EU (CJEU) has delivered a number of landmark decisions that mark a significant victory of data privacy vis-à-vis modern electronic surveillance, confirm the extraterritorial application of EU data privacy rights, and show big tech companies, such as Google and Facebook that data protection rights are taken seriously in the EU.

Primary and secondary data EU protection law is surrounded by an impressive amount of soft law, reports, guidelines and recommendations by independent authorities and bodies specialising on data protection both at the national level (the national Data Protection Authorities or 'DPAs'); and at the EU level, the European Data Protection Supervisor ('EDPS') and the European Data Protection Board ('EDPB', previously known as Article 29 Working Party). EU data protection law is further complemented by an extensively rich legal academic scholarship that spans across several hundreds of EU data protection books and textbooks, thousands of journal articles, data privacy studies, blogposts and specifically dedicated data protection conferences and workshops.

Yet, despite this rich body of law (both hard and soft) and the complementing academic literature, there are a number of uncertainties that remain about EU data protection law- both theoretical and practical. The centrepiece of EU data protection law, the GDPR, has modernised data privacy law but it has also brought forward new questions and problems.

A first set of questions concerns the relationship of the GDPR with its legislative predecessors, in particular, the Data Protection Directive (DPD). What has the GDPR changed in this respect and are the changes it introduced significant? Questions about foundational issues remain as well. What is the relationship between the fundamental right to privacy and the fundamental right to data protection and what role is each of these rights expected to play?

While the extent of the changes the GDPR introduced and how much these depart from the DPD are interesting points for discussion, it is fairly undisputed that both legal instruments are quite complex. The complexities of the GDPR are numerous and they can be seen throughout its long text. They even concern basic definitions such as 'controller', 'processor' and now 'joint controllers' that are the main actors held accountable for the implementation of data protection responsibilities, principles and rules. A further area that remains contentious concerns the interrelations between data protection law and other forms of legal regulation such as competition law or consumer law. Can data protection law be used to advance competition law objectives, for instance to control the market power of big tech? Can competition law be used to protect data privacy? How can competition law and data protection law work together to deal with big tech problems?

A third set of questions refers to the relationship between hard law data protection instruments, such as the GDPR, and soft law measures, such as the privacy-related standards adopted by the International Organization for Standardisation ('ISO'). What is the purpose of these soft law rules, how they interrelate with the GDPR and what can they add in this respect? Can the GDPR 'learn' anything from soft law tools and their mechanisms or there is a risk that these could undermine its human rights centred core?

Once more, questions also arise about the relationship between data protection law and new technologies. The GDPR is clear of its aims to address modern technological challenges. Recital 6 states:

Rapid technological developments and globalisation have brought new challenges for the protection of personal data. The scale of the collection and sharing of personal data has increased significantly. Technology allows both private companies and public authorities to make use of personal data on an unprecedented scale in order to pursue their activities... Technology has transformed both the economy and social life, and should further facilitate the free flow of personal data within the Union and the transfer to third countries and international organisations, while ensuring a high level of the protection of personal data.

In this regard, the GDPR contains a series of substantive provisions that concern the impact of new technologies on personal data processing. It imposes an obligation on controllers to undertake data protection impact assessments (DPIAs) 'where a type of processing in particular using new technologies, ...is likely to result in a high risk to the rights and freedoms of natural persons' and attempts 'to address the risks arising from profiling and automated decision-making' by establishing a general prohibition for decision-making based solely on automated processing that produces legal effects concerning the data subject or significantly affects her. While the aspirations of the GDPR to address challenges brought by new technologies, such as big data, Artificial Intelligence (AI) and machine learning are remarkable, it remains to be seen whether as a regulatory measure it is up to this task. More importantly perhaps, it remains to be seen whether data protection legal instruments, such as the GDPR, are appropriate tools to deal with AI and big data problems. The GDPR purports to do so by containing rules, as seen above, among others on automated decision -making including profiling, but can its scope and concept be stretched so much so that it becomes the 'law of everything' (Koops, 2014; Purtova, 2018)?

A further set of issues concerns the protection of data privacy rights in different jurisdictions across the globe. It is worth noting that the EU's GDPR is one model for data protection regulation (applicable throughout the European Union), but many countries worldwide are adopting new rules on data privacy that might or might not be inspired by the GDPR. The quest to acquire the precious 'adequacy finding' is a strong motivation to incorporate the GDPR principles in other jurisdictions, but we should avoid adopting a mainly 'Eurocentric' perspective of data protection law. It is dangerous to assume that data privacy laws cannot be done differently from the EU's model.

Furthermore, while the GDPR has been widely applauded for strengthening data privacy protections in Europe and even worldwide and the EU presents itself as a 'global force' of good in data privacy, at the same time it is adopting all the more invasive measures that monitor and put under pervasive surveillance non-EU citizens. Third Country Nationals (TCNs) are treated as suspicious or criminals by default and as a result their personal information, including their unique identifying biometric data are collected, processed, analysed and stored in EU large interoperable databases. This illustrates the differential distribution of EU data privacy rights: additional levels of surveillance are imposed for TCNs with measures that often contravene basic principles of the GDPR. Paradoxically, this is not considered problematic; it is presumed that TCNs should expect by default diminished levels of data privacy. The disparate impact of data protection has attracted little attention in the popular data privacy narrative, but it is a problem that should be taken seriously.

Finally, a variety of perspectives, methodologies and disciplinary lenses that go beyond legal analysis is needed for studying data protection. Data protection will not achieve its objectives and will remain a dead letter if it is limited to traditional, black-letter legal debates. New perspectives and methodologies are needed, and data protection should be examined in a variety of different contexts involving problems that legal scholars often fail to consider.

Jurisprudential developments are at the heart of EU data privacy law. The right to be forgotten is an example of an impressive amount of case-law originating from both EU and national courts. A form of this right is included in the GDPR, but the CJEU in its seminal decision in *Google Spain* that was delivered before the entry into force of the GDPR, had already taken the opportunity to introduce such a right in the EU legal order with respect to search engines. Yet, the Court's landmark decision in *Google Spain* seems to be raising more questions than answering them. Uncertainties still remain regarding the scope of this right and these can be seen both in recent CJEU and national court judgments. It certainly appears that the right to be forgotten will remain an area that generates complex theoretical and practical questions for the time to come.

This book engages with these questions from a variety of perspectives and disciplinary lenses. Data protection is a constantly evolving body of law that aims to deal with several technological and societal problems, while addressing its internal gaps and uncertainties. This very idea connects the chapters in this book.

The contributions that follow engage to this open dialogue, by offering new theoretical considerations and a taxonomy of data protection related problems as well as solutions, proposals and models. The present volume is divided in five sections, all of them encountering some of the most pressing and significant debates concerning data privacy in the EU.

Section 1 considers the foundational questions regarding privacy and data protection examined within the context of the main data protection legislative instrument in the EU, the GDPR.

Chapter 1 examines the substantive, procedural and organisational changes that the GDPR introduced and reflects on how these achieve the aims of protecting the right to the protection of personal data and further fundamental rights and freedoms. Ana Neves argues that such examination is necessary in order to fully understand the different dimensions of the right to data protection and be able to deal with the implications of the use of information and personal data within complex technological frameworks.

In Chapter 2, Dimosthenis Lentzis investigates whether the widespread belief that the GDPR has a much broader material and territorial scope than the Data Protection Directive it has replaced is correct. Having analysed the relevant rather obscure provisions of the GDPR that raise a number of complex questions, the Chapter concludes that this is only partially true. According to Lentzis, the truly revolutionary features of the new legal framework should be searched elsewhere and not in its rules concerning its material and territorial scope.

Konstantina Samara explores in Chapter 3 the potential validity of a personal data vending transaction between the data subject and the controller under the scope of the GDPR. The analysis, which is undertaken through a fundamental rights perspective, finds that forced disclosure of personal information as a prerequisite for the enjoyment of Information Society services is an oxymoron under the GDPR's opt-in requirements. Samara argues that the GDPR's opt-in clause should be perceived not only as granting a 'positive will power' to data subjects to enter into a personal data processing relationship; it should be seen as offering a positive discretionary power in choosing the types of 'currency' for the enjoyment of information society services. According to Samara, data subjects' real control over their personal data could be enhanced if the latter are legally recognised as forms of 'assets' or 'currencies'. This could also increase awareness of the economic and proprietary values of personal data, lead to a 'monetary equity' and, thus, potentially a stronger protection of personal information.

While Section 1 of the book revisits basic concepts and assumptions, Section 2 focuses on a plethora of complex questions that arise when considering the GDPR. These concern the uncertainties regarding basic definitions, such as 'controllers' and 'processors'; the challenges that new technologies such as AI and profiling present; the purposes of EU data privacy law; the problems of its implementation at the national level; and, its relationship with other instruments.

In Chapter 4, Yordanka Ivanova critically examines the GDPR's provisions on the concepts of 'controller', 'processor', and 'joint controller', in the light of relevant non-binding guidelines and case law and the corresponding data protection responsibilities of different data processing actors through the prism of the new accountability principle. The Chapter finds that the definition of these concepts creates significant legal uncertainties regarding both application and compliance. Ivanova goes on to propose a new value chain method for allocating responsibilities among joint controllers that is more effective and appropriate for the technology and data-driven world.

Chapter 5 considers whether the GDPR provides adequate and effective protection to problems that arise from profiling. Elena Georgiou investigates the application of the GDPR to data processed for profiling purposes; the potential protective mechanisms that exist in this respect; the problematic of group profiles; and whether the data protection principles can effectively minimise the asymmetries of knowledge and the unbalanced distribution of powers between controllers and individual subjects resulting from the use of profiling. The Chapter argues that the GDPR provides limited solutions to all these problems, thus, leaving individuals with unsatisfactory protections.

Chapter 6 reflects on the interrelationship between data protection and competition law. Arletta Gorecka argues that privacy concerns have a multidimensional impact on competition law; nevertheless, they do not require any legal changes within the remits of competition law. The Chapter distinguishes three phases in the EU legal development of data assessment in competition law: i) ignorance of personal data protection; ii) identification of parallel pathways between competition law and data protection; and iii) a third that has emerged from certain member states recognising the importance of personal data in the competition law sphere. Gorecka submits that competition authorities should base their assessments solely on competition law rules as these appear flexible enough to incorporate data privacy concerns.

Chapter 7 focuses on the Portuguese law that implements the GDPR (Law 58/2019) and the judgment of the Portuguese Comissão Nacional de Proteção de Dados (CNPD) (National Commission for Data Protection) declaring that nine articles of this law were incompatible with EU Law and cannot, therefore, be applied in the future. Graça Canto Moniz examines the reasoning behind this peculiar decision and assess its consequences. She considers that given the absence of an *erga omnes* effect of this decision, it is possible that Portuguese courts might, in future cases, ask the CJEU to clarify its understanding regarding the provisions disapplied by the CNPD. This is regarded as the best option that can solve the problems and uncertainties that arose from the CNPD's decision.

Athena Christofi, Pierre Dewitte, Charlotte Ducuing and Peggy Valcke explore in Chapter 8 the interplay between the GDPR and 'private' regulatory instruments of data processing, such as the International Organization for Standardisation ('ISO') standards in the field of privacy. At the centre of their analysis is the risks-based approach enshrined in the GDPR, which culminates with the obligation to conduct a DPIA in cases of high-risk processing. At the same time, the authors find that risks-based methodologies are also at the core of privacy-related standards adopted by ISO. The Chapter maps the misalignments between the two instruments and warns that the GDPR's objective to protect fundamental rights should not be undermined by embracing a risks-based approach.

Section 3 addresses another issue of increasing importance, data privacy at and beyond the EU's borders. The EU has established over the years digital, 'smart' borders through the operation of large databases which store the personal -including the biometric- data of TCNs. While the GDPR has strengthened data protection standards, the latter protections do not apply to TCNs. Beyond the EU's borders, it is worth noting that many countries are adopting their own data protection laws and it is important to also pay attention to these developments as well.

Chapter 9 discusses the EU's 'smart borders'. These refer to several information systems containing data related to migrants, asylum seekers and travellers managed through the use of digital systems. Sarah Progin-Theuerkauf, Margarite Zoeteweij-Turhan and Ozan Turhan examine the existing and future information systems containing data related to migrants, asylum seekers and TCNs by focusing on their modus operandi, access rights and specific data protection issues. They go on to analyse the importance of the two new interoperability regulations adopted in 2019 by taking a look at their potential effects on the protection of fundamental rights of the TCNs affected. The authors contend that while digital borders remain invisible, they raise in practice higher boundaries than physical borders and render migrants from third countries increasingly transparent. More importantly, blanket assumptions about the alleged 'dangerous nature' of TCNs result to unjustifiable discrimination.

Chapter 10 focuses on the processing of biometric data that is often taking place in the EU's large-scale IT border management systems. Simone Casiraghi and Alessandra Calvi argue that biometric data is expected to play a key role to make these systems interoperable by creating common search portals and by establishing common repositories with biographic data of the persons whose data are stored in these systems. Chapter 10 demonstrates the discrepancy between the status of biometric data in border management instruments and the new status granted to biometric data in the General Data Protection Regulation (GDPR) and the Law Enforcement Directive (LED).

Chapter 11 scrutinises the stimulus the GDPR initiated on the enactment of official privacy laws in jurisdictions other than the European Union and analyses, using a comparative approach the privacy laws enacted in the Kingdom of Bahrain, one of the Gulf Cooperation Council (GCC) countries by examining its similarities and differences with the GDPR. Maria Casoria and Eman Mahmood AlSarraf find that the regulatory process in the GCC region is still at its inception and, thus, it is interesting to investigate the GDPR's influence in this respect.

Section 4 introduces two studies of data protection that depart from a traditional legal analysis.

Chapter 12 aims to provide a holistic perspective on what happens when organizations try to protect personal data. Ine van Zeeland and Jo Pierson investigate how an interdisciplinary framework for the study of factors that influence personal data protection in practice can be constructed by collecting research results from the various disciplines in which this subject has been studied, as well as from different jurisdictions beyond the EU. As the authors argue, there is a clear need for an all-round perspective on data protection 'on the ground' that can provide valuable insights to different stakeholders in the digital economy – policy makers, watchdogs, privacy and consumer advocates, industries, technology developers- and inform policies and hands-on approaches at the macro (societal), meso (sectoral), and micro levels (organizational).

Chapter 13 examines how the implementation of the GDPR changed the ways in which personal data of EU customers are processed. Tomáš Pikulík and Peter Štarchoň explore the links between the rights of customers as data subjects and related aspects of customer satisfaction. They note that data-driven marketing puts data at the centre of additional value creation and brings new insights and perspectives. According to the authors, the impact of the GDPR on customer-centric information and communication technologies can increase consumer awareness of data protection rights and create new pathways to customer centricity and the legal and technical aspects of data processing within the digital economy ecosystem.

Section 5 focuses on case law developments regarding the right to be forgotten by taking a closer look both at the EU and the Member States' level.

Chapter 14 explores two underdeveloped in the literature aspects of the right to be forgotten: its unexpected consequences on search engines and the difficulties of its implementation in practice by the latter. Maria Tzanou argues that the horizontal application of EU privacy rights on private parties, such as internet search engines -as undertaken by the CJEU- is fraught with conceptual gaps, dilemmas and uncertainties that create confusions about the enforceability of the right to be forgotten and the role of search engines. The Chapter goes on to propose a comprehensive legal framework for the implementation of this right, which aims to ensure a legally certain and proportionate balance of the competing interests online in the light of the GDPR.

In Chapter 15, Federica Casarosa and Dianora Poletti examine the jurisprudence of the Italian Supreme Court on the right to be forgotten and in particular a case recently decided by the Grand Chamber that addressed the application of the right to be forgotten to printed press. While the Grand Chamber could have clarified how far the criteria identified by the CJEU in *Google Spain* would be applicable to factual circumstances involving printed press, the court did not evaluate the right to be forgotten as a single concept, but rather it provided for a set of distinctions which resulted in different rights to be forgotten. Chapter 15 considers that this classification barely fits with the EU's approach and potentially hinders the harmonisation objectives of the GDPR.

This section concludes with Evelyn Kirkwood's chapter which focuses on the legacy of *Google Spain* and its impact on some recent cases within different EU Member States regarding the right to be forgotten. Chapter 16 examines in detail the UK joined cases of *NT1* and *NT2* and the questions that arise with regard to the right to be forgotten when criminal convictions are at issue.

Overall, the aim of this book is to provide readers with new perspectives on data protection and the more recent developments in the field from a variety of different backgrounds and disciplines. It is certainly a peculiar time to be reflecting about data privacy in the COVID-19 era of imposed quarantines and 'self-isolation'. This can be seen, on the one hand, as a form of what Anita Allen has called 'unpopular privacy' (Allen, 2011). On the other hand, and while everyone in the society is asked to endure these forms of unpopular privacy, data protection is suffering again under current, COVID-19 related measures that require the monitoring for instance of phone location data to track phone users' movements. Data privacy scholarship needs to remain awake and ready to speak up against these new and ongoing privacy threats. We must make sure that these extraordinary circumstances and the measures they require do not become the new ordinary as far as our fundamental rights and freedoms are concerned.

Keeping these thoughts in mind, I hope that the following pages with their broad coverage of a diverse range of data protection problems and perspectives will provide the reader with interesting and thought-provoking discussions about the present and the future of (EU) data privacy law.

Maria Tzanou
Keele University, UK

REFERENCES

Allen, A. L. (2011). *Unpopular Privacy: What Must We Hide?* New York: Oxford University Press. doi:10.1093/acprof:oso/9780195141375.001.0001

Koops, B.-J. (2014). The trouble with European data protection law. *International Data Privacy Law*, *14*(4), 250–261. doi:10.1093/idpl/ipu023

Purtova, N. (2018). The law of everything. Broad concept of personal data and future of EU data protection law. *Law, Innovation and Technology*, *10*(1), 40–81. doi:10.1080/17579961.2018.1452176

Tzanou, M. (2017). *The Fundamental Right to Data Protection: Normative Value in the Context of Counter-Terrorism Surveillance*. Oxford, UK: Hart Publishing.

Acknowledgment

The editor would like to acknowledge the help of all the people involved in this project and, more specifically, to the authors and reviewers that took part in the review process. Without their support, this book would not have become a reality.

First, the editor would like to thank each one of the authors for their contributions. My sincere gratitude goes to the chapters authors who contributed their time and expertise to this book.

Second, the editor wishes to acknowledge the valuable contributions of the reviewers regarding the improvement of quality, coherence, and content presentation of chapters. Most of the authors also served as referees; I highly appreciate their double task.

Maria Tzanou
Keele University, UK

Section 1
GDPR: The Foundational Questions

This section considers the foundational questions regarding privacy and data protection examined within the context of the main data protection legislative instrument in the EU, the GDPR.

Chapter 1
Protection of Personal Data Regulation and Public Liberties:
A Polyhedron With Unexpected Effects

Ana Neves
School of Law, University of Lisbon, Portugal

ABSTRACT

The Regulation (EU) 2016/679 on the protection of natural persons with regard to the processing of personal data and on the free movement of such data is much more than a personal data regulation. It has a wide range of impacts, of different nature: substantive, procedural, and organisational ones. In each of these dimensions, it is the personal autonomy and the equilibrium of the relationship of individuals with those processing their data that are at stake, hence, the centrality that individual rights over their own data shall have. Nonetheless, the access, the flow, and the free movement of information, including personal data, are the essential foundations of a free and democratic society in which the freedoms and rights of individuals are guaranteed. Despite having the necessary premises to guarantee it, the GDPR carries the risk of being used by public authorities to condition the space for public freedoms.

INTRODUCTION

The Regulation 2016/679 (GDPR) lays down rules on the protection of natural persons with regard to the processing of personal data and on the free movement of such data within the European Union. It intends to achieve a common protection of fundamental rights and freedoms of natural persons, in particular of their right to the protection of personal data, and to guarantee the free flow of data within the European Union (e.g., Recitals (1) and (2) and Article 1 of GDPR). On the one hand, it stresses the rights of data subjects that enable them to have more control over their own personal data, reducing *power and information asymmetries between ordinary citizens and those who control the processing of their personal data* (Orla Lynskey, 2020, p. 82). On the other hand, it specifies *the obligations of those who process or determine the processing of personal data* and reinforces the compliance and enforcement framework (e.g., Recital (11)).

DOI: 10.4018/978-1-5225-9489-5.ch001

However, the GDPR is much more than a personal data regulation. It has a wide range of different types of impacts, of diversified nature, substantive, procedural and organisational ones. Processing of personal data takes place in different dimensions of individuals' lives, on various grounds and in different ways. It intertwines with rights that *enable people to have a value as a human being in public and social life[1]*, like the right to freedom of expression and information, the right to freedom of peaceful assembly and to freedom of association and freedom of thought, conscience and religion[2]. It is about protection of fundamental rights and freedoms of natural persons, mobilised either within the same protective framework or as competitors. This aspect is highlighted by the GDPR and it renews the need to discuss the scope of the right to data protection[3]. It also justifies renewed attention to some classic categories of law disciplines, as responsibility and consent.

The GDPR involves organisational changes. These relate to the monitoring and enforcement architecture of personal data regulation, to the internal organisation of controllers and processors and to the *collaborative governance regime* (Kaminski, 2019, p. 195) that it involves. The GDPR implies also procedural modifications related to the way personal data are processed in the light of its structural principles and with the exercise of procedural rights, like the right to rectification or the right to erasure. The organisational and procedural aspects are designed to guarantee the protection of personal data, but they correspondingly shape the guarantee of the right of data protection, the balancing with other rights, and also the way to understand it.

The present study aims to highlight the cross-cutting effect of the GDPR, the triple and interrelated substantive, procedural and organisational impacts of it and how considering these is important to understand the right to the protection of personal data and to safeguard the exercise of fundamental rights and freedoms. Firstly, the main differences between the GDPR and the repealed Directive 95/46/EC of the European Parliament and of the Council of 24 October 1995 (DPD) are outlined. Then, organisational and procedural aspects are considered, stressing its role towards the substantive dimension of data protection. In third place, the focus is on the substantive aspects, mainly, looking at the GDPR clarification of the nature of the right to protection of personal data, and at the relevance of its core principles. Both are an important tool for protection of fundamental rights and freedoms of natural persons.

BACKGROUND

The right to data protection has autonomous provisions on some constitutions[4] and in some international instruments[5]; and has been considered in the scope of Article 8 of the Convention on Human Rights, which provides about the right to respect for private and family life.[6] Orla Lynskey underlines that [t]*he right to data protection set out in Article 8 of the EU Charter of Fundamental Rights had played a pioneering role in the development of EU fundamental rights jurisprudence* (2020, p. 80), pointing out cases like Schecke and Eifert[7], Digital Rights Ireland[8] and Google Spain[9]. These cases predate Regulation 2016/679, but come after the Commission proposal which triggered the reform of the Directive 95/46/EC of the European Parliament and of the Council of 24 October 1995, repealed by the GDPR[10], proposal which stated as its objective the building the *a stronger and more coherent data protection framework in the EU, backed by strong enforcement that will allow the digital economy to develop across the internal market, put individuals in control of their own data and reinforce legal and practical certainty for economic operators and public authorities.[11]*

The GDPR can be said *an extension and refinement of existing requirements imposed by the 1995 Data Protection Directive* (Hoofnagle, p. 98). Among other changes, the following stand out:

1. The GDPR characterizes itself – in Article 1, dedicated to the *subject-matter and objectives* – as an act that *protects fundamental rights and freedoms of natural persons and in particular their right to the protection of personal data*, as well as states that *the free flow of personal data within the Union is neither restricted nor prohibited on grounds relating to the protection of individuals with regard to the processing of personal data*. The repealed Directive 95/46/EC, in Article 1, under the title *object of the Directive*, stated in similar but not quite so affirmative terms. It paid less attention to fundamental rights and freedoms of natural persons than the GDPR. For instance, it had not an article about access to official documents[12] and it was more laconic about the conciliation between processing of personal data and freedom of expression.[13]

2. The GDPR fosters the information duties towards the data subject, like the duty to inform about data transfers to third countries or international organisations [14]; the duty to inform about the purpose for processing; the duty to inform about the existence of automated decision-making and, in this case, to give meaningful information about the logic involved and its meaning and scope[15]; and the duty to inform users without delay in case of harmful data breach.[16]

3. The GDPR strengthens the rights of the data subject, like the right to data portability; clarifies the right to erasure data (where a person no longer allows his data to be processed and there are no legitimate grounds for keeping the data, it will be deleted), and the right to have easy access to his/her own data.[17]

4. The GDPR pays more detailed attention to the automated decision-making[18], requiring the adoption of new or adapted procedural safeguards (such as the right to a statement of reasons or the right to an explanation of the underlying logic and scope of automated decisions).

5. It reinforces the integrated nature of data protection institutional system, by giving a central role to the European Data Protection Board. It, namely, provides guidance and interpretation, adopts some binding decisions; and functions as counterpoint to the intervention of the national supervisory authorities, which, in addition, must fulfil more demanding independence requirements.[19]

6. It determines that, in general, the controller and the processor shall designate a data protection officer, as a «guardian» of data protection law and as an adviser.[20]

7. Among the duties of the controller, it introduces the duty to carryout a data protection impact assessment where processing operations are likely to result in a high risk to the rights and freedoms of natural persons[21]; and the duty to maintain records of processing activities under its responsibility.[22]

8. It defines a strong enforcement framework[23], namely it makes the system of enforcement more concrete and as so reduces the margin of discretion of States to apply it. Penalties including administrative fines should be imposed for specified infringements in addition to, or instead of, appropriate measures adopted by the supervisory authority.[24]

9. It removes most of the notification obligations to the supervisory authority.[25]

10. The GDPR readjusts its territorial scope to the fact that it is a directly applicable text and adopts two main criteria to ascertain it: the 'establishment' criterion - according to which the GDPR applies to processing *in the context of an establishment* of a controller or processor in the EU[26] - and the 'targeting' criterion -, according to which the GDPR applies to non-EU controllers or processors in certain specific circumstances.[27]

The summary of the main changes does not reflect the real impact of the GDPR. It has organisational, procedural and substantive effects on data protection law, which bring with them a better conceptual delimitation of the right to data protection and the consequent need to understand it within a broader framework of fundamental rights and freedoms that must be guaranteed in a democratic, transparent State, governed by the rule of law.

ORGANISATIONAL AND PROCEDURAL IMPACTS OF THE GDPR AND THEIR SUBSTANTIVE RELEVANCE

Data protection regulation is about the collection and other performing operations on personal data and about empowering individuals to be aware and control their personal data. The core principles of GDPR as well as various of its provisions demand organisational and procedural changes, some of which go beyond the data protection dimension.

The GDPR obliges institutions to think about the information they gathered or asked for and about the way they organise, control, secure, correct, transmit, erase personal data. It demands that inherent *appropriate technical or organisational measures* are taken. These shall be *designed to implement data-protection principles, such as data minimisation, in an effective manner and to integrate the necessary safeguards into the processing* and ensure *that, by default, only personal data which are necessary for each specific purpose of the processing are processed.*[28] The GDPR obliges also to pay attention to information needs of clients or citizens and institutions, namely, due to the portability right, which is favoured by the use of interoperability systems and by the use of technology.

Apart from the effect on the number and the kind of organic-functional structures, it must be high-lighted the existence of a data protection officer GDPR in public authorities (except for courts acting in their judicial capacity) and in other controllers or processors in the case of processing specific data or doing so in specific terms[29]. It shall secure the implementation of GDPR, by carrying out specified tasks (notably as a register[30]), with wide technical autonomy, and as such he has a special position towards the controller or processor even if he is a staff member[31]. The public authorities or bodies, given their organisational structure and size, may designate a single data protection officer[32], arrangement that promotes cooperative relationships. The existence of a data subject, whose contact details shall be known, is a guarantee of the rights of data subjects, inasmuch it shall *monitor compliance with this Regulation, with other Union or Member State data protection provisions.*[33]

Data subjects shall benefit from a homogeneous protection independently of his/her geographical location.[34] In this perspective, national public authorities responsible for monitoring the application of the GDPR[35] must be worth of the same reliability and work easily in coordination and cooperation. In the GDPR, there is a more precise definition of its features and less autonomy of Members States to provide about them[36]. Each supervisory authority shall have complete independence in performing its tasks and exercising its powers, namely towards national authorities. Nevertheless, there is a functional centrality of European Data Protection Board, as it shall contribute to the consistent application of data protection rules throughout the European Union, and promote cooperation between the data protection national supervisory authorities[37], which is endeavoured, besides under the general cooperative duties[38], by the possibility of adopting legally binding decisions in clearly specified cases[39] and by the 'one-stop-shop mechanism'.[40]

The processing of personal data principles (Article 5), like the purpose limitation principle, the data minimisation and the accuracy principles[41], gained a renewed importance that manifests itself in procedural duties. On the one hand, controller has precise duties to provide information in a certain form and terms[42] and to document and to organize records (see, e.g., Article 20 of GDPR). On the other hand, there shall adopt procedural measures to secure the exercise of the rights of data subjects, like the right of access to the personal data, the right to rectification, the right to erasure and the right to data portability.[43]

The right to data portability is an important tool for data subjects to control their personal data. It enables *individuals to maximise the advantages of big data and to benefit from the value created by the use of their personal data* (I. van Ooijen and H.U. Vrabec, 2019, p. 102) and it could also favour the information interchange. The data subject, not only have *the right to receive the personal data concerning him or her, which he or she has provided to a controller* and *have the right to transmit those data to another controller without hindrance from the controller to which the personal data have been provided* (Article 20(1)[44]), but also *have the right to have the personal data transmitted directly from one controller to another, where technically feasible* (Article 20(2). This is of the interest of the data subject and seemingly of the interest of the controller to which the data are transmitted.[45] In the case of *performance of a task carried out in the public interest or in the exercise of official authority vested in the controller*[46], the right does *not apply to processing necessary for the exercise of them*[47], but the transmission between public authorities of personal data that is in the interest of the his or her holder[48] may hardly be hindered by the public authority addressed.

Another relevant effect coming from the GDPR is the emphasis on the importance of accurate data and on the data subjects right *to access and correct data.*[49] In the case of public authorities, it reinforces, and are reinforced by, the duty to act diligently, *which is inherent in the principle of sound administration* and *requires that administration act with care and caution.*[50] This may demand them *to consider information supplied by other competent authorities under a duty to inform or entered into a database when carrying out their activities*[51] [52], which is facilitated by interoperability solutions in which public authorities and private are many times necessarily participants[53] and by the only once principle.[54] In this context, the 'purpose limitation' and the 'lawfulness, fairness and transparency'[55] principles help to build reliable and useful relationships. The 'transparency', 'accuracy' and 'integrity' principles[56] favours the exercise of the right to information.

The 'transparency' and 'fairness' principles entail renewed attention to automated decision--making systems (e.g. article 22 and recital 71).[57] On the one hand, the extent and scope of the guarantees provided for in the GDPR are very much discussed.[58] On the other hand, the GDPR is motivating the search for new guarantees to deal with the use of algoritms.[59] [60] In both cases, the GDPR is being called upon to incorporate the reasoning behind judgments on the matter.[61]

At intra and inter-administrative cooperative and collaborative level, the GDPR calls for a greater dialogue between the data protection national supervisory authority and the national supervisory authority responsible for securing the Directive (EU) 2019/1024 of the European Parliament and of the Council of 20 June 2019 on open data and the re-use of public sector information.[63] And as Kaminski points out, the GDPR *is full of broad standards, to be given specific substance over time through ongoing dialogues between regulators and companies, backed eventually by courts. Both the Recitals and the Working Party guidelines, along with numerous mechanisms ranging from a formal process for establishing codes of conduct to less formal impact assessment requirements, are part of this collaborative approach* (2019, p. 195).[64]

SUBSTANTIVE ASPECTS

The adoption of appropriate technical and organisational measures and the protection of rights of data subjects under the GDPR are interconnected. Those measures influence or affect the exercise of the right to data protection. The interlinked nature of the substantive and the organisational and procedural dimensions is present in the set of principles relating to personal data processing (Article 5).[65] For instance, the 'accuracy" principle demands that *every reasonable step must be taken to ensure that personal data that are inaccurate, having regard to the purposes for which they are processed, are erased or rectified without delay.*[66]

Moreover, the procedural aspects fall within the scope of the very understanding of the right to data protection. Within the GDPR, it has gained a new or a more precise and clear content. The right to data protection consists of a number of «sub-rights», like the right to rectification, the right to erasure ('right to be forgotten')[67], the right of access by the data subject[68] and the right to restriction of processing.[69] They serve the aim of enhancing the individual's control over personal data and of reducing the asymmetries between individuals and those who process their data (Lynskey, 2014). The RGPDP helps to clarify the concepts and to understand the distinction between the right to personal data protection and the right to privacy. These rights have diverse material objects[70], different subject scope[71] and restrictive grounds or logics[72] (Kokott and Sobotta, 2017; Tzanou, 2017, p. 40[73]). With the GDPR, the distinction between the right to data protection and the right to privacy emerges more clearly. The first one is about trustful (reliable and accurate) information related to all aspects of an individual's life. As such, it concerns the protection of the personal identity. In sociable, political and administrative life, people should be treated in a fair way, which means in accordance with their own facts and deeds, as they are represented by accurate ledgers. Therefore, it is not in its essence a negative right. Otherwise, it demands an effective transparency from the controllers of personal data: without this one it is not possible to discuss and guarantee the above-mentioned rights.[74]

In this perspective, it must be underlined that it cannot be used or exercised to humper other fundamental rights, namely civil liberties. On the contrary, the GDPR *protects fundamental rights and freedoms of natural persons* (Article 1(2)).[75] For instance, pursuant to art. 85, the right to the protection of personal data must be reconciled with the right to freedom of expression and information, including processing for journalistic purposes and the purposes of academic, artistic or literary expression.[76]

The correct understanding of the procedural dimension of the right to data protection and the correct implementation of data protection regulation prevent it from being used to hinder the exercise of rights such as the freedom of expression, the freedom of assembly (for instance, by denying publicity to citizens' Assemblies or by collecting unlawful information about individuals assembled in a public places), the right to access official documents.[77] The value of receiving information from public authorities and to impart it is of particular significance as it relates directly to democracy and to citizenship.[78] From the open government standpoint, there is a risk, of the data protection regulation being used by public authorities to hide information about the way they manage public resources, conflict of interest situations and illegal practices.[79] The nature of data and access to it are different things. The more difficult is to access information, less trust is placed in public authorities and the greater the negative influence on the representative democratic legitimacy. The contrapuntal effect of, for instance, the Directive on the Protection of Persons Reporting on Breaches of Union Law (Directive (EU) 2019/1937 of the European Parliament and of the Council of 23 October 2019)[80] reveals the existence of an insufficient flow of relevant information. The relationship between the right to data protection and transparency should not be an antinomic one.[81] The former demands a proportional, objective and entirely clear processing of personal data of data subjects. The effectiveness of the lawful, fair and transparent data processing and, therefore, of data minimization, requires the development of information systems that ensure it; and may improve the sharing of data, and remove reasons to hinder the exercise of the respective rights.

Related to the guarantee of exercise of rights provided in the GDPR, some concepts or categories used therein are of particular importance and justify renewed attention. It is the case of consent, responsibility and non-discrimination categories. The data protection regulation questions the place of consent as a data processing title, which is a central concept of law of obligations (Debet, 2016, pp. 22-24). Indeed, only the expression of a free, informed and specific will can be considered as a consent, assessed in the concrete contexts and by reference to real alternatives and to the degree of transparency.[82] The recital 74 of the GDPR states that the *responsibility and liability of the controller for any processing of personal data carried out by the controller or on the controller's behalf should be established*. This means, in particular, that the controller shall *implement appropriate and effective measures and be able to demonstrate the compliance of processing activities* with GDPR, *including the effectiveness of the measures*. It also means that they shall *maintain records of processing activities under its responsibility* and that they shall *cooperate with the supervisory authority* (Recital 82[83]). Within the GDPR, regarding automated decision-making, the controller has the responsibility to secure that the algorithm used is the computational translation of the normative premises relevant to the decision and, therefore, that it is legally sound.[84] In addition, namely due to the importance of accuracy data and the cooperative duties, the responsibility for factual errors and for the respect of impartiality principle can emerge more clearly. Concerning non-discrimination, the GDPR stresses the need that processing of personal information and the decision-making process be free of pre-bias and, in automated decision-making, the importance of using reliable or certified algorithms and of impact assessment tools.[85]

CONCLUSION

The GDPR can be said a *detailed regulatory regime* about information, *the most consequential regulatory development in information policy in a generation* (Hoofnagle et al., 2019, p. 65). Purtova argues (2018, p. 40) that [w]*hen the hyperconnected onlife world of data-driven agency arrives, the intensive compliance regime of the General Data Protection Regulation (GDPR) will become 'the law of everything', well-meant but impossible to maintain*. As a data protection regime and as an inherent discipline about processing information, the GDPR has necessarily a cross-cutting character. This, on the one hand, at first, obliges to be attentive to the objective and scope of the right to data protection. This means not to turn it into a right to privacy and to be aware of the importance and substantive relevance of procedural dimensions of the former. On the other hand, it is important to keep in mind that the GDPR is an act about protection of fundamental rights and freedoms of natural persons (Article 1(2)). This means that *it must be considered in relation to its function in society and be balanced against other fundamental rights, in accordance with the principle of proportionality* (Recital 4). Here, public authorities have a special responsibility. They must respect the rights of the data subjects they interact with and they must not use the GDPR to make the exercise of public power and private institutions opaque. Unduly confusion between data protection and privacy can be used to hamper the exercise of fundamental freedoms which are the ground of liberal democratic society. At the same time, public authorities as regulators seem not be doing enough to help individuals understand and deal with *the implications of the use of information and personal data*[86] and to ensure the exercise of data protection rights[87] , namely, in the context of the relations they establish through technology (Mantelero, 2017).

REFERENCES

Abreu, J. C. (2017). Digital Single Market under EU political and constitutional calling: European electronic agenda's impact on interoperability solutions. *UNIO - EU Law Journal*, *3*(1), 123-140. Retrieved January 30, 2020 from https://revistas.uminho.pt/index.php/unio/issue/view/25

Carloni, E., & Falcone, M. (2017). L'equilibrio necessario. Principi e modelli di bilanciamento tra trasparenza e privacy. *Diritto Pubblico*, *23*(3), 723-777.

Charter of Fundamental Rights of the European Union, 2016/C 202/02, Official Journal of the European Union C 202/389, 7.6.2016.

Cobbaut, E. (2019). Article 11 - Freedom of Expression and Information. In F. Dorssemont, K. Lörcher, S. Clauwaert, & M. Schmitt (Eds.), *The Charter of Fundamental Rights of the European Union and the employment relation* (pp. 295–313). Oxford: Hart Publishing. doi:10.5040/9781509922680.ch-014

Communication of the Commission to the European Parliament, the Council, the European Economic and Social Committee and the Committee of Regions (2016). Online Platforms and the Digital Single Market – opportunities and challenges for Europe, Brussels, COM(2016) 288 final.

Consiglio di Stato, Judgment of 13 of December 2019, N. 02936/2019 REG.RIC.

Convention for the Protection of Individuals with regard to Automatic Processing of Personal Data, adopted on 28 January 1981, ETS No 108;

Council of Europe. (2017). Consultative Committee of the Convention for the Protection of Individuals with Regard to Automatic Processing of Personal Data (T-PD). *Guidelines on the Protection of Individuals with regard to the Processing of Personal Data in a World of Big Data*. Retrieved December 15, 2019, from https://www.coe.int/en/web/data-protection/-/new-guidelines-on-artificial-intelligence-and-personal-data-protection

Council of Europe. (2017). *Guidelines on the protection of individuals with regard to the processing of personal data in a world of Big Data, 2017, No. 9*. Retrieved December 16, 2019, from https://rm.coe.int/16806ebe7a

Council of Europe. (2018). *Study on the human rights dimensions of automated data processing techniques (in particular algorithms) and possible regulatory implications*. Retrieved December 16, 2019 from https://edoc.coe.int/en/internet/7589-algorithms-and-human-rights-study-on-the-human-rights-dimensions-of-automated-data-processing-techniques-and-possible-regulatory-implications.html

Data Protection Working Party, Guidelines on consent under Regulation 2016/679, adopted on 28 November 2017, as last revised and Adopted on 10 April 2018, 17/EN, WP259 rev.01

Debet, A. (2016). La protection des données personnelles, point de vue du droit privé. *Revue du Droit Public*, *1*, 17–34.

Decision (EU) 2015/2240, of the European Parliament and of the Council, 25th November 2015, establishing a programme on interoperability solutions and common frameworks for European public administrations, businesses and citizens (ISA2 programme) as a means for modernizing the public sector.

Demirbolat, A. O. (2018). *The Relationship Between Democracy and Education*. Bentham Science Publishers.

Directive 2003/4/EC of the European Parliament and of the Council of 28 January 2003 on public access to environmental information and repealing Council Directive 90/313/EEC.

Directive 95/46/EC of the European Parliament and of the Council of 24 October 1995 on the protection of individuals with regard to the processing of personal data and on the free movement of such data.

Directive (EU) 2019/1024 of the European Parliament and of the Council of 20 June 2019 on open data and the re-use of public sector information.

Directive (EU) 2019/1937 of the European Parliament and of the Council of 23 October 2019 on the protection of persons who report breaches of Union law.

ECJ, Judgment of the Court (Grand Chamber) of 9 November 2010, Volker und Markus Schecke GbR (C-92/09) and Hartmut Eifert (C-93/09) v Land Hessen.

ECJ, Judgment of the Court (Grand Chamber) of 4 of April 2014, Digital Rights Ireland Ltd (C-293/12) and Kärntner Landesregierung (C-594/12).

ECJ, Judgment (Ninth Chamber) of 22 March 2017, C-665/15, Commission v Portugal (failure of the Member State to use of and connect to the EU network within the EU driving licence network).

ECJ Judgment of the Court (Grand Chamber), 8 April 2014, Digital Rights Ireland, Joined Cases C-293/12 and C-594/12.

ECJ, Judgment of the Court (Grand Chamber), 13 May 2014, Google Spain SL and Google Inc. v Agencia Española de Protección de Datos (AEPD) and Mario Costeja González, C-131/12.

ECJ, Judgment of the Court (Grand Chamber) of 4 April 2017, European Ombudsman v Claire Staelen, Case C-337/15 P.

ECJ, Judgment (Tenth Chamber) of 5 October 2016, Commission v Portugal, C-583/15.

ECtHR, S. and Marper v. the United Kingdom, Judgment (Grand Chamber) of 4 December 2008.

ECtHR, I v. Finland, Judgment of judgment of 17 of July 2008 (Fourth Section) Application 20511/03.

ECtHR, Sérvulo & Associados – Sociedade de Advogados, RL and others c. Portugal, Judgment of 3 September 2015 (First Section), Application 27013/10.

ECtHR, Antović and Mirković v. Montenegro, Judgment of 28 of November 2017, Application no 70838/13.

ECtHR, Magyar Helsinki Bizottság *versus* Hungary, Judgment of 8 November 2016 (Grand Chamber) Application no. 18030/11.

Edwards, L., & Veale, M. (2018). Enslaving the algorithm: From a 'right to an explanation' to a 'right to better decisions'? *IEEE Security and Privacy, 16*(3), 46–54. Retrieved December152019. doi:10.1109/MSP.2018.2701152

European Commission (2012). COM(2012) 11 final, 2012/0011, (COD) C7-0025/12, Proposal for a Regulation of the European Parliament and of the Council on the protection of individuals with regard to the processing of personal data and on the free movement of such data.

European Commission. (n.d.). *Digital4EU 2016 – Stakeholder Forum Report*. Retrieved December 16, 2019, from https://ec.europa.eu/digital-single-market/en/news/digital4eu-2016-report

European Parliament. (2019). *Understanding algorithmic decision-making: Opportunities and challenges*. Study elaborated by Claude Castelluccia and Daniel Le Métayer at the request of the Panel for the Future of Science and Technology and managed by the Scientific Foresight Unit within the Directorate-General for Parliamentary Research Services of the Secretariat of the European Parliament. Retrieved December 15, 2019, from https://www.europarl.europa.eu/thinktank/en/document.html?reference=EPRS_STU(2019)624261

European Union Agency for Fundamental Rights. (2019). *Fundamental Rights Report 2019*. Retrieved January 30, 2020 from https://fra.europa.eu/en/publication/2019/fundamental-rights-report-2019

Federal Constitutional Court, Order of 6 November 2019, 1 BvR 276/17 -Right to be forgotten II and Order of 6 November 2019, 1 BvR 16/13 - Right to be forgotten I.

Felzmann, H., Villaronga, E. F., Lutz, C., & Tamò-Larrieux, A. (2019). Transparency you can trust: Transparency requirements for artificial intelligence between legal norms and contextual concerns. *Data & Society*, 1-14. Retrieved January 30, 2020, from journals.sagepub.com/home/bds

Granger, M.-P., & Irion, K. (2018). The right to protection of personal data: the new posterchild of European Union citizenship? In Civil Rights and EU Citizenship. Cheltenham: Edward Elgar Pub. doi:10.4337/9781788113441.00019

Hendrickx, F. (2019). Article 8 – Protection of Personal Data Frank. In F. Dorssemont, K. Lörcher, S. Clauwaert, & M. Schmitt (Eds.), *The Charter of Fundamental Rights of the European Union and the employment relation* (pp. 249–271). Oxford: Hart Publishing.

Hoofnagle, C. J., & Sloot, B. (2019). The European Union general data protection regulation: What it is and what it means. *Information & Communications Technology Law, 8*(1), 65–98. doi:10.1080/13600834.2019.1573501

Kędzior, M. (2019). GDPR and beyond - a year of changes in the data protection landscape of the European Union. *ERA Forum, 19*(4), 505–509. Retrieved December 15, 2019, from https://link.springer.com/article/10.1007/s12027-019-00549-x

Kaminski, M. E. (2019). The Right to Explanation, Explained. *Berkeley Technology Law Journal, 34*, 189–209.

Kokott, J., & Sobotta, C. (2017). The distinction between privacy and data protection in the jurisprudence of the CJEU and the ECtHR. *International Data Privacy Law, 7*(4), 222–228. doi:10.1093/idpl/ipt017

Lepage, A. (2017). La protection contre le numérique: les données personnelles à l'aune de la loi pour une République numérique. In Le Droit Civil à L'Ère Numérique, Actes du colloque du Master 2 Droit privé général et du Laboratoire de droit civil - Paris II - 21 avril 2017 (pp. 35-39). La Semaine Juridique, LexisNexis SA.

Lynskey, O. (2020). Delivering Data Protection: The Next Chapter. German Law Journal, 21, Special Issue 1 (20 Challenges in the EU in 2020), 80-84. Retrieved February 24, 2020, from https://www. cambridge.org/core/journals/german-law-journal/issue/20-challenges-in-the-eu-in-2020/3F9E1FEE4C 3CFAC8A84DE1431108C9CC

Lynskey, O. (2014). Deconstructing data protection: The 'added-value' of a right to data protection in the EU legal order. *The International and Comparative Law Quarterly*, *63*(3), 569–597. doi:10.1017/ S0020589314000244

Malgieri, G. (2019). Automated decision-making in the EU Member States: The right to explanation and other 'suitable safeguards' in the national legislations. *Computer Law & Security Review*, *39*, 1-26. Retrieved December 08, 2019, from http://creativecommons.org/licenses/by/4.0/

Mantelero, A. (2016). Personal data for decisional purposes in the age of analytics: From an individual to a collective dimension of data protection. *Computer Law & Security Review*, *32*(2), 238–255. doi:10.1016/j.clsr.2016.01.014

Mantelero, A. (2017). Regulating big data. The guidelines of the Council of Europe in the context of the European data protection framework. *Computer Law & Security Review*, *33*(5), 584–602. doi:10.1016/j. clsr.2017.05.011

Netherlands's Constitution of 1815 (with amendments through 2008). (n.d.). Retrieved from https:// www.constituteproject.org/

Obserdorff, H. (2016). L'espace numérique et la protection des données personnelles au regard des droits fondamentaux. *Revue du Droit Public*, *1*, 41–54.

Ooijen, I., & Vrabec, H. U. (2019). Does the GDPR Enhance Consumers' Control over Personal Data? An Analysis from a Behavioural Perspective. *Journal of Consumer Policy*, *42*(1), 91-107. Retrieved December 15, 2019, from https://link.springer.com/article/10.1007/s10603-018-9399-7

Pajuste, T. (2019). The Protection of Personal Data in a Digital Society: The Role of the GDPR. In M. Susi (Ed.), *Human Rights, Digital Society and the Law: A Research Companion* (pp. 303–315). London: Routledge. doi:10.4324/9781351025386-21

Pfisterer, V. (2019). The Right to Privacy – A Fundamental Right in Search of Its Identity: Uncovering the CJEU's Flawed Concept of the Right to Privacy. *German Law Journal*, *20*(5), 722–733. doi:10.1017/ glj.2019.57

Purtova, N. (2018). The law of everything. Broad concept of personal data and future of EU data protection law. *Law, Innovation and Technology*, *10*(1), 40–81. doi:10.1080/17579961.2018.1452176

Recommendation Rec(89)2 of the Committee of Ministers to member States on the protection of personal data used for employment purposes.

Recommendation Rec(97)5 of the Committee of Ministers to member States on the protection of medical data.

Regulation (EU) 2016/679 of the European Parliament and of the Council of 27 April 2016 on the protection of natural persons with regard to the processing of personal data and on the free movement of such data, and repealing Directive 95/46/EC.

ReNEUAL. (2014). *Model Rules on EU Administrative Procedures, Book VI – Administrative Information Management, Drafting Team: Diana-Urania Galetta and al.* Retrieved December 15, 2019, from http://www.reneual.eu/

Richard, J. (2016). Le numérique et les données personnelles: quels risques, quelles potentialités? *Revue du droit public*, *1*, 87-100.

Scholta, H., Mertens, W., Kowalkiewicz, M., & Becker, J. (2019). From one-stop shop to no-stop: An e-government stage model. *Government Information Quarterly*, *36*(1), 11–26. doi:10.1016/j.giq.2018.11.010

Spanish Constitution of 1978 with Amendments through 2011. (n.d.). Retrieved from http://www.senado.es/web/conocersenado/normas/constitucion/index.html?lang=en

Switzerland's Constitution of 1999 (with amendments through 2014). (n.d.). Retrieved from https://www.constituteproject.org/

Tambou, O. (2018). National Adaptations of the GDPR. Opening Remarks. In *National Adaptations of the GDPR* (pp. 24-27). Blogdroiteuropéen. Retrieved December 15, 2019, from https://wp.me/p6OBGR-3dP

Tzanou, M. (2017). *The Fundamental Right to Data Protection: Normative Value in the Context of Counter-Terrorism Surveillance*. Oxford: Hart Publishing.

United States Supreme Court. (1976). United States v. *Miller*, *425*, 437.

Wachter, S., Mittelstadt, B., & Floridi, L. (2017). Why a Right to Explanation of Automated Decision-Making Does Not Exist in the General Data Protection Regulation. *International Data Privacy Law*, *7*, 76-99. Retrieved December 15, 2019, from https://academic.oup.com/idpl/article/7/2/76/3860948

ENDNOTES

1   Demirbolat, 2018, p. 70.
2   Recital 4, Article 1.° 85 GDPR.
3   E.g., Nadezhda Purtova, 2018; and Lynskey, 2020.
4   E.g. Section 18 (3) of Spanish's Constitution of 1978 (with amendments through 2011); Article 13(2) of Switzerland's Constitution of 1999 (with amendments through 2014); and Article 10 (2) and (3) Netherlands's Constitution of 1815 (with amendments through 2008) - https://www.constituteproject.org/.
5   E.g., at the Council of Europe level, the Convention for the Protection of Individuals with regard to Automatic Processing of Personal Data, adopted on 28 January 1981, ETS No 108 and the Amending Protocol to the Convention for the Protection ofIndividuals with Regard to the Processing of

Personal Data, adopted by the Committee of Ministers at its 128th Session in Elsinore on 18 May 2018; and the Recommendation Rec(89)2 of the Committee of Ministers to member States on the protection of personal data used for employment purposes; and the Recommendation Rec(97)5 of the Committee of Ministers to Member States on the protection of medical data.

[6] See, for instance, ECtHR, *S. and Marper v. the United Kingdom,* Judgment (Grand Chamber) of 4 December 2008, application nos. 30562/04 and 30566/04, § 103:

The protection of personal data is of fundamental importance to a person's enjoyment of his or her right to respect for private and family life, as guaranteed by Article 8 of the Convention. The domestic law must afford appropriate safeguards to prevent any such use of personal data as may be inconsistent with the guarantees of this Article.

[7] Judgment of the Court (Grand Chamber) of 9 November 2010, Volker und Markus Schecke GbR (C-92/09) and Hartmut Eifert (C-93/09) v Land Hessen.

[8] Judgment of the Court (Grand Chamber), 8 April 2014, Digital Rights Ireland, Joined Cases C-293/12 and C-594/12.

[9] Judgment of the Court (Grand Chamber), 13 May 2014, Google Spain SL and Google Inc. v Agencia Española de Protección de Datos (AEPD) and Mario Costeja González, C-131/12.

[10] COM(2012) 11 final, 2012/0011, (COD) C7-0025/12, Proposal for a Regulation of the European Parliament and of the Council on the protection of individuals with regard to the processing of personal data and on the free movement of such data.

[11] Context of the proposal, no. 1, last paragraph.

[12] It has a reference in Recital 72.

[13] Article 9.

[14] E.g., Articles 13(1)-(f), 14(1)-(f), and 15(2) of GDPR; and Recitals 20, 56, 57 and 59 and Article 25 of DPD.

[15] Articles 13(2)-(f), 14(2)-(f), and 15(1)-h of GDPR and Recitals 71; and Article 12(a) and Article 15 of DPD.

[16] E.g., Recitals 85-87 and Article 33 of GDPR.

[17] Articles 15 to 20 of GDPR.

[18] Article 22 of GDPR and Article 15 of DDPR.

[19] Articles 51-54, 37, 35 and 42.

[20] Articles 37-39.

[21] E.g. Recitals 84 and 90 and Article 35.

[22] Recital 82 and Article 19 of GDPR.

[23] Recital 7.

[24] Recital 148 and Articles 83 and 84 of GDPR.

[25] Article 18 of DPD.

[26] Article 3(1)

[27] Article 3(2). In addition, Article 3(3) confirms the application of the GDPR to the processing of personal data where Member State law applies by virtue of public international law. Moreover, while Article 4 of the DPD made reference to the 'use of equipment' in the Union's territory as a basis for bringing controllers who were *not established on Community territory* within the scope of EU data protection law, such a reference does not appear in Article 3 of the GDPR.

[28] E.g., Article 25 (1) and (2); see, also, e.g., recital 78 and article 5(1) (d) GRPD). See still Carloni and Falcone, 2017, pp. 727-728; and p. 732.

²⁹   Article 37 of GDPR.

³⁰   As Hoofnagle, Sloot and Borgesius highlight, the data protection officer has the task of documenting what actually happens with data, and so data depredations will be more difficult to hide and, in enforcement proceedings, the accounting that companies have to undertake will provide the proof of noncompliance (2019, p. 68).

³¹   Article 37 (6) and Article 38(4).

³²   Article 37 (1)). A group of undertakings may appoint a single data protection officer provided that a data protection officer is easily accessible from each establishment (article 37 (2)).

³³   Article 39(1) -b).

³⁴   Recital 13 states that it is important to "provide natural persons in all Member States with the same level of legally enforceable rights and obligations and responsibilities for controllers and processors, to ensure consistent monitoring of the processing of personal data".

³⁵   ECJ Judgment 4 April 2014, Digital Rights Ireland Ltd (C-293/12) and Kärntner Landesregierung (C-594/12), para. 68.

³⁶   For instance, the general conditions for the members of the supervisory authority, some rules on the establishment of the supervisory authority and the competence, tasks and powers are set in the GDPR (Article 52 to Article 59).

³⁷   See, for instance, Recital 139. See also Article 63, about consistency mechanism, and Articles 60-62, respectively about *cooperation between the lead supervisory authority and the other supervisory authorities concerned*, mutual assistance and about *joint operations of supervisory authorities.*

³⁸   See, for instance, Article 52(4), Recitals 123 and 139, and Article 51(2)-(4).

³⁹   See, for instance, Kędzior, 2018, p. 506; and Tambou, 2018, p. 24. See, also, for instance, Recital 136.

⁴⁰   A cooperative relationship is, for instance, implied in the *one-stop-shop mechanism* (e.g., Recitals 127 and 128). About the 'one-stop-shop', see Scholta and al., 2019.

Under the one-stop shop mechanism, businesses only have to deal with one supervisory authority (in the EU country where they have their main establishment) in the case of cross-border processing (Articles 56 and 60 of GDPR).

⁴¹   Article 5(1) (a)-(d).

⁴²   E.g., Article 12(1), (4) and (7) of GDPR.

⁴³   Article 19 and 20 of GDPR.

⁴⁴   Article 20 (1) GDPR states that the data subject has the right to transmit the personal data concerning him or her data to another controller without hindrance from the controller to which the personal data have been provided, where (…) the processing is based on consent…or on a contract and the processing is carried out by automated means.

⁴⁵   Article 20 (2) GDPR.

⁴⁶   Article 20.° (3).

⁴⁷   Bearing in mind the conditions stated for the exercise of the right of portability: the processing shall be based on consent, regarding general data and special categories of personal data, or on a contract, regarding general data, and the processing shall be carried out by automated means (Article 20-(1)).

⁴⁸   The objective of the data portability is to *further strengthen the control* of the data subject over *his or her own data* (Recital 68).

⁴⁹   *E.g.* Hoofnagle, Sloot and Borgesius, 2019, p. 69.

⁵⁰ Judgment of the Court (Grand Chamber) of 4 April 2017, European Ombudsman v Claire Staelen, Case C-337/15 P, para. 34. See also Article 41 of the Charter of Fundamental Rights of the European Union, (2016/C 202/02).

⁵¹ For instance, see Article VI-20 of Book VI (Administrative Information Management) of *ReNEUAL Model Rules on EU Administrative Procedures,* Book VI – Administrative Information Management, Drafting Team: Diana-Urania Galetta and al., 2014, p. 254 *(*http://www.reneual.eu/*).* See also Communication of the Commission to the European Parliament, the Council, the European Economic and Social Committee and the Committee of Regions, Online Platforms and the Digital Single Market – opportunities and challenges for Europe, Brussels, 25 May 2016, COM(2016) 288 final.

⁵² The Recital 5 clearly mentions: National authorities in the Member States are being called upon by Union law to cooperate and exchange personal data so as to be able to perform their duties or carry out tasks on behalf of an authority in another Member State.

⁵³ Article 2(1) of Decision (EU) 2015/2240, of the European Parliament and of the Council, 25th November 2015, establishing a programme on interoperability solutions and common frameworks for European public administrations, businesses and citizens (ISA2 programme) as a means for modernizing the public sector. Member States must implement all necessary measures to promote interoperability under the ISA2 programme so that electronic registrations, IT tools and Social Media can work to benefit the complete implementation of a Digital Single Market. At a sector level, see Judgment of ECJ (Ninth Chamber) of 22 March 2017, C-665/15, Commission v Portugal (failure of the Member State to use of and connect to the EU network within the EU driving licence network); and Judgment of ECJ (Tenth Chamber) of 5 October 2016, Commission v Portugal, C-583/15 (failure of Portugal "to create a national electronic register of road transport undertakings and by failing therefore to establish the interconnection with the electronic registers of other Member States").

⁵⁴ *Public administrations should ensure that citizens and businesses supply the same information only once to a public* administration. See, for instance, "Digital4EU" 2016 – Stakeholder Forum Report: https://ec.europa.eu/digital-single-market/en/news/digital4eu-2016-report.
Joana Covelo de Abreu (2017, p. 129) argues that *the evolvement of this principle includes not only data that has severe importance to governmental matters (such as the name, the address, the employment) but also concerning all data provided on proceedings that were set in motion by individuals.*

⁵⁵ Article 5(1)-a) and b) of GDPR.

⁵⁶ Article 5(1)-a), d) and f), of GDPR.

⁵⁷ Rights related to the use of technology (Richard, 2016, p. 99). See also, e.g., Malgieri, 2019.

⁵⁸ E.g., Malgieri and Comandé, 2017; and Wachter, Mittelstadt and Floridi, 2017.
Edwards and Veale (2018, p. 7) argue: *Rights become dangerous things if they are unreasonably hard to exercise or ineffective in results, because they give the illusion that something has been done while in fact things are no better.* They claim that there is a risk of the right to explanation turning into an empty right similar to what happens to consent of the data subjects.

⁵⁹ See, for instance, European Parliament, in March 2019, *Understanding algorithmic decision-making: Opportunities and challenges,* p. VII (and p. 78), whose authors are Castelluccia and Le Métayer. It is highlighted that *transparency and explainability may allow for the discovery of deficiencies, but do not provide absolute guarantees for the reliability, security or fairness of an ADS* (algorithmic

decision systems). It is argued that *accountability is the most important requirement as far as the protection of individuals is concerned* and that this *can be achieved via complementary means such as AIAs* [algorithmic impact assessments], *auditing and certification.*

[60]   As decision-making processes by human beings are not necessarily 'better' than but simply different automated decision-making systems, different kinds or bias, risk or error are likely to develop in automated decision-making – Council of Europe (2018). Study on the human rights dimensions of automated data processing techniques (in particular algorithms) and possible regulatory implications, p. 43.

[61]   Consiglio di Stato, Judgment of 13 of December 2019, N. 02936/2019 REG.RIC; and Federal Constitutional Court, Order of 6 November 2019, 1 BvR 276/17 -Right to be forgotten II and Order of 6 November 2019, 1 BvR 16/13 - Right to be forgotten I.

[62]   E.g., Article 52(4).

[63]   Directive 2003/4/EC of the European Parliament and of the Council of 28 January 2003 is repealed with effect from 17 July 2021.

[64]   See, for instance, the definition of binding corporate rules and the expected engagement of the group of undertakings, or group of enterprises to ensure compliance with them (e.g., Articles 47(2)-j) and l) of GDPR); and the role that a*ssociations or other bodies representing categories of controllers or processors can play by drawing up codes of conduct.*(Recital 98).

[65]   As Hoofnagle, Sloot and Borgesius state that they are an appealing set of substantive and procedural protections against the power of data intensive companies (2019, p. 77).

[66]   Article 5(1)-d).

[67]   Article 17 and Judgment of ECJ (Grand Chamber) of 13 May 2014, Google Spain SL and Google Inc. v Agencia Española de Protección de Datos (AEPD) and Mario Costeja González.

[68]   Article 15.

[69]   Article 18.

[70]   Some personal data are, by their nature, tendentially private, but the data protection right is not, structurally, a right about privacy. The right to informational self-determination is somewhat between the two and relates to the decision of an individual to let others know information about him/her, in an informed and conscious manner - Lepage (2017, p. 38) highlights that informational self-determination *results in particular in better information for the person, prior to any well-considered decision.*

The ECtHR case-law ensures the protection of personal data within the scope of the right to privacy, which is the result of the lack of a specific provision in the European Convention on Human Rights, as well as of the fact that many personal data relate to personal life, to expectation of keeping it reserved. See, for instance, US Supreme Court case of United States v. Miller, 425, 437 (1976); Obserdorff, 2016, p. 48 (refers the use of data subjects' personal data to have a social or a public life); Judgment Antović and Mirković v. Montenegro, 28 of November 2017, Application no 70838/13, para. 42.

[71]   Legal persons are excluded from data protection but they can rely on the right to privacy (e.g. ECtHR Judgment 3 September 2015, Sérvulo & Associados – Sociedade de Advogados, RL and others c. Portugal, application 27013/10).

[72]   Data protection is in general about licit, fair, and purposing processing. The interference with private life is about justifications.

[73] As the author said, the view that any type of processing of personal data interferes with the right to data protection, besides introducing a cyclical argument, is counter-intuitive because it also includes lawful processing that complies with all the requirements of Article 8 EUCFR.

[74] According to Margot E. Kaminski, transparency is a basic principle of the GDPR. She writes:, it may be surprising to an American audience how many of GPDP's rights look like open government laws rather than reasons for traditional privacy actions' (2019, p. 209).

[75] Recital 4 states that GDPR respects all fundamental rights and observes the freedoms and principles recognised in the Charter as enshrined in the Treaties, in particular the respect for private and family life, home and communications, the protection of personal data, freedom of thought, conscience and religion, freedom of expression and information, freedom to conduct a business, the right to an effective remedy and to a fair trial, and cultural, religious and linguistic diversity.

[76] It is possible to say that both constitute a limit to each other (Hendrickx, 2019, p. 252).

[77] Judgement of ECtHR, GC, of 8 November 2016, Magyar Helsinki Bizottság *versus* Hungary, Application no. 18030/11.

[78] The right to data protection shall be seen as an *EU citizens' right* (Granger and Irion, 2018).

[79] See, for instance, Carloni and Falcone, 2017, pp. 733 and 744; and European Union Agency for Fundamental Rights, Fundamental Rights Report 2019, p. 50: In Belgium, for instance, Article 29 of the draft Act concerning the processing of personal data establishes an exception to data protection when journalistic, academic, artistic or literary forms of expression are at stake. In an opinion on the draft Act, the Council of State underlined that the exceptions in its Article 29 lead to a more restrictive definition of the freedom of expression than Article 11 (freedom of expression and information) of the Charter would allow. The law was ultimately adopted without taking the Council of State's opinion into account.

[80] Cobbaut (2019, p. 313) states that the Directive on the protection of persons reporting on breaches of Union law persons, as well as the Trade Secret Directive, *even if they might constitute restrictions on freedom of expression, are also opportunities to extend the field of application of Article 11.*

[81] Carloni and Falcone, 2017, pp. 735-736.

[82] See, for instance, Mantelero, 2014; Felzmann et al., 2019 (they show *the critical relations between transparency* and *informed consent*); and Data Protection Working Party, *Guidelines on consent under Regulation 2016/679*, adopted on 28 November 2017.

[83] And Article 30.

[84] ECtHR judgment of 17 of July 2008, I v. Finland, Application 20511/03. Controllers have a positive duty not to include impertinent or unnecessary information in individual files or records and to ensure that access to it must take place in compliance with the purposes for which it was collected and processed.

[85] Member States' laws that have implemented the GDPR in the field of automated decision-making provide some additional measures to safeguard the data subject's rights and freedoms and legitimate interests (Malgieri, 2019, p. 2).

[86] Council of Europe, Guidelines on the protection of individuals with regard to the processing of personal data in a world of Big Data, 2017, No. 9 (https://rm.coe.int/16806ebe7a).

[87] As significantly establishes the Article 9(2) of the Spanish Constitution: It is the responsibility of the public authorities to promote conditions ensuring that freedom and equality of individuals and of the groups to which they belong are real and effective, to remove the obstacles preventing

or hindering their full enjoyment, and to facilitate the participation of all citizens in political, economic, cultural and social life.

Chapter 2
Revisiting the Basics of EU Data Protection Law:
On the Material and Territorial Scope of the GDPR

Dimosthenis Lentzis

Aristotle University of Thessaloniki, Greece

ABSTRACT

It is often said that the EU General Data Protection Regulation (GDPR) has a much broader material and territorial scope than the EU Data Protection Directive it has recently replaced. This chapter tries to find out if (and, if so, to what extent) this assumption is correct. To this end, it analyzes, in the light of the existing case-law of the Court of Justice of the EU, the relevant provisions of the GDPR, namely Articles 2 and 3. It comes out that the GDPR has a slightly different (but not necessarily broader) material scope and a broader (but not as broad as one would expect) territorial scope than the old EU Data Protection Directive.

INTRODUCTION

May 25, 2018, marked the beginning of a new era in the protection of personal data in Europe and beyond (Albrecht, 2016). It was the date the EU General Data Protection Regulation (hereinafter, GDPR) became fully applicable, replacing the 22-year-old EU Data Protection Directive which had long ceased to meet the challenges of the constantly evolving online environment (Lambert, 2017, pp. 35-36). The GDPR is intended to provide a stronger and more coherent legal framework for the protection of personal data in the EU *in order to create the trust that will allow the digital economy to develop across the internal market* in a way combining human rights protection (GDPR, Recital 7); it gives data subjects new rights, including the right to portability and the right to be forgotten, and imposes new obligations on data controllers and data processors, including notice and privacy by design requirements. There is a widespread belief that the new regulation has a much broader material and territorial scope than the EU

DOI: 10.4018/978-1-5225-9489-5.ch002

Data Protection Directive it has replaced. This chapter tries to find out if (and, if so, to what extent) this assumption is correct. To this end, it analyzes the unfortunately rather obscure relevant provisions of the GDPR, namely Art. 2 on the different types of processing of personal data to which the GDPR applies or does not apply (part A) and Art. 3 on the conditions under which a data controller or data processor established or not established in the EU is bound to comply with the GDPR (part B).

Four preliminary remarks should be made at this point.

First, in the EU, the protection of natural persons in relation to the processing of their personal data is recognized as a fundamental right (CJEU, Case C-275/06, *Promusicae*, judgment of the Court, para. 63) – a fundamental right independent from (although closely connected with) the fundamental right to privacy or private life from which it originates (Tzanou, 2011). Art. 16(1) TFEU, which is the legal basis of the GDPR, and Art. 8(1) of the EU Charter of Fundamental Rights stipulate that everyone has the right to the protection of personal data concerning him or her. Along the same line, the GDPR affirms in its very first Art. that it protects fundamental rights and freedoms of individuals and in particular the right to the protection of personal data. The fundamental nature of the right to the protection of personal data must always be taken into account when interpreting the GDPR's provisions.

Second, the existing case-law on the interpretation of the EU Data Protection Directive is in principle relevant for the interpretation of the GDPR. In numerous occasions over the past 22 years, the provisions of the EU Data Protection Directive have been interpreted by the Court of Justice of the EU (hereinafter, CJEU) in the context of the preliminary reference procedure of Art. 267 TFEU, the formal mechanism of judicial dialogue between the CJEU and national courts that ensures the uniform interpretation and application of EU law in the Member States. In all these occasions, the CJEU has opted for a teleological interpretation guided by the aim to offer enhanced protection of personal data and resulting to a dynamic approach of the relevant concepts. The EU legislature has endorsed, and thus legitimized, almost every solution adopted by the CJEU, with the formal recognition of a right to erasure (also known as right to be forgotten, right to oblivion and right to delete) being the most striking example.

Third, the GDPR was incorporated into the European Economic Area (EEA) Agreement by the EEA Joint Committee in Brussels on July 6, 2018, and entered into force in all three EEA European Free Trade Association States (Norway, Iceland and Liechtenstein) a few days later. In the present chapter, all references to the EU, EU Member State(s) or Member State(s) should be understood to include the EEA European Free Trade Association States.

Finally, this chapter makes extensive use of the GDPR's recitals. In EU law, recitals provide the reasons the articles of a legal act have been adopted; they can be used to resolve ambiguity in related legislative provisions, but since they have no binding legal force they can never be relied on either as a ground for derogating from those provisions or for interpreting them in a way clearly contrary to their wording (Klimas & Vaičiukaité, 2008).

MATERIAL SCOPE OF THE GDPR

The rules on the material scope of the GDPR are contained in Art. 2 thereof. Art. 2(1) specifies the situations in which the GDPR applies (section 1), whereas Art. 2(2) lists the situations excluded from its application (section 2).

Types of Processing Covered by the GDPR

According to Art. 2(1), the GDPR applies *to the processing of personal data wholly or partly by automated means and to the processing other than by automated means of personal data which form part of a filing system or are intended to form part of a filing system*. This provision is identical to that of Art. 3(1) of the EU Data Protection Directive. For the GDPR to apply it does not matter if the data processor is a public authority or a private party. However, it should be noted that the GDPR is addressed solely to the Member States; the processing of personal data by EU institutions, bodies, offices and agencies has always been governed by a separate EU legal act, Regulation 45/2001 in the past and Regulation 2018/1725 since December 2018.

Processing of personal data wholly or partly by automated means is admittedly the *raison d'être* of any modern legislation on the protection of personal data. Even before the time of the internet, it was clear to everyone that all major threats to personal data were coming from the unprecedented processing capabilities offered by computers. Today, the changes in social life that technology has brought about must also be considered. Indeed, not only private companies and public authorities have now, thanks to technology, an almost unlimited capacity to collect, analyze and use personal data in order to pursue their activities, but also natural persons willingly share more and more personal information through social media (GDPR, Recital 6). Therefore, and since the GDPR is, by design, technology neutral in order to avoid becoming obsolete (Castro-Edwards, 2017, p. 4), the term *automated means* should be interpreted broadly to include all the different technology options used to process personal data (computers, smartphones and other smart devices, etc). The CJEU has ruled that processing of personal data by automated means includes placing information on an internet page because it entails the operation of loading that page onto a server and the operations necessary to make it accessible to people who are connected to the internet (CJEU, Case C-101/01, *Lindquist*, judgment of the Court, paras. 26-27), surveillance in the form of a video recording of persons (CJEU, Case C-212/13, *Ryneš*, judgment of the Court, para. 25) and filming and recording of public officials carrying out their duties at their place of work and the subsequent publication of the video recording on the internet (CJEU, Case C-345/17, *Buivids*, judgment of the Court, para. 47). Processing of personal data by automated means is the rule for private companies, even for small ones, and public authorities.

In order to prevent the risk of circumvention, the GDPR also applies to the manual processing of personal data, but only if these data are contained or are intended to be contained in a filing system. Contrary to automated processing, manual processing is being entirely executed by humans without using machines (Voigt & von dem Bussche, 2017, p. 10). *Filing system* is defined in Art. 4(6) of the GDPR as *any structured set of personal data which are accessible according to specific criteria, whether centralized, decentralized or dispersed on a functional or geographical basis*. This definition is much broader than that of the EU Data Protection Directive (Kelleher & Murray, 2018, p. 62). HR files organized according to names of employees are a typical example of a filing system. In a recent judgment, the CJEU held that the set of personal data collected, otherwise than by automated means, by members of a religious community, in the context of door-to-door proselytizing, on the basis of a specific geographical allocation and for the purposes of preparation for subsequent visits to people with whom a spiritual dialogue has been begun, is capable of constituting a filing system (CJEU, Case C-25/17, *Jehovan todistajat*, judgment of the Court, paras. 53-62). Files that are not structured according to specific criteria were excluded from the material scope of the GDPR most probably because of the very high degree of processing necessary to extract personal data from them. Manual processing of personal data, generally on paper, is sometimes done by private companies and public authorities for back-up purposes, but much more often by natural persons as part of their personal or household activities.

Types of Processing Not Covered by the GDPR

There are overall four types of processing of personal data to which the GDPR does not apply. More specifically, pursuant to Art. 2(2), the GDPR is not applicable to the processing of personal data, (a) in the course of activities that fall outside the scope of EU law, (b) by the Member States when carrying out activities that fall within the scope of Chapter 2 of Title V of the TEU, (c) by natural persons as part of purely personal or household activities, and (d) by competent authorities for the purpose of the prevention, investigation, detection or prosecution of criminal offences or the execution of criminal penalties. Although the corresponding provision of the EU Data Protection Directive, Art. 3(2), had a somewhat different wording, in essence, it provided for exactly the same exceptions. The inapplicability of the GDPR in the above cases does not necessarily mean that natural persons enjoy no protection at all; other acts of EU law, national law or public international law on the protection of personal data may apply.

Despite the fact that, as a principle, the EU has only the competences conferred upon it by the Member States and that competences not conferred upon it remain with the Member States (TEU, Art. 5), the division of competencies between the EU and its Member States has always been a complex issue – and one that has led to many disputes before the CJEU. The only example of activities falling outside the scope of EU law the GDPR gives is that of activities concerning national security (GDPR, Recital 16). This reference reflects not only Art. 4(2) TEU, which explicitly states that national security remains the sole responsibility of each Member State, but also Declaration no. 20 annexed to the Treaty of Lisbon, which urges that *whenever rules on protection of personal data to be adopted (…) could have direct implications for national security, due account will have to be taken of the specific characteristics of the matter.* Other competencies that have beyond any doubt not been conferred upon the EU and thus remain with the Member States include the conditions for the acquisition and loss of nationality, family law, inheritance law, the content of teaching and the organization of educational systems, and direct taxation. In any event, the exception covers activities of the Member States or the authorities of the Member States and not of individuals (CJEU, Case C-101/01, *Lindquist*, judgment of the Court, paras. 43-44, CJEU, Case C-73/07, *Satakunnan Markkinapörssi and Satamedia*, judgment of the Court, paras. 40-42, and CJEU, Case C-73/16, *Puškár*, judgment of the Court, para. 36).

Chapter 2 of Title V of the TEU governs the common foreign and security policy (CFSP) of the EU. The CFSP covers all areas of foreign policy and all questions relating to the EU's security, including the progressive framing of a common defence policy that might lead to a common defence (TEU, Art. 24). Hence, when Member States process personal data for the needs of the CFSP, the GDPR does not apply. This is primarily the case of the processing of personal data in order to establish the lists of natural persons that will be the subjects of EU targeted sanctions – most usually restrictive measures such as asset freezing and prohibition of entry into or transit through the territories of the Member States – with a view to combat international terrorism. According to Art. 39 TEU, the Council is under an obligation to adopt a decision laying down special rules relating to the protection of individuals with regard to the processing of personal data by the Member States when carrying out activities falling within the scope of the CFSP, but, almost ten years after the entry into force of the Treaty of Lisbon, no such decision has been adopted. It is therefore important to bear in mind that the CFSP constitutes only one aspect of the EU's multi-faceted action on the international scene. Consequently, whenever processing personal data in the context of the common commercial policy (Arts. 206-207 TFEU), development cooperation (Arts. 208-211 TFEU), economic, financial and technical cooperation with third countries (Arts. 212-213 TFEU), and humanitarian aid (Art. 214 TFEU), Member States have to comply with the GDPR.

The term *personal or household activities* refers to activities with no connection at all to a professional or commercial activity; it does not cover activities that are partly personal or household and partly professional or commercial (Voigt & von dem Bussche, 2017, p. 16). The exception was originally introduced to include the holding of addresses, E-mail addresses, phone numbers, birthdays etc., as well as the processing of various data for hobbies and vacation or entertainment purposes. Today, the main issue lies in the placing of personal data on social media. Could just tweeting *at* another person trigger the applicability of EU data protection legislation? In contrast with the EU Data protection Directive which was adopted at a time when social media simply did not exist, the GDPR is aware of the problem but does very little to tackle it. Recital 18 merely explains that personal or household activities also include *social networking and online activity undertaken within the context of such activities*. Moreover, in an effort to avoid misunderstandings, the same Recital adds that the GDPR does apply *to controllers and processors which provide the means for processing personal data for (...) personal of household activities*. From its part, the CJEU has repeatedly pointed out that, since this exception relates only to activities carried out in the course of private or family life of individuals, it does not apply to the processing of personal data consisting in publication on the internet so that those data are made accessible to an *indefinite number of people*, even if this publication is privately motivated, thus expanding the criterion of "space" as far as the notion of household is concerned (CJEU, Case C-101/01, *Lindquist*, judgment of the Court, para. 47, and CJEU, Case C-73/07, *Satakunnan Markkinapörssi and Satamedia*, judgment of the Court, paras. 43-44). It is submitted that the Court's conclusion, which is valid for any other form of public communication of personal data (Erdos, 2015, p. 124), allows the assumption that if personal data are made available through social media only to a limited number of people (e.g. only to a limited number of friends on Facebook), the exception will apply. This assumption is corroborated by two recent judgments of the CJEU. More specifically, in a case concerning the use of CCTV, the CJEU ruled that, to the extent that video surveillance covers even partially a public space and is accordingly directed outwards from the *private setting* of the person processing the data in that manner, it cannot be regarded as an activity which is a purely personal or household one (CJEU, Case C-212/13, *Ryneš*, judgment of the Court, para. 33), whereas in another one concerning door-to-door preaching by members of the Jehovah's Witnesses Community it stressed that the proselytizing in the course of which the personal data of the persons visited are collected goes beyond the household setting of the person processing the data because this person leaves his or her private and family setting in order to meet, in their homes, people who are not in their *inner circle* (CJEU, Case C-25/17, *Jehovan todistajat*, judgment of the Court, paras. 42-44). It seems that for the CJEU the actual or virtual setting of the person processing the data and the nature of the relationship between that person and the group of people to whom the data was communicated are just as important as the purpose of the processing (Butler, 2015, p. 2).

The protection of natural persons with regard to the processing of personal data by competent national authorities for the purpose of the prevention, investigation, detection or prosecution of criminal offences or the execution of criminal penalties, including the safeguarding against and the prevention of threats to public security, has early on been the subject of a separate EU legal act. In the past, there was Framework Decision 2008/977, today there is Directive 2016/680. The need for special rules on the protection of personal data in the fields of judicial cooperation in criminal matters and police cooperation has also been acknowledged in Declaration no. 21 annexed to the Treaty of Lisbon, in which reference is made to the sensitive nature of these activities. The rules contained in Directive 2016/680 are intended to be applied by judicial authorities, the police and other law enforcement agencies. Obviously, however, it is the purpose of the processing of personal data and not the nature of the national authority processing them that matters. Therefore, it goes without saying that, when a national authority, like the Prosecutor's Office, processes personal data for purposes other than those described in Directive 2016/680, it is the GDPR that applies (GDPR, Recital 19, Directive 2016/680, Recital 11).

It is clear from the above that the material scope of application of the GDPR is particularly wide. On the one hand, the types of processing covered by the GDPR are defined in a broad way, broad enough to ensure that the new legal framework will be applied even to the collection of personal data through wearables. On the other hand, the fundamental nature of the right to the protection of personal data and the existing case-law of the CJEU leave no doubt that all the exceptions the GDPR provides for are meant to be – and will be – strictly interpreted. But there is nothing new in all this. The only real difference with the repealed EU Data Protection Directive lies is the modest attempt to adapt to the reality of social networks (Feiler, Forgó & Weigl, 2018, p. 49). Actually, the main question regarding the material scope of application of the GDPR is how strictly the exception for data processing related to personal or household activities will be interpreted in cases concerning the disclosure of personal data on social networks.

TERRITORIAL SCOPE OF THE GDPR

The rules on the territorial scope of the GDPR are contained in Art. 3 thereof. Art. 3(1) lays down the conditions under which the GDPR applies to data controllers and data processors established in the EU territory (section 1), whereas Art. 3(2) those under which the GDPR applies to data controllers and data processors established outside the EU territory (section 2). Note that, pursuant to Art. 3(3), the GDPR also applies *to the processing of personal data by a controller not established in the Union, but in a place where Member State law applies by virtue of public international law*. Recital 25 provides the example of Member States' diplomatic missions or consular posts; another one is that of ships or offshore constructions carrying the flag of a Member State.

Data Controllers and Data Processors Established in the EU

According to Art. 3(1), the primary factor that gives rise to the territorial applicability of the GDPR is *the processing of personal data in the context of the activities of an establishment of a controller or a processor in the Union* (CJEU, Case C-131/12, *Google Spain*, opinion of AG Jääskinen, point 60). The same provision goes on to clarify that, in that case, the GDPR is applicable *regardless of whether the [data] processing takes place in the Union or not*. The provision of Art. 3(1) of the GDPR is essentially identical to that of Art. 4(1)(a) of the EU Data Protection Directive, with the exception of the reference to *the territory of the Member States* which has been replaced by the requirement that the data controller or data processor must be established *in the Union*. This was done because, as a Regulation, the GDPR does not need transposition into the legal systems of the Member States, but is applied uniformly in the entirety of the EU territory (Gömann, 2017, p. 574). There are two key questions related to this provision.

The first key question is the following: When is a data controller or data processor established on the EU territory?

The answer to this question is not as straightforward as it may seem at first glance. Recital 22 of the GDPR explains that the term *establishment* implies *the effective and real exercise of activity through stable arrangements* and that *the legal form of such arrangements, whether through a branch or a subsidiary with a legal personality, is not the determining factor in that respect.* This is the same wording as in Recital 19 of the EU Data Protection Directive. In his opinion in the *Weltimmo* case, Advocate General Cruz Villalón suggested that, by using this wording, the EU legislature has opted for a flexible definition of the concept of establishment, which departs from a formalistic approach whereby undertakings are established solely in the place where they are registered (CJEU, Case C-230/14, *Weltimmo*, opinion of AG Cruz Villalón, point 28). The CJEU agreed with the Advocate General and concluded that, in order to determine whether the data processor or data controller has an establishment in the EU, both the degree of stability of the arrangements and the effective exercise of activities in the EU must be interpreted in the light of the specific nature of the economic activities and the provision of services concerned (CJEU, Case C-230/14, *Weltimmo*, judgment of the Court, para. 29). In other words, the existence of an establishment depends to a large extent on a case-by-case analysis (Voigt & von dem Bussche, 2017, p. 23).

For undertakings offering services exclusively over the internet, the above means that the presence of only one representative could, under certain circumstances, constitute a stable arrangement if that representative acts with a sufficient degree of stability through the presence of the necessary equipment for provision of the specific services in the EU (CJEU, Case C-230/14, *Weltimmo*, judgment of the Court, paras. 30-33). Thus, an undertaking with a representative serving as a point of contact, a bank account and a letter box in a Member State was deemed to have an establishment in the EU from the moment it pursued a real and effective activity – even a minimal one – there (in that particular case it was the running of a property dealing website containing advertisements of properties situated in a Member State, which were written in the language of that Member State and were subject to a fee after an initial period of one month). However, the mere fact that an undertaking's website is accessible in a Member State cannot suffice to constitute an establishment in the EU in the absence of other factors capable of showing that it has stable arrangements there (CJEU, Case C-191/15, *Verein für Konsumenteninformation*, judgment of the Court, para. 76), although, as we will see below, the GDPR may still be applicable via Art. 3(2)(a) on the offering of goods and services to data subjects in the EU by data controllers or data processors established outside the EU.

The second key question is: When is the processing of personal data taking place in the context of the activities of the establishment?

Again, the answer to this question is not as simple as one might think. The only thing that is certain is that there in no need for the establishment to curry out any data processing activities itself. Of course, if it does curry out such activities, the GDPR will definitely apply. But even if it does not, the GDPR will still be applicable as long as there is a close and preferably economic connection between the data processing taking place somewhere outside the EU and the activities of the EU establishment (Feiler, Forgó & Weigl, 2018, p. 52, Voigt & von dem Bussche, 2017, p. 24). This was made clear in the *Google Spain* case. The case was about Google Inc., a US based company which operates Google Search, and one of its subsidiaries in the EU, Google Spain SL; the latter was intended to promote and sell in Spain advertising space offered by the first's search engine in order to make the service offered by that engine profitable. It was not disputed that the processing of the personal data at issue in that case was curried out exclusively by Google Inc., without any intervention on the part of Google Spain. Yet, the CJEU held that processing of personal data is also carried out *in the context of the activities of an establish-*

ment of a data controller or data processor in the EU when the operator of a search engine established outside the EU (in that case Google Inc.) sets up in a Member State a branch or subsidiary (in that case Google Spain SL) which is intended to promote and sell advertising space offered by that engine and which orientates its activity towards the inhabitants of that Member State (CJEU, Case C-131/12, *Google Spain*, judgment of the Court, paras. 52-60). This very broad reading of the words *in the context of the activities of an establishment* is to be attributed to the fundamental nature of the right to the protection of personal data.

In fact, as it has been rightly observed, with *Google Spain* the requirement of processing *in the context of the activities of an establishment* was virtually set aside (Gömann, 2017, p. 574). This allowed the CJEU to avoid *the odd situation whereby the EU data protection rules would not apply to a Spanish citizen who, through a Spanish website, searches on his own name, and finds a link to a Spanish website of a Spanish newspaper which published his personal data on something that happened in Spain* (Kranenborg, 2015, p. 76), but, combined with the fact that the threshold for being established in the EU is very law (Kelleher & Murray, 2018, p. 113), it also resulted to the EU Data Protection Directive and today the GDPR having extraterritorial effect. For example, the GDPR will be also applicable to the processing of personal data done by a Canadian company that has an office in Paris, whether the data subjects are French, Canadian or American, whether they accessed the company's services from France, Canada or the USA, and even if all the processing occurs in Canada, if the supporting activity of the Paris office is connected, no matter how loosely, to the processing taking place in Canada (Taylor, 2018). To many this has no sense and this is why it is suggested that, in order to determine whether the GDPR applies, one must also look at the nationality or location of the data subject. Accordingly, only citizens of the EU, regardless of their place of residence, and residents in the EU Member States, regardless of their nationality, should be able to rely on the provisions of the GDPR. However, neither the actual wording of Art. 3(1) of the GDPR nor the relevant case-law of the CJEU supports this view. Nationality and place of residence of data subjects are not decisive in the context of this provision.

The extraterritorial effect resulting from the CJEU's reading of the requirement at issue, apart from not being easily identifiable as such, faces a major challenge: to respect international comity. International comity requires national law creating cross-border obligations to be interpreted and applied in a manner that minimizes the risk of conflict with foreign law. This leads to a presumption against extraterritoriality. Sometimes, however, extraterritoriality is justified under the so-called *effects doctrine* developed in the USA. In the EU, this doctrine is usually linked with EU competition law, the extraterritorial application of which is recognized so long as the economic effects of the anticompetitive conduct are experienced on the domestic (: European) market (Torremans, 1996; for other examples of extraterritorial reach of EU law see Scott, 2014). In the case of processing of personal data in the context of the activities of an establishment of a controller or a processor in the EU, the actual conduct could be the processing of personal data outside the EU territory. But what is the effect of that conduct in the EU when the data subject is neither an EU citizen nor a resident of a Member State? And even if there is an effect in the EU, is it substantial and foreseeable enough, as the effects doctrine requires, to support jurisdiction? The answers to the aforementioned questions will determine whether the extraterritorial reach of the GDPR in such cases is respectful of international comity or not. Suffice to say here that more and more commentators suggest that both these questions should be answered in the negative (Taylor, 2017, Tene & Wolf, 2013).

Data Controllers and Data Processors Established Outside the EU

Art. 3(2) of the GDPR provides for two instances in which it applies to data controllers and data processors not established in the EU. More specifically, the GDPR applies to such data controllers or data processors if the data subjects are in the EU and the processing activities are related to (a) the offering of goods or services or (b) the monitoring of the data subjects' behavior. No similar provisions were to be found in the EU Data Protection Directive.

(a) In the first case, the case of *targeting*, for the GDPR to apply it should be apparent that the data controller or data processor established outside the EU envisages offering goods or services to data subjects in one or more Member States in the EU. The GDPR contains a non-exhaustive list of criteria that can be useful in revealing the data controller's or data processor's intentions. More specifically, Recital 23 of the GDPR clarifies that *whereas the mere accessibility of the controller's, processor's or an intermediary's website in the Union, of an email address or of other contact details, or the use of a language generally used in the third country where the controller is established, is insufficient to ascertain such intention, factors such as the use of a language or a currency generally used in one or more Member States with the possibility of ordering goods and services in that other language, or the mentioning of customers or users who are in the Union, may make it apparent that the controller envisages offering goods or services to data subjects in the Union.* Interestingly enough, the CJEU uses the same criteria in cases concerning jurisdiction over consumer contracts in order to determine whether a trader's activity is directed to the Member State of the consumer's domicile, together with other factors, like the use of a top-level domain name of a Member State, targeted advertising to consumers in a Member State and the mentioning of the possibility of delivery of the goods or services in a Member State (CJEU, Case C-585/08 and Case C-144/09, *Pammer and Hotel Alpenhof*, judgment of the Court, paras. 75-84). The extraterritorial application of the GDPR under this provision mostly affects international corporations doing business through the Internet (Voigt & von dem Bussche, 2017, p. 26). Nevertheless, the provision expressly states that the GDPR applies irrespective of whether a payment by the data subject is required, even if, that is to say, the goods or services are offered to the data subject for free (Kelleher & Murray, 2018, p. 114).

(b) The GDPR is also applicable when data processing is related to the *monitoring* of a person's behavior. According to Recital 24 of the GDPR, in order to determine whether a data processing activity can be considered to monitor the behavior of data subjects, it should be ascertained *whether natural persons are tracked on the internet including potential subsequent use of personal data processing techniques which consist of profiling a natural person, particularly in order to take decisions concerning her or him or for analyzing or predicting her or his personal preferences, behaviours and attitudes.* In fact, any form of web tracking allowing website providers to analyze the behavior of the website's users, inter alia, by measuring how long, how often or on what way the website was visited, such as via cookies or social media plug-ins and tags, falls within this rather vague description of monitoring (Voigt & von dem Bussche, 2017, p. 28). The extraterritorial application of the GDPR under this provision concerns the processing operations of data controllers or data processors that are not directly market-oriented (Gömann, 2017, p. 586). Furthermore, it concerns employers monitoring their employees, e.g. by installing software that maintains and analyses the use of Internet and e-mail traffic, by recording phone calls or instant messaging or by tracking data of company cars and equipment. In any event, the reason behind monitoring the data subjects' behaviour is irrelevant.

Art. 3(2) of the GDPR asserts a global jurisdiction for EU data protection legislation (Kelleher & Murray, 2018, p. 112) and, at least in Europe, it was widely welcomed as a necessary step towards a more comprehensive protection of a fundamental right. And, indeed, in the case at hand, the claims for extraterritorial reach are reasonable and well-founded, because if the EU did not extend its data protection to the conduct of foreign parties, it would not be providing effective protection for data subjects under its own jurisdiction. It should be reminded that, pursuant to Art. 3(2), data controllers and data processors not established in the EU are obliged to comply with the GDPR only when and only for as long as they are targeting or monitoring data subjects in the EU, in other words only when and for as long as their conduct is having a substantial and foreseeable effect in the EU. It does not matter that the words *data subjects in the EU* most probably imply that it is sufficient for a person to be in the territory of a Member Sate even for a very short period of time (and, adversely, that a person does not need to be a permanent resident of a Member State) to merit the high level of protection guaranteed by the GDPR; the requirements of the effects doctrine are met anyway. Therefore, it is safe to conclude that the extraterritorial reach of the GDPR under Art. 3(2) raises no questions regarding the respect of international comity.

Needless to say, the extraterritorial reach of the GDPR is one thing, the effective enforcement of the obligations stemming form it is quite another. A good example of the difficulties that may arise in a number of challenging cases would be a judgment by a Member State court or a decision by a Member State administrative authority ordering a third country search engine operator (with or without an EU establishment, it makes little difference in this context) to remove links to webpages displayed following the search of an individual's name, in accordance with Art. 17 of the GDPR which guarantees the right to erasure (right to be forgotten). As it is well-known, the right to be forgotten is not recognized in most jurisdictions outside the EU, including the USA, Japan and China, the EU's largest trade partners. Even in the EU itself, the right has a rather short history (Singleton, 2015). Consequently, the order of the Member State court or administrative authority would almost certainly not be enforceable in the third country where the search engine operator is based. True, the CJEU has always made a clear distinction between adjudicative jurisdiction on the one hand and enforcement on the other, in the sense that exercise of jurisdiction does not automatically guarantee effectiveness of enforcement (van Calster, 2015). Lack of enforcement would nonetheless be a problem not only for the data subject seeking erasure of personal data that is no longer relevant to him or her, but also for the effectiveness and reputation of the EU legal system in general.

CONCLUSION

There is a widespread belief that the GDPR has a broader material and territorial scope than the EU Data Protection Directive it has replaced. It should be clear by now that this is only partly true.

As far as the material scope of the GDPR is concerned and contrary to what one might have expected, there are no substantial changes compared to the 22-year-old EU Data Protection Directive. Despite the fact that the EU legislature was fully aware of the fundamental changes the social media revolution has brought about over the last decade and sincerely wanted to adjust the EU data protection rules to the new reality, the outcome of the 4-year-long ordinary legislative procedure (the European Commission's original proposal was published on January 25, 2012) was rather poor in this respect. A few references in the preamble of the GDPR to social networking and related online activities constitute only a small step forward and leave a lot of room for interpretation by the CJEU, which is not actually a bad thing, but it certainly does not offer the high degree of legal certainty natural persons and businesses in the industry would wish for.

Turning to the territorial scope of the GDPR, what stands out in comparison with the EU Data Protection Directive is no doubt the introduction of Art. 3(2) which makes data processing by data controllers or data processors not established in the EU subject to the GDPR under certain conditions (Castro-Edwards, 2017, p. 6). The fact that the GDPR was specially designed to have extraterritorial reach is important in many aspects and should not be underestimated. However, and leaving aside the fact that it is not uncommon for states to make extraterritorial jurisdictional claims in areas such as data privacy and related fields (Svantesson, 2012), the territorial scope of the EU Data Protection Directive had also been expanded in that sense following the CJEU's judgment in the *Google Spain* case and the abandonment of the requirement of *processing in the context of the activities of an establishment*. As a result, the difference turns out to be less revolutionary than it looks at first glance (Gömann, 2017, pp. 588-589).

In conclusion, although the provisions on the material and territorial scope of the GDPR are rather obscure and raise some difficult questions, the truly revolutionary features of the new legal framework for the protection of personal data in the EU are to be found elsewhere.

REFERENCES

Albrecht, J. P. (2016). How the GDPR will change the world. *European Data Protection Law Review*, *2*(3), 287–289. doi:10.21552/EDPL/2016/3/4

Butler, O. (2015). *The expanding scope of the Data Protection Directive: The exception for a purely personal or household activity*. University of Cambridge Legal Studies Research Papers, no. 54.

Castro-Edwards, C. (2017). *EU General Data Protection Regulation: A guide to the new law*. London: The law. *Society*.

Erdos, D. (2015). From the Scylla of restriction to the Charybdis of license? Exploring the scope of the 'special purposes' freedom of expression shield in European data protection. *Common Market Law Review*, *52*(1), 119–154.

Feiler, L., Forgó, N., & Weigl, M. (2018). *The EU General Data Protection Regulation (GDPR): A Commentary*. New York, NY: Globe Law and Business.

Gömann, M. (2017). The new territorial scope of EU data protection law: Deconstructing a revolutionary achievement. *Common Market Law Review*, *54*(2), 567–590.

Kelleher, D., & Murray, K. (2018). *EU data protection law*. Dublin: Bloomsburg Professional.

Klimas, T., & Vaičiukaité, J. (2008). The law of recitals in European Community legislation. *ILSA Journal of International & Comparative Law*, *15*(1), 61–93.

Kranenborg, H. (2015). Google and the right to be forgotten. *European Data Protection Law Review*, *1*(1), 70–79. doi:10.21552/EDPL/2015/1/13

Lambert, P. B. (2017). *Understanding the new European data protection rules*. Boca Raton, FL: CRC Press.

Scott, J. (2014). Extraterritoriality and territorial extension in EU law. *The American Journal of Comparative Law*, *62*(1), 87–125. doi:10.5131/AJCL.2013.0009

Singleton, S. (2015). Balancing a right to be forgotten with a right to freedom of expression in the wake of Google Spain v. AEPD. *Georgia Journal of International and Comparative Law, 44*(1), 165-193.

Svantesson, D. (2012). Extraterritoriality in the context of data privacy regulation. *Masaryk University Journal of Law and Technology, 7*(1), 87–96.

Taylor, M. (2017). The Misunderstood Implementation of a Landmark Decision and How Public International Law Could Offer Guidance. *European Data Protection Law Review, 3*(2), 196–208.

Taylor, D. (2018). *GDPR – territorial scope and the need to avoid absurd and inconsistent results.* Retrieved from http://www.circleid.com/posts/20180214_gdpr_territorial_scope_need_to_avoid_absurd_inconsistent_results/

Tene, O., & Wolf, C. (2013). *Overextended: Jurisdiction and applicable law under the EU General Data Protection Regulation.* The Future of Privacy Forum White Papers, no. 1.

Torremans, P. (1996). Extraterritorial application of E.C. and U.S. competition law. *European Law Review, 21*(4), 280–293.

Tzanou, M. (2011). Data protection in EU law: An analysis of the EU legal framework and the ECJ jurisprudence. In C. Akrivopoulou & A. Psygkas (Eds.), *Personal data privacy and protection in a surveillance era: Technologies and practices* (pp. 273–297). Hershey, PA: Information Science Reference. doi:10.4018/978-1-60960-083-9.ch016

Van Calster, G. (2015). *Regulating the Internet: Prescriptive and jurisdictional boundaries to the EU's right to be forgotten.* Retrieved from https://papers.ssrn.com/sol3/papers.cfm?abstract_id=2686111

Voigt, P., & von dem Bussche, A. (2017). *The EU General Data Protection Regulation (GDPR): A practical guide.* Cham: Springer International Publishing. doi:10.1007/978-3-319-57959-7

KEY TERMS AND DEFINITIONS

Data Controller: The natural or legal person, public authority, agency or other body which, alone or jointly with others, determines the purposes and means of the processing of personal data; where the purposes and means of such processing are determined by Union or Member State law, the controller or the specific criteria for its nomination may be provided for by Union or Member State law (GDPR, Art. 4(7)).

Data Processor: A natural or legal person, public authority, agency or other body which processes personal data on behalf of the controller (GDPR, Art. 4(8)).

Data Subject: An identified or identifiable natural person. An identifiable natural person is a person that can be identified, directly or indirectly, in particular by reference to an identifier such as a name, an identification number, location data, an online identifier or to one or more factors specific to the physical, physiological, genetic, mental, economic, cultural or social identity of that natural person.

Manual Filing System: Any structured set of personal data which are accessible according to specific criteria, whether centralised, decentralised or dispersed on a functional or geographical basis (GDPR, Art. 4 (6)).

Personal Data: Any information relating to a data subject.

Processing: Any operation or set of operations which is performed on personal data or on sets of personal data, whether or not by automated means, such as collection, recording, organisation, structuring, storage, adaptation or alteration, retrieval, consultation, use, disclosure by transmission, dissemination or otherwise making available, alignment or combination, restriction, erasure or destruction (GDPR, Art. 4(2)).

Profiling: Any form of automated processing of personal data consisting of the use of personal data to evaluate certain personal aspects relating to a natural person, in particular to analyse or predict aspects concerning that natural person's performance at work, economic situation, health, personal preferences, interests, reliability, behaviour, location or movements (GDPR, Art. 4(4)).

APPENDIX I: LEGAL SOURCES

Regulation 2018/1725/EU of the European Parliament and of the Council, of 23 October 2018, on the protection of natural persons with regard to the processing of personal data by the Union institutions, bodies, offices and agencies and on the free movement of such data (...), OJ L 295, 21.11.2018, p.39.

Regulation 2016/679/EU of the European Parliament and of the Council, of 27 April 2016, on the protection of natural persons with regard to the processing of personal data and on the free movement of such data (...), OJ L 119, 4.5.2016, p. 1.

Directive (EU) 2016/680 of the European Parliament and of the Council of 27 April 2016 on the protection of natural persons with regard to the processing of personal data by competent authorities for the purposes of the prevention, investigation, detection or prosecution of criminal offences or the execution of criminal penalties, and on the free movement of such data (...), OJ L 119, 4.5.2016, p. 89. It should be mentioned that three Member States, namely the United Kingdom, Ireland and Denmark, have an opt-out from that Directive.

Proposal for a Regulation of the European Parliament and of the Council on the protection of individuals with regard to the processing of personal data and on the free movement of such data (General Data Protection Regulation), COM (2012) 011 final.

Council Framework Decision 2008/977/JHA of 27 November 2008 on the protection of personal data processed in the framework of police and judicial cooperation in criminal matters, OJ L 350, 30.12.2008, p. 60.

Decision 1247/2002/EC of the European Parliament, of the Council and of the Commission of 1 July 2002 on the regulations and general conditions governing the performance of the European Data-protection Supervisor's duties, OJ L 183, 12.7.2002, p. 1.

Regulation 45/2001/EC of the European Parliament and of the Council of 18 December 2000 on the protection of individuals with regard to the processing of personal data by the Community institutions and bodies and on the free movement of such data, OJ L 8, 12.1.2001, p. 1.

Directive 95/46/EC of the European Parliament and of the Council of 24 October 1995 on the protection of individuals with regard to the processing of personal data and on the free movement of such data, OJ L 281, 23.11.1995, p. 31.

APPENDIX II: TABLE OF CASES BEFORE THE COURT OF JUSTICE OF THE EU

Case C-345/17, *Buivids*, judgment of the Court, 14 February 2019, ECLI:EU:C:2019:122.

Case C-25/17, *Jehovan todistajat*, judgment of the Court, 10 July 2018, ECLI:EU:C:2018:551.

Case C-73/16, *Puškár*, judgment of the Court, 27 September 2017, ECLI:EU:C:2017:725.

Case C-191/15, *Verein für Konsumenteninformation*, judgment of the Court, 28 July 2016, ECLI:EU:C:2016:612.

Case C-230/14, *Weltimmo*, judgment of the Court, 1 October 2015, ECLI:EU:C:2015:639.

Case C-230/14, *Weltimmo*, opinion of AG Cruz Villalón, 25 June 2015, ECLI:EU:C:2015:426.

Case C-212/13, *Ryneš*, judgment of the Court, 11 December 2014, ECLI:EU:C:2014:2428.

Case C-131/12, *Google Spain*, judgment of the Court, 13 May 2014, ECLI:EU:C:2014:317.

Case C-131/12, *Google Spain*, Opinion of AG Jääskinen, 25 June 2013, ECLI:EU:C:2013:424.

Cases C-585/08 and C-144/09, *Pammer and Hotel Alpenhof*, judgment of the Court, 7 December 2010, ECLI:EU:C:2010:740.

Case C-73/07, *Satakunnan Markkinapörssi and Satamedia*, judgment of the Court, 16 December 2008, ECLI:EU:C:2008:727.

Case C-275/06, *Promusicae*, judgment of the Court, 29 January 2008, ECLI:EU:C:2008:54.

Case C-101/01, *Lindquist*, judgment of the Court, 6 November 2003, ECLI:EU:C:2003:596.

Chapter 3
Selling Personal Data:
The Legal Framework and Nature of Personal Data Selling Transactions Under GDPR

Konstantina Samara

University of Macedonia, Greece & Democritus University of Thrace, Greece

ABSTRACT

The prevalent and currently unanimous European legal system regarding personal data comprises a set of protective rules, enshrining, amongst others, the prerequisites for lawful processing. The venture of the ensuing aims to examine, under the scope of both constitutional rules and the ius cogens provisions of the Regulation (EU) 2016/679, the validity of a transaction pertaining to the processing of personal data. The objective of the herein argumentation specifically focuses on the juridical act of selling personal data, in accordance with the principle of contractual freedom and its compatibility with the core of constitutional provisions, which safeguard human value. The correlations examined below are referred to the contractual interaction between the subject of the personal data and the data controller under the scope of a double facet approach of GDPR, as a legal system both personal and property oriented.

INTRODUCTION

The prevailing perception in the literature of personal data law tends to trace as a common denominator of all European respective legislation a human right, dignity-based approach. As expected, the currently set in effect Regulation (EU) 2016/679 (hereinafter GDPR) has been founded on terms of core human rights, for the safeguard of which provides for accordingly. Through this lens, the interpretation of data subject's "consent" seems to be limited to the mere operational aim of "consent" as a legal base for processing; as a consequence, the predominant normative value of "consent" has been delimited to a ground precluding the initially unlawful character of processing, which constitutes a harmful act against protected human rights. However, this unilateral perception of "consent" disregards every thought relating to its precise constituent compounds, according to which consent can be perceived as a *statement of will*

DOI: 10.4018/978-1-5225-9489-5.ch003

aiming to an act with lawful consequences, or in other words, as a *legal transaction*. Hence, according to Christodoulou (2013, pp. 50-54), consent is a unilateral judicial act, whilst it is argued, hereinafter, that consent is manifested as a bilateral judicial act and specifically as a contract, since it constitutes the acceptance of a prior contracting proposal. For this reason, the author of this chapter strictly believes that the prevalent human right approach is deficient because it fails in thoroughly depicting the current data-driven economy, where personal data are traded as "assets", "goods" and "commodities". Simultaneously, "human right approach" does not guarantee an accurate construe of the GDPR provisions, which imply the existence of a "proprietorial" relationship between data subjects and their personal data. The herein chapter ventures a dual-based interpretation of GDPR, as a set of legal provisions deriving from the anxiety to safeguard both, personal and property nature of personal data, as well as the respective rights, stemming from them.

The basic underlying argument of this chapter consists in the thought that the mere fact of regulative intervention causally linked to the protection of a right does not, by definition, prohibit a potential commercial exploitation of the right in question; thus, regulative rules do not always indicate an "inalienable" character of the regulated right. Therefore, having considered that the regulative initiative of GDPR comprises a set of provisions safeguarding the individual interests during the processing of their personal data, it can be inferred that these inherently mandatory rules may also govern every potential relevant contractual relation, expressed as a manifestation of the contractual freedom principle. In the context of individual autonomy "consent" can connote the expression of data subject's "power of disposal", in a way that the data subject itself capitalizes or adversely withholds their data.

In other words, the herein chapter ventures to examine the validity of a personal data vending transaction between the data subject and the controller, under the scope of GDPR provisions which mirror fundamental constitutional principles regarding privacy, personhood and human value. In order to probe the legal accuracy of the aforementioned venture, the author estimate that the most expedient method should initially encompass the conceptual and normative approach of personal data right in the light of core constitutional values, and subsequently the systemic linkage of personal data right with "family" notions. The ultimate undertaking of this method is to mine the personal and property-based elements of GDPR, which as a whole comprise the idiosyncratic nature of personal data right, both as a right important for human dignity and personality and as a right of economic nature. Blending the "duality" of the right with "de facto personal data marketplaces", this chapter aims to question the inalienability of personal data *per se*.

BACKGROUND

The Rationale of "Human Right Approach"

The divergent approaches regarding personal or property nature of personal data rights are founded on different perceptions of privacy across the two sides of Atlantic: the prevailing approach in Europe argues that privacy constitutes a fiduciary of *dignity* and therefore it is inalienable, whereas in America privacy is construed under the light of *liberty* and, thus, it is alienable in the context of the contractual freedom principle. Moreover, both aspects are reflected in the accordingly adopted legislative policy, with Europe seeing in internet –the current threat of privacy by technology- the natural continuance of a long tradition in protecting the right to privacy; this is the reason for which EU creates *ex-ante* severe rules leaving only a little space to self-regulating competence of enterprises, contrary to American policy (Tassis, 2013). The viewpoint of European legislatures mirrors especially a "dignity approach", according to which the sanctity of dignity is incompatible with vending personal data in the marketplace and thus, privacy should not be seen as a service because it is a fundamental human right. Consequently, the intrinsic value of privacy does not allow personal data to become the subject matter of trade, because their rationale is laid in ensuring a threshold of respect and evolving in an environment of "intimacy".

Conceptualizing Privacy as the Framework for Constructing a Personal Data Protection Right

The perception of privacy, as a legal ancestor of the right to personal data, is based on the interpretation of "privacy" and in its dynamic correlation with "family" constitutional liberties and values, such as family life, inviolability of home, privacy of communication and personality. Commencing from the main semantic and normative conceptualization of privacy, it is observed that the historical perception of private life has passed through the traditional approach of privacy as the outcome of a contrasted interrelation between public and private life. The Greek scholar Dagtoglou has defined accordingly "public life" as the social or professional life to the degree that encompasses individual interaction with a broad circle of persons, or aims to influence public affairs; (…) private life, on the contrary, is limited to the person itself, the family, the narrow circle of friends and acquaintances, as well as to individual sexual activities and relations (2012, p. 273, own translation). The above definition reflects a by contrast conceptualization of private life since it is inferred that private life is life lacking public attributes.

However, privacy can be defined by deploying a novel "conceptual design" appearing in the scholar discourse; based on *dialectic and interactive approach,* this aspect argues that public and private life interact in a dialectical means which limits their "spatial" normative capacity (Akrivopoulou, 2012, pp. 69-115). More explicitly, it has been argued that dichotomizing the two notions, in an absolute way, although initially necessary, does not seem to follow the extroverted facet of privacy stemming from social and technological evolution. Thus, the need for relativizing the dogmatic distinction of both notions emerges as a necessity; the interlinking of private life to the "extramural world" has been ventured through the doctrine of "intimacy", in a twofold semantic meaning.

According to the "intimacy" theory, as analyzed by Akrivopoulou, privacy develops its dynamic content under the notion of *intimacy of oneself,* by encompassing moral autonomy and liberty conditions and by safeguarding that leading one's life is unaffected by governmental parenting; in that sense, intimacy bulletproofs a course of moral choices of the individual regarding their sexuality, sentimental and family life and uniqueness (2012). Concurrently, under Akrivopoulou, intimacy also presents a societal manifestation, since individuals enjoy the freedom of communicating their "uniqueness" to their peers; hence, a community of privacy is being created (2012, p. 65). This exact thought leads the same scholar to aptly argue that, "intimacy guarantees even how a person enjoys being "autonomous" in the social (*societal privacy*) and public space (*public privacy*)" (2012, p.15). Ergo, perceiving privacy, under the scope of this approach, is vividly illustrated in the ECtHR case-law Niemietz v. Germany, according to which *it would be too restrictive to limit the notion to an "inner circle" in which the individual may live his own personal life as he chooses and to exclude therefore entirely the outside world not encompassed within that circle. Respect for private life must also comprise to a certain degree the right to establish and develop relationships with other human beings* (Raab, 2013, p.41).

The practical value of the novelty in perceiving "privacy" as a confliction-originated right lies in the fact that it solves the dilemma regarding the "political" or "natural" quality of privacy, in favour of the "political" approach; moreover, it paves the way for the discourse on the alienability or inalienability of this right. Hence, it can be argued that the operational objective of privacy, in claiming moral autonomy into an "extroverted" context, portrays the definition of a "political" and therefore tradable right. Specifically, privacy due to its dynamic and evolving character seems rather "political" than "natural'", that is, an inherent of human nature, right. The intrinsic tendency of privacy to be developed through a constant socio-political dialogue reaffirms that its normative scope extends over the narrow perception of the private sphere and underlines the elasticity of its content. This is the reason why Akrivopoulou argues that the normative sign of privacy cannot be described, but it can be defined only through the normative conflicting of this right with other lawfully vested objectives and interests (2012).

The analysis so far leads to the conclusion that privacy combines in a *sui generis* way two attributes, by being a self-efficient right and, concurrently, constituting a "precondition" for the shaping and the protection of human uniqueness. These attributes seem to be engaged in a bidirectional relationship while perceiving privacy both as a "right" and as a "condition" reaffirms the necessity in conceptualizing privacy under the scope of a broad personal sphere (Akrivopoulou, 2012). Therefore, the absolute distinction between the private and public sphere appears to be "anachronistic" in a normative and socio-technological point of view.

Privacy and Family Rights: Assuring the Individual's Self Determination

Approaching the conceptual and normative frame of privacy cannot be accomplished with legal certainty, without correlating privacy to "family" rights, such as the right to family life, the inviolability of home, the freedom of communication and the protection of personality; although these emerging interlinkages tend to raise the difficulty level of conceptually and normatively understanding privacy, they highlight the core argumentation of human right approach. The analysis ensuing is founded on the interpretation of family rights in couples, to the formulation of which the right to privacy takes part as an invariant.

Venturing these correlations, it can be notably argued that apprehending privacy as a defence umbrella of individual's moral autonomy and self-determination, against paternalistic governmental intervention, illustrates family life as a typical example of claiming moral freedom and self-determination; in this sense, family life is schematically depicted as a concentric circle of privacy. Characteristically, it has been noted that the conjunction between private and family life impacts the latter since it demoralizes and emancipates the content of family life from the legal framing of wedlock. To this context, family life encompasses even de facto forms of symbiosis or family, including the novel or the divergent ones (Spiropoulos, Kontiadis, Anthopoulos, Gerapetritis, 2017, p. 206); under Solove "The shrinking of the size of the family (…), the core transformation of family as institution, the changing architecture of the home (….) and numerous other changes in the quality and nature of life had profound effects for the perception of what the private life entailed" (2002, p. 1141). As a result, the configuration of a person's moral choices according to their absolute and unbiased volition affects amongst others and the shaping of their family choices.

By the same token, the correlation between privacy and inviolability of home highlights that privacy is a broader right, for the reason that inviolability contributes only to the mere spatial perception of privacy and safeguards rights emerging in the untouchable home environment. On the contrary, the altering perception of privacy as a dual right, with introvert and extrovert expression, induces to conceptualize privacy as a figuratively spatial notion, that is, as a "sphere", "zone" or "territory of the self" (Akrivopoulou, 2012, p. 111); at the same time, this approach, by deploying both literally or figuratively the spatial criterion, achieves a vivid distinction between privacy and inviolability of home.

Partly similar to inviolability of the home, freedom of communication also originates from the natural environment of the house, as a privacy "district", and sequentially it expands beyond the narrow spatial boundaries of the house. Thus, it can be accordingly cited that Akrivopoulou reasons the enhanced protection of communication freedom as follows: "(…) it is because private life encloses all of the private relationships of a person with their peers, the necessity for protecting private sphere during the transition of the message to the extramural world is rendered more obvious" (2012, p.111, own translation). As a consequence, freedom of communication seems to contribute to the expression of extrovert, societal privacy.

The last dynamic correlation to be ventured, towards the conceptual and normative disambiguation between privacy and "family" liberties, is referred to the couple "privacy-personality". This issue is scrutinized by Akrivopoulou, according to whom "the relation of privacy and the personal sphere is dual faceted, analyzed in two sequences" (2012, p. 283, own translation). The underlying argument of this approach comprises the thought that privacy constructs an "ecosystem" for the formulation of personality, and operates as the *beginning* of the individual; sequentially, privacy is modified to a right and to a protective condition of the individual, as well (Akrivopoulou, 2012). From the aforementioned viewpoint, personality seems to descend from a privacy "ecosystem" which, evolutionally, safeguards its own creation by reframing it protectively. To sum up, Solove highlights the bidirectional interrelation of privacy and personality by quoting Jeffrey Riemann's wording: "the right to privacy (...) protects the individual's interest in becoming, being and remaining a person" (2002, p. 1116).

However, distinguishing the two notions is not always uncomplicated; should privacy manifests an extrovert tendency, issues seem to arise. Thus, the implied herein question is referred to the difference amongst the extrovert aspect of privacy and the inherently extrovert personality. Reasoning this phenomenon, it has been cited that this prescribed blur distinction finds its roots to the *"human continuum"*, that is, perceiving human action as a whole and not as a sum of divided phases. An attempt in tackling this issue should be the thought that the point of distinction between the two notions lies in their disparate functioning: privacy aims to protect and enhance individual autonomy and authenticity of the identity, whilst, personality safeguards the individualizing of the person (Akrivopoulou, 2012).

Privacy and Personal Data: Constructing the Right to Informational Self Determination

The completion of the venture to clarify the difference between privacy and family notions paves the way, sequentially, to question the interrelationship between privacy and personal data. A catalytic criterion for finding the parities and the disparities of these two rights lies in the argument of "pursued goal". Briefly, privacy creates and protects the conditions of an individual's autonomy for the person to make individualized moral choices, whilst personal data safeguard "the right to informational self-determination". The core notion of this newcomer right lies in the perception of privacy "(…) as an expectation in a certain degree of accessibility of information" and thus secrecy does not constitute a conceptual compound of privacy (Solove, 2002, p. 1152). Bearing that in mind, it can be inferred that the mere conceptual relativity of the terms "autonomy" and "self-determination" is indicative of their normative relativity as well; furthermore, this insight reveals that both rights are parts of the human continuity distinctly. In other words, the main concern of privacy, that is, the authenticity of the individual[1] and their choices, acquires a more "tangible" nature, by being embodied in the form of personal data, controlled, as naturalistically expected, by the person to whom data indicate. This is the reason why Igglezakis argues that the right to informational self-determination does not constitute an "absolute" right but a right functioning against rendering individuals "mere informational subject matters" (2004, p. 54, own translation). To summarize, it can be argued that personal data constitute an intangible "carrier" of individuals' private sphere information; with the aid of this argument, it is aptly described, as well, the foundation of the rationale for granting data subjects control over their personal data.

By the aforementioned analysis, it is safely deduced that personal data right "follows" sequentially the right to privacy; indeed, the existence of an "incubating personal data environment" seems to be the prerequisite for awarding lawful importance to data mined information. However, it is observed that, due to the dynamic character of privacy, the initially one-way connection between privacy and personal data evolves into bidirectional. In that sense, it could be argued that the dynamic context of privacy governs both creation and evolution of personal data, the latter manifested by "triggering" privacy to continuously demonstrate new aspects, which may potentially become the content of new personal data. The justification of this interdependence emerges when hypothetically reflect upon a scenario, where data subjects lack autonomous data control; the unlimited flow of personal data may tarnish *autonomy* and influence *individual's moral choices*, whilst, it may lead to "biased" personal data since total absence of data control affects the "incubating personal data environment" of privacy.

Personal Data and Their Specific Content: The Individualization of the Individual's Identity

So far, it has been highlighted that personal data "carry" information about a person's private life; the private sphere, nevertheless, does not occupy the full extent of the multi-facet personal data range. Since personal data do not only reveal information about an individual's authenticity but also encompass details for the individualization of a person's identity, it is inferred that personal data content reflects the information of partly private and partly personal sphere. More detailed, whilst the general function of personal data entails in identification, the information that data "carry" may especially relate to authenticity or individuality of the person; schematically, it can be claimed that the main function of personal data aims in identifying the person, whereas other separate concentric functions of personal data are categorized on the base of their specific content; ergo, personal data "imprint" information regarding "authenticity" or "individuality" of a living human being.

Precisely, the legislative distinction of personal data to "simple" and "sensitive" conduces to the conclusion that both categories embed information relating to both private and personal sphere. Hence, without claiming that the ambition of the herein chapter aims to conceptually match "privacy" and "personhood" with the inherent distinction of data into "simple" and "sensitive" respectively[2], the ensuing venture is to reveal the nature of personal data's content by exploiting GDPR itself.

More specifically, to illustrate this, it suffices to mention that data are encompassing sensitive information of private sphere, like those relating to religious belief, which enjoy enhanced protection, under Ar. 9 of GDPR; however, the same article provides also for the augmented protection of data, connected to personhood, such as joining in a trade union organization. Similarly, data not falling within GDPR's provisions about "sensitive data" are being protected as "simple" although they usually enclose information stemming from a private sphere; hence, it is observed that, "simple" data concurrently can mirror both extrovert privacy and personality. To sum up, the conjunction of Ar. 4(1) and 9 of GDPR leads to the inference that personal data right stands amongst personality and privacy rights; in other words, one could argue that the personal data right originates from traditional rights, from which it borrows its moral and normative foundation, henceforth it evolves into a defence line against the ubiquitous technological threat.[3]

The analysis so far has underlined that the contemporary perception of privacy on the grounds of synthetic analysis between public and private life constitutes a flexible theoretical channel for conceptualizing privacy as a non-static right; on the contrary, privacy is proved to be a right, which "receives" constant feedback from the current social and technological evolution, in a way that underpins the "plasticity" of its conceptual and normative value. Hence, in the era of Information Society, processing personal data illustrates the reality of a constantly enriched perception of privacy. The argument that personal data are "entities" enclosing information, which *inter alia* converge with aspects of an introvert and extrovert private sphere, elucidates the demand for a plasticity-based conceptualization of privacy. Thus, it can be claimed that the close interconnection between information and individuals renders personal data the subject matter of legitimate protection since the operational aim of the right in question is to function as "an external defence line of the private sphere" (Akrivopoulou, 2012). In other words, the neophyte right to personal protection emerges as the evolved outcome of traditional preexisting rights, with its practical value lying in interlinking information to a person, in such a way that information and person constitute "an aggregate of the human self".

MAIN FOCUS OF THE CHAPTER

The Rationale of Property Right Approach: Legislative "Hints" of a *Quasi* Proprietary Right

The previous synopsis of personal data right normative value, under the scope of "human right approach", reflects the prevalent inclination in interpreting the regulative initiative of GDPR; similarly, it underlines that the foundational reason for such a statute lies in the mere existence of an extremely vulnerable and threatened right. According to this tendency, the European legislator has recently argued in the preamble 24 of the Directive EU (2019/770) (hereinafter DCDS Directive) that "(…) personal data cannot be considered as a commodity (…)", whilst the EDPS had already expressed in the Opinion 4/2017 serious doubts about the use of the notion of "counter-performance" and of "actively provided data" in the context of the relationships between the consumers and the suppliers (…)"

However, the herein arising question deals with the rectitude of this unidirectional aspect. On the one hand, the factual perception of personal data, as a tradable and fruitful entity in the context of *de facto* personal data marketplaces, provides the outlook for a progressive approach of GDPR; on the other hand, legislative subtle hints, such as those lying in GDPR and DCDS Directive, should be taken into consideration when reflecting upon the current normative, conceptual and financial value of personal data right and its compromises.

Briefly, it can be argued that the currently set in effect GDPR comprises a framework of provisions, potentially applicable to the transactional harnessing of personal data, in a way which highlights the *sui generis* nature of data as of both personal and property quality, concerning its mandatory provisions and to the core community doctrine of respecting human value. To illustrate this thought, it is necessary to cite Victor who argues that "the Regulation draft (…) includes three elements that lend themselves to a property-based conception: consumers are granted clear entitlements to their own data; the data, even after it is transferred, carries a burden that "runs with" it and binds third parties; and consumers are protected through remedies grounded in "property rules" " (2013, p. 515). Furthermore, the DCDS Directive encompasses provisions, which attribute the quality of "consumer" to data subjects in contracts where the latter are supplied with digital content or digital services for a set price or by granting access to their personal data. These aforementioned legislative hints are ventured be unfolded in the ensuing sections after a brief factual representation of the digital economy and the current position that personal data have inevitably occupied therein.

De Facto Personal Data Marketplaces: The Emergence of Digital Economy and the Appearance of Personal Data as New Species of Asset

The growing convergence of innovative technological evolution, such as artificial intelligence, cloud computing, big data and internet of things, with everyday human activity has been leading to mass production of great data volume. The intrinsic value of personal data is depicted in the data ecosystem where personal data are initially produced and sequentially infused into the administrative and private sector. The current exploitation of personal data consists in commercializing mined information in absentia of data subjects, who happen to be either data producers or data consumers. Hence, it has been interestingly argued that the interaction amongst humans, computational systems and information describes the phenomenon of "Human-Data Interaction" (Mortier, Haddadi, Hendenson, Mcauley & Crowford, 2014). This term stems from the ubiquitous computational presence in everyday life and poses the question of the way according to which human should interact with data. Inherently, this perspective does not focus on the general issue of the interrelation between human and computational systems; it shifts, instead, the scientific interest to the specified field of human-data interaction, in the context of an idiosyncratic eco-system.

Hence, it is commonplace that since data are *de facto* attributed financial sigh across their entire dynamic course, their attribute as the "moving force" of the global economy is fully justified. More relevantly, Mortier et al., maintain that they do not consider data to be static but dynamic; they also argue that "… the algorithms and processes that consume data often emit other data as outputs that are fed into other processes as inputs of equal validity to raw "observed" data" (2014, p. 5). Historically, personal data's value has been described under the terms of various financial approaches: ergo, it has been aptly argued that personal data constitute a new species of "oil", a "currency" of the digital world and a novel category of "asset". This economic approach has led to the financial conceptualization of data as follows: «...data is becoming a new type of raw material that's on par with capital and labour" (World Economic Forum, 2011, p. 7); in other wording, "(...) personal data has become the *de facto* currency of the Internet Age, subsidizing everything from free search engines to cheap cell phones" (Tannert, 2016). Similarly, it has been documented that data, in general, represent a tradable good, which inaugurates an innovative kind of economy, the so-called "data economy". The aforementioned attributes enhance the widespread sense that personal data are inherently carriers of economic value, even in the embryonic stage of raw data.

The types of personal data commercialization are subdivided into two major categories: the first one acknowledges personal data as a good *per se*, whereas the other one aims in granting access to personal data as a data-based rendered service. Hence, whilst in the first category the transactional subject matter is raw data, in the second category personal data are commercialized indirectly. Analytically, the transactional good in the field of data as a service is not data itself but a service based on collected and processed data (i.e Google Maps). Consequently, data as a service method represents the most widespread and profitable means of personal data commercialization. Due to that reason, companies are credited with the emergence of multi-sided platforms. According to this phenomenon, consumers enjoy digital services for free (sic) while their data are collected and monetized in the other side of the platform through practices of targeted advertisement (Surblyte, 2016, pp.18-19). Moreover, the multi-sided platform phenomenon highlights the *modus operandi* of services like those rendered by Facebook and Google and establishes a new kind of labour, the so-called digital labour (Rimbert, 2016).

Furthermore, even though data subjects unwittingly grant access to their personal data, it is observed that they do not profit accordingly by the commercialization of their own data; this is the reason why Stathopoulos (2000) argues that data subjects can bring a claim for unjust enrichment. In respect to this phenomenon, Rimbert (2016) maintains that social networks convert gratuitously friendships, emotions, desires and anger into data subjectable to being commercialized by algorithms; with this insight, it is explicitly reasoned why data subjects are usually referred to foreign literature as "end users". Similarly, the wording "If you are not paying for the product, you are the product" attributes the quality of "prosumer" to individuals, since they consume the product they create themselves. To conclude, according to Rimbert' s vivid illustration, "Economic historians may credit the casually dressed bosses of Silicon Valley with the creation of a world-group of cheerfully dispossessed labourers, willing co-producers of the services they consume" (2016).

On the contrary, data brokers, data analytics companies and advertisers benefit from redeeming the personal data mined information for cash (Stathopoulos, 2003, p. 3), to which they have gained access with the use of take-it-or-leave its tactics. To recapitulate, acknowledging financial value to information does not seem to be an innovative invention; the mere function of the stock market is founded on the intrinsic monetary value of information. Therefore, it could be figuratively claimed that information deriving from collected and processed personal data is "infused" into a new species of "stock market", the "personal data stock market", which reflects the essence of everyday online experience in web 2.0.

Property Right Approach: The Intellectual Property Insight

The previous digressional depiction of the data-driven economy gives its place to the analysis of the property nature of personal data. This approach comprises two separate aspects, *id est*, full property and intellectual property viewpoint; ergo, the full property approach treats personal data as intangible goods and fluctuates from the utmost –for the European standards- scenario of data infusion in a free and self-regulated market to the secure –according to the author- perspective of infusing personal data into the markets under a regulatory state supervision. Nevertheless, it has been argued that vesting personal data with a full proprietary character is dogmatically incompatible with the core values governing intellectual property law, to which personal data law presents obvious parities. Towards this perspective, Prins mentions in respect to a personal data property right that it "(…) might have to be inalienable only and waivable only in certain limited circumstances comparable to the moral rights under intellectual property law" (2006, p. 247).

This approach seems to reflect the idiosyncratic nature of personal data, as data "produced" whenever human acts in the frame of private and personal sphere. As already mentioned, some personal data seem to reflect specified expressions of a person's "authenticity" and other "individualize" data subjects personality; in other words, personal data seem to engage a *sui generis* "paternity status" analogically similar to the provisions of intellectual property law. This "paternity status", indeed, is reminiscent of the connection bond between a creator and their creation. Respectively, Prins implies that the common denominator of intellectual property and personal data lies in information; however, Prins points out that their differentiator resides in the mere existence of consciousness during the production of information (2006, p. 223).

Analytically, since moral right attributed to creator, under intellectual property law, reasons the unacceptability of absolute alienation between creator and creation, it is inferred that exercising access power to "creation" is guaranteed by granting rights which "run with" creation; additionally, the same kind of rights is granted, as detailed below, through GDPR provisions. Hence, by drawing analogies from intellectual property law, it could be argued that the *quasi* paternal relationship between data subjects and their own data is compatible with constant enjoyment of the inalienable "moral right" on data; similarly, taking into consideration that, under intellectual property doctrine, moral right does not preclude benefit from the financial fruit of creation, it could be argued that data subject's moral right does not preclude commercialization of personal data by their own "creators".

The Hybrid Nature of Personal Data and of the Rights Stemming Therefrom: Both Personal and Proprietary

The perspective that the herein chapter aspires to introduce conceives personal data and the rights arising therefrom as of dual nature, representing an equilibrium of a personal and proprietary based approach. The specific disadvantages of a unidirectional conception of personal data and the rights resulting therefrom, either as solely personal or as fully proprietary, arise because these aspects disregard respectively that the cornerstone of "personal data" is data subjects' individuality and authenticity and, thus, the ontological reality of *de facto* personal data marketplaces seems to be ignored. As a result, the novel conceptual design in perceiving personal data right as a *sui generis right*, combining personal and proprietary qualities, serves a double-facet function: on the one hand, it satisfies the technological and financial demand for the lawful acknowledgement of personal data as "asset" motivating internal and global economy; on the other hand, it regulates the secure infusion of this brand new "asset" into the markets and protects the -by default- "weak" contracting party. Hence, the spirit of GDPR can be construed under the progressive and dynamic scope of designing a regulated union marketplace, where personal data can be also sold under state guarantee towards the equilibration of conflicted rights regarding the protection of personal data and free movement of information.

However, the mere factual depiction of personal data marketplaces does not suffice to "baptize" personal data as a partially proprietary "good" endowed with respective powers; legislative volition is also sought after. Studying GDPR in the light of civil law dogma reveals some dispersed hints of core property approach doctrine; as Victor has argued, the fact that *data subjects are granted clear entitlements to their own data and that data, even after it is transferred, carry a burden that "runs with" it and binds third parties,* reflects significant traditional civil law doctrines (2013, p. 515). Nevertheless, the widespread construe of GDPR -about processing personal data- disregards these doctrines, since the mainstream perception of GDPR's venture is merely demarcated to granting data subjects new authorities and to threatening severe penalties in case of a data breach.

Still, implementing these doctrines to *de facto* personal data marketplaces leads to the conclusion that GDPR implicitly acknowledges personal data as partially proprietary right; the aforementioned interpretative framework, appears to be leading to the conclusion, that GDPR could pave the way for raising a collective awareness regarding personal data value[4], whereas, at the same time, it officially hails the neophyte "transactional good" of personal data. Towards this perspective, the DCDS Directive provides for an implicit fictional equation between the function of paying a price and providing personal data, in contracts where data subjects are supplied with digital content or digital services, despite clearly avoiding to use the wording "counter-performance".

Venturing a further analysis of the abovementioned doctrines and commencing from "entitlement" issues, it is advisable to highlight that the discourse about the entitled to fruitfully commercialize personal data is not new; this topic has mainly concerned American literature. More specifically, the issue, in question, is vividly addressed by Kang and Buchner (2004), in their study, "Privacy in Atlantis", where the two prevalent tendencies in the discourse regarding personal data's nature, stemming from "dignity" and "property approach" accordingly, are thoroughly portrayed. Analytically, the authors hypothetically reflect upon a scenario of vending herbs between a merchant and a consumer and question –amongst others- the beneficiary of the information mined from a bilateral contract. Towards the same reasoning, Solove's respective argumentation is succinctly expressed with the phrase: "(…) personal information is often formed in relationships with others" (2002, p. 1113). In this regard, the implied issue questions the exclusivity of personal data ownership.

According to the author's opinion, the topic covered by the two scholars is twofold and encompasses two distinct subject areas. The first one is referred to acknowledging the entitled of property right in personal data amidst a consumer and a merchant, that is –in terms of personal data law- between a data subject and a controller. Dealing with this issue, in the context of a bilateral agreement, an apt answer would have taken into consideration that the primal foundational components of personal data protection right are "dignity-based"; ergo, the mere fact that personal data embed information about the individual's private and personal sphere resolves the problem towards the equitable allocation of the right-holder to the data subject. The opposite option would ironically signify the trading of data retrieval at the expense of data subjects, who, although identifiable through their data, are deprived of data control since their personal data are subjected to controller's dominance (Kang & Buchner, 2004, p. 239). In practice, data subjects would be oxymoronically forced to pay the price for preserving the "classified" nature of the information mined by their own data; Schwartz has respectively coined the term "threat value" which connotes the price that someone would have to place on not disclosing their personal information (2003, p. 2077). The contradiction of this aspect is apparent since personal data retrieval would reverse the way informational self-determination right is being exercised and, finally, it would eliminate the essence of self-determination.

The second subject area constitutes a modified version of the first and refers to occasions where the same quantity of herbs has been sold by the same vendor to multiple buyers; in other words, this issue extends to the nature of the internal relationship amongst more than one data subjects-consumers in the same contract. This case is successfully dealt with civil law provisions regarding co-ownership in conjunction with GDPR provisions. Consequently, when personal data seem to be the result of "joint creation", data subjects will be co-beneficiaries of the jointly created personal data. This phenomenon is cited in foreign literature as co-ownership (or joint ownership) and joint authorship, depending on the perspective adopted accordingly in the context either of full property or intellectual property approach (Kang and Buchner, 2004).

To sum up, personal data right and the individual powers resulting therefrom seem -under the light of GDPR- to constitute, upon their emergence, "objects of enjoyment" by data subjects. The rationale of this conclusion lies in the thought that personal data is a "marker" of the data subject, which explains why granted powers to data subjects "run with" their personal data; accordingly, it highlights the idiosyncratic "ownership" status attributed to data subjects. Therefore, it seems that the practical value of data subjects' legal entitlement entails in the economic entitlement of the consenting subjects, as well; during decision making process data subjects should have the right whether to opt for granting access, as a *quasi* counter-performance or to abstain from divulging personal information to join the Information Society[5].

The Data Subject's Idiosyncratic "Ownership" Status: Do Data Subjects Own in an Absolute Way the Personal Data They "Produce"?

More profoundly, to investigate the nature of this idiosyncratic "ownership" status as of falling into the provisions either of obligation or property law, it would seem appropriate to venture a dynamic correlation between this "ownership" status and the traditional perception of ownership. The endeavour, that follows, seeks to exploit the "anatomical" interpretative tools of property law by deliberately disregarding that personal data cannot be considered as "thing", because they lack tangibility. Hence, according to general principles of property law, the main authorities granted to owners, comprise possession, *usus*, *fructus*, and consumption of the owned; similarly, the owner is entitled to transfer, mortgage or pledge the thing, or even waive ownership right. Consequently, the combination of the "ownership" compound elements is conducive to articulate the following definition: ownership is the lawful power over a thing, exercised against all, following owner's absolute volition; in other words, ownership manifests an aspect of *dominative* "absoluteness", since it grants the authority of excluding any third party's interaction with the thing (Georgiades, 2010; Anthimos et. al, 2010).

In personal data law, GDPR provision does not seem to grant data subject an absolute power over their personal data; this conclusion is induced by the fact that "consent" is merely just one of the six legal bases for processing. Consequently, when processing personal data is conducted for the sake of the overriding public interest (Ar. 6 (1)(e)), there is no need for a concurrent consent; in this case, data subject's consent, as a way of expressing "dispositive will" over data, is lacking, therefore, the "absolute" character of ownership is becoming "relativized". In this regard, the herein chapter argues that, *in abstracto*, there is no "dominion" right over personal data, since the same data can be processed under another legal base, but for "consent". Furthermore, from a legislative point of view, the GDPR lacks this proprietary "absoluteness", since it aims not only to protect personal data from being unlawfully processed but also to ensure free movement of personal data; the balanced coexistence and the sought-after cooperation of these colliding goals render personal data "relativized", for the mere reason that the protected rights are inherently subjected to restrictions and compromises.

From the aforementioned analysis, it follows that the kind of "ownership" status attributed to data subjects, advocates in favour of an "obligational" nature of the right, without disregarding the *"in rem"* effect stemming from individual powers, that data subjects are endowed with. Specifically, the rights to rectification (Ar. 16), erasure (Ar. 17), restrict processing (Ar. 18) and data portability (Ar. 20) seem to reflect an *in rem* effect of these powers deriving from personal data protection right, similar to those of a traditional right *in rem*. Particularly, these individual rights "run with" personal data, in a way that it could be reasonably argued that both personal data *per se* and personal data protection right develop, indeed, a *quasi in rem* effect; moreover the same rights are granted even if processing is not consent-based. Emphatically, it needs to be highlighted that the legislative objective of enhanced protection, served by *in rem* powers over personal data, seems to be identical with the objective pursued by traditional "real rights". Hence, in both cases, these special rights "run with" the "thing", regardless of potential succession in the "interacting" persons; therefore, by drawing analogies in personal data law, it can be inferred that data subjects exercise their *in rem* powers against any data controller, irrespective of succession on behalf of the latter, in a "tracking" manner over their personal data.

To summarize, the aiming point of the foregoing approach is to trigger the emergence of personal data qualities resembling traditional rights *in rem* and to sequentially submit these qualities to a *quasi in rem* effect of personal data right. Moreover, the findings of this correlation can be summarized into the conclusion that data subject's *quasi in rem right* is reminiscent of usufructuary; this is specifically reasoned by the fact that, since data subject cannot totally transfer or waive their right, due to its partially "moral" nature, the only "disposable" power over personal data is granting *usus* and *fructus* for some time; consequently, acknowledging this idiosyncratic "dominative" authority of data subjects over their personal data, implies the underlying possibility of actualizing this power by "commercializing" personal data upon volition as a manifestation of contractual freedom principle in the context of everyday digital reality. This idiosyncrasy can be reasoned by quoting Schwartz's wording "…property can be felt as a bundle of interests rather than a despotic dominion over a thing" (2004, pp. 2059-2060). Towards this perspective, the following analysis ventures to shed light on the blur function of personal data in the current digital ecosystem, where digital content and digital services are served for money or personal data.

Directive 2019/770: Data Subject as a Customer of Online Services for the Supply of Digital Content and Digital Services. Personal Data in Position of "Counter Performance"

The Convergence Between the Directive 2019/770 and GDPR: A Brief Depiction

The Directive 2019/770 (henceforth DCDS Directive) launches a primary European legislative initiative for the protection of data subjects-consumers, who wish to enjoy digital content or digital services. Briefly, the DCDS Directive constitutes a consumer-centric statute laying down rules regarding the conformity of digital content or digital service with the contract, the remedies in the event of lack of such conformity, the failure to supply, the modalities for the exercise of those remedies as well as the modification of digital content or digital service (pr. 11). The main ambition of this Directive is to strike a fair balancing between a high level of consumers protection and the promotion of enterprises' competitiveness.

The regulatory field of the DCDS Directive appears to be partially convergent with the field of its personal data legislative counterpart. This convergence, in particular, arises in case of contracts where the trader supplies, or undertakes to supply, digital content or digital service to the consumer, and the consumer provides or undertakes to provide personal data (pr. 24). A typical example of such a conjunction, taking place in our daily digital routine, is given at the end of the 24th preamble of the Directive, as follows: "(…) this Directive should apply where the consumer opens a social media account and provides a name, an email address that are used for purposes other than solely supplying the digital content or digital service, or other than complying with legal requirements" and continues by mentioning that the Directive "should equally apply when the consumer gives consent for any material that constitutes personal data, such as photographs or posts that the consumer uploads, to be processed by the trader for marketing purposes (…)". In terms of personal data law, it is conspicuous that should personal data be processed in the abovementioned contractual framework, the legal base for processing is founded on "contract" (Ar. 6 (1) b) and/or "consent" (Ar. 6 (1) a).

The Implicit Interchangeable Role of Personal Data and Price as "Means of Payment" in the Field of DCDS Directive. The Reservations of EDPB

The aforementioned analysis leads us to the conclusion that the DCDS Directive seems to regulate -amongst others- a *sui generis* contractual species, where granting access to personal data is fictionally equated to paying a price for rendered services. This equation, indeed, reveals that the consumers' act of granting access to their personal data, serves functionally as an *ex lege* "means of payment instead of performance", in a contractual framework where: a) digital content or digital service is the furnishment and b) the access to personal data may be regarded as constituting a *quasi* counter-performance for the supplied digital content/service.

Emphatically, one could argue that although from a definition point of view "personal data" are not treated as conceptually equal to "price" (Ar. 2(7) and (8)), however, it is implicitly acknowledged that the access to personal data may function as an idiosyncratic type of "counter-performance" in contracts falling within the scope of Ar. 3 (1). In other words, personal data seem to function, within the Directive's material scope, as "means of payment"; hence, granting access to personal data is currently attributed a contractual obligation dimension. Bearing that in mind, the European legislator clarifies that "While fully recognizing that the protection of personal data is a fundamental right and that therefore personal data cannot be considered as a commodity, this Directive should ensure that consumers are, in the context of such business models, entitled to contractual remedies" (pr. 24). To this point, we argue that the aforementioned explicit personal data exemption from "commodities" constitutes an endorsed interpretative guidance in order to venture the balancing between the "fundamentality of personal data protection" and the subsequent *de facto* waiving of this right, which is functionally manifested as a contractual performance; this balancing is portrayed in Ar. 3 (1), which *equally covers contracts with a monetary and a data-based compensation* (Hacker. P, 2019), as following: "This Directive shall apply to any contract where the trader supplies or undertakes to supply digital content or a digital service to the consumer, and the consumer pays or undertakes to pay a price. This Directive shall also apply where the trader supplies or undertakes to supply digital content or digital service to the consumer and the consumer provides or undertakes to provide personal data to the trader (…)".

Preceded the analysis of that contradiction and venturing to draw some conclusions, one could maintain that the DCDS Directive, while primarily regulates certain aspects concerning contracts for the supply of digital content and digital services, it also defends the inalienability threshold of personal data protection right, in the light of the prevalent "personal right approach"[6] . However, the Directive inaugurates, at the same time, the discussion about personal data "atypical monetary value", since it implicitly acknowledges "granting access to personal data" as, in practice, "means of payment". Consequentially, it could be stressed that personal data, under the scope of the DCDS Directive, could be conceptualized as the "subject-matter" of a dispositive legal transaction and as a functional equivalent to "money".

The Interaction Between GDPR Data Subjects' Rights and DCDS Directive Consumers' Rights

In order to illustrate the interplay between the two statutes and in case of rival rights' emergence, it is critical to highlight that, from a personal data law perspective, the Directive seems to pay due respect to every GDPR provision regarding lawful processing. In this context, preamble 38 notes that the Directive should not regulate the conditions for the lawful processing of personal data, as this issue is exclusively addressed by the GDPR.

Sequentially, preamble 38 mentions several cases, where Directive should apply, without prejudice to the provisions of GDPR; thus issues regarding e.g. the legal grounds for processing, the conditions for assessing that consent under Ar. 6 (1)(a) is freely given and valid, or that processing is necessary for the contract under Ar. 6 (1)(b), and the exercise of data subjects' rights such as data erasure and data portability, fall exclusively into the material scope of GDPR, even when they happen to arise in the context of a contract for digital content and digital services, pursuant to Ar. 3 (1) of the Directive. Furthermore, the same preamble reaffirms that DCDS Directive should be without prejudice to those rights, which apply to any personal data provided by the consumer to the trader or collected by the trader in connection with any contract falling within the scope of this Directive, and in case where the consumer has terminated the contract in accordance with this Directive (pr. 38).

Respectively, in the following preamble, it is clarified that "… the consumer's right to withdraw consent for the processing of personal data should fully apply in contracts covered by this Directive". Towards this approach, it is also underlined that "The right of the consumer to terminate the contract in accordance with this Directive should be without prejudice to the consumer's right under Regulation (EU) 2016/679 to withdraw any consent given to the processing of the consumer's personal data" (pr. 39). Hence, the issue to be dealt at this point regards the correlation between the exercise of the right to withdraw "consent" in processing and its repercussions to a contract, where the data subject is a consumer of digital services who has firstly "consented" and sequentially granted access to their personal data as a *quasi-contractual* counter-performance.

Furthermore, it is essentially questionable whether the case of unlawful processing affects the validity and the legality of the interrelated DCDS contract, in which granting access to personal data functions as a "counter-performance". Towards this academic field, Hacker P. (2019) has made an interesting analysis commencing with an axiomatic statement that "in almost every case, only a fraction of the envisaged processing activities are unlawful". More profoundly, Hacker ponders on the practical implementation of that partial legality to the contractual frame of a DCDS contract, to conclude that "the promise to provide the service, for example, access to a social network, cannot be partially invalidated: either access is granted or not". Sequentially, Hacker also scrutinizes the interdependence between the withdrawal of consent or other "family incidents", such as the exercise of data portability right, and the launching of a data-based *quasi* counter-performance counterpart, by venturing an essential distinction; for that reason, Hacker develops a well-documented theory by commencing from the self-evident fact that, "the transfer of one piece of personal data is put to multiple uses, some of which may be legal and some illegal" (2019). In that manner, Hacker interestingly concludes that service provider's claim to gain access to personal data is not enforceable against consumers when the intended processing would violate data protection law. However, he argues that when such a transfer has been made there is no practical way of retroactively invalidating the transfer; in other words, transferring personal data to the service provider instantly function as a "counter-performance", and this fact cannot be altered upon the occurrence of personal data law violation. The rationale of this approach lies -amongst others- in the thought that data subjects enjoy enhanced protection when the DCDS contract remains untouched despite the violation incident. For this reason, Hacker argues that if "data subjects who already face unlawful processing would be denied contractual rights, this would seem to run counter precisely to the interests of those the GDPR initially intends to protect" (2019).

The aforementioned analysis ventured to achieve a brief understanding of the issue regarding the interrelation of the so-called conflicted rights, stemming from the two intersect statutes. The following sections are consisted in epitomizing the specific characteristics of personal data protection right and in proposing an alternative construe of "consent" into the everyday contractual digital experience.

SOLUTIONS AND RECOMMENDATIONS

The Specific Hybrid Characteristics of Personal Data Protection Right: A Sui Generis Right Emerges

It is a commonplace that personal data protection right launches a new category of lawful powers, which made their appearance in the rule of law since communications technology has been rapidly evolving and penetrating every field of human action. Understanding these neophyte rights cannot be achieved with watertight criteria, such as those applied in "traditional" legal rights and the powers stemming from them. However, exploiting the classical principles of law science could provide some of the "anatomical" needed tools for this attempt. Towards this perspective, the herein chapter aspires to shed light on the nature of multiple manifestations of personal data protection right.

The outcome of this venture is articulated with the form of a conclusion, according to which the right to personal data protection can be described as a *sui generis* "right of obligation" with the effect of an *in rem* right, characterized by a peculiar legal nature of both personal and proprietary origin; moreover, it is worth mentioning again that the right to personal data protection resembles in nature to the intellectual property right.

According to the author, this alternative conceptual design of "personal data" leads to a harmonic conjunction of "personal" and "property" based approach of personal data protection right, in a way that not only respects the twofold nature of the right, and its historical personal-based *ratio* but also empowers the current role of data subjects when it comes to privacy self-management choices as the result of a decision making process. The specific characteristics of "personal data" and the powers stemming from them are briefly the following:

1. The right to personal data protection is a personal right since its historical emergence was assigned to safeguard rights, values and liberties, pertaining to private and personal sphere, from technological menace. In this regard, the GDPR shelters the personal nature of the right, by enforcing data subjects with *in rem* powers over their personal data, as prescribed in other absolute rights, such as the right to personality.
2. The right to personal data protection is also claimed to be a *property right,* without disregarding the fact that the dawn of the right was in the context of an anthropocentric approach; hence, it is critical to underline that property-based approach seems to highlight the duality of the right and to reinvent the rationale in protecting personal data, because of their quality to be a vulnerable good, "traded" in *de facto* personal data marketplaces. Particularly, it could be argued that the *in rem effect* of granted powers, such as portability, highlights the "proprietary relation" between data subjects and their data, in a divergent sense from the classical "dominative" perception of property. Hence, the proprietary nature of personal data can be perceived under the notion of a "right to

obligation", referring to an intangible asset, which is protected through granting *in rem* powers; that is, by enhancing personal data right with a quota of "absoluteness".

3. Perceiving personal data protection right under the dual scope of a combined personal and property-based approach is reminiscent of its counterpart prototype right stemming from the intellectual property law field. However, the right in question seems rather to be a *quasi-intellectual* property right, since it only borrows the rationale of intellectual property law, adjusted accordingly to its very idiosyncratic nature. A sharp distinction between the two notions is ventured by Prins, as already mentioned, who baptizes personal data as "Humanistic Property" and defines the neophyte term, by using Steve Mann's wording: "Humanistic property is that which we give without conscious thought or effort, and differs from Intellectual Property which is what we consciously produce for the purpose of disclosing it to other people" (2006, p. 223). Conceptually, from the abovementioned definition it is inferred that the common denominator between Humanistic and Intellectual Property is "information", whilst their differentiator –amongst others- lies in the "consciousness of producing information".

4. Normatively, one could argue in favour of data subjects' "moral right" reflected in every protective GDPR provision. Under this scope, it is imposed to take into consideration the fact that pure property rights are inherently alienable and, consequentially, being traded means that the initially entitled should be alienated from the good. However, this alienation does not occur in case of "selling" personal data, since "data subject-seller" is granted rights, that confirm the perpetual bond between the seller and the "sold", even after processing takes place; the lack of total alienation reaffirms data subjects' "moral right" on their data. As a consequence, the "tracking" character of granted powers fortifies the thought that personal data right is a *quasi-intellectual property right* since even during processing data subject does not fully alienate from their personal data.

5. Both personal and property nature of personal data protection right necessitates data subjects initially being entitled; this entitlement is brought into fruition on the base of the contractual freedom principle, where "consent" can be perceived as a statement of will for the dispositive "judiciary act" of processing personal data. According to Calabresi and Mohamed, who define property by contrasting it to the liability rules, "An entitlement is protected by a property rule to the extent that someone who wishes to remove the entitlement from its holder must buy it from him in a voluntary transaction in which the value of the entitlement is agreed upon by the seller"; whereas the two scholars support that, "(…) whenever someone may destroy the initial entitlement if he is willing to pay an objectively determined value for it, the entitlement is protected by a liability rule" (Purtova, 2009, p. 516).

From the abovementioned, it is inferred that data subject could enjoy the fruit of commercializing their personal data in the context of contractual freedom, by disclosing them for a set price to third parties, under the *ius cog*ens provisions of GDPR governing data subject's information, consent and processing of their personal data. Adversely, data subject could *de lege ferenda* abstain from every act of data commercialization in the context of a negative manifestation of contractual freedom principle, according to which data subjects should have the right to decide freely and not coercively whether to dispose their personal data as a type of "counter-performance" in order to join Information Society services or not. Data subjects should be practically endowed with an efficient and alternative way of compensating their service provider, distinct from granting access to personal data; this right has recently appeared in the literature as a right of "data-free" option for concluding a contract in the field of digital economy

(Hacker P., 2019); according to Hacker, to acknowledge the necessity of such a right "(…) would imply that traders are under one obligation, as a matter of principle, to provide consumers at least the option to pay for the product with their money instead of their data, potentially with two buttons, one for "paying with money" and one for "paying with data". Pursuant to Hacker "(…) such a right to a data-free option would respect the privacy preferences of consumers on the other side of the U-shaped distribution: those who value privacy and data protection highly".

The Alienability of Personal Data: A Brief Estimation of the Conditions Under Which Consenting to Personal Data Processing May Be Deemed as a Valid Dispositive or Even "Selling" Transaction

Reflecting on the constituent components of GDPR consent in the context of a civil law dogma approach induces to the finding that "consent", *per se,* encompasses the two following distinct phases: i) data subject's statement of will, which is addressed to a third party (controller) and consists in licensing personal data access and processing, and ii) the material action of granting access to data. These compound elements of "consent", conceptualized as a current juridical act, are reminiscent of the constituent compounds of Ar. 1034 of the Greek Civil Code, which is a typical example of transferring the ownership of a movable tangible good. This article sets particularly two prerequisites for the aiming transfer: i) delivery of occupancy and ii) respective prior agreement that the ownership is transferred. Ergo, under an interdisciplinary approach, where personal data law meets contract law, consumer law and intellectual property law as well, "consent" to processing personal data seems to be a *dispositive legal transaction,* the *causa* of which may be, *inter alia,* laid in the prior data subject's legal bind to exchange or even "sell" their own data.

After all, entering into digital contracts, not only under the *stricto sensu* meaning of the DCDS Directive (Ar. 3 (1)) but also in the *lato sensu* framework either of consent under Ar. 6 (1)(a) or of a contract under Ar. 6(1)(b), connotes an act of demonstrating the dispositive power that data subjects exercise over their personal data. This kind of disposal, although in a position of *quasi* counter-performance, is not exclusively regulated by contract or consumer law, -as already mentioned- but seems to be also subjected to the same prerequisites, required by GDPR for lawful processing under the legal base of consent or contract. In this regard, the herein subsection questions the difference between "transactional consent" and "GDPR consent" and argues that consent under Ar. 6(1)(a) and (b) is functionally externalized in the digital world as an "expression of dispositive power" over personal data, in the exact way "transactional consent" is externalized in a contractual framework. Therefore, and having taken into consideration the aforementioned analysis regarding not only personal data protection right but also personal data *per se,* this chapter firmly maintains that "consent", in both cases of Ar. 6 (1)(a) and (1)(b), seems to require the existence of a lawfully entitled stakeholder, attributed legal powers, in order to manage their data at their very interest; these powers are reminiscent of those granted in the framework of a *quasi* ownership status.

Characteristically, it is entailed that in personal data protection right the "ownership" status may be altered only upon the volition of the person entitled, according to the general rule of contractual freedom and individual autonomy; in other words, it is claimed that the informational value mined from personal data cannot be disposed without data subject's will, as it is the case in every property right (Kang and Buchner, 2004). At this point, after having ventured to cast light on the twofold nature of personal data protection right, and especially to the property nature this right manifests, it follows that 'transactional" and "GDPR" consent appears to be the same single notion, since they are both manifestations of dispositive power, and, as such, they depend on the fulfilment of two prerequisites: the existence of a "proprietary right" over a good and of a person entitled to its enjoyment. Bearing that in mind, it can be argued that the phenomenical difference between the two "types" of consent does not exist, since there is only one single conceptual and normative meaning of "consent" in the crossroad of contract and personal data law. Interestingly, Strahilevitz O. (2017) has argued that "privacy is not *sui generis*; it is instead a valuable laboratory to examine the evolution of contract law in the digital era".

In order to illustrate the abovementioned phenomenical duality, it suffices to reflect upon two different cases. The first one is depicted in every day numerous digital transactions, where social media users enjoy online services by consenting to the processing of their personal data; this kind of consent is lawfully manifested in the context of Ar. 6(1)(b). In that scope, granting access to certain personal data consists a necessary prerequisite for the fulfilment of controller's contractual obligation towards data subjects-consumers (e.g., granting access to certain demographic or other data for the creation of an account in order to enjoy e-mail services). However, in a plethora of cases, these platforms do not simply undertake to render the digital service they provide, but they also stealthily take advantage of the established interaction with the data subject, so as to sequentially usurp data subject's "consent", in a context of a growing "necessity".

More profoundly, it could be argued that in such cases this kind of "consent" has been propagated for many years as "lawful" by controllers, claiming that it falls under the scope of Ar. 6(1)(a). Fortunately, this myth gets debunked by acknowledging that "consent" in many cases is extracted without due respect of the minimum content requirements for "informed consent"; the greatest example that could portray this violation is blur information about the processing purposes, including cases of "enhancing user's experience". Towards this reasoning, it is observed that social media platforms, for instance, factually depend on the deliverance of their services, or the quality of the latter, on gaining access to as many, "necessary" and "not necessary" personal data, by using the "necessity" notion as a Trojan horse to mine as much as possible personal data. Respectively the Berlin Court of Appeals has stated that consumers' decision to agree to data processing as a pre-condition for being able to use a service could be considered as a transactional decision in the sense of the Unfair Commercial Directive (hereinafter UCD); therefore the lawfulness of this decision should be scrutinized not only under GDPR but also in the sense of the UCD since this decision is of contractual nature (Helberger, Borgesius, Reyna, 2017).

Moving on to the second and more imaginative case study, this chapter reflects upon "consent" by perceiving it to be detached from the fruitful enjoyment of a "free" digital service; hence, in a fictional case study, a gym owner wishes to examine the working out habits of the locals with the intention of expanding their enterprise in a new area. The aiming target of the gym owner is to render personalized services; therefore, to create customized working out programs, the gym owner proposes to the inhabitants of the particular area to grant him access to their training habits for an agreed price, by filling a questionnaire. In this hypothetic scenario, "consent" protests actively in favour of individual and transactional autonomy and falls within the scope of Ar. 6 (1)(a), for the mere reason that the "necessity" of Ar. 6(1)(b) is not met. Analytically, having in mind that individuals' participation to these training programs is not granted nor did they have the initiative of a request in the context of potentially entering into contract, it is concluded that in the respective case the "necessity" prerequisite of Ar. 6 (1)(b) is not met. However, the answer would be quite different when reflecting that granting access to this kind of personal data would function as a concurrent obligation in a wider contractual field between a trainer and a trainee, as that prescribed in Ar. 6 (1)(b); according to Guidelines 2/2019 of the EDPB "The important issue here is the nexus between the personal data and processing operations concerned, and the performance or non-performance of the service provided under the contract".

Although the aforementioned examples ventured to illustrate some typical contractual expressions of consent under Ar. 6(1) (a and b), an exhaustive distinction between their similarities and differences would transcend the scope of the herein chapter. Nevertheless, the preceded analysis aimed to underline that, in both cases, "consent", perceived under the legal ideal of the notion, produces the results of a juridical act, since data subject's expression of will triggers the legal consequence of granting access to personal data, as an idiosyncratic means of exchange or counter-performance, otherwise, as a way of harnessing the fruitful economic power of one's "digital asset". In a more advanced level, data subjects should be acknowledged to have the contractual freedom not only to exchange or "sell" their data but also to seclude information about themselves and alternatively pay a "fee" in plain money for joining Information Society services.

After all, "consideration" does not purport to be an adequate criterion to divide "consent" into two distinct notions, in correspondence to GDPR and transactional consent, respectively. Hence, pursuant to the Guidelines 2/2019 of EDPB on the processing of personal data under Ar. 6(1)(b) GDPR it is claimed that "(…) Ar. 6(1)(b) cannot provide a lawful basis for online behavioural advertising simply because such advertising indirectly funds the provision of the service". Furthermore, it is clarified that "Although such processing may support the delivery of a service, this in itself is not sufficient to establish that it is necessary for the performance of the contract at issue". The aforementioned guideline stresses that "necessity" of Ar. 6(1)(b) should be detached from controllers' financial interests; at the same time, the Directive does not preclude funding through personal data, so long as it is GDPR-abiding. The same rationale could apply when it comes to implementing Ar. 6(1)(a), where "free will" plays a key role in weighting the legality of "consent" (instead of "necessity" of Ar. 6(1)(b)).

The reason why the herein chapter strongly stands in favour of a single perception of "consent", lies in the mere fact that GDPR sets the rules for regulated processing, without forbidding, a potential transactional background of consent. Emphatically, it could be stated otherwise that GDPR seems to implicitly acknowledge this potentiality, by the fact that it imposes obligations to mutual parties' concessions in order to balance conflicting rights; *id est*, GDPR provides for actions of "disposing", or "waiving" a lawful interest for the sake of personal data protection's conflicting counterpart. This conclusion seems to be fortified by the secondary objective of GDPR to ensure the free flow of personal data within the EU (Ar. 1 (3)). To conclude, from a legal point of view, a data subject's bind to "sell" their personal data, as *causa* of consent to processing their data, does not introduce additional parameters regarding the legality of "transactional consent", different than those governing "GDPR consent"; this argument seems to be verified with the thought that both kinds of consent should actually meet only one severe boundary, which is essentially respect for human value and dignity.

On the one hand, property approach opponents axiomatically argue that the perspective of data subjects selling their personal data guarantees little autonomous data-control, therefore, the pertinent contract must be considered invalid; indeed, the justification of this argument lies amongst others in the fact that a person cannot assess the ramifications of divulging a set of personal data in the context of a contractual relationship (Kang & Buchner, 2004). However, the causal ground of this viewpoint rests on arguments of legal policy and asserts so-called exclusive interconnectivity between consent and safeguarding personal data. Nevertheless, this approach disregards the fact that GDPR also provides for others, distinct from consent, legal bases for processing; in practice, from this point of view, GDPR has been currently confronting the risk of little autonomous data control.

In other words, the herein chapter argues that GDPR has already reckoned with inevitable phenomena of "information asymmetry" and "power inequality" when configuring "consent" as a legal base for processing personal data. Hence, it would be accurate to argue that GDPR "consent" currently deals with the abovementioned risks, manifested so far in a traditional contract field. Informed and freely given consent is indeed the cornerstone of contractual lawfulness but at the same time, an absolute demand for such qualities seems to become a utopia. Currently, these phenomena are given a new, digital, territory to acquire, linked to the decision-making process with respect to privacy and constitute a reality which cannot be fully altered and controlled because of algorithmic opacity.

On the other hand, from a personal-based approach, one could argue that the great importance ascribed by the GDPR to issues concerning the functional aim, the nature, and the particular content of personal data in view of processing, reflects weightings regarding the human value, privacy, personality and individual autonomy. The same weightings are mainly reflected on settled legal values, which govern contracts holistically and verify the lawfulness of "consent", as a manifestation of contractual freedom principle. A typical legislative example reflecting contract legality and validity lies in Ar. 178 and 179 of the Greek Civil Code; thus, according to Ar. 178, the judicial act that contravenes "moral rights" is invalid, whereas pursuant to Ar. 179 the main species of such invalid transactions, encompass indicatively cases of extremely restricting individual freedom and unduly exploiting the need and inexperience of the contracting counterpart, in order to abstract a legally binding promise to perform an act, or a furnishment obviously disproportionate to the consideration given. These core values are also reflected in consumer law and play a key role in balancing the negotiating power between consumers and providers of digital services, by helping regulators and courts to develop and modernize the existing catalogue of fair and unfair practices (Helberger, Borgesius, Reyna, 2017).To conclude, setting the conditions for the expression of unbiased and free will and the elimination of every undue influence, constitute the limits of the contractual freedom principle whilst it also cross-checks processing purpose in the light of human value; towards this direction, it is noted that data protection law could also provide an additional benchmark to assess the fairness of contractual conditions (Helberger, Borgesius, Reyna, 2017), without exempting GDPR consent from the transactional field.

CONCLUSION

Safeguarding dignity of data subjects constitutes the cornerstone of "digital ethics" which emerge as the contemporain transformation of traditional ethics into the context of a digital data ecosystem. Just as "moral rights" curb contracting parties' freedom in formulating contractual terms, so do "digital ethics" undertake a similar role in "digital transactions". By drawing analogies from traditional non-digital customs in the field of personal data processing, it is inferred that the principles introduced by the aforementioned provisions are directly applicable to a personal data processing contract, as well. Hence, in the Information Society, respect for free and unaffected will power and proper information regarding data processing should constitute the cornerstone of the digital ecosystem. To this end, GDPR perceives "consent" only as positively- stated action, defined and expressed through opt-in clause; this clause practically signifies the dynamic quality of consent, needed across the data life cycle. In the context of the current legislative inclination for enhancing data subjects' control, the idea of the herein chapter is that property approach will contribute to a holistic enforcement of data subjects, which derives from raising awareness regarding the monetary value of personal data and the sequential acknowledging of property rights over them; as Spiekermann-Hoff and Novotny argue "The main reason for establishing an ownership claim to PI is a psychological one: "ownership" of PI creates asset awareness in the minds of all stakeholders" (2015, p.7).

Consequently, recognizing a partial property nature of personal data right draws the attention to the realization that processing upon consent is proven to be transactional, whilst it renders the stakeholders-data subjects more prudent during managing their data. In other words, the duality of personal data protection right, as of both personal and property quality, conduces to piercing the "inalienability" (sic) veil of personal data; at the same time, it provokes the legal community to deal with the conspicuous *de facto* trading practice, in which the majority of "digital inhabitants" participate unconsciously. In fact, personal data are daily traded, since data subjects are typically "obliged" to enter into "exchange" transactions in order to enjoy digital services, where granting access to personal data has been unilaterally set as the only way of performing the furnishment for an online experience. This policy, however, is inconsistent with the doctrine of "digital ethics" and seems to be incompatible with the legislative prioritization of safeguarding free individual will power as the basis of voluntary choice.

To sum up, forced disclosure of personal information as a prerequisite for the enjoyment of Information Society services is an oxymoron under the light of currently established "opt-in status". The true meaning of GDPR opt-in clause, according to the author, should be perceived not only in the sense of granting a "positive will power" to data subjects for them to enter into a personal data processing relationship; it should be also perceived in the sense of a "positive discretion power" in choosing the species of "currency" during performing the contractual obligation stemming from the enjoyment of information society services. For this reason, legal recognition of personal data as "asset" and "currency", under the light of a GDPR partially property-based approach, could validate personal data as "means of payment"; consequently, it could enhance data subjects' authority of real control over their personal data and provoke a raise of awareness on the exact economic and proprietary value personal data reflect. Acknowledging "monetary equity" between money and personal data could pave the way to more realistic and reinforced protection of personal data right since it preconditions the further acknowledging of a binary option regarding granting or not granting access to personal data when joining Information Society.

REFERENCES

Akrivopoulou, X. M. (2011). The right to data protection via the lens of the right to privacy. *Theory and Practice of Administrative Law*, *7*, 679–691.

Akrivopoulou, X. M. (2012). *The right to privacy: From its genesis to its current development and protection*. Athens, Greece: Sakkoulas Publications.

Anthimos, A., Avgitides, D., Valtoudis, A., Varela, M., Vervesos, N., & Georgiades, A. (Eds.). (2010). A brief interpretation of the Greek Civil Code, 2. Athens, Greece: Law & Economy- P.N. Sakkoulas.

Bauer, C., Korunovska, J., & Spiekermann, S. (2012). On the Value of Information –What Facebook Users are Willing to Pay. *ECIS 2012*, *Proceedings*, 197. Available at: https://aisel.aisnet.org/ecis2012/197

Ben-Shahar, O., & Strahilevitz, L. J. (2016, June). Contracting over Privacy: Introduction. *The Journal of Legal Studies*, *45*(S2), S1–S11. doi:10.1086/690281

Bix, B. H. (2010). Contracts. In The Ethics of Consent: Theory and Practice, (pp. 251-279). Oxford University Press. doi:10.1093/acprof:oso/9780195335149.001.0001

Christodoulou, K. N. (2013). *Personal data protection Law*. Athens, Greece: Nomiki Bibliothiki Group.

Dagtoglou, P. D. (2012). *Constitutional Law: Civil Rights* (4th ed.). Athens, Greece: Sakkoulas Publications.

European Data Protection Board. (2019). *Guidelines 2/2019, On the Processing of Personal Data under Article 6 (1)(b) in the Context of the Provision of Online Services to Data Subjects, version 2.0.* Retrieved from https://edpb.europa.eu/our-work-tools/our-documents/smernice/guidelines-22019-processing-personal-data-under-article-61b_en

European Data Protection Supervisor. (2017). *Opinion 4/2017, On the Proposal for a Directive on certain aspects concerning contracts for the supply of digital content.* Retrieved from https://edps.europa.eu/sites/edp/files/publication/17-03-14_opinion_digital_content_en.pdf

Georgiades, A. S. (2010). *Corporeal property law* (2nd ed.). Athens, Greece: Sakkoulas Publications.

Hacker, P. (2019), Regulating the Economic Impact of Data as Counter-Performance: From the Illegality Doctrine to the Unfair Contract Terms Directive, In: Sebastian Lohsse, Reiner Schulze and Dirk Staudenmayer (eds.), Data as Counter-Performance: Contract Law 2.0? (Hart/Nomos, forthcoming). Available at: Regulating the Economic Impact of Data as Counter-Performance: From the Illegality Doctrine to the Unfair Contract Terms Directive by Philipp Hacker:: SSRN

Igglezakis, I. D. (2004). *Sensitive personal data.* Athens, Greece: Sakkoulas Publications.

Kaisis, A. G., & Paraskevopoulos, N. A. (2001). *Personal data protection.* Athens, Greece: Sakkoulas Publications.

Kang, J., & Buchner, B. (2004). Privacy in Atlantis. *Harvard Journal of Law & Technology, 18,* 229–267. Available at: https://www.researchgate.net/publication/228189643_Privacy_in_Atlantis

McDerpott, Y. (2017). Conceptualizing the right to data protection in an era of Big Data. *Big Data &Society (BD&S), 4*(1). Available at https://journals.sagepub.com/doi/full/10.1177/2053951716686994

Mortier, R., Haddadi, H., Henderson, T., McAuley, D., & Crowcroft, J. (2014). *Human-Data interaction: The human face of the data-driven society.* Available at SSRN: https://ssrn.com/abstract=2508051

Prins, C. (2006). Property and Privacy: European Perspectives and the Commodification of Our Identity. *Information Law Series, 16,* 223-257. Available at SSRN: https://ssrn.com/abstract=929668

Purtova, N. (2009). Property rights in personal data: Learning from the American discourse. *Computer Law & Security Review, 25*(6), 507–521. doi:10.1016/j.clsr.2009.09.004

Raab, C. D. (2013). *Privacy as a security value. Jon Bing: En Hyllest A Tribute.* Available at SSRN: https://ssrn.com/abstract=3057433

Rimbert, P. (2016). Socialize our digital labour: No such thing as free data. How do the world's suppliers of online data –anybody using a smartphone- get to share in the wealth they generate? (C. Goulden, Trans.). *Le Monde Diplomatique.* Retrieved from https://mondediplo.com/2016/09/09digitallabor

Schwartz, P. M. (2003). Property, Privacy and Personal Data, 117. *Harvard Law Review*, 2056–2128. Retrieved from https://pdfs.semanticscholAr.org/8d8d/e4cb107a627c7c7b0da9076248ed1e3b28b4.pdf

Solove, D. J. (2002). Conceptualizing Privacy. *California Law Review*, *90*(4), 2. doi:10.2307/3481326

Spiekermann-Hoff, S., & Novotny, A. (2015). A vision for global bridges: Technical and legal measures for international data markets. *Computer Law and Security Review, 31*(2), *181-200*. Available at: https://epub.wu.ac.at/5485/

Spiropoulos, F., Kontiadis, X., Anthopoulos, X., & Gerapetritis, G. (Eds.). (2017). *The Constitution: Articles' Interpretation*. Athens, Greece: Sakkoulas Publications.

Stathopoulos, M. (2000). The usage of personal data and the combat in the field of liberties acknowledged both to controllers and to data subjects. *Legal Pontium, 48,* 1–19.

Surblyte, G. (2016). *Data as a Digital Resource.* Max Planck Institute for Innovation & Competition Research Paper No. 16-12. Available at SSRN: https://ssrn.com/abstract=2849303

Tannert, C. (2016). *Could your personal data subsidize the cost of a new car?* Retrieved from http://www.thedrive.com/tech/4457/could-your-personal-data-subsidize-the-cost-of-a-new-car

Tassis, S. (2013). Privacy as a field of a commercial dispute between the EU and USA. *Media and Communication Law, 1,* 46–57.

Victor, J. M. (2013). The EU General Data Protection Regulation: Toward a Property Regime for Protecting Data Privacy. *The Yale Law Journal, 23,* 513–528. Available at: https://digitalcommons.law.yale.edu/ylj/vol123/iss2/5

World Economic Forum (Ed.). (2011). *Personal data: The emergence of a new asset class.* Retrieved from: https://www.weforum.org/reports/personal-data-emergence-new-asset-class

Zech, H. (2017). Data as a tradeable commodity – Implications for contract law. In *Proceedings of the 18th EIPIN Congress: The New Data Economy between Data Ownership, Privacy and Safeguarding Competition.* Edward Elgar Publishing. Available at SSRN: https://ssrn.com/abstract=3063153

ADDITIONAL READING

Acquisti, A. (2010). *The economics of personal data and the economics of privacy.* Retrieved from: https://pdfs.semanticscholAr.org/e4ae/9f8b13fab5c5ce1e1e820b64bce196f60c53.pdf

Baitaineh, A. S., Mizouni, R., Barachi, M. E., & Bentahar, J. (2016). Monetizing personal data: A two-sided market approach. *Procedia Computer Science, 83,* 472–479. doi:10.1016/j.procs.2016.04.211

Basho, K. (2000). The licensing of our personal information: Is it a solution to internet privacy? *California Law Review, 88*(5), 1507–1546. doi:10.2307/3481264

Lund, J. (2011). Property Rights to Information. *Northwestern Journal of Technology and Intellectual Property, 10*(1), 1–18. Available at: https://scholarlycommons.law.northwestern.edu/njtip/vol10/iss1/1

Parra- Arnau. J. (2017). Optimized, direct sale of privacy in personal data marketplaces. *Information Sciences,* 354-384. Retrieved from: https://arxiv.org/abs/1701.00740

Riederer, C., Erramilli, V., Chaintreau, A., Krishnamurthy, B., & Rodriguez, P. (2011). *For Sale: Your Data. By: You.* Retrieved from: http://conferences.sigcomm.org/hotnets/2011/papers/hotnetsX-final85.pdf

Samuelson, P. (1999). Privacy as Intellectual Property? *Stanford Law Review, 52*(5), 1125–1173. doi:10.2307/1229511 PMID:11503653

Voss, G. (2017). Internet, New Technologies and Value: Taking Share of Economic Surveillance. *Journal of Law, Technology and Policy, 2017,* 469-485. Available at: https://papers.ssrn.com/sol3/papers.cfm?abstract_id=3086632

KEY TERMS AND DEFINITIONS

De Facto Personal Data Marketplaces: A marketplace (usually a platform) which enables convenient buying and selling of data between data brokers and companies.

End-Users: Individual consumers, citizens or persons about and from whom personal data are created. The term resembles its "family" term "prosumer", currently used to attribute to a person the quality of a producer and consumer at the same time.

Individualization of Person's Identity: The enclosing of information related to human personality, in the exact way privacy embodies data regarding the individual's authenticity; the term is not used as interchangeable of «Identifiable», which is a compound element of the notion of personal data in general.

Juridical Act: A lawful act or expression of will intended to have legal consequences. It may be unilateral, bilateral and multilateral. "Legal transaction" is an interchangeable term for a juridical act.

Obligational Right: A right related to personal obligation. An obligational right, when not "ex lege", is linked with the legal doctrine of privity, according to which contracts bind only the contracting parties; hence, no third party can take legal action with regard to the contract in favour or against the contracting parties. The term is contracted to the term *"right in rem"* or its interchangeable "real right".

Personal Right: A right pertaining to the quality of persons as "individuals". The claims deriving from personal rights aim to compensate the claimant for non-pecuniary (moral) damages.

Property Right: A right in favour or against specific property. The claims deriving from property rights aim to compensate the claimant for pecuniary damages.

Raw Data: Data that hasn't undergone processing. This term is herein used in contradiction to the term "inferred data" in order to underline the financial value that even a single raw datum embodies and to emphasize the dynamic economic sign of personal data across their evolving course.

Right in Rem Effect: The effect of legal powers over a tangible thing, which "run with" the thing and being exercised "erga omnes". These powers stem from a "dominative" ownership relation between a person and a (usually) tangible thing.

ENDNOTES

[1] The importance of free choice is highlighted by Solove quoting that according to the philosopher Stanley Benn, "privacy amounts to respect for individuals as choosers" (2002, p. 1116).

[2] The distinction of data into "simple" and "sensitive" does not always reflect accordingly the "simple" or "sensitive" content of enclosed information; sometimes, instead, it serves political or social interests. Igglezakis illustrates this thought with the argument that the Directive 95/46EC had exempted financial personal data from the category of "sensitive" even though they relate to the core private life, in order to enhance financial transparency and tackle money laundering (2013, p.94, own translation).

[3] See Akrivopoulou, (2011, 2012); McDermott (2017, p. 2) has also argued that "(…) the creation of the right could be traced to several distinct values inherent in the pre-existing data protection framework, namely privacy, autonomy, transparency and non-discrimination (…)".

[4] It is notably maintained by Buer C., Kuronovksa J., & Spiekerman S. (2012), that asset consciousness and psychology of ownership seem to drive data subjects' personal data management tactic.

[5] See Hacker (2019) claiming the necessity of the introduction of a right to a "data-free option".

[6] The rationale of exempting personal data from the commodity genre seems to serve, besides personal data law dogma, the avoidance of bulk of legal issues quite technical in nature, which arise upon the transfusion of personal data into markets. A profound analysis of them would transcend the scope of the herein chapter.

Section 2
A Closer Look at the GDPR: Basic Definitions, Purposes, New Technologies, Implementation, and Its Relationship With Other Instruments

This section focuses on a plethora of complex questions that arise when considering the GDPR. These concern the uncertainties regarding basic definitions, such as 'controllers' and 'processors', the challenges that new technologies such as AI and profiling present, the purposes of EU data privacy law, the problems of its implementation at the national level, and its relationship with other instruments.

Chapter 4

Data Controller, Processor, or Joint Controller:
Towards Reaching GDPR Compliance in a Data- and Technology-Driven World

Yordanka Ivanova

Sofia University, St. Kliment Ohridski, Bulgaria & Vrije Universiteit Brussel, Belgium

ABSTRACT

This chapter aims to examine critically the existing legal provisions on the concepts of controller, processor, and joint controller, as interpreted by the relevant non-binding guidelines and case law, and to propose a new "value chain" method for allocating responsibilities among joint controllers that is more effective and appropriate for the technology- and data-driven world. It also examines the corresponding data protection responsibilities of different data processing actors, in particular through the prism of the new accountability principle, which arguably includes not only obligations for means but also result-oriented obligations for compliance in terms of data subjects' effective and complete protection.

INTRODUCTION

Defining the capacity of an organization processing personal data and its counterparts constitutes an obligatory first step in every action plan for reaching compliance with the General Data Protection Regulation (GDPR). This task is, however, not straightforward due to the short definitions in the GDPR of the key concept of *data controller*, who determines the purposes and means of the data processing and *data processor*, who is only acting on behalf of the controller. The GDPR largely inherits these concepts from the repealed Directive 95/46/EC without additional guidance except for clarifying their new responsibilities (e.g., GDPR art. 24–28). This cannot, however, answer the pre-existential question of how to define correctly the legal capacity of the actor, which is of key importance to correctly assign the tasks, responsibilities and liability under GDPR. Legal uncertainty is further increased due to sometimes conflicting guidelines given by Working Party Article 29 (WP29, 2010) and the guidelines of

DOI: 10.4018/978-1-5225-9489-5.ch004

some national data protection authorities (DPAs) how to apply these notions in practice. The importance of this question becomes even more pressing with the introduction of the new accountability principle, which shifts the burden on controllers and processors to put in place appropriate measures and be able to demonstrate compliance with their incumbent data protection responsibilities.

Not surprisingly, disputes on the concepts of controller and processor and their responsibilities have already reached the Court of Justice of the EU (CJEU), which is solely competent to interpret with binding force these notions that have autonomous meaning within the EU legal order and must be applied uniformly in all EU Member States. With its recent jurisprudence,[1] CJEU has importantly developed new principles and criteria in assessing the capacity of an organization processing personal data. On a positive side, this case- law brings certain clarity and significantly enlarges the scope of application of the EU data protection legislation. It also puts the under-explored concept of *joint controllers* in the spotlight, which becomes the primary legal instrument for ensuring the collective responsibility of various controllers who use the same personal data in an often obscure and unaccountable manner. Still, this case-law fails to fill in all legal gaps and opens at the same time new challenges for the effective protection of the data subjects' rights, in particular with the new phase-oriented approach where responsibilities are limited only in respect of the processing phase in which the joint controller is involved, thus disregarding the risks and adverse impacts from the subsequent processing, once the data is transferred to another (joint) controller.

In the context of these doctrinal developments, the purpose of this chapter will be two-fold. First, it will aim to critically examine the existing legal provisions on the concepts of (joint) controller and processor, as interpreted by the relevant non-binding guidelines and case law, and to propose a new "value chain" method for allocating responsibilities among (joint) controllers. Secondly, the chapter will examine the corresponding responsibilities of the different data processing actors, in particular through the prism of the new accountability principle, which arguably includes not only obligations for means, but also result-oriented obligations for compliance in terms of effective and complete protection of the data subjects.

BACKGROUND

The attribution of responsibility of data controllers and processors has been already examined by a number of scholars. Alsenoy (2016) has compared the two regimes of liability under the repealed Directive and the GDPR, concluding that they remain unchanged and are in compliance with the European Tort Law Principles. On the other hand, many scholars have already emphasized the difficulties in applying the linear concepts of controller and processor to the new economic and technology reality, including *inter alia* Tene (2013); De Hert and Papakonstantinou (2016); Gürses and Hoboken (2017); Mahieu, Hoboken, and Asghari (2019). While GDPR does not change these concepts, it does clarify the responsibilities of the data processing actors and their accountability, which become more flexible and scalable according to the risks to the individuals' rights. This new risk-based approach is perceived by Quelle (2017) as changing the nature of the obligations with a possibility for calibration according to the level of risk and other relevant factors such as scope and context of processing.

This chapter contributes a review of the most recent CJEU case-law on the concepts of (joint) controller and processor and an analysis of the new criteria developed by the Court for attributing data protection responsibilities. As Mahieu et al. (2019) have pointed out, it will be argued that the CJEU has extensively used the concept of the (joint) controller to enlarge the scope of the data protection legislation and impose responsibilities on entities and persons who have been so far considered exempt. However, the chapter will analyze critically the new phase-oriented approach developed by the CJEU and propose instead a new value chain method for delineating the scope of the pluralistic control and allocating responsibilities among joint controllers. Contrary to Quelle (2017) and Alsenoy (2016), the controller's responsibility under GDPR will also be analyzed as obligations for outcomes, considering the requirement for effectiveness of the measures put in place by the controller to achieve the objectives of the GDPR. Arguments will also be presented why the risk involved in the processing should not serve as a defense for the controller to escape or reduce its civil liability. Contrary to the prevailing opinion (e.g., Bygrave, 2017 and EDPB, 2019), it will also be argued that recent case law gives grounds for considering the new "by design" principle obligatory also for the technology designers and developers as joint controllers together with the users of their products or services.

DEFINING THE CAPACITY OF A DATA PROCESSING ACTOR

This section will present the existing distinct model for compliance with the GDPR, where data processing actors are assigned different responsibilities depending on whether they act as a controller, joint controller, or processor. These concepts are crucial because they allocate responsibilities for compliance with data protection law and determine how data subjects can exercise their rights, which is the applicable national law and how effective are the enforcement powers of the DPAs (WP29, 2010). The definitions in the GDPR will be analyzed in the context of the key criteria used by the WP29 and the CJEU and the controversies due to the different interpretative approaches.

Definition of Data Controller

Data controllers are the main actors who bear the most stringent obligations for compliance with data protection law. GDPR art. 4 (7) defines a *data controller* as:

The natural or legal person, public authority, agency or other body which, alone or jointly with others, determines the purposes and means of the processing of personal data; where the purposes and means of such processing are determined by Union or Member State law, the controller or the specific criteria for its nomination may be provided for by Union or Member State law.

This definition consists of the following three elements.

Natural Person, Legal Person, Public Authority, Agency or Other Body

The first element refers to the personal side: who can be a controller, ranging from natural to legal persons, public authorities and any other body, thus creating a harmonized legal regime for both public and private actors. In the strategic perspective of allocating responsibilities, WP29 (2010) has advocated that it must be the legal entity or body considered ultimately responsible for data processing within the realm of its activities, "unless there are clear elements indicating that a natural person shall be responsible." Still, as evident from the definition, natural persons could also act as controllers, for example, when processing data with connection to a professional or commercial activity (GDPR Recitals 18 and

91), employees using personal data outside the control of the employer (WP29, 2010, p. 17), or when processing data which is not purely personal or household in nature (art. 2 (2) (c); GDPR Recital 18). In particular, the CJEU has ruled that the household exemption from the data protection legislation does not apply when the purpose of the processing is to "make the data accessible to an unrestricted number of people or where that activity extends, even partially, to a public space and is accordingly directed outwards from the private setting of the person processing the data in that manner."[2] *Bodil Lindqvist*[3] and *Bilvius*[4] thus demonstrate that internet users posting online information relating to other individuals to an unrestricted number of people are also data controllers. Such strict interpretation of the household exemption significantly enlarges the notion of data controller and shows that many users of internet or third-party services processing personal data can be subject to the full GDPR application.

Determine the Purpose and Means of Processing

The determination of the purposes and means of data processing is a crucial element, as this is essentially what distinguishes any controller from a processor. WP29 (2010) rephrases this requirement into replying to the questions of who determines *why* and *how* the processing takes place. It has essentially advocated for a functional concept of controllership that allocates "responsibilities where the factual influence is, and thus based on a factual rather than a formal analysis." To ensure predictability, some rules of thumb are provided how to establish who "determines the purposes and means," which may follow from explicit or implicit legal competence (e.g., provided in Member State or EU law or following from common civil or commercial relationships) or factual influence exercised over the processing, for instance, when there is no legal provision or contract in place, or there is a provision or contract, but the factual situation does not correspond with its stipulations.

In its case law, the CJEU has also upheld this functional concept and has applied a rather broad interpretation of controllership. The Court has done so essentially with the help of the principle of "effective and complete protection of data subjects"[5], an expression of the general principle of effectiveness, which has played a key role in a series of important rulings where the broad interpretation of the notion of the controller was enforced and new criteria for defining its capacity developed. First, in *Google Spain*, the CJEU has ruled that a controller may determine the purposes and means of the processing even if it does not exercise control over the data.[6] In *Facebook fan page*, the Court ruled that a controller "who exerts influence over the processing of personal data for his own purposes,[…] participates, as a result, in the determination of the purposes and means of that processing."[7] Thus, even if Facebook alone designs the whole of Facebook's technical possibilities and system of ends that it can be used for, any Facebook fan page administrator was found to play a role in determining both the purposes and the means of the processing by defining the type of statistics and the objectives of managing and promoting its activities.[8] The CJEU also confirmed that "no actual control or access to the personal data" is necessary for an entity to be qualified as a controller.[9] In the subsequent *Yehovah's witnesses* case,[10] this broad interpretation was further applied in practice with the religious community found a controller only because the processing of personal data of persons contacted by door-to-door preachers "help to achieve the objective of the religious community" and because it "organises and coordinates the preaching activities of its members." In the most recent *Fashion ID* judgment,[11] the Court went even further by concluding that the Fashion ID company is a controller because it has embedded on its website the Facebook "Like" social plugin. The CJEU ruled that by simply choosing to integrate a third-party service processing personal data, the website operator "exerts a decisive influence over the collection and transmission of the personal data of visitors to that website' to the third party service provider," which would not have occurred without that service, thus determining "the 'means' at the origin of the collection and transmission of personal data."[12] As regards the purposes of processing, the CJEU concluded that these are jointly determined because the processing operations are performed "in the economic interests" of both Fashion ID and Facebook.[13]

While "purposes and means" is consistently used in the case law as one noun-phrase, influencing somehow the processing (or agreeing to the processing and making it possible) appears to be enough to qualify as determining both the purposes and the means of that processing operation. As highlighted by Mahieu et al. (2019, p. 86), the crucial step the Court takes to arrive at this broad interpretation is that, instead of only looking at the general purposes and means of Facebook, it looks at the individual data processing operations within the system and the value chain. This move from a "macroscopic" to a "microscopic view" of data processing operations is characterized by them as a significant expansion of the interpretation of "determines the purposes and means" beyond WP29's opinion (2010).

Alone or Jointly

The third element concerns the possibility of determining the purposes and means "alone or jointly" with others, which presupposes two types of controllers.

Independent Controller(s)

According to WP29:

The mere fact that different subjects cooperate in processing personal data, for example in a chain, does not entail that they are joint controllers in all cases, since an exchange of data without sharing purposes or means in a common set of operations should be considered only as a transfer of data between separate controllers. (2010, p.16)

This interpretation is, however, questioned by the recent *Fashion ID* judgment,[14] where simply agreeing to use third-party services was ruled to involve joint controllership for the collection and transmission of the personal data when both controllers have (economic) interests in the processing.

An example of independent controllers could be found in the *Google Spain* case where the Court found that the search engine's processing of personal data "can be distinguished from and is additional" to that of the original publisher and that its "data processing . . . affects the data subject's rights additionally."[15] As suggested by Mahieu et al. (2019), two criteria could be established for two controllers to qualify as independent. They must carry out distinct data processing operations and each of these operations should affect the data subject(s) separately. The author of this chapter also adds that there must be no legal relationship between the controllers as this may make them joint controllers or processors for parts of the processing operations.

Joint Controllers

The concept of joint controllership implies the idea of "pluralistic control," where a controller determines the purpose(s) and means of the processing not alone but "jointly with others." Applying the functional approach, WP29 has argued that joint control should not be primarily determined by what the contract between the parties states, but by the factual control they yield over the purposes and means of processing (2010, pp. 18–20). Given the many different forms and combinations of joint control, it has further argued that it is not necessary that the different parties determine the purposes and means equally. Joint control is thus said to follow from various circumstances, including:

- Use of centralized or shared infrastructure/databases, e.g., common internet platform, shared database of customers;
- Social platforms and their users, if the household exemption is not applicable (WP29, 2009);
- Joint purpose(s) pursued at macro-level of separate data processing operations, e.g., controllers across the whole adverting ecosystem collaborating for the common objective of behavioral advertising (WP29, 2010a);
- Processor or employees not respecting the instructions of the controller and acting outside the scope of its control or processing the data for their own purposes, e.g., in the SWIFT case (WP29, 2006).

Although these examples give some guidance when a joint controllership may exist, WP29 "remains unclear to what extent and to which part of the processing a party needs to be involved in order to be classified as a joint controller" (Mathieu et al., p. 90). An answer to this question can be found in the CJEU case law that interestingly classified all recent cases as joint controllership. In applying the broad definition of controller to ensure 'effective and complete protection of data subjects', the Court has also confirmed that:

The existence of joint responsibility does not necessarily imply equal responsibility of the various operators engaged in the processing of personal data. On the contrary, those operators may be involved at different stages of that processing of personal data and to different degrees, so that the level of responsibility of each of them must be assessed with regard to all the relevant circumstances of the particular case.[16]

Based on the Court's case law, it can be concluded that two or more controllers determine the "purpose(s) of processing" jointly when they are pursuing a common purpose,[17] a purpose of their own,[18] or have some legitimate interest (economic or other) in the processing of the personal data.[19] Two or more controllers determine the "means of processing" jointly when they are organizing or coordinating the activity of other controllers processing personal data[20] or when they exert some influence over the processing operation,[21] including by simply initiating the collection or transmission of the data when using the service of another controller.[22] As highlighted by Mathieu et al. (2019), an important consequence of this broad interpretation is that in many situations, one personal data processing operation will have a large variety of joint controllers. While applying such a wide interpretation of joint controllership indeed helps to protect the data subjects better, it also leads to legal uncertainty about its exact scope of application and the extent to which each joint controller is responsible for the actions of the other joint controller(s).

The Court has attempted to bring some clarity and limit the application of joint controllership in its most recent *Fashion ID* ruling. In a stark contrast with the WP29's macroscopic interpretation of what it means to determine the purpose and means jointly, the Court has ruled that joint controllership must be limited only to the set of operations in which the joint controllers are actually involved (e.g., collection and transmission of data), while for any preceding or subsequent data processing operation Facebook should be considered an independent controller.[23] As suggested by Mathieu and Hoboken (2019), the Court has thus introduced a phase-oriented approach in determining the purposes and means of processing and, hence, delineating the scope of application of joint controllership from the individual responsibility of each controller which may in fact contradict with the WP29's broader interpretation above.

Definition of Data Processor

Data processors are secondary actors in data protection law with lower responsibility in comparison with controllers. GDPR art. 4 (8) defines *processor* as "a natural or legal person, public authority, agency or other body which processes personal data on behalf of the controller." The main purpose of this concept is therefore to distinguish between those responsible as controller(s) and those that are only acting on their behalf. Based on this definition, the following elements must be present for an entity to qualify as a processor.

A Natural or Legal Person or Any Other Body

Similar to the definition of controller, processors can be also a broad range of actors, including "a natural or legal person, public authority, agency or any other body." Considering the rationale of this concept to enable controllers to outsource data processing activities, WP29 (2010, p. 25) has argued that the first basic condition for qualifying as a processor is to be a separate legal entity with respect to the controller. *A contrario*, controller's employees must not be considered processors since they are characterized instead as distinct "persons" who are authorized to process personal data under the authority of the controller as staff in its own organizational structure.[24]

Acting on Behalf of the Controller

The second basic condition is that the processor must act on behalf of the controller which in WP29's opinion should mean serving someone else's interests, thus recalling the legal concept of *delegation*. According to WP29 (2010, p.25), the delegated processing activity may be limited to a very specific task or context or may be more general and extended. The legal requirements for the mandate of the processor are now provided in GDPR Article 28, which requires a written contract to specify the subject matter of the delegation and the processor's obligations. The processor must act only within the mandate and on the instructions given by the controller with regard to the purpose of the processing and the means.

No Role in Determining the Purpose and Means of Processing

A third basic condition may be deduced a contrario from the notion of controller, notably that the processor must not play any role in determining the purposes and means of the data processing mandated by the controller since then it would become a (joint) controller rather than a processor. For example, if a processor uses the data provided by the controller for its own purposes or outside the mandate, then it automatically becomes a controller in respect of that processing.[25] While determining the means certainly turns the processor into a (joint) controller, WP29 (2010, p. 25) has argued that the delegation may imply a certain degree of discretion about how to best serve the controller's interests, allowing the processor to choose the most suitable means of processing as long as these are non-essential (e.g., not defining the categories of data, retention period etc.). Such understanding is also shared by the European

Data Protection Supervisor (EDPS, 2019), although in the cited above case law the CJEU does not draw such distinction between essential and non-essential means and adopts instead a wide interpretation of the notion of controller.

WP29 (2010) has also provided a list of examples of potential processors, e.g., mailing services, payroll, hosting or cloud providers, computer grids, operation of video surveillance, call centers acting on behalf of a controller, accounting services acting under the strict supervision of controllers. Still, these service providers are sometimes very differently qualified by national DPAs and it is often their interpretation which is generally followed on the ground by companies to avoid enforcement actions. For example, according to the UK Information Commissioner's Office (ICO, 2016) accounting firms act always as independent controllers given that they have specific professional obligations, while the Bulgarian DPA (2016) has issued guidelines that accounting firms should be considered instead processors.

These very different and often contradictory interpretations of the capacity of service providers are further questioned in the light of the recent CJEU case law which has enforced a rather broad interpretation of the concept of (joint) controller and what it means to "determine the purpose and means of processing." In applying the new criteria, as analyzed above, the concept of processor thus seems to be of increasingly limited application. A list of additional criteria suggested by WP29 (2010, p. 28) also implies a more limited application of *processor*, which must be arguably judged based on factual circumstances such as:

- Level of prior instructions given by the controller, which determines the margin of manoeuvre left to the processor;
- Monitoring by the controller of the execution of the service with a constant and careful supervision of the processor providing an indication that the controller is still in full control of the processing;
- Visibility given to the data subjects and their expectations on this basis;
- Expertise of the service provider where traditional roles and prevailing professional expertise may entail its qualification as a controller (e.g., accountants, attorneys-at-law, auditors).

Thus, even if the concept of *processor* is still preserved in the GDPR, the recent broad interpretation of the concept of (joint) controllership in the CJEU case law, the increasing specialization of the processes and the growing information and technology imbalances among certain service providers and business users may eventually lead to the inapplicability and gradual extinction of the concept of processor, as advocated by De Hert and Papakonstantinou (2016).

ACCOUNTABILITY AND RESPONSIBILITY OF (JOINT) CONTROLLERS AND PROCESSORS

The distinction between (joint) controllers and processors is crucial as it aims first and foremost to allocate different data protection responsibilities that are further enhanced now with the new accountability principle—one of the most important changes introduced with the GDPR with a view to bridging the existing compliance gap. The new accountability principle essentially aims to foster data protection in practice by obliging controllers to put in place appropriate and effective measures for compliance with the GDPR and to be able to demonstrate so.[26] As pointed out by WP29 (2010b, p. 9–10), the purpose of accountability is at ensuring *de facto* effective compliance with existing principles and obligations and moving data protection from theory to practice. With less bureaucracy and reporting, controllers bear now enhanced responsibility and the burden to prove compliance of their operations with the GDPR. Given that the emphasis of accountability is on showing how responsibility is exercised and making this verifiable, responsibility and accountability are hence said to be two sides of the same coin and both essential elements of good governance and compliance.

In essence, accountability consists of two main elements: (a) the obligation for a controller to take appropriate and effective measures to ensure compliance with GDPR and (b) the obligation to demonstrate compliance and provide evidence thereof. It also involves *proactive* responsibilities on behalf of the controller as well as *reactive* liability (administrative and civil) for any failure to comply with its obligations. While systematically accountability is placed only as part of the controller's obligations, WP29 (2010b) and other national DPAs (e.g., ICO, 2016) have confirmed that this principle is also applicable to processors. The next subsections will examine what are the specific responsibilities of (joint) controllers and processors in the light of the new GDPR provisions and the accountability principle.

Controller's Accountability

GDPR Article 24 now clarifies that it is controller's responsibility to "implement appropriate technical and organizational measures to ensure and to be able to demonstrate that processing is performed in accordance with this Regulation." Article 5 (2) also stipulates that the controller must ensure and be able to demonstrate compliance with the data processing principles, referring explicitly to the principle of accountability. More specific data protection obligations incumbent on the controller are spread across various provisions of the GDPR, including responsibility for:

- Adoption of internal binding policies and procedures,[27] which should ensure "data protection governance" and assign clear roles and responsibilities at all levels within the organization from the top management to the lowest data processing levels.
- Compliance with data processing principles,[28] including lawfulness, fairness, transparency, minimization, purpose and storage limitation, accuracy, confidentiality and integrity as well as accountability, which must be all operationalized into the controller's internal policies and procedures.
- Compliance with the data subjects' rights to information, access, correction, deletion, etc.,[29] which aim to enhance the data subject's control over their personal data and constitute an essential second prong of the binary accountability framework established by the GDPR where controllers can be held accountable not only by the DPAs, but also by individual data subjects (Kaminski, 2019).
- Embedding the new 'data protection by design and by default principle"[30] (DPbDD) into controller's operations, services and organizational culture with these well recognized ethical principles becoming now fully-fledged legal obligations so as to ensure the least possible interference with individuals' rights and effective integration and respect of the data processing principles and the data subjects' rights from the design stage right through the lifecycle.
- Integration of the risk-based approach into controller's operations,[31] supported with a new obligation to carry out Data Protection Impact Assessment[32] (DPIA) for processing operations likely to result in high risk to individuals' fundamental rights as a new ex-ante tool for assessment and prevention of risks and harms to the individuals' rights and the society at large.
- Maintenance of a register of data processing operations.[33]

- Implementation of security measures appropriate to the level of risk to guarantee the confidentiality, integrity and availability of personal data, including new obligations for reporting data breaches.[34]

- Appointment of a Data Protection Officer (DPO)[35] in certain cases with a key independent compliance and accountability role.

- Exercise of effective control over staff and data processors,[36] so that employees and processors acting under the authority of the controller process personal data according to its instructions and in compliance with the GDPR.

- Respect of specific rules for international transfers outside the EU/EEA.[37]

- Evaluation of the effectiveness of the measures[38] by monitoring, testing, regular review, internal and external audits. In case of larger, more complex, or high-risk data processing, the effectiveness of the measures adopted should be verified regularly and may also include periodic transparent audits by qualified and preferably independent parties (WP29, 2010b).

- Ability to demonstrate compliance[39] by providing evidence that the policies and measures have been adopted, actually implemented and evaluated periodically for their effectiveness. Adherence to approved codes of conduct or approved certification mechanisms can be also a way to demonstrate compliance[40] but would not shield the controller from liability.

- Liability for non-compliance which includes 'strict' civil liability for damages resulting from an infringement of the Regulation, including solidary liability with other controllers and processors involved in the data processing jointly responsible for the full damages sustained by affected data subjects.[41] The controller bears also administrative liability for non-compliance (GDPR, Article 83) with potential sanctions of up to 20 million euro or 4% of the controller's global turnover.

The overview above shows that there is certain scalability of controller's responsibilities in accordance also with the principle of proportionality, which requires that the legal burden on controllers should not go beyond what is strictly necessary to achieve the objective of the EU legislation.[42] While some of the measures are 'staples' that will have to be implemented in most data processing operations (e.g., procedures, security measures, compliance with data subjects' rights; WP29, 2010b, p. 13), others are obligatory only in specific cases, in particular for operations perceived as high risky (e.g., obligations for DPO and DPIAs). It is also important to highlight that the stringency and comprehensiveness of the measures should also depend on the facts and circumstances of each particular case, taking into account "the nature, scope, context and purposes of processing as well as the risks . . . for the rights and freedoms of data subjects."[43] In principle, the more complex and riskier is the processing, the stronger the safeguards must be and the greater accountability from the controller may be sought to demonstrate compliance (WP29, 2010b, p. 4).

The state of the art of the technology and the cost of implementation are other relevant factors that controllers should consider when determining the suitability and the effectiveness of the measure.[44] As the European Data Protection Board (EDPB, 2019, p.8) has argued, state of the art of technology should not only require taking into account the current progress in the technology in terms of data protection compliance measures available on the market, but also thorough knowledge about the emerging risks that new technologies pose to individuals' fundamental rights and consideration of existing standards about the necessary measures to prevent and mitigate those risks. Recent case law[45] also confirms that greater safeguards must be in place for risky processing, in particular through automated means or processing of sensitive data. In *GC v CNIL,* the CJEU has further ruled that '*specific features of the processing carried out may [...] have an effect on the extent of the operator's responsibility and obligations.'*[46] The Court has thus introduced new criterion in interpreting the obligations, notably *"the responsibilities, powers and capabilities of the controller"* which led to the conclusion that the restrictions for processing sensitive data[47] are applicable to Google only *"on the basis of a request by the data subject"* and not prior to that.[48]

This scalability and adaptability of controller's obligations raises, however, important questions if this does not eventually diminish the level of protection and *de facto* changes the nature and extent of the controller's responsibility. According to Quelle (2017, pp. 17 and 22), even if the risk-based approach requires measures that protect against potential interferences with the rights of the individuals (as an outcome), it may be also used to calibrate even hard-to-reconcile result-oriented obligations such as compliance with data subjects' rights. This conclusion is also drawn in the context of the differences perceived in the literature between the new risk-based approach as opposed to the traditional rights-based approach in data protection (Gellert, 2017). Alsenoy (2016) has also argued that GDPR mostly imposes obligations of means and not results (e.g., implementing security measures, DPIAs) and that the assessment of risk may be a decisive factor for engaging controller's civil liability. By contrast, the author of this paper claims that the responsibility of the controller should be interpreted as responsibility for both 'means' and 'outcomes'.

Arguments in support of the result-based responsibility can be found in the controller's obligation to comply with the data processing principles,[49] which remain rights-based (WP29, 2014). These principles, even if inherently involving certain proportionality assessment (Kuner, 2008; Gellert, 2016; Quelle, 2017), are arguably 'result' focused – they require certain outcome in the sense that the personal data must be processed in a lawful, fair, and transparent manner for specific purposes, preserving its confidentiality and integrity etc. WP29 (2010b, p.17) has also argued that because accountability puts emphasis on certain outcomes to be achieved in terms of good data protection governance, the GDPR obligations are said to be result-focused. Furthermore, it has specifically emphasized that fulfilling the accountability principle does not necessarily mean that a data controller complies with the substantive principles or obligations in the GDPR. But probably one of the strongest arguments for interpreting the controller's responsibility in terms of outcomes is the requirement that the measures must be 'effective', and the controller is obliged to regularly test and evaluate them to demonstrate so.[50] Arguably, effectiveness requires that these measures should effectively and in practice prevent and mitigate the risks and harms and be appropriate to achieve the objective of the GDPR to ensure high protection of the data subjects' rights. Effectiveness is also a key requirement in the new DPbDD principle—the measures and safeguards should protect the individual "by design" all along the full cycle and "be implemented in an effective manner [...] in order to meet the requirements of this Regulation and protect the rights of data subjects."[51] Such result-oriented interpretation of the controller's responsibility is also fully supported by the legal principle of effective and complete protection of data subjects.[52]

Considering all these arguments and irrespective of the scalability of the means chosen by the controller and its margin of discretion, the controller should be arguably also responsible to guarantee as outcomes the respect of the data processing principles and the rights of the data subjects in order to achieve the objective of the GDPR and ensure effective and complete protection of the data subjects. Contrary to Alsenoy (2016), this paper thus argues that the risk involved in the processing cannot be a defense of the controller to evade or reduce its civil liability because it should have been aware about that risk (EDPB, 2019) and already assessed it as part of its obligation to do a risk assessment and the DPIA (Article 24(1) and Article 35). Hence, by deciding to undertake the risky processing in its own benefit it has obviously accepted the risk, thus assuming responsibility for any consequences as a result of its materialization. The strict liability regime, which does not require any fault on behalf of the controller in correctly foreseeing or assessing the risk,[53] means that the controller should be liable for all damages resulting from the risky data processing except where it can prove it is not in any way responsible for the event giving rise to the damage, e.g., due to force majeure.[54]

Joint Controllers' Accountability

Joint controllers have all above-mentioned responsibilities as controllers, which, however, must be clearly allocated among them in respect of the data processing operations for which they are jointly responsible. For this purpose, GDPR Article 26 now imposes on joint controllers three main additional obligations for:

- Allocation of responsibility by means of an arrangement between the joint controllers unless, and in so far as, the respective responsibilities of the controllers are determined by Union or Member State law to which the controllers are subject. The arrangement shall duly reflect the respective roles and relationships of the joint controllers *vis-à-vis* the data subjects and it may also designate a contact point for data subjects.
- Transparency *vis-à-vis* the data subjects who should be informed about the essence of the arrangement and how they can exercise their data subjects' rights.
- Responsibility of each joint controller to ensure compliance with the data subjects' rights at their request irrespective of the internal arrangements and distribution of tasks among the joint controllers.

WP29 (2010, pp. 22–24) has also opined that factual circumstances should be considered with a view to assessing whether the arrangements between joint controllers reflect the reality of the data processing. Arguably, this functional approach could also be used in case joint controllers have not concluded an arrangement and there is no legal framework that explicitly or implicitly allocates data protection responsibilities.

The Court has also made an attempt to apply such a functional approach in *Fashion ID* where it had to identify the joint controller responsible for notifying and collecting informed consent from the website visitors in the absence of any arrangement between Fashion ID and Facebook. By applying the new phase-oriented approach, the Court has essentially ruled that Fashion ID in its capacity of a joint controller operating the website is best placed to inform website visitors and collect their informed consent, since "it is the fact that the visitor consults that website that triggers the processing of the personal data and the consent must be given prior to the data processing."[55] However, once the data is transmitted, Facebook also becomes responsible for informing the data subjects about the subsequent purposes of use for which it should be considered an independent controller.[56] An important consequence of the phase-oriented restrictive interpretation of joint controllership is that it excludes responsibility on behalf of the website operator for any subsequent processing undertaken by Facebook,[57] thus significantly limiting also the website operator's civil liability[58] only to the collection and transmission of the personal data.

Data Processor's Accountability

While controllers are in principle obliged to ensure compliance with all provisions under GDPR, processors are obliged to process the data according to the controller's instructions and comply with a more limited number of obligations, listed now in Article 28, including:

- Provision of sufficient guarantees that appropriate measures are implemented within the processor so as the processing will meet the GDPR requirements and ensure the protection of the data subjects' rights. The adherence to approved code of conduct and certification mechanism may serve as a way to provide such guarantees.
- Having a clear mandate for processing on behalf of the controller by means of a written contract or other legal act, which is binding on the processor with regard to the controller and sets out the modalities of the mandate (e.g., the purpose of processing, categories of data, etc.) and processors' obligations.
- Processing personal data only on documented instructions from the controller, including with regard to international transfers. The processor is obliged to immediately inform the controller if, in its opinion, an instruction infringes GDPR or other Union or Member State data protection provisions.
- Ensuring that persons authorized to process the data have committed themselves to confidentiality or are under an appropriate statutory obligation of confidentiality and that they do not process the data except on instructions from the controller.[59]
- Taking all measures required to ensure the security of the processing pursuant to Article 32.
- Engaging another subprocessor only on the basis of a contract with identical obligations and subject to prior specific or general written authorization of the controller; the processor should still remain fully liable to the controller for the performance of that other subprocessor's obligations.
- Assisting the controller for fulfilling its obligations to respond to requests for exercising data subject's rights, carrying out DPIAs, and ensuring the security of the processing and reporting data breaches.
- Deleting or returning all personal data to the controller after the end of the provision of the services.
- Making available to the controller all information necessary to demonstrate compliance with the obligations in Article 28 and allow for and contribute to audits, including inspections.
- Maintaining a record of all categories of processing activities carried out on behalf of each controller.[60]
- Appointing a DPO, where obligatory.[61]
- Liability for non-compliance (administrative and civil).[62] The civil liability of the processor is also strict and solidary with other processors and controllers involved in the processing but proportionate - only if the processor has not complied with GDPR obligations specifically directed to processors or if it has acted outside or contrary to the controller's lawful instructions.[63]

CHALLENGES TO THE CONCEPTS OF CONTROLLER/PROCESSOR AND ACCOUNTABILITY IN THE TECHNOLOGY AND DATA DRIVEN WORLD

The primary objective of the reform with the GDPR was to adapt the data protection legislation to the new technological and economic reality. The section above has shown that the new obligations under GDPR have managed partially to achieve this by creating a new model of accountability that aims at effective, proactive compliance on behalf of (joint) controllers and processors and *ex-ante* prevention of risks to the data subjects' rights. Despite these positive developments and the adjudicative broad interpretation of the concept of (joint) controller, this section will argue that there are still challenges and legal gaps in the allocation of responsibilities, especially in light of the latest CJEU case law and the phase-oriented approach, which is considered inadequate for the contemporary context of processing and ultimately resulting in ineffective attribution of control and protection of data subjects.

Legal Uncertainty Regarding Application and Compliance

A first major challenge is the inconsistent interpretation of the notions of (joint) controller and processor, given by the WP29 (2010) and the CJEU, which creates significant legal uncertainty for data processing actors how to apply these concepts in practice. As shown above, this contradiction is even further complicated as companies may also be subject to divergent interpretations given by the national DPAs regarding their legal capacity as well as the scope and nature of their responsibilities.

While GDPR has specified the responsibilities of the (joint) controllers and processors, it has not helped to clarify the meaning of these concepts and their consistent interpretation. In addition, the high-level principles and the obligation for accountability enshrined in the broad provisions give room for flexibility and scalability of the controller's obligations but may also result in significant legal uncertainty in the absence of more detailed guidelines. As a result, roles and responsibilities may be subject to divergent interpretation in the different Member States, which may not only create compliance problems for the data processing actors but also put at risk the uniform and effective enforcement of the GDPR. This may also allow amoral calculators to contest the DPA's interpretation of the provisions and assessment of compliance, especially when there has been no further specific guidance on how to solve the existing controversies and how to apply these high-level provisions in practice (Black, 2001). As Mahieu et al. (2019) point out, there is also no legal rule what happens if joint controllers have not delineated the scope of their joint operations or do not arrange appropriately their responsibilities for compliance with the GDPR. The most recent *Fashion ID* judgment poses the question whether the new phase-oriented approach adopted by the Court will be the only mechanism to delineate the scope of joint controllership or other mechanisms may also be used, for example, assessment of whether common macro objective(s) are pursued, as recommended by WP29 (2010) or as it could be deduced from of the *Yehovah's witnesses* judgment.

Another unclear issue is how far the obligation for DPbDD is legally binding on designers, developers, and manufacturers of software and other data processing technologies as these actors most often do not process personal data. Article 25 places this obligation only on controllers, and the GDPR states that:

When developing, designing, selecting and using applications, services and products that are based on the processing of personal data or process personal data to fulfil their task, producers of the products, services and applications should be encouraged to take into account the right to data protection . . . to make sure that controllers and processors are able to fulfil their data protection obligations. (GDPR Recital 78)

This gives the impression that these technology providers are not legally obliged and remain outside the scope of the GDPR—an understanding also shared by EDPB (2019, p. 25) and the EDPS (2018). In the light of the recent CJEU's wide interpretation of what it means to determine "the purpose and means of processing" even in the absence of access to or processing of personal data, it can be argued though that these actors do exercise influence over the means of processing for their own economic benefit, considering that they are in fact the persons designing, developing or manufacturing these means. These service or product providers can hardly be considered simply processors, considering their specialized technical expertise, know-how, information, and technology capabilities, which challenge the idea that an ordinary controller could solely determine the means of processing without their decisive contribution to this process. To recognize these actors as joint controllers is also in line with the principle for placing responsibility and liability to the persons best positioned to do something about it (e.g., similar to product liability). If this interpretation is correct, their role as (joint) controllers should be legally recognized and their responsibilities for compliance with the GDPR clarified, as recommended below in this chapter.

Inapplicability to Non-linear and Technology-Driven Contexts

Many authors (cited in Mathieu et al., 2019, p. 88) have already argued that the traditional concepts of (joint) controller and processor inherited from the repealed directive are obsolete and difficult to apply in the contemporary technology and economic reality where the way and the extent to which personal data is being processed across multiple actors has changed dramatically in comparison with 1995. While the dichotomy of controller-processor relationship may have been appropriate in a "linear" environment of centralized data processing with controllers acting as the main architects of the systems and in command of the control (Tene, 2013), this is not anymore the case with the growing specialization of the processes, outsourcing of the services to third parties and extensive use of ICT built out of service modules of third-party software which make the processing highly non-linear, interdependent and dynamic (Mathieu et al., 2019).

The latest CJEU case law points to the conclusion that the concept of joint controllership will gain much greater application instead of the controller-processor relationship, which has prevailed up to now. While this may seem good news at first sight, the lack of clear legally binding mechanism for attribution of responsibility in the absence of an arrangement between the joint controllers in combination with the new single-phase approach applied by the Court can severely limit the benefits of this concept and make it highly ineffective as an instrument for accountability in today's interdependent data-driven world. Moreover, distinguishing the phases and types of data processing operations may turn out to be particularly difficult in certain circumstances or outright inadequate. In particular, this may be quite irrelevant when all operations actually pursue a common objective or are part of an integrated service or product involving many different actors.

It is, therefore, argued that because the phase-oriented approach focuses only on the set of operations or phases of processing, it inherently entrenches the Court's analysis in examining only the joint means of processing, but disregarding the common overarching objective(s) which may ultimately connect the various data processing phases along the full data value chain. Thus, while WP29 (2010a) reached the conclusion that all actors involved in the behavioral advertising ecosystem should be joint controllers, the CJEU remained blind about this common objective and concluded that joint controllership should be limited only to the collection and transmission of personal data by the website operator, but not to the subsequent processing undertaken by Facebook even though this processing culminates with the website visitors' micro-targeting with ads which is also in the interests of the website operator who maximizes its profits by using Facebook's illegal services. The current legal framework, as interpreted by the Court with its reductionist approach in delineating the scope of joint controllership, may thus prove to be highly inadequate for the complex, interdependent, and non-linear context of contemporary data processing.

Ineffective Attribution of Responsibilities

As noted by WP29 (2010, p. 18), in a complex environment it is even more important that "responsibilities can be easily allocated, so as to ensure that the complexities of joint control do not result in an unworkable distribution of responsibilities which would hamper the effectiveness of data protection law." It appears, however, that the new phase-oriented approach will lead exactly to such unworkable and ineffective attribution of responsibilities in *prima facie* violation of the GDPR. To illustrate, in *Fashion ID,* the Court has made essentially the website operator responsible for informing and collecting the consent of the website visitors even if the operator does not know for what purposes the data will be later used by Facebook. This is, however, in contradiction with the requirement that consent must be given only for specific purposes, and the data subject must be informed about these purposes prior to the collection,[64] thus making any consent obtained by the website operator invalid in practice. The Court has indeed ruled that Facebook should afterward provide notice to the website visitor for the subsequent uses, but these uses would be illegal if the consent on the basis of which the data has been collected and transferred is invalid.

This approach is also in stark contradiction with the DPbDD principles because website operators as controllers could choose a service provided by a third party but remain absolved from responsibility immediately after the data are transferred to the service provider. Paradoxically, the website operator can use a service for which it is not responsible for ensuring that once transferred, the personal data will be processed in the most privacy-friendly manner "by design and by default" in violation of Article 25 GDPR. The obligation for designing the appropriate means for informing the data subjects and collecting their informed consent is also wrongly placed on the website operator instead of Facebook as a service provider who is solely determining the purposes and designing the technical means for the provision of its services, while the website operator as a joint controller only accepts these standard terms and make use of the services for its own benefit. Finally, this ineffective delineation of tasks will prevent the website operator from adequately assessing *ex-ante* the risk of the processing operations, as the latter will not have information about the potential impact and risks of the subsequent processing undertaken by Facebook in violation of GDPR Articles 24(1) and 35.

Unjust Regime for Liability

Delineating the joint responsibilities according to the phases of processing would also exempt a joint controller from liability about the actions of the other joint controller, once the latter has obtained the data and further processed it.[65] The regime for solidary liability of the website operator under GDPR Article 82 (4) would thus only cover damages from the illegal collection and transmission of the data to Facebook, but not what Facebook has subsequently done with this data, even if the website operator has gained an economic advantage by using the Facebook service. This will certainly not help to achieve the rippling effect of GDPR compliance, as advocated by AG Bot,[66] because business users could continue to use non-compliant services and be absolved from liability under GDPR as long as they have lawfully collected and transferred the personal data to the service provider.

Such a regime of liability is also highly unjust for the affected data subjects who will not be able to claim full compensation from the website operator for its use of the non-compliant services given that Article 82 (4) would not be applicable for the subsequent illegal profiling and micro-targeting performed by Facebook. Except where national rules specifically provide so, the Court practically absolves the website operator from liability about the actions of Facebook in contradiction with the traditional tort law principles of Member States (codified in the Principles of European Tort Law, 2005), according to which multiple tortfeasors should be jointly liable for the *full* damage with a right to regress against the other tortfeasor(s) for their respective part(s) in the damages incurred.

Detrimental to Individuals' Fundamental Rights

The phase-oriented approach is detrimental not only to the individuals' rights to effective and complete compensation but also to their fundamental right to data protection, which aims to grant them greater control over how their personal data are processed. In contradiction with the objective of the GDPR and the principle of effective and complete protection, this approach in practice significantly deteriorates the position of the data subjects. Individuals will, hence, not know for what purposes their personal data will be exactly collected and used once transmitted to the service providers and will not be able to form reasonable expectations and exercise meaningful control over the subsequent processing. The processing operations along the value chain will also be surrounded in opacity as the data subject will be informed only later and individually by each controller responsible for the subsequent processing(s). Such an obligation for separate notifications will eventually flood the individuals with privacy notices and possibly requests for consent, which will overwhelm them and further diminish their control over the processing (in this sense, Solove, 2013). Finally, there is a clear risk of dilution and constant shift of responsibility between the different controllers across the value chain which will significantly hamper data subjects to exercise their rights to access, correction etc. While Article 26(5) GDPR allows that these requests may be sent to any joint controller, the data subject will have to send them now to numerous controllers at the same time, also facing serious difficulties in identifying the correct controller and its role in the chain of processing.

SOLUTIONS AND RECOMMENDATIONS

The challenges highlighted above could be overcome to some extent with a radical change in the Court's approach in delineating the scope of joint controllership switching from "single phase" to "value chain." Hence, this chapter suggests that the Court should first and foremost assess whether the set of operations are interconnected and interdependent as contributing ultimately to an overarching common objective and/or the provision of an integrated service or product. If so, joint controllers should be in principle all actors involved in the value chain from the initial collection of the data right through the data lifecycle, if they pursue an economic or other interest and to the extent that they agree with the processing even if done by other controllers.

With DPbDD, it is also critically important that this value chain approach starts from the very design stage of the product or service and also encompasses designers, developers or manufacturers of data processing products/services who should be recognized as fully fledged joint controllers, as argued above. Their roles should be further clarified with respect to the requirements for DPbDD (e.g., obligatory testing and evaluation, periodic auditing etc.) and the obligation to carry out a service/product DPIA. Considering that this service DPIA should be available for business and consumer users acting arguably as joint controllers to tailor it to their specific data processing context and risks (to this effect EDPB, 2019, p. 9), there are strong arguments to make the service DPIA public after removing confidential information and trade secrets. Importantly, such interpretation would help to overcome one of the greatest shortcomings in Article 35 which does not mandate publicity of the DPIA.

More concrete rules of thumb will also be necessary for the attribution of responsibilities in the absence of an arrangement between the joint controllers or when this arrangement does not correspond to the factual circumstances. In this respect, it is suggested that instead of the phase-oriented approach in allocating responsibilities, the Court should use another criterion, notably the "responsibilities, powers and capacities" of the joint controllers as recently upheld in the *Google Spain*[67] and *GC*[68] rulings. All requirements for DPbDD would be thus placed directly on the service provider within whose "powers and capacities" solely remain the provision of a GDPR compliant service, including designing the appropriate arrangement for the allocation of data protection responsibilities which users of the service must only accept and implement accordingly. Such interpretation will certainly ensure more effective, systematic, and uniform enforcement of the obligations of the GDPR, while the responsibility of the users as joint controllers will be to verify whether the proposed arrangement and the product/service is indeed GDPR compliant and only use it if so.

In addition to these general interpretative rules, more specific legally binding obligations should be imposed on joint controllers that must be incorporated in the arrangement or be directly applied in its absence. In addition to what is already specified in GDPR Article 26, this may include obligations for the following:

- Using only (joint) controllers who can provide sufficient guarantees for compliance with the GDPR (similar to the obligation for processors in GDPR Article 28 [1]). To avoid a "chilling effect" on the market and facilitate buying-in of the certification as a compliance mechanism, it may be reasonable to envisage 'safe harbor' for business and consumer users using certified services/products who may shift liability towards the service/product provider, if they have not contributed to the damage with their own behavior (e.g., non-compliance with the arrangement or additional influence exercised over the processing).
- Ensuring granular transparency of all data flows and responsibilities of (joint) controllers for compliance in carrying out the specific data processing operations. Each joint controller should also be transparent about any data processing operations that are planned to be performed outside the scope of the common objective pursued and/or the joint means of the processing.
- Duty for coordination and cooperation between joint controllers in exercising their responsibilities (e.g., for informing data subjects, obtaining consent, complying with requests for the exercise of data subjects' rights). Such a general obligation for cooperation may also help to address power and information asymmetries between joint controllers and give the parties a right to immediately terminate the contract if the other joint controller is not meeting its contractual obligations or is in some other way contravening the data protection legislation.

- Ensuring traceability of the data processing operations with immutable, auditable trails at key decision and disclosure points, so as to verify compliance with the respective obligations and attribute liability in case of non-compliance.
- Providing data subjects with an integrated privacy notice and control management system to provide a clear understanding of all data flows, legal grounds, and purposes pursued in each stage with a designation of the responsible joint controller(s). This system should also enable the data subject to exercise control over the processing across the whole data value chain, including managing consent, granting or withdrawing access to their data to joint controllers, and exercising their data subjects' rights to access, correction etc.
- Continuously monitoring the compliance of the service/product and the risks posed to the data subjects' rights and freedoms. This may include an obligation for the product or service user to promptly inform the service provider about any changes in the assessed risks.
- Right to request all necessary information from a joint controller to demonstrate and verify compliance, including an obligation to allow for and contribute to inspections and audits.

FUTURE RESEARCH

The viability of the value chain approach recommended above could be tested in future CJEU case-law or in guidelines of the European Data Protection Board, which are highly needed to solve existing controversies. Future research may also analyze the pros and cons of this method and make recommendations for its improvement or propose other methods for delineating the scope and attribution of responsibilities between joint controllers.

CONCLUSION

Recent CJEU case law has made joint controllership the primary legal concept applicable to many data processing actors who should now increasingly share responsibilities for compliance with the GDPR. To make this concept effective and workable in practice, the present paper has proposed a new value chain method in delineating its scope to replace the existing phase-oriented approach currently applied by the Court. Arguably, such a value chain approach is more incentivizing and suited to the current economic and technological reality and more appropriate to ensure effective protection of the data subjects and enhanced accountability of the multiple actors involved. The stage is now open for a change in the Court's approach or proposition of other methods to address the deficiencies identified in this chapter, so as to make the existing model for the distribution of data protection responsibilities fit for the contemporary reality.

ACKNOWLEDGMENT

This research received no specific grant from any funding agency in the public, commercial, or not-for-profit sectors. Disclaimer: the paper reflects author's personal opinion as a researcher and is in no way engaging or presenting the position of the EU Institutions.

REFERENCES

Alsenoy, B. (2016). Liability under EU data protection law: from Directive 95/46 to the General Data Protection Regulation. *JIPITEC, 7*(271).

Article 29 Working Party. (2006). Opinion 10/2006 on the processing of personal data by the Society for Worldwide Interbank Financial Telecommunication (SWIFT), WP 128.

Article 29 Working Party. (2009). Opinion 5/2009 on online social networking, WP 163.

Article 29 Working Party. (2010). Opinion 1/2010 on the concepts of "controller" and "processor", 00264/10/EN WP 169.

Article 29 Working Party. (2010a). Opinion 2/2010 on online behavioural advertising, 00909/10/EN WP 171.

Article 29 Working Party. (2010b). Opinion 3/2010 on the principle of accountability, 00062/10/EN WP 173.

Article 29 Working Party. (2014). Statement on the role of a risk-based approach in data protection legal framework, 14/EN WP 218.

Black, J. (2001). Managing Discretion. *ARLC Conference Papers*. www.lse.ac.uk/collections/law/staff%20 publications%20full%20text/black/alrc%20managing%20discretion.pdf

Bulgarian Commission for Personal Data Protection. (2016). *Guidelines on the GDPR*. Retrieved https:// www.cpdp.bg/index.php?p=element&aid=1163

Bygrave, L. A. (2017). Data Protection by Design and by Default: Deciphering the EU's Legislative Requirements. *Oslo Law Review*, *4*(2), 2017. doi:10.18261/issn.2387-3299-2017-02-03

De Hert, P., & Papakonstantinou, V. (2016). The new General Data Protection Regulation: Still a sound system for the protection of individuals? *Computer Law & Security Review*, *32*(2), 179–194. doi:10.1016/j. clsr.2016.02.006

European Data Protection Board. (2019). Guidelines 4/2019 on Article 25 Data Protection by Design and by Default.

European Data Protection Supervisor (2018). Opinion 5/2018 Preliminary Opinion on privacy by design

European Data Protection Supervisor (2019). Guidelines on the concepts of controller, processor and joint controllership under Regulation (EU) 2018/1725.

European Group on Tort Law. (2005). *Principles of European Tort Law*. Retrieved from http://www. egtl.org/petl.html

Gellert, R. (2016). We have always managed risks in data protection law. Understanding the similarities and differences between the rights-based and the risk-based approaches to data protection. *European Data Protection Law Review*, *2*(4), 481–492. doi:10.21552/EDPL/2016/4/7

Gürses, S., & Hoboken, J. (2017). Privacy after the Agile Turn. In J. Polonetsky, O. Tene, & E. Selinger (Eds.), *Cambridge Handbook of Consumer Privacy. Cambridge University Press.*

Information Commissioner's Office. (2016). *Guide to the General Data Protection Regulation (GDPR).* Retrieved from https://ico.org.uk/for-organisations/guide-to-data-protection/guide-to-the-general-data-protection-regulation-gdpr/accountability-and-governance/

Kaminski, M. (2019). Binary governance: Lessons from the GDPR's approach to algorithmic accountability. *Southern California Law Review, 92*(6), 1529. doi:10.2139srn.3351404

Kuner, C. (2008). Proportionality in the European Data Protection Law and its importance for data processing companies. *Privacy and Security Law Report, 7*(1615).

Mahieu, R., & Hoboken, J. (2019). *Fashion-ID: introducing a phase-oriented approach to data protection?* Retrieved from https://europeanlawblog.eu

Mahieu, R., Hoboken, J., & Asghari, H. (2019). Responsibility for data protection in a networked world: On the question of the controller, "effective and complete protection" and its application to data access rights in Europe. *JIPITEC, 10*, 85.

Quelle, C. (2017). The risk revolution in EU data protection law: We can't have our cake and eat it, too. In R. Leenes, R. van Brakel, S. Gutwirth, & P. De Hert (Eds.), *Data protection and privacy: The age of intelligent machines* (1st ed.). Hart Publishing.

Solove, D. (2013). Privacy self-management and the consent dilemma. *Harvard Law Review*, 126, 1880.

Tene, O. (2013). Privacy law's midlife crisis: A critical assessment of the second wave of global privacy laws. *Ohio State Law Journal*, 74, 1217.

ADDITIONAL READING

Alsenoy, B. (2019). *Data Protection Law in the EU: Roles, Responsibilities and Liability. 6.* KU Leuven Centre for IT & IP Law Series. doi:10.1017/9781780688459

Edwards, L. (2016). Privacy, Security and Data Protection in Smart Cities: A Critical EU Law Perspective. 2(1) *European Data Protection Law Review* 28.

Edwards, L. (2018). Data Protection: Enter the General Data Protection Regulation. Forthcoming in L. Edwards (ed.). Law, Policy and the Internet. Hart Publishing.

European Union Agency for Network and Information Security (ENISA). (2015) Privacy by Design in Big Data. Retrieved from https://www.enisa.europa.eu/publications/big-data-protection

Gellert, R. (2015). Data Protection: A Risk Regulation? Between the Risk Management of Everything and the Precautionary Alternative. 5 *International Data Privacy Law* 3, 13.

Koops, B. J., & Leenes, R. (2014). Privacy regulation cannot be hardcoded. A critical comment on the "privacy by design" provision in data-protection law. 28. *International Review of Law Computers & Technology, 159*, 168.

Kuner, C., Bygrave, L., Docksey, C., & Drechsler, L. (2020). The General Data Protection Regulation. Forthcoming in Oxford, Oxford University Press.

Lynskey, O. (Ed.). (2015). *The Foundations of EU Data Protection Law*. Oxford: Oxford University Press.

KEY TERMS AND DEFINITIONS

Accountability: Responsibility of data processing actors to put in place appropriate and effective measures to ensure compliance with the GDPR and be able to demonstrate so.

Data Controller: Any natural or legal person, public authority, agency or other body which, alone or jointly with others, determines the purposes and means of the processing of personal data.

Data Processing: Any operation or set of operations which is performed on personal data or on sets of personal data, whether or not by automated means, such as collection, recording, organisation, structuring, storage, adaptation or alteration, retrieval, consultation, use, disclosure by transmission, dissemination or otherwise making available, alignment or combination, restriction, erasure or destruction.

Data Processor: A natural or legal person, public authority, agency or other body which processes personal data on behalf of the controller.

Data Subject: Identified or identifiable natural person.

Joint Controller: A controller who determines the means and purposes of data processing jointly with other controller(s).

Phase-Oriented Approach: An approach used to delineate the scope of responsibility of a (joint) controller only to the set of data processing operations in which the controller actually participates as determining the means and purposes.

Value Chain Approach: An approach used to delineate the scope of responsibility of a (joint) controller for the whole set of data processing operations starting from the very design phase of the data processing product or service right through the whole data lifecycle with the irreversible deletion of the personal data.

ENDNOTES

[1]   Case C-210/16 Wirtschaftsakademie Schleswig-Holstein (Facebook fan page), EU:C:2018:388; Case C-40/17 Fashion ID GmbH & Co. KG, ECLI:EU:C:2019:629; Case C-25/17 Tietosuojaval-tuutettu Jehovan todistajat (Yehovah's witnesses), ECLI:EU:C:2018; Case C-136/17, GC and others v CNIL, ECLI:EU:C:2019:773.

[2]   C-101/01 *Lindqvist*, EU:C:2003:596, para. 47; C-73/07 *Satakunnan Markkinapörssi and Satamedia*, EU:C:2008:727, para. 44; C-212/13 *Ryneš*, EU:C:2014:2428, paras. 31 and 33, Case C-25/17 *Tietosuojavaltuutettu Jehovan todistajat (Yehovah's witnesses)*, ECLI:EU:C:2018, para. 40.

[3]   CJEU, C-101/01, *Bodil Lindqvist*, EU:C:2003:596.

4   C-345/17 *Buivids,* ECLI:EU:C:2019:122.

5   Case C-131/12, *Google Spain*, ECLI:EU:C:2014:317, paras. 34 and 38; Case C-210/16 *Wirtschaft-sakademie Schleswig-Holstein (Facebook fan page)*, EU:C:2018:388, para. 28; Case C-40/17 *Fashion ID GmbH & Co. KG*, ECLI:EU:C:2019:629, para. 66.

6   Case C-131/12, *Google Spain*, para. 34.

7   Case C-210/16 *Facebook fan page*, para. 68.

8   Case C-210/16 *Facebook fan page*, para. 39.

9   Case C-210/16 *Facebook fan page*, para. 38; Case C-25/17 *Yehovah's witnesses*, para. 69.

10   Case C-25/17 *Yehovah's witnesses*, ECLI:EU:C:2018:551, para. 71.

11   Case C-40/17 *Fashion ID GmbH & Co. KG*, ECLI:EU:C:2019:629.

12   Case C-40/17 *Fashion ID GmbH & Co. KG*, ECLI:EU:C:2019:629, paras. 78–79.

13   Case C-40/17 *Fashion ID GmbH & Co. KG*, ECLI:EU:C:2019:629, para. 80.

14   Case C-40/17 *Fashion ID,* paras. 78–80.

15   Case C-131/12, *Google Spain*, paras. 35 and 83.

16   Case C-210/16 *Facebook fan page*, paras 28, 43, and 44; Case C-25/17 *Yehovah's witnesses*, para.66; Case C-40/17 *Fashion ID*, para. 70.

17   Case C-25/17 *Yehovah's witnesses*, para. 71.

18   Case C-210/16 *Facebook fan page*, para. 68.

19   Case C-40/17 *Fashion ID*, para.80.

20   Case C-25/17 *Yehovah's witnesses*, para.71.

21   Case C-210/16 *Facebook fan page*, para.36.

22   Case C-40/17 *Fashion ID*, paras.78–79.

23   Case C-40/17 *Fashion ID*, paras.76.

24   GDPR art. 29.

25   GDPR art. 28 (10).

26   GDPR art. 5 (2) and 24 (1).

27   GDPR art. 24 (2).

28   GDPR art. 5–10.

29   GDPR art. 12–21.

30   GDPR art. 25.

31   GDPR art. 24 (1) and 25.

32   GDPR art. 35–36.

33   GDPR art. 30.

34   GDPR art. 32–34.

35   GDPR art. 37–39.

36   GDPR art. 28, 29, and 32 (4).

37   GDPR art. 44–49.

38   GDPR art. 24 (1) and 32 (1) (d).

39   GDPR art. 5 (2) and 24 (1).

40   GDPR art. 24 (3), 25 (3), and 32 (3).

41   GDPR art. 82.

42   Treaty of the Functioning of the EU art. 5 (4).

43   GDPR art. 24 (1).

44   GDPR art. 25 (1).

45 Joined Cases C-293/12 and C-594/12 *Digital Rights Ireland*, ECLI:EU:C:2014:238, para. 55.

46 Case C-136/17, *GC and others v CNIL*, ECLI:EU:C:2019:773, para. 45.

47 GDPR art. 9–10.

48 Case C-136/17, *GC and others v CNIL*, para. 47.

49 GDPR art. 5 (1).

50 GDPR recital 74 and art. 32 (1).

51 GDPR art. 25.

52 Case C-131/12, *Google Spain*, ECLI:EU:C:2014:317, paras. 34 and 38; Case C-210/16 *Wirtschaftsakademie Schleswig-Holstein (Facebook fan page)*, EU:C:2018:388, para. 28; Case C-40/17 *Fashion ID GmbH & Co. KG*, ECLI:EU:C:2019:629, para. 66.

53 GDPR art. 82 (2).

54 GDPR art. 82 (3).

55 Case C-40/17 *Fashion ID,* paras. 102–103.

56 Case C-40/17 *Fashion ID,* para. 101.

57 Case C-40/17 *Fashion ID*, para. 76.

58 Case C-40/17 *Fashion ID*, para. 74.

59 GDPR art. 29 of the GDPR.

60 GDPR art. 30 (2).

61 GDPR art. 37–39.

62 GDPR art. 82–84.

63 GDPR art. 82 (2) and (4).

64 GDPR art. 7.

65 Case C-40/17 *Fashion ID*, para. 85.

66 Opinion of AG Bot in Case C-210/16 *Facebook fan page*, para. 74.

67 Case C-131/12, *Google Spain*, para. 83.

68 Case C-136/17, *GC and others v CNIL*, para. 48.

Chapter 5

GDPR in Between Profiles and Decision–Making:
How the General Data Protection Principles Under Article 5 GDPR Are Engaged With Profiling

Elena Georgiou
University College London, UK

ABSTRACT

The creation and application of profiles may affect individuals and their lives. The lack of transparency and accuracy that may result from these profiles can cause asymmetries of knowledge and unbalanced distribution of powers between business entities and individual subjects. As such, profiling challenges the protection of individuals and generates concerns over the individuals' privacy and data protection. In using profiling practices, every business entity must comply with data protection legislation. The purpose of the chapter is to examine the effectiveness of the GDPR to ensure protection for individuals within the context of profiling. It identifies and analyses, from a profiling point of view, a number of strengths and weaknesses associated with the general data protection principles as adopted under the Article 5 GDPR. The author argues that profiling contradicts the transparent nature of data protection principles, and thus of the GDPR. In practice, the law is ineffective to ensure fair, lawful, and transparent profiling activities to safeguard individuals and their rights.

INTRODUCTION

New technological developments and the large amount of databases nowadays enable the use of profiling practices which collect, combine, analyse and automatically categorise data into groups. This automatic categorisation and identification of individuals' data enables business entities to classify individuals into certain profiles. Although such resulting profiles can help business entities to identify current or potential targets for their own benefits and decision-makings (e.g. build their business models, improve

DOI: 10.4018/978-1-5225-9489-5.ch005

their services or organise their marketing strategies), profiling is likely to generate certain prejudicial treatments for the individuals, which may threaten their privacy and data protection rights, as personal and sensitive information may be revealed.

The creation and application of profiles may affect individuals and their lives. This is because profiling enables business entities to discover new knowledge about their current or potential customers by creating new personal data about individuals (e.g. a customer's previous purchases habits may reveal information about his/her economic situation), from data relating to other individuals (e.g. members of the group profiles to which the individuals belong), or even generating sensitive personal data from non-sensitive data (e.g. a customer's home address may reveal information about his/her ethnicity or religion). By attributing to individuals personal data which in fact belong to other individuals with whom they share some common characteristics (e.g. same purchase habits), there is a possibility of classifying them in a category – profile – in which they do not belong (e.g. an individual may mistakenly be classified as a high income customer because he/she likes to view expensive watches). As a result, individuals are given new (incorrect) characteristics and values, based on which business entities decide whether to include or exclude them from certain services (e.g. receiving a low premium for insurance coverage or being hired for a job).

Consequently, the lack of transparency and accuracy that may result from these profiles can cause asymmetries of knowledge and unbalanced distribution of powers between business entities (who obtain new knowledge about individuals from the created profiles) and individual subjects (who are not aware of the profiles applied to them). Knowledge asymmetry may affect the level of power between business entities and customers (Schermer, 2011). The effect of this imbalance of powers may lead to unfair treatments for the customers (e.g. different prices for different types of customers) and unfair manipulation of a person's future choices or actions (e.g. customers are forced to buy products that they are not initially interested in) (Schermer, 2013). As such, profiling challenges the protection of individuals' fundamental rights and values and generates concerns over the individuals' privacy and data protection.

As a result, these challenges exhibit the importance and the necessity of ensuring privacy and data protection rights and of questioning the applicability and effectiveness of the law to protect these rights within the context of profiling. Both these rights are necessary instruments for a democratic society. Privacy underpins human dignity and other key values of human life (i.e. autonomy, integrity, self-determination and identity) and has become one of the most important human rights of the modern age. Personal data refers to any kind of information that can be used to identify an individual, either directly or indirectly, using a combination of different information. For this reason, data protection encompasses also protection for other fundamental rights like freedom of expression, freedom of religion and conscience and the right to equality and non-discrimination (Ferraris, Bosco and D'Angelo, 2013a).

In order to protect individuals' rights to privacy and data protection, every business entity (controller) must comply with data protection legislation. Data protection legislation has always been approached within the notion of transparency. This is why data protection legislation does not prohibit processing of personal data but regulates it. In this way, the law tries to defend personal data while, at the same time, it protects the legitimate interests of controllers in processing such data for social and economic purposes.

Until recently, the major legislative instrument for data protection in Europe was the Data Protection Directive 96/45/EC (DPD).[1] However, new technological developments have created new legal challenges for data protection legislation that go beyond the ones considered under the DPD. Therefore, in January 2012, the European Commission drafted the General Data Protection Regulation ('GDPR' or the 'Regulation') which has been applied directly to all Member States since 25th May 2018.[2] The entry into force of the GDPR (on 24th May 2016) constitutes a pivotal development for the protection of personal data: the Regulation sets out specific rules governing profiling. In this way, the GDPR aims to strengthen the protection of individuals in relation to profiling, whereas it imposes on controllers more obligations to ensure their accountability and transparency in the profiling process. Highly significant in the GDPR is the requirement that profiling is subject to the data protection principles of the Regulation as adopted uinder Article 5 GDPR (and the provisions regulating the lawfulness of the processing of data). This means that profiling must be fair, lawful and transparent.

However, in a profiling-based environment, with personal data being collected and analysed at an unprecedented level, the effective application of the GDPR is questionable. Yet, it is questionable whether the general data protection principles of the Regulation can fulfil the demands of a profiling-based environment, by effectively and adequately minimising the asymmetries of knowledge and the unbalanced distribution of powers between the controllers and the individual subjects, resulting from the use of profiling, and thus maintaining individuals' abilities to exercise control over their data.

Bearing in mind the above considerations, the purpose of the chapter is to examine whether, in practice, the protection provided under the GDPR is adequate and effective to ensure fair, lawful and transparent profiling activities in order to safeguard the protection of individuals' rights to privacy and data protection within the context of profiling. In particular, it identifies and analyses, from a profiling point of view, a number of strengths and weaknesses associated with the new data protection principles as adopted under Article 5 GDPR as well as with the applicability of the GDPR in general. The chapter will answer the following questions: Does the GDPR effectively apply to the processing of data with to regard profiling? Does the GDPR protect individuals from group profiles? Does the GDPR (in particular Article 5 GDPR) effectively minimise the asymmetries of knowledge and the unbalanced distribution of powers between the controllers and the individual subjects, resulting from the use of profiling?

The chapter is organised as follows: in the first part, the chapter examines the possible problems that may arise in relation to the applicability of the GDPR in the context of profiling. The analysis is extended by the detailed examination of the problems arising in relation to the use of group profiling. The second part discusses the protection offered to individuals against profiling and the problems that may arise when the GDPR applies. In particular, the section examines whether the applicability of data protection principles as provided under Article 5GDPR is effective in view of profiling.

Regulating Profiling Under the GDPR

Up until recently, EU data protection legislation had not provided an explicit definition of the term *profiling* nor had it included any reference to the word profiling. The DPD only provides rules for the processing of personal data in general. The only provision that could be seen to deal with profiling is Article 15 DPD.[3]

Article 15 DPD provides the right for every person not to be subject to a decision based solely on the automated processing of data intended to evaluate personal aspects relating to him/her, unless such a decision is taken in the course of entering into or of performance of a contract, or is authorised by law.[4] The primary focus of this article is on the 'automatisation of decisions about individuals' (Bygrave, 2001, p.18) resulting from the processing of their data. The article does not create a direct prohibition on a particular type of decision-making, but rather it confers to individuals a right to prevent them from being subjected to automated decision-makings (Bygrave, 2001). Therefore, decisions based on profiling are considered to be within the scope of Article 15 DPD to the extent that there is no human involvement in the process (decisions should be based entirely on the results produced by the profile).[5] One of the problematic aspects of Article 15 DPD is that it is only applied to the application of the profiles (decision-making process) and not to the process of creating the profiles. Thus, the DPD did not regulate the creation of profiles but only set out restrictions on the way those profiles are to be used.

For this reason, the GDPR regulates not only the decision-making resulting from the application of the profiles but also the creation of the profiles (Vermeulen, 2013). In this respect, the Regulation sets out specific rules for profiling and indicates that the processing of data for profiling purposes is subject to the data protection principles under Article 5 GDPR and the provisions regulating the lawfulness of the processing under Article 6 GDPR.[6] Additionally, Article 4(4) GDPR provides an explicit definition of profiling.[7] In this way, the Regulation affirms that the processing of personal data for profiling is undoubtedly subject to the scope of the new data protection legislation.

Further, one of the significant changes of the GDPR is that, as a Regulation, the new data protection legislation aims to eliminate the legal divergence between EU Member States by providing a greater degree of uniformity for data protection in Europe. Such uniformity entails that the level of protection for the data process for profiling and the application of the provisions of the Regulation should be the same in all EU Member States. The scope of the application of the Regulation is broadened to cover processing activities concerning European data subjects, not only by EU but also by non-EU based controllers and processors.[8] In this way, the Regulation increases the level of data protection for individuals who are subject to profiling activities outside the EU. In addition, for the profiling to be lawful, the GDPR provides that there must be a legal basis to justify it. For this reason, the GDPR strengthens the requirement of consent by demanding that consent must be also the unambiguous indication of the individual and that it must be given for specific profiling purposes. Moreover, the Regulation requires that individuals must consent not only to the creation of a profile but also to its application.

All of the aforesaid changes create a feeling of innovation and give the idea that the new data protection legislation intends to adopt a very different approach to that of the DPD by adopting more modernised, globalised and uniform principles for the protection of personal data in the context of profiling. The actual effectiveness of the new data protection legislation, however, can only be determined by examining the degree to which the provisions of the GDPR achieve its respective objectives in relation to profiling. The next sections, therefore, examine how and to what extent, in practice, the provisions of the GDPR are applicable within the context of profiling.

The Problem With the Applicability of the GDPR

One of the most disputed issues in the GDPR is the scope of its application. The Regulation applies only to the processing of personal data.[9] The processing of data that are not qualified as personal is excluded from the scope of the Regulation. In addition, Article 4(4) GDPR defines profiling as any form of automatic processing of personal data for the purpose of evaluating, analysing or predicting certain personal aspects relating to a natural person. Therefore, for the profiling to be subject to the scope of the Regulation there must be processing of personal data. That is, the data of an identified or an identifiable natural person.[10]

According to the European Data Protection Board (the "Board'), previously the Article 29 Working Party, the main criterion for identifiability is whether the individual can possibly be singled out, directly or indirectly, within a group of people (i.e. he/she can be distinguished from all other members of the group profile).[11] Therefore, an identifiable individual is one who can be identified, directly (e.g. the collected data are directly related to a named individual) or indirectly (e.g. the collected data do not enable the identification of a particular individual unless additional data are collected about that individual), from data based on certain identifiers.[12] To determine whether an individual is identifiable or not, it is necessary to consider all the means which are reasonably likely to be used either by the controller or by any other person to identify the said individual (it is not relevant who can identify the individual).[13] In other words, as long as the data can reasonably be linked to an identifiable individual, they are considered to be personal data and thus within the scope of the GDPR. In the absence of a reasonable possibility of linking the data to an identifiable individual, the data are not personal and are excluded from the scope of the Regulation (Schreurs, Hildebrandt, Kindt, & Vanfleteren, 2008). This exclusion also includes cases where personal data are rendered anonymous in such a way that the individual is no longer identifiable.[14]

With regard to profiling, however, such exclusions are questionable since (as it will be seen below) profiling may apply to an individual even if that individual is not identifiable within the meaning of the Regulation (Gutwirth and Hildebrandt, 2010; Schreurs et al., 2008).

Identifiability and Profiling

Personal data is defined in Article 4(1) GDPR as any information relating to an identified or identifiable natural person (data subject). According to Lee Bygrave, this definition incorporates two elements: (a) the data must facilitate the identification of the individual (identifiability elements) and (b) the data must relate to or concern that individual (data–person relation elements) (Bygrave, 2002, p.42). If either of the two elements is not fulfilled, the data are not personal and the GDPR is not applicable. The question, therefore, is whether the data being processed for profiling satisfy these two elements.

The first case to be examined is that of individual or personalised profiling. A personalised profiling concerns a set of correlated data (profile) that identifies and represents one particular individual (the data are collected in connection with one single person).[15] The profile is based on the characteristics and behaviour of that particular individual (e.g. his/her shopping habits or product preferences). Applying, therefore, the concept of personal data, personalised profiling seems to satisfy both elements: the profile identifies one particular individual (identifiability element) and relates to the data about that individual (data–person relation element). However, identification in personalised profiling does not necessarily mean that the individual is identifiable within the meaning of the GDPR (Schreurs, Hildebrandt, Gasson, & Warwick, 2005, FIDIS Deliverable D7.3). In the case of biometric behavioural profiling, for instance, the use of facial recognition technologies can collect real-time (anonymous) information about an audience's emotional reactions towards a product, a speech or a campaign and create personalised, emotional profiles without linking the profiles to identifiable individuals.[16] In this case, although the profile may continuously identify the individual as the same person over a period of time, the individual is not identified by his/her name but by the serial number assigned to him/her. In this context, the profile is not considered to be the personal data of an identifiable individual. It follows, therefore, that although personalised profiling normally satisfies both elements of personal data, there may be cases where the profile contains no personal or anonymous data and so cannot facilitate the identification of the individual and thus the GDPR is not applicable (Schreurs et al., 2005, FIDIS Deliverable D7.3). In such a case, the GDPR is not applicable and the individual has no rights upon his/her data.

The second case to be examined is that of group profiling. Identification in group profiles does not imply the knowledge of the actual identity of the individual. The profile identifies and represents a group (community or category) of individuals sharing one or more common characteristics.[17] The profile is not interested in the characteristics of a particular individual. It reveals knowledge about the habits, preferences, behaviour and lifestyle of a certain group of people (e.g. reading habits of lawyers or shopping preferences of Spanish customers) (Hildebrandt, 2009; Schermer, 2013). Thus, the purpose of the profile is to identify the individual as a member of a particular group, rather than to distinguish him/her from the other members of the group (as a specific individual).[18] In other words, identification in group profiling refers to the knowledge that the individual is a member of a particular group rather than the knowledge of his/her actual identity. As such, for group profiling it is not necessary for the individual to be identifiable in the sense of the GDPR. The profile applies to those individuals (identifiable or not) whose data match the characteristics of the profile.[19]

This means that the data used for the profile may not be the personal data of the individual to whom the profile is applied. As a result, there may be cases where group profiles do not satisfy either the element of identifiability nor the element of data–person relationship (that is the case for non-distributive group profiles).

So viewed, the concept of personal data limits the applicability of the GDPR in relation to profiling practices (Gutwirth and Hildebrandt, 2010; Schreurs et al., 2008). Firstly, because many profiles (especially group profiles) can be created without the use of personal data but rather with the use of non-personal data and, in particular, of anonymous personal data to which the GDPR does not apply (Schreurs et al., 2005, FIDIS Deliverable D7.3); and secondly, because group profiles do not necessarily apply to an identifiable individual (Hildebrandt, 2009; Hildebrandt, Gutwirth and De Hert, 2005, FIDIS Deliverable D7.4). In this regard, two issues are at stake in relation to the protection of individuals: the application of group profiles and the use of anonymous data.

The Problem with Group Profiling

The first issue to be considered is the protection of individuals against group profiles. As it is explained above, a group profile does not demand the identifiability of individuals in the meaning of the GDPR. Identification, in this case, refers to the knowledge that the individual is a member of a particular group rather than to the knowledge of his/her actual identity. For this reason, a group profile may either apply to an identifiable individual or to a non-identifiable individual. Obviously, from a legal perspective, this situation creates problems.

If the group profile applies to an identifiable individual (i.e. the profile is based on personal data), the GDPR applies which means that the profiling is subject to the rules of the Regulation and that the rights of the individual and the obligations of the controller with regard to the data are activated. If, however, the group profile applies to a non-identifiable individual (i.e. the profile is based on non-personal or anonymous data), the GDPR does not apply and the individual has no rights and the controller no obligations with regard to the data. The most problematic type of group profiling is that of non-distributive group profiles.

A non-distributive group profile is a group profile where not all the members share the same characteristics.[20] This means that the characteristics assigned to the group (and to the individual as a member of the group) may not be applicable to each individual in the group (de Andrade, 2011; Leenes, 2008). As a result, an individual may be identified as a member of the group but he/she cannot be identified as a single entity. This is because the creation of a non-distributive group profile is not based on the personal data of identifiable individuals but on the data (often anonymous) of other individuals (de Andrade, 2011). In other words, the data used to create the profile are not the personal data of the classified individual but rather derive from the categorisation and generalisation of a large amount of data collected from a number of other individuals. As a result, the knowledge inferred from the profile is probabilistic: the characteristics assigned to the members of the group are derived from the probability that the members belong to that group and not from the data belonging to them (Poullet, 2010). If, for example, a group of people with certain genetic characteristics indicates that there is 80% probability that its members will suffer from a particular type of disease, this does not mean that every individual in the group has an 80% possibility of suffering from this disease. The fact that an individual has an 80% possibility of suffering from the disease does not result from the data collected about him/her, but from the fact that the individual is a member of that group (in which its members have an 80% possibility of suffering from this disease). As a result, characterising an individual in the group as having this type of disease may not be true (Custers, 2004).

In this respect, the use of such data cannot qualify as the personal data of an identifiable individual since neither of the two elements of personal data can be satisfied. Consequently, non-distributive profiles are not considered to be within the scope of the GDPR (Georgiou, 2018, pp.174–179). This implies that not only the individuals whose (personal) data were used to create the profile but also the individuals to whom the profile applies are not protected under the GDPR. In this case, therefore, individuals have no access to and no control over their profiles. Moreover, since the data are not personal, the controller has no obligation to ensure the protection of the data as provided by the GDPR. This, of course, raises questions in relation to the fairness, lawfulness and transparency of group profiles.

Thus, the issue in the case of non-distributive group profiles is not whether the GDPR adequately protects individuals but whether there is any protection at all. Considering the material scope of the Regulation, the answer is obvious: the GDPR, just like the DPD, does not provide protection against the creation and application of non-distributive group profiles (Georgiou, 2018).

Having examined when the GDPR is applicable, and also the problems that arise from the applicability of the Regulation, the following section considers the protection of individuals against profiling and its challenges when the GDPR applies. The analysis is made under the assumption that the data processed constitute the personal data of an identifiable individual as explained above and is merely concentrated on the general data protection principles of the Regulation.

Problems Arising When the GDPR Applies

When the GDPR applies, the processing of data for profiling must be in accordance with the rules of the Regulation. These rules do not prevent the processing of data or the use of profiling, but they set out the conditions for fair and lawful profiling activities. In other words, they try to balance the interests of the parties involved by establishing boundaries between the rights of individuals and the obligations of business entities. However, in practice, the effective application of those rules may lack certainty. For this reason, the following subsections examine how the general data protection principles of the Regulation engage with profiling.

a) The Problem with the General Data Protection Principles

The Regulation creates rights and responsibilities from the moment personal data are collected and processed (Schreurs et al., 2008). Article 5 GDPR defines a number of general principles which regulate the lawfulness of the collection and processing of personal data: (a) lawfulness, fairness and transparency principle; (b) purpose limitation principle; (c) data minimisation principle; (d) accuracy principle; (e) storage limitation principle; and (f) integrity and confidentiality principle (Article 5(1) GDPR). In addition, Article 5(2) GDPR provides for the accountability principle which requires controllers' compliance with these principles in order to ensure their accountability and liability in the profiling process.

Purpose Limitation: Collecting and Re-Processing of Data

A specific point of attention concerns the purpose limitation principle. The goal of this principle is to ensure that the processing of data is lawful, fair and transparent. In determining, therefore, whether profiling fulfils these requirements, the way data are collected and how they are intended to be used are important elements.

The principle consists of a two-part test: firstly, the data should only be collected for specified, explicit and legitimate purposes and secondly, these data should not be further processed in a way that is incompatible with those purposes.[21] This means that the controller must explicitly specify the purposes for which he/she intends to use profiling before the collection of the data (general purposes such as for 'marketing strategies' or 'improving user experience' are not sufficient) and that the purposes must be communicated in an intelligible and transparent form for the individual and be lawful under one of the legal bases required by the Regulation.[22]

However, the correct application of this principle is questionable in the context of profiling since the purpose of the profiling may not be known at the time of the collection of the data. As Viktor Mayer-Schönberger and Yann Padova describe it, the collection of the data is 'opportunistic rather than purposeful' (Mayer-Schönberger and Padova, 2016, p.320). This is because it is after the analysis stage (after the collection) that the real value of the data will be discovered (Mayer-Schönberger and Padova, 2016).

One of the basic elements of profiling is that it constitutes a hypothesis in the sense that it does not only give answers to existing questions but it also creates answers to new questions that the controller did not know to ask in advance (before the collection) (Hildebrandt, 2008; Mayer-Schönberger and Padova, 2016). In fact, profiling as a hypothesis is neither an examination nor a further investigation of a particular subject or phenomenon. It is the mining of the data that provides the controllers with knowledge they did not intend to uncover. In other words, profiling enables the identification of hidden patterns and correlations in the data that the controller did not intend to discover when collecting the data. In this way, profiling produces new knowledge about individuals which gives new value to the data and thus creates new purposes.

Consider, for example, a supermarket that is collecting customers' data (e.g. name, date of birth, contact details, marital or work status, etc.) for the purpose of its loyalty card programme. By analysing these data, the supermarket discovers that the majority of its customers who shop on Sundays are university students and young professionals who prefer frozen food. In light of these findings, the supermarket decides to offer discount coupons on certain products (e.g. baby food or birthday cakes) every Sunday, in order to attract other customers as well. This new pattern between the customers was not something that the supermarket intended to discover when collecting the customers' data. Its only intention was to provide the customers with loyalty cards. It follows, therefore, that unless the collected data are analysed, the controller does not know the real value of the data and where such value – new knowledge – will be useful in order to assess the purposes of its collection (i.e. how to apply the profile).

Thus, even if the purposes of the profiling are known in advance, they may change after the analysis stage because new unexpected patterns are found in the data that lead to additional purposes that could not be considered in the first place (Roosendaal, 2013). In the above example, while the customers' data were collected for the loyalty card programme, the analysis of the data reveals information that the supermarket can use for its marketing strategies.

The next issue, therefore, that needs to be considered is the further use of data for other purposes. As indicated above, the second part of the principle does not expressly prohibit re-processing of data for new purposes. It only requires that the data should not be further processed in an incompatible way.[23] This means that where the data are to be used for an incompatible purpose, a new legal basis is required (e.g. an individual should be asked again for his/her consent). Thus, as long as the new purposes are compatible with the initial ones, further profiling is allowed. In such a case, no new legal basis is required for the profiling to be lawful (e.g. an individual should not be asked again for his/her consent).[24] In this way, the GDPR creates for controllers the flexibility to process data for any other purpose which may be considered as compatible with their initial profiling activities.

In order to determine whether the further profiling is compatible with the initial one, the controller should assess whether such profiling goes beyond the scope of the purposes for which the data were collected. In doing so, the controller must consider the following factors (compatibility test): (a) the link between the initial and the intended further purposes; (b) the context of the collection of the data and the reasonable expectations of individuals based on their relationship with the controller; (c) the nature of the data, the consequences for the individuals and the existence of security measures (e.g. encryption or pseudonymisation).[25]

The first two factors are of particular importance here. There must be some sort of relationship between the initial and further purposes, and the individual can reasonably expect, based on his/her relationship with the controller (e.g. seller–customer or doctor–patient relationship), that his/her data may be used in this way. This seems to suggest that any further profiling activity which is deemed to be reasonable for the individual because of his/her relationship with the controller would satisfy the requirements of the compatibility test and thus be lawful (Kotschy, 2014). For example, the customers of the supermarket mentioned above may have reasonable expectation that their loyalty card data may be used by the supermarket for its marketing strategies. Thus, the re-use of the data to provide discount coupons for the customers can reasonably be seen as a usual activity between the supermarket and its customers. Moreover, it could be argued that there is a link between the use of data for providing loyalty cards and the re-use of data for providing discount coupons. This, however, does not mean that every time the supermarket uses the customers' loyalty card data for its marketing strategies, that such use will be within the expectations of the customer and thus considered compatible.

If the processing of data is unexpected, inappropriate or does not meet the expectations of a reasonable person in the situation of the individual, it is likely to be considered incompatible.[26] For example, the use of loyalty card data to provide personalised discounts to customers of a specific region (i.e. racial profiling), or to assess when a female customer is likely to be pregnant in order to send her targeted baby products or pregnancy offers in advance, is unlikely to be the reasonable expectation of the customer (Information Commissioner's Office (ICO), 2014). Moreover, the use of data on an individual's social media accounts to make decisions about him/her may also not constitute the reasonable expectation of the individual. If, for instance, a business entity is going to use information that the individual has posted on his/her social media account (e.g. links, photos or video uploads) to assess his/her suitability for a job or credit worthiness, this is unlikely to be either within the expectation of the individual or to satisfy the compatibility test (Information Commissioner's Office (ICO), 2014).

Another issue that makes the application of the principle problematic is the predictive-future character of profiling. Profiling does not only provide knowledge about an individual's past and current conditions but it also makes predictions about the probable future situation of the individual (i.e future condition, behaviour and activities of the individual who is being profiled) (Hildebrandt, 2009). This knowledge can result in unexpected future purposes (e.g. five or ten years after the initial purposes). Consider the example of a student loan company which is collecting information about its student loan holders. By using profiling, the company can use information about its current student loan holders to discover, for instance, their future financial situations. Such knowledge can be used by business entities to offer certain services to them in the future (e.g. a student with future high credit worthiness may be offered a high rate for a future home loan). The question that arises is whether such future purposes can satisfy the compatibility test. In other words, can the students have a reasonable expectation that their data (collected for a student loan application) can be used to assess their future suitability for a home loan or to calculate their rate for a future loan, or should such purposes be considered to be incompatible with the initial purpose to grant a student loan (e.g. five or ten years before)?

In analysing the purpose limitation principle, the Board directly addresses the issue of the compatibility test in relation to profiling and big data analytics. It identifies two types of compatible further purposes: firstly, when profiling is done to predict general trends and correlations in the data, and secondly, when profiling is done to analyse or predict the preferences, behaviour and attitudes of individuals in order to make decisions affecting them (e.g. to provide personalised offers or targeted advertisements).[27] In this context, it can be argued that the Board allows a broad range of profiling activities to be considered compatible.

In the first case, emphasis is given to the technical and organisational measures the controller should apply in order to ensure the security and confidentiality of the data (e.g. anonymisation or pseudonymisation). In the second case, the Board requires that the free, specific, informed and unambiguous opt-in consent of the individual is necessary in order for the further profiling to be lawful, and demands that the controllers provide individuals with access to their profiles.[28] Additionally, the Board states that further processing for different purposes does not automatically render the profiling incompatible but that it should be assessed on a case-by-case basis.

The meaning of *incompatible purposes* is not further defined in the GDPR. However, the Regulation sets out the conditions under which further profiling is permitted, even if the purpose of such profiling is incompatible with the initial one. The first way for controllers to process data for incompatible purposes is by obtaining the individual's consent for the profiling or if the profiling is based on an EU or Member State law.[29] The second way is when the profiling is for archiving purposes in the public interest or for scientific, historical research or statistical purposes (hereafter 'statistical purposes').[30]

Under the DPD, further processing for statistical purposes could only take place if the Member States adopted suitable legal measures which permit such processing.[31] The GDPR does not follow this supposition but it creates an exception to the principle (Kotschy, 2014): further profiling for statistical purposes is allowed without the need for a new legal basis (e.g. the individual's consent is not required) as long as the controller adopts 'appropriate safeguards'.[32] This shows that, on the one hand, the GDPR tries to restrict the flexibility of controllers to process data for any other purposes and, on the other hand, it attempts to narrow such restrictions.

The term 'statistical purposes', although not further explained in the Regulation, can be seen as having a broad meaning, including the processing of data for public and commercial interests alike.[33] In the Regulation, statistical purposes are defined as 'any operation of collection and the processing of personal data necessary for statistical surveys or for the production of statistical results'.[34] In the dictionary, *statistical* is defined as '(…) consisting of, or based on statistics';[35] and *statistics* is defined as 'the science that deals with the **collection**, **classification**, **analysis**, and **interpretation** of numerical facts or data, and that, by use of **mathematical theories** of **probability**, imposes order and regularity on aggregates of more or less disparate elements'.[36]

Arguably, the definition of *statistics* coincides with the meaning of profiling and the six steps of the Knowledge Discovery in Databases (KDD) process. KDD is the process of the 'nontrivial extraction of implicit, previously unknown, and potentially useful information from the data' (Schermer, 2011, p. 27) which enables the creation of profiles. The process of KDD involves six steps: (1) *data recording* – the collection of the relevant data by offline or online activities; (2) *data preparation* – the organisation, or warehousing, and cleansing of the data in order to be ready for use; (3) *data mining* – the use of mathematical algorithms to automatically discover patterns and correlations in the data; (4) *data interpretation* – the examination and interpretation of the results (patterns and correlations) derived from the mining of the data; (5) *data evaluation* – the evaluation of the usefulness of the profile; (6) *application of profiles* – the controller decides how the profile will be used and for what purposes (Georgiou, 2018, p.43; Hildebrandt and Backhouse, 2005, FIDIS Deliverable D7.2). Accordingly, profiling involves the collection and (statistical) analysis of data, with the use of data mining techniques (i.e. mathematical algorithms), in order to identify and classify probable patterns and correlations of behaviour in profiles.

Clearly, therefore, profiling reflects what *statistics* is all about (Georgiou, 2018, p.186). So viewed, it seems difficult not to argue that the processing of data for profiling would not form (in almost all cases) processing for statistical purposes under the GDPR (Georgiou, 2018, p.186). Interestingly, this would mean that any further profiling activity can fall within the exception of statistical purposes of the GDPR and thus be considered to be compatible and lawful, without the need for individuals' additional consent.[37] In this way, it can be argued that the GDPR gives *authorisation* to business entities to re-process data for profiling, for any other purposes and without restrictions, by simply claiming the exception of statistical purposes (Georgiou, 2018, p.186). In light of this argument, however, it is questionable whether the exception of statistical purposes will remain an exception or whether it is becoming the general rule, allowing business entities to legitimise their otherwise incompatible profiling activities.

According to Article 5(1)(b) GDPR, further profiling for statistical purposes must be in accordance with the conditions and safeguards referred to in Article 89(1) GDPR. Article 89(1) GDPR provides that the controller must adopt technical and organisational measures in order to ensure the rights of individuals and, in particular, the principle of data minimisation. However, it does not further clarify what these measures should be. It only states that such measures may include the use of pseudonymisation or anonymisation, provided that the statistical purposes can be fulfilled in this way. Unlike anonymous data, pseudonymous data continue to be protected under the GDPR. In contrast, where data are anonymised, they fall outside the protection of the Regulation (unless the individual can be re-identified with the use of reasonable effort). This enables the controller to use the data for a longer period of time without being subject to the rules of the Regulation.

Nevertheless, if statistical purposes cannot be fulfilled by processing pseudonymous or anonymous data, the article permits the processing of personal data for those purposes. In this case, the GDPR authorises Member States to adopt measures to ensure that the processing of personal data does not affect a particular individual, as well as to provide derogations for the rights of individuals (as provided under Articles 15, 16, 18, 19, 20 and 21 of the GDPR) if the exercise of such rights 'seriously impair the achievement of the specific purposes, and such derogations are necessary for the fulfilment of those purposes'.[38] In this way, it is to be contended that the protection of individuals is overridden by the priority of controllers to process data for statistical purposes (or otherwise profiling) (Kotschy, 2014).

Consequently, therefore, Article 89 GDPR does not effectively ensure the efficacy of the Regulation to protect individuals where the exception of statistical purposes applies (Kotschy, 2014). This is, firstly, because as long as the controller uses anonymous data, these data can be further processed for statistical purposes (meaning, for a broad range of profiling activities); secondly, because the article permits the use of personal data without requiring the consent of the individual; and thirdly, because the article does not state who can re-process the data for such purposes: is it only the controller who initially collects the data or can the data also be transferred to a third party for these purposes? In the first case, the controller is chosen by the individual and is likely to be someone he/she trusts (e.g. credit scoring carried out by the individual's bank), while in the second case, the controller is unknown to the individual (e.g. credit scoring carried out by a credit scoring agency) (Kotschy, 2014).

Additionally, the fact that Article 89(1) GDPR does not define the types of measures that should be adopted, but leaves it up to the choice of each Member State, is problematic. This is because some Member States may adopt flexible measures in order to encourage profiling activities while others may adopt more restrictive ones (Mayer-Schönberger and Padova, 2016). As a result, controllers will have to deal with different measures across the EU and individuals with different levels of data protection. Arguably, this will impair the effect of the GDPR as a harmonised data protection legal instrument for profiling in Europe (Mayer-Schönberger and Padova, 2016).

Minimisation and Accuracy of the Data

The next problem concerns the principles of data minimisation and accuracy. According to the general data protection principles, controllers should limit the amount of data they collect and process and must keep the data accurate. In particular, the GDPR requires that data must be 'adequate, relevant, and limited to what is necessary in relation to the purposes for which they are processed' (data minimisation principle) and that the data must be 'accurate and kept up to date' (accuracy principle).[39]

Like the DPD, the GDPR maintains the data minimisation principle but it attempts to make it stronger by requiring that the data should be 'limited to what is necessary' for the purpose of the profiling. In short, no more data than are necessary should be used. In terms of profiling, however, this is antithetic. The idea of profiling is to collect, combine and analyse vast amounts of different types of data from a variety of data sources. In essence, profiling is about collecting and analysing as many data as possible (Information Commissioner's Office (ICO), 2014).

Viktor Mayer-Schönberger, a professor at Oxford University, and Kenneth Cukier, the senior editor for Data and Digital at *The Economist*, speak about the 'N=all' approach which requires the analysis of all the data in the database(s) (Duhigg, 2012). They argue that '[i]n order to fully investigate an individual, analysts need to look at the widest possible penumbra of data that surrounds the person – not just whom they know, but whom those people know too, and so on' (Information Commissioner's Office (ICO), 2014, p.23). This means that business entities do not use a sample of data to make their analysis (e.g. to identify a customer's preference) but rather all the data available about a particular individual. For example, if an internet service provider wants to automatically offer to its users discount coupons for stores and restaurants based on their current geographical locations, it needs to have a wider picture of its users, not just to know their current locations but also their preferences and lifestyle (e.g. food preferences, shopping and spending habits, most visited restaurants and stores, etc.).

From a data minimisation perspective, however, this creates questions as to whether the data processed are (unreasonably) excessive and also whether all these data are relevant to what is necessary for the purpose of the profiling (e.g. to provide discount coupons for stores and restaurants in the users' current geographical locations) (Information Commissioner's Office (ICO), 2014). This is especially an issue in the case of autonomic profiling (i.e. Ambient Intelligence environments such as smart houses or smart restaurants and Internet of Things networks which connect smart devices such as TVs, washing machines, lamps etc.) where, by default, every piece of data is collected and stored somewhere (Rouvroy, 2008).

Yet, profiling may reveal new unexpected patterns and correlations that may give new personal data about individuals and their lives. The use of facial recognition technology, for example, to assess the emotional reactions of customers during the demonstration of a product, may disclose correlations between customers' clothing tastes and their emotional reactions. This information is not necessarily relevant to what is necessary for the purpose of creating customers' emotional profiles related to the product.

The question, therefore, that arises is: what constitutes necessary collection of data in the case of profiling? The GDPR does not clarify what the term *relevant and limited to what is necessary* means. Is, for example, the continuous tracking of all individuals' activities through the internet 'limited to what is necessary' for an online store to offer targeted advertising for its products?; is the collection of data from individuals' social media accounts 'relevant' to the bank for assessing their suitability to pay their debts?; or is the collection of an employee's data relating to his/her visits to a psychologist 'relevant and limited to what is necessary' for the employer to determine if the employee is suitable for a job or a promotion? One way for the controllers to know what data are relevant and not excessive to the profiling is to identify the purposes of the profiling before the collection of the data. However, as it is explained above, the purpose of profiling cannot be known unless the data are analysed. Consequently, if the controller cannot determine the purposes of the profiling before the collection of the data, how can he/she assess what data will be relevant for a certain profiling?

Furthermore, the accuracy of the profiling may also be an issue. The GDPR provides that the data must be 'accurate and kept up to date' (accuracy principle).[40] Theoretically, for a profile to be accurate the controller must collect as many data as possible about the individual subject. By contrast, data minimisation requires the limitation of the data to the extent necessary. As a consequence, such limitation may create problems as to the accuracy of the profiles. In terms of profiling, therefore, the application of the data minimisation principle is debatable since the more data are collected for the creation of profiles the more accurate the result of the profiling will be (i.e. the application of the profile will be more precise) (Hildebrandt, 2009; Schermer, 2013).

As a result, the strict application of the principle may create less accurate profiles which may lead to false inclusions or false exclusions of a person in a profile. In particular, inaccurate profiles may increase the false positive and false negative results of profiling and thus facilitate unfair treatments of individuals (e.g. discrimination, stigmatisation, stereotyping and de-individuation). Classifying individuals in the wrong profiles means that individuals are assigned with incorrect 'worth' or 'risk' values that can affect their options and choices (e.g. being excluded or included from certain services). In this context, it can be argued that the GDPR cannot be seen as an effective legal instrument against discrimination because the data minimisation principle will not necessarily prohibit or eliminate the discriminatory effects of profiling.

Retention of the Data

A third problem relates to the storage limitation principle. According to this principle, controllers should also limit 'to a strict minimum' the period of time they store the data.[41] The GDPR, however, does not further explain what the term *strict minimum* means or how it should be assessed. It only provides that the data must be kept 'for no longer than is necessary for the purposes for which the personal data are processed'.[42] In other words, the data can only be retained for the period necessary for the completion of the initial profiling for which they have been collected. In this way, the Regulation gives flexibility to controllers to determine for themselves what is the 'strict minimum' period for each of their profiling activities. In addition, further storage of the data for other purposes presupposes a new legal basis (e.g. an individual must give his/her consent or the retention must be in the legitimate interest of the controller) (Mayer-Schönberger and Padova, 2016).[43]

In the same way as with the purpose limitation principle, the GDPR provides an exception to the storage limitation principle. It allows for further retention of data, for longer than is necessary and without the need of new legal basis, insofar as the data will be processed solely for statistical purposes and in accordance with the safeguards of Article 89(1) GDPR (as well as of the security measures adopted by the Member States as provided under Articles 89(2) and (3) GDPR). Once more, the Regulation leaves room for controllers to retain the data for longer periods for statistical purposes.

Bearing in mind, however, that the majority (if not all) of profiling activities constitute processing for statistical purposes, it is obvious that the GDPR encourages business entities to retain the data beyond the initial period and (re-) use these data for their future profiling activities (Mayer-Schönberger and Padova, 2016). Take, for instance, the example of the student loan company mentioned above. By arguing the statistical exception, the company can retain the data of its current student loan holders (collected for student loan applications) and (re-) use these data for any future profiling activity, without the consent of the student loan holders. Considering, therefore, the statistical purposes exception as well as the capacity of profiling technologies to store a large amount of data with almost no cost, the flexibility of further retention may lead controllers to keep the data forever.

To summarise, the data protection principles aim to ensure that profiling is lawful, fair and transparent. For this reason, the principles attempt to safeguard the individuals' right to control who is going to process their data, for how long and for what purposes as well as to enhance the accountability and transparency of controllers in the profiling. However, following the above analysis, it can be argued that the effective application of data protection principles is not objective in the context of profiling since, as it is shown, it is difficult to ensure total compliance with those principles.

The GDPR requires controllers to limit the collection, (re-) processing and retention of data to what is strictly relevant and necessary for the purposes for which they are collected. By contrast, profiling involves the collection and retention of as many data as possible and for longer periods of time. In addition, the transformative nature of the value of the data makes the purposes of the profiling unforeseeable at the time of the collection. As such, it is uncertain how these principles will be correctly and effectively applied, especially in the case of autonomic profiling (i.e. AmI and IoT environments) where, by default, every piece of data is collected and stored somewhere (Rouvroy, 2008).

To mitigate, however, this contradiction, the GDPR provides for controllers a number of flexibilities for the re-processing and retention of data. It allows the controllers to keep and process data for longer periods and for a number of different purposes, provided that these purposes are compatible with the initial ones or fall within the exception of statistical purposes. This suggests, however, that as long as the profiling is compatible or done for statistical purposes, the data can be kept and processed forever. Bearing in mind that 'statistical purposes' reflects what profiling is all about, the GDPR indirectly gives to controllers the *authority* to use the retained data for any of their profiling activities and without the additional consent of the individual. Moreover, if the controller complies with consent or other legal basis or if he/she includes the new (incompatible) purposes or the further retention of the data within the context of statistical purposes, the limitation requirements are abolished. What is more, if he/she chooses to anonymise the data, he/she will be free, from any obligation under the GDPR, to retain and process the data for an unlimited period. In the end, the GDPR does not intend to restrict profiling activities but rather to offer ways to enable further profiling.

The principles that have been analysed above show that the GDPR presents many gaps and cannot create a symmetry between the business entities and the individual data subjects. Obviously, all the above open-ended restrictions, in relation to further processing and retention of data, leave room for different interpretations of the principles and create problems as to the transparency, lawfulness and fairness of profiling (Kohnstamm, 2014).

CONCLUSION

In the context of profiling, therefore, it is difficult to effectively apply the Regulation. As shown from the above findings, the applicability of the Regulation is limited in view of profiling because there may be cases in which the profile contains non-personal data or anonymous data that cannot facilitate the identification of the individual within the meaning of Article 2(1) GDPR. This is mostly the case with group profiling, and especially of non-distributive group profiles, although in personalised profiling there may also be cases in which the individual subject is not identifiable within the meaning of Article 2(1) GDPR. In these cases, the GDPR does not apply and the individuals do not have any rights upon their data whereas the controllers have absolute control over the data with no obligation to comply with the provisions of the Regulation. So viewed, group profiling is perhaps the most problematic issue under the GDPR since the members of a non-distributive group profile continue to be unprotected under the new data protection regime.

Furthermore, where the identifiability factor is satisfied, which means that profiling is governed by the rules of the Regulation, the situation is not prosperous either. As shown from the above findings, the GDPR neglects to achieve a level of symmetry between individuals and controllers, either in terms of knowledge or in terms of power (control). On the one hand, the general data protection principles of Article 5 GDPR do not effectively apply to ensure the transparency and accountability of controllers. The restrictions on further processing and retention of data indirectly give the *authority* to business entities to re-use the data for further profiling, and for any other purposes, without the additional consent of the individual by simply arguing the statistical purpose exception. Moreover, as mentioned above, the data minimisation principle is inconsistent with profiling because, firstly, the more data that are collected and analysed the better for the accuracy of the profiles and, secondly, it is difficult for business entities to assess, at the collection stage, which data are likely to be relevant for the profiling since the purpose of the profiling cannot be determined before the collection of the data.

As a result, the Regulation is unsuccessful in achieving a balanced distribution of powers between the business entities and their data subjects. Indeed, it is to be argued that the distribution of powers, as created under Article 5 of the GDPR, is at the expense of individuals and in favour of the controllers, both in terms of knowledge and in terms of power, and thus how they exercise that power. Therefore, without the right level of balance of powers between the parties involved, the protection provided under the Regulation and in particlar under Article 5 GDPR cannot be satisfactory for the individuals.

REFERENCES

Bygrave, L. (2001). Automated profiling: Minding the machine: Article 15 of the EC Data Protection Directive and automated profiling. *Computer Law & Security Report, 17*(1), 17–24. doi:10.1016/S0267-3649(01)00104-2

Bygrave, L. (2002). Data protection law: approaching its rationale, logic and limits. The Hague: Kluwer Law International.

Custers, B. H. M. (2004). The power of knowledge: Ethical, legal and technological aspects of data mining and group profiling in epidemiology. Nijmegen: Wolf Legal Publishers (WLP).

Cuthbertson, A. (2016, August 16). *Is your sex toy spying on you?* Retrieved January 15, 2017, from https://www.newsweek.com/your-sex-toy-spying-you-489328

de Andrade, N. N. G. (2011). Data protection, privacy and identity: Distinguishing concepts and articulating rights. In *Privacy and identity management for life 6th Ifip Wg 9.2, 9.6/11.7, 11.4, 11.6/PrimeLife International Summer School, Helsingborg, Sweden, August 2-6, 2010, revised selected papers* (Vol. 352). Berlin: Springer.

Dictionary.com. (n.d.a). *Statistical.* Retrieved November 27, 2016, from https://www.dictionary.com/browse/statistical

Dictionary.com. (n.d.b). *Statistics.* Retrieved November 27, 2016, from https://www.dictionary.com/browse/statistics

Directive 2002/58/EC of the European Parliament and of the Council of 12 July 2002 concerning the processing of personal data and the protection of privacy in the electronic communications sector (Directive on privacy and electronic communications), OJ L 201, 31/07/2002 P. 0037-0047

Directive 2009/136/EC of the European Parliament and of the Council of 25 November 2009 amending Directive 2002/22/EC on universal service and users' rights relating to electronic communications networks and services, Directive 2002/58/EC concerning the processing of personal data and the protection of privacy in the electronic communications sector and Regulation (EC) No 2006/2004 on cooperation between national authorities responsible for the enforcement of consumer protection laws. (Directive on privacy and electronic communications), OJ L 337/11, 18/12/2009 P. 0011–0036.

Directive 95/46/EU of the European Parliament and of the Council of October 1995 on the protection of individuals with regard to the processing of personal data and on the free movement of such data, OJ L 281, 23/11/1995 P. 0031-0050

Duhigg, C. (2012, February 16). *How companies learn your secrets.* Retrieved October 10, 2016, from https://www.nytimes.com/2012/02/19/magazine/shopping-habits.html

Emmons, A. (2016, August 4). *Microsoft pitches technology that can read facial expressions at political rallies*. Retrieved August 18, 2016, from https://theintercept.com/2016/08/04/microsoft-pitches-technology-that-can-read-facial-expressions-at-political-rallies/

Ferraris, V., Bosco, F., Cafiero, G., D'Angelo, E., & Suloyeva, Y. (2013a). *The impact of profiling on fundamental rights* (Working Paper 3 of the EU Profiling Project). Retrieved May 13, 2014, from http://www.unicri.it/special_topics/citizen_profiling/PROFILINGproject_WS1_Fundamental_1110.pdf

Ferraris, V., Bosco, F., Cafiero, G., D'Angelo, E., & Suloyeva, Y. (2013b). *Defining profiling* (Working Paper 1 of the EU Profiling Project). Retrieved May 13, 2014, from: http://profiling-project.eu/wp-content/uploads/2013/07/PROFILINGproject_WS1_definition_2607.pdf

Georgiou, E. (2018). *The law of commercial profiling* (Unpublished doctoral thesis). Brunel University, London, UK.

Gutwirth, S., & Hildebrandt, M. (2010). Some caveats on profiling. In S. Gutwirth, Y. Poullet, & P. De Hert (Eds.), *Data protection in a profiled world*. Dordrecht: Springer. doi:10.1007/978-90-481-8865-9_2

Hildebrandt, M. (2006). Profiling: From data to knowledge. *Datenschutz und Datensicherheit, 30*(9), 548–552. doi:10.100711623-006-0140-3

Hildebrandt, M. (2008). Defining profiling: A new type of knowledge? In M. Hildebrandt & S. Gutwirth (Eds.), *Profiling the European citizen: Cross-disciplinary perspectives*. Dordrecht: Springer. doi:10.1007/978-1-4020-6914-7_2

Hildebrandt, M. (2009). Who is profiling who? Invisible visibility. In S. Gutwirth, Y. Poullet, P. de Hert, C. de Terwangne, & S. Nouwt (Eds.), *Reinventing data protection?* Dordrecht: Springer Netherlands. doi:10.1007/978-1-4020-9498-9_14

Hildebrandt, M., & Backhouse, J. (2005). D7.2: Descriptive analysis and inventory of profiling practices. *FIDIS consortium*. Retrieved July 14, 2014, from http://www.fidis.net/resources/deliverables/profiling/

Hildebrandt, M., Gutwirth, S., & De Hert, P. (2005, September 5). D7.4: Implications of profiling practices in democracy. *FIDIS consortium*. Retrieved July 15, 2015, from http://www.fidis.net/resources/deliverables/profiling/

Information Commissioner's Office (ICO). (2014). *Big Data and Data Protection 20140728 version: 1.0*. Retrieved July 1, 2018 from https://www.huntonprivacyblog.com/wp-content/uploads/sites/28/2016/11/big-data-and-data-protection.pdf

Kohnstamm, J. (2014). Privacy by debate: The European Data Protection Supervisor's contribution to collaboration between National Data Protection Authorities. In H. Hijmans & H. Kranenborg (Eds.), *Data protection anno 2014: How to restore trust? Peter Hustinx, European Data Protection Supervisor (2004–2014)*. Cambridge: Intersentia Publishing Ltd.

Kotschy, W. (2014). The proposal for a new General Data Protection Regulation—Problem solved? *International Data Privacy Law, 4*(4), 274–281. doi:10.1093/idpl/ipu022

Leenes, R. (2008). Regulating profiling in a democratic constitutional state. Reply: Addressing the obscurity of data clouds. In M. Hildebrandt & S. Gutwirth (Eds.), *Profiling the European citizen: Cross-disciplinary perspectives*. Dordrecht: Springer.

Mayer-Schönberger, V., & Padova, Y. (2016). Regime change? Enabling big data through Europe's new data protection regulation. *The Columbia Science and Technology Law Review*, *XVII*, 319.

Poullet, Y. (2010). About the e-Privacy Directive: Towards a third generation of data protection legislation? In S. Gutwirth, Y. Poullet, & P. De Hert (Eds.), *Data protection in a profiled world*. Dordrecht: Springer. doi:10.1007/978-90-481-8865-9_1

Regulation (EU) 2016/679 of the European Parliament and of the Council of 27 April 2016 on the Protection of Natural Persons with Regard to the Processing of Personal Data and on the Free Movement of Such Data, and Repealing Directive 95/46/EC (General Data Protection Regulation) Article 29 Working Party, 'Opinion No. 03/2013 on Purpose Limitation' adopted on 2nd April 2013 (00569/13/EN WP 203) Article 29 Working Party, 'Opinion No. 4/2007 on the Concept of Personal Data', adopted on 20th June 2007 (01248/07/EN, WP 136)

Roosendaal, A. (2013). Digital personae and profiles in law: Protecting individuals' rights in online contexts. Nijmegen: Wolf Legal Publishers (WLP).

Rouvroy, A. (2008). Privacy, data protection, and the unprecedented challenges of ambient intelligence. *Studies in Ethics, Law, and Technology*, *2*(1). doi:10.2202/1941-6008.1001

Schermer, B. (2011). The limits of privacy in automated profiling and data mining. *Computer Law & Security Review*, *27*(1), 45–52. doi:10.1016/j.clsr.2010.11.009

Schermer, B. (2013). Risks of profiling and the limits of data protection law. In B. Custers, T. Calders, B. Schermer, & T. Zarsky (Eds.), *Discrimination and privacy in the information society: Data mining in large databases*. Dordrecht: Springer. doi:10.1007/978-3-642-30487-3_7

Schreurs, W., Hildebrandt, M., Gasson, M., & Warwick, K. (2005). D7.3: Report on actual and possible profiling techniques in the field of ambient intelligence. *FIDIS consortium*. Retrieved July 3, 2018, from http://www.fidis.net/resources/deliverables/profiling/

Schreurs, W., Hildebrandt, M., Kindt, E., & Vanfleteren, M. (2008). Cogitas, ergo sum: The role of data protection and non-discrimination law in group profiling in the private sector. In M. Hildebrandt & S. Gutwirth (Eds.), *Profiling the European citizen: Cross-disciplinary perspectives*. Dordrecht: Springer. doi:10.1007/978-1-4020-6914-7_13

Vermeulen, M. (2013, September 1). Regulating profiling in the European Data Protection Regulation: An interim insight into the drafting of Article 20. EMSOC Working Paper. *SSRN Electronic Journal*. Available from SSRN: https://ssrn.com/abstract=2382787

ENDNOTES

[1]   Directive 95/46/EC of the European Parliament and of the Council of October 1995 on the protection of individuals with regard to the processing of personal data and on the free movement of such data, OJ L 281, 23/11/1995 P. 0031-0050.

[2]   Regulation (EU) 2016/679 of the European Parliament and of the Council of 27 April 2016 on the Protection of Natural Persons with Regard to the Processing of Personal Data and on the Free Movement of Such Data, and Repealing Directive 95/46/EC (General Data Protection Regulation).

[3]   It should be noted that the e-Privacy Directive 2002/58/EC as it was amended by the Directive 2009/136/EC, although it does not explicitly refer to profiling, allows the use of cookies and other tracking devices that can be used for profiling activities where the controller has informed the user about the purpose of profiling and where he/she has obtained the user's consent (Article 5(3)).

[4]   Article 15(1) DPD: 'Member states shall grant the right to every person not to be subject to a decision which produces legal effects concerning him or significantly affects him and which is based solely on automated processing of data intended to evaluate certain personal aspects relating to him, such as his performance at work, creditworthiness, reliability or conduct etc.'

[5]   Article 15 DPD is closely related to the rights conferred under Articles 10, 11 and 12 of the DPD which provide to individuals the rights to be informed for the collection of their personal data and to obtain knowledge of the logic involved in any processing of such data, in particular in the case of automated decision-makings.

[6]   Recital 72 GDPR.

[7]   Profiling is defined as 'any form of automated processing of personal data consisting of the use of personal data to evaluate certain personal aspects relating to a natural person, in particular to analyse or predict aspects concerning that natural person's performance at work, economic situation, health, personal preferences, interests, reliability, behaviour, location or movements;'.

[8]   Article 3 GDPR.

[9]   Article 2(1) GDPR.

[10]   Article 4(1) GDPR.

[11]   Article 29 Working Party, 'Opinion No. 4/2007 on the Concept of Personal Data', adopted on 20th June 2007 (01248/07/EN, WP 136).

[12]   Article 4(1) GDPR considers identifiers such as names, identification numbers, location data or data related to physical, physiological, genetic, mental, economic, cultural or social identity, as well as online identifiers (IP addresses, cookies or RFID-tags) to be personal data. Recital 30 GDPR states that online identifiers may allow the indirect identification of an individual because when combined with unique identifiers they can be used to create profiles about individuals and thus enable individuals to be singled out even when their real names are not known.

[13]   Recital 26 GDPR.

[14]   Recital 26 GDPR.

[15]   An individual profile, for example, is the personal profile of Mr 'X' who is 45 years old, divorced, has two children and is a lawyer with a mortgage and one credit card.

[16]   A good example is Microsoft's 'Realtime Crowd Insights' software (an Application Programming Interface (API) that connects web applications to Microsoft cloud computing services) which can read the facial expressions of the crowds at political campaigns and create personalised emotional profiles for each participant. With the use of camera, the software collects the face image of each

person in the crowd and sends them to Microsoft servers. Microsoft then analyses the images and returns with a profile for each person. Each profile includes an assigned serial number (e.g. 'b2ff') and several pieces of information about the person such as an estimation of his/her age, gender, ethnicity, clothing style, time of attention and any emotions detected (e.g. anger, fear, happiness etc.). The persons are not identified by their names but only by their serial numbers (Emmons, 2016).

17   A group may consist of either a community – existing group of people – (e.g. members of a specific religion or team), or a category of people that have no connection between them but who share one or more common characteristics (e.g. a group of women with black hair and green eyes) (Custers, 2004; Hildebrandt, 2006).

18   Group profiles can be classified as distributive and non-distributive profiles. A *distributive group profile* is a group where all the members share the same characteristics (e.g. a group of lawyers working in the UK). A *non-distributive group profile* is a group where the members do not share all the characteristics of the group (e.g. a group of people with a high risk of depression is profiled according to a list of risk factors such as economic situation, stressful conditions at work, losing a job etc.) (Ferraris et al., 2013b).

19   In group profiling, a person may be identifiable (in the case of distributive group profiles) where the profile applies to the group as a whole but also to each single member of the group in the form of individual profile. For instance, if all the individuals in a certain group are London citizens having a specific type of sun allergy, then if an individual is known to be a member of that group (he/she is a London citizen having that specific type of sun allergy), he/she can easily be distinguished from the group.

20   For example, a group of people with a high risk of depression is profiled according to a list of risk factors (e.g. economic situation, stressful conditions at work, family history of depression, losing a job, etc.). A person may be identified as a member of that group because he/she lost his/her job, while another person may be identified as a member of that group because he/she is getting divorced.

21   Article 5(1)(b) GDPR.

22   Article 29 Working Party, 'Opinion No. 03/2013 on Purpose Limitation' adopted on 2nd April 2013 (00569/13/EN WP 203).

23   Recital 50 and Article 6(4) GDPR.

24   Recital 50 GDPR.

25   Article 6(4) and Recital 50 GDPR; See also note 22.

26   See note 22.

27   See note 22.

28   See note 22.

29   Article 6(4) GDPR.

30   Article 5(1)(b) GDPR and Recital 50; see also Recitals 159, 160 and 162 for the meaning of scientific, historical and statistical research. It should be noted that the public health research is treated as a subject of scientific research.

31   Recital 29 DPD.

32   Article 89(1) GDPR.

33   Recital 159 GDPR.

34   Recital 162 GDPR.

35   Dictionary.com, 'http://www.dictionary.com/browse/statistical' (accessed 27 November 2016).

36   Dictionary.com, 'http://www.dictionary.com/browse/statistics' (accessed 27 November 2016).

37   A good example is that of a company producing internet-connected sex toys. The company, by using the argument of 'market research purposes', has continuously collected data about the temperature and vibration intensity of the toys while they are being used by the users (without their consent) in order to understand what settings and levels of intensity are most preferable (Cuthbertson, 2016).

38   Recital 156 and Article 89(2)–(3) GDPR.

39   Article 5(1)(c) and (d) GDPR.

40   Article 5(1)(d) GDPR.

41   Recital 39 GDPR.

42   Article 5(1)(e) GDPR.

43   Article 6(4) GDPR.

Chapter 6
Is "Privacy" a Means to Protect the Competition or Advance Objectives of Innovation and Consumer Welfare?

Arletta Gorecka
https://orcid.org/0000-0001-6555-4264
University of Strathclyde, UK

ABSTRACT

The relationship between competition law and privacy is still seen as problematic with academics and professionals trying to adequately assess the impact of privacy on the competition law sphere. The chapter looks at the legal development of the EU merger proceedings to conclude that EU competition law is based on the prevailing approach and assesses decisions involving data through the spectrum of keeping a competitive equilibrium in hypothetical markets. Secondly, it considers the legal developments in the EU Member States' practice, which acknowledges the apparent intersection between the phenomena of competition law and privacy. This chapter attempts to propose that privacy concerns appear to hold a multidimensional approach on competition legal regime; nevertheless, it does not result in the need of legal changes within the remits of competition law, as the privacy concerns are already protected by the data protection and consumer protection law.

INTRODUCTION

The debate on the intersection of competition law and privacy acts as a challenge for the existing competition law framework. The notion of privacy has achieved attention from academics and adjudicators, indicating its dynamic nature (EDPS, 2016). The unprecedented magnitude of data collection could raise challenges for both society and legislation, since personal data functions as a tradable commodity (World Economic Forum, 2011). The personal data protection concerns have had a numerous impact on the framework of competition law — from the anticompetitive agreements to abuse of dominance

DOI: 10.4018/978-1-5225-9489-5.ch006

or merger control. The merger control and abuse of dominance related to competitive harm through the access to substantial customer data; the irretraceable algorithms replaced the price-fixing cartels. Arguably, the breaches of privacy could act as reducing competitive process, or as a proxy to abuse, since the competition, the harm could take forms of misuse of power which harm consumer and competition.

THE CHAPTER OBJECTIVES AND ITS OUTLINE

This chapter considers privacy impact on competition law. The term privacy will be used interchangeably with data protection. The author proposes that privacy concerns appear to hold a multidimensional approach to competition legal regime; nevertheless, it does not result in the need for legal changes within the remits of competition law. The first part discusses the legal background. The second part of the chapter distinguishes three phases in the EU legal development of data assessment in competition law: ignorance of data, identification of parallel pathways between competition law and data protection, and the third phrase recognized by the EU Member State practice — recognition of data in the competition sphere (the third part). The fourth part analyzes whether privacy could act as an element enhancing innovation, consumer welfare or the competitive process, based competition law goals. In conclusion, the author recapitulates the findings and assesses privacy impact on competition law.

LEGAL BACKGROUND

EU law, by its foundation, aims to promote peace, well-being of its citizens, freedom, sustainable and economic development (Art 1, TEU). The rules adopted on competition law and data protection law reflect on the fundamental goals under the Treaty on the Functioning of the European Union's (TFEU, 2008) separate legal bases. Hence, the purpose of these areas intersect. The focus of this section is to offer a brief explanation of competition and data protection rules.

EU Competition Law

EU competition law pursues a multitude of different aims that include the protection for market structures, economic freedom, consumer welfare and the promotion of efficiency (Guidelines on the Commission's Enforcement, 2009). Article 101-106 TFEU (2008) sets out the rules on competition law, which aim at prevention or distortion of competition, or abuse of a dominant position. EU competition law applies to any 'economic activity' that might 'affect trade between the Member States' (Guidelines on the effect on trade concept contained in Articles 81 and 82 of the Treaty (2004)). The emphasis is placed on Article 102 TFEU (2008), since the privacy infringements, i.e. unfair data acquisition on an unprecedented scale, allow for the abuse of dominance (see the later discussion of Facebook case).

Article 102 TFEU (2008), which prohibits the abuse of a domination position in a relevant market, could apply to the anticompetitive actions of online platforms, which operate on the data acquisition. Yet, a mere dominance in a relevant market is not prohibited. An abuse under 102 TFEU is understood as taking forms of exclusionary abuse and exploitative abuse (Commission guidance, 2009). The exclusionary and exploitative abuses are discussed in depth in the section of the Facebook case, here only a brief discussion is presented.

The exploitative conduct refers to an action which harms consumers (in most cases the victims were companies, and not end consumers) (Hubert, Combet, 2011) and includes an application of excessive prices or unfair discrimination. According to *United Brands* (1972), the Commission, to determine whether an action amounted to an exploitative abuse, is required to determine whether: (i) the price is unfair in itself or unfair whether compared with competing products, and whether (ii) the profit margin amount is excessive by comparing product cost with price. The type of exclusionary conduct refers to the abuse by which the market structure is damaged (Commission guidance, 2009, paras 5, 19), and includes specific forms of tying, bundling, refusal to supply, market squeeze, and predation (Commission Guidance, 2009). The actions of exclusionary abuse are deemed to be harmful to consumers and have an impact on consumer welfare.

Furthermore, the competition law also applies to mergers (Merger Regulation, 2004), which by its nature bring structural changes to the market. Hence, the mergers tend to impact the structure of a relevant market, and often goes beyond the national borders of a Member State. The nature of the merger review falls within the scope of regulation and is appraised by the Commission. Hence, merger control aims at controlling of undertakings activity, accounting its effect on competition, taking into account the factors like including its interest on consumers. (Commission Guidance, 2009).

EU Data Protection Law

EU law offers extensive data protection recognition, offering protection for personal data of legal and/or natural persons and public and/or private bodies. The data protection is, amongst others, protected by several primary and secondary law, including the Charter of Fundamental Rights and the General Data Protection Regulation (2008). Article 16 TFEU (2008) provides a basis for EU data protection.

Within the scope of the Charter (2010), Article 8 recognizes personal data as a proactive right, which goes beyond the protection of individuals against a state's intervention (see Article 7 of the Charter (2010)). By the virtue of Article 8, individuals might expect their information to be proceeded by anyone, including the State. Yet, Article 8 is subject to Article 8(2) and (3), which requires for such a proceeding to lawful, fair and transparent for individuals; the right is also subject to control by an authority.

The GDPR, replacing the Data Protection Directive (1995), is an instrument which governs how companies are allowed to process personal data. By Article 4(2) GDPR (2016), the 'processing' involves any activity that might be undertaken about 'personal data'. The term 'personal data', defined in Article 4(1) GDPR, refers to any acquired information relating to natural persons, which allows them to be identified (including IP, or location). Furthermore, the GDPR refers to 'data subject' and 'data controller' to enhance the clarity of its regime. Article 4(1) GDPR defines a 'data subject' as persons to whom personal data relates, whereas Article 4(7) explains 'data controllers' are any person (natural or legal) who proceeded the acquired data.

Under the GDPR's regime, consent plays a vital role: a data controller could only process personal data under lawful bases set out in Article 6(1) GDPR and includes consent, public interest, legitimate interests, and contract. Data subject's consent has to be informed, specific, unambiguous and freely given. Furthermore, data controllers have to collect consent in an affirmative action. The GDPR enhanced the supervisory power and strengthened the protection of personal data and simultaneously the protection of users privacy.

DATA PROTECTION WITHIN THE EU COMPETITION LAW PROCEEDINGS

Empirically, the EU legal practice contributed to the identification of different phases of the development of the intersection between competition law and data protection. Primarily in *Asnef-Equifax* (2006), the CJEU rejected the interplay between competition law and data protection rules by stressing that data protection law is outside the scope of competition law. At the same time, the vertical merger of *TeleAtlas/ TomTom* (2008) did not raise any data issues and kept a prudent approach in excluding data protection arguments in its assessment. Nevertheless, the EU Commission defined a narrow market product of digital maps, which could be potentially acknowledging the digital data in market definition.

With an increased appetite for data, the subsequent enforcement abandoned isolation of data protection principles from anticompetitive assessments. The merger of *Google/DoubleClick* (2008) could indicate parallel pathways between competition and data protection rules. The Commission, adopting *Asnef-Equifax* (2006) ratio, concluded the case "without prejudice to the obligations imposed onto the parties by Community legislation concerning the protection of individuals and the protection of privacy about the processing of personal data" (*Google/DoubleClick*, 2008, para 368). Nevertheless, the Commission was conscious that the acquisition of users' data might result in targeted advertisement and restrictions of privacy rules. The potential anticompetitive conduct concerned exploitative and exclusionary abuse, diminishing consumer experience and lessening competition on a relevant market. The Commission considered the case by applying well-established competition law principles and cleared off the merger.

The later merger proceedings acknowledged the increasing importance of data. In *Telefonica UK/ Vodafone UK/Everything Everywhere* (2012), a decision on joint venture creation, the Commission mentioned that personal data acted as a commodity, as consumers tend to surrender their data to market players (para 543). However, the *Microsoft/LinkedIn* (2016) offered a more mature approach to data within EU competition law, as the Commission relied on that the users' privacy protection to assume the impact of combining the two companies' databases. Interestingly, the decision referred to the GDPR (2016), which at the time of the assessment had not been applicable, and announced that the GDPR (2016) would empower individuals with control over their data and limit Microsoft ability to access and process personal data of the users (*Microsoft/LinkedIn*, 2016, para 178). Nevertheless, the Commission did not preclude Microsoft's access to LinkedIn's data after the merger. Yet, the Commission defined two horizontal issues following the merger. Firstly, there was no distortion to competition as pre-merger the companies were competitors on the hypothetical market. Secondly, Microsoft and LinkedIn after a merger would combine their database and achieve market power, resulting in higher barriers to entry (*Microsoft/LinkedIn*, 2016, para 178). Yet, the Commission focused on securing a competitive process and did not provide any guidance on data protection within competition law sphere.

Hence, no consensus remains as to an optimal method of evaluating data in EU competition law. It is apparent that EU competition law supports the prevailing approach and assesses decisions involving personal data through the spectrum of protecting a competitive equilibrium in hypothetical markets. Nevertheless, the concept of privacy appears to be a multi-dimensional and dynamic issue (Bergkamp, 2002), requiring careful considerations of all dimensions and interests of parties on relevant markets (Thibodeau, 2014). Both data protection and competition legal orders seek the advancement of market integration and share a concern for the welfare of individuals, with consumers benefiting from the collection of their data in a wide array of free services, products or contents. Thus, data protection and competition law could intersect with each other, and kept balanced during an assessment of anticompetitive misconducts. Yet, although data protection principles begin to influence competition authorities, the protection of the individuals' rights as consumers and market participants is already protected by the data protection and consumer protection authorities. Yet, it remains unclear how to encompass data protection principles into competition law assessments. Initially, the assessment should be based on restoring effective competitive processes. all other protections only to ensure that there were no gaps in the type of protection.

THE EU MEMBER STATES COMPETITION AUTHORITIES' PRACTICE ACKNOWLEDGING DATA PROTECTION IMPLICATIONS

German's Bundeskartellamt Case of Facebook

The BKA launched an investigation against Facebook due to suspicions that Facebook has abused its dominant position in the social media market. The initial suspicion was that Facebook's T&Cs had violated data protection provisions, which could amount to an imposition of unfair condition on users; Facebook's dominant position allowed the platform to collect and use the user's data from Facebook's owned platforms, including WhatsApp, Instagram, Oculus and Masquerade as well as from any websites/apps that use 'Facebook Business Tools'. The BKA proceeding against Facebook is undoubtedly an explicit example where competition authority applied the data protection infringement as the ground of intervention.

Market Definition

The BKA began in a traditional way in defying narrowly the relevant market as the social network market in Germany (*Facebook*, case summary, 2019, p. 4). The BKA, based on the criterion for demand-side substitution, exhibited two sides of the market (*Facebook*, case summary, 2019, p.3). Firstly, there is a market for social media, from the perspective of the private users', based on terms of application, price and characteristics (*Facebook*, case summary, 2019, p.4). The second, opposing side, was the private end-users' market using Facebook free of charge (*Facebook*, case summary, 2019, p.4). The non-price access to Facebook was not seen as a problem since section 18(2a) GWB states that the market assumption would not be invalidated due to free service provided (*Facebook*, case summary, 2019, p.4). The relevant market amounted to around 95% of daily social network users in the territory of Germany (*Facebook*, case summary, 2019, p.4), which evidently indicated Facebook's dominant position in these markets. Unquestionably, the dominant position is not itself prohibited; dominant companies are subjected to special obligations, which include adequate terms of service. For services such as Facebook, which based its products through advertising-financed profits, personal data is a key aspect. Yet, although competition on the social network market was not high, the BKA focused on the fact that Facebook's market share was exceptionally high, based on the assessment of factors including indirect network effect, innovation, and access to data (*Facebook*, case summary, 2019, p.4)

Dominant Position and Abuse of Dominance

The BKA considered that key elements which further prove Facebook's dominant position on the market. Firstly, Facebook's users might potentially not switch to another social network (*Facebook*, case summary, 2019, p.5), creating a lock-in effect. This was evidenced by a poor competition within this sector, with a small number of social networks being available. Due to Google+ being shut down, there have been no alternative social platform available to be compared with Facebook. Furthermore, the behavioral element of the users' nature might influence Facebook's dominant position, as the users are unlikely to switch to different providers which are not used by their family members or friends. Hence, other competitors experienced a decrease of their active users.

The BKA considered that key elements which further prove Facebook's dominant position. Firstly, Facebook's users might not switch to another social network (*Facebook*, case summary, 2019, p.5), creating a lock-in effect. This was evidenced by a poor competition within this sector, with a small number of the social network being available. Due to Google+ being shut down, there has been no alternative social platform available to be compared with Facebook. Furthermore, the behavioral element of the users' nature might influence Facebook's dominant position, as the users are unlikely to switch to different providers which are not used by their family members or friends. Hence, other competitors experienced a decrease in their active users.

The BKA determined that Facebook's conduct was a clear manifestation of market power (*Facebook*, case summary, 2019, p.6). This is a crux of theories of harm. The BKA was concerned with two antitrust issues: the accumulation of the data allowed Facebook to entrench the dominant position and the single catch-all consent of Facebook users to be unfair under Art 102(a) TFEU. Such an approach might be pictured dividing the theories of harm into two spectrums: exploitative and exclusionary theories of harm. Although the BKA based its decision relying on German law, the chapter considers the wider EU competition law implication.

Considering the exploitative theories of harm, the BKA assessed that:

[I]mplementing Facebook's data policy, which allows Facebook to collect user and device-related data from sources outside of Facebook and to merge it with data collected on Facebook, constitutes an abuse of a dominant position [...] in the form of exploitative business terms. (Facebook, case summary, 2019, p.7).

Furthermore, the exploitative abuse in question amounts to Facebook manifesting its market power and implementing abuse T&Cs; any T&Cs are inappropriate given the constitutional rights, including the right to informational self-determination (*Facebook*, case summary, 2019, p.8). Generally, under EU law, exploitative abuses are prohibited under Article 102 TFEU (2008). The exploitative abuses include a prohibition of unfair trading conditions, unfair pricing, or predatory pricing (*United Brands*, 1978, para 248; *Jean-Louis Tournier,* 1989, para 34; *Tetra Pak II*, 1996, para 41-44). It remains accepted that a price or trading terms might be unfair as to its effect on competitors. Yet, the case law affirmed that excessive trading conditions and/or prices could amount to abuse of dominance due to its effects on consumers welfare (*United Brands*, 1978, para 248).

For many, the Commission practice is capable of supporting the privacy concern as a parameter for anticompetitive abuse under Article 102(a) TFEU (2008), due to its disproportionate nature (Nazzini 2019). Therein, the case of the exploitative trading condition, *BRT v SABAM* (1974), which considered whether a Belgian collecting society abusing its dominant position by demanding authors to give up their copyright in the name of the society, points that the 'fairness' of the clause requires an assessment of all relevant interests, which is necessary to achieve proportionate assessment ensuring a balance. Furthermore, in *Tetra Pak II*, the Commission raised an interesting point regarding applicability of the proportionality test in exploitative abuse assessments (*Tetra Pak II*, 1996, para 106). According to the

Commission, such clauses imposed "additional obligations which have no connection with the purpose of the contract and which deprive the purchaser of certain aspects of his property rights" (*Tetra Pak II*, 1996, para 107). Comparing these cases to the Facebook case, the BKA deduced that Facebook's privacy policy was not required to offer social network to its users, nor for monetizing the network through targeted advertising (*Facebook*, case summary, 2019, p.10). Also, the BKA applied a broad proportionality test, which balanced all relevant interests (*Facebook*, case summary, 2019, p.8); the BKA, relying on section 19(1) GWB, examined closely the relationship between competition law and data protection law. In the BKA's view, the GDPR was based on constitutional rights of a uniform level of data protection and, hence, was appropriate to be assessed under competition law.

In the Facebook case, arguably, the GDPR infringement might constitute a basis for an exploitative abuse. This approach would require a case-by-case analysis, as the mere infringement of the GDPR would not amount to an exploitative abuse. Under Article 7(4) GDPR (2016), the performance of the contract is taken into the account, when assessing whether consent has been freely given. This suggests that a consent to the processing of the data is of utmost importance and the performance of a contract is conditional regardless of a data controller holding a dominant position. The BKA took great care to justify the GDPR's reliance to establish an infringement of competition law. Although the general position of EU competition law is to disregard the privacy-related concerns, the BKA relied on the German Federal Court of Justice case, which pointed that the protection of constitutional rights might be justified by application of competition rules, as a dominant-market position dictated special, unlawful, privilege to abolish the contractual autonomy of the users (*Facebook*, case summary, 2019, p.7). The GDPR infringement, in itself, might not be seen as competitive harm. Yet, the BKA pointed out that the GDPR infringement was relevant from the competition law perspective, as Facebook's market position was significant to consider corporate the infringement circumstances. Therefore, the BKA took an accumulative approach and regarded the GDPR infringement as a strong indicator of the abuse of dominance, both recognized in section 19(1) of German Competition Act and Article 102 TFEU. Yet, it is not easy to understand the precise meaning of the BKA reasoning, as Facebook's exploitative claims will not have a solid basis under EU competition law. Yet, the privacy standard might potentially be seen as relevant for the assessment of anticompetitive unilateral conduct in Germany. Any GDPR infringement will not be seen as competitive harm but the firm in question must bargain its market power both in the name of end-users and competitive process than other firms would not commit similar breaches.

Moreover, the title of the Facebook's case summary, "Facebook, Exploitative business terms pursuant to Section 19(1) GWB for inadequate data processing" (*Facebook*, case summary, 2019) might deceive that the BKA focused solely on exploitative abuses. However, the section of the case summary, titled "Manifestation of market power" points out that, arguably, Facebook's conduct also falls within the meaning of the exclusionary abuse (*Facebook*, case summary, 2019, p.11). The BKA indicated that Facebook's conduct:

[I]mpedes competitors because Facebook gains access to a large number of further sources by its inappropriate processing of data and their combination with Facebook accounts. It has [...] gained a competitive edge over its competitors in an unlawful way and increased market entry barriers [...]. (Facebook, case summary, 2019, p.11)

Additionally, article 102 TFEU prohibits exclusionary practices. In light of the Facebook case summary, the case might have not brought any explicit reference to exclusionary abuses. Yet, it is insightful to mention the concept exclusionary abuses within the *Facebook* case. Within the ratio of *Post Danmark I* (2012), Facebook's conduct would be considered as being exclusionary, since the conduct amounted "to the detriment of consumers, of customers hindering the maintenance of the degree of competition existing in the market or the growth of that competition" (para 24). Therein, the healthy competition or competition on the merits would require an undertaking to obtain data by the voluntary consent, as per the GDPR; any effect of unlawful conduct by the dominant undertaking would have a detrimental effect both on consumers and competition and, in principle, be seen as abusive. The restriction of the effective competitive process might result in consumer harm as well as foreclosure of competitors on social media and the online advertising markets. Thereby, Facebook's GDPR infringement attaches competitive weight, as poor privacy protection might involve lower quality, higher prices, or reduced innovation. Yet, the competitive weight of Facebook's conduct would have a foreclosure effect rather than simply relying on the GDPR infringement. Additionally, Facebook's GDPR breach might impact the competitive processes; based on *AstraZeneca* (2006), where the infringement of other legal principles could amount to exclusionary practices. Generally, all the elements of abuse of dominant position must be identified to ascertain the impact of the GDPR infringement on the anticompetitive assessment. It might become acceptable that the unlawful acquisition of data might have an impact on barriers to entry, making it difficult or impossible. Generally, the 'data asymmetry' might result in hindering of competitive growth. Thus, to a certain extent, privacy concerns and competition principles might have exclusive competence. However, this could only be effective as a further indicator of competitive abuse.

French Competition Authority's Report on the Online Advertising Sectors

French Competition Authority (FCA) published a report on a sector enquiry into online advertising two months before the GDPR came in force (Online Advertising sector inquiry, 2018). The report identifies possible competition concerns in the online advertising sector (Online Advertising sector inquiry, 2018, p 4). The online advertising sector has been rapidly growing since the last decade due to the new improved digital capabilities, which enable end-users tracing.

The report mapped out that the sector is characterized by "fragile competitive equilibrium" since there are only two significant global players (Facebook and Google) in the sector (Online Advertising sector inquiry, 2018, p.6). To picture this efficiently, zero-priced platforms collect the users' data and then exchange the data to advertising services in return for profit, which permits a zero-priced platform to innovate. The FCA noted that, in consequence, these players benefit from competitive advantages, including vertical integration of advertising services and data analysis (Online Advertising sector inquiry, 2018, p 10). Moreover, the FCA added that this multidimensional relationship might have potentially a negative impact on other market players, as the overall market growth might be available only to players with an access to the best quality of data and algorithms. The report indicated list practices which might be detrimental to a competitive process, such as (i) leveraging effects, (ii) discrimination, (iii) anticompetitive strategies involving low prices, and (iv) restrictions on access to data or interoperability (Online Advertising sector inquiry, 2018, p.102). Nevertheless, assessment of the comparability of these conducts with competition legal order was not the objective of the report, and only aimed to provide a market analysis.

The FCA report provided a comprehensive description of the advertising ecosystem and provided an important contribution to the debate on the interplay between data protection and competition law, proposing that the free advertising services could be subjected to competition law. Nonetheless, their functionalities offered to users are distinctive to the type of ads, or demands for intermediation. Although the report might be viewed as disregarding privacy concerns in competition legal regime, the FCA's approached indicated an apparent priority to fight with anticompetitive data-related behaviors.

Impact of German and French Developments on EU Competition Law

The above discussion indicates the intensity of the debate. It is beyond the scope of this research to discuss every aspect, arising from the French and German developments. Consequently, a brief discussion of key aspects will be presented.

The first question is whether a case involving unilateral conduct abusing data protection is relevant to competition law. The French and German assessments were an expression of understanding of the role of the Big Data within the meaning of competition enforcements. For many, the process of digitalization remarks the 'end of the competition as we know it' (Gal & Elkin-Koren, 2016, p.44). A handful of technology undertakings exercise control over a large quantity of personal data and its processing, with a focus on personal practices. Big Data's treatment under EU competition law amounts to the absorbing debate, with the differing points available regarding how to analyze Big Data. Davila (2015) claims it is a nebulous topic. Some academics declare that Big Data is a crucial barrier to entry since data are problematic to collect, replicate and process (Rubinfield & Gal, 2017, p.350). Yet, an accepted consensus remains that data protection within competition law is itself problematic.

The French and the German competition authorities, in attempt to bring clarity over this nebulous topic, published a joint report, which aimed to identify key issues in assessing a relationship between data, competition law and market power (Joint paper of the French Competition Authority and the Bundeskartellamt, 2016.) The Report acknowledged that 'data is everywhere' (Joint paper of the French Competition Authority and the Bundeskartellamt, 2016, p.44). It requires a case-by-case examination of competition law to assess substitutability between data and competition law, as data advantage might amount to competition law risk. This approach might be criticized due to the lack of predictability. Also, the French/German approach relied on their national laws, which by the rule can be stricter than the rules imposed by EU law. Furthermore, this might create further uncertainty as the EU Commission pursues its Digital Single Market Strategy (Brotman, 2016). Yet, the French/German study reflected a determination amongst the EU Member States competition authorities to address the effects data collection and its usage by companies and to reflect on the boundaries between data protection and competition law. Nevertheless, the appeal on the Facebook case is pending (Lamadrid, 2019), and different national competition authorities are currently investigating further interferences of data protection within the competition law. There are two sides of coins attached to data analysis within the competition law spectrum, which might arise from the French and German legal developments — data seen as a positive competitive constraint and more prevailing approach recognizing data as being beyond the scope of competition rules.

Firstly, any GDPR infringement does not automatically imply on the competition law applicability. In *Facebook* case, the BKA justified Facebook's anticompetitive behavior by the GDPR. Yet, the Higher Regional Court of Düsseldorf raised serious doubts regarding such assessment, as the BKA's focused too much on the data protection law and disregarded the application of antitrust law. Arguably, privacy is a complex matter from the competition law perspective, and it is clearly beyond the scope of competition law to assess all potential public policy infringements. Crucially, there are difficulties in asserting what classifies as a competitive level of privacy. Besides, the BKA failed to assess the counterfactual, which functions as a cornerstone for any theory of harm assessment (*Société Technique Minière,* 1966).

The acquisition of the data is an important parameter of a business model, as the Court stressed that Facebook's business model is based on offering free service which is financed through tailored advertising. Importantly, consumers are not obliged to use Facebook, if they are unsatisfied with the platform; the consent to use Facebook is solely voluntary. The BKA incorrectly indicated that FB's users do not read the T&Cs offered by the platform. Yet, realistically, the users are just indifferent - they do not wish to devote their time and effort to read the T&Cs. The Court concluded that there was no evidence that their consent was obtained through pressure or coercion. However, consumer welfare is a recognizable goal of competition law, it is probably not the most important one. Furthermore, the EU merger assessment, which could allow for a dynamic policy-making approach, abstained from taking data consideration into the merger control cases. Potential reason to justify such action is an inability to extend competition law to direct assess privacy law pitfalls. Besides, privacy concerns could be associated with informational asymmetry rather than market power. Hence, it is another reason why competition law should not intervene in privacy law.

The debate around the data relates only to the common cliches, arguing that data is a factor contributing to market power, increasing market transparency, and acting as a competitive instrument (Lassierre & Mundt, 2017), as affirmed in the Facebook case. Yet, this raises a further question: should competition law make end-users better? The competition law should not be 'instrumentalized,' as it is beyond the scope of the competition legal enforcement to broader macroeconomic agenda (Lamadrid, 2019). According to Lamadrid (2019), the privacy-concerns were not a problem for competition law. Additionally, the BKA's case has not developed this idea any further, analyzing the privacy-concerns as a mere, additional feature in the antitrust assessment, which asserted Facebook's abuse of dominance. The BKA proceeding might be thus seen as targeting all data-run companies, essentially since data is an important parameter of their business models (Lamadrid, 2019). Thus, Lamadrid (2019) argued that investigations might be interpreted as granting an omniscient power to competition authority which could consider different policies when assessing anticompetitive conducts of dominant undertakings. This would create even more ambiguity, as competition law enforcement should only focus on protecting competitive processed within a relevant market. Such an argument would be supported by an argument *non bis in idem* — there shall be no legal action put in motion twice over the same conduct of action (Lamadrid, 2019).

These are just assumptions as to impact of the German and French approaches on competition law. Under Regulation 1/2003 (2003), national competition authorities (NCA) have become the primary enforcer of EU competition law (arts.1-13). Hence, since 2004, the Commission has adopted only 15% of the enforcement decisions (Aziewicz, 2015, p.263). In accordance, the harmonization is a key feature (Gauer, 2001, pp.187-201). According to Article 4(2) Treaty on European Union (TEU) (2010), the Member States are responsible to take relevant steps to safeguard responsibilities arising from the EU Treaties. More frequently, markets are measured locally, and proceedings are time-consuming. Therefore, it appears that there is a possible point for the reform, making sure that the NCAs are more effective enforcers. Such an approach might increase predictability of competition law enforcement and better integration between national decisions and standards might result in consistency of competition law enforcement within the EU Member States. Although the BKA's case indicated an apparent "a connection between such an infringement and market dominance" (Lamadrid 2019). The causality link between disapproved behavior and dominance is required under both German and EU law. Also, more broadly, the Court indicated that the data relevant for generating revenues is 'incomprehensible' and requires closer examination by antitrust authorities as to the barriers to entry (Lamadrid 2019). BKA's decision has not demonstrated how market entry could be affected by the data. Evidently, the matters regarding privacy could be beyond the scope of competition law interventions. In this respect, it is difficult to conclude the future of the relationship between data protection and competition law. The BKA's Facebook case did not contribute to developing the relationship between data protection and competition law, as the assessment relied primarily on consideration of the GDPR infringement: the Higher Regional Court of Düsseldorf concluded that privacy as a public policy is not a matter for competition law and arguably is a matter outside the realms of competition law (Lamadrid 2019). At the time of writing this chapter, the appeal on Facebook case is pending with a possible good chance of success.

IS PRIVACY A MEAN TO SUPPORT EFFECTIVE COMPETITION AND INNOVATION OR INFLUENCE CONSUMER PROTECTION?

Although the BKA proceeding indicated that Article 102(a) TFEU (2008) appeared to, arguably, including privacy-concerns into the range exploitative and exclusionary abuses, it remains uncertain whether privacy-concerns could expand theories of harm. Potentially, the recognized theories of harms in the digital economy include, amongst others, targeted advertising and imposition of unfair T&Cs. The main emphasis is given on defying the general impact of privacy concerns in competition law.

With the development of digitalization, issues relating to Big Data remains the key priority for the Commission and national competition authorities (Crofts & Newman, 2016, pp 380-381). Many have inquired whether conduct such as imposing unlawful contractual terms that do not affect price or quality could be deemed as anticompetitive considering other parameters (Ezrachi & Stucke, 2014, p.8). The discussion above indicated that there are two opposing arguments present: the EU competition law perspective disregards the applicability of data protection in the competition law assessments whereas the French/German approaches supported the integration of data protection into competition law paradigm. Consequently, consumer welfare, in the short run, could be determined by prices, whereas in, in the long run — by the quality and innovation (Schneider, 2018, p. 219).

Privacy, Competition and Innovation

Data has become a key input for online service providers, allowing them to monetize their services and improve their quality. Vestager (2015) claimed that data acquisition does not immediately result in anticompetitive conducts. However, data acquisition on an unprecedented scale could put end-users' privacy into danger. This section would assess whether privacy can be seen as broadening competition law horizons.

Competition law and data protection law are two distinctive legal orders, which aims at remediating different violations at the core. EU competition law, based on its ordo-liberal foundation, is a tool to safeguard competition, consumers, and market structure (*GlaxoSmithKline Services Unlimited*, 2009). Although EU competition agenda might be applied in other policy concerns, including consumer protection, investment, transportation or public health (Ezratchi, 2016), privacy-concerns were noted to be outside the scope of EU competition law (*Asnef-Equifax*, 2006). Data protection is a problematic concern in competition assessment, due to ambiguities concerning the economic assessment of privacy. Although the Facebook case recognized privacy as a competitive face, if one considered this case from competition law perspective, the BKA analyzes the T&Cs, which acted as a contract between Facebook and the end-users, to assess that it represented an abuse of dominant position; potentially also referring to concept of fairness (Vestager, 2018). Hence, the references to privacy are, arguably, irrelevant for competition law. Privacy was merely referred to as an argument to further the argument based on the established principles of competition law. There are some situations when privacy concerns and competition law would not act mutually, for example, an undertaking might breach data protection law without beaching competition law.

There is a consensus that the scope and measurement of efficiency gains play a crucial part in the competitive assessment (Guidelines on the assessment of horizontal mergers, 2004). The concepts of efficiencies play a vital role in Article 101(3) TFEU (2008); the Commission indicated that the main goal of Article 101 TFEU (2008) is to protect market competition as a means to ensure resources' efficient allocation of resources (General Guidelines, 2004, para. 13). However, there is no alternative to Article 101(3) TFEU (2008) defence recognized under Article 102, the role of allocation is, arguably, considered under this provision, as a dominant undertaking could justify its foreclosure of competition on the no-harm to consumers ground. Categorically, Lamadrid argued that provisions violating Article 102 TFEU (2008) might be mitigated if an abuse contributes to increasing efficiency. In the wider specter, the protection of effective competition anatomy bears important implications on the digital economy context (Ezratchi, 2018). The data acquisition might offer a mandate for intervention without considering an effect on consumers, which potentially enables for an efficient consideration on the effects of the digital market (Ezratchi, 2018). Furthermore, the data protection concerns might indicate potential issues concerning barriers to entry or increase of rival's cost. Yet, data significantly influence a market shape and its development, highlighting that it is a relevant fact in the assessment of market process and competition order. Nevertheless, relying on the BKA's case, there is no similar precedent in the EU competition legal order. It can be difficult to assess the competitive level of privacy and it is still uncertain whether data protection might serve as supporting competition assessment. Interestingly, data protection could introduce baseline for individuals' protection which competition law could further enhance; these two distinctive fields of law share normative features and are concerned with market power asymmetries, simultaneously protecting consumer welfare throughout the data processing cycle and against abuse of undertakings' market power, which deviates from their preferences. The recently published report by the EU Commission on the relationship between competition law and data protection did not put forward any solution to weight up the data privacy element as a part of the competitive assessment (Vestager, 2019). The report indicated that it is too early to contemplate any changes to competition law enforcement (Vestager, 2019); potentially a case-by-case analysis would be required to weight up the importance of data as an element lessening competition or an extension to the theories of harms. Hence, in the author's view, the future debate would focus on clarifying the goals of competition which are itself very flexible and adaptable to societal changes, since the competitive edges of the GDPR breaches require careful consideration. Interestingly, greater competition on privacy could result in better products/services provided to consumers.

This paper suggests that Big Data should not be contradistinguished, as it might lower commercial freedom; the Commission might accept speculative ideas on non-horizontal issues resulting from the accession of data (Davilla, 2017, p.379). Innovation might be seen as normatively positive if it allows for more efficient fulfillment of consumer preferences, which might lead to their utility increase. Innovation does not solely contribute to the development of particular companies but also acts as an important economic prerogative. Innovation could be regarded as an important factor in encouraging companies to develop or improve products and services. On the other hand, there also must be a reasonable prospect of being rewarded for the innovative endeavors of companies, which could result in higher profits or a temporary increase in market power. Within the digital economy, the treatment of efficiencies, especially of dynamic efficiencies — innovation — is significant. Innovation stimulates dynamics market as well as enhance consumers welfare, and in turn, might offset diminishing marginal returns.

Competition law fosters competition in innovation by enhancing efficiency maximization, supporting free market and market integrity ('Guidelines on the applicability of Article 101 TFEU, 2011, para 119-122). In the innovation and data protection assessment, the Schumpeterian and the Arrowian hypothesis play an important role. The former understands market concentration to enable internalization of the rewards resulting from the efforts of innovation, which potentially might create negative correlation between innovation processes and competition, as supporting creative destruction where old technologies are replaced by the new (Schumpeter, 1954) whereas the latter understands competitive pressure as an innovation parameter (Arrow, 1962). Therefore, these U-shaped relationships suggest that innovation increase results in competitive pressure, whereas market power decreases investment in innovation (Aghion, 2005). The uncertainty surrounding data protection within the competition legal order calls for cautious intervention, due to difficulties to apprehend the quickly changing environment of the digital market. The scope of markets, existing competition and future players might change with modern waves of innovation. This supports the protection of competition as an independent objective for the sake of the protection of innovation and efficiencies (Larouche & Schinkel, 2013).

Furthermore, in the author's opinion, the services and apps which are offered at the zero-cost must have enough profit to keep the innovative grown, to make the services to be attractive for the consumers. Therefore, a reasonable scenario includes packages offered to end-users, respecting their internet anonymity. The first package would be based on zero-price and, hence, require users' voluntary consent to data acquisition. The data functions, then, as an asset and enables service providers to sell off the data to third parties. In this respect, a service provider would gain a profit for selling the data, whereas a consumer would be subjected to the advertisement. The second package might be based on a subscription fee which profits a service provider. Consequently, a service provider receives profit which might be used for innovative purposes, whereas consumers enjoy privacy protection.

Privacy and Consumer Welfare

Promotion of consumer welfare is undoubtedly protected by competition law and the GDPR, which is more akin to consumer protection than competition law. The 'ultimate' goal of competition law is to ensure the effectiveness of competition in the internal market, which aims at increasing consumers welfare (*Österreichische Postsparkasse and Bankfür Arbeitund Wirtschaft* 2006, para 115), whereas data protection, like consumer protection law, aims at protecting the effective exercise of consumer choice (Averrit, Lande, 2007). Hence, competition law and data protection are interchangeably influencing each other, protecting the market at different aspects of the identical spectrum. There is an increased consensus that a consumer's decision making might be potentially influenced by privacy. Nevertheless, the law and its interpretation depend on the ideological roots and is unlikely to rapidly reshape its roots to encompass the societal changes. In the author's view, the hybrid nature of EU law reinforces the possibility of counterbalancing competition law and privacy protections. In the light of the French and German legal development, privacy could be only seen as an additional feature which expanded the theories of harms under Article 102 TFEU (2008). Therefore, as competition law seeks to protect competitive specifications to which consumers respond, including price, quality, innovation and choice, data protection parameters could also reflect on innovation, quality and choice. Hence, data protection to certain extend could act as a benchmark for competition law, only if applied holistically: both protect individuals and market integration.

Data functions as a non-economic activity since it aims at benefiting all members of society. The concept of social welfare could capture problems that lead to a market, creating goods which are not considered as improving the general welfare. In the author's view, consumer welfare can provide a workable benchmark for intervention in digital markets, as allowing to address any exploitative and/ or exclusionary practices to restrict competition. Within the digital economy, the concept of consumer welfare might be used to tackle the welfare effect on numerous groups of consumers. The Commission acknowledged that the notion of 'consumers' covered all direct and indirect, covered by an agreement, product users, incorporating producers, retailers, wholesalers and final consumers (Ezrachi, 2018, p.6). The application of consumer welfare is heterogeneous, as comprising all members of the society. In the digital economy, the behavioral element supports an increase the users consumption; consumers are likely to use platforms used by their family and friends, often unaware of maintaining competitive pricing because of their increased consumption. Furthermore, considering a price-centric method to consumer welfare, according to Ezrachi (2018), a distorted picture might be provided. The digital market usually provides ostensibly free for consumer services, hence, quality forms an important competitive parameter. Bringing an example of the *Facebook* case, the distortion of privacy was seen as harming consumer welfare, despite the lack of price effects. Hence, the privacy might enforce a range of, not easily quantifiable, variables impacting on consumer welfare.

Yet, privacy might potentially introduce new challenges to the consumer welfare sphere (Ezrachi, 2018, p.5), including targeted advertising, or increased prices. Consequently, the changing economic landscape brings uncertainty to the nature of the competition pressures, with an emphasis being given on the normative scope of competition enforcement — mainly as to whether the EU competition law could be viewed as a societal norm also advancing the wealth. The objectives of Article 102 TFEU (2008) are necessary for functioning internal market and consumers (*Deutsche Telekom AG v Commission,* 2010). This would thereby ensure the EU's legal and functional well-being. The goals of the EU, according to Advocate General Kokott, recognized 'equality of opportunity' of the EU aims (*Motosykletistiki Omospondia Ellados NPID (MOTOE)*, 2008, p. 29). In this respect, the use of asymmetric information might give rise to abuses which adversely impact consumers well being and, hence, may require intervention. According to Lassierre and Mundt (2017), the concept of Big Data cannot be expressed by the terms 'privacy' or 'personal data' as it is a much broader phenomenon. In this context, the digital economy might affect the democratic values, informational flows and itself influence the competitive process.

Despite the deontological approach in this context, EU competition law should contribute to a fairer society (Lamadrid 2017, pp.147-148), as the objective of the market integration (*Sot. Lélos Kai Sia,* 2008), a key element of the EU foundation, accounts the consumer welfare. Undoubtedly, this might also be seen as a feature of data protection law. Vestager (2016) referred to the fair market importance, claiming that competition enforcement pursued the objectives of fairness, for which the public authorities also to defend the interests of the consumers. The competition amongst the undertakings relates to the price, wider choice of product, or better quality. As noted by a vertical merger of *TeleAtlas/TomTom* (2008), this merger could improve consumer welfare as the TomTom's large consumer base would have improved the maps provided by TeleAtlas. Nevertheless, there is the possibility that merging undertakings would acquire a large volume of consumer data, which would result in anticompetitive conduct (Holles de Peyer, 2017, p.769). Yet, the contemporary regulations applicable to mergers provides adequate flexibility to capture any anticompetitive acts (Holles de Peyer, 2017, p.790). Contrarily, there are risks associated with the creation of large networks, which impact barriers to entry, innovation and elimination of potential competition and market tipping, might be indicatives to call for careful consideration. Thus, this follows that the existing competition rules are itself adaptable to apprehend the events in the social, political or economic sphere, and privacy might be relevant only as a proxy to competition lessening.

The consumer welfare benchmark is useful in addressing competition law infringement's effect on the consumers' groups. Yet, social welfare might function as a separate stream, to which different criteria apply (*Albany*, 1999). Townley (2009) argued that the structure of EU Treaties demands an assessment of wider public policy concerns in competition law. Arguably, it is beyond the scope of competition law to assess all potential public policy infringement. Data protection law, which is designed to provide optimal protection of personal data, might only act as normative support, which would guide competition law about non-price parameters. Furthermore, privacy protection, acting as a part of the contract between the user and the platform provider, might create potentially exclusionary or exploitative practices if the contractual clause is unfair on the consumers. Assessing this through a prism of competition law might potentially create novel forms of theory of harms, which requires intervention. However, the key issues lay in apprehending these claims within the established goals of competition law. Undoubtedly, weighting the goals and values, theories of harm, and economic analysis is a foundational proof of evidence on which a decision is founded (Ezrachi, 2018, p.29). It is deducible that privacy concerns might not revolute the competition law itself, but might only provide an insight into the anticompetitive activity. The established competition law rules are adaptable to provide adequate remedies to bring a competitive equilibrium on a relevant market. Hence, the mere privacy violations which only brings detriment of consumer welfare will be answered by data protection or consumer protection law, and not by competition law.

CONCLUSION

This chapter presented a legal overview of the relationship between data protection and competition law debate. The EU practice might be analyzed through three different phases: ignorance of data, identification of parallel pathways between competition law and data protection, and the third phrase recognized by the EU Member State practice — recognition of data in the competition sphere. However, to the present day, the EU Commission disregards the application of the data protection by placing a great emphasis on the correctness of the application of competition law. The fundamental grasp of competition policy is that an efficient competition amongst market players attempts at achieving better goods, services, and lower prices for consumers. The French and Germany developments placed further issues in recognizing the data protection in competition law assessment. It is certain that with a rapidly evolving world, competition authorities pay attention to companies within the sector of the digital economy. However, there is still a debate as to whether competition law can adapt to the rapidly evolving digital market.

Having considered all of the relevant arguments, it might be seen that data should be regarded as a part of the competitive process. The competition authorities should solely base its assessment on the remits of competition law. The paper presented two sides of the argument: privacy as a competitive and innovative parameter, and — a consumer welfare parameter. To a certain extent, the acquisition of data could create competition law infringement, data violation might also harm consumers as they are objected to unfair trading practices, competition and upset innovation processes. Nevertheless, according to the arguments presented, the existing competition rules are itself adaptable to apprehend the events in the social, political or economic sphere.

REFERENCES

Aghion, P. (2005). Competition and Innovation: An Inverted-U Relationship. *The Quarterly Journal of Economics*, 701.

Arrow, K. J. (2016) Welfare and the Allocation of Resources for Invention. In R. Nelson (Ed.), The Rate and Direction of Economic Activities: Economic and Social Factors. NBER Books.

Autorité de la Concurrence, Avis no 18-A-03 portant sur l'exploitation des donnees dans le secteur de la publicite sur internet, 6 March 2018

Averitt, N., & Lande, R. (2007). Using the 'consumer choice' approach to antitrust law. *Antitrust Law Journal*, 74.

Aziewicz, A. (2015). Due Process Rights in Polish Antitrust Proceedings. Case comment to the Judgment of the Polish Supreme Court of 3 October 2013 – PKP Cargo S.A. v. President of the Office of Competition and Consumers Protection (Ref. No. III SK 67/12, *YASS* 261. Bergkamp, L. (2002). The Privacy Fallacy: Adverse Effects of Europe's Data Protection Policy in an Information-Driven Economy. *Computer Law & Security Report*, 31.

BKA. (2019). *Case B6-22/16 Facebook, Exploitative business terms pursuant to Section 19(1) GWB for inadequate data processing.* Retrieved August 28, 2019 <https://www.bundeskartellamt.de/SharedDocs/Entscheidung/EN/Fallberichte/Missbrauchsaufsicht/2019/B6-22-16.html?nn=3600108>

BKA & Autorite de la concurrence. (2016). *Competition Law and Data.* Retrieved September 30, 2019 https://www.bundeskartellamt.de/SharedDocs/Publikation/DE/Berichte/Big%20Data%20Papier.pdf?__blob=publicationFile&v=2

Brotman, S. N. (2016). *The European Union's Digital Single Market Strategy: A conflict between government's desire for certainty and rapid marketplace innovation?* Retrieved November 12, 2019 https://www.brookings.edu/wp-content/uploads/2016/07/digital-single-market.pdf

BRT v SABAM; ECLI:EU:C:1974:25, 27/03/1974

C-49/07 Motosykletistiki Omospondia Ellados NPID (MOTOE) v Elliniko Dimosio, [2008] ECR I-4863

Case M.8124 Microsoft/LinkedIn, 14 October 2016

Case 27/76 United Brands Company and United Brands Continentaal BV v. Commission, [1978], ECR 207

Case 395/87 Ministère public v. Jean-Louis Tournier, [1989] ECR 2521

Case C-209/10 Post Danmark A/S v Konkurrencerådet ECLI:EU:C:2012:172

Case C-235/08 Asnef-Equifax v Asociación de Usuarios de Servicios Bancarios ECR I-11125. [2006].

Case C-333/94P Tetra Pak International SA v. Commission (Tetra Pak II), [1996] ECR I-5951

Case C-468/06 Sot. Lélos Kai Sia v. GlaxoSmithKline [2008] ECR I-7139

Case C-67/96 Albany EU:C:1999:430

Cases C-501/06 P etc GlaxoSmithKline Services Unlimited v Commission and Others [2009] ECR I-9291

Charter of Fundamental Rights of the European Union 2010 OJ C 83/02

Consolidated Version of the Treaty on European Union, 2010 OJ C 83/01

Consolidated Version of the Treaty on the Functioning of the European Union, 2008 OJ C 115/47

Council Regulation (EC) No 1/2003 of 16 December 2002 on the implementation of the rules on competition laid down in Articles 81 and 82 of the Treaty

Council Regulation (EC) No 139/2004 of 20 January 2004 on the control of concentrations between undertakings

Crofts, L., & Newman, M. (2016). Data abuses could be targeted by antitrust regulators as Vestager weights new law. *MLex*. Retrieved October 23, 2018 <www.mlex.com/GlobalAntitrust/DatailView.aspx?cid=831793&siteid=190&rdir=1>

Davilla, M. (2017). Is Big Data a Different Kind of Animal? The Treatment of Big Data Under the EU Competition Rules. *JECL & Pract*, (8), 370.

Deutsche Telekom AG v Commission (2010) C-280/08

EDPS. (2016). *On the coherent enforcement of fundamental rights in the age of big data* (Opinion 8/2016). Retrieved July 22, 2019 https://www.huntonprivacyblog.com/wp-content/uploads/sites/28/2016/10/14-03-26_competitition_law_big_data_EN.pdf

EU General Data Protection Regulation (GDPR). *Regulation*, *2016*(679).

European Commission (1992) XXIInd Report on Competition Policy

European Commission, (2004). Guidelines on the Application of Article 81(3) of the Treaty. OJ C101/97

European Commission, (2004) Guidelines on the assessment of horizontal mergers under the Council Regulation on the control of concentrations between undertakings. OJ C 31/5.

European Commission, (2004). Commission Notice Guidelines on the effect on trade concept contained in Articles 81 and 82 of the Treaty, 2004/C 101/07.

European Commission (2009). Guidelines on the Commission's enforcement priorities in applying Article 82 of the EC Treaty to abusive exclusionary conduct by dominant undertakings, (OJ C45/02)

European Commission, (2011). Guidelines on the applicability of Article 101 of the Treaty on the Functioning of the European Union to horizontal cooperation agreements. OJ C 11/1

Ezrachi, A. (2018). The Goals of EU Competition Law and the Digital Economy. *BEUC*. Retrieved October 13, 2019 https://www.beuc.eu/publications/beuc-x-2018-071_goals_of_eu_competition_law_and_digital_economy.pdf

Ezrachi, A., & Stucke, M. (2014). *The Curious Case of Competition and Quality' The curious case of competition and quality.* Oxford Legal Studies Research Paper 64/2014.

Ezratchi, A. (2017). Sponge. *Journal of Antitrust Enforcement, 5*, 49.

Gal, M. S., Elkin-Koren, N. (2016). Algorithmic consumers. *Harv JL & Tech, 44.*

Gauer, C. (2001). Does the Effectiveness of the EU Network of Competition Authorities Require a Certain Degree of Harmonisation of National Procedures and Sanctions? In C. D. Ehlemann & I. Atanasiu (Eds.), *European Competition Law Annual: The Modernisation of EC Antitrust Policy* (pp. 187–201). Hart.

Google/DoubleClick, COMP/M.4731, OJ 2008 C184/10

Holles de Peyer, B. (2017). EU Merger Control and Big Data. *JCL& E, 767,* 769.

Hubert, P., & Combet, L. (2011). Exploitative abuse: The end of the Paradox? *Doctrines l Concurrences, 1,* 44-51.

Joined Cases T-213/01 and T-214/01 Österreichische Postsparkasse and Bankfür Arbeitund Wirtschaft v Commission [2006] ECRII-1601

Lamadrid, A. (2017). Competition Law as Fairness. *JIPLP, 147,* 147–148.

Lamadrid, A. (2019). *The Bundeskartellamt's Facebook Decision- What's not to like? Well....* Received October 30, 2019 https://chillingcompetition.com/2019/02/27/the-bundeskartellamts-facebook-decision-whats-not-to-like-well/

Larouche, P., & Schinkel, M. P. (2013). *Continental Drift in the Treatment of Dominant Firms: Article 102 TFEU in Contrast to § 2 Sherman Act.* TILEC Discussion Paper No. 2013-020.

Nazzini, R. (2019) Privacy and Antitrust: Searching for the (Hopefully Not Yet Lost) Soul of Competition Law in the EU after the German Facebook Decision. *CPI.* Retrieved October 23, 2019 <https://www.competitionpolicyinternational.com/wp-content/uploads/2019/03/EU-News-Column-March-2019-4-Full.pdf>

Rubinfield, D., & Gal, M. (2017). Access Barriers to Big Data. *Arizona Law Review, 340,* 350.

Schneider, G. (2018). Testing Art. 102 TFEU in the Digital Marketplace: Insights from the Bundeskartellamt's investigation against Facebook. *Journal of European Competition Law & Practice.*

Schumpeter, J. (1954). *Capitalism, Socialism, and Democracy.* George Allen & Unwin.

Telefónica UK/Vodafone UK/Everything Everywhere/JV, No COMP/M.6314, 4 September 2012

Thibodeau, P. (2014). *The Internet of Things Could Encroach on Personal Privacy.* Retrieved October 2, 2019 https://www.computerworld.com/article/2488949/emerging-technology/the-internet-of-things-could-encroach-on-personal-privacy.htm

TomTom/Tele Atlas, Case No COMP/M.4854, Decision of 14.5.2008

Townley, C. (2009). *Article 81 EC and Public Policy.* Oxford: Hart Publishing.

Vestager, M. (2016). Competition for a Fairer Societ. *10th Annual Global Antitrust Enforcement Symposium.*

Vestager, M. (2016). Competition in a big data world. *DLD 16*. Retrieved September 23, 2019 https://ec.europa.eu/commission/2014-2019/vestager/announcements/competition-big-data-world_en

Vestager, M. (2018). *Fair markets in a digital world*. Retrieved September 26, 2019 https://ec.europa.eu/commission/commissioners/2014-2019/vestager/announcements/ fair-markets-digital-world_en

Vestager, M. (2019). *Defending Competition in a Digitised World*. Bucharest: In the European Consumer and Competition Day.

World Economic Forum. (2011). *Personal Data: The Emergence of a New Asset Class*. Retrieved August 29, 2014 http://www3.weforum.org/docs/WEF_ITTC_PersonalDataNewAsset_Report_2011.pdf

KEY TERMS AND DEFINITIONS

Big Data: The gigantic digital databases, held, acquired, and used by governments, companies or other organizations, and later analyzed through the use of algorithms.

Competitive Process: An action to provide an open and equal opportunity to parties on a market.

Consumer Welfare: One of the goals of competition law, which refers to individual benefit obtained from goods/services consumption.

Digital Market: An internet-based structure where demand and supply forces operate, which allow sellers and buyers interact. In digital market, the marketing of services or products also might rely on digital advertising, mobile phones and any another digital platform. Chanels on digital market are based on data acquisition.

Innovation: A method allowing an undertaking to create a new service/product. In digital market, digital platforms, which offers free service to their users, may only finance innovation through selling data to advertising platforms.

Privacy: A right recognized in the Charter of Fundamental Rights (2010), and the GDPR. For many, it is a dynamic rights. The latest practice of the EU Member States indicated that privacy could be potentially used as expanding the theorems of harms.

Theories of Harm: A measurement of competitive process harm, recognized by Article 102 TFEU. Competition law recognizes exploitative and exclusionary theory of harm. From a digital economy angle, privacy might be seen as expanding both exploitative and exclusionary theories of harm.

Chapter 7

Is There Anything Left of the Portuguese Law Implementing the GDPR?
The Decision of the Portuguese Supervisory Authority

Graça Canto Moniz
Lusofona University, Portugal & Nova School of Law, Portugal

ABSTRACT

The entry into force of the General Data Protection Regulation (GDPR) was expected to cause difficulties to data controllers and data processors mostly due to the practical consequences of the accountability principle and the role of risk. However, in Portugal, there were supplementary problems triggered by two events: the long legislative process of the national law implementing the GDPR and the decision of the national supervisory authority to disapply nine provisions of it. In August 2019, the Portuguese Parliament adopted the law implementing the GDPR, Law 58/2019, and one month later, the Portuguese supervisory authority, Comissão Nacional de Proteção de Dados, decided that nine articles of the recently adopted national law were incompatible with European Union Law. This chapter aims to address this chain of events, to understand the reasoning behind the decision of the Portuguese authority, and to tackle its practical consequences to day-to-day data-processing activities of data controllers and data processors. Overall, it also aims to evaluate what is left of the national piece of legislation after this decision.

INTRODUCTION

In August 2019, after a long legislative process, the Portuguese Parliament adopted the Law 58/2019 (hereinafter *national law*) that implements the General Data Protection Regulation (GDPR). A month later, the Portuguese supervisory authority, *Comissão Nacional de Proteção de Dados* (CNPD) (National Commission for Data Protection), decided that 9 articles of the recently adopted law were incompatible

DOI: 10.4018/978-1-5225-9489-5.ch007

with the European Union (EU) Law. Hence, those provisions would not be applied in the future (CNPD, 2018).

This article aims to explain the reasoning behind this decision and assess its consequences. The first section briefly outlines the birth of the national law. The second section sets out the arguments presented by the Portuguese supervisory authority. The third section examines the exact provisions ruled out by the CNPD and identifies their inconsistent nature with the EU law. Finally, the fourth section measures the impact and the consequences of this decision.

THE BIRTH OF THE PORTUGUESE LAW IMPLEMENTING THE GDPR

The Government's Draft

The applicability of the GDPR, according to article 99 (2), started on May 25, 2018. In Portugal, the legislative process for its implementation began in August 2017, when the Government designated a special group (Presidency of the Council of Ministers, 2017) to prepare the first draft of its proposal (hereinafter *government's proposal*). This draft would be presented and approved by the Portuguese Parliament (article 197 of the Portuguese Constitution).

However, in May 2018, the document (Presidency of the Council of Ministers, 2018) prepared by this committee failed to pass the Portuguese Parliament. Indeed, among others, it was impossible to reach an agreement in the following issues (Portuguese Parliament, 2018): a) the broad possibility, for public authorities and bodies, to process personal data for a purpose other than that for which the personal data have been collected (articles 6 (4) (1) (e) and 9 (2) (g) of the GDPR); b) the conditions applicable to children's consent regarding information society services (article 8 (1) of the GDPR); c) the rules on whether and to what extent administrative fines could be imposed on public authorities and bodies from the sanction's regime (article 83 (7) of the GDPR); and d) the rules governing processing personal data and the right to freedom of expression and information (article 85 of the GDPR).

The Discussion at the Portuguese Parliament

Under this circumstances, the Parliament had the power to amend and detail the government's proposal. In addition, all political parties understood that, given the relevance of the topic, it deserved an in-depth discussion in a special commission for constitutional issues and fundamental rights (Portuguese Parliament, 2018).

Consequently, from May 2018 until the end of the legislative process, by June 2019, members of Parliament auditioned several entities and received legal opinions from different stakeholders (private entities, associations, trade unions) and sectors (education, health, insurance, technology). As Cordeiro explains, this draft was criticized by the largest Portuguese business association, *Confederação Empresarial de Portugal* (Cordeiro, 2019). In particular, the national supervisory authority issued an opinion (CNPD, 2018) underlying that several provisions of the government's proposal were incompatible with the EU law and directly contradicted the GDPR, namely: a) article 2 of the government's proposal, stating the scope of the national law; b) the provisions regarding the functioning of the supervisory authority (articles 4, 6, 7, 8 of the government's proposal); c) the role and functions of the data protection officer (articles 9, 11 and 12 of the government's proposal); d) the right to data portability (article 18 of the government's proposal); e) the limits for the right to access and for the right to information (article 20 government's); f) data retention periods (article 21 of the government's proposal); g) processing personal data by public entities for a new purpose, (article 23 of the government's proposal); g) data transfers (article 22 of the government's proposal); h) processing personal data in the employment context (article 28 of the government's proposal); and i) the penalties for infringement of the GDPR (articles 37 to 45 of the government's proposal), among other provisions. It is important to note that a considerable number of the issues underlined by the national supervisory authority were remarks common to other stakeholders' opinions. This was especially the case when considering the scope of application of the national law, the limits on the right to access and information, processing personal data by public entities for new purposes, the employee consent, and the infringements regime of the GDPR (Portuguese Parliament, 2018).

The Approval and Signing of the National Law

In June 2019, the Parliament's proposal was adopted with the votes in favour by the Social Democrats, *Partido Social Democrata,* and the Socialists, *Partido Socialista*, with several other parties abstaining and no votes against. After this electoral procedure, by the end of July, the President signed the law, which was published in the Official Journal in August. Ultimately, some of the concerns highlighted by several stakeholders during the legislative process were, at least partially, attended by the Portuguese members of Parliament such as the conditions applicable to children's consent regarding the information society services (article 8 (1) of the GDPR), the rules on whether and to what extent administrative fines from the sanctions regime could be imposed on public authorities and bodies (article 83 (7) of the GDPR), among others. Nevertheless, it is also accurate to state that other concerns, reflected in the CNPD decision, were ignored without any explicit reason. As it will be explained in the next section, this was one of the arguments that the CNPD put forward to substantiate its reasoning.

THE REASONING OF THE PORTUGUESE DATA PROTECTION AUTHORITY

On September 3rd 2019, the Portuguese supervisory authority issued an opinion with two main goals (CNPD, 2019, p. 2): to formalize and to set the understanding that 9 of the 62 articles of the Portuguese law implementing the GDPR were incompatible with the EU law; and to clarify that future cases those provisions would not be applied. In order to reach this decision, the CNPD mainly presented substantive arguments, related to the exact solutions adopted by the national legislator, and one formal argument, linked to the legislative process of this piece of law.

1.1. Substantive Arguments

The main argument of the Portuguese supervisory authority is the principle of precedence or primacy of EU law. According to this principle, the laws issued by EU institutions are to be integrated into the legal systems of Members States, which are obliged to comply with them. Therefore, if a national rule contradicts a EU law provision, Member States must apply the EU law provision (Claes, 2015, p. 178). As with the direct effect principle, the primacy of EU law was not inscribed in the Treaties, but has been developed by the Court of Justice of the European Union (ECJ) in its case law during the 1960s and

1970s. The principle of primacy was articulated in the *Costa Enel* case (1964) and further developed in other cases, such as *Simmenthal* (1978) and *Fratelli Constanzo* (1989). Literature summarizes the ECJ case law on this topic in the following key issues (Kwiecien, 2006, p. 67): (i) the prohibition on national agencies to challenge the validity of the EU law; (ii) the prohibition to apply national provisions that contradict the EU law; (iii) the prohibition to enact provisions that contradict the EU law; and (iv) the obligation to rescind national legislation contrary to the EU law.

In its decision, the Portuguese supervisory authority relies, among others, on the *Fratelli Constanzo* case to substantiate its reasoning. In this case, the ECJ stated that administrative bodies and authorities are under the same obligation as national courts to apply the provisions of the EU law and to refrain from applying provisions of national law which conflict with it (CNPD, 2019, p. 2). According to this reasoning, the ECJ has equated administrative bodies and authorities of Member States with national courts, transforming them into European administrative bodies of direct and immediate application of EU law to the detriment of national law. The general terms used by the Court indicate that, in principle, the obligation to comply with EU law is applied to all its instruments. A necessary prerequisite for this situation is that the concerned provision must be directly effective in the sense that courts and administrative bodies are able to apply it. As De Witte (2011, p. 333) explains, this obligation is quite curious. Indeed, in national law, administrative bodies and authorities are normally subordinated to the legislator and cannot set aside, by their own initiative, legislative norms conflicting with the constitution. Only adequate courts can do so.

The second legal argument presented by the CNPD is the nature of the GDPR. Since the GDPR is a Regulation, it is a legal act that is automatically and uniformly applied to all EU countries as soon as it enters into force and without the need for integration into national law. Additionally, the GDPR seeks to enhance the consistency in the application and legal certainty of the rules applied to processing personal data across EU Member States. This is expressed in new legal solutions such as the one-stop-shop (article 56 of the GDPR) and the consistency mechanism (article 63 of the GDPR). The CNPD sustains that the adoption of national law in contradiction with the GDPR not only violates the primacy of EU law, but also seriously undermines the adequate functioning of the consistency mechanism. Instead, it places the national authority at risk of violating the national law or the EU law (CNPD, 2019, p. 1).

The third argument presented by the CNPD is that its ruling aims to contribute to the legal certainty and to boost the transparency of future proceedings and positions of the Portuguese supervisory authority. Lastly, the CNPD states that the only possible solution is not to apply the 9 provisions of the national law. The argument is that the contradictions with the GDPR could not be "saved" with a consistent interpretation, given the high degree of the contradictions at stake with the its text. This approach is in line with the "three-step model" as developed by Prechal (2007). According to this model, the first step is that administrative authorities and bodies are primarily obliged to apply the EU law. The second step consists of an attempt to solve the conflict by using consistent interpretation of the concerned national laws. Lastly, when consistent interpretation cannot resolve the incompatibility, the third step, as a last resort, is the "disapplication" of the conflicting provisions of the national law (Prechal, 2007, p. 40).

Formal Argument

During the legislative process, some members of the Portuguese Parliament (Portuguese Parliament, 2018) noted the absence of the national supervisory authority from the first special committee designated by the Government to formulate its draft proposal to the Parliament. The inclusion of the CNPD was not legally compulsory and its exclusion is arguably a legitimate choice of the Government, even one justified with a potential conflict of interest. Nonetheless, the reason why the Portuguese Parliament did not consider the concerns of the supervisory authority, as well as those of other stakeholders – which was explained in its legal opinion in May 2018 –, is not clear. As a matter of fact, the 9 provisions disapplied by the Portuguese authority were previously pointed out and "[The CNPD] highlighted all these issues in its Opinion 20/2018 (…) having reasonably set out the rules which it considered to be in breach of the European Union law and, in particular, of the GDPR" (CNPD, 2019, p. 2).

THE CONFLICTS WITH THE EU LAW

When a national authority comes across incompatibilities between the provisions of national law and the provisions of the EU law, the literature distinguishes two types of collision – indirect collision and direct collision (Verhoeven, 2009, p. 67). The first type of collision takes place when "the EU law provides substantive rules on the concerned case, whereas the application of these rules depend on the national procedural law, which may limit the effects of the substantive provisions of the EU law". The second type of collision "exists when a provision of the national law conflicts with a provision of the EU law, and when the two cannot be applied simultaneously because that would lead to incompatible legal consequences. This is often the case when both provisions have a substantive character" (Verhoeven, 2009).

Relying on the legal arguments of the CNPD, the author believes that the case at stake is a direct collision since there is no national procedural law implicated. Therefore, the following section will focus on the national provisions considered incompatible with the EU law, in particular with the GDPR. As already mentioned, there are 9 articles disapplied by the CNPD: article 2 (scope of application); article 20 (1) (restrictions to the right of information and access); article 23 (the application of the purpose limitation principle to public bodies); article 28 (3) (a) (employee consent); articles 37, 38 and 39 (penalties); article 61 (2) (consent forfeiture); and article 62 (2) (previously authorized processing of personal data).

The Scope of Application of the National Law: Article 2

Unlike the GDPR, the Portuguese legislator adopted the geographical place criterion of processing personal data in article 2 to state the scope of the national law. In fact, article 3 of the GDPR establishes its territorial scope of application according to the location of the establishment of the data controller or processor and not the location of processing.

Article 2 (1) of Law 58/2019 extends its scope to all "(…) processing personal data carried out on national territory (…) with the exception of the situations excluded in article 2 of the GDPR". Number 2 of the same provision states that: "This law shall be applied to processing personal data carried out outside the national territory when: a) processing is carried out in the context of the activities of an establishment located in the national territory; (…)".

The main problem identified by the CNPD in this provision concerns the application of GDPR rules to allocate the jurisdiction among supervisory authorities in cases of "cross-border processing" (article 4 (23) of the GDPR). This type of processing occurs in two cases: (a) when processing personal data takes place in the context of the activities of establishments in more than one Member State of a controller or processor in the Union, where the controller or processor is established in more than one Member State; or (b) when processing personal data takes place in the context of the activities of a single establishment of a controller or processor in the Union, but which substantially affects or is likely to substantially affect data subjects in more than one Member State. In addition, article 56 (1) provides that "without prejudice to Article 55, the supervisory authority of the main establishment or of the single establishment of the controller or processor shall be competent to act as the lead supervisory authority for the cross-border processing carried out by that controller or processor in accordance with the procedure provided in Article 60".

As the CNPD explains, when the data controller or data processor has "more than one establishment in the EU, article 56 (1) of the GDPR determines the criteria to find the supervisory authority responsible for leading the procedure and issue the final decision in order to ensure the functioning of the one-stop-shop mechanism (…)". Additionally, as the CNPD clarifies, "this lead authority will apply its national law (…)" (CNPD, 2019, p. 3). In fact, according to that same provision, as a general rule, the lead supervisory authority is the one where the main establishment of the data controller or data processor is located. Therefore, article 2, by stating that the national law is applicable to processing personal data performed in national territory, when that processing concerns activities of the main establishment of the controller or processor located in another Member State, is incompatible with the rule set by article 56 (1) of the GDPR. The same is applied to processing personal data in the context of the activities of an establishment located in Portugal when this establishment is not the main establishment of the data controller or data processor. It seems that the reasoning of the Portuguese authority assumes that the lead supervisory authority will never apply legislation from another Member State. However, this is clearly a matter of choice of law in cross-border processing which the GDPR does not explicitly solve.

Lastly, article 2 (3) of the national law states that it applies to the processing of personal data performed outside the national territory when the data of Portuguese data subjects residing abroad is inscribed at consular posts. The CNPD understands that this provision restricts the scope of application of article 3 (3) of the GDPR addressing specific situations, such as (but not only) diplomatic missions or consular posts, where Member State laws are applied by virtue of public international law.

1.2. Restrictions to the Right to Information and Access: Article 20

Article 20 (1) of the national law states that "the rights to information and access to personal data provided for in articles 13 and 15 of the GDPR shall not be exercised when the law imposes a duty of confidentiality on the data controller or processor opposable to the data subject".

In its reasoning, the CNPD distinguishes two cases. First, concerning the right to information when personal data have not been obtained from the data subject (article 14 of the GPDR), the CNPD sustains that only such provision establishes legitimate restrictions to its scope, specially number 5, stating that the right to information does not apply where and insofar as "the personal data must remain confidential, subject to an obligation of professional secrecy regulated by Union or Member State law, including a statutory obligation of secrecy". In fact, the Portuguese authority quotes the EU Commission to clarify that "the national legislator cannot copy the text of the GDPR when it is not necessary (…) neither interpret it nor add additional conditions to rules that are directly applicable according to the Regulation" (CNPD, 2019, p. 1).

The second case concerns the right to information when the personal data were obtained from the data subject (article 13 of the GDPR), as well as the right of access (article 15 of the GDPR). The supervisory authority explains that those rights can only be restricted according to article 23 of the GDPR (Restrictions). This provision states that Member States can "restrict the scope of the obligations and rights by way of a legislative measure provided for in articles 12 to 22 when such a restriction respects the essence of the fundamental rights and freedoms and is a necessary and proportionate measure in a democratic society to safeguard: national security; public security; the prevention, investigation, detection or prosecution of criminal offences or the execution of criminal penalties; the protection of judicial independence and judicial proceedings; the prevention, investigation, detection and prosecution of breaches of ethics for regulated professions", among others.

As the national authority notes, article 20 of the national law does not specify the purpose or purposes, among those listed above, of the restriction that it aims to pursue. Furthermore, it does not respect the additional criteria presented in article 23 (2) of the GDPR, concerning the processing purposes or processing categories; the personal data categories; the scope of the restrictions introduced; the safeguards to prevent abuse or unlawful access or transfer; the specification of the controller or controllers categories; the storage periods and the applicable safeguards taking into account the nature, scope and processing purposes or processing categories; the risks to the rights and freedoms of data subjects; and the right of data subjects to be informed about the restriction, unless that may be prejudicial to the restriction purpose. (CNPD, 2019, p. 4).

The Application of the Purpose Limitation Principle to Public Entities and Bodies: Article 23

The GDPR establishes an "omnibus regime" (Lynskey, 2015, p. 14) in the sense that it states the application of data protection rules to public and private actors. However, the legislative history of article 23 of the GDPR illustrates the debate, at EU level, surrounding this option (Lynskey, 2015, p. 21). At national level, in Portugal, article 23 (1) of the national law admits that processing personal data by public bodies can be performed for purposes other than those for which the personal data were initially collected. However, this hypothesis "is exceptional in nature and must be duly substantiated with a view to ensure the pursuit of public interests that cannot otherwise be safeguarded according to articles 6 (1) (e), 6 (4) and 9 (2) (g) of the GDPR".

As the CNPD underlines, the GDPR does not recognize Member States the power to broadly assert deviations from the original processing purpose performed by public bodies. In fact, article 6 (4) of the GDPR only allows this power when it is "necessary and proportionate in a democratic society to safeguard the objectives considered in article 23 (1)". Therefore, the national law should explain the purpose of the public interest that allows public entities to further process personal data, or re-use them. Rather, it extends such possibility to any public interest. In addition, the CNPD states that this general concession to public bodies cannot be considered a "necessary and proportionate" measure since this presupposes an analysis and consideration of each individual purpose, according to recital 50 of the GDPR (CNPD, 2019, p. 4).

By allowing personal data to be processed by public authorities and bodies for any purpose other than the original, article 23 (1) of the national law, also allows a departure from the reasoning of compatibility of purposes, thus contradicting the purpose limitation principle as established in articles 5 (1) (b) of the GDPR and 8 (2) of the Charter of Fundamental Rights of the European Union. According to both provisions, personal data can be "collected for specified, explicit and legitimate purposes and not further processed in a manner that is incompatible with those purposes".

Employee Consent: Article 28

Processing personal data in the employment context is one of the many areas where the GDPR, in article 88, expressly grants Member States the power to decide on specific data protection rules. According to article 28 (3) (a) of the national law, "unless otherwise stated by law, the employee consent cannot be a legal ground for processing personal data: a) if processing generates a legal or economic advantage for the employee (…)".

Recalling the definition of consent, in article 4 (11) of the GDPR, its role as a legal basis for processing, according to article 6 (1) (a) and article 9 (2) (a) of the GDPR, as well as the work of the Article 29 Working Party, the CNPD understands that this solution excessively restricts the relevance of the consent by erasing any margin of free will for workers even when there are conditions for it, mostly in cases without any risk to their rights and interests. In fact, the Portuguese authority argues that "notwithstanding the non-equal nature of the employment relationship, it follows from the principle of the dignity of the human person the need to recognize the minimum of free will for individuals to enjoy their fundamental right to control their personal data, even in the context of social and legal relations where, as a general rule, they need protection from the other party (CNPD, 2019, p. 5). For this reason, the Portuguese supervisory authority sustains that this provision does not correspond to an appropriate national legislative measure safeguarding the dignity, fundamental rights and legitimate interests of the worker.

Therefore, article 28 (3) (a) is an unjustified and disproportionate restriction of articles 6 (1) (a) and 9 (2) (a) of the GDPR.

Penalties: Articles 37, 38 and 39

The Portuguese supervisory authority identifies inconsistencies with the general conditions for imposing administrative fines set out in article 83 (4) and (5) of the GDPR. Number 4 sets out infringements "subject to administrative fines up to 10 000 000 EUR, or in the case of an undertaking, up to 2% of the total worldwide annual turnover of the preceding financial year, whichever is higher". Number 5 sets out infringements "subject to administrative fines up to 20 000 000 EUR, or in the case of an undertaking, up to 4% of the total worldwide annual turnover of the preceding financial year, whichever is higher". The problematic provisions of the national law are articles 37, 38 and 39.

Article 37 (1)

The first contradiction with the GDPR concerns the option of the Portuguese law, in article 37 (1) (a), to exempt certain conducts (negligent ones) from administrative fines, violating the principles of article 5 of the GDPR. According to the CNPD, article 83 (5) (a) of the GDPR does not distinguish between any types of conducts and the Member States do not have the power to lawfully perform such a distinction.

Additionally, article 37 (1) (h) of the national law only sanctions situations where the data controller does not provide "relevant information". This is another example of a distinction that is absent from the wording of article 83 of the GDPR and one that unlawfully restricts the scope of this article.

Lastly, the sanction for violating the duty to cooperate with the national supervisory authority, stated in article 37 (1) (a) (k) of the national law, should have heavier sanctions in order to respect article 83 (4) (a) of the GDPR. This provision includes, among the infringements subject to administrative fines up to 10 000 000 EUR, or in the case of an undertaking, up to 2% of the total worldwide annual turnover of the preceding financial year, the violation of the obligations of the data controller and the data processor pursuant to several articles, including article 31 of the GDPR stating that "the controller and the processor and, where applicable, their representatives, shall cooperate, on request, with the supervisory authority in the performance of its tasks".

Article 37 (2) and 38 (2)

These provisions assert, for the types of infringements expressed in article 83 (4) and (5) of the GDPR, different sanctioning frames based on the dimension of the undertaking and the nature of the subject (natural or legal person) performing processing personal data.

The CNPD understands that if the GDPR aims to harmonize the EU's legal framework applicable to processing personal data and to foster the consistency of its application across Member States, the maximum limits provided in article 83 for administrative fines cannot be dismissed by Member States. "The setting of limits in national law that are lower than those provided for in article 83 (4) and (5) of the GDPR constitute a breach" and "from the principle of the primacy of the EU law, as reflected in article 288 TFEU, it follows that the regulations have binding value and are directly applicable in all Member States, thereby ruling out any possibility of a Member State to unilaterally nullify its effects by means of a legislative act different from the EU's (CNPD, 2019, p. 7). Additionally, in article 83, or in the recitals relating to the sanctions regime of the GDPR, there is no room for the autonomous consideration of the size of the undertaking when applying administrative fines. Therefore, the criterion adopted by the national law to distinguish small and medium-sized undertakings and to restrict the maximum administrative fines only to large companies is, in itself, a violation of the GDPR. In fact, the CNPD recalls that, in the GDPR, the relevance recognised to small and medium-sized undertakings is very strict, as opposed to the original proposal of the GDPR, since the EU institutions understood that the impact on data subjects from the conduct of data controllers and data processors does not rely on the number of employees in these organizations but rather on the nature of the activity carried out (categories of data processed, volume of data processed, categories of data subjects, among others) and the risk this activity poses to the rights and interests of data subjects.

The Portuguese supervisory authority applies the same reasoning to the distinction provided by the national law for the sanctions regarding natural persons (CNPD, 2019, p. 8).

Article 39 (1) and (3)

Article 39 (1) of the national law provides that "when determining the measure of the fine, in addition to the criteria in article 83 (2) of the GDPR the supervisory authority takes into account: (a) the economic situation of the agent, in the case of a natural person, or the turnover and the annual balance, in the case of a legal person; (b) the continuing character of the infringement; (c) the size of the entity, taking into account the number of employees and the nature of services provided.". As the CNPD notes exhaustively throughout its decision, the GDPR leaves no room for Member States to add criteria to those provided for in article 83 (4) and (5) of the GDPR. This is the reason why the Portuguese authority disapplies article 39 (1) of the national law, which unduly sets out three criteria for the determination of the fine in addition to those set out in article 83 (2) of the GDPR (CNPD, 2019, p. 8).

In article 39 (3), the national law imposes on the Portuguese supervisory authority a previous compulsory step for the decision to sanction certain conducts which, according to CNPD, creates, once more, a special regime for that kind of conduct which is not compatible with the GDPR (CNPD, 2019, p. 9).

Article 61 (2): Consent Forfeiture

Article 61 (2) states that "when the consent forfeiture gives rise to the termination of a contract of which the data subject is part, processing personal data is lawful until the consent forfeiture occurs". The CNPD explains that this solution was introduced to solve a specific problem, felt mostly by the insurance sector, in cases where the contract is not a lawful ground for processing of special categories of data. Nevertheless, this provision mistakes two grounds for processing personal data since it states that the consent forfeiture implies the termination of a contract or, as the Portuguese authority explains, "admits that the consent for processing personal data is a prerequisite for the lawfulness of the contract of which the data subject is part" (CNPD, 2019, p. 9). In fact, consent is only used for processing personal data when those data are not necessary for the performance of a contract.

The author agrees with the Portuguese authority when it explains that "the cause of this clear distinction in the GDPR is the requirement for freedom to express consent imposed by article 4 (11) of the GDPR. If consent was necessary for the processing related to the performance of a contract, the conditions for freedom could not be safeguarded" (CNPD, 2019, p. 10). This is also stated by the Article 29 Working Party: "If the controller wishes to process personal data that is actually necessary for the performance of the contract, consent is not the legal basis" (Article 29 Working Party, 2018, p. 9).

By confusing and establishing a dependency relationship between these two grounds for processing personal data, the national law violates the GDPR, especially article 4 (11) and recital 42 when these provisions clarify that "consent should not be regarded as freely given if the data subject has no genuine or free choice, or is unable to refuse or withdraw consent without detriment" (CNPD, 2019, p. 10).

Article 62 (2): Previously Authorized Processing Personal Data

The last article ruled out by the national supervisory authority, article 62 (2), establishes that "all the [valid] authorizations or notifications of processing to the CNPD (…) cease to be in force since the entry into force of the GDPR". Regarding this matter, the GDPR stipulates, in article 99, its entry into force on the 20th day after its publication (the 4th of May 2016), and its applicability starting on 25th of May 2018. Recalling this specific schedule, the CNPD understands that article 62 (2) of the national law, by retroacting its effects to the entry in force of the GDPR, is clearly asserting the retroactive application of the GDPR itself, thus violating article 99 (2) (CNPD, 2019, p. 11).

CONSEQUENCES OF THE DECISION OF THE PORTUGUESE SUPERVISORY AUTHORITY

In the past, scholars noted the lack of evidence that administrative authorities and bodies actually abide by the *Constanzo obligation* (Verhoeven, 2009, p. 66 and Witte, 2011, p. 323). This trend has been changing, with ECJ decisions such as the *Workplace Relations Commission* (2018) case and with positions such as the one adopted by the Portuguese supervisory authority.

The consequences of the CNPD decision can be understood according to two main different perspectives: a theoretical perspective, concerning the relationship between EU Law and national law, and a practical perspective, focused on the impact of this decision on data processing activities of data controllers, data processors and on the interests and rights of data subjects.

From a theoretical point of view, the *de facto* application of the *Constanzo obligation* by administrative bodies and authorities does not mean that the obligation is unproblematic and indisputable. Firstly, there is no previous intervention of the ECJ on incompatibility. In fact, unlike national courts, this is arguably a possibility available for administrative bodies and authorities. However, given the competence, tasks and powers and, above all, the imposition of independence upon national supervisory authorities in the GDPR (Chapter 4), one could ask if the acknowledgement of the preliminary ruling for administrative bodies and authorities in those circumstances would not be useful to avoid uncertainties surrounding the *Constanzo obligation*. In addition, three main fundamental principles are at stake when administrative bodies unilaterally disapply national law: the principle of the separation of powers; the principle of legality; and the requirement of uniform application of EU law in connection with the principle of legal certainty (Bombois, 2009, p. 169). It must be noted that the CNPD recognizes this, not only by assuming that its decision has practical consequences, but also by quoting a Portuguese scholar (Martins, 2018) who expressly states that the *Constanzo obligation,* when followed by administrative authorities and bodies, poses many challenges to the principle of legality, especially in its dimensions of precedence and prevalence of the law (Martins, 2018, p. 84 e 85).

Additionally, in this particular case, the decision to disapply the national law challenges the understanding that this mechanism is a "negative rule of instruction" (Verhoeven, 2009, p. 69) in the sense that it only denotes the disapplication of the national law in a concrete case. In fact, the Portuguese authority decision was not prompted by a particular case. Instead, it is a general statement for the future of the activity of that authority. This is problematic since some scholars only foresee the possibility of an administrative authority to declare a provision unlawful and not applicable in general as *ultima ratio,* in a specific case, or even when it has been explicitly empowered to do so by a statutory provision (Verhoeven, 2009, p. 76). Despite the absence of a doctrinal consensus on this broad possibility, on the one hand, the existence of a straightforward prohibition is not clear. On the other hand, it is unquestionable that this decision clarifies the position of the supervisory authority, leaving no doubts towards its reasoning and conduct when applying the 9 articles in future cases. Thus, one could understand this decision as a preventive measure towards future direct conflicts between EU and national law and, as such, a contribution to the transparency of the work and supervision of the national authority.

In terms of practical consequences of the CNPD's decision, it seems that, given its position on article 2, a choice of law rule is still missing in cases of cross-border processing. In fact, this is an old question, highlighted by the European Data Protection Supervisor (EDPS) during the GDPR legislative discussions (EDPS, European Data Protection Supervisor opinion, 2012, p. 17). This might have a serious impact when the data controller has more than one establishment and needs to understand what law should be applied, for example, to the children's consent. On the other side, the national Parliament does not have the power to restrict the scope of application of the GDPR. Therefore, the extension, in article 2 (3) of the national law, of its scope of application to all processing personal data of Portuguese data subjects residing abroad and inscribed at consular posts, is unlawful. In this case, considering that the GDPR is very clear on this issue, the consequences arising from the disapplication of article 2 for data controllers, data processors and data subjects are minor.

Problems for data controllers, data processors and data subjects could also arise concerning articles 20, 23, 37, 38 and 39 of the national law. Indeed, despite the fact that CNPD's decision is a general disapplication of national law, it does not have an *erga omnes* effect. This implies that the non-application by the CNPD of the national law does not mean that the provisions concerned are rendered invalid or null and void, so they can be applied, for instance, by national courts. Henceforth, one could say that there is a theoretical risk of divergences between the national courts and the supervisory authority regarding the incompatible nature of those provisions with the EU law, mostly in cases related to restrictions to the right to information and access (article 20 of the national law) and the re-use of personal data for new purposes by public entities (article 23 of the national law). For example, in theory, a data controller can reject a petition for access to personal data based on article 20 of the national law. In addition, according to article 79 of the GDPR, the application of the data subject can directly reach a national court without any previous intervention of the national supervisory authority. The same can be said for the judicial interpretation of article 23 of the national law and the reading of national courts of articles 37, 38 and 39 of that law. However, if a national court has doubts about the interpretation or validity of the EU Law it should ask the ECJ for clarification, according to article 267 of the Treaty on the Functioning of the EU. The same mechanism can be used to determine whether a national law or practice is compatible with EU law. This hypothesis could put an end to the problems that arise for the legal system when an administrative body or authority applies the *Constanzo obligation.*

It is the author's opinion that the incompatible nature of the provisions of the national law identified by CNPD, in particular those regarding the lawfulness of the employee consent, the relationship between the grounds for processing personal data and the retroactivity of the GDPR, are so manifest that the ECJ most likely would agree with the reasoning of the CNPD. On another note, there is a broad consensus surrounding those topics, not only among the stakeholders who expressed concerns similar to those of the CNPD during the legislative process of Law 58/2019, but also in the work and opinions of the Article 29 Working Party, considered by the national supervisory authority to substantiate its reasoning.

CONCLUSION

The GDPR is not a Directive. However, as a Spanish scholar highlighted, it has "the body of a Regulation but the soul of a Directive" (Mexía, 2016, p. 34). This means that many provisions in the GDPR allow the national legislator to develop specific solutions for certain issues. Thus, one could expect that a decision to disapply the national law implementing the GDPR would be catastrophic for the day-to-day activities of data controllers and data processors.

It is still soon to assess all the consequences of such decision but it seems that the catastrophe is, at least, not imminent. Firstly, the CNPD's decision applies only to 9 articles in a total of 62 and excludes important provisions from its scope, such as the data protection officer, the children's consent, data retention periods, administrative and judicial remedies available to the data subject, among others. Secondly, the arguments forwarded by the national supervisory authority to disapply articles 2, 28, 61 and 62 seem reasonable enough to deserve a broad agreement since its strongly based in legitimate sources, such as the Article 29 Working Party and in other stakeholders' opinions. Lastly, this decision was adopted immediately after the entry into force of the national law implementing the GDPR. So, its impact on specific processes adopted to ensure compliance with the national law was, most likely, very low.

Nevertheless, given the absence of an *erga omnes* effect of this decision, it is possible that national courts will, in future cases, ask the ECJ to clarify its understanding regarding the provisions disapplied by the CNPD. Since a new legislative process to amend the national law is not foreseeable, this is the best option to solve the problems and uncertainties that arose when the CNPD applied the *Constanzo obligation.*

REFERENCES

Bombois, T. (2009). L'administration "juge" de la légalité communautaire – Réflexions autor des arrêts *Fratelli Costanzo* et *Abna* de la Cour de Justice de Luxembourg. *Journal des tribunaux, 128*, 169-174.

Claes, M. (2015). The Primacy of EU Law in European and National Law. In A. Arnull & D. Chalmers (Eds.), *The Oxford Handbook of European Union Law* (pp. 178–211). Oxford, UK: Oxford University Press.

Cordeiro, A. (2019). Portugal: A Brief Overview of the GDPR Implementation. *European Data Protection Law Review, 5*(4), 533–536. doi:10.21552/edpl/2019/4/12

Kwiecien, H. (2006). The Primacy of European Union Law Over National Law Under the Constitutional Treaty. In P. Dann & M. Rynkowski, (Eds.), The Unity of the European Constitution (pp. 67-86). Springer. doi:10.1007/978-3-540-37721-4_5

Lynskey, O. (2015). *The Foundations of EU Data Protection Law*. Oxford, UK: Oxford University Press.

Martins, P. (2018). *National Public Administrations and European Union Law. Essential Questions and Case Law*. Lisbon, Portugal: Universidade Católica Editora. (in Portuguese)

Mexía, P. (2016). La singular naturaleza jurídica del reglamento general de protección de datos de la UE. Sus efectos en acervo nacional sobre protección de datos. In J. Mañas (Dir.), Reglamento General De Protección De Datos. Hacia un nuevo modelo europeo de privacidade. Madrid: Reus.

Prechal, S. (2007). Direct Effect, Indirect Effect, Supremacy and the Evolving Constitution of the European Union. In C. Barnard (Ed.), *The Fundamentals of EU Law Revisited: Assessing the Impact of the Constitutional Debate* (pp. 35–71). Oxford, UK: Oxford University Press. doi:10.1093/acprof:oso/9780199226221.003.0003

Verhoeven, M. (2009). The 'Costanzo Obligation' of National Administrative Authorities in the Light of the Principle of Legality: Prodigy or Problem Child? *Croatian Yearbook of European Law and Policy, 5*(5), 65–92. doi:10.3935/cyelp.05.2009.81

Witte, B. (2011). Direct Effect, Primacy and the Nature of Legal Order. In *P. Craig & G. de Búrca (Eds.), The Evolution of EU Law* (pp. 323–362). Oxford, UK: Oxford University Press.

ADDITIONAL READING

Article 29 Working Party (2018), *Guidelines on consent under Regulation 2016/679*

Comissão Nacional de Proteção de Dados (2018), *Opinion 6275/2018*

de Proteção de Dados, C. N. (2019).. . *Decision (Washington, D.C.)*, *2019*(494).

European Data Protection Supervisor (2012), *Opinion of the European Data Protection Supervisor on the data protection reform package*

Portuguese Parliament. (2018), *Hearings for the approval of Law 58/2019*. Retrieved from: http://debates. parlamento.pt/catalogo/r3/dar/01/13/03/080/2018-05-03/13?pgs=7-16&org=PLC&plcdf=true

Presidency of the Council of Ministers (2017), *Decision 7456/2017*

Presidency of the Council of Ministers (2018), *Proposal 120/XIII*

KEY TERMS AND DEFINITIONS

Data Controller: The natural or legal person, public authority, agency or other body which, alone or jointly with others, determines the purposes and means of processing personal data; where the purposes and means of such processing are determined by Union or Member State law, the controller or the specific criteria for its nomination may be provided for by Union or Member State law.

Data Processor: The natural or legal person, public authority, agency or other body which processes personal data on behalf of the controller.

Personal Data: Any information relating to an identified or identifiable natural person ('data subject'); an identifiable natural person is one who can be identified, directly or indirectly, in particular by reference to an identifier such as a name, an identification number, location data, an online identifier or to one or more factors specific to the physical, physiological, genetic, mental, economic, cultural or social identity of that natural person;

Processing: Any operation or set of operations which is performed on personal data or on sets of personal data, whether or not by automated means, such as collection, recording, organization, structuring, storage, adaptation or alteration, retrieval, consultation, use, disclosure by transmission, dissemination or otherwise making available, alignment or combination, restriction, erasure or destruction.

APPENDIX: TABLE OF CASES

- Case C-106/77, *Amministrazione delle Finanze dello Stato v Simmenthal SpA,* Judgement of 9 March 1978
- Case C-103/88, *Fratelli Costanzo SpA v Comune di Milano,* Judgement of 22 June 1989
- Case C-224/97, *Erich Ciola v Land Vorarlberg*, Judgement of 29 April 1999
- Case C-118/00, *Gervais Larsy v Institut national d'assurances sociales pour travailleurs indépendants (INASTI)*, Judgement of 28 June 2001
- Case C-198/01, *Consorzio Industrie Fiammiferi (CIF) v Autorità Garante della Concorrenza e del Mercato,* Judgement of 9 september 2003
- Case C-378/17, *Minister for Justice and Equality, Commissioner of An Garda Síochána v Workplace Relations Commission,* Judgement of 4 december 2018

APPENDIX: LEGISLATION

Law 58/2019 guarantees the implementation in Portugal of Regulation EU 2016/679 of the European Parliament and of the Council of April 2016 on the protection of natural persons with regard to processing personal data, and repealing Directive 95/46/EC (General Data Protection Regulation).

Regulation EU 2016/679 of the European Parliament and of the Council of April 2016 on the protection of natural persons with regard to processing personal data, and repealing Directive 95/46/EC (General Data Protection Regulation).

Chapter 8

Erosion by Standardisation:
Is ISO/IEC 29134:2017 on Privacy Impact Assessment Up to (GDPR) Standard?

Athena Christofi
https://orcid.org/0000-0002-4506-6324
KU Leuven, Belgium

Pierre Dewitte
https://orcid.org/0000-0003-4204-7467
KU Leuven, Belgium

Charlotte Ducuing
https://orcid.org/0000-0003-1160-0637
KU Leuven, Belgium

Peggy Valcke
https://orcid.org/0000-0002-8456-430X
KU Leuven, Belgium

ABSTRACT

This chapter examines the interplay between the GDPR and parallel private regulation in the form of privacy-related standards adopted by the International Organisation for Standardisation (ISO). Focusing on the understanding of 'risks' in the GDPR and ISO respective ecosystems, it compares the GDPR requirement for Data Protection Impact Assessments (DPIAs) with ISO/IEC 29134:2017, a private standard on Privacy Impact Assessment explicitly referred to by EU Data Protection Authorities as relevant in the context of DPIA methods. The resulting gap analysis identifies and maps misalignments, critically reflecting on whether the parallel form of ISO regulation, in the context of DPIAs, could support or rather blurs GDPR's objective to protect fundamental rights by embracing a risks-based approach.

DOI: 10.4018/978-1-5225-9489-5.ch008

INTRODUCTION

In the era of relentless technological developments with an ambivalent potential to both advance the common good and undermine individuals' rights and freedoms, regulating the processing of personal data is by no means a simple task. Focusing on the European Union ('EU') legal order, this Chapter explores the interplay between the General Data Protection Regulation ('GDPR'),[1] including GDPR-based soft-law instruments, and 'private' regulatory instruments of data processing adopted over the past years, such as ISO standards in the field of privacy. At the centre of the analysis is the risks-based approach enshrined in the GDPR, which culminates with the obligation to conduct a Data Protection Impact Assessment ('DPIA') in cases of high-risk processing. At the same time, risks-based methodologies are also at the core of privacy-related standards adopted by the International Organization for Standardisation ('ISO'). The Chapter juxtaposes the two strands of regulation focusing on the provisions of the GDPR on DPIAs on the one hand, and ISO's counterpart ISO/IEC 29134:2017 Information technology — Security techniques — Guidelines for privacy impact assessment (hereinafter ISO/IEC 29134) on the other. By mapping misalignments, the aim is to assess and critically reflect on whether the parallel form of ISO regulation could support or rather blurs the GDPR's objective to protect fundamental rights by embracing a risks-based approach.

The Chapter falls into three main parts. The first part revolves around the GDPR's regulatory model for data protection, laying out regulatory challenges and the solutions envisaged by the EU legislator. It begins with what constitutes a major challenge for today's regulators: the pacing problem of the law in light of constant technological developments. In the authors' view, any critical analysis of the regulation of privacy and data protection should acknowledge this challenge and the fact that it can put to test the traditional 'command and control' regulatory model to favour 'new' regulation focused on risk and on a decentralised approach. Second, it lays down the key regulatory characteristics of the EU data protection legal framework, namely: (i) GDPR's omnibus nature and fundamental rights objective; (ii) the law's focus on general data processing principles that ought to be operationalised by regulated entities on a case by case basis and; (iii) the risks-based approach coupled with the accountability principle. It explains that, while those characteristics were devised with the desire to bring regulatory flexibility, they may impact legal certainty as regulated entities are faced with broad notions whose scope and incumbent obligations may be unclear. The Chapter then argues that the lack of legal certainty has been acknowledged by the EU legislator, even if perhaps only implicitly. The third section introduces the soft law tools foreseen under the GDPR, which are expected to supplement and consolidate the latter's objectives by providing guidance on how to achieve compliance. It sketches the characteristics of the GDPR's co-regulatory model and limitations of the envisaged soft law tools that one may already see three and a half years after the Regulation's adoption and one and a half year after its entry into force.

The second part explores the emergence and pitfalls of the parallel form of private regulation through ISO privacy-related standards, notably ISO/IEC 29134. With the GDPR co-regulatory model still in its infancy, it is indeed extra-GDPR soft law instruments that keep gaining traction. Because of their worldwide recognition and fast development, ISO standards can be particularly popular amongst companies as a means to demonstrate compliance with the GDPR. The sheer amount of work on privacy-related standards by ISO over the past few years echoes businesses' growing concern for data protection and need for tools to orient their compliance efforts. After a brief introduction to ISO and its standardisation work, the Chapter discusses ISO's willingness to play a role as a relevant actor in the regulation of privacy and data processing globally – more importantly in the EU market – as well as Article 29

Working Party's ('WP29')[2] – now European Data Protection Board ('EDPB') – willingness to embrace the work of ISO on privacy impact assessments.

This brings us to the core of the paper, which consists of an evaluative gap analysis between DPIAs under the GDPR, grounded in risks-based approach and fundamental rights objectives, and ISO/IEC 29134 dealing with privacy impact assessments. Although the latter instrument is mentioned by WP29 as a relevant methodology to carry out a DPIA, the authors identify some misalignments. The first relates to ISO's focus on data *security*, in contrast with the – significantly broader – GDPR's focus on data *protection*. The second is about ISO/IEC 29134's preoccupation with 'privacy risk' contrasted with the notion of 'risks to the rights and freedoms' of individuals which is central in the GDPR. In the pursue of quantification of 'privacy risk' based on the notion of harm, it is also argued that ISO/IEC 29134 falls short of providing a method that genuinely takes into consideration the rights and freedoms that might be at stake, which can be very high-level, unquantifiable, yet crucial to consider when developing a project entailing the processing of personal data. Moreover, ISO/IEC 29134 includes provisions inviting organisations to consider risks to the organisation, in contrast with the GDPR where risk ought to be assessed solely on the basis of the individual whose rights may be impacted as a result of the processing.

The gap analysis is followed by a discussion on why the misalignments were in fact to be expected given the different mindset and ecosystem where the GDPR and ISO are respectively placed. The third part of the Chapter critically reflects on the risk of the risks-based approach, an issue that has already been raised by academic scholarship, and how it may have opened the door to a quantitative and information security-centric approach that seems alien to the GDPR's fundamental rights objective and falls short of providing for a comprehensive, meaningful DPIA. The endorsement by EU DPAs of ISO/IEC 29134 can thus be viewed as problematic.

Definitions of different terms are provided in the related sub-sections, at their first occurrence. Abbreviations are used only upon prior use of the entire expression.

PART I: THE CHALLENGE OF REGULATING DATA PROCESSING

Regulating New Technologies: The Pacing Problem of the Law

Ensuring the efficient and meaningful regulation of rapidly evolving technologies has become a major challenge for law- and policy-makers across the globe (Fenwick et al., 2016, pp. 562–567). What is referred to as the 'pacing problem' of the law can be attributed to several factors. First, to the sluggishness inherent to the traditional legislative apparatus. Simply put, technological progresses have largely outpaced the capacity of regulators to keep up with the latest innovations (Marchant, 2011, pp. 20–22). The institutional intricacies and political dialogues that come bundled with any democratic system have cluttered the decision-making process, broadening the gap between the product of the legislative procedure and the reality on the ground. In other words, "while technology changes exponentially, social, economic and legal systems change incrementally" (Downes, 2009, p. 2).

Second, to the ever-increasing complexity of new technologies. Not only is the legislative process intrinsically slow, but policymakers are not always equipped with the necessary expertise to understand and – to a larger extent – regulate emerging technologies. This is all the more apparent in the case of AI and machine learning – a subset of the former (Genç, 2019) –, both of which will bring their share of disruptive applications (Turner, 2018). As a result, regulators find themselves in a bit of a predicament: either regulating and running the risk of hindering innovation or missing the point, or staying idle and paving the way for a lack of legal certainty and potential detrimental effects the application of such technologies might have. Neither scenario is optimal; in both cases, "it makes it harder for new technologies to reach the market in a timely or efficient manner" (Fenwick et al., 2016, pp. 561; 582). This is reinforced by the fact that, while a given technology might be mature enough for adoption, it is nonetheless incredibly difficult to prospectively assess its impact on society. It is therefore equally challenging for regulators to proactively enact a future-proof regulatory framework that appropriately addresses all the issues raised by such fast-evolving sectors without stifling innovation. In that sense, that pacing problem echoes the so-called 'Collingridge dilemma' (Thierer, 2018), according to which, "by the time desirable consequences are discovered, the technology is often so much part of the economic and social fabric that its control is extremely difficult" (Collingridge, 1981, p. 19).

That pacing problem is particularly significant in the context of privacy and data protection law, since emerging technologies often rely on the processing of large amounts of datasets, or ultimately interfere with these two fundamental rights. Ensuring a high level of data protection in a constantly-evolving environment is a daunting task. Given the wide variety of situations governed by data protection law, a rigid command-and-control regulatory approach would drastically lower the level of congruence between the objectives pursued by the regulator and the impact on the regulated entities' behaviour (Decker, 2018).

Unravelling GDPR's Key Regulatory Characteristics

Omnibus Regulation With a Fundamental Rights Objective

In an era where every organisation collects, accesses or otherwise processes personal data, regulating data processing essentially touches upon the day to day management of countless public and private entities. Data protection regulation not only becomes the law of everything – as Purtova argued in relation to the broad definition of personal data under EU law (Purtova, 2018) – but a law for everyone to be mindful of as it triggers extensive compliance obligations. Yet, there are considerable differences among organisations in terms of the scope, context and potential for harmful impact of their processing operations on the individual and society. Regulators across the world have opted for different solutions to address the pervasiveness and heterogeneity of data processing and its privacy implications, mostly a sectorial approach on the one hand, and an *omnibus* regime on the other.[3] The EU follows the *omnibus* approach, with a catch-all act providing legal requirements that are technology- and sector-neutral and that – in principle – bind both private and public authorities (Lynskey, 2015, pp. 15–30), striving for coherence and a high level of protection among Member States. In such an *omnibus* regime, there is an inherent need for flexibility. The GDPR should be fit for purpose to regulate behaviours as diverse as the extensive profiling for assessing a person's creditworthiness and the sending of a micro-enterprise's promotional catalogue to its customers. An overtly prescriptive rule-based framework would risk to overburden organisations where data processing is mainly a low risk by-product of operating their (physical) business, or – in an attempt to avoid such scenario – to enable the most digitally savvy ones to benefit from compromise-based rules of limited ambition. On the contrary, legal frameworks enshrining broad principles and a scalable approach towards compliance based on the risks presented by a given behaviour can provide both comprehensiveness and flexibility.

A second point to stress is that the GDPR is a law with a fundamental rights objective. Article 1(1) GDPR starts by stating that the Regulation "lays down rules relating to the protection of natural persons with regard to the processing of personal data and rules relating to the free movement of personal data". This provision captures the essence of what makes the GDPR a transversal piece of legislation, which goes far beyond the protection of individuals' fundamental rights to privacy and data protection. Rather, it aims at protecting all the fundamental rights of natural persons in any instance where their personal data are processed. As such, the GDPR positions itself as a catalyst operationalizing – through a secondary piece of legislation – the various safeguards necessary to achieve its regulatory objective (Clifford & Ausloos, 2018, pp. 23–25).

A Principles-Based Approach to Ensure Flexibility

The GDPR – like its predecessor – was designed following a principles-based approach, rather than a rules-based one.[4] Article 5 sets the general principles governing the processing of personal data, the scope and interpretation of which are not clearly specified in the text but depend on a case-by-case analysis. Those principles are essential in order to ensure legitimate processing of personal data, which cannot be achieved by mere procedural and prescriptive provisions. Principles and rules thus coexist and, while principles-based regulations have been criticised for their lack of legal certainty and their over-reliance on regulatees' good will (Allen, 2014, pp. 380–381; Quelle, 2018, pp. 504–508), they nonetheless remain essential to ensure a flexible and future-proof regulatory framework. This has always been at the forefront of the data protection reform, with the WP29 emphasising on multiple occasions the necessity to move away from the conception of compliance as a mere 'ticking-the-box' exercise (Article 29 Working Party, 2009, pp. 13–15, 2013, p. 2; Quelle, 2018, p. 514).

The GDPR fine-tunes, complements and explicitly names the various principles already introduced by the Convention 108[5] and the Data Protection Directive, namely: lawfulness, fairness, transparency, purpose limitation, data minimisation, accuracy, storage limitation, integrity and confidentiality and accountability.[6] While some of these are more prescriptive than others – *e.g.* the obligation to pair each processing activity with a specified, explicit and legitimate purpose – Article 5 GDPR leaves controllers a wide margin of appreciation when it comes to actually complying with these requirements. What makes a processing operation *fair* or *unfair*? Should a controller wish to re-use personal data, what distinguishes a compatible new purpose from a non-compatible one? As regards the lawfulness principle, further specified in Article 6, when is processing *necessary* for a public interest task, or for a private entity's legitimate interests, and when would the latter interests be overridden by the interests of the individual whose personal data are at stake? Controllers are called to address those questions with regard to the specific processing operation(s) they envisaged. To do so, they essentially need to operationalise broad (legal) notions like *necessity* and *proportionality* and the balancing of interests that those entail (Clifford & Ausloos, 2018). In the day-to-day practice, by requiring controllers to comply with broad principles, the GDPR essentially entrusts them with important decision-making powers. Principles-based regulation is thus particularly demanding for regulated entities as it 'responsibilises' them (Martin Lodge & Wegrich, 2012, pp. 63–70).

A Risks-Based Approach to Ensure Scalability

Among the general principles enshrined in the GDPR, *accountability*[7] requires controllers to "be responsible for, and be able to demonstrate compliance with" those general principles. In that sense, the GDPR builds on an obligation that was already laid down in its predecessor,[8] and adds the requirement of demonstrability. Not only does the GDPR confirm the responsibility of the controller as a general principle, but it also details how controllers should behave when actually implementing their obligations. Article 24 (1) GDPR compels them to "implement appropriate technical and organisational measures to ensure and demonstrate compliance", while Article 25 (1) GDPR requires them to do so "both at the time of the determination of the means for processing and at the time of the processing itself". The GDPR also provides a list of criteria in light of which the said measures are to be evaluated, which explicitly includes "risks of varying likelihood and severity for rights and freedoms of natural persons" posed by the processing. The notion of risk is closely connected to this of accountability, as "risk control is materialising through [a] new enforced self-regulation model" (Macenaite, 2017). Controllers must therefore tailor the extent of their compliance efforts to the actual risks posed by their processing operations throughout the entire personal data processing life cycle.

Read together, these provisions of the GDPR form the prism through which all the other provisions of the Regulation must be interpreted. Such risks-based approach ensures the flexibility necessary to go from a rigid to a scalable regulatory framework able to encompass a wide variety of different situations. It "provides a way to carry out the shift to accountability that underlies much of the data protection reform, using the notion of risk as a reference point in light of which we can assess whether the organisational and technical measures taken by the controller offer a sufficient level of protection" (Quelle, 2018, p. 505). The accountability principle grounded in risks-based scalability culminates with the obligation to conduct a DPIA. While, at first sight, DPIAs are only *formally* required "where a type of processing in particular using new technologies […] is likely to result in a high risk to the rights and freedoms of natural persons",[9] the authors nonetheless consider such an assessment as the cornerstone of any compliance exercise, regardless of the type of processing involved. In that sense, Article 35 GDPR should be interpreted as minimum requirements for *riskier* processing operations rather than a provision limiting DPIA to only a subset of activities.

In the Pursuit of Legal Certainty: The GDPR's Soft-Law Ecosystem

While the principles-based approach based on the accountability principle certainly brings regulatory flexibility, it nonetheless impacts legal certainty, which is already undermined by the fast pace of technological developments. Aware of such challenges, the EU legislator introduced a wide array of soft-law instruments in the GDPR, the purpose of which is to offer regulatees more legal certainty by providing interpretation on how to achieve compliance *with respect to specific situations*, e.g. specific scenarios, specific sectors, specific processing activities (Kamara & De Hert, 2018).

Guidance from Supervisory Authorities

As conceived in the GDPR, the role of supervisory authorities is to sanction violations but also to guide regulated entities into compliance. According to the GDPR, supervisory authorities shall promote "public awareness and understanding of the risks, rules, safeguards and rights in relation to processing [of personal data]"[10] as well as "awareness of controllers and processors of their obligations".[11] The GDPR introduces a new mechanism of prior opinion of the supervisory authority to the controller, in case of data processing activities whose DPIA showed a high risk for the rights and freedoms of individuals.[12] Guidance can also be provided by the EDPB, following the practice of its predecessor WP29, with the purpose to try and ensure consistent interpretation of the legal provisions throughout the EU.[13]

Instruments of Co-Regulation

Co-regulation has been described by the European Commission as part of its Better Regulation agenda as the "mechanisms whereby a [European Union] legislative act entrusts the attainment of the objectives defined by the legislative authority to parties which are recognised in the field".[14] More generally, it can be defined as a "model that combines both legislation and self-regulatory instruments in support of the law" (Kamara, 2017, p. 2). Such model has been given much prominence in EU data protection law.

Codes of Conduct

Under the GDPR, just like under the previous Data Protection Directive, codes of conduct can be drafted by associations and bodies representing categories of controllers or processors, with the purpose to "specif[y] the application of the GDPR" with respect to a sector's characteristics. Draft codes must be submitted to the competent supervisory authority, who shall provide an opinion on whether a draft code complies with the GDPR. Should it be so and should the draft code provide "sufficient appropriate safeguards", the supervisory authority shall "approve" the draft code (or further amendments or extension of a previous code).[15] "Approved" draft codes should be published by the supervisory authority.[16] Approval and publicity of draft codes concerning data processing in several Member States also implies an opinion of the EDPB, which may trigger an implementing act of the European Commission to grant the approved Code "general validity within the Union".[17] Adherence to an approved code of conduct can serve to demonstrate compliance with GDPR obligations.[18] Notwithstanding the competences of supervisory authorities, the code of conduct "shall contain mechanisms" which enable an independent expert body, accredited by the supervisory authority, to monitor compliance with the GDPR.[19] As part of the accreditation requirements, the independent expert body shall in particular be equipped to handle complaints and take enforcement actions vis-à-vis controllers or processors who have adhered to the code of conduct in case of infringement (e.g. "suspension or exclusion" from the code of conduct).[20]

Certification Mechanisms

The GDPR sets out provisions to incentivise – and in certain cases legally recognise – mechanisms of certification, seals and marks, with respect to processing operations. There is no definition of certification in the GDPR, but the EDPB defined it as "a statement of conformity" (EDPB, 2019a, p. 18). Such mechanisms can be used by controllers and processors to demonstrate compliance with the respective provisions of the GDPR, although without "reducing the[ir] responsibility for compliance" and "without prejudice to the tasks and powers of the supervisory authorities".[21] Upon documented assessment of the processing activities, certification may be granted either by the supervisory authority or by a body accredited by the latter or by a national accreditation body, provided they comply with conditions laid down in the GDPR.[22] Just like codes of conduct, certification mechanisms and data protection seals and marks shall be collated in a register and made publicly available.[23] While ascribing some legal value to certification mechanisms is far from novel, the GDPR was said to take these mechanisms a step further by extending their scope to the enforcement of fundamental rights (Lachaud, 2018, pp. 245–251).[24] Figure 1 illustrates the certification mechanisms ecosystem as detailed in the GDPR.

Figure 1. Overview of the GDPR certification mechanisms ecosystem

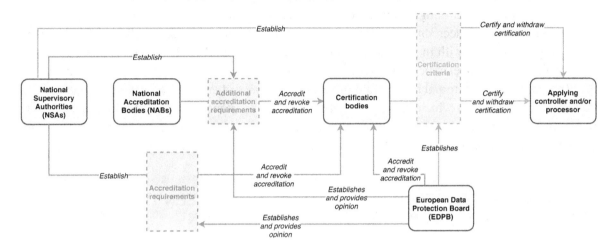

Limitations of GDPR's Soft-Law Mechanisms

Guidelines from supervisory authorities are welcome, but generally remain high-level and still require to be operationalized by the regulated entities. As to co-regulatory mechanisms, whether they are capable of bringing the expected legal certainty and of channelling regulatees into compliance remains debated within legal scholarship (on the GDPR certification mechanisms, see (Kamara & De Hert, 2018; Lachaud, 2016)). Since they require market uptake, it remains to be empirically seen whether businesses will embrace them in the future and to what extent, while they remain for the time being rather scarce. Responses to the public consultation the EDPB launched on its (draft) Guidelines on codes of conduct and monitoring bodies (EDPB, 2019b) and Guidelines on certification (EDPB, 2019a) point to certain challenges. As regards codes of conduct, it has been argued, for instance, that their development entails a significant organisational and financial burden for the industry association (Insurance Europe, 2019) and that in the absence of EU-wide codes, the emergence of national ones could in fact lead to a fragmented European market (DIGITALEUROPE, 2019). The same could be said about certification mechanisms. Although the GDPR grants the European Commission the competence to adopt implementing acts laying down mechanisms to recognise them,[25] no such act has been adopted yet. While the European Commission may exercise its competence in the future, the very purpose of certification mechanisms – namely to bring legal certainty to regulatees – is affected by the time lag, which may hinder their uptake by the market. Mutual recognition of national certification schemes may also raise consistency issues (Lachaud, 2016), which the European Commission would struggle to fix.[26] GDPR certification schemes have to be implemented in national legal frameworks,[27] which takes time before they can genuinely be used by companies, while the latter are concurrently bound to comply with GDPR requirements.

This slow development pace is related to the co-regulatory nature of both codes of conduct and GDPR certification mechanisms. While giving the power to non-state entities to authoritatively specify and monitor how GDPR notions should apply (e.g. with a sectorial code of conduct), the co-regulatory framework was carefully crafted to ensure compliance and consistency of 'soft' rules with the 'hard law', public rules established in the GDPR. The former should serve to enhance the latter's objectives, rather than pursue a de-regulatory agenda. Two factors illustrate this point. First, the strong involvement of public regulators in the adoption of soft law rules, in particular of the EDPB and national supervisory authorities.[28] Among other things, they approve the criteria forming the basis for certification as well as the requirements for the accreditation of certification bodies.[29] They can also sanction or revoke them, should they not comply with their accreditation mandate.[30] Second, the GDPR also includes transparency requirements, with reference to both the *process* for adopting co-regulatory mechanisms (including by accreditation of the external bodies) and the *content* of codes of conduct, certification schemes and the substantive norms on which the latter are grounded.[31] This stands in contrast with purely private mechanisms, which are inherently opaquer. For instance, most of standards developed by ISO are not publicly available since they are for sale.

PART II: ISO TO THE RESCUE? THE INTERPLAY BETWEEN THE GDPR AND PARALLEL PRIVATE PRIVACY REGULATION

Historical and Methodological Background

A Brief Introduction to ISO

Established in 1947, ISO is a private, global standard-setting body. ISO presents itself as an "independent, non-governmental international organisation with a membership of 164 national standards bodies",[32] one per country. Even though its members ("national standards bodies") are often established by statutory and/or publicly supported, ISO primarily remains "a forum for coordinating standardisation efforts by private business", rather than an intergovernmental organisation (Wirth, 2009, p. 81). ISO played an important role in broadening the scope of standards, from their original focus on products to processes and to 'management standards', as the ISO 9000 series of standards on quality management illustrates.[33] Such a shift paved the way to a great variety of management standards, ranging from environmental aspects to risk management, social responsibility (Higgins & Hallström, 2007) or personal data processing as further discussed below. Such pattern has resulted in what could be called the 'standardisation of everything', again recently illustrated by the increased interest of ISO in standardising artificial intelligence ('AI')[34] while, at the same time, the High-Level Expert Group on AI commissioned by the European Commission envisaged standardisation efforts as a means to deliver 'Trustworthy AI' label (High-level Expert Group on Artificial Intelligence (AI HLEG), 2019).

At global level, the broadening of the scope of (ISO) standards in the 1990s was analysed as occurring along with two other phenomena. First, companies were going global and, second, public regulation "governing corporate life" withdrew, while being partially compensated by increased reporting obligations (Higgins & Hallström, 2007, p. 696), what others have called a trend towards the "responsibilisation" of companies, core to the neoliberal paradigm (Renaud & and al., 2018, pp. 199–200; Shamir, 2008). With respect to the European context, the growth of (ISO) standards was generally found to go along with the construction of the internal market and the 'new approach' to technical harmonisation, which resulted in the need for products' technical specifications to be recognised across Member States. Management – or processes – standards are used by companies to demonstrate compliance, which has resulted in an emphasis placed on the formal auditability and 'certifiability', rather than – or even to the detriment of – the substantive outcome (Higgins & Hallström, 2007, pp. 696–698). In other words, the offer has followed the demand for standards, so that the characterisation of standardisation as market regulation has induced biases on the very substance of the regulation.[35]

ISO's Attempt to Address Privacy in a Market in Demand of Legal Certainty

ISO's willingness to enter the market for privacy is evidenced from the sheer amount of work put in the last few years in the development of standards dealing among other things with privacy engineering, privacy architecture, the conduct of privacy impact assessments, privacy information management, security and privacy in the context of big data, the Internet of Things and smart cities.[36] The willingness of ISO to play a role in GDPR implementation – but also more generally in data protection technical implementation – shows from the reading of privacy-related standards, primarily with the ISO 29xxx series (Macenaite, 2017, p. 531). ISO/IEC 29134 standard (further discussed below) notes that PIA reporting, assuming it follows the ISO standard, aims to "communicate assessment results to stakeholders", such as regulators, as PIA reporting can serve as "evidence supporting compliance with applicable legal requirements".[37] The standard further explains that, "in some jurisdictions, a PIA may be necessary to meet legal and regulatory requirements",[38] which obviously includes the EU GDPR. The standard also highlights in several instances the usefulness of PIA to demonstrate compliance with privacy and data protection legal requirements vis-à-vis customers and citizens.[39] Yet, the most explicit sign of willingness of ISO to be entrenched in the GDPR environment can be found in the recent standard ISO/IEC 27701:2019 – which explicitly links to the GDPR and includes in annex a correlation table, mapping and matching the standard's clauses with the relevant GDPR provisions.[40]

For entities subject to the GDPR, ISO standards could constitute an additional source of regulation to help operationalise vague concepts and bridge the gap between principles and their contextual application. By doing so, they would meet regulated entities' need for legal certainty and serve to demonstrate compliance, based on the reputation, capacity, technical expertise and global reach of ISO. The GDPR obligation to conduct DPIAs is a prime illustration of how ISO standards are expected to play such role.

ISO and GDPR Meet: DPIAs, Risks-Based Approach and WP29 Endorsement

The introduction in the GDPR of an obligation to conduct a DPIA was described as closely related to the notion of risk as regulatory yardstick, with the regulatory novelty that the legal obligations shall be tailored according to the risks to fundamental *rights and freedoms* of individuals (Macenaite, 2017, pp. 522–525). However, the GDPR gives little guidance on how to conduct such assessments. Although with 75 occurrences, the term 'risk' is not defined in the GDPR nor is it explained what it concretely means to manage risks to fundamental rights. Similarly, the GDPR remains silent on the methodology that should be followed to manage the risks identified along the way.

Supervisory authorities have therefore engaged in filling that gap. In 2017, WP29 adopted Guidelines on DPIAs with the aim to provide a more detailed, explanatory overview of the objectives and process envisaged in the GDPR (Article 29 Working Party, 2017). The Guidelines clarify that the controller is free to choose a methodology, but, reciprocally, *must* choose one that meets the common criteria identified in Annex 2 of the Guidelines. They also provide examples of methodologies developed by national supervisory authorities, which could be used to assist in the implementation of the basic requirements of the GDPR, however without arbitrating as for their relevance.

Importantly, the Guidelines mention certain ISO standards, and hence render them particularly relevant in the context of GDPR compliance with the obligation on DPIA. Annex 1 "Examples of existing EU DPIA frameworks" mentions the (at the time still upcoming) ISO/IEC 29134 standard as "[a]n international standard [that] will also provide guidelines for methodologies used for carrying out a DPIA". The same standard is also referred to in the introductory part of the Guidelines as one of the documents that WP29 had taken into account when developing the Guidelines. Further, the Guidelines observe that recital 90 of the GDPR, outlining components of the DPIA, would "overlap with well-defined components of risk management (e.g. ISO 31000)" (Article 29 Working Party, 2017, p. 17).

ISO/IEC 29134 constitutes guidelines and does not anticipate certification, but advises "organisations" to have their PIA review and/or audited by independent reviewers, with the possible involvement of "any relevant organization charged with the administration of the privacy legislation, such as data protection authorities or privacy commissioners".[41] There is thus no doubt that WP29 views ISO standards related to risk management, and particularly ISO/IEC 29134, as tools for regulatees to fulfil their GDPR obligations with respect to DPIA. In particular, when it comes to operationalising the vague notion of risk, which pervades the GDPR and especially its provisions on DPIAs, there may be synergies with ISO, which is well-accustomed to risk management methodologies. By referring to ISO's work, WP29 essentially welcomes such synergies as a means to provide more legal certainty to regulatees when implementing the GDPR.

However, bearing in mind the substantially different nature of the GDPR and ISO standards, one should be cautious that they may not provide a similar understanding of the notion and role of risk. By attempting to map alignments and misalignments, the following sections aim to assess whether the parallel form of ISO regulation could support or rather blurs GDPR's objective to protect fundamental rights by adopting a risks-based approach. ISO/IEC 29134 is at the centre of the analysis, as it stands at the crossroads between the willingness of both ISO and EU supervisory authorities to provide guidance on DPIA methodology. The following sections aim to put the endorsement of this standard by WP29 to the GDPR test.

Gap Analysis: Testing ISO/IEC 29134 against the Risks-Based Approach in the GDPR

This section identifies the main misalignments of ISO/IEC 29134 with the GDPR, particularly with the risks-based regulation of DPIAs. It should also be added at the outset that the GDPR and the standard are using diverging terminology, as ISO aims for a global reach and is not EU-specific. For instance, while the GDPR refers to "DPIA" and "data subject", the standard speaks of "Privacy impact assessment" ('PIA') and "Personal Identifiable Information Principal" ('PII Principal'). The relationship between the two fundamental rights of, respectively, 'data protection' on the one hand and 'privacy' on the other, remains an open discussion. While it has been convincingly argued that the notion of privacy is broader in scope than this of data protection, discussing such conceptual misalignment is beyond the scope of this chapter.[42] Additionally, the title "PIA" within the meaning of the ISO ecosystem may not capture the extent of the concept as defined in other contexts. Yet, terminology gap lies beyond the scope of this paper, which focuses on the *substantive scope* of the assessment and on the notion of risk (management).

From Information Security Risk Management to…
Information Security Risk Management?

The risks-based approach in the GDPR originates from the Data Protection Directive,[43] where it played a role in tailoring obligations to ensure *security* of data processing (Macenaite, 2017, pp. 518–522).

ISO/IEC 29134 undoubtedly reflects an information security mindset. While expressly acknowledging that PIA may be performed by an organisation "as an independent function",[44] the standard mostly views PIA *as part of* the information security management system ('ISMS') of an organisation.[45] Similarly, most of the examples of privacy risks and respective mitigation measures listed in the standard, are related to information security. Illustrations of privacy risks are typically "data breaches", such as "unauthorised access to PII (loss of confidentiality), unauthorised modification of the PII (loss of integrity), loss, theft or unauthorised removal of the PII (loss of availability)", although other examples are also provided, such as "failure to consider the rights of the PII principal (e.g. loss of the right of access)".[46] Similarly, illustrations of criteria for evaluating the "significance of the privacy risks" are "vulnerabilities of the supporting assets and capabilities of the risk sources to exploit the vulnerabilities".[47]

The GDPR's take on the notion of risk is distinct from its information security counterpart, as also recognised by WP29 in its Guidelines on DPIA. The latter underlines that, "conversely [to] risk management in other fields (*e.g. information security*) […] focused on the organisation, the GDPR] takes *their* perspective [n.b.: of data subjects]" (emphasis added) (Article 29 Working Party, 2017, p. 17). The misalignment between ISO/IEC 29134 and the GDPR is twofold. First, a focus on security alone falls short of ensuring that personal data are indeed protected in compliance with the law as the GDPR's notion of risk to rights and freedoms is significantly *broader* than the risk's understanding in information security. Second, a focus on information security *within the meaning of* the ISMS of an organisation would inherently mainly focus on the organisation, rather than on data subjects, as WP29 warned against. The contentious issue of *whose perspective* is being taken into account in the DPIA, or in other words 'whose risks' are being managed is further discussed in the remainder of this section.

Risks to Rights and Freedoms of Natural Persons vs. Privacy Risks

The GDPR is preoccupied with the risk to the rights and freedoms of natural persons posed by the processing of personal data. This rights-based focus of the notion of 'risk' in the GDPR links to the fundamental right's understanding of personal data protection in the EU – manifested with the recognition of a standalone right to the protection of personal data in the EU Charter of Fundamental Rights[48] and to the objective of the GDPR to provide a high level of protection of (all) fundamental rights (Clifford, 2019, pp. 122–140). Recital 75 explains that the risk to the rights and freedoms of individuals can be "of varying likelihood and severity" and "may result from personal data processing which could lead to physical, material or non-material damage", including situations where the processing "gives rise to discrimination, financial loss, damage to the reputation, loss of confidentiality of personal data protected by professional secrecy, any other significant economic or social disadvantage; where data subjects might be deprived of their rights and freedoms or prevented from exercising control over their personal data; where personal data of vulnerable natural persons, in particular of children, are processed; or where processing involves a large amount of personal data and affects a large number of data subjects." WP29 stressed that, while concerning "primarily the rights to data protection and privacy[,] other fundamental rights may also [be] involve[d], such as freedom of speech, freedom of thought, freedom of movement, prohibition of discrimination, right to liberty, conscience and religion" (Article 29 Working Party, 2014, p. 4).

In contrast, ISO/IEC 29134 standard narrows down the scope of the impact assessment to privacy entitlements, with the term 'privacy' not being specifically defined in the ISO ecosystem. As from the introduction, ISO/IEC 29134 standard clarifies that a PIA is understood as "an instrument for assessing the potential impacts on privacy of a process, information system, programme, software module, device or other initiative which processes [PII]" (emphasis added).[49] When substantiating what should be understood by "harm to users of the product, service or system", as part of the components to define risk criteria, the standard broadly refers to "physical, financial, reputational harm, embarrassment and invasion of domestic life [and, further,] different types of privacy such as bodily privacy, location and space privacy, behavioural privacy, privacy of communications, privacy of data and image, privacy of thoughts and feelings and privacy of associations".[50] Such list of harms sounds both extensive and narrow. *Extensive*, since it refers to any kinds of "harm" ("physical, financial, reputational", etc.), *Narrow*, because the focus is obviously placed on privacy and there is not explicit reference to other fundamental rights and freedoms *per se*. The two last "privacy of", namely "privacy of thoughts and feelings and privacy of associations", also seem to *broaden* the scope of what is commonly understood as privacy, not only to various sub-categories of "privacy harms" as a literal reading of the text would suggest, but also, supposedly, to the instrumental role that privacy plays with respect to other rights and freedoms of individuals. One can only assume that this unusual wording constitutes an attempt to bridge the gap between the narrow approach of ISO based on privacy – and even mostly on information security –, and the broad approach of the GDPR, based on a non-exhaustive list of rights and freedoms. It is also complemented by a catch-all reference to "legal and regulatory requirements [...]".

The focus on sole *harm* is, again, narrower than the GDPR approach. WP29 expressly clarified that "the risks-based approach goes beyond a narrow 'harm-based-approach' that concentrates only on damage and should take into consideration every potential as well as actual adverse effect, assessed on a very wide scale ranging from an impact on the person concerned by the processing in question to a general societal impact (e.g. loss of social trust)" (Article 29 Working Party, 2014, p. 4).

Risk Quantification Under ISO's Approach vs. Unquantifiable Risks to Rights

The GDPR's risks-based approach calls for determining the likelihood and severity of the risk to the rights and freedoms of individuals by reference to the nature, scope, context and purposes of the processing.[51] At the same time, a crucial part of ISO/IEC 29134 methodology on performing a PIA relates to the assessment of privacy risk. According to the standard, the risk must be identified (step 1), analysed (step 2) and evaluated (step 3) – the ultimate objective being to mitigate that risk.[52] As part of this process organisations are called to evaluate both the level of impact and the likelihood of the risk. This risk analysis "can be qualitative, semi-quantitative or quantitative, or a combination of these, depending on the circumstances".[53] It is explained that a qualitative analysis is usually first used to shed light on major risks and allows to "obtain a *general* indication of the level of risk" yet "*when possible and appropriate* [organisations] should also undertake more *specific* and *quantitative* analysis of the risk" (emphasis added): risk estimation entails "assigning values to the potential consequences (level of impact) and the threats (likelihood) of a risk".[54]

This is arguably a call to *quantify* privacy risk, which is supported by Annex A, an informative annex setting forth "example scales and criteria for estimating the impact and likelihood" that any organisation should take into consideration when performing risk analysis. The *level of impact* can be classed as Negligible (scale 1), Limited (scale 2), Significant (scale 3) and Maximum (scale 4) based on the consequences on the individual.[55] For instance, the level of impact is 'Limited' if individuals "may encounter significant consequences, which they should be able to overcome despite a few difficulties (extra costs, denial of access to business services, fear, lack of understanding, stress, minor physical ailments, etc.)".[56] Examples of consequences that would render the impact 'Significant' include "misappropriation of funds", "blacklisting by banks", "loss of employment" and "worsening of state of health"; 'Maximum' entails "financial distress such as unserviceable debt or inability to work, long-term psychological or physical ailments, death".[57] The same scales (Negligible – Limited – Significant – Maximum) apply when it comes to classifying the risk *likelihood*. Annex A refers to the "likelihood of each threat being exploited", which should be estimated by considering "the vulnerabilities of the supporting assets and the capabilities of risk sources to exploit them". For instance, the likelihood is 'Negligible' when it comes to the "theft of paper documents stored in a room protected by a badge reader *and* access code", but would become 'Maximum' when the said papers are simply stored at an organisation's lobby.[58] Selecting the value of the level of impact and the value of likelihood should enable organisations to create a privacy risk map and place both values into a matrix.[59]

Such an approach, that strives to meaningfully quantify privacy risks, comes with inherent limitations. One may be able to quantify a system's vulnerabilities, the likelihood of external attacks and certain consequences of a data breach, e.g. as regards the number of individuals affected and the sensitivity of the personal information at stake. It is much more difficult – if not impossible – to quantify potential harms on 'rights and freedoms', which are of course intangible. Moreover, in the pursue of quantification, ISO's approach (strictly) focuses on possible consequences for the *individual* data subjects, lacking a *collective* dimension. Yet in the GDPR understanding, while the holders of the right to data protection are individuals, data protection must also "be considered in relation to its functions in society" meaning that it should be contrasted and balanced against other rights and interests in a proportionate manner. The reference in the GDPR and in particular in the DPIA provisions on "risks to the rights and freedoms of natural persons" is wide enough to call for assessing the impact of a processing operation on both a specific individual, e.g. in case sensitive information about him or her would be compromised, but also individuals as a whole, e.g. in case cameras deployed in public spaces would cultivate a – justifiable or unjustifiable – fear of surveillance.

Artificial Intelligence and many other disruptive technologies keep emerging and may gradually unfold expected and unexpected impacts. In this era of constant development, uncertainty and experimentation, it is important that risk assessments are preoccupied not only with system security and a list of concretely identified reputational or financial consequences for individuals, which are of course important considerations. They should equally address 'high-level' impacts and risks to rights, which can be nebulous and *where a quantification logic cannot fit*. It is data processing's potential – and often unintentional and hidden – discriminatory biases, the potential for chilling effects on democracy and even ethical considerations on whether and how a certain technology will affect life at work, at the city, human behaviour and human interaction that seem closer to the requirement to assess 'risks to rights and freedoms' in a comprehensive manner. In *Digital Rights Ireland*, the Court of Justice of the European Union ('CJEU') annulled a piece of legislation requiring telecommunication operators to retain traffic data of customers considering among other things that "the fact that data are retained and subsequently used without the subscriber or registered user being informed is likely to generate in the minds of the persons concerned the feeling that their private lives are the subject of constant surveillance" (*Digital*

Rights Ireland, 2014, para. 37). Concerned with the (potential and definitely uncertain) creation of a 'chilling effect' the court's and supervisory authorities' reasoning was high level, admittedly lacking evidence or any attempt to quantify the threat's impact or likelihood.[60] Case law[61] and guidelines on necessity (EDPS, 2017) and proportionality (EDPS, 2019) of measures entailing the processing of personal data can be valuable to include in the risk assessment process, since high-level risks to rights are implicitly assessed in the fair balance exercise (advantages/disadvantages) undertaken by legislators, courts and supervisory authorities. An approach focused on risks quantification risks to overshadow such qualitative assessments.

An Exclusive Focus on Risks to Individuals vs Risks to Organisations

ISO/IEC 29134 notes that "the organisation's management should examine separately privacy risks from a PII principals [data subject]'s point of view and privacy risks from the organisation's point of view".[62] Seemingly unclear at first read, this sentence can be understood as suggesting that an organisation conducting a PIA, should analyse the risks to data subjects independently from the specific risks of the organisation therein (e.g. in terms of reputation). Such interpretation is supported by informative Annex A, which estimates the level of impact of privacy threats from the perspective of "PII principals".[63]

Such independence of the analysis of risks to data subjects constitutes a prerequisite for the PIA to comply with the requirements of the GDPR, which obviously disregards the risks *for the controller* therein, with its focus being exclusively placed on the risks to the rights and freedoms of natural persons". WP29 already clarified that "the legitimate interest pursed by the controller or a third party *is not relevant* to the *assessment* of the risks for the data subjects" (emphasis added) (Article 29 Working Party, 2014). While the DPIA shall include the purposes of the processing,[64] such item should not be confused with the *identification of risks* (of data subjects), but rather plays a role in the analysis of the necessity and proportionality of the envisaged data processing activities.[65]

Yet, ISO/IEC 29134 then brings together risks incurred by both individuals and controllers, when describing what the "definition of the risk criteria" should be based on, namely "stakeholder expectations and perceptions, and negative consequences for goodwill and reputation".[66] While the former seems to point to expectations of data subjects, the latter obviously links it to risks to the organisation. Similarly, the same list includes "the strategic value of the information process" and "the present value and future opportunity made by the information process, aka 'strategic value'". Both seem to point to the same item, which unquestionably refers to interests of the organisation (with respect to the data processing) rather than to these of individuals. The concrete impact arises at the latter stage of "privacy risk evaluation", which "involve[s] prioritization of privacy risks, based on the severity of privacy impact on PII principals as well as the overall impact to the organisation".[67] On this basis, nothing seems to prevent the "organisation" from counter-balancing the severity of risks to individuals with a potential overall positive impact on itself or, alternatively, to prioritise "privacy risks" incurred to the organisation over these incurred by individuals (or 'PII principals'). The result of the "relative prioritisation of privacy risks" is the prioritisation in the "allocation of resources for their treatment".

The analysis conducted in this section displays significant misalignments between the two regulatory systems, with a potential impact on the protection of rights and freedoms of individuals as a result. Such conclusion may sound surprising, given the willingness of both ISO and WP29 to leverage ISO risk management tools to support operationalisation of GDPR obligations with respect to DPIAs. The following section sets up to critically explain this situation.

PART III: CRITICAL REFLECTIONS ON THE MISALIGNMENTS: WHO IS TO BLAME?

In order to critically explain the misalignment, the present section first looks at ISO and its ecosystem. It then turns to the GDPR environment, with respect, first, to its risks-to-rights-approach and, second, to the role played by supervisory authorities therein.

ISO as an Ecosystem with Strong Information Security Roots

Part of the above-mentioned misalignments can be attributed to the fact that – as it is similarly the case for legislation developed in a broader regulatory framework – ISO/IEC 29134 does not operate in a vacuum. Rather, ISO standards must be interpreted in light of the ecosystem they fit in. Figure 2 introduces the most relevant ISO standards in the field of privacy and highlights some of the dependencies between those documents. In that sense, ISO/IEC 29134 is anchored into a broader framework that comes with its own semantic and conceptual background. This already appears from the Introduction, where the document highlights that "controls deemed necessary to treat the risks identified during the privacy impact analysis process may be derived from multiple sets of controls, including ISO/IEC 27002 (for security controls) and ISO/IEC 29151 (for PII protection controls) or comparable national standards".[68] In turn, this fragmented ecosystem – where every situation is subject to a specific set of documents cross-referencing one another – raises several issues.

The first issue is linked to ISO's longstanding focus on information security rather than privacy, or at least, not on privacy and data protection as interpreted under EU law. As explained above, the notion of 'risk' under the GDPR is drastically different from its ISO counterpart. This impacts not only the

Figure 2. Overview of the privacy-related ISO standards

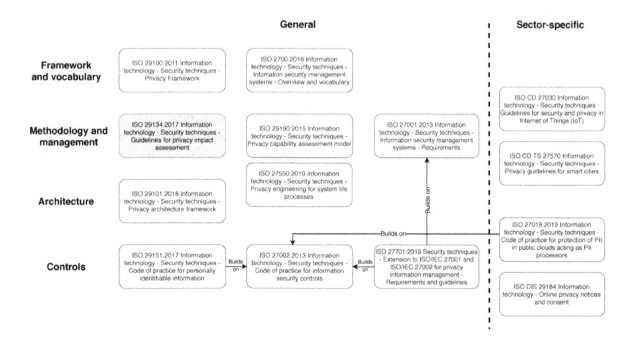

methodology deployed to identify risks and assess their likelihood and severity, but also the controls that are suggested to efficiently mitigate them. While the list of examples of privacy risks provided in ISO/IEC 29134 was described above as of limited relevance when it comes to capturing all the risks to data subjects' rights and freedoms, ISO/IEC 29134 laconically evacuates that dimension in a note stating that "those possibilities of non-implementation or bad implementation of fundamental rights could only be checked and improved". Quite ironically, however, the same note also concludes that "not implementing those fundamental rights is not an option".[69] When it comes to mitigating those risks, ISO/IEC 29134 refers to the measures substantiating the principles detailed in ISO/IEC 29100 as well as to other sets of controls "defined in recognized international standards or issued by recognized institutions".[70] In doing so, it goes back to its security roots and explicitly references ISO/IEC 27001,[71] ISO/IEC 27002[72] and ISO/IEC 29154.[73] The anchoring of ISO/IEC 29134 in ISO ISMS ecosystem also explains its difficulty in departing from an organisation-focused approach to risks. Coupled with that, such cross-references to standards grounded in information security are symptomatic of the fact that ISO is stepping slightly out its comfort zone when trying to address fundamental rights issues while continuing to use essentially its old toolbox. This being said, ISO's extensive legacy in ISMS is also an unprecedented advantage when it comes to developing a methodology to substantiate the shift towards Data Protection by Design and accountability. This, thanks to years of expertise in the field of risks identification, quantification and mitigation. In other words, the ecosystem in which ISO/IEC 29134 evolves is both a *forte* and a limiting factor.

The second issue – more pragmatic and deriving directly from the first – has to do with the number of documents one has to purchase in order to benefit from a comprehensive risks management framework. Figure 2 is, in that sense, self-explanatory. The repeated mentions, in ISO/IEC 29134, that the conduct of a PIA does not require the setting up of an ISMS, as identified in the gap analysis conducted in the previous section, sounds thus rather like a disclaimer, as the methodology is not likely to yield much results *on its own*. The methodological framework offered by ISO/IEC 29134 has indeed to be supplemented with the appropriate controls and mitigation strategies detailed in other standards. This can be illustrated with the recent ISO/IEC 27701 standard which, while "designed to permit the addition of sector specific requirements without the need to develop a new Management System" – is nonetheless positioned as an extension to ISO/IEC 27001 and ISO 27002 and entails a dependency to the 27xxx family of standards dealing with ISO's ISMS (*ISO/IEC 27701 Security Techniques — Extension to ISO/IEC 27001 and ISO/IEC 27002 for Privacy Information Management — Requirements and Guidelines*, 2019). Annexes E (Mapping to ISO/IEC 27018 and ISO/IEC 29151) and F (How to apply ISO/IEC 27701 to ISO/IEC 27001 and ISO/IEC 27002) are particularly indicative of the need to articulate various documents.

The fact that ISO is willing to enter the privacy market is not a problem in itself. From the perspective of using ISO/IEC 29134 to demonstrate compliance with EU data protection law, the challenge rather arises from the false impression of alignment given to the standard users. While merely extending or reusing ISMS *mutatis mutandis* to DPIAs within the meaning of the GDPR sounds daunting without *substantial methodological changes*, it does not mean that ISO methods have no merit for GDPR compliance. ISO/IEC 29134 should be designed and used for what it can really provide rather than be subtly re-branded as a DPIA methodology. This implies to recalibrate its scope and ambit throughout the whole standard. Failure to do so essentially fails to deliver a standard's expected outcome, namely legal certainty for regulatees.

GDPR as a Principles- and Risks-Based Law: Are the Risks of the 'Risk to Rights' Approach Coming True?

Several authors have voiced concerns on the effectiveness of GDPR's risks-based approach. In a thorough analysis of the notion of 'risk to a right', van Dijk et al. pointed to the importance of introducing legal insights in DPIAs when assessing risk, while risk can take various forms (pecuniary, social, moral, psychological and physical). Although risk assessment methodologies are not legal *per se*, one should remember that case law on privacy and data protection – to which we would add case law on fundamental rights more broadly – has for long dealt with such issues (van Dijk et al., 2016, pp. 299–303). A mere IT systems-engineering approach to risk assessment would indeed fail to meet the GDPR requirements. The notion of risk as regulatory yardstick for the application of rights of data subjects was already found to come with a shift from "the nature of rights" to a quantitative risks-based approach which is becoming overwhelming (van Dijk et al., 2016, pp. 292–293). Such shift towards assessing the likelihood of occurrence of certain circumstances constitutes a topic of legal concern (Macenaite, 2017). It appears indeed simpler for an organisation "to articulate a number of more measurable 'harms' concerning data security breaches" than to reflect on the fundamental rights that might be impacted from the processing and assess proportionality – as eloquently put by Quelle "[i]t is a challenge to operationalise the notion of risk in the GDPR while doing justice to its broad meaning" (Quelle, 2018, p. 505). The study of ISO/IEC 29134 in this Chapter arguably proves that the scholars' criticisms on the GDPR's risks-based approach, or rather on the risks inherent to the risks-based approach, were right.

An Informal Delegation of Power from Supervisory Authorities to ISO?

WP29 Guidelines on DPIAs were an opportunity to clarify the 'risk to rights' approach and the way it can be operationalised through DPIAs. Yet, the Guidelines do not further clarify how the *nature* of rights and freedoms of individuals should impact the conduct of a DPIA. Additionally, when laying down the criteria for an "acceptable DPIA", Annex 2 refers to the management of "risks to the rights and freedoms of data subjects". However, the examples of risks listed in the annex all pertain to information security, namely "illegitimate access, undesired modification, and disappearance of data", as already observed by (Quelle, 2018, p. 506).

The reference to ISO/IEC 29134 – and to ISO standards more generally – in the DPIA Guidelines brings further confusion. As mentioned above, "International standards", namely ISO 31000:2009 on risk management and "ISO/IEC 29134 (project)" are referred to in the introduction of the Guidelines as part of the building blocks on which the Guidelines are based.[74] WP29 indeed considers that the components of the DPIA, as outlined in Recital 90 of the GDPR, partially overlap with the scope of ISO 31000. ISO/IEC 29134 is also referred to in Annex 1 of the Guidelines ("Examples of existing EU DPIA frameworks") as an "international standard [that] will provide guidelines for methodologies used for carrying out a DPIA". Such references beg a number of questions. The first relates to their legal value: Should such references be interpreted as an endorsement by the WP29 (now EDPB) – which is in fact the highest EU administrative authority in charge of data protection enforcement – of the standard on which regulatees could thus legitimately rely? While it seems to be the case, the fact that the standard was still in development at the time, and hence not officially adopted nor published, raises the question of whether and how WP29 has conducted a due diligence assessment of its alignment with GDPR requirements, or whether the endorsement has rather been a blank cheque. Indeed, the gap analysis between the GDPR's risks-based approach and ISO/IEC 29134 in this Chapter shows misalignments, which have the potential to be detrimental to the protection of rights and freedoms of individuals with respect to the processing of their personal data.

The second question relates to what could constitute, in the authors' view, an unintended circumvention of the GDPR approach and spirit with respect to co-regulation. As it stands, the reference to ISO/IEC 29134 standard in the Guidelines appears to amount to a delegation of regulatory authority to a private body, without the involvement of a *public* regulator, which, as outlined in Part I on the co-regulatory system of soft law instruments envisaged in the GDPR, is an important feature of the latter's certification/codes of conduct ecosystem. Indeed, it should be stressed that ISO/IEC 29134 standard is not meant to be certifiable within the GDPR, as it is an extra-GDPR instrument that has not been formally approved by a supervisory authority as required by Articles 42 and 43. Yet, it is well expected that the standard may be used in practice as a methodology to conduct DPIAs, practically serving as means to demonstrate compliance –or at least, compliance best-efforts- with GDPR obligations. It should be recalled that GDPR essentially mandates certification criteria to be formally adopted by supervisory authority(ies) and made publicly available.[75] In contrast, ISO/IEC 29134 standard is only available upon payment of a fee. The latter points to a third problem related to the ISO ecosystem. As discussed above, ISO/IEC 29134 is not a standalone product but implies the use of other related ISO standards. Endorsing ISO/IEC 29134 essentially opens the door to the broader ISO privacy ecosystem, as purchasing only ISO/IEC 29134 standard would be of limited value. There is however no sign that WP29 took these circumstances into account when endorsing it in the Guidelines, in terms of the extent of such endorsement.

CONCLUSION

With the adoption of the GDPR, the EU prides itself on the most comprehensive legal framework on the protection of personal data in the world. The GDPR is an omnibus regulation of personal data processing aimed at protecting fundamental rights of individuals, and particularly data protection and privacy. It mandates data controllers to operationalise general principles like fairness, lawfulness, proportionality, giving due regard to the risks to the rights and freedoms of individuals that the data processing activities entail. Though it has enriched the GDPR with flexibility and sustainability, reliance on principles and risks may also have an impact on legal certainty, to the detriment of regulatees. Well-aware of this situation, the EU legislator designed various soft law and co-regulatory mechanisms that may bridge the gap between principles and their operationalisation, such as guidance from supervisory authorities and certification as means for regulatees to demonstrate compliance. Although efforts for the establishment of GDPR soft-law tools so far undertaken should be praised, they alone do not meet regulated entities' need for legal certainty.

In particular, the new obligation for controllers to conduct DPIAs in order to assess and mitigate risks to rights and freedoms of individuals begs many questions as to how such assessments should be carried in practice, given that the GDPR itself only provides high-level requirements without attempting to define risks or provide a methodology for this assessment. WP29 has attempted to answer some of these questions in its DPIA Guidelines of 2017, where it notably referred to the (at the time still up-coming) ISO/IEC 29134 as a – relevant – methodology to conduct DPIAs. On its part, ISO seems to be willing to enter the privacy standards business, and ISO/IEC 29134 is obviously designed as a means for companies to demonstrate compliance with the obligation to conduct a DPIA, with the advantage to rely on ISO reputation and track-record in risk management.

In light of the above, the Chapter sought to put ISO/IEC 29134 to the GDPR test. The analysis identified several misalignments, likely to have a detrimental impact on the rights and freedoms of individuals, should it be used as a methodology to conduct DPIAs within the meaning of the GDPR. ISO/IEC 29134 has a narrow 'privacy' – and even ISMS – mindset, which fails to truly recognise the risks to rights and freedoms of individuals. Moreover, the standard aims to quantify risk, viewed as the likelihood of 'harm' to individuals, which is a reductionist understanding of the DPIAs under the GDPR focused on 'risks to rights'. The ISMS pattern of the standard may also explain the 'organisation-angle' adopted throughout the standard, which is likely to clash with the DPIA's purpose to solely assess the risks to individuals, independently from the risks that may be occurred by the controller.

To understand the causes for the misalignments between ISO/IEC 29134 and the GDPR requirements, the Chapter critically looked at both sides, namely the ISO ecosystem on the one hand, and the GDPR environment on the other. The ISO fragmented ecosystem was found to explain the ISMS path dependency and the challenge for ISO to genuinely embrace a GDPR mindset. The problem does not arise from the narrow privacy and ISMS approach of ISO to PIA as such, but rather from the prospect to apply such a methodology to DPIAs *without the substantial methodological changes required to do so*. In the authors' view, the blame should however mostly be borne on the GDPR side. The 'risk to rights' approach at the core of the obligation to conduct DPIAs is a challenging one, and supervisory authorities have not yet provided controllers with the necessary guidance as to how to meaningfully integrate a rights-based assessment in DPIA methodologies. The reference to ISO/IEC 29134 in the Guidelines of WP29 on DPIAs was certainly aimed to fill that gap. However, it rather looks like a short-sighted blank cheque given to a private standards body, taking EU data protection regulation – rooted in a fundamental rights tradition- back to a narrow information security understanding. A narrow approach that fails to consider rights and freedoms may fail to meet the most important challenge of regulating data processing: tackling the uncertain impact of disruptive technologies on our lives, thoughts, cities and societies.

Against this backdrop, regulators – more specifically supervisory authorities – would be well-advised to be more careful when referring to private initiatives for compliance with GDPR obligations in their soft law documents. With respect to the methodology for conducting DPIAs, the misalignment of ISO/IEC 29134 standard should not be viewed as a deadlock, but should rather invite practitioners, scholars and regulators alike to further investigate avenues for elaborating methodologies in an interdisciplinary manner. This chapter calls into question the (implicit) assumption that there should be a 'one-size-fits-all' methodology for conducting DPIAs. Rather, there could be a variety of methodologies depending on the sectors and categories of data and data processing purposes, but also on the amount of affected individuals and on the nature of rights and freedoms at stake. As scholars have already highlighted, DPIAs within the meaning of the GDPR should be inclusive vis-à-vis data subjects (Kloza et al., 2017). Research should thus further investigate how best to have data subjects participating in DPIAs – including from a methodology perspective - as it could serve to better account for risks to their social and collective rights and freedoms, this area being yet under-researched (Mantelero, 2016, 2019). Methodologies entailing data subjects' participation in the DPIA exercise could constitute a valid alternative where risks to rights and freedoms are not easily quantifiable.

While, as illustrated throughout this chapter, ISO/IEC 29134 is no silver bullet, one should nonetheless acknowledge its added value in the current data protection landscape. In that sense, it allows controllers and processors – provided that they are willing to bear the costs associated with such an exercise – to initiate their compliance journey on the basis of an integrated set of guidance documents that nicely complements the efforts deployed by national supervisory authorities. Ultimately, this also paves the way for the alignment of software engineering and legal practices, a goal that has been – and will remain for the next few years – one of the cornerstones of the data protection reform.

ACKNOWELDGEMENT

This research was supported by the Research Association Flanders [SPECTRE project- FWO reference number S006318N] and the KU Leuven [PRiSE project – project number C24/17/005]. The authors would like to thank Eric Lachaud, Tilburg University, for the insightful discussions on the GDPR certification schemes and helpful comments on an earlier draft version. All errors remain solely the authors' responsibility.

REFERENCES

Allen, J. P. (2014). Rules- or Principles-Based Regulation—Factors for Choosing the Best Language Strategy. *Canadian Business Law Journal*, *56*(3), 375–394.

Article 29 Working Party. (2009). *Joint contribution to the Consultation of the European Commission on the legal framework for the fundamental right to protection of personal data.* https://ec.europa.eu/justice/article-29/documentation/opinion-recommendation/files/2009/wp168_en.pdf

Article 29 Working Party. (2013). *Statement of the Working Party on current discussions regarding the data protection reform package.* https://ec.europa.eu/justice/article-29/documentation/other-document/files/2013/20130227_statement_dp_reform_package_en.pdf

Article 29 Working Party. (2014). *Statement on the role of a risk-based approach in data protection legal frameworks, 14/EN WP 218.*

Article 29 Working Party. (2017). *Guidelines on Data Protection Impact Assessment (DPIA) and determining whether processing is "likely to result in a high risk" for the purposes of Regulation 2016/679—17/EN WP 248 rev.01.*

Clifford, D. (2019). The legal limits to the monetisation of online emotions. KU Leuven, Faculty of Law.

Clifford, D., & Ausloos, J. (2018). Data Protection and the Role of Fairness. *Yearbook of European Law*, *37*, 130–187. doi:10.1093/yel/yey004

Collingridge, D. (1981). *The Social Control of Technology.* Palgrave Macmillan.

Council of Europe. (1981). *Convention for the Protection of Individuals with regard to Automatic Processing of Personal Data.* https://www.coe.int/en/web/conventions/full-list/-/conventions/treaty/108/signatures

Decker, C. (2018). *Goals-based and rules-based approaches to regulation.* BEIS Research Paper Number 8, 67.

DIGITALEUROPE. (2019). *Response to public consultation on draft EDPB Guidelines on codes of conduct and monitoring bodies.* https://www.digitaleurope.org/resources/response-to-public-consultation-on-draft-edpb-guidelines-on-codes-of-conduct-and-monitoring-bodies/

Downes, L. (2009). *The Laws of Disruption: Harnessing the New Forces That Govern Life and Business in the Digital Age.* Basic Books.

EDPB. (2019a). *Guidelines 1/2018 on certification and identifying certification criteria in accordance with Articles 42 and 43 of the Regulation Version 3.0.* https://edpb.europa.eu/our-work-tools/public-consultations/2019/guidelines-12018-certification-and-identifying_en

EDPB. (2019b). Guidelines 1/2019 on Codes of Conduct and Monitoring Bodies under. *Regulation, 2016*(67). https://edpb.europa.eu/our-work-tools/our-documents/guidelines/guidelines-12019-codes-conduct-and-monitoring-bodies-under_en

EDPS. (2017). *Assessing the necessity of measures that limit the fundamental right to the protection of personal data: A Toolkit.* https://edps.europa.eu/sites/edp/files/publication/17-06-01_necessity_toolkit_final_en.pdf

EDPS. (2019). *Assessing the proportionality of measures that limit the fundamental rights to privacy and to the protection of personal data.* https://edps.europa.eu/sites/edp/files/publication/19-12-19_edps_proportionality_guidelines2_en.pdf

Europe, I. (2019). Response to the EDPB's draft-guidelines on Codes of Conduct & Monitoring Bodies, Position Paper referring to Guidelines 1/2009 on Codes of Conduct & Monitoring Bodies under. *Regulation, 20116*(679). https://www.insuranceeurope.eu/sites/default/files/attachments/Response%20to%20EDPB%20draft-guidelines%20on%20codes%20of%20conduct%20%26%20monitoring%20bodies.pdf

European Court of Human Rights. (2019). *Guide on Article 8 of the European Convention on Human Rights.* https://www.echr.coe.int/Documents/Guide_Art_8_ENG.pdf

Fenwick, M., Kaal, W. A., & Vermeulen, E. P. M. (2016). Regulation Tomorrow: What Happens When Technology Is Faster Than the Law? *American University Business Law Review, 6*(3). doi:10.2139srn.2834531

Genç, Ö. (2019, February 5). Notes on Artificial Intelligence (AI), Machine Learning (ML) and Deep Learning (DL)…. *Medium.* https://towardsdatascience.com/notes-on-artificial-intelligence-ai-machine-learning-ml-and-deep-learning-dl-for-56e51a2071c2

Higgins, W., & Hallström, K. T. (2007). Standardization, Globalization and Rationalities of Government. *Organization, 14*(5), 685–704. doi:10.1177/1350508407080309

High-level Expert Group on Artificial Intelligence (AI HLEG). (2019). Ethics Guidelines for Trustworthy AI.

ISO/IEC 27701 Security techniques—Extension to ISO/IEC 27001 and ISO/IEC 27002 for privacy information management—Requirements and guidelines, (2019). https://www.iso.org/standard/71670.html

ISO/IEC 29134 Information technology—Security techniques—Guidelines for privacy impact assessment, (2017). https://www.iso.org/standard/62289.html

Kamara, I. (2017). Co-regulation in EU personal data protection: The case of technical standards and the privacy by design standardisation "mandate.". *European Journal of Law and Technology*, *8*(1). http://ejlt.org/article/view/545

Kamara, I., & De Hert, P. (2018). Data Protection Certification in the EU: Possibilities, Actors and Building Blocks in a Reformed Landscape. In R. Rodrigues & V. Papakonstantinou (Eds.), Privacy and Data Protection Seals (pp. 7–34). T.M.C. Asser Press. doi:10.1007/978-94-6265-228-6_2

Kloza, D., Van Dijk, N., Gellert, R. M., Borocz, I. M., Tanas, A., Mantovani, E., & Quinn, P. (2017). *Data protection impact assessments in the European Union: Complementing the new legal framework towards a more robust protection of individuals*. Brussels Laboratory for Data Protection & Privacy Impact Assessments Policy Brief.

Kokott, J., & Sobotta, C. (2013). The distinction between privacy and data protection in the jurisprudence of the CJEU and the ECtHR. *International Data Privacy Law*, *3*(4), 222–228. doi:10.1093/idpl/ipt017

Lachaud, E. (2016). Why the certification process defined in the General Data Protection Regulation cannot be successful. *Computer Law & Security Review*, *32*(6), 814–826. doi:10.1016/j.clsr.2016.07.001

Lachaud, E. (2018). The General Data Protection Regulation and the rise of certification as a regulatory instrument. *Computer Law & Security Review*, *34*(2), 244–256. doi:10.1016/j.clsr.2017.09.002

Lodge & Wegrich. (2012). *Managing Regulation: Regulatory Analysis, Politics and Policy* (1st ed.). Palgrave Macmillan.

Lynskey, O. (2015). *The Foundations of EU Data Protection Law*. Oxford University Press.

Macenaite, M. (2017). The "Riskification" of European Data Protection Law through a two-fold Shift. *European Journal of Risk Regulation*, *8*(3), 506–540. doi:10.1017/err.2017.40

Mantelero, A. (2016). Personal data for decisional purposes in the age of analytics: From an individual to a collective dimension of data protection. *Computer Law & Security Review*, *32*(2), 238–255. doi:10.1016/j.clsr.2016.01.014

Mantelero, A. (2019). Comment to Articles 35 and 36. In GDPR Commentary. Edward Elgar Publishing.

Marchant, G. E. (2011). The Growing Gap Between Emerging Technologies and the Law. In G. E. Marchant, B. R. Allenby, & J. R. Herkert (Eds.), *The Growing Gap Between Emerging Technologies and Legal-Ethical Oversight* (Vol. 7, pp. 19–33). Springer Netherlands; doi:10.1007/978-94-007-1356-7_2

Purtova, N. (2018). The law of everything. Broad concept of personal data and future of EU data protection law. *Law, Innovation and Technology*, *10*(1), 40–81. doi:10.1080/17579961.2018.1452176

Quelle, C. (2018). Enhancing Compliance under the General Data Protection Regulation: The Risky Upshot of the Accountability- and Risk-based Approach. *European Journal of Risk Regulation*, *9*(3), 502–526. doi:10.1017/err.2018.47

Regulation (EU) 2016/679 of the European Parliament and of the Council of 27 April 2016 on the protection of natural persons with regard to the processing of personal data and on the free movement of such data, and repealing Directive 95/46/EC, OJ L 119/1, European Parliament, Council (2016). https://eur-lex.europa.eu/eli/reg/2016/679/oj

Renaud, K., Flowerday, S., Warkentin, M., Cockshott, P., & Orgeron, C. (2018). Is the responsibilization of the cyber security risk reasonable and judicious? - ScienceDirect. *Computers & Security*, *78*, 198–211. doi:10.1016/j.cose.2018.06.006

Shamir, R. (2008). The age of responsibilization: On market-embedded morality. *Economy and Society*, *37*(1), 1–19. doi:10.1080/03085140701760833

Solove, D. (2015, November 13). *The Growing Problems with the Sectoral Approach to Privacy Law*. https://teachprivacy.com/problems-sectoral-approach-privacy-law/

Thierer, A. (2018, August 16). The Pacing Problem, the Collingridge Dilemma & Technological Determinism. *Technology Liberation Front*. https://techliberation.com/2018/08/16/the-pacing-problem-the-collingridge-dilemma-technological-determinism/

Turner, J. (2018). *Robot rules*. Springer Berlin Heidelberg.

van Alsenoy, B. (2019). *Data Protection Law in the EU: Roles, Responsibilities and Liability*. Intersentia. doi:10.1017/9781780688459

van Dijk, N., Gellert, R., & Rommetveit, K. (2016). A risk to a right? Beyond data protection risk assessments. *Computer Law & Security Review*, *32*(2), 286–306. doi:10.1016/j.clsr.2015.12.017

Wirth, D. (2009). The International Organization for Standardization: Private Voluntary Standards as Swords and Shields. *Boston College Environmental Affairs Law Review. Boston College. Law School*, *36*(1), 79.

Zapatero Gómez, V. (2019). A Soft Law. In V. Zapatero Gómez (Ed.), *The Art of Legislating* (pp. 83–100). Springer International Publishing. doi:10.1007/978-3-030-23388-4_6

ENDNOTES

[1] Regulation (EU) 2016/679 of the European Parliament and of the Council of 27 April 2016 on the protection of natural persons with regard to the processing of personal data and on the free movement of such data, and repealing Directive 95/46/EC, OJ L 119/1 (*GDPR*, 2016).

[2] Article 29 Data Protection Working Party was an advisory body created by (*Directive 95/46/EC*, 1995) (no longer in force). It comprises of representatives of national supervisory authorities. Since the entry into force of the GDPR it has been replaced by the European Data Protection Board.

[3] The US for instance has followed a sectoral approach by adopting various federal and state laws directed to specific industry sectors (*e.g.* financial services, telecommunications) or protective of particular types of data and data subjects (*e.g.* Children's Online Privacy Protection Act – COPPA, Health Information Portability and Accountability Act –HIPAA). While the aim is to offer more nuanced regulation focusing on particular challenges faced in a given sector, the sectoral approach

has been met with criticism from the industry itself for leaving gaps of protection or for making enterprises subject to several overlapping laws (Solove, 2015).

4   To be accurate, the GDPR follows a hybrid approach as some of the obligations are fairly clear-cut and prescriptive. Art. 28 and 30, which respectively require a contract to ground the controller-processor relationship and the keeping of records of processing activities, and specify the contracts' and records' contents, are notable examples of prescriptive provisions. At the same time though, the core of the GDPR is principles-based.

5   Convention for the Protection of Individuals with regard to Automatic Processing of Personal Data, ETS No 108, 1987 (*Convention No. 108*, 1981).

6   For a concise historical account of these, and other data protection law instruments that are relevant in the European context, see, (van Alsenoy, 2019, p. 155 ff.).

7   GDPR, Art. 5 (2).

8   Data Protection Directive, Art. 6 (2).

9   GDPR, Art. 35 (1).

10   GDPR, Art. 57 (1) (b).

11   GDPR, Art. 57 (1) (d).

12   GDPR, Art. 35, 36 (1) and (2) and Art. 57 (1) (l).

13   GDPR, Art. 70 (1). An overview of Guidelines, Opinions and Recommendations issued over the years by the European forum of supervisory authorities (EDPB and its predecessor, WP29 can be found at the website of the EDPB, <https://edpb.europa.eu/our-work-tools/general-guidance/gdpr-guidelines-recommendations-best-practices_en> (last accessed 23/12/2019).

14   Inter-institutional Agreement between the European Parliament, the Council of the European Union and the European Commission on Better Law-Making, OJ L 123/1, pt. 18 (*Inter-Institutional Agreement*, 2003).

15   GDPR, Art. 40.

16   GDPR, Art. 40 (6).

17   GDPR, Art. 40 (7), (8) and (9).

18   GDPR, Art. 24 (3) and 28 (5).

19   GDPR, Art. 40 (4) and 41. See also (EDPB, 2019b).

20   GDPR, Art. 41 (2) (c) and Art. 41 (4).

21   GDPR, Art. 42.

22   GDPR, Art. 43 (2) and (3).

23   GDPR, Art. 42 (8).

24   The adherence to an approved code of conduct and to approved certification mechanisms is considered as "mitigating factor", to be taken into account by supervisory authorities when deciding whether or not to impose an administrative fine and of what amount, as part of the obligation for supervisory authorities to take into account the context of the infringement (GDPR, Art. 83 (2) (j) and (k))

25   GDPR, Art. 43 (9).

26   Another question lies in the unclear legal value of certification mechanisms designed at national level with respect to obligations of the GDPR, but *outside* the scope of the certification mechanisms provided by Article 42 (1) of the GDPR. This was expressly confirmed in (EDPB, 2019a). In this respect, the CNIL – French supervisory authority – adopted regulation in 2018 on the certification of Data Protection Officers ('DPOs'); however, such certificates do not – and cannot – be vested

with any kind of legal recognition in other Member States. Not only is it likely to hinder uptake, but it may also add a detrimental extra-layer of complexity to this matter and aggravate confusion.

27   GDPR, Art. 42 and 43.

28   Concerning certification mechanisms under Arts. 42 and 43 GDPR, the fact that supervisory authorities are key actors in the certification ecosystem is illustrated in Figure 1 (above) mapping the relevant actors in the certification process.

29   GDPR, Art. 57 (1) (n) and (p).

30   GDPR, Art. 43 (7).

31   GDPR, Art. 41 to 43.

32   Website of ISO, https://www.iso.org/about-us.html.

33   Or the "ISO 9000 family of standards", as named on the ISO website, https://www.iso.org/iso-9001-quality-management.html, last visited 11.12.2019.

34   See the headline of ISO website, on the date of 12.12.2019, on AI and standardisation: https://www.iso.org/news/ref2451.html, last visited 13.12.2019.

35   On the non-neutrality of standards markets with respect to the substantive content of the standard, see also (Zapatero Gómez, 2019).

36   For a comprehensive overview and introduction to ISO standards related to privacy, see https://ipen.trialog.com/wiki/ISO (last visited 22.12.2019). See also Figure 2.

37   (*ISO/IEC 29134*, 2017) Clause 5.2 (Objectives of PIA reporting).

38   ISO/IEC 29134, Introduction.

39   ISO/IEC 29134, Clause 5.1 (Benefits of carrying out a PIA) and Clause 5.2 (Objectives of PIA reporting).

40   ISO/IEC 27701:2019, Security techniques — Extension to ISO/IEC 27001 and ISO/IEC 27002 for privacy information management — Requirements and guidelines, Annex D (informative).

41   ISO/IEC 29134, Clause 6.5.4 (Review and / or audit of the PIA).

42   See on that point (Kokott & Sobotta, 2013).

43   Data Protection Directive, Art. 17 (2). See also (Article 29 Working Party, 2014).

44   ISO/IEC 29134, Introduction. See also the "note" that "a PIA does not necessarily require an ISMS", Clause 6.4.5.2 (Determine controls), Note 4.

45   ISO/IEC 29134, Introduction.

46   ISO/IEC 29134, Clause 6.4.4.1 (Privacy risk identification). See also Table B.1 of Annex B.

47   ISO/IEC 29134, Clause 6.3.1 (Set up the PIA team and provide it with direction).

48   Art. 8 (*EU Charter*, 2012).

49   ISO/IEC 29134, Introduction. See also the definition of PIA in Clause 3.7.

50   ISO/IEC 29134, Clause 6.3.1 (Set up the PIA team and provide it with direction).

51   GDPR, Rec. 75-77.

52   ISO/IEC 29134, Clauses 6.4.4 (Assess privacy risk) and 6.4.5 (Prepare for treating privacy risks).

53   ISO/IEC 29134, Clause 6.4.4.2 (Privacy risk analysis).

54   *Ibid.*

55   ISO/IEC 29134, Annex A (Informative) (Scale criteria on the level of impact and on the likelihood).

56   *Ibid.*

57   *Ibid.*

58   *Ibid.*

[59]   An exemplary matrix can be found in ISO/IEC 29134, Annex D (Illustrated examples supporting the PIA process – D.2 Example of a privacy risk map).

[60]   The 'chilling effect' is typical for fundamental rights assessments. This notion is also core to the jurisprudence of the European Court of Human Rights, see for instance with respect to the freedom of expression.

[61]   In addition to (*Digital Rights Ireland*, 2014), assessments on necessity and proportionality are prominent in: (*Google Spain*, 2014, paras. 80–81); (*Tele2 Sverige AB*, 2016, paras. 82–112). There is also ample case law from the European Court of Human Rights clarifying the 'necessity' criterion as regards limitations on the right to privacy under Art. 8(2) of the European Convention on Human Rights; see: (European Court of Human Rights, 2019, p. 8).

[62]   ISO/IEC 29134, Clause 6.3.1 (Set up the PIA team and provide it with direction).

[63]   ISO/IEC 29134, Annex A "(information) – Scale criteria on the level of impact and on the likelihood".

[64]   GDPR, Art. 35 (7) (a).

[65]   GDPR, Art. 35 (7) (d).

[66]   ISO/IEC 29134, Clause 6.3.1 (Set up the PIA team and provide it with direction).

[67]   ISO/IEC 29134, Clause 6.4.4.3 (Privacy risk evaluation).

[68]   ISO/IEC 29134, Introduction.

[69]   ISO/IEC 29134, Note under Clause 6.4.4.1.

[70]   ISO/IEC 29134, Clause 6.4.5.2, Note 2.

[71]   ISO/IEC 29134, Introduction and Clause 6.4.5.2, Note 3.

[72]   ISO/IEC 29134, Introduction.

[73]   ISO/IEC 29134, Introduction and Clause 6.4.5.2, Note 3.

[74]   See above, Part II.

[75]   GDPR, Art. 42 (5) and 43 (6).

APPENDIX 1: TABLE OF LEGISLATION

Charter of Fundamental Rights of the European Union *OJ C 326/391.*, European Parliament, Council and Commission.

Convention for the Protection of Individuals with regard to Automatic Processing of Personal Data, ETS No 108, 1987 (Convention No. 108, 1981).

Directive 95/46/EC of the European Parliament and of the Council of 24 October 1995 on the protection of individuals with regard to the processing of personal data and on the free movement of such data, *OJ L 281/31.*

Inter-institutional Agreement between the European Parliament, the Council of the European Union and the European Commission on Better Law-Making, *OJ L 123/1* (no longer in force).

Regulation (EU) 2016/679 of the European Parliament and of the Council of 27 April 2016 on the protection of natural persons with regard to the processing of personal data and on the free movement of such data, and repealing Directive 95/46/EC (General Data Protection Regulation), *OJ L 119/1.*

APPENDIX 2: TABLE OF CASE LAW

CJEU, Digital Rights Ireland v Minister for Communications, Marine and Natural Resources [...], *Digital Rights Ireland,* Joined Cases C-293/12 and C-594/12, 8 April 2014.

CJEU, Google Spain SL, Google Inc. V Agencia Española de Protección de Datos (AEPD), Mario Costeja González, *Google Spain,* Case C-131/12, 13 May 2014.

CJEU, Tele2 Sverige AB v Post- och telestyrelsen, and Secretary of State for the Home Department v Tom Watson, Peter Brice, Geoffrey Lewis, *Tele2 Sverige AB,* Joined Cases C-203/15 and C-698/15, 21 December 2016.

Section 3
Data Privacy at and Beyond the EU's Borders

The EU has established over the years digital, 'smart' borders through the operation of large databases that store the personal—including the biometric—data of TCNs. While the GDPR has strengthened data protection standards, the latter protections do not apply to TCNs. Beyond the EU's borders, it is worth noting that many countries are adopting their own data protection laws and it is important to also pay attention to these developments as well.

Chapter 9
Smart Borders and Data Protection

Sarah Progin-Theuerkauf
Fribourg University, Switzerland

Margarite Zoeteweij
Fribourg University, Switzerland

Ozan Turhan
Swiss Refugee Council, Switzerland

ABSTRACT

In May 2019, the elections to the European Parliament and the political consequences of the new composition of the Parliament, as well as the never-ending Brexit debate, in which there seems to be a new dramatic turn every week, received a lot of media attention. So, it is perhaps not surprising that two regulations adopted by the Council on 20 May 2019 have so far gone almost unnoticed. However, this is completely unjustified, as they will have far-reaching consequences. Specifically, the chapter concerns regulations 2019/817 and 2019/818, establishing a framework for the interoperability (i.e. linkage) between EU information systems in the field of borders and visa and in the area of freedom, security, and justice. The regulations are part of the EU's idea to create smart borders (i.e., borders that can be better and more easily controlled by using new digital systems). This chapter critically analyses the establishment of the individual databases and their interoperability, with a particular focus on data protection issues that result from them.

INTRODUCTION

In May 2019, the elections to the European Parliament and the political consequences of the new composition of the Parliament, as well as the never-ending Brexit debate, in which there seemed to be a new dramatic turn every week, received a lot of media attention. Thus, it is perhaps not surprising that two regulations adopted by the Council on 20 May 2019 have so far gone almost unnoticed. However, this is

DOI: 10.4018/978-1-5225-9489-5.ch009

completely unjustified, as they will have far-reaching consequences: Regulations 2019/817[1] and 2019/818[2] establish the framework for the interoperability (i.e. linkage) between EU information systems in the field of borders and visa and in the Area of Freedom, Security, and Justice. (Two different regulations were needed because data collection within Schengen cooperation and data collection outside Schengen are based on different legal bases.) The regulations are part of the EU's plan to create Smart Borders, i.e. borders that can be better and more easily controlled by using new digital systems.

Three of the databases integrated into the system of the new regulations have been in existence for many years and have proved their worth, such as the Schengen Information System (SIS II), the Visa Information System (VIS) and Eurodac, while the other three, the Entry Exit System (EES), the European Criminal Records Information System for third country nationals (ECRIS-TCN) and the European Travel Information and Authorisation System (ETIAS), have not yet been set up or are in operation.[3] The new interoperability regulations were presented as measures that are urgently needed to improve security in the EU, e.g. because they enable more efficient controls of persons at the external borders or improve the detection of multiple identities and thus contribute to the fight against illegal migration.[4]

However, the increasing availability of stored data, brought about by the interoperability of databases, raises questions about the adequate protection of fundamental rights of the individuals concerned. It is doubtful whether compliance with fundamental rights is sufficiently guaranteed and whether the current EU data protection framework is sufficient in practice.

Since the entire system of interoperability of the various databases is based on the principle of mutual trust - trust in the legitimacy of the data collection and decision-making processes of the Member States and the work of the authorities that have access to the databases - there are only limited legal possibilities to challenge the storage of personal data in those data bases. This seems problematic.

After setting out the legal standards on data protection in the EU (II.), this chapter gives an overview on the existing or future information systems containing data related to migrants and asylum seekers in the EU, their modus operandi, access rights and specific data protection issues (III.). Subsequently, the novelties introduced by the two new interoperability regulations will be analyzed. In particular, their (possible) effects on the protection of fundamental rights of the individuals whose data are collected, stored and used, will be explained (IV.). The chapter ends with a conclusion (VI.).

THE EU DATA PROTECTION STANDARD

The databases that are the subject of this chapter provide for the storage and use of a range of personal data on migrants: This is information on identified or identifiable natural persons who are third-country nationals and who have entered or wish to enter the Schengen area. The general legal framework for the protection of such data in Europe is fragmented (FRA, 2019).

The first – and, so far, only – international instrument dealing with data protection is the 1981 Council of Europe Convention on Data Protection.[5] The Convention contains basic data protection rights. An Additional Protocol to the Data Protection Convention was adopted in 2001.[6] Among other things, it contains the obligation to establish national data protection authorities. A revised version of the Data Protection Convention was adopted in May 2018, of which the Additional Protocol of 2001 is an integral part.[7] However, to date, the revised Convention has only been ratified by Bulgaria and Croatia.[8]

The European Convention on Human Rights[9] is also of high relevance for this topic. Although the ECHR does not contain an explicit right to the protection of personal data, the European Court of Human Rights (ECtHR) has derived this right from the right to respect for private life according to Art. 8 ECHR.[10] In particular, according to the ECtHR, fingerprints "containing unique information about the data subject which enables accurate identification in a wide variety of circumstances" belong to a special category of sensitive data to which stricter criteria can be applied.[11]

In this context, the ECtHR stressed that "...the need for such safeguards is all the greater as it concerns the protection of personal data subject to automatic processing, not least when such data are used for police purposes. In particular, national law should ensure that such data are relevant and not excessive for the purposes for which they are stored and should be kept in a form which does not permit identification of data subjects longer than necessary for the purpose for which they are stored. [...] It must also provide adequate safeguards to ensure that the personal data stored are effectively protected against misuse and abuse".[12]

Since 2009, the Charter of Fundamental Rights of the European Union[13] has protected the fundamental right to data protection within the European Union (EU). Art. 7 contains a parallel norm to Art. 8 ECHR. In addition, Art. 8 establishes an explicit right to the protection of personal data. This is repeated in Art. 16 (1) TFEU.[14]

Art. 16 (2) TFEU forms the legal basis for a comprehensive data protection system. Based on the predecessor of this article, the EU data protection directive issued in 1995[15] on the basis of the competence for the internal market of Art. 100a EC Treaty (later Art. 95 EC) was revised and a new general data protection regulation (GDPR)[16] was adopted, which has been in force since May 2018 (for more details see Albrecht & Jotzo, 2017; Epiney & Kern, 2016; Kühling & Buchner, 2017).

According to the regulation, authorities are also subject to the regulations of the GDPR when processing personal data of natural persons (Article 5 GDPR). Art. 5 of the GDPR sets out the main principles that must be observed when processing such data. These include in particular:

- the **principle of legality**, i.e. the fair and lawful processing of data;
- the **principle of purpose limitation**, i.e. the use of the data in accordance with the purpose for which they were obtained;
- the **principle of data minimization**, i.e. the limitation to data that is relevant and relevant to the purpose.

The GDPR is complemented by a directive containing specific provisions on the protection of personal data and the free movement of personal data in the field of judicial cooperation in criminal matters and police cooperation.[17] In order to extend the principles of the general data protection regulation to EU institutions and bodies, a further regulation was finally issued in October 2018.[18] These regulations form the basic framework of data protection in the EU (FRA, 2019), which must also be observed in the area of migration. In addition, however, all instruments analyzed below contain provisions on data protection that are specific to the respective legal act.

In institutional terms, it is worth noting that the European Agency for the Operational Management of Large IT Systems (eu-LISA) was set up in 2012.[19] Eu-LISA is responsible for the operational management of SIS, VIS and Eurodac and will also be responsible for EES, ETIAS and ECRS-TCN. The main task of eu-LISA is to ensure the smooth operation of the information technology systems. However, the Agency is also responsible for the security of the systems and the data stored in them. Furthermore, the Agency may also be given responsibility for the design, development and operational management of other large-scale IT systems to be created in the future.

The qualitative and quantitative expansion of the use of data in the various databases in the migration area provided for by EU law and the interoperability of the databases considerably increase the risk of data protection violations. Moreover, as mentioned above, the principle of mutual trust, which forms the basis of EU law, makes it particularly difficult to ensure effective monitoring of the implementation of the relevant rules.

MIGRATION RELATED EU DATABASES

The following paragraphs separately analyze the EU databases that contain migration-related data, so as to better identify the sticking points that creating and operating these databases interoperable will entail.

SIS

SIS I

In 1985, the Schengen Agreement was signed by five Member States of the then European Economic Community (Germany, France, Belgium, the Netherlands and Luxembourg), which agreed on the gradual dismantling of common borders and increased border controls at the external borders. The Schengen Information System (SIS) was set up by Article 92 of the Convention Implementing the Schengen Agreement (Schengen Convention)[20], signed in 1990, to compensate for the security deficit caused by the loss of the possibility of carrying out checks on persons at internal borders.

Initially, the Schengen cooperation took place entirely outside the framework of the European Economic Community, which had no competence in the field of border controls. It was not until the Maastricht Treaty of 7 February 1992 that a number of competences in the policy areas of migration and asylum was conferred to the European Community. With the incorporation of the Schengen acquis in the legal structure of the EU by the Treaty of Amsterdam of 1997, the Schengen Agreement and the Schengen Convention finally became binding for all EU Member States – unless Member States had opted out from the cooperation in this policy area. As a result, each legal act was given a legal basis in different "pillars" of EU law. A large part of the former Schengen acquis (external border controls, parts of visa policy, refugee and asylum policy, immigration policy and judicial cooperation in civil matters) was integrated into Title IV of the EC Treaty (and thus into the first pillar of the EU); only police and judicial cooperation in criminal matters remained at the intergovernmental level, and were thus part of the third pillar (Title VI of the EU Treaty). From a legal point of view, it should be noted that EU law has since taken precedence over Schengen law, i.e. the provisions of the Schengen Agreement and the Implementing Convention continue to apply only to the extent that no newer EU law has been adopted. Indeed, many provisions of the Schengen Agreement and the Implementing Convention have now been replaced by EU acts.

The SIS enables competent Member State authorities to enter and consult alerts on persons or objects for the purpose of border checks and other police and customs controls, as well as in the case of the specific category of alerts referred to in Article 96 of the Schengen Convention for the purposes of issuing visas, residence permits and administering legislation on foreigners.

The SIS now contains more than 80 million data records. [21] Most data concern objects, only 1% of data concern persons. Most of the personal data entered in the SIS concern third-country nationals who are to be refused entry pursuant to Article 96 of the Schengen Convention[22] (now Article 24 of the SIS II Regulation)[23]. Such a refusal of entry or residence may be issued by a competent national authority if that authority considers a third-country national to be a threat to public policy, public security or national security, in particular if the third-country national has been sentenced in a Member State to a term of imprisonment of at least one year, or if there are serious grounds for suspecting that he has committed a serious criminal offence, or if there are clear indications that he intends to commit such an offence on the territory of a Member State, or if the third-country national has been subject to an expulsion, refusal of entry or removal measure involving an entry ban because of failure to comply with Union or national rules on the entry or stay of third-country nationals (Article 24(2)(a) and (b) of the SIS II Regulation, previously Article 96(2) and (3) of the Schengen Convention).

The refusal of entry or a visa is based on Article 5 of the Schengen Convention (now Article 6 of the Schengen Borders Code[24]), which provides that a person for whom an alert has been issued in the SIS for the purpose of refusing entry must be refused entry into the Schengen territories. Only on humanitarian grounds, for reasons of national interest or because of international obligations may the national authorities derogate from this obligation to refuse entry (Article 6(5c) of the Schengen Borders Code).

Once the competent authority of the Member State considers it appropriate to enter an alert for a particular person in the SIS, the Schengen Convention stipulates that this person's first name and surname, particular physical characteristics, place and date of birth, sex, nationality, the reason for issuing an alert and the action to be taken in respect of that person shall be entered in the system by this Member State authority (Article 94 Schengen Convention).

As the SIS functions exclusively on a "hit/no hit" basis, the network of national SIRENE[25] Bureaus was set up to complement it. This allows the exchange of additional information – not entered in the SIS - such as fingerprints and photographs. The SIRENE Bureau, set up by each Member State participating in the SIS, is responsible for the exchange of additional information and the coordination of activities relating to SIS alerts.[26]

SIS II

The SIS was established as an intergovernmental information system for the exchange of information by a relatively small group of states. With the enlargement of the EU and the rapid development of information technologies, the need to replace the SIS with a more advanced, centralized system quickly became clear. In December 2006, the Council adopted Regulation 1987/2006 on the establishment of SIS II. [27] However, the development of appropriate technical solutions took longer than expected. After a transitional phase (SISone4all), SIS II finally became operational in 2013.

SIS II consists of a central system (C-SIS) managed by the EU agency eu-LISA and the national systems of the Schengen States (N-SIS), as well as a communication network between the systems. The database, which is accessible to national border control authorities, police, customs, judicial and vehicle registration authorities, Europol and Eurojust, now also stores and uses biometric data such as fingerprints and photographs (Article 20 Regulation 1987/2006, now Article 20 Regulation (EU) 2018/1861).

Fingerprints were initially used only to confirm the identity of a person found as a result of a search, usually by name and date of birth. This one-to-one search compares the person's fingerprints with a set of prints stored in the SIS. The ability to identify a person by their fingerprints, on the other hand, requires the comparison of that person's fingerprints with all the fingerprints present in the system - a so-called "one-to-many" search. The legal basis for such a "one-to-many" search based on fingerprints was created in Art. 22(c) of the SIS II Regulation (see also Art. 33 (2) Regulation (EU) 2018/1861). This feature requires the implementation of an automatic fingerprint identification system (AFIS). The required technology was developed until 2016, and after an almost two-year pilot phase, AFIS for SIS II became operational in March 2018.[28]

The SIS II Regulation was reformed once again in November 2018.[29] The use of SIS II AFIS is now mandatory (Article 43(2) SIS II Regulation), but Member States have two years from the entry into force of the new Regulation to implement the AFIS function in SIS II (Article 74(8) SIS II Regulation). Several Member States have already established the necessary legal and technological infrastructure and use the possibility to identify persons in SIS II by means of their fingerprints; other participating States plan to introduce it before long.[30]

Both the SIS II Regulation and the SIS II Decision contain specific data protection provisions. The SIS II Regulation provides, inter alia, that sensitive categories of data as defined in Article 9(1) of the General Data Protection Regulation[31] may not be processed (Article 40 SIS II Regulation). It also provides for specific rights for the data subject, such as the right of access to personal data, the right to rectify factually inaccurate data, the right to erase unlawfully stored data and the right to information in the event of an alert against the data subject (Article 41 SIS II Regulation). This information must be in writing and accompanied by a copy or reference to the national decision on the alerts.

However, there is no obligation to provide information if national law permits a restriction based, inter alia, on the protection of national security or the prevention of criminal offences (Article 42(2) SIS II Regulation).

Critical Assessment

Although the criteria for the entry of an alert in the SIS, as laid down in the Convention, were clear and aimed at a uniform implementation, there were significant differences in the relevant national legislation and practice. While in some Member States, minor offences could already lead to an alert in the SIS, in others the same offence was far from sufficient to result in a refusal of entry and a subsequent entry in the SIS (Brouwer, 2008). With the SIS II Regulation, the conditions for the admission of a third-country national pursuant to Article 96 of the Convention were supplemented by the explicit obligation to make an individual assessment of proportionality and subsidiarity (Article 24(1)(a) and Article 21 SIS II Regulation). In addition, the Regulation provides for the obligation to create the possibility to appeal to a national court against such the decision to impose an entry ban.

Even if these provisions, which were incorporated into the SIS II Regulation in 2006, limited the discretion of the Member State in deciding whether or not to issue an alert for a particular third-country national, the review of the limits of discretion constitutes an obstacle which may be insurmountable for many of the third-country nationals concerned by an alert decision. Third-country nationals registered in the SIS II for reasons of public order and security will normally only be informed of the existence of the alert if they are confronted with a refusal of a visa or entry, the (renewal) of a residence permit or a removal. This makes it difficult to challenge SIS warnings timely.

Even if, on the basis of Article 53 and Article 54 of the SIS II Regulation, a person is entitled to access, rectification of inaccurate data and erasure of unlawfully stored data and to bring an action to obtain compensation in connection with an alert concerning him or her, some Member States have yet to implement the necessary national legal framework to provide for such a legal procedure.[32] Challenging and correcting false or unlawful warnings therefore remains a difficult right to practice in these Member States.

With regard to alerts resulting from an entry ban following the application of a return decision under the Return Directive, which provides for common standards and procedures for the return of third-country nationals residing illegally in their territory, the third-country national concerned is aware of this entry ban.[33] The proposed recast of the Return Directive[34] is intended to establish a link between the national return systems and SIS II, so that all national return decisions associated with an entry ban are also automatically visible in SIS II. This means, however, that the Return Directive does not leave Member States any margin of discretion in deciding whether or not to impose an entry ban. Article 11 of the Return Directive provides that expulsion decisions are to be accompanied by an entry ban if the obligation to return is not fulfilled or if no deadline for voluntary departure has been set (Progin-Theuerkauf, 2019). In such cases, there is hardly any room for the application of the principle of proportionality in the decision to issue an entry ban – although according to the SIS II Regulation, this is a prerequisite that applies to all entries in SIS II (Meijers Committee, 2012).[35]

Therefore, the mechanisms to protect individuals against the misuse of their personal data or against erroneous results from the use of such data appear to be comparatively weak and function poorly.

Eurodac

Eurodac 2000

The 1990 Dublin Convention[36] introduced a system for the allocation of responsibility for asylum applications, ensuring that asylum seekers have their material asylum application examined in only one Member State and at the same time are entitled to effective access to the asylum procedure in that Member State. The Dublin Convention replaced Chapter VII of the Schengen Convention, which provided for similar arrangements based on the principle of the "safe third country", which by the end of the 1990s had been implemented by virtually every Western European state (Costello, 2006) - the cause of the phenomenon of "refugees in orbit". The Dublin system – then and now - is based on a hierarchy of provisions determining responsibility, such as the legal presence of family members of the asylum seeker in a Member State, a Member State having issued a visa that was valid at the time of the application for asylum, or the illegal entry into a Member State. Once established in accordance with the Dublin Regulation, cessation of the responsibility is only possible in a limited number of scenarios.

The application of the Dublin Convention encountered considerable difficulties in practice as it resulted in asylum seekers often destroying travel documents or other documents that could disclose information about their itinerary in order to avoid the determination of responsibility of a particular Member State. This problem was only partially solved by requiring travel agencies and airlines to keep a copy of the identity documents of passengers on certain flights (Brouwer, 2008b).

At a meeting of migration ministers in 1991, the ministers agreed to conduct a feasibility study on the establishment of a system for the storing and comparing of dactyloscopic data of asylum seekers. After this study was completed, the ministers asked the Council's Legal Service for its opinion on whether Article 15 of the Dublin Convention could be used as the legal basis for the creation of such a system, which would be called 'Eurodac'.[37] Article 15 provided the States Parties to the Convention with a legal basis for the exchange of data necessary for the application of the Convention. While the Legal Service confirmed that the article could, in principle serve as a legal basis for the establishment of such a system, its Opinion also underlined that such a system, once established, should not be used for other purposes, such as the facilitation of the implementation of other international instruments or the initiation of criminal proceedings against asylum seekers.[38] This reservation was repeated by the European Parliament resolution of 1998 on the draft Eurodac Convention.[39] The Parliament stated – without it having a decisive say in the decision-making process at the time – that "[t]he use of the system pursuant to the preceding paragraphs must be regarded as subject to very strict limits. The use of the Eurodac system must on no account be extended to cover wider areas or other purposes."[40]

After lengthy discussions in the Council (Aus, 2006; Peers & Rogers, 2006), and only after the entry into force of the Amsterdam Treaty, the Eurodac Regulation was adopted in 2000[41] – without, however, the article that was proposed by the European Parliament. The Eurodac Regulation was the first instrument adopted on the basis of Title IV of the EC Treaty. Its sole objective, according to the preamble, was to facilitate the application of the Dublin criteria in order to determine which State is responsible for an asylum application lodged in a Member State. For this reason, Eurodac only contained fingerprints of asylum seekers and persons apprehended while illegally crossing a border. While an identification number and the place and date of arrival were linked to the fingerprints stored in the system, Eurodac did not store any personal data such as name, address or date of birth (Meijers Committee, 2007).

The information collected in relation to asylum seekers could be stored for ten years, information in relation to irregular border crossings for two years. Fingerprints of third-country nationals illegally present in one of the Member States could be compared with those of asylum seekers and irregular border crossers, but could not be stored.

Eurodac 2013

As early as 2006, Germany - the Member State which had insisted on the introduction of the possibility of checking the fingerprints of illegally staying third-country nationals with data stored in the Eurodac Regulation - proposed making Eurodac accessible to police and law enforcement authorities, arguing that "asylum seekers and foreigners residing illegally in the EU are often involved in the preparation of terrorist crimes".[42]

In the context of an evaluation of the Dublin system – which included a review of the functioning of the Eurodac system in the first three years of its existence - the Commission agreed that "although the main objective of the Eurodac Regulation is to support the rapid identification of the Member State responsible for an asylum application [...] the information contained in the database may also have other useful applications. ... [T]he Commission will [examine] the possibility of extending the scope of Eurodac with regard to the use of its data for law enforcement purposes".[43]

In September 2009 and again in May 2012 (after the entry into force of the TFEU), the Commission presented a proposal[44] providing for access to Eurodac by law enforcement authorities. The Commission argued that this was necessary as part of the agreement on negotiations on the Common European Asylum System (CEAS) package. The Eurodac Regulation was recast as part of the Asylum package of 2013.[45] The 2013 recast Regulation now contains the legal basis for access of national authorities and EU agencies entrusted with the implementation of the EU's anti-terrorism policy and the fight against organized crime to data collected in Eurodac, if this is necessary in a particular case and if the comparison with Eurodac data will contribute significantly to the prevention, detection or investigation of terrorist offences or other serious criminal offences. Access can only be granted if no match has been found in the national databases and national databases of other Member States and if no match has been found in the Visa Information System. This access includes data on recognized and subsidiary protected refugees for up to three years after the granting of status, as these are part of the data that are stored in Eurodac.

Eu-LISA keeps records of all data processing operations, in order to monitor data protection and ensure data security, while national supervisory authorities should assist and advise data subjects in the exercise of their rights (Articles 28 and 29 recast Eurodac Regulation). The handling of the central Eurodac system by eu-LISA (Article 31 recast Eurodac Regulation) is governed by the Data Protection Regulation, applicable to the EU institutions, and supervised by the EDPS. The home Member State ensures data security and data protection before and during the transfer to the Central System (Article 34(1) recast Eurodac Regulation). As far as Eurodac is used for law enforcement purposes, the Data Protection Directive applicable to police and law enforcement authorities is relevant, while data used for the main purpose of the database (the facilitation of the Dublin Regulation) is covered by the General Data Protection Regulation (FRA, 2019).

The Commission intends to extend the scope of the Eurodac Regulation even further in the future.[46] The aim is to enable Member States to store and retrieve data of third-country nationals and stateless persons who have not applied for international protection but are found to be present irregularly in the EU. Furthermore, the storage of additional personal data (e.g. name, date of birth and photographs) shall be permitted. Also, the circle of authorities that are given access to Eurodac shall be further extended. From the perspective of data protection, these developments give rise to serious reasons for concern.

Critical Appraisal

Already in the original version of 2000, the Eurodac Regulation raised questions as to its legality. In particular, the possibility of systematically checking the fingerprints of third-country nationals who are found to be present irregularly in a Member State was criticized as going beyond what was necessary for the proper implementation of the Dublin Regulation and therefore without a legal basis.

Interferences in fundamental rights, including the right to private life in accordance with Art. 8 ECHR, must comply with the principle of proportionality. However, there is only an inadequate link between the fingerprint data of illegal residents and the application of the Dublin Regulation, unless there is reason to believe that the person concerned has previously lodged an asylum application in another Member State.

Furthermore, the responsibility of a Member State for the illegal crossing of its borders under the Dublin Regulation ends one year after such crossing (Art. 13 para. 2 of the Dublin III Regulation). The retention of fingerprints of persons registered as irregularly crossing a border for more than one year is therefore not necessary. This, also, constitutes a violation of the principle of proportionality (Peers and Rogers, 2006).

Recital 8 to the recast Eurodac Regulation of 2013 maintains that law enforcement authorities' access to the information stored in Eurodac is necessary for the prevention, detection or investigation of terrorist offences and other serious criminal offences, without further substantiating this statement. The recitals of the Regulation are clearly based on the premise that there is a link between security and the residence of foreigners, whereas in fact this is a controversial statement (Guild, 2009). The European Data Protection Agency also argued in this context that it "had not seen any evidence from the Commission that such access was necessary [for national authorities and EU agencies entrusted with the implementation of EU anti-terrorism policy and the fight against organized crime]".[47] Therefore, there is no justification for the discriminatory treatment of third-country nationals, which is further enabled by the recast Eurodac Regulation.

That discrimination by default will be the result of the recast Eurodac Regulation may be clear from the following example: Whereas fingerprints of an asylum seeker found at a crime scene can lead to identification via a Eurodac hit, this is not possible for other categories of persons (especially the Member States own nationals), whose data is not stored systematically in a database. Therefore, it seems obvious that more links will be established between asylum seekers registered in Eurodac and organized crime than between Member State nationals and organized crime. The more links are established between Eurodac data and organized crime or terrorism, the more fertile ground there will be for the idea that asylum seekers are inextricably linked to such crimes. This, in turn, will lead to increased stigmatization of asylum seekers.[48]

The new version of the Eurodac Regulation of 2013 exposes asylum seekers to even more far-reaching infringements of fundamental rights, even though they are a particularly vulnerable group in society and therefore actually would need a higher level of protection.

VIS

Development and Scope

In 1993, the Schengen Executive Committee adopted instructions relating to visas, on the basis of Article 132 of the Schengen Convention, including criteria to be applied when examining visa applications.[49] The essence of these instructions was that diplomatic missions and consulates should carefully examine whether the person applying for a visa could pose a security or immigration risk. To this end, a Visa Information System (VIS) would be developed (Brouwer, 2008b).

The establishment of a Visa Information System became a priority for the EU following the attacks of 11 September 2001. In the conclusions of the Justice and Home Affairs Council of 20 September 2001, the Council invited the European Commission to submit a proposal for the establishment of a network for the exchange of information on visas issued by Member States.[50] The need to set up a Visa Information System was subsequently addressed in a number of EU documents and communications, stressing the multiple uses of the data provided, e.g. for "solving problems with regard to returns".[51]

In June 2004, the Council adopted a Decision enabling the Commission to start the technical preparations for the establishment of the VIS. A proposal for a VIS Regulation was presented in December of the same year.[52] However, it took until June 2008 for the VIS Regulation to be adopted.[53] Even at this stage, the system was not yet technically operational.

The VIS is an essential building block of the common visa policy, but it is much more than that. The conditions and guarantees for access to VIS data by national police authorities and Europol for the purpose of the prevention, detection and investigation of terrorist offences and of other serious criminal offences are laid down in Council Decision 2008/633/JHA.[54] The VIS contains not only alphanumeric data on each short-stay visa issued and extended,[55] but also on each visa refused, annulled or revoked for third-country nationals of countries whose nationals need a visa. In addition, photographs, fingerprints and links to other visa applications of the applicant or persons travelling with him may be recorded. The competent national authorities have the primary responsibility for ensuring that the data are lawfully collected, processed and transmitted. Each record is to be kept for five years.

The data can only be entered, erased or modified by visa authorities, but other authorities can also access the data for purposes foreseen in the Regulation. Chapter III of the Regulation lays down the conditions for the use of the VIS by other authorities. The VIS can be used by authorities at external borders and immigration authorities on the territory of a Member State to verify the identity of a person (individual consultation) and to confirm that entry conditions are met. Immigration authorities or border guards can also send a query to the VIS to identify a person by his fingerprints. In addition, national asylum authorities can search the VIS, using fingerprints, for the application of the Dublin Regulation and for the examination of the merits of an asylum application. In all these cases, the national authorities only have access to the data to which they are entitled in the event of a "hit".

In principle, data cannot be transferred to third countries or international organizations. Third States or international organizations listed in the Annex to the Regulation (UNHCR, IOM, ICRC) are exempted if this is necessary to prove the identity of third-country nationals, including for the purpose of return (Article 31(1) and (2) VIS Regulation).

The data protection rights of data subjects are governed by the VIS Regulation itself. The Regulation provides for the right to information (for the purposes of data collection and storage, access and contact with the competent authority to exercise this right, see Article 37 VIS Regulation), access to data stored in the VIS, rectification of inaccurate data and deletion of unlawfully stored data (Article 38 VIS Regulation).

Critical Appraisal

Due to the enormous number of visa applications submitted annually to the representations of Member States, and the length of the period for which the collected data is kept, VIS will soon become the largest biometric database in the world (Peers, 2016). To date, however, hardly any critical scientific analyses of the VIS have been carried out - unlike on the SIS II. One of the reasons could be that the VIS rules on access to data and the reasons for deciding to enter data into the system are much clearer (Peers, 2016). Access by other authorities to the data collected in the VIS, as proposed in the interoperability regulations, is likely to have a negative impact on this point.

Entry/Exit-System (EES)

Development and Scope

The EU Commission first mentioned the idea of establishing an Entry/Exit System (EES)[56] in February 2008, in its Communication "Preparing the next steps for border management in the European Union".[57] The idea was repeatedly floated in several other communications.[58] The European Council also signaled its support for the proposal.[59] In the European Migration Agenda[60] of 13 May 2015, the European Commission called for a transition to a new phase of "intelligent borders", of which the establishment of such an Entry/Exit System would be part. Finally, in November 2017, two regulations[61] were adopted foreseeing the creation of an EES. Its introduction is, for now, planned for the third quarter of 2021. It is being developed by eu-LISA (Art. 5 EES Regulation).

It will consist of a central system, a unified national interface, a secure communication channel with the VIS, a secure communication channel with the unified national interfaces, a web service and a data register (Art. 7 EES Regulation). The web service is intended to enable third-country nationals, but also carriers, to check the remaining permitted stay of a certain third-country national at any time (Art. 13 EES Regulation). For this purpose, the EES becomes interoperable with the VIS (Art. 8 EES Regulation).

The EES Regulation also establishes a link between foreigners and criminal offences and points out that the EES should contribute to the prevention, detection and investigation of terrorist or other serious stratagems (recital 15, Art. 6 (2) EES Regulation).

The Regulation applies to third-country nationals who are admitted for a short stay in the territory of the Member States and who undergo border checks at the borders. Family members of Union citizens (or other third-country nationals entitled to freedom of movement) who are third-country nationals and who do not hold a residence card or residence title are also to be registered (Art. 2 EES Regulation).

The EES will be operated at the external borders. It will cover all entries and exits of third-country nationals entering the Schengen area for a short stay. The EES registers the time and place of entry and calculates the duration of the permitted stay (Art. 1 (1) (a) and (b) EES Regulation). The system should replace the obligation on Member States to stamp passports of third-country nationals. It issues warnings to the Member States when the permitted stay has come to an end (Art. 1 (1) (c) and Art. 12 EES Regulation). The competent national authorities receive a list of "overstayers" (i.e. persons who have not yet left the country despite an expired visa).

Data of third-country nationals who have been refused entry for a short stay will also be stored. The system stores the time and place of the refusal of entry, the authority and the reasons (Art. 1 (1) (d) and Art. 18 EES Regulation). The storage of data of these persons should make it possible to discover "overstayers" and travelers without identity papers more easily during checks within the Schengen area with the help of biometric identifiers (facial image and fingerprints).

According to Art. 9 EES Regulation, only national border authorities, visa authorities or immigration authorities, which must be designated by the Member States, have access to the EES. Data may only be entered, changed, deleted or queried by duly authorised personnel. Access must be limited to the necessary extent and must be proportionate to the objectives pursued (Art. 9 para. 1 EES Regulation).

Art. 10 EES Regulation establishes general principles, in particular the principle of proportionality.

An individual file is created for each third-country national whose data will be collected in the EES, either by border authorities or through a self-service system (Art. 14 EES Regulation). The file will be updated if necessary. Facial images are taken live when the file is created or when it is necessary to update the image stored in the file (Art. 15 EES Regulation). There are differences between the dossiers that are created for third-country nationals subject to visa requirements (Art. 16 EES Regulation) and those that are exempt from visa requirements (Art. 17 EES Regulation). The stored data include at least the name, travel documents, facial image and fingerprint data of the right hand. In the case of third-country nationals exempt from visa requirements, fingerprints will only be collected from the age of 12 (Art. 17(3) EES Regulation).

Border authorities have access to the EES in order to verify the identity of the third-country national. Verification takes place via facial images or fingerprints (Art. 23 EES Regulation). Other authorities such as visa authorities (Art. 24 EES Regulation) also have access to the EES. In individual cases, data from the EES may be kept in national files for as long as is strictly necessary (Art. 28 EES Regulation).

Finally, designated Member States' authorities active in the field of security and criminal prosecution may also consult data from the EES (Art. 29 EES Regulation), but only for the purpose of preventing, detecting and investigating terrorist offences and other serious criminal offences, and in compliance with the principle of proportionality, i.e. if the national databases have been consulted beforehand and fingerprints have been verified via AFIS. Europol's access to EES data is also provided for and regulated by the Regulation (Art. 33 EES Regulation).

Data are retained for three years (Art. 34 EES Regulation). Data of third-country nationals who are family members of Union citizens will only be stored for one year. If no date of exit has been entered at or before the end of the permitted stay, data can be stored for five years; this applies to all third-country nationals, including the family members of EU citizens. In case third-country nationals (not family members of EU citizens) have not left, the data will be kept for five years. At the end of the retention period, the data will be automatically deleted.

Any Member State responsible may correct, complete or delete data (Art. 35 EES Regulation). Each Member State designates a responsible authority (Art. 39 EES Regulation). The data collected and recorded in the EES must be processed lawfully. An explicit reference to the human dignity of the third-country national concerned can be found in Art. 39 para. 1 lit. a EES Regulation.

The Member State that has alphanumeric data in the EES may keep this data also in its national entry/exit system or in equivalent national files (Art. 40 EES Regulation). Art. 41 EES Regulation expressly prohibits the transfer of data stored in the EES to third countries, international organizations or private bodies. Nevertheless, there are exceptions, in particular with regard to return procedures.

The Member States are liable for material and immaterial damage suffered by persons or Member States as the result of an unlawful processing operation or any act not compliant with the Regulation (Art. 45 EES Regulation).

The data protection rights are set out in Art. 50 et seq. of the EES Regulation. In particular, every third-country national has a right to information, access to, rectification, completion and erasure of personal data, and – providing the conditions are fulfilled – also to the restriction of the processing thereof. The Regulation also provides for a directly enforceable right to bring an action or a complaint before the competent authorities or courts of Member States. The national supervisory authorities and the European Data Protection Supervisor ensure coordinated supervision (Art. 57 EES Regulation).

Critical Appraisal

The EES is particularly criticized with regard to its potential effects on data protection.[62] The European Data Protection Supervisor (EDPS) focused in particular on the fact that there is no uniform European policy on dealing with "overstayers", whereas the creation of large databases in the EES could actually only be created to support a common EU policy anchored in Union law.[63] The mere facilitation of the calculation of the length of stay and the compilation of statistics are not purposes that justify an interference in the right to private life. Terrorist attacks by third-country nationals who have stayed in the EU for three months - whether with or without a visa - are also unknown. Furthermore, the EDPS doubts whether it is appropriate to set up a system such as the EES without thoroughly evaluating the functioning of the existing databases (SIS, VIS, Eurodac). In particular, working with biometric data is a massive encroachment on the personal rights of those concerned.

Additionally, it is not clear how errors due to an automated decision based on the EES can or will be avoided. Finally, the possibility of data queries by law enforcement authorities and the possible transfer of data to third countries or international organizations is criticized. Finally, also the length of the period for which data of overstayers can be retained (5 years) is found to be too long.

The points of criticism are justified and raise many questions, especially since the EU Commission estimates that the number of border crossings will increase; in 2025, about 300 million border crossings are to take place by third country nationals alone.[64]

European Travel Information and Authorisation System (ETIAS)

Establishment and Content

In May 2016, the EU Commission warned that border authorities at the Schengen external borders do not have any information on travelers who are not subject to visa requirements, and that this lack of information needed looking into.[65] Two years later, in September 2018, two regulations, which provide for the introduction of a European Travel Information and Authorisation System (ETIAS), were adopted.[66]

ETIAS is to apply to third-country nationals who are exempt from the visa requirement in order to check whether the presence of these third-country nationals could pose a risk to security, a risk of illegal immigration or a high risk of epidemics (Art. 1 ETIAS Regulation). Like the EES, the system should be operational in the third quarter of 2021.

The objectives of ETIAS are manyfold: Among other things, the system should lead to greater security, combat illegal immigration, contribute to the protection of public health and increase the effectiveness of border controls (Art. 4 ETIAS Regulation). Thus, the Regulation establishes a link between the presence of third country nationals and terrorist offences and other serious crimes (Art. 4(f)). On the other side, Article 14 of the ETIAS Regulation emphasizes the applicability of the principle of non-discrimination and other relevant fundamental rights.

ETIAS will consist of the ETIAS information system, a central office to be located at Frontex and the national ETIAS offices. Eu-LISA is to develop the system and ensure its technical management (Article 5 in conjunction with Articles 6, 7 and 8 of the ETIAS Regulation).

The ETIAS central unit should be operational 24/7. Interoperability with the other EU information systems should exist (Art. 11 ETIAS Regulation), in order to verify whether, for example, the travel document used for he application is listed as stole, or whether the person carrying the travel document is subject to a SIS alert (Article 20 of the Regulation).

Access to ETIAS should be restricted to staff of the ETIAS Central Unit and the ETIAS national units. However, border authorities, immigration authorities and transport companies will also be allowed to make certain enquiries (Art. 13 ETIAS Regulation).

The ETIAS is expected to function as follows. Citizens from third countries who are exempt from visa obligations will henceforth nevertheless have to be able to show a travel authorization, that they can obtain through ETIAS. In order to obtain this authorization, they should fill in an online application form (via a website or a mobile application) as early as possible. In the form, applicants must provide a range of personal data, including name, nationality(ies), travel documents, e-mail address, education, current occupation and Member State of intended stay (Art. 17(2) ETIAS Regulation). In addition, the applicant must answer questions such as whether he has been convicted of a criminal offence in the last ten years or even twenty years in the case of terrorist offences, whether he has spent the last ten years in a war or conflict zone or whether a return decision has been issued against him. If the applicant answers one of these questions in the affirmative, he must then answer a number of additional questions. The IP address from which the application form was submitted is also recorded.

A travel authorisation fee of EUR 7 is payable per application; applicants under 18 or over 70 years of age are exempt from the fee (Art. 18 ETIAS Regulation).

The ETIAS automatically processes the application data sets and compares the data with the SIS, EES, VIS, Eurodac, Europol data and Interpol data. In particular, the system checks whether travel documents have been reported stolen, whether an alert for refusal of entry has been issued with regard to the applicant, whether an arrest warrant has been issued against him/her, etc. If the automated processing does not produce a hit in any of the aforementioned systems, the ETIAS central system issues the travel authorization (Article 21 ETIAS Regulation). This does not, however, give any automatic right of entry or residence. Furthermore, travel authorisations can be cancelled or revoked (Art. 40 and 41 ETIAS Regulation).

Certain ETIAS screening rules, or algorithms, are laid down which make it possible to identify risks to security, illegal immigration or an epidemic. These algorithms are based on statistics and other sources of information. Various risks are established by the Commission in an implementing act, based on which the ETIAS Central Unit will then establish a set of specific risk indicators such age, sex or nationality, country or place of residence, level of education or professional activity (Art. 33 ETIAS Regulation). Added to these risk indicators is an ETIAS watchlist of persons

ETIAS establishes a watch list of data relating to persons who are suspected of having committed or taken part in a terrorist offence or other serious criminal offence or persons regarding whom there are factual indications or reasonable grounds, based on an overall assessment of the person, to believe that they will commit a terrorist offence or other serious criminal offence. These data are based on information related to terrorist offences or other serious criminal offences, as entered by the Member States or Europol (Art. 34 ETIAS Regulation).

If the application form, processed by ETIAS, produces one or more hits, the ETIAS Central System consults the ETIAS Central Unit. It then has access to the application file and can carry out further checks (Art. 22 ETIAS Regulation). In case of a hit, the application is processed manually by the national ETIAS office in accordance with Art. 26 ETIAS Regulation. Other Member States or Europol may be consulted (Art. 28 and 29 ETIAS Regulation). Records of incorrect hits are to be deleted.

Specific rules apply to family members of Union citizens or other third-country nationals who enjoy a right to free movement under Union law (Art. 24 ETIAS Regulation). They do not have to answer all of the questions on the application form, and the application fee is waived.

Within 96 hours of the submission of an application, the applicant will be informed whether his or her entry permit has been granted or refused or whether he or she must provide further information (Art. 30 ETIAS Regulation).

ETIAS can be used by authorities at the external borders (Article 47), objection authorities (Article 48) or law enforcement and security authorities of the Member States (Article 50). Europol can also have access (Art. 53 ETIAS Regulation).

Each application is retained for the duration of the validity of the travel authorisation or for five years in the event of refusal, cancellation or withdrawal of the travel authorisation (Art. 54 ETIAS Regulation). In case the travel authorization was issued, the applicant can choose to have his data retained for three years to facilitate the submission of a new application.

The ETIAS central unit and the national ETIAS units shall have the obligation to update the data stored in the ETIAS central system and ensure that they are correct (Art. 55 ETIAS Regulation). The Regulation also contains rules on liability for damages (Art. 63 ETIAS Regulation) and data protection (Art. 56 ETIAS Regulation). As with the EES, there are rules on the possibility of communicating personal data to third countries, international organisations and private bodies (Art. 65 ETIAS Regulation). The national supervisory authorities and the European Data Protection Supervisor will cooperate to supervise ETIAS and the national border infrastructures (Art. 68 ETIAS Regulation).

Critical Appraisal

The ETIAS has also attracted criticism for having the potential to lead to data protection issues, but not only.[67] The questions in the authorization application form about professional training and current employment, which applicants have to answer, may not lead to data protection issues but to discriminatory profiling based on (access to) education and employment. In this respect, the EDPS questioned the ETIAS algorithms and the identification of risks. With regard to data protection, the long retention period of five years for refused, cancelled or revoked travel authorizations seems problematic. The possible transfer of data to third countries is also criticized. Last but not least, the Regulation does not make it sufficiently clear that the travel authorization will not affect the right to make an asylum application.

European Criminal Records Information System for Third Country Nationals (ECRIS-TCN)

Development and Scope

The European Criminal Records Information System (ECRIS), which allows the exchange of information on criminal convictions handed down in another Member State, has been in place since 2009.[68]

In April 2019 it was decided to set up ECRIS-TCN, a centralised system for identifying Member States where information on convictions of third country nationals and stateless persons is available.[69] The system is intended to make it possible to exchange information on convictions of third-country nationals in other Member States in order to take them into account in new criminal proceedings or prevent new criminal offences.

ECRIS-TCN consists of a central system, a national central access point in each Member State, interface software and a communication infrastructure (Art. 4 ECRIS-TCN Regulation). The central system is located at eu-LISA.

For each convicted third-country national, the central authority of the convicting Member State creates a data record in the Central System. In addition to alphanumeric data such as name, date of birth, sex, nationality, etc., this data record also contains fingerprint data and, where appropriate, facial images (Article 5 of the ECRIS-TCN Regulation). The fingerprint data are collected if the third-country national has been sentenced to a custodial sentence of at least six months or if the third-country national has been convicted of an offence punishable under the law of the Member State by a custodial sentence of a maximum of at least twelve months.

The central authorities use ECRIS-TCN to identify the Member States where criminal records information on a third-country national is held in order to obtain information on previous convictions, if information on this person is needed in the Member State concerned for the purposes of criminal proceedings or for any other purpose mentioned in Article 7 of the Regulation, where national law so provides. These purposes include security checks or inspections when obtaining an authorisation or recruiting staff, or when carrying out voluntary work in contact with children, but also visa, naturalisation and migration procedures, including asylum procedures.

Europol, Eurojust and the EUStA shall be entitled to query the ECRIS-TCN. The competent authorities may use all or only some of the data for the search.

Union citizens can also be checked to see whether criminal records information exists against them in a Member State as third-country nationals.

In the event of a hit, the Central System shall automatically provide the competent authority with information. If there is no hit, the competent authority is automatically informed (Art. 7 ECRIS-TCN Regulation).

Each data record is stored in the central system for as long as the data on the conviction(s) are stored in the criminal records. All data, including fingerprints and facial data, will be deleted at the latest one month after the end of the storage period (Art. 8 of the Regulation on the ECRIS-TCN Regulation).

Member States may modify or delete the data they have entered in the ECRIS-TCN (Art. 9 of the ECRIS-TCN Regulation).

Third countries and international organizations may use a form for the purpose of criminal proceedings to request information on the information stored in the ECRIS-TCN on a third-country national (Art. 17 ECRIS-TCN Regulation). The transmission of data to private parties is not permitted (Art. 18 ECRIS-TCN Regulation).

Data protection rights are regulated in Art. 23 ff. of the ECRIS-TCN Regulation. Data subjects have the right to information, correction, deletion and restriction of processing. An appeal is also provided for (Art. 27 ECRIS-TCN Regulation).

Supervision is carried out by the national data protection authorities and the European Data Protection Supervisor (Art. 28, 29 and 30 ECRIS-TCN Regulation).

Eu-Lisa is responsible for the development of ECRIS-TCN.

Critical Appraisal

ECRIS-TCN has also been criticized in some aspects, although less so than EES and ETIAS.[70] In particular, it was demanded that disproportionate consequences of criminally relevant violations of objection standards should be avoided. The "carte blanche" given to the Member States by the reference to national law in Article 7(1) of the ECRIS-TCN Regulation with regard to the retrieval of ECRIS data is particularly problematic here (Brouwer, 2019). ECRIS-TCN can also be used, if national law so provides, for the withdrawal or refusal of a residence permit. In view of the considerable differences between the Member States, particularly with regard to the prosecution of offences against immigration laws, this does not appear to be expedient.

The possible transfer of data to third countries was also criticized, as this could lead to violations of fundamental rights or persecution of the data subject in the third country.

The use of fingerprint data also received a negative response. Alternatives such as the storage of residence permits or travel documents had not been sufficiently examined.

INTEROPERABILITY

Development and Structure of the New System

As early as 2016, the Commission called for the improvement of the Union's data management architecture in the field of border control and security and for the adoption of the legal framework providing for the interoperability between EU information systems.[71] The Council expressed its support for these plans.[72] In December 2017, the Commission presented two proposals for regulations on interoperability[73], which were presented once more but in an amended version in June 2018.[74]

In May 2019, the Council and Parliament agreed with the proposals that would make above analyzed six databases in the area of asylum, migration and security, namely SIS, VIS, Eurodac, EES, ETIAS and ECRIS-TCN, interoperable.[75] Regulation 2019/817 applies to EES, VIS, ETIAS and SIS (Article 3 of Regulation 2019/817). It refers to the Schengen acquis on borders and visas and is therefore based on Articles 16(2), 74 and 77(2)(a), (b), (d) and (e) TFEU. Regulation 2019/818 applies to Eurodac, SIS and ECRIS-TCN, as well as to Europol data to the extent necessary to allow simultaneous consultation of the three other information systems (Article 3 of Regulation 2019/818). It concerns the areas of police and judicial cooperation, asylum and migration (i.e. areas outside Schengen) and is based on Articles 16(2), 74, 78(2)(e), 79(2)(c), 82(2)(d), 85(1), 87(2)(a) and 88(2) TFEU.

The regulations are structured in parallel.[76] In terms of content, both regulations provide for the same components:

- A **European Search Portal** (ESP) and a **Biometric Matching Service** (BMS) (yet to be established);
- The alphanumeric core data will be collected in a **Common Identity Repository** (CIR).
- In addition, a **Multiple Identity Detector** (MID) will be created.

The European Search Portal (ESP) will provide Member State authorities and Union bodies with rapid access to EU information systems, Europol and Interpol data. The search portal will be designed to allow for a simultaneous consultation of all databases.

Use of the ESP is reserved to Member State authorities and Union bodies which have access to at least one of the EU information systems in accordance with the legal instruments applicable to those EU information systems, the CIR and MID, Europol data or Interpol databases. Member State authorities and Union bodies may only use the ESP and the data it provides for the purposes and objectives laid down in the relevant legal bases.

ESP users shall enter alphanumeric and/or biometric data in the ESP in order to make searches. When carrying out a query, the ESP shall, on the basis of the data entered by the ESP user and according to the user profile, simultaneously consult the EES, ETIAS, VIS, SIS, Eurodac, ECRIS-TCN, CIR, Europol data and Interpol databases. As soon as data is available from one of the EU information systems, Europol or Interpol databases, the user will receive replies via the ESP. These replies shall only contain the data to which the user is entitled to have access under Union and national law. The reply issued by the ESP shall specify the EU Information System or database from which the data concerned originate.

The common service for the comparison of biometric data (common BMS) has the task of storing biometric templates generated from the biometric data stored in the CIR and the SIS and of enabling cross-system consultation of several EU information systems using biometric data.

An individual file containing the data referred to in Article 18 (surname, forename(s), date of birth, place of birth, nationality(ies), sex, previous names, pseudonyms and/or aliases where available, and information on travel documents where available) shall be created in the common identity data memory (CIR) for each person recorded in the EES, VIS, ETIAS, Eurodac or ECRIS-TCN.

Whenever data are added, amended or deleted in Eurodac or in the ECRIS-TCN, the data stored in the individual files in the CIR shall automatically be amended accordingly automatically in accordance with Article 18.

Searches in the CIR shall be carried out in accordance with Articles 20, 21 and 22, and only for the purposes of identification, detection of multiple identities, or prevention, detection or investigation of terrorist offences or other serious criminal offences. The individual files shall be stored in the CIR only for as long as the corresponding data may be stored in at least one of the EU information systems of which data is contained in the CIR.

In order to support the functioning of the CIR and the objectives of the EES, VIS, ETIAS, Eurodac, SIS and ECRIS-TCN, a Multiple Identity Detector (MID) shall be established to create and store identity confirmation files as referred to in Article 34, to establish the links between data contained in the EU information systems, including the CIR and the SIS, and to enable the detection of multiple identities. The identity confirmation files and the data contained in them, including the links, shall be stored in the MID only as long as the linked data are stored in two or more EU information systems. They are automatically erased from simultaneously from the MID with the deletion of the data from the databases on which they were originally entered.

The processing of data in the common BMS is the responsibility of the Member State authorities responsible for processing in Eurodac, SIS and ECRIS-TCN. The Member State authorities responsible for processing data in the CIR are those responsible for processing in Eurodac and in the ECRIS-TCN. The European Border and Coast Guard Agency and the Member State authorities are responsible for the processing of data in the MID.

The persons concerned have a right to information (Art. 47) and of access to, rectification and erasure of personal data stored in the MID as well as to a restriction of their processing (Art. 48). In order to facilitate the exercise of the rights of access to personal data or the rectification, erasure or restriction of the processing of personal data, a web portal will be established (Art. 49).

Personal data stored, processed or accessed by the interoperability components shall not be transferred or made available to third countries, international organisations or private parties (Art. 50). Supervision in terms of data protection is carried out by the supervisory authorities of the Member States and the EDPS (Art. 51-53).

The following graphic gives a schematic overview of how the information stored in the individual databases will flow into the new instruments and how the interoperability will work in theory.

Critical Appraisal

The impact that the interoperability of the information systems is difficult to assess at this stage, as the three new systems are still being established. The whole interoperable system will have a large number of "moving parts"[78] in the six databases.

However, various points of criticism can already be identified:

- The Union legislator seems to assume that third-country nationals are by definition a threat to security. In this context, the EDPS called for a clarification of the extent to which identity fraud is a real issue among third country nationals in order to assess the proportionality of the database.[79] This call from the EDPS does not seem to have been answered.

- Due to the size of the central database CIR and the nature of the data stored in it, any violation of data protection rules can cause immense damage, potentially for millions of people. [80]

- Biometric databases are also an attractive target for hackers. The expansion and interconnection of these databases makes them more attractive to attack.

- The conditions for querying the central database to facilitate identity checks (Art. 20) are rather vague; it is not clear when exactly there is a reason to doubt a person's identity or the authenticity

Figure 1. [77]

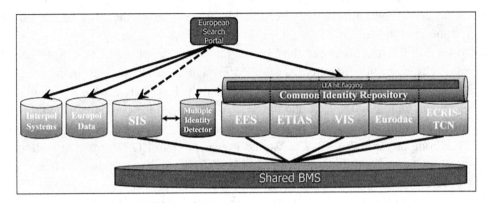

of documents. Routine consultation of the data would be a serious breach of the purpose limitation principle. [81]

- Facilitating access of law enforcement authorities to information systems that have nothing to do with law enforcement in the classic sense of the word (Article 22) is problematic. [82]
- Last but not least, the interoperability of the information systems and the exchange of data is based on the principle of mutual trust, a fundamental pillar of Union law (Leboeuf, 2016). However, in view of corruption[83], shortcomings in the rule of law[84] and the independence of individual authorities in the Member States[85], this trust appears to be currently shaken, at least in some aspects. The individuals whose data are concerned, however, have inadequate options to exercise their rights to a lawful use of their data (Brouwer, 2019).

OVERALL ASSESSMENT AND CONCLUSION

The interoperability regulations demonstrate a noticeable trend in the EU towards the collection and storage of ever more data relating to third-country nationals, thereby moving closer and closer to the US border control system. Digital borders remain invisible, but create in practice higher boundaries than physical borders. On the other hand, migrants from third countries are increasingly becoming transparent. Security considerations can only justify some of the developments analyzed in this chapter. Since there is no evidence that third-country nationals represent a security risk per se, the blanket assumption of their dangerous nature leads to an unjustifiable discrimination. The constant widening of the circle of authorities and actors who are authorized to access data should also reviewed critically. Violations of the earmarking principle seem likely as a result. Finally, the principle of data minimization is also increasingly being disregarded, with more and more data being stored for longer periods of time, without a clear and convincing justification.

Overall, the trend towards interoperable large-scale IT systems must be regarded as very worrying for data protection and fundamental rights reasons.

ACKNOWLEDGMENT

This research was supported by Aargauer Stiftung (Switzerland).

REFERENCES

Additional Protocol to the Convention for the Protection of Individuals with regard to Automatic Processing of Personal Data, regarding supervisory authorities and transborder data flows, ETS 181.

Albrecht, J. P., & Jotzo, F. (2017). Das neue Datenschutzrecht der EU. Grundlagen, Gesetzgebungsverfahren, Synopse.

Aus, J. P. (2006). Eurodac: A Solution Looking for a Problem? European Integration online Papers, 10(6).

Brouwer, E. (2008a). *The other side of the Moon*. Center for European Policy Studies.

Brouwer, E. (2008b). Digital Borders and Real Rights: Effective Remedies for Third-Country Nationals in the Schengen Information System. Academic Press.

Brouwer, E. (2019). *Interoperability and Interstate Trust: a Perilous Combination for Fundamental Rights*. https://eumigrationlawblog.eu/interoperability-and-interstate-trust-a-perilous-combination-for-fundamental-rights/

Cathryn Costello. (2006). *The European Asylum Procedures Directive in Legal Context*. UNHCR Research Paper No. 134. https://www.refworld.org/docid/4ff14e932.html

Charter of Fundamental Rights of the European Union, OJ C 83/391, 30.3.2010.

Commission Delegated Regulation (EU) 2019/946 of 12.3.2019 supplementing Regulation (EU) No 515/2014 of the European Parliament and of the Council as regards the allocation of funds from the general budget of the Union to cover the costs of developing the European Travel Information and Authorisation System, OJ L 152, 11.6.2019, p. 41-44.

Convention for the Protection of Human Rights and Fundamental Freedoms of 4 November 1950, ETS 006.

Convention for the Protection of Individuals with regard to Automatic Processing of Personal Data, ETS No.108.

Convention implementing the Schengen Agreement of 14 June 1985 between the Governments of the States of the Benelux Economic Union, the Federal Republic of Germany and the French Republic on the gradual abolition of checks at their common borders, OJ L 239, 22.09.2000, pp. 19-62.

Council Decision 2008/633/JHA of 23.6.2008 concerning access for consultation of the Visa Information System (VIS) by designated authorities of Member States and by Europol for the purposes of the prevention, detection and investigation of terrorist offences and of other serious criminal offences, OJ L 218, 13.8.2008.

Council Decision 2009/316/JHA of 6.4.2009 on the establishment of the European Criminal Records Information System (ECRIS) in application of Article 11 of Framework Decision 2009/315/JHA, OJ L 93, 7.4.2009, p. 33-48.

Council of the European Union (2008);

Council Regulation (EC) No 2725/2000 of 11.12.2000 concerning the establishment of "Eurodac" for the comparison of fingerprints for the effective application of the Dublin Convention, OJ L 316, 15.12.2000, p. 1-10.

Directive 2008/115/EC of the European Parliament and of the Council of 16.12.2008 on common standards and procedures in Member States for returning third-country nationals residing in the Community, OJ L 348, 24.12.2008, p. 98-107.

Directive 95/46/EC of the European Parliament and of the Council of 24.10.1995 on the protection of individuals with regard to the processing of personal data and on the free movement of such data, OJ L 281, 23.11.1995, p. 31-50.

Directive (EU) 2016/680 of the European Parliament and of the Council of 27.4.2016 on the protection of individuals with regard to the processing of personal data by the competent authorities for the purpose of the prevention, investigation, detection or prosecution of criminal offences or the execution of criminal penalties and on the free movement of such data and repealing Council Framework Decision 2008/977/JHA, OJ L 119, 4.5.2016, p. 89-131.

Dublin Convention of 15.6.1990 determining the State responsible for examining applications for asylum lodged in one of the Member States of the European Communities, OJ C 254, 19.8.1997, p. 1.

ECtHR, Leander v. Sweden, No. 9248/1981, judgment of 26.3.1987.

ECtHR, S. and Marper v. United Kingdom, nos. 30562/04 and 30566/04, judgment of 4.12.2008.

Epiney, A., & Kern, M. (2016). Zu den Neuerungen im Datenschutzrecht der Europäischen Union. Datenschutzgrundverordnung, Richtlinie zum Datenschutz in der Strafverfolgung und Implikationen für die Schweiz. In Die Revision des Datenschutzes in Europa und die Schweiz / La révision de la protection des données en Europa et la Suisse, Zürich et al., 39 et seq.

European Commission, Proposal for a Regulation of the European Parliament and of the Council concerning the Visa Information System (VIS) and the exchange of data between Member States on short-stay visas, COM(2005) 0835 final.

European Commission. Amended proposal for a Regulation of the European Parliament and of the Council concerning the establishment of 'EURODAC' for the comparison of fingerprints for the effective application of Regulation (EU) No (establishing the criteria and mechanisms for determining the Member State responsible for examining an application for international protection lodged in one of the Member States by a third-country national or a stateless person) and requests for comparison with EURODAC data made by law enforcement authorities of the Member States and Europol for the purpose of prosecution and amending Regulation (EU) No 1077/2011 establishing a European Agency for the operational management of large-scale IT systems in the area of freedom, security and justice, COM (2012)254 final, p. 3.

European Commission, Proposal for a Regulation of the European Parliament and of the Council concerning the establishment of Eurodac for the comparison of fingerprints for the effective application of [Regulation (EU) No Regulation (EU) No 604/2013 establishing the criteria and mechanisms for determining the Member State responsible for examining an application for international protection lodged in one of the Member States by a third-country national or a stateless person], for establishing the identity of illegally staying third-country nationals or stateless persons and for determining the identity of applicants for comparison with Eurodac data by the security and law enforcement authorities of the Member States and Europol for the purposes of security and law enforcement (recast), COM(2016) 272 final.

European Commission, Proposal for a Regulation of the European Parliament and of the Council establishing a framework for interoperability between EU information systems (borders and visas) and amending Council Decision 2004/512/EC, Regulation (EC) No 767/2008, Council Decision 2008/633/JHA, Regulation (EU) 2016/399 and Regulation (EU) 2017/2226, COM(2017) 793 final.

European Commission, Proposal for a Regulation of the European Parliament and of the Council establishing a framework for interoperability between EU information systems (police and judicial cooperation, asylum and migration), COM(2017) 794 final.

European Commission, Amended proposal for a proposal for a European Parliament and Council Regulation establishing a framework for interoperability between EU information systems (police and judicial cooperation, Asylum and Migration) and amending [Regulation (EU) 2018/XX [Eurodac Regulation], Regulation (EU) 2018/XX [Regulation on the SIS in the field of law enforcement], Regulation (EU) 2018/XX [ECRIS-TCN Regulation] and Regulation (EU) 2018/XX [eu-LISA Regulation], COM(2018) 480 final.

European Commission, Amended proposal for a Regulation of the European Parliament and of the Council establishing a framework for interoperability between EU information systems (borders and visas) and amending Council Decision 2004/512/EC, Regulation (EC) No 767/2008, Council Decision 2008/633/JHA, Regulation (EU) 2016/399, Regulation (EU) 2017/2226, Regulation (EU) 2018/XX [ETIAS Regulation], Regulation (EU) 2018/XX [Regulation on the SIS in the field of border checks] and Regulation (EU) 2018/XX [eu-LISA Regulation], COM(2018) 478 final.

European Commission, Proposal for a Directive of the European Parliament and of the Council on common standards and procedures in Member States for returning illegally staying third-country nationals (recast), COM(2018) 634 final.

European Commission, Proposal for a Regulation of the European Parliament and of the Council amending Regulation (EC) No 767/2008, Regulation (EC) No 810/2009, Regulation (EU) 2017/2226, Regulation (EU) 2016/399, Regulation (EU) 2018/XX [Interoperability Regulation] and Decision 2004/512/EC and repealing Council Decision 2008/633/JHA, COM(2018) 302 final.

FRA. (2019). *Handbook on European Data Protection Law*. Luxembourg: FRA.

Guild, E. (2009). Security and Migration in the 21st Century. Cambridge.

Kühling, J., & Buchner, B. (2017). Datenschutz-Grundverordnung. Kommentar.

Leboeuf, L. (2016). *Le droit européen de l'asile au défi de la confiance mutuelle*. Limal.

Meijers Committee (2007). Note on the proposal of the JHA Council to give law enforcement authorities access to Eurodac, CM0712-IV, 18.9.2007.

Meijers Committee (2012). Note on the coordination of the relationship between the Entry Ban and the SIS-alert. An urgent need for legislative measures. CM 1203.

Peers, S. (2016). *EU Justice and Home Affairs Law* (4th ed.). Oxford. doi:10.1093/acprof:oso/9780198776840.001.0001

Peers, S., & Rogers, N. (2006). EU Immigration and Asylum Law: Text and Commentary. Academic Press.

Progin-Theuerkauf, S. (2019). The EU Return Directive - Retour à la "case depart"? *Sui-generis*, p. 32. https://sui-generis.ch/article/view/sg.91/1026

Protocol amending the Convention for the Protection of Individuals with regard to Automatic Processing of Personal Data, ETS No. 223.

Regulation (EC) No 1987/2006 of the European Parliament and of the Council of 20.12.2006 on the establishment, operation and use of the second generation Schengen Information System (SIS II), OJ L 381, 28.12.2006, p. 4-23.

Regulation (EC) No 562/2006 of the European Parliament and of the Council of 15.3.2006 establishing a Community Code on the rules governing the movement of persons across borders (Schengen Borders Code), OJ L 105, 13.4.2006, p. 1.

Regulation (EC) No 767/2008 of the European Parliament and of the Council of 9.7.2008 concerning the Visa Information System (VIS) and the exchange of data between Member States on short-stay visas (VIS Regulation), OJ L 218, 13.8.2008, p. 60-81.

Regulation (EU) 2016/679 of the European Parliament and of the Council of 27.4.2016 on the protection of individuals with regard to the processing of personal data, on the free movement of such data and repealing Directive 95/46/EC (general data protection regulation), OJ L 119, 4.5.2016, p. 1-88.

Regulation (EU) 2017/2226 of the European Parliament and of the Council of 30.11.2017 on an entry/exit system (EES) for the collection of entry and exit data and data on refusal of entry of third-country nationals at the external borders of the Member States and laying down the conditions for access to the EES for security and law enforcement purposes and amending the Convention implementing the Schengen Agreement and Regulations (EC) No 767/2008 and (EU) No 1077/2011, OJ L 327, 9.12.2017, 20; Regulation (EU) 2017/2225 of the European Parliament and of the Council of 30.11.2017 amending Regulation (EU) 2016/399 as regards use of the entry/exit system, OJ L 327, 9.12.2017, 1.

Regulation (EU) 2018/1240 of the European Parliament and of the Council of 12.9.2018 concerning the establishment of the European Travel Information and Authorisation System (ETIAS) and amending Regulations (EU) No 1077/2011, (EU) No 515/2014, (EU) 2016/399, (EU) 2016/1624 and (EU) 2017/2226, OJ L 226, 30.9.2018, p. 1. OJ L 236, 19.9.2018, p. 1-71.

Regulation (EU) 2018/1241 of the European Parliament and of the Council of 12.9.2018 amending Regulation (EU) 2016/794 for the purpose of establishing a European Travel Information and Authorisation System (ETIAS), OJ L 236, 19.9.2018, p. 1-71.

Regulation (EU) 2018/1725 of the European Parliament and of the Council of 23.10.2018 on the protection of individuals with regard to the processing of personal data by the Union institutions, bodies, offices and agencies, on the free movement of such data and repealing Regulation (EC) No 45/2001 and Decision No 1247/2002/EC (Text with EEA relevance), OJ L 295, 21.11.2018, p. 39-98.

Regulation (EU) 2018/1860 of the European Parliament and of the Council of 28.11.2018 on the use of the Schengen Information System for the return of illegally staying third-country nationals, OJ L 312, 7.12.2018, p. 14-55. OJ L 312, 7.12.2018, p. 1-13.

Regulation (EU) 2018/1861 of the European Parliament and of the Council of 28.11.2018 on the establishment, operation and use of the Schengen Information System (SIS) as regards border controls, amending the Convention implementing the Schengen Agreement and amending and repealing Regulation (EC) No 1987/2006, OJ L 312, 7.12.2018, p. 14-55.

Regulation (EU) 2018/1862 of the European Parliament and of the Council of 28.11.2018 on the establishment, operation and use of the Schengen Information System (SIS) in the field of police cooperation and judicial cooperation in criminal matters, amending and repealing Council Decision 2007/533/JHA and repealing Regulation (EC) No 1986/2006 of the European Parliament and of the Council and Commission Decision 2010/261/EU, OJ L 312, 7.12.2018, p. 56-106.

Regulation (EU) 2019/816 of the European Parliament and of the Council of 17.4.2019 establishing a centralized system for the identification of Member States where information on convictions of third country nationals and stateless persons (ECRIS-TCN) is available, supplementing the European Criminal Records Information System and amending Regulation (EU) 2018/1726, OJ L 135, 22.5.2019, p. 1-26.

Regulation (EU) 2019/817 of the European Parliament and of the Council of 20 May 2019 establishing a framework for interoperability between EU information systems in the fields of borders and visas and amending Regulations (EC) No 767/2008, (EU) 2016/399, (EU) 2017/2226, (EU) 2018/1240, (EU) 2018/1726 and (EU) 2018/1861 of the European Parliament and of the Council, Council Decision 2004/512/EC and Council Decision 2008/633/JHA, OJ L 135/27.

Regulation (EU) 2019/818 of the European Parliament and of the Council of 20 May 2019 on establishing a framework for interoperability between EU information systems in the field of police and judicial cooperation, asylum and migration and amending Regulations (EU) 2018/1726, (EU) 2018/1862 and (EU) 2019/816, OJ L 135/85.

Regulation (EU) No 1077/2011 of the European Parliament and of the Council of 25.10.2011 establishing a European Agency for the operational management of large-scale IT systems in the area of freedom, security and justice, OJ L 286, 1.11.2011, p. 1-17. The Regulation has since been replaced by Regulation (EU) 2018/1726 of the European Parliament and of the Council of 14 November 2018, p. 39.11.2018 on the European Union Agency for the operational management of large-scale IT systems in the area of freedom, security and justice (eu-LISA), amending Council Regulation (EC) No 1987/2006 and Decision 2007/533/JHA and repealing Regulation (EU) No 1077/2011, OJ L 295, 21.11.2018, p. 99-137.

Regulation (EU) No 603/2013 of the European Parliament and of the Council of 26 June 2013 on the establishment of 'Eurodac' for the comparison of fingerprints for the effective application of Regulation (EU) No 604/2013 establishing the criteria and mechanisms for determining the Member State responsible for examining an application for international protection lodged in one of the Member States by a third-country national or a stateless person and on requests for the comparison with Eurodac data by Member States' law enforcement authorities and Europol for law enforcement purposes, and amending Regulation (EU) No 1077/2011 establishing a European Agency for the operational management of large-scale IT systems in the area of freedom, security and justice, OJ L 180, 29.6.2013, p. 1–30

Sirene Manual, Commission Decision 2017/115/EU of 31.8.2017 replacing the Annex to Decision 2013/115/EU on the Sirene Manual and other implementing measures for the second generation Schengen Information System (SIS II), OJ L 231, 7.9.2017, p. 6-51.

Treaty on the Functioning of the European Union (TFEU), consolidated version, OJ C 326/47.

ENDNOTES

[1]   Regulation (EU) 2019/817 of the European Parliament and of the Council of 20 May 2019 establishing a framework for interoperability between EU information systems in the fields of borders and visas and amending Regulations (EC) No 767/2008, (EU) 2016/399, (EU) 2017/2226, (EU) 2018/1240, (EU) 2018/1726 and (EU) 2018/1861 of the European Parliament and of the Council, Council Decision 2004/512/EC and Council Decision 2008/633/JHA, OJ L 135/27.

[2]   Regulation (EU) 2019/818 of the European Parliament and of the Council of 20 May 2019 on establishing a framework for interoperability between EU information systems in the field of police and judicial cooperation, asylum and migration and amending Regulations (EU) 2018/1726, (EU) 2018/1862 and (EU) 2019/816, OJ L 135/85.

[3]   As the three most recent databases are so new, legal literature on their scope and possible dangers is almost non-existent.

[4]   See recital 9 of Regulation 2019/818 and Regulation 2019/817.

[5]   Convention for the Protection of Individuals with regard to Automatic Processing of Personal Data, ETS No.108.

[6]   Additional Protocol to the Convention for the Protection of Individuals with regard to Automatic Processing of Personal Data, regarding supervisory authorities and transborder data flows, ETS 181.

[7]   Protocol amending the Convention for the Protection of Individuals with regard to Automatic Processing of Personal Data, ETS No. 223.

[8]   For the status of the ratifications see https://www.coe.int/en/web/conventions/full-list/-/conventions/treaty/223/signatures (last accessed on 04.02.2020).

[9]   Convention for the Protection of Human Rights and Fundamental Freedoms of 4 November 1950, ETS 006.

[10]   ECtHR, Leander v. Sweden, No. 9248/1981, judgment of 26.3.1987, para. 48.

[11]   ECtHR, S. and Marper v. United Kingdom, nos. 30562/04 and 30566/04, judgment of 4.12.2008, para. 84.

12   Ibid, para. 103.

13   Charter of Fundamental Rights of the European Union, OJ C 83/391, 30.3.2010.

14   Treaty on the Functioning of the European Union (TFEU), consolidated version, OJ C 326/47.

15   Directive 95/46/EC of the European Parliament and of the Council of 24.10.1995 on the protection of individuals with regard to the processing of personal data and on the free movement of such data, OJ L 281, 23.11.1995, p. 31-50.

16   Regulation (EU) 2016/679 of the European Parliament and of the Council of 27.4.2016 on the protection of individuals with regard to the processing of personal data, on the free movement of such data and repealing Directive 95/46/EC (general data protection regulation), OJ L 119, 4.5.2016, p. 1-88.

17   Directive (EU) 2016/680 of the European Parliament and of the Council of 27.4.2016 on the protection of individuals with regard to the processing of personal data by the competent authorities for the purpose of the prevention, investigation, detection or prosecution of criminal offences or the execution of criminal penalties and on the free movement of such data and repealing Council Framework Decision 2008/977/JHA, OJ L 119, 4.5.2016, p. 89-131.

18   Regulation (EU) 2018/1725 of the European Parliament and of the Council of 23.10.2018 on the protection of individuals with regard to the processing of personal data by the Union institutions, bodies, offices and agencies, on the free movement of such data and repealing Regulation (EC) No 45/2001 and Decision No. 1247/2002/EC (Text with EEA relevance), OJ L 295, 21.11.2018, p. 39-98.

19   Regulation (EU) No 1077/2011 of the European Parliament and of the Council of 25.10.2011 establishing a European Agency for the operational management of large-scale IT systems in the area of freedom, security and justice, OJ L 286, 1.11.2011, p. 1-17. The Regulation has since been replaced by Regulation (EU) 2018/1726 of the European Parliament and of the Council of 14 November 2018, p. 39.11.2018 on the European Union Agency for the operational management of large-scale IT systems in the area of freedom, security and justice (eu-LISA), amending Council Regulation (EC) No 1987/2006 and Decision 2007/533/JHA and repealing Regulation (EU) No 1077/2011, OJ L 295, 21.11.2018, p. 99-137.

20   Convention implementing the Schengen Agreement of 14 June 1985 between the Governments of the States of the Benelux Economic Union, the Federal Republic of Germany and the French Republic on the gradual abolition of checks at their common borders, OJ L 239, 22.09.2000, pp. 19-62.

21   See SIS II annual statistics 2018, https://www.eulisa.europa.eu/Publications/Reports/SIS%20 2018%20statistics.pdf.

22   The majority of alerts on persons (54%) at the end of 2018 concerned alerts in accordance with Article 24 of the SIS II Regulation (i.e. persons to be refused entry or stay in the Schengen area), see https://www.eulisa.europa.eu/Publications/Reports/SIS%202018%20statistics.pdf.

23   Regulation (EC) No 1987/2006 of the European Parliament and of the Council of 20.12.2006 on the establishment, operation and use of the second generation Schengen Information System (SIS II), OJ L 381, 28.12.2006, p. 4-23.

24   Regulation (EC) No 562/2006 of the European Parliament and of the Council of 15.3.2006 establishing a Community Code on the rules governing the movement of persons across borders (Schengen Borders Code), OJ L 105, 13.4.2006, p. 1.

25   SIRENE stands for "Supplementary Information Request at the National Entries".

26   See also Sirene Manual, Commission Decision 2017/115/EU of 31.8.2017 replacing the Annex to Decision 2013/115/EU on the Sirene Manual and other implementing measures for the second generation Schengen Information System (SIS II), OJ L 231, 7.9.2017, p. 6-51.

27   See note 23.

28   See https://www.eulisa.europa.eu/Newsroom/News/Pages/AFIS-deployment-March-2018.aspx.

29   Regulation (EU) 2018/1861 of the European Parliament and of the Council of 28.11.2018 on the establishment, operation and use of the Schengen Information System (SIS) as regards border controls, amending the Convention implementing the Schengen Agreement and amending and repealing Regulation (EC) No 1987/2006, OJ L 312, 7.12.2018, p. 14-55. See also Regulation (EU) 2018/1860 of the European Parliament and of the Council of 28.11.2018 on the use of the Schengen Information System for the return of illegally staying third-country nationals, OJ L 312, 7.12.2018, p. 14-55. OJ L 312, 7.12.2018, p. 1-13; Regulation (EU) 2018/1862 of the European Parliament and of the Council of 28.11.2018 on the establishment, operation and use of the Schengen Information System (SIS) in the field of police cooperation and judicial cooperation in criminal matters, amending and repealing Council Decision 2007/533/JHA and repealing Regulation (EC) No 1986/2006 of the European Parliament and of the Council and Commission Decision 2010/261/EU, OJ L 312, 7.12.2018, p. 56-106.

30   See https://www.eulisa.europa.eu/Newsroom/PressRelease/Pages/eu-LISA-successfully-launches-SIS-II-AFIS-Phase-One.aspx.

31   This concerns data revealing racial or ethnic origin, political opinions, religious or philosophical beliefs or trade union membership, as well as the processing of genetic data, biometric data uniquely identifying a natural person, health data or data concerning the sexual life or sexual orientation of a natural person.

32   Helsinki Foundation for Human Rights, Statement in case of detained head of Open Dialogue Foundation, 22.08.2018, https://www.hfhr.pl/en/hfhr-issues-statement-in-case-of-detained-head-of-open-dialogue-foundation/.

33   Directive 2008/115/EC of the European Parliament and of the Council of 16.12.2008 on common standards and procedures in Member States for returning third-country nationals residing in the Community, OJ L 348, 24.12.2008, p. 98-107.

34   European Commission, Proposal for a Directive of the European Parliament and of the Council on common standards and procedures in Member States for returning illegally staying third-country nationals (recast), COM(2018) 634 final, Preamble, para. 37 et seq.

35   Although the issue was raised in the context of the SIS II Regulation of 2006, the same applies to the SIS II Regulation of 2018.

36   Dublin Convention of 15.6.1990 determining the State responsible for examining applications for asylum lodged in one of the Member States of the European Communities, OJ C 254, 19.8.1997, p. 1.

37   SN 1419/93 WGI 1365.

38   5546/93, JUR 25.

39   A4-0402/97 of 15.1.1998.

40   Draft Council Act drawing up the Convention concerning the establishment of 'Eurodac' for the comparison of fingerprints of applicants for asylum and the Convention drawn up on the basis of Article K.3 of the Treaty on European Union, concerning the establishment of 'Eurodac' for the

comparison of fingerprints of applicants for asylum, (11079/97 - C4-0506/97 - 97/0915(CNS)), Amendment 7, 'Article 1(3a) (new)'.

41 Council Regulation (EC) No 2725/2000 of 11.12.2000 concerning the establishment of "Eurodac" for the comparison of fingerprints for the effective application of the Dublin Convention, OJ L 316, 15.12.2000, p. 1-10.

42 Council of the European Union, Presidency Programme on Police and Judicial Co-operation, Council doc. 17102/06, 22.12.2006, p. 6.

43 European Commission, Report from the Commission on the evaluation of the Dublin system, COM(2007) 299 final, p. 11.

44 European Commission, Amended proposal for a Regulation of the European Parliament and of the Council concerning the establishment of 'EURODAC' for the comparison of fingerprints for the effective application of Regulation (EU) No (establishing the criteria and mechanisms for determining the Member State responsible for examining an application for international protection lodged in one of the Member States by a third-country national or a stateless person) and requests for comparison with EURODAC data made by law enforcement authorities of the Member States and Europol for the purpose of prosecution and amending Regulation (EU) No 1077/2011 establishing a European Agency for the operational management of large-scale IT systems in the area of freedom, security and justice, COM (2012)254 final, p. 3.

45 Regulation (EU) No 603/2013 of the European Parliament and of the Council of 26 June 2013 on the establishment of 'Eurodac' for the comparison of fingerprints for the effective application of Regulation (EU) No 604/2013 establishing the criteria and mechanisms for determining the Member State responsible for examining an application for international protection lodged in one of the Member States by a third-country national or a stateless person and on requests for the comparison with Eurodac data by Member States' law enforcement authorities and Europol for law enforcement purposes, and amending Regulation (EU) No 1077/2011 establishing a European Agency for the operational management of large-scale IT systems in the area of freedom, security and justice, OJ L 180, 29.6.2013, p. 1–30

46 European Commission, Proposal for a Regulation of the European Parliament and of the Council concerning the establishment of Eurodac for the comparison of fingerprints for the effective application of [Regulation (EU) No Regulation (EU) No 604/2013 establishing the criteria and mechanisms for determining the Member State responsible for examining an application for international protection lodged in one of the Member States by a third-country national or a stateless person], for establishing the identity of illegally staying third-country nationals or stateless persons and for determining the identity of applicants for comparison with Eurodac data by the security and law enforcement authorities of the Member States and Europol for the purposes of security and law enforcement (recast), COM(2016) 272 final.

47 European Data Protection Supervisor, Eurodac: Creeping erosion of fundamental rights continues, press release of 5.9.2012.

48 UNHCR, Comments on Eurodac, November 2012, https://www.unhcr.org/protection/operations/50adf9749/unhcr-comments-eurodac.html.

49 Common Consular Instructions, Annex A to Council Decision 1999/435/EC, OJ L 176, 10.7.1999, p. 1-16.

50 SN 3926/6/01 REV 6, 20.9.2001, under 26.

[51]   See European Commission, Green Paper on a Community return policy on illegal residents, COM (2002) 175.

[52]   European Commission, Proposal for a Regulation of the European Parliament and of the Council concerning the Visa Information System (VIS) and the exchange of data between Member States on short-stay visas, COM(2005) 0835 final.

[53]   Regulation (EC) No 767/2008 of the European Parliament and of the Council of 9.7.2008 concerning the Visa Information System (VIS) and the exchange of data between Member States on short-stay visas (VIS Regulation), OJ L 218, 13.8.2008, p. 60-81.

[54]   Council of the European Union (2008); Council Decision 2008/633/JHA of 23.6.2008 concerning access for consultation of the Visa Information System (VIS) by designated authorities of Member States and by Europol for the purposes of the prevention, detection and investigation of terrorist offences and of other serious criminal offences, OJ L 218, 13.8.2008.

[55]   In the future, the Commission intends to include also long-stay visas and residence permits in the VIS, see the proposal for a Regulation of the European Parliament and of the Council amending Regulation (EC) No 767/2008, Regulation (EC) No 810/2009, Regulation (EU) 2017/2226, Regulation (EU) 2016/399, Regulation (EU) 2018/XX [Interoperability Regulation] and Decision 2004/512/EC and repealing Council Decision 2008/633/JHA, COM(2018) 302 final.

[56]   Together with the EES proposal, the Commission proposed a Registered Traveller Programme (RTP) as part of the Smart Borders Package, which will be presented in 2013, to provide frequent travellers from third countries with the possibility of prescreening so that they can use automated border control systems in the same way as nationals of Member States. The proposal for RTP was withdrawn by the Commission in 2016.

[57]   Communication from the Commission to the European Parliament, the Council, the European Economic and Social Committee and the Committee of the Regions - Preparing the next steps in border management in the European Union, COM(2008)69 final, point 3.

[58]   Communication from the Commission to the European Parliament and the Council, An area of freedom, security and justice serving the citizen, COM(2009) 262 final; Communication from the Commission to the European Parliament and the Council, Intelligent borders: options and the way forward, COM(2011) 680 final.

[59]   EUCO 23/11, Conclusions of 23 and 24 June 2011, para. 24; EUCO 19/14, Conclusions of 26 and 27 June 2014, para. 9.

[60]   Communication from the Commission to the European Parliament, the Council, the European Economic and Social Committee and the Committee of the Regions, The European Migration Agenda, COM(2015) 240 final.

[61]   Regulation (EU) 2017/2226 of the European Parliament and of the Council of 30.11.2017 on an entry/exit system (EES) for the collection of entry and exit data and data on refusal of entry of third-country nationals at the external borders of the Member States and laying down the conditions for access to the EES for security and law enforcement purposes and amending the Convention implementing the Schengen Agreement and Regulations (EC) No 767/2008 and (EU) No 1077/2011, OJ L 327, 9.12.2017, 20; Regulation (EU) 2017/2225 of the European Parliament and of the Council of 30.11.2017 amending Regulation (EU) 2016/399 as regards use of the entry/exit system, OJ L 327, 9.12.2017, 1.

[62]   See e.g. https://www.greens-efa.eu/en/article/document/data-retention-under-the-proposal-for-an-eu-entry-exit-system-ees/; European Data Protection Supervisor, Opinion of the European Data

Protection Supervisor on the proposals for a Regulation on an Entry/Exit System (EES) and for a Regulation on a Passenger Registration Programme (RTP), https://edps.europa.eu/sites/edp/files/publication/13-07-18_smart_borders_de.pdf; European Data Protection Supervisor, Opinion 6/2016, EDPS Opinion on the Second EU Smart Border Package, https://edps.europa.eu/sites/edp/files/publication/16-09-21_smart_borders_en.pdf.

[63] European Data Protection Supervisor, Opinion of the European Data Protection Supervisor on the proposals for a Regulation on an Entry/Exit System (EES) and for a Regulation on a Passenger Registration Programme (RTP), https://edps.europa.eu/sites/edp/files/publication/13-07-18_smart_borders_de.pdf.

[64] European Commission, Executive Summary, Impact Assessment on the Establishment of an EU Entry Exit System, SWD(2016) 115 final, https://ec.europa.eu/home-affairs/what-we-do/policies/borders-and-visas/smart-borders_en.

[65] European Commission, Communication to the European Parliament and the Council, Towards more robust and intelligent information systems for border management and security, COM(2016) 205 final.

[66] Regulation (EU) 2018/1240 of the European Parliament and of the Council of 12.9.2018 concerning the establishment of the European Travel Information and Authorisation System (ETIAS) and amending Regulations (EU) No 1077/2011, (EU) No 515/2014, (EU) 2016/399, (EU) 2016/1624 and (EU) 2017/2226, OJ L 226, 30.9.2018, p. 1. OJ L 236, 19.9.2018, p. 1-71 and Regulation (EU) 2018/1241 of the European Parliament and of the Council of 12.9.2018 amending Regulation (EU) 2016/794 for the purpose of establishing a European Travel Information and Authorisation System (ETIAS), OJ L 236, 19.9.2018, p. 1-71. See also Commission Delegated Regulation (EU) 2019/946 of 12.3.2019 supplementing Regulation (EU) No 515/2014 of the European Parliament and of the Council as regards the allocation of funds from the general budget of the Union to cover the costs of developing the European Travel Information and Authorisation System, OJ L 152, 11.6.2019, p. 41-44.

[67] See e.g. the opinion of the FRA, The impact on fundamental rights of the proposed Regulation on the European Travel Information and Authorisation System (ETIAS), 30.6.2017, and the opinion of the European Data Protection Supervisor 3/2017 on the proposal for a European Travel Information and Authorisation System (ETIAS), https://edps.europa.eu/sites/edp/files/publication/17-03-070_etias_opinion_de.pdf.

[68] Council Decision 2009/316/JHA of 6.4.2009 on the establishment of the European Criminal Records Information System (ECRIS) in application of Article 11 of Framework Decision 2009/315/JHA, OJ L 93, 7.4.2009, p. 33-48.

[69] Regulation (EU) 2019/816 of the European Parliament and of the Council of 17.4.2019 establishing a centralized system for the identification of Member States where information on convictions of third country nationals and stateless persons (ECRIS-TCN) is available, supplementing the European Criminal Records Information System and amending Regulation (EU) 2018/1726, OJ L 135, 22.5.2019, p. 1-26.

[70] See FRA, Opinion on the exchange of information on third-country nationals under a possible future system complementing the European Criminal Records Information System, https://fra.europa.eu/en/opinion/2015/fra-opinion-exchange-information-third-country-nationals-under-possible-system; EDPS, Opinion 11/2017 on the Proposal for a Regulation on ECRIS-TCN, https://edps.europa.eu/sites/edp/files/publication/17-12-12_opinion_ecris_tcn_2017_0542_de_1.pdf.

[71] European Commission, Communication to the European Parliament and the Council, Sounder and smarter information systems for border management and security, COM(2016) 205 final.

[72] Council of the European Union, Roadmap to improve the exchange and management of information, including interoperability solutions in the area of Justice and Home Affairs, 9-10.6.2016, https://www.consilium.europa.eu/de/meetings/jha/2016/06/09-10/.

[73] European Commission, Proposal for a Regulation of the European Parliament and of the Council establishing a framework for interoperability between EU information systems (borders and visas) and amending Council Decision 2004/512/EC, Regulation (EC) No 767/2008, Council Decision 2008/633/JHA, Regulation (EU) 2016/399 and Regulation (EU) 2017/2226, COM(2017) 793 final, and Proposal for a Regulation of the European Parliament and of the Council establishing a framework for interoperability between EU information systems (police and judicial cooperation, asylum and migration), COM(2017) 794 final.

[74] Amended proposal for a Regulation of the European Parliament and of the Council establishing a framework for interoperability between EU information systems (borders and visas) and amending Council Decision 2004/512/EC, Regulation (EC) No 767/2008, Council Decision 2008/633/JHA, Regulation (EU) 2016/399, Regulation (EU) 2017/2226, Regulation (EU) 2018/XX [ETIAS Regulation], Regulation (EU) 2018/XX [Regulation on the SIS in the field of border checks] and Regulation (EU) 2018/XX [eu-LISA Regulation], COM(2018) 478 final and Amended proposal for a proposal for a European Parliament and Council Regulation establishing a framework for interoperability between EU information systems (police and judicial cooperation, Asylum and Migration) and amending [Regulation (EU) 2018/XX [Eurodac Regulation], Regulation (EU) 2018/XX [Regulation on the SIS in the field of law enforcement], Regulation (EU) 2018/XX [ECRIS-TCN Regulation] and Regulation (EU) 2018/XX [eu-LISA Regulation], COM(2018) 480 final.

[75] Regulation 2019/817 (note 1) and Regulation (EU) 2019/818 (note 2).

[76] The references to articles in the following paragraphs refer to articles in both aforementioned regulations.

[77] Figure provided by the European Commission, used by the Commission in its assessment of the impact on identity documents, together with document Proposal for a Regulation of the European Parliament and the Council on establishing a framework for Interoperability of 12 December 2017; SWD/2017/0473 final - 2017/0351 (COD).

[78] EDPS, Opinion on the proposals for two Regulations establishing a framework for interoperability of large-scale EU IT systems, 2018/C 233/07.

[79] Ibid.

[80] Ibid.

[81] Ibid.

[82] Ibid.

[83] See https://www.corruptioneurope.com/.

[84] See infringement proceedings against Poland, ECJ, Case C-619/18, European Commission v Republic of Poland, see also European Commission, press release IP/19/1957; European Commission, press release IP/19/1912 and https://ec.europa.eu/info/policies/justice-and-fundamental-rights/effective-justice/rule-law/rule-law-framework_de.

[85] ECJ, Cases C-508/18 and C-82/19 PPU, OG and PI, ECLI:EU:C:2019:456, in which the Court found that the German public prosecutors were not sufficiently protected from the influence of politics. In particular, the right of the Minister of Justice (as part of the executive) to issue individual

instructions was criticised. As a result, the current 5'600 or so European arrest warrants issued by German public prosecutors' offices will probably have to be reviewed and reissued if necessary. See https://www.lto.de/recht/justiz/j/eugh-europaeischer-haftbefehl-deutsche-staatsanwaelte-nicht-unabhaengig/.

Chapter 10
Biometric Data in the EU (Reformed) Data Protection Framework and Border Management:
A Step Forward or an Unsatisfactory Move?

Simone Casiraghi
(iD) https://orcid.org/0000-0001-6708-9175
Vrije Universiteit Brussel, Belgium

Alessandra Calvi
Vrije Universiteit Brussel, Belgium

ABSTRACT

Biometrics technologies have been spreading cross-sector in the public and private domains. Their potential intrusiveness, in particular regarding privacy and data protection, has called the European legislators, in the recent EU data protection reform, to introduce a definition of "biometric data," and to grant biometric data specific protection, as a "special category of data." Despite the reformed framework, in the field of border management, the use of biometric data is expected to increase steadily because it is seen as a more efficient and reliable solution. This chapter will look into the reformed data protection and border management legal frameworks to highlight discrepancies between the two, and ultimately assess to what extent the new data protection reformed regime for biometric data is satisfactory.

DOI: 10.4018/978-1-5225-9489-5.ch010

INTRODUCTION

Biometrics technologies, and the consequent processing of biometric data, have been spreading cross-sector and across Europe in recent years, although the use of fingerprints in criminal and civil matters dates back to the 19th Century (Kindt, 2013). The word "biometrics" originates from the Greek "*bios*" (life) and "*metron*" (measurement) and indicates, roughly, a set of technologies that process biological or behavioral traits for purposes of recognition.[1]

A paradigmatic use case of biometrics in the public sector in Europe is that of border management, where processing biometric data for the identification and the verification of the identity of individuals is portrayed as a more secure, efficient and reliable solution, as it is shown by e.g. the "Smart Border Package" proposed by European Commission (EC) in 2013 and by the revision of the European Union (EU) large-scale information technology systems (IT systems) in the area of asylum and migration. Large-scale IT systems are just one of the many border management instruments to enable and facilitate the exchange of information between authorities within the EU. This is done through, *inter alia*, the processing of different types of biometric data on top of more traditional alphanumeric data (i.e. data represented by letters, digits, special characters, spaces, and punctuation marks).[2]

In recent years, new rules on EU large-scale IT systems were introduced or proposed, and in 2017 the EC proposed to make these information systems interoperable at the EU level. As a result, in early 2019, two regulations for large-scale IT systems interoperability were adopted, one for the EU information systems in the field of borders and visa, and one for the field of police and judicial cooperation, asylum and migration.[3] In both frameworks, biometric data is expected to play a key role, to make these systems "interoperable" by, for instance, creating a common search portal and by establishing a common repository with biographic data of the persons whose data are stored in the different IT system (Fundamental Rights Agency [FRA], 2018, p. 20).

This chapter aims to show the discrepancy between the status of biometric data in these border management instruments and the new status granted to biometric data in the so-called data protection reform package, which includes the General Data Protection Regulation (GDPR) and the Law Enforcement Directive (LED) - other than the Regulation 2018/1725 on the protection of natural persons concerning the processing of personal data by the Union institutions, bodies, offices and agencies and on the free movement of such data (EUDPR).

The chapter will argue that, despite the efforts to standardize the definition and legal regime of biometric data across the EU, and the safeguards that are in place to protect them in the GDPR, in the LED, and the EUDPR, this is not sufficiently reflected in the case of border management instruments. The main research question will be: to what extent is the new definition and status of biometric data introduced in the reformed data protection framework consistent with the legal framework on the interoperability of EU large-scale IT systems?

The scope of the article is limited to the European Union's data protection framework, although the authors acknowledge the importance of the Council of Europe's instruments for privacy and data protection such as the European Convention of Human Rights and the modernized Convention 108.

To support the argument, the structure will be as follows.

In the next section, the chapter will provide an overview of the reformed EU data protection landscape concerning biometric data. The section will briefly sketch the situation before the entry into force of the GDPR, the LED and the EUDPR, the reasons why the legislator took this initiative (high risks to rights and freedoms of data subjects) and then move to the new definition and the legal status of biometric data in those frameworks.

In the following section, the status of biometric data in border management instruments (i.e. large-scale IT systems and interoperability regulations) will be outlined. Afterward, a short comparison between the GDPR, the LED, and the EUDPR on the one hand and border management instruments, on the other hand, will be drawn, to pinpoint how the rigorous definition and safeguards of the former are less clear in the latter.

Finally, the authors will provide some practical recommendations for the European regulators and policymakers based on the previous analysis, to address some of the inconsistencies outlined. In line with these recommendations, future research paths will be suggested, with particular regard to the increasing attention given by the EC to "contactless" or "seamless" border crossing technologies, which combine different types of biometric data to identify travelers.

OVERVIEW OF THE DATA PROTECTION REFORM PACKAGE ON BIOMETRIC DATA

In recent years, EU Institutions and bodies, such as the European Data Protection Supervisor (EDPS) and the Article 29 Data Protection Working Party (WP29) - now European Data Protection Board (EDPB) – have been using the words "biometrics", "biometric data", "biometric systems" and "biometrics technologies" in an interchangeable way, which can be misleading. To avoid confusion, it is important to distinguish from the start between biometric data and biometrics technologies (or simply biometrics) (Jasserand, 2016b, p. 66). The term "biometrics technologies" refers to a wide range of devices like fingerprint scanners or iris scanners, and socio-technical systems, like facial recognition systems or smart gates at the airport. Instead, biometric data are the types of data that are processed by such technologies, such as fingerprints (or dactyloscopic data), palmprints, facial images or blood samples for DNA analysis.

As a second step, another distinction can be made between biometric data from a technical and from a legal perspective. In the first case, biometric data refer to a type of technical processing that leads from biometric information or characteristics to a (digital) format (e.g. a template) that can be used to recognize individuals (Jasserand, 2016b, p. 70). In its legal meaning, biometric data are conceived as a type of *personal data* related to body characteristics and linked to the identifiability of an individual (Jasserand, 2016b, p. 71). In this latter sense, it is important to note that a definition of biometric data is a legal *construction* resulting from negotiations among the members of the data protection community, as a way to look at biometrics through "legal lenses" and adapt data protection concepts to such technologies to find an "optimal match" (Gutwirth, 2016, p. 19).

A New Definition of Biometric Data

The introduction of the concept of biometric data is relatively recent in the EU data protection landscape. Before the data protection reform package, there was no specific reference to biometric data in EU hard law. In the Directive 95/46/EC, i.e. the former Data Protection Directive, and the Framework Decision 2008/977/JHA, i.e. the "precursor" of the LED, biometric data did not have a specific definition, nor were they given a status of sensitive data. The only references to biometric data could be found in soft law instruments.

In 2003, the WP29 provided guidelines to member states to encompass biometric data in the broader category of personal data (Article 29 Working Party, 2003). An attempt to define biometric data in the EU context was made later also by the WP29 Opinion 4/2007 (Article 29 Working Party, 2007, p. 8), that considered them as "biological properties, behavioural aspects, physiological characteristics, living traits or repeatable actions where those features and/or actions are both unique to that individual and measurable, even if the patterns used in practice to technically measure them involve a certain degree of probability".

After the entry into force of the data protection reform package in 2018 (including GDPR, LED and the EUDPR), two main new elements concerning the rules applicable to biometric data were introduced. First, a standardized legal definition of biometric data; second, a specific legal regime, or status, applicable to biometric data, that is nowadays included in the "special categories" of personal data.

To begin with, biometric data are now defined either in the GDPR, in the LED and the EUDPR as "personal data resulting from specific technical processing relating to the physical, physiological or behavioural characteristics of a natural person, which allow or confirm the unique identification of that natural person, such as facial images[4] or dactyloscopic data" (Art. 4(14) GDPR, Art. 3(13) LED and Art. 3(18) EUDPR).

It is worth unpacking the definition of biometric data are in its three main components. Biometric data are personal data:

1. "resulting from specific technical processing" (first element),
2. "relating to the physical, physiological or behavioural characteristics of a natural person" (second element)
3. "which allow or confirm the unique identification of that natural person" (third element) (Art. 4(14) GDPR, Art. 3(13) LED and Art. 3(18) EUDPR).

The three elements have to exist cumulatively. Indeed, not all personal data "relating to the physical, physiological or behavioural characteristics of a natural person" are biometric data, but only when, cumulatively, they result from specific technical processing and they allow or confirm the unique identification of that natural person (Ducato, 2019, p. 1301).

This first element of the definition makes it clear that biometric data are interlinked but distinct from biometrics technologies, referred to as "specific technical processing". Albeit there is no common understanding of what "specific technical processing" means, most likely the choice to provide such a generic reference was made to comply with technological neutrality (Recital 15 GDPR).

Secondly, the reference to the physical, physiological or behavioral characteristics of a natural person enables the legislator to include within the category of biometric data not only the data collected through first-generation biometrics (e.g. fingerprints) but also through the so-called "second-generation biometrics" or "biometrics-at-the-distance". Second-generation biometrics, unlike first-generation ones, besides being more and more automated and integrated, measure also behavioral or "weak" biometric identifiers (less unique and stable as opposed to "strong" ones), such as gait (manner of walking), voice, body odor, ECG (electrocardiography), EEG (electroencephalography), body temperature, or pupil dilation, when used to uniquely identifying a natural person (Mordini & Tzovaras, 2012, p. 9). This is particularly relevant, given the fact that, unlike first-generation biometric traits, second-generation ones may be obtained without the subject being aware of that, even from low-quality video footage, making them ideal for use in surveillance applications (Reid et al., 2013). The use of second-generation biometrics is also interlinked with the recent (debated) rise in deployment of multi-modal biometric systems (which combine physiological and behavioral traits) and facial recognition technologies (FRA, 2019; Fussey & Murray, 2019).

The third element of the definition (i.e. "which allows or confirms the unique identification of the natural person"), has been related by Jasserand to the three-steps process of biometric recognition (2016a, p. 304). In short, the first phase is the enrolment of biometric characteristics in a biometric system and biometric characteristics are captured in the form of an image (biometric sample). The second phase is the feature extraction, where the sample is extracted, reduced and transformed into labels or numbers, i.e. a mathematical representation of the characteristic (biometric template), via an algorithm. In the third phase, a biometric sample is presented at a sensor and compared with a previously recorded template or sample. Jasserand (2016a) defends the idea that the terms "allowing" refers to, technically speaking, the *identification* (i.e. the one-to-many process whereby the system compares the captured template with all the available templates to determine the individual's identity), whereas "confirming" refers to the *verification* (i.e. the one-to-one process whereby an individual claims an identity and the system compares the captured biometric template with the stored template corresponding to the claimed identity) (p. 305).

In sum, a clear and standardized definition of biometric data is of crucial importance. Having multiple definitions of biometric data or lacking a distinction between the latter and biometrics technologies (or systems), might determine the uncertainty in the applicability of the new regime introduced by the data protection reform package.

A Special Regime for Biometric Data

Besides the definition, the second novelty introduced by the data protection reform package regarding biometric data is that they are included within the "special categories of personal data", that capture data "revealing racial or ethnic origin, political opinions, religious or philosophical beliefs, or trade union membership, genetic data, biometric data for the purpose of uniquely identifying a natural person, data concerning health or data concerning a natural person's sex life or sexual orientation" (Art. 9(1) GDPR, Art. 10 LED, Art. 10 (1) EUDPR and Art. 76 EUDPR). Processing these special categories of data may pose high risks to the data subjects (see below), hence requiring enhanced protection. Therefore, only when biometric data are processed "for the purpose of uniquely identifying a natural person" they are subject to a prohibition principle (Art. 9(1) GDPR) unless a limited number of conditions is met (10 in total, listed in Art. 9(2) GDPR).

Similarly, in the LED, the processing of special categories of data "shall be allowed only where strictly necessary, subject to appropriate safeguards for the rights and freedoms of the data subject, and only:

1. Where authorised by Union or Member State law;
2. To protect the vital interests of the data subject or of another natural person; or
3. Where such processing relates to data which are manifestly made public by the data subject" (Art. 10 LED).

In the EUDPR, there is also a distinction between the rules on the processing of biometric data by union bodies, offices and agencies when carrying out activities falling within the police and judicial cooperation in criminal matters, and other types of activities. In the former, the processing of biometric data "shall be allowed only where strictly necessary for operational purposes, within the mandate of the

Union body, office or agency concerned and subject to appropriate safeguards for the rights and freedoms of the data subject. Discrimination against natural persons on the basis of such personal data shall be prohibited" (Art. 76 EUDPR). In the latter, there is a general prohibition of processing of biometric data (Art. 10(1) EUDPR), unless certain conditions - that recall those listed in Art. 9(2) GDPR - are met (Art. 10(2) EUDPR).

In sum, the data protection reform package introduced a special regime for biometric data, but it does not include an absolute ban on their processing. Instead, there is a wide list of exceptions, which are different in the GDPR, LED and EUDPR, where the processing of biometric data is still allowed.

Why Was a Special Regime Introduced? Risks to Rights and Freedoms

The choice of EU legislators to introduce a special legal regime for biometric data - and a special category of data in general - is because "the context of their processing could create significant risks to the fundamental rights and freedoms" (Recital 51 GDPR). To provide a sketch of what could be the risks involved while processing biometric data, it is useful to refer to the typology elaborated by Kindt (2013, p. 275). According to her, risks can relate to the nature of biometric data themselves; to the architecture of biometric systems; to the use of biometric systems.

Risks Related to the Nature of Biometric Data Themselves

Being biological and/or behavioral characteristics (allegedly) unique, biometric data permit almost ubiquitous and more accurate identification of individuals both by the public and the private sector. The identification of individuals by public authorities or private companies can have many benefits, for instance, it allows citizens to enjoy services provided by the government or to do bank transactions. At the same time, it can lead to unwanted identification, thus compromising the possibilities to remain anonymous and the control people have on their identities, for example in the case of police investigations using facial recognition in public spaces. Biometric data are more vulnerable compared to other types of personal data: they can be visible and leave traces, thus making them easily capturable from a distance without the data subject being aware of it. The intrusiveness in people's privacy is even higher while different types of biometric data are combined, such as in the case of multi-modal biometric systems. Moreover, biometric samples could reveal information related to one's ethnic group (e.g. skin color or other morphometric differences) or health (e.g. to infer certain diseases). Finally, the fact that they are unique does not prevent them from being forged or stolen, leading to identity theft crimes like document fraud (Kindt, 2013, p. 143).

Risks Related to the Architecture of Biometric Systems

Risks do not only concern the nature of biometric data, but also the architecture or design of biometric systems. The architecture of the system enables and restricts the uses of biometric data, and as a consequence, it also poses a different set of risks (Kindt, 2013, p. 352). To simplify, an important distinction can be made between systems that store biometric data in a centralized way (e.g. in a database) or in devices under the control of data subject (e.g. a chip in the passport). In the latter case, the exclusive storage of data on a local device under control of the data subjects may reduce the risks related to the processing. Still, it is possible that, for instance, biometric data are nevertheless copied, or the device containing them is lost. In the case of centralized storage by contrast, which is more related to the scope of this chapter, the risks at stake are higher. Firstly, central databases are more vulnerable than local devices to security risks, like unauthorized access or attacks, which can have different risks for each part of the biometric system (e.g. the sensors, the storage medium or other sub-components). Secondly, the storage of biometric data in a central database might permit that such data are (re-)used for other purposes not initially foreseen ("function creep"), like profiling or criminal investigations. An example related to border management is when Interpol and law enforcement agencies were granted access to the information stored in the Visa Information System (VIS, see below) (Kindt, 2013, p. 358). In 2004, VIS was established to improve the management of a common EU visa policy and to enhance the security of visas. However, in 2008 access was granted for detection and investigation of terrorist offenses, a purpose that was not foreseen in the regulation of 2004 (Kindt, 2013, p. 386).

Risks Related to the Use of Biometric Systems

The third category of risks is related to the use of biometric systems. In this sense, there may be difficulties related to the enrolment of biometric characteristics, which might be easier for certain categories of people but more difficult for others, thus causing episodes of discrimination. There are also risks linked to the lack of accuracy of certain biometric systems, which could generate a disproportionate number of false positives or false negatives, which rates are higher when identifying certain categories of very young, old or disabled people, depending on the system (Kindt, 2013, p. 363). Based on the threshold that is set, a high rate of false positives could lead to, for instance at an airport, wrong flagging of people and would, in general, affect the interpretation of the human operator supervising the biometric machines (Macnish, 2012).

To sum up, processing biometric data bears the risk of affecting different rights and freedoms enshrined in the Charter of Fundamental Rights of the European Union (CFR), beyond privacy and data protection (Art. 7 and 8 CFR). Some examples include the right to human dignity (Art. 1 CFR) and to integrity of the person (Art. 3 CFR), freedom of expression and information (Art. 11 CFR) and freedom of assembly and association (Art. 12 CFR), the right to asylum (Art. 18 CFR), the rights of the child (Art. 24 CFR) and the right to good administration (Art. 41 CFR) (FRA, 2018). To prevent the consequences posed by high-risk processing activities, the data protection reform package introduced, *inter alia*, some methods and approaches that aim to tackle the risks in advance, before they materialize (i.e. the so-called risk-based approach). One approach is Data Protection by design and by default (Art. 25 GDPR, Art. 20 LED, Art. 27 EUDPR), which require the data controller to "embed" or inscribe data protection principles in the design of the systems, and would help to address the risks related to the architecture of the biometric systems listed above. Another approach is the process of Data Protection Impact Assessment (DPIA, Art. 35 GDPR, Art. 27 LED and Art. 39 and 89 EUDPR), which would help to identify and provide advice on the risks and impacts related to the use, nature, and architecture of biometric systems listed above. DPIA is particularly relevant when it comes to processing biometric data: for example, all the three cases enumerated in the GDPR when a DPIA is required (Art. 35(3) GDPR) are likely to apply to large-scale biometric systems.

As a preliminary conclusion, it appears that the novelties introduced by the data protection reform package were aimed at granting extra protection to biometric data, forbidding their processing or limiting it only to the strictly necessary, and accompanying the processing of biometric data to other specific safeguards (such as DPIA). This can be confirmed, for instance, by the recent case where the first fine for biometrics use under the GDPR was issued by the Swedish data protection authority in 2019.[5] However, the trend towards the processing of biometric data seems to be different in the context of border management.

BIOMETRIC DATA IN THE EU BORDER MANAGEMENT

To show this contrast, this section aims to briefly analyze the definition and status of biometric data in specific border management instruments (large-scale IT systems and interoperability) to then point out possible discrepancies between the two instruments later in the chapter. The first step to build this argument is to highlight what is the relation between border management instruments and the EU data protection legal framework more generally.

EU Data Protection Legal Framework Applicable to Border Management

Overview of Border Management Legal Instruments

Due to the complexity of the border management regulatory landscape in the EU, this sub-section will briefly outline the main legal frameworks and components of the EU architecture that governs border management. Art. 3(2) of the Treaty on the European Union (TEU) explains the general goals of the EU in this sector: "The Union shall offer its citizens an area of freedom, security and justice without internal frontiers, in which the free movement of persons is ensured in conjunction with appropriate measures with respect to external border controls, asylum, immigration and the prevention and combating of crime". It is with this goal in mind that:

- the internal borders checks in the European Union have been abolished and an integrated management system for external border has been created, together with a common policy on visa;
- certain aspects of asylum process and immigration were harmonized;
- efforts against illegal immigration and other forms of international crimes were intensified;
- EU large-scale IT systems were created (Engström & Heikkilä, 2014).

The resulting legal landscape for border management in the EU is highly complex, including instruments that were originally part of intergovernmental agreements and were later incorporated in EU Treaties or codified in EU regulations and directives.

A primary example is the *Schengen acquis,* a set of rules integrated in European Law to regulate the abolition of border controls within the Schengen area and strengthen border checks at external borders. The Schengen Agreement of 1985 established the Schengen Area,[6] in which internal border checks were largely abolished. The agreement was implemented by the Schengen Implementing Convention of 1990 and then incorporated into the European Union Law through the Schengen Protocol attached to the Treaty of Amsterdam, which entered into force in 1999. Since then, as no more checks are performed at the borders within the Schengen area,[7] EU states have been joining forces to improve security and efficiency at external borders. In this context, the Schengen Borders Code, first introduced in 2006, provides EU member states with a set of rules that govern how external border checks are carried out on people, duration of stay in the Schengen area and entry requirements.

To ensure European cooperation on border management, several Union-wide instruments have been established over the years. Some of the instruments are devoted to the exchange of information (e.g. the Prüm decision, the Advanced Passenger Information directive, the Passenger Name Record directives, the Eurosur framework, the EU large-scale IT systems), others discipline identity cards and passports, others again regulate certain European bodies and agencies involved in border management (e.g. the European Border and Coast Guard (Frontex)).

The chapter will focus exclusively on the information exchange systems, and in particular on the large-scale IT systems, which are managed by the European Union Agency for the Operational Management of Large-Scale IT Systems in the Area of Freedom, Security and Justice (eu-LISA) (Regulation (EU) 2018/1726). Most of these large-scale IT-systems focus on the *identification* (one-to-many process, see above) of a specific person by matching alphanumeric data and biometric data with the information already in the system. In this context, the types and quantity of biometric data is expected to increase in the upcoming years (FRA, 2018). At the time of writing, these are the large-scale IT systems that already contain (or will contain) biometric data:

- The Schengen Information System (SIS). Nowadays called SIS II, it contains alerts for missing/wanted objects and people, and it allows information exchanges between national border control, customs, and police authorities.
- Eurodac (European Dactylography). Its main purpose is to determine which Member State is responsible for examining an application for asylum and assist the control of irregular immigration.
- VIS (Visa Information System). Its scope is to facilitate the exchange of information on visa applications between the Schengen Member States.
- EES (Entry-Exit Systems). Its goal is to calculate and monitor the duration of authorized stays of third-country nationals and to identify over-stayers.
- ECRIS-TCN (European Criminal Records Information System for Third Country Nationals). Its purpose is to share information on previous convictions of third-country nationals.[8]

With the entry into force of the two regulations on interoperability, one for the EU information systems in the field of borders and visa (i.e. Regulation (EU) 2019/817, applicable to the EES, VIS, ETIAS, and SIS) and one in the field of police and judicial cooperation, asylum and migration (i.e. Regulation (EU) 2019/818 applicable to Eurodac, SIS and ECRIS-TCN), those databases will become interoperable.

More particularly, the regulations establish:

- A European Search Portal (ESP), allowing competent authorities to search multiple EU information systems simultaneously (including Europol data and Interpol databases), using both biographical and biometric data (Art. 6 Regulation (EU) 2019/817);
- A shared biometric matching service (BMS), which would re-group and store all the biometric templates currently used for other large-scale information systems (and future ones) in one single location, therefore allowing and facilitating e.g. cross-system comparisons (Art. 12 Regulation (EU) 2019/817);
- A common identity repository (CIR), containing biographical and biometric data of third-country nationals available in several EU information systems (Art. 17 Regulation (EU) 2019/817);

- A multiple identity detector (MID), checking whether the biographical identity data contained in the search exists in other systems covered, to enable the detection of multiple identities linked to the same set of biometric data.

The new regulations do not modify the rights of access by competent authorities as set out in the legal basis relevant for each European information system. The European search portal will flag where data or links exist in relation to a query, but the system will only show each authority the data to which they already have a right of access under previous legislation setting up the different databases.

To recap, border management related legal instruments have their own (data protection) rules but, for what is not expressly regulated in the single instrument, they explicitly refer to the GDPR, the LED and the EUDPR. That is why they can be considered *lex specialis* with respect to them. On top of that, they need to comply with the fundamental rights enshrined in the CFR.

Border Management Legal Instruments and Data Protection Reform Package

After the entry into force of the Lisbon Treaty, the right to personal data protection became a fundamental right under EU law, recognized by the CFR) and by the Treaty on the European Union (TEU) and the Treaty on the Functioning of the European Union (TFEU), giving the EU now a specific legal basis to adopt legislation to protect this fundamental right.

More in detail, Art. 16 TFEU prescribes ordinary legislative procedure for rules relating to the protection of individuals with regard to the processing of personal data by Union institutions, bodies, offices and agencies, and by the Member States when carrying out activities which fall within the scope of Union law. Art. 39 TEU waivers this rule, setting a special legislative procedure (whose outcome is a Council decision) in the field of common foreign and security policy. Therefore, depending on the policy sectors, data protection rules are adopted with different legislative procedures.

Among the reasons that determined the adoption of the reform there are:

- for the GDPR, to reduce the fragmentation in the implementation of personal data protection in the European Union, to reduce the legal and practical uncertainty for markets operators and public authorities. At the same time, the goal is to increase trust in online activities to unleash the potential digital economy to develop across the internal market, putting at the same time individuals in control of their own.
- For the LED, to protect the fundamental rights and freedoms of natural persons and in particular their right to the protection of personal data while guaranteeing a high level of public safety, and to ensure the exchange of personal data between competent authorities within the Union.
- For the EUDPR, the need to align to the GDPR and the LED also the processing of personal data by the Union institutions, bodies, offices and agencies.

The fact that different rules are depending on the policy sector is physiological, but the overlapping of different policy goals and the existence of grey areas (especially in the field of migration and law enforcement), together with the participation of different entities in border management (e.g. both national and European) create uncertainty about the proper legal regime applicable (e.g. GDPR, LED, EUDPR). In relation to the data protection reform package, and the new rules on processing biometric data, the interoperability regulations and the regulations of large-scale IT systems fall under the GDPR for what concerns processing of personal data (and, *a fortiori*, biometric data), unless the purpose is the "the prevention, detection or investigation of terrorist offences or of other serious criminal offences" (in this case the LED applies). Additionally, coordinated supervision should be ensured in accordance with the EUDPR, which also applies to the processing of personal data by eu-LISA.

Biometric Data in the Large-Scale IT Systems

Definitions and Legal Regime of Biometric Data in the Large-Scale IT Systems Regulations

One of the main safeguards concerning the risks to rights and freedoms deriving from the processing of biometric data in the GDPR, in the LED and in the EUDPR is the limitation of their processing, which is conversely one the core elements necessary for the functioning of the large-scale IT systems and their interoperability. To support this case, by giving an overview of the definitions and legal regime of biometric data in large-scale IT systems, it is useful to distinguish between those who were updated *after* the data protection reform package (SIS II, ECRIS-TCN, EES) and those who are not yet but will be soon (Eurodac, VIS).

As for the latter case, the Eurodac database includes, at the time of writing, only fingerprints, but it is planning to include facial images too. The Regulation (EU) 603/2013 does not mention biometric data, but it refers only to fingerprint data (Art. 2) as "data relating to fingerprints of all or at least the index fingers, and if those are missing, the prints of all other fingers of a person, or a latent fingerprint". While it is said that fingerprints constitute an effective element to establish an identity of the person, there is no mention of the sensitivity of the data extracted from them.

The VIS database also includes only fingerprints. However, besides defining fingerprint data, current rules on VIS (Regulation (EC) 767/2008) do mention "biometric data" and "biometrics" (three times in total) but neither do they define what they are, nor do they make a distinction among the two (see above).[9]

It is understandable that, in line with the fact that biometric data were not explicitly defined by the EU legislator before 2016 (see above), neither the Eurodac nor the VIS regulations contain specific definitions or a legal regime for biometric data. However, in the proposals to update Eurodac and the VIS, there is still no definition of biometric data, nor a reference to their special status.

Regarding the regulations that were updated after the entry into force of the data protection reform package, the SIS, which was reformed in 2018, will contain palm prints, fingerprints, facial images and DNA concerning, for example, missing persons to confirm their identity. The SIS Regulation 2018/1861 in the field of border checks defines biometric data as "personal data resulting from specific technical processing relating to the physical or physiological characteristics of a natural person, which allow or confirm the unique identification of that natural person, namely photographs, facial images and dactyloscopic data" (Art. 3(13)). The definition is almost equivalent to that of the GDPR, the LED, and the EUDPR, except for the "behavioural" characteristics which are not mentioned. Then, the regulation defines also "dactyloscopic data" as "data on fingerprints and palm prints which due to their unique character and the reference points contained therein enable accurate and conclusive comparisons on a person's identity" and "facial image" as "digital images of the face with sufficient image resolution and quality to be used in automated biometric matching" (Art. 3(14-15)). The Art. 3 of SIS Regulation 1862/2018 in the field of police and judicial cooperation, echoes the definition of biometric data contained in Regulation 2018/1861, adding to them "DNA profile" (Art. 3(15)). Chapter 9 and Chapter

16 of the two SIS regulations are on Data Protection, and they include data subject rights and judicial remedies, but they do not specify the special regime for biometric data nor the need for safeguards like data protection by design or DPIA.

The EES will include facial images and fingerprints, as stated in Regulation 2017/2226. Art. 3(18) defines biometric data only in a closed way, as "fingerprint data and facial image", which are further specified at Art. 3(17-18). However, such regulation has two important characteristics about the legal regime of biometric data. First, it is the only one, among large-scale IT systems, that mentions the impact of biometric data processing on privacy as follows:

"The use of biometrics, *despite its impact on the privacy of travellers*, is justified for two reasons: biometrics are a reliable method of identifying third-country nationals who are present on the territory of the Member States but not in possession of travel documents or any other means of identification, a common situation for irregular migrants. Second, biometrics allow for a more reliable matching of entry and exit data of bona fide travelers." (Recital 20) (italics added). Concerning privacy, it is important to note that the regulation states also that eu-LISA should perform a security risk assessment and follow principles of privacy by design and by default "during the entire lifecycle of the development of the EES" (Art. 37(1)(a-b)).

ECRIS-TCN will include also fingerprints and facial images. The Regulation (EU) 2019/816 on the ECRIS-TCN does not include "biometric data" in its list of definitions (Art. 3), although it contains the definition of fingerprints and facial images. The terms "biometrics", "biometric matching", "biometric identifier" and "biometric performance" are also mentioned but not further defined in the regulation. Chapter 5 is dedicated to data protection rights and supervision, and it contains important provisions inspired by the data protection reform package and in general the EU data protection framework, but it does not address the specific sensitive status of biometric data. The regulation also mentions that "The use of biometrics is necessary as it is the most reliable method of identifying third-country nationals within the territory of the Member States, who are often not in possession of documents or any other means of identification, as well as for more reliable matching of third-country nationals data" (Recital 25).

The same trend about the status and definition of biometric data observed in the large-scale IT systems can be found in the interoperability regulations. Both interoperability regulations 2019/817 and 2019/818 introduce closed or technical definitions of biometric data. Biometric data "means fingerprint data, facial images or both" (Art. 4(11) in both regulations). In turn, "fingerprint data" means "fingerprint images and images of fingerprint latents, which due to their unique character and the reference points contained therein enable accurate and conclusive comparisons on a person's identity". In terms of definitions, the novelty of the frameworks is that, in both interoperability regulations, the notion of "biometric template", as different from "biometric data", is introduced. A biometric template means "a mathematical representation obtained by feature extraction from biometric data limited to the characteristics necessary to perform identifications and verifications" (Art. 4(12)).

The approach towards biometric data is evident also in the recitals of the interoperability legal frameworks. For example, in both interoperability regulations, biometric data are associated with effectiveness, efficiency (Recital 9) and reliability: "Biometric data, such as fingerprints and facial images, are unique and therefore much more reliable than alphanumeric data for the purposes of identifying a person" (Recital 18). These features and advantages are thoroughly explained, while the topic of sensitivity of biometric data is just quickly mentioned with no further explanation: "Biometric data constitute sensitive personal data. This regulation should lay down the basis and the safeguards for processing such data for the purpose of uniquely identifying the persons concerned" (Recital 20).

In sum, it can be concluded that biometric data play an important role in the legal frameworks for large-scale IT systems. However, there is a mismatch between the tendency of the EU legislator to protect biometric data on a general level but to allow its increasing use in the context of border management at the same time. The following section will summarize where the mismatches lie to then provide some specific recommendations.

Biometric Data in the Data Protection Reform Package and Border Management Instruments: A Comparison

A Comparison at the Definitional Level

At a definitional level, in the light of this short overview, it appears that the definitions of biometric data are fragmented in the various legal instruments for large-scale IT systems. On the one hand, the definitions of biometric data are often closed and refer to specific types of biometric data included in the various databases, often without referring to the standardized and technologically neutral definition introduced by the data protection reformed package. This can be comprehensible considering that the large-scale databases contain only those biometric data expressly mentioned, but it may be misleading in so far as national authorities might process other types of biometric data that are not then transferred in the databases. On the other hand, an oscillation between the terms "biometrics" or "biometric identifiers", "biometric template" or "biometric data" can be observed, but without further clarification. Additionally, the notion of facial image is defined differently across different instruments, since in SIS new rules (i.e. Regulations 1861 and 1862 of 2018) there is the extra condition that there should be "sufficient image resolution and quality to be used in automated biometric matching" for a facial image to be considered biometric data (Art. 3(15) and Art. 3(14)). It appears that this criterion is not applicable, or at least not made explicit, for the other databases.

Additionally, comparing the definitions of biometric data of the above with that of the GDPR, the LED, and the EUDPR, behavioral characteristics are excluded. This can be justified by the fact that behavioral characteristics are not data contained in the databases (yet), but it becomes problematic since second-generation biometrics are being used (or at least tested) in border control for identification purposes in the European landscape, at least at a research-level. Facial recognition technologies are being combined with behavioral traits, such as in the case of iBorderCtrl project, where face-matching tools and automatic deception systems are being combined to help border guards detecting whether travelers are "telling the truth" (FRA, 2019, p. 17). These types of data may not be stored on EU large-scale IT systems (again, yet), but still may be contained in national ones.[10]

In general, it seems that the effort made by the EU legislator in the data protection reform package to distinguish between a legal and a technical sense of biometric data (Jasserand 2016b, see above) is not yet reflected in these instruments. The underlying reasons for mentioning biometric data is often descriptive or technical (quality standards and technical specifications), and not to warn controllers and processors against possible fundamental rights infringements from the processing of biometric data.

A Comparison at the Level of the Legal Regime

At the level of the status of biometric data, it is more or less made explicit that biometric data are not only desirable but *necessary* for their reliability and accuracy, as opposed to alphanumeric data. Therefore, their processing *must* be permitted to achieve the goals of security, justice and prevention and combating of crime (Art. 3(2) TEU). However, the risks that biometric data processing could bring about to data subjects is hardly mentioned. Additionally, the role of eu-LISA in monitoring the systems mostly regards security and cost-effectiveness, which can be achieved by carrying out risk analyses, vulnerability assessments or financial impact assessment. These are undoubtedly important goals for the functioning of the databases, but from a data protection perspective, they risk overshadowing the impact of these systems on data subjects. To protect them, safeguards introduced in the data protection reform package like data protection by design or DPIA are not explicitly referred to. Only in one instrument (the EES Regulation) the possible impact on privacy is mentioned, but this is again overstepped by the possible benefits biometrics could bring about. This aspect is crucial since, under the data protection regime, eu-LISA is not obliged to implement privacy by design and by default or to carry out a DPIA, given its designated status of data processor, and not of data controller, in the interoperability regulations (Art. 41 Regulation 2019/817 and 2019/818) (see below).

SOLUTIONS AND RECOMMENDATIONS

When the Smart Border Package and the interoperability proposals were advanced by the European Commission in 2013 and 2017, concerns were raised by various stakeholders (e.g. EDPS, FRA, NGOs, academia, etc.) about the negative impacts that the new rules would have had on fundamental rights in general and privacy/data protection in particular. It was pointed out how interoperability is not just a technical choice, but it entails a political approach that somehow blurs the lines between various policy goals (e.g. asylum, migration management, law enforcement or counterterrorism), risking equating, for instance, the notions of terrorists and criminals with foreigners (European Data Protection Supervisor [EDPS], 2018). Interoperability entails much more than interconnecting IT-systems: it has technical, semantic, social, cultural, economic, organizational and legal dimensions (De Hert & Gutwirth, 2006). These aspects of interoperability are extremely important but are beyond the scope of this article. This is why the recommendations and solutions by the authors are limited to the uncertainties related to the definition and status of biometric data and to reconcile the two approaches followed in the GDPR and the LED legal frameworks on the one hand, and on the EU large-scale IT systems and interoperability, on the other hand.

Among the many options, the authors recommend the following:

1. Regulatory initiatives in border management, especially the updates of large-scale IT databases, should also include more uniform definitions of "biometric data" in line with that provided by the data protection reform package. If other terms such as biometrics, biometric identifier or biometric template are introduced, these should be also defined properly, to avoid uncertainties in the application of the special regime.
2. In border management instruments, a clearer distinction between biometrics processing for verification and identification purposes should be made because, in the second case, there is a higher risk of interference with fundamental rights (FRA, 2019, p. 33).
3. From the short overview of the regulations on large-scale IT systems and interoperability, it seems that the legislators did not pay adequate attention to the sensitive status of biometric data and safeguards that are needed to protect rights and freedoms of data subjects. This aspect could be made

clearer by adding to the requirements that eu-LISA and member states should carry out not only risk assessments, vulnerability assessments, and cost-benefit analyses, but also data protection by design and by default (Art. 25 GDPR, Art. 20 LED) and a DPIA (Art. 35 GDPR, Art. 27 LED).

4. To ensure the interests of the data subjects are taken into account, and the risks coming from the processing of biometric data are properly considered, legislative proposals to regulate biometric data in border management should be discussed not only with data controllers but with all interested parties.

5. As outlined by the EDPS (2018), eu-LISA and member states should implement privacy (or data protection) by design and by default in designing biometric systems to ensure their compliance with data protection principles. In short, such tools require that technical and organizational measures are implemented at an early stage of the development and implementation of a technological system (Art. 25 GDPR and Art. 20 LED). Similarly, the FRA refers to the two methods as "relevant in the development of technical solutions for IT systems" (2018, p. 72), especially to ensure purpose limitation.

6. In the GDPR, large-scale processing of biometric data for the purpose of uniquely identifying a natural person (Art. 35(3)(b)) is a trigger for data controllers to perform a Data Protection Impact Assessment (DPIA). The LED, by contrast, does not refer to specific cases, but only points out that a DPIA is required "where a type of processing, in particular, using new technologies, and taking into account the nature, scope, context and purposes of the processing is likely to result in a high risk to the rights and freedoms of natural persons" (Art. 27(1) LED). Processing of biometric data in EU large-scale IT systems is also sufficient to trigger the safeguard in the LED.

7. Such an obligation is provided in the GDPR, in the EUDPR, and the LED (although not in all cases of biometric data processing) but it is missing in large-scale IT systems and interoperability regulations. What is also problematic is that DPIA is an obligation only on data controllers. In relation to the personal data in the shared BMS, CIR, MID of the interoperability regulations (see above), eu-LISA is considered data processor (Art. 41 Regulation 2019/817 and 2019/818). This means that eu-LISA, *inter alia,* is exempted from the legal obligation to carry out a DPIA. The European Court of Justice or the EU legislators could intervene to qualify eu-LISA as joint-controller to bind it to conduct a DPIA.

8. It could be clarified to what degree border management is governed by the GDPR and or the LED or by national laws. In addition to border management instruments, Member States are also free to maintain and introduce further conditions and limitations with regard to the processing of genetic data, biometric data and data concerning health (Art. 9(4) GDPR). In the Netherlands, for instance, Art. 29 of the Dutch GDPR implementation act, the UAVG (Uitvoeringswet Algemene Verordening Gegevensbescherming, 2018), states that biometric data can be processed for identification of an individual if the processing is necessary for authentication or security purposes. The CNIL in France also adopted a specific regulation on the use of biometric data in the workplace (on 10 January 2019). Although this solution is consistent with the attempt of the GDPR to safeguard the different data protection traditions in the Member States, the level of protection of biometric data risks to be inhomogeneous in the various Member States.

9. When it is not possible to review regulatory frameworks, recurring to soft law instruments (such as guidelines) is advisable, especially to clarify which categories of biometric data are more intrusive, when a DPIA is warranted when processing biometric data or how to handle the concerns raised by second-generation biometrics.

FUTURE RESEARCH DIRECTIONS

The authors decided to focus on the recommendations above because the EC has been investing in research and development on biometrics technologies for border management, to cope with the increasing number of travelers crossing European borders. One example is the number of projects funded within the framework Horizon 2020 program for Secure Societies 2018-20 (FRA, 2019, p. 17). While the EC is pushing for more and more "invisible", "seamless" or "contactless" solutions to increase efficiency, these solutions, which make large use of biometric data, bear the risk of infringing fundamental rights. Therefore, solid legal frameworks about how to handle (future generation) biometric data, as well as careful application of those already in place, are needed.

How can legal scholars and experts contribute to this new trend in the use of biometric data at the borders, which seems in contrast with the data protection reform package? This is indeed also a political question. The authors believe that legal scholars could contribute to clarify what sort of issues could emerge from new biometrics technologies and how to address them. Critical analyses of the current definition of biometric data in GDPR, LED and EUDPR, and concrete proposal to improve it, were not addressed in this chapter but would be nevertheless very welcome. At the same time, the field of biometrics, which includes many different disciplines (from computer science to law) that do now always dialogue with each other, require legal experts also to come out of their "bubble" and be open to discussion, even if this requires learning a different vocabulary about biometrics. Initiatives in this direction are being taken, for example, by the European Association for Biometrics.

On a practical level, broadening the scope of Data Protection Impact Assessment could be advisable when dealing with biometrics technologies, to make sure that the special regime for biometric data is taken into account at the border management level. Critics of DPIA have already noted how the scope of such a tool would not encompass the range of societal and human rights issues raised by biometrics technologies and the processing of biometric data. It can be argued how surveillance at a distance (which can be translated into "biometrics at a distance") involve mechanisms to categorize or profile people on the basis of stereotypes and prejudices. Following David Lyon (2003), "given that surveillance now touches all of us who live in technologically "advanced" societies in the routine activities of everyday life, on the move as well as in fixed locations, the risks presented go well beyond anything that quests for "privacy" or "data protection" can cope with on their own" (p. 2). Moreover, DPIA could be criticized for not being driven by social values and it might be interpreted as a mere compliance assessment of data protection law (Clarke, 2016).To tackle these shortcomings, resorting to forms of human rights or social impact assessment (Vanclay, 2015), whenever possible (especially in the case of biometrics used for identification purposes) would allow actors involved in biometrics and border management to become more aware of conflicts and negotiations in the design of the technology, and create a broader space for discussion. As noted by the FRA (2019), public authorities need to obtain all necessary information to carry out such an assessment from the industry, and trade secrets or confidentiality issues should not hinder the effort (p. 34).

CONCLUSION

To conclude, the present inquiry started with the question "to what extent is the new definition and status of biometric data introduced in the reformed data protection framework consistent with the legal framework on the interoperability of EU large-scale IT systems?"

To answer the question, the chapter started by sketching what the current definition and status of biometric data in the data protection reform package is and what was the reason for introducing it (i.e. the higher risks posed by the processing of special categories of data). Secondly, the chapter overviewed the definitions and status of biometric data in large-scale IT systems and interoperability regulations. Third, the authors confronted the two frameworks and highlighted some discrepancies.

After confronting the frameworks, it can be noted that the data protection reform package has brought some undeniable improvements in the definition, regulation, and protection of biometric data in the EU. The introduction of the new concept of biometric data and the inclusion of it in the "special categories" of personal data are a sign of the attempt to look closely and limit, whenever possible, the processing of biometric data in the light of the recent rise in the deployment of biometrics technologies. This pioneering move, which was very much needed in the EU, could serve as an example for other jurisdictions and work as a deterrent for the processing of biometric data in different sectors.

Nevertheless, the sector of the EU border management, especially the large-scale IT systems and their interoperability, seems to go in a different direction. This is an instance of a double-faced policy of the EU's data protection law. On the one hand, a stricter approach towards biometric data is promoted, but on the other, its enforcement is made more difficult by creating initiatives that seem in contrast with data protection principles.

It is difficult for now, given the fact that the data protection reform package came into force only in 2018, to fully assess the effectiveness of the introduction of a special regime for biometric data in hard law. For example, relevant case law, at the time of writing, still refers to the old data protection regime. However, it was shown how it is possible to argue that, in the light of the analysis conducted in the field of border management, the new regime for biometric data in GDPR and LED is not fully satisfactory, especially from the perspective of the data subjects.

To begin with, there are still unclarities within the regime of the GDPR and LED. The nature of biometric templates and samples needs further clarification. The different rules on biometric data processing in the field of law enforcement, the grey areas of application between the LED and the GDPR in border management and border control can be problematic. Moreover, the broadness of the exception to the special discipline ex Art. 9 GDPR, casts doubts on the EU data protection reform's success to create a homogenous system for biometric data protection in the European Union.

Secondly, there are loopholes across GDPR, LED, EDUPR and large-scale IT and interoperability systems. Specifically, despite the attempt to standardize the definition of biometric data in the data protection reform package, the definitions of biometric data in the various instruments of border management are fragmented and not in line with the data protection reform package. Besides, it is not clear how "second generation" biometric data will be treated by such systems, whether they will be stored and where, and whether they will become operational soon. All in all, despite the stress on the sensitivity of biometric data brought forward by the data protection reform package, biometric data are still processed widely in border control, and this trend is expected to continue in the near future, in contrast with the definition and status provided by the data protection reform package and in general by the EU data protection legal framework.

ACKNOWLEDGMENT

This research was made possible through funding from the European Union's Horizon 2020 Research and Innovation Programme under Grant Agreement No 787123 (Privacy, Ethical, Regulatory and SOcial No-gate crossing point solutions Acceptance).

The information and views set out in the chapter are those of the authors and do not necessarily reflect the official opinion of the project, the European Commission or other European institutions.

REFERENCES

Article 29 Working Party. (2003). *Working document on biometrics*. Retrieved from https://ec.europa. eu/justice/article-29/documentation/opinion-recommendation/files/2003/wp80_en.pdf

Article 29 Working Party. (2007). *Opinion No 4/2007 on the concept of personal data*. Retrieved from https://ec.europa.eu/justice/article-29/documentation/opinion-recommendation/files/2007/wp136_en.pdf

Clarke, R. (2017). *The distinction between a PIA and a Data Protection Impact Assessment (DPIA) under the EU GDPR*. Paper presented at the Computers Privacy and Data Protection Conference (CPDP), Brussels, Belgium.

De Hert, P., & Gutwirth, S. (2006). Interoperability of police databases within the EU: An accountable political choice? *International Review of Law Computers & Technology, 20*(1-2), 21–35. doi:10.1080/13600860600818227

Ducato, R. (2019). I dati biometrici. In R. D. Vincenzo Cuffaro (Ed.), *I dati personali nel diritto europeo* (pp. 1285–1321). Torino: Giappichelli.

Engström, V., & Heikkilä, M. (2014) *Fundamental rights in the institutions and instruments of the Area of Freedom, Security and Justice*. Frame Deliverable 11.1. Retrieved from http://www.fp7-frame.eu/wp-content/uploads/2016/08/09-Deliverable-11.1.pdf

European Commission. (2016). Proposal for a regulation of the European parliament and of the council on the establishment of 'Eurodac' for the comparison of fingerprints for the effective application of [Regulation (EU) No 604/2013 establishing the criteria and mechanisms for determining the Member State responsible for examining an application for international protection lodged in one of the Member States by a third-country national or a stateless person], for identifying an illegally staying third-country national or stateless person and on requests for the comparison with Eurodac data by Member States' law enforcement authorities and Europol for law enforcement purposes. Retrieved from https://ec.europa. eu/transparency/regdoc/rep/1/2016/EN/1-2016-272-EN-F1-1.PDF

European Data Protection Supervisor. (2018). *EDPS Opinion 4/2018 on the Proposals for two Regulations establishing a framework for interoperability between EU large-scale information systems*. Retrieved from https://edps.europa.eu/sites/edp/files/publication/2018-04-16_interoperability_opinion_en.pdf

Fundamental Rights Agency. (2018). *Under watchful eyes – biometrics, EU IT-systems and fundamental rights*. Luxembourg: Publications Office of the European Union.

Fundamental Rights Agency. (2019). *Facial recognition technology: fundamental rights considerations in the context of law enforcement.* Luxembourg: Publications Office of the European Union.

Fussey, P., & Murray, D. (2019). *Independent Report on the London Metropolitan Police Service's Trial of Live Facial Recognition Technology.* Academic Press.

Gutwirth, S. (2016). Le droit n'est pas une science mais la science juridique existe bel et bien. In G. Azzaria (Ed.), *Les nouveaux chantiers de la doctrine juridique* (pp. 1–39). Montreal: Yvon Blais /Thomson Reuters Canada.

Jasserand, C. A. (2016a). Legal Nature of Biometric Data: From 'Generic' Personal Data to Sensitive Data. *European Data Protection Law Review, 3*(3), 297–311. doi:10.21552/EDPL/2016/3/6

Jasserand, C. A. (2016b). Avoiding terminological confusion between the notions of 'biometrics' and 'biometric data': An investigation into the meanings of the terms from a European data protection and a scientific perspective. *International Data Privacy Law, 6*(1), 63–76.

Kindt, E. J. (2013). *Privacy and Data Protection Issues of Biometric Applications.* Dordrecht: Springer. doi:10.1007/978-94-007-7522-0

Kloza, D., Van Dijk, N., Casiraghi, S., Vazquez Maymir, S., Roda, S., Tanas, A., & Konstantinou, I. (2019). *Towards a method for data protection impact assessment: Making sense of GDPR requirements. d.pia.lab Policy Brief No. 1/2019.* Brussels: Vrije Universiteit Brussel.

Lyon, D. (2003). Surveillance as Social Sorting: Computer Codes and Mobile Bodies. In D. Lyon (Ed.), *Surveillance as Social Sorting. Privacy, Risk and Digital Discrimination* (pp. 13–30). London: Routledge.

Macnish, K. (2012). The Unblinking Eye: The Ethics of Automated Surveillance. *Ethics and Information Technology, 14*(2), 151–167. doi:10.100710676-012-9291-0

Mordini, E., & Tzovaras, D. (2012). *Second Generation Biometrics: The Ethical, Legal and Social Context.* Dordrecht: Springer Netherlands. doi:10.1007/978-94-007-3892-8

Reid, D. A., Samangooei, S., Chen, C., Nixon, M. S., & Ross, A. (2013). Soft Biometrics for Surveillance: An Overview. In V. G. C. R. Rao (Ed.), *Handbook of Statistics* (pp. 327–352). Amsterdam, The Netherlands: Elsevier.

Vanclay, F. (2015). *Social Impact Assessment: Guidance for assessing and managing the social impacts of projects.* Fargo, ND: International Association for Impact Assessment.

Wayman, J. L. (2007). The Scientific Development of Biometrics Over the Last 40 Years. In K. de Leuw & J. Bergstra (Eds.), *The History of Information Security: A Comprehensive Handbook* (pp. 263–274). Amsterdam, The Netherlands: Elsevier. doi:10.1016/B978-044451608-4/50011-0

Wiles, P. (2018). *Annual Report 2018.* Office of the Biometrics Commissioner.

ADDITIONAL READING

Brouwer, E. (2008). *Digital Borders and Real Rights. Effective Remedies for Third Country Nationals in the Schengen Information System.* Leiden: Martinus Nijhoff Publishers. doi:10.1163/ej.9789004165038.i-568

De Hert, P. (2013). Biometrics and the Challenge to Human Rights in Europe. Need for Regulation and Regulatory Distinctions. In P. Campisi (Ed.), *Security and Privacy in Biometrics* (pp. 369–413). Dordrecht: Springer. doi:10.1007/978-1-4471-5230-9_15

European Parliament. (2019). Interoperability between EU borderand security information systems. Retrieved from https://www.europarl.europa.eu/RegData/etudes/BRIE/2018/628267/EPRS_BRI(2018)628267_EN.pdf

European Parliament. (2019). Protection of EU external borders. Retrieved from https://www.europarl.europa.eu/RegData/etudes/BRIE/2018/630316/EPRS_BRI(2018)630316_EN.pdf

Gates, K. A. (2011). *Our Biometric Future. Facial Recognition Technology and the Culture of Surveillance.* New York: New York University Press. doi:10.18574/nyu/9780814732090.001.0001

Gutwirth, S. (2007). Biometrics between opacity and transparency. *Annali dell'Istituto Superiore di Sanita, 43*(1), 61–65. PMID:17536155

Johnson, P., & Williams, R. (2007). European Securitization and Biometric Identification: The Uses of Genetic Profiling. *Annali dell'Istituto Superiore di Sanita, 43*(1), 36–43. PMID:17536152

Marciano, A. (2019). Reframing biometric surveillance: From a means of inspection to a form of control. *Ethics and Information Technology, 21*(2), 127–136. doi:10.100710676-018-9493-1

Swanlund, D., & Schuurman, N. (2018). Second Generation Biometrics and the Future of Geosurveillance: A Minority Report on FAST. *ACME: An International Journal for Critical Geographies, 17*(4), 920–938.

Yue, L. N. (2013). *Bio-Privacy. Privacy Regulations and the Challenge of Biometrics.* New York: Routledge.

KEY TERMS AND DEFINITIONS

Biometric Data: In a technical sense, biometric data refer to technical processing that leads from biometric information or characteristics to a (digital) format (e.g. a template) that can be used to recognize individuals. In a legal sense, biometric data are a type of personal data extracted from physical, physiological and behavioral characteristics.

Data Protection Impact Assessment (DPIA): DPIA can be defined as "an evaluation technique used to analyse the possible consequences of an initiative for a relevant societal concern or concerns (i.e. a matter or matters of interest or importance), if this initiative could present danger to these concerns, with a view to supporting an informed decision on whether to deploy the initiative and under what conditions, and it constitutes in the first place a means to protect those concerns" (Kloza et al., 2019, p. 1).

First-Generation Biometrics: First-generation biometrics are more traditional biometrics technologies that rely on physical features like fingerprints or facial image to recognize an individual.

Function Creep: The use of (biometric) data for another purpose than that for which it was originally processed.

Identification: Identification refers to the one-to-many process whereby the system compares the captured template with all the available templates to determine the individual's identity.

Interoperability: Interoperability refers to the functionality of (large-scale) information systems to exchange data and to enable the sharing of information. In the context of border control, the goal of the EU is to improve its data management architecture by ensuring that border guards, customs authorities, police officers and judicial authorities have the necessary information at their disposal to perform their functions, by overcoming structural shortcomings that impede their work (European Data Protection Supervisor, 2018). Biometric data are a key enabler of interoperability because they are seen as a much more reliable means to identify a person than alphanumeric data (i.e. "data represented by letters, digits, special characters, spaces and punctuation mark").

Second-Generation Biometrics: Second-generation biometric technologies are those biometrics that require less human cooperation and can be run in a transparent and "invisible" way to the subjects. This has led to a shift from human eye performed identification (e.g. traditional fingerprint analysis) to increasingly automated, digital and "smart" biometrics. Examples are technologies that measure "motor skills", electromagnetic body signals or human-computer interaction patterns (Mordini & Tzovaras, 2012, p. 9).

Verification: Verification is the one-to-one process whereby a person claims an identity and the system compares the captured biometric template with the stored template corresponding to the claimed identity.

ENDNOTES

[1] The use of the term as indicating a unified field of scientific inquiry has become common, in the English literature, only from the early 1980s (Wayman, 2007, 263). The spectrum of what is usually referred to as "biometrics" is, in fact, wide and includes disciplines from distinct scientific traditions.

[2] The Schengen Informative System (SIS), the Entry-Exit System (EES), the European Travel Information System (ETIAS) and the European Criminal Records Information System on Third Country Nationals (ECRIS-TCN); or, at a proposal stage, in the case of Visa Information System (VIS) and Eurodac (European Asylum Dactyloscopy database).

[3] I.e. the Regulation (EU) 2019/817, applicable to the EES, VIS, ETIAS, and SIS and the Regulation (EU) 2019/818 applicable to Eurodac, SIS and ECRIS-TCN

[4] With a clarification that "The processing of photographs should not systematically be considered to be processing of special categories of personal data as they are covered by the definition of biometric data only when processed through a specific technical means allowing the unique identification or authentication of a natural person." (Recital 51 GDPR).

[5] In this case, the Swedish Data Protection Authority issued a fine of SEK 200 000 to a school for using biometric facial recognition systems to record the attendance of students, in violation of Art. 5 GDPR.

[6] The area included originally five of ten then EC members. Today, it comprises 26 European states.

[7] Except in cases of temporary reintroduction of border control at internal borders in case a serious threat to public policy or internal security is in place.

8   For a deeper overview of biometrics, large-scale IT systems and fundamental rights see the report by the Fundamental Rights Agency (2018).

9   Reading the various provisions in combination, it is possible to infer that biometric data encompass fingerprint data (and possibly photographs) (Art. 5), but this is not made explicit.

10   See how the biometrics commissioner in the UK is pushing to govern the use and retention by the police of second-generation biometrics (Wiles, 2018).

Chapter 11
The Impact of the GDPR on Extra–EU Legal Systems:
The Case of the Kingdom of Bahrain

Maria Casoria
Royal University for Women, Bahrain

Eman Mahmood AlSarraf
Al Zayani Investments, Bahrain

ABSTRACT

The chapter discusses the influence of the General Data Protection Regulation (GDPR) on legal systems extra-EU and particularly the Kingdom of Bahrain, country member to a regional organisation located in the Arabian Gulf denominated Gulf Cooperation Council (GCC), which is exclusive to six states (i.e., Saudi Arabia, United Arab Emirates, Oman, Qatar, and Kuwait in addition to Bahrain). Amongst these countries, Bahrain is the only one that has recently enacted its own separate Personal Data Protection Law (PDPL) mostly resembling the GDPR due to the ever-increasing commercial relationship with business undertakings in Europe. Moreover, the adoption of the data protection law counts as a huge leap forward taken by the kingdom in reforming its legal framework, since it is the state's striving strategy to grow into a midpoint for data centre, just on time for the launch of data centres opening in Bahrain that are endorsed by Amazon Web Services.

INTRODUCTION

The recent unprecedented increase in data production stemming from the propagation of the digital economy has led to the worldwide proliferation of regulations seeking to protect data owners and providers, supervise the collection of data, and minimise data security breaches. This is primarily true in the States members of the Gulf Cooperation Council (GCC), regional organisation founded in 1981 and exclusive to six States located on the shores of the Arabian Gulf - Bahrain, Saudi Arabia, United Arab Emirates, Oman, Qatar, and Kuwait (Borea, 2019) -, due to the lack of an advanced rule of law for

DOI: 10.4018/978-1-5225-9489-5.ch011

privacy in most of them, despite their progressive shift from economies relying on the exploitation of natural sources to data-driven societies.

With the constant rejuvenation occurring to technology and its accessories, the development of privacy laws has become crucial and therefore most countries are now amending their laws and regulations to best fit the global epidemic occurring. As reported on the official website of the United Nations Conference on Trade and Development, 107 countries (of which 66 are developing or transition economies) have put in place a legislation to secure the protection of data and privacy. In this area, Asia and Africa show a similar level of adoption, with less than 40 per cent of the countries having a law in place (UNCTAD, 2019). In percentages, this means that:

- 57% of the countries have passed laws on data protection and privacy.
- 10% of the countries has just draft legislations.
- 21% of the countries does not have a legislation at all.
- 12% no data are available.

As far as the European Union (EU) framework is concerned, since the enactment of the General Data Protection Regulation (GDPR) there have been many discussions about its impact and repercussions. In economic and statistical terms, scholars pointed out that the GDPR might have a rather negative effect on the European Union's internal market and economy (Allen, DWE, Berg A, Berg C, Markey-Towler, B and Potts, J, 2019). Nonetheless, from a legal perspective, the impact that the GDPR is producing on other legal systems is remarkable. Indeed, protecting individuals' personal data has become of critical importance in the 21st century, due to the phenomenon of digitalisation, a wide-ranging motion that affects all individuals with no exception. Consequently, laws and regulations are constantly amended and modified in order to match the innovative digitalisation endangerments. In our times, technology is administering most facilities and services, artificial intelligence is spreading like wildfire, and business undertaking are trying to take advantage of the technological disruption while trying to cope with the need for securing information (Francis L. & Francis J, 2017).

This chapter dwells around two focal pillars. Firstly, it scrutinises the stimulus the GDPR initiated on the enactment of official privacy laws in jurisdictions other than the European Union; secondly, it analyses, with a comparative approach, the privacy laws enacted of the GCC countries, with focus on the Kingdom of Bahrain, while parallelly shedding light on similarities and differences with the GDPR. Indeed, if on the one side the European Union legal framework seems to be quite advanced, the regulatory process in the GCC region is still at its inception and, thus, it seems interesting to investigate how the European Union is influencing the legal changes in other legal systems. Moreover, unlike the EU, the GCC as a regional organisation does not yet have in place a common rule of law for the protection of personal data. Considering the above reasons, the Kingdom of Bahrain followed the footsteps of the GDPR, mirroring, to a large extent, the methodology adopted by the GDPR, as this is the Kingdom's first law dealing exclusively with this legal phenomenon.

SETTING THE SCENE: THE IMPACT OF THE GDPR INTERNALLY AND EXTERNALLY

The GDPR, enforced since 25th May 2018, in a relatively short time span is evidently astounding the magnitude of impact the Regulation had on the country's Member States to the European Union and its firms. There is rather a disagreement when it comes to the question of whether the GDPR reformed the shape of privacy laws and how personal data was processed. If one spectrum is that the GDPR aligned a cohesive legal framework that promotes the awareness of European nationals in relation to their rights and strengthening the enforcement of safeguarding data protection (Press Corner, 2019); the other end of the spectrum are the numbers and statistics that point towards the hindrance of the GDPR on enterprises, digital modernisation, employment and the customers (Chivot & Castro, 2019).

Such hindrance has extended to various sectors and aspects. Firstly, the GDPR is said to be exhausting company resources vis-a-vis capital, budget and assets. Reports indicate that more than 40 percent of companies have spent about $10.1 Million (9 Million Euros) in compliance efforts exclusively, this includes US firms that have a data presence in the EU region (PricewaterhouseCoopers, 2017). In 2017, an average of $1.3 Million (1.2 Million Euros) was spent on GDPR compliance according to companies reports. This amount increased up to $1.8 Million (1.6 Million Euros) in the year of 2018 (Ernst & Young, 2018). Roughly 500 companies were estimated to have spent about $7 Billion in compliance costs for GDPR (Forbes, 2018). A survey conducted in October 2018 showed that about 52 percent of companies, with an appointed data protection officer, claimed that the only reason they have this position in their companies is for compliance purposes as they believe that it does not add any value to the company (Ernst & Young, 2018). In an effort to weaponize the GDPR against companies, electronic tools have been developed. An example includes piling GDPR-authorised data requests on companies that requires addressing within a 30-day period to avoid wasting the companies' time (GrowRevenue, 2019).

Another critical aspect of GDPR is that its implementation is allegedly harming EuropeanTech Startups. The amounts of deals and investments in young EU ventures have decreased noticeably due to the implementation of GDPR. The GDPR was estimated to result in the loss of 30,000 jobs in the EU on a yearly basis (Jia, Jin, & Wagman, 2019). Studies showed that between the period of May 2018 and April 2019 there was a decrease of $14.1 Million (12.5 Million Euros) per month per Member State, in the venture funding of the EU tech firms. The amount of monthly venture deals has decreased by 26.1 percent, whereas the amount of money raised to said firms decreased by 33.8 percent. For firms that are between three to six years old, so called 'Young Ventures', the number of venture deals per month have decreased by 20.5 percent in addition, a decrease of $4.4 Million (3.9 Million years) was recorded for monthly investment per Member State. Moreover, firms that are less than three years old, so called 'New Ventures', have witnessed a decrease of 30.3 percent in the amount of monthly deals as well as a decrease of $5.2 Million (4.6 Million Euros) in the amount of monthly investment per Member State.

During the same period, the financial, health, and the IT sectors were also affected. The health sector recorded a decrease of 26.1 percent in the number of deals and a decrease of $7.9 Million (7 Million Euros) in the amount of monthly investment per Member State. The financial sector showed a decrease in the number of deals by 21.3 percent and a decrease of $6.8 Million (6 Million Euros) in the amount of monthly investment per Member State. The IT sector was impacted the most as the records show a decrease of 32.4 percent in the number of deals and $8.2 Million (7.3 Million Euros) in the amount of monthly investment per Member State (Jia, Jin, & Wagman, 2019).

Lastly, it has also been stated that the GDPR minimises competition in digital advertising. After the implementation of the GDPR, the number of advertising vendors in the EU has decreased by 3.4 percent across all websites, whereas the US websites witnessed an increase of 8.3 percent. In the EU, advertising vendors have lost their market reach especially the smaller entities, they lost somewhere between 18 to 31 percent between the period from April to July 2018 (WhoTracks.Me, 2018). The period between May and July 2018 displayed that Google's tracking code appeared on slightly more websites but Facebook appeared 7 percent fewer. The smaller companies were the ones that suffered the most as they recorded a decrease of 32 percent (Wall Street Journal, 2018).

Despite the concern on whether the GDPR revolutionised the future of data protection in the European Union or not, the fact that the GDPR paved the way for countries outside the EU to update their domestic legal framework remains factual and cannot be overlooked. The enactment of the GDPR promoted the enactment of privacy laws in extra-EU countries as well as the establishment of national data protection watchdogs. While it is true not all states headed towards the path of modifying their laws to best match the GDPR and its modernised provisions, the GDPR stimulated a handful of states and reach a step closer to harmonisation (Ius Laboris, 2019). Below is a list of countries (apart for those part to the Gulf Cooperation Council) which will be scrutinised in the following sections to support the aforesaid statement.

Argentina

As an outcome of the GDPR, Argentina has newly commenced a legislative procedure to update the National Data Protection system. Early this year in 2019, a new resolution was adopted on selected methods for, among others, access to private data, retaining biometric data, categories of giving consent to entry of personal data treatment, as lastly the Argentinian Congress took the initiative and began examining their Personal Data Protection Law No. 25, 326 (Ius Laboris, 2019).

Brazil

After the initiative the European Union began with the GDPR, the Brazilian Authorities have initiated their own innovative regulation managing such matter. Following the GDPR that was implemented in May 2018, Brazil started ratifying their own version of the law, the Brazilian General Data Protection Law Federal Law No. 13,709/2018 (LGPD). The Regulation was signed on the 14th of August 2018 and is expected to be enforced in August 2020 (DLA Piper, 2019).

Brazil's General Data Protection Law simulates, to a certain extent, the GDPR, as they both primarily share the key objective of strengthening personal data protection, enacting rigid but necessary penalties on those who infringe on the rights of individuals and on processing agents. They both also comparably regulate controllers and processors of personal data, govern the extra-territoriality principle and share the stern approach of high penalties to non-compliance to the regulation. However, while the GDPR's penalties can reach up to 20 Million Euros or 4% of the global turnover if it is a case of undertaking (GDPR, 2018), according to the Brazil's LGPD the fine can go as high as 2% of Brazilian revenues reaching a maximum at 50 Million Brazilian Real (BRL). (Brazilian General Data Protection Law 2018). In general terms, this is deemed to be a significant move by Brazil as they only recently entered the movement of data protection and its regulations in 2009. Until that point, the monitoring framework of data protection was sector-centered and predominantly governed— among other laws — by the Brazil's Civil Rights Framework for the Internet.

Norway

Norway, one of the Member States to the European Economic Area but not to the EU, has incorporated the GDPR as a part of their national law. The GDPR is subjected on all individuals Member State to the European Union and the European Economic Area. Hence, since Norway is a Member State to the European Economic Area, the GDPR is applicable thereof. The principles of GDPR has been merged into the European Economic Area since the 20th of July 2018, a couple of months after the GDPR was officially enforced in the European Union, followed by the incorporation of Norway in their domestic laws (Lexology, 2019).

Before the enforcement of the GDPR, Norway examined and studied its own laws in preparation of the implementation to begin. The new amendments included a new legislative Privacy Act, modifications to the 'camera monitoring' in establishments and organisations, and access to workers correspondences (Global Legal Group, 2019). In any case, Norway must comply with the GDPR to an extent for the objective of the GDPR to succeed which is the harmonisation and to guarantee the free flow of personal information throughout the EU and the EEA (Wikborg Rein, 2018).

Panama

Given that Panama is considered one of the countries with a thriving business and a main attraction for international establishments, it is only practical that several European Union enterprises branched out or have subsidiaries in Panama. Accordingly, Panama has adjusted their privacy law in the attempt to comply with the GDPR and prolong their affairs with the European Union.

Panama passed the Law No/ 81 of 26 March 2019 promulgating Personal Data Protection, which is expected to be enforced on 29th of March 2021 (Morgan & Morgan, 2019). While Panama did in fact enact a new legislation in line with the GDPR criteria, it the law is not a verbatim adoption of the EU rule of Law. In fact, Panama did not follow the strict penalty policy of GDPR, but rather went in a different yet lower standard policy, whereas the maximum penalty for breaching or non-compliance to Law 81 is US$10,000, which vastly differs from the penalty imposed by the GDPR (Lexology, 2019).

While it is too soon to be certain, the major difference in penalties imposed by the two laws could plausibly lead to a greater challenge in the upcoming future vis-à-vis firms whether they will act in accordance with the law or if they will use the rather low penalty as a loophole for deviating (Interact Law, 2019).

The above overview demonstrates how extensive the impact GDPR has been on other jurisdictions since its enforcement, whereby some states have implemented requirements similar to GDPR, where others were 'inspired' by the Regulation and accordingly amended their domestic privacy laws. Many other countries are progressively heading towards either establishing or amending their existing privacy law, be it in any shape or form, an example such as the California Consumer Privacy Act, which is said to be the most innovate regulation in the field expected to be enforced in 2020. Another example is the Japan Act on the Protection of Personal Information that was modified in May 2017 (PrivSec Report, 2018).

While it is true that there have been various amendments internationally and that not all of them can considered as a direct outcome of the emergence of the GDPR, the significance of the EU regulation cannot be overlooked or taken for granted. Therefore, one can easily conclude that the impact of the GDPR has extended throughout different jurisdictions and states, reflecting deeply the importance of privacy law in every country to ensure an individual's security.

DATA PROTECTION IN THE GULF COOPERATION COUNCIL WITH A SPECIAL EMPHASIS ON THE KINGDOM OF BAHRAIN

As aforementioned, the Kingdom of Bahrain is a member of the Gulf Cooperation Council, regional organisation established primarily to achieve harmony and create a sturdy political, economic, legislative coalition among States sharing similar political, cultural, and Islamic bonds. At regional level, some laws in sectors relating to Commerce, IP rights and Arbitration, have been passed in the past few years for the sake of harmonisation, but the stalemate of the regional block has made harmonisation difficult to achieve. The lack of common rules is also due to the current status of the economic integration in the GCC, which is still a customs union despite all the past attempts to move towards a common market and a monetary union that have been unsuccessful. Nevertheless, when it comes to the national regulation of sectors relating to commerce and market, one can observe some similarities in the approach taken by the local legislators in issuing rules for their respective countries.

A Regional Overview on Privacy Laws

At the outset it shall be clarified that in the Arabian Gulf region there is no one cohesive and synchronised law for data protection, but instead some of the Member States have enacted a number of domestic laws to regulate data protection and, even when a state does not have a separate law on the matter, the constitution grants at least the right to privacy to the citizens. Consequently, the terms of comparison relate to the national privacy laws passed in some of the countries concerned. It is of utmost importance to highlight that only very recently the GCC countries have realised the importance of protecting personal data. Therefore, many, if not all, the GCC Member States are on the route of adopting new laws to advance the development of their rules in this specific field of law.

Until July 2018, and with one exception (namely, Qatar – Law No. 13 of the year 2016 concerning Privacy and Protection of Personal Data), none of the GCC Member States had a modern, nationally applicable data protection law. Legal issues relating to privacy and data protection were typically analysed in terms of general, and ill-fitting, criminal provisions relating to the unauthorized disclosure of secrets, or, in appropriate circumstances, industry-specific obligations relating to healthcare or credit data, or telecommunications sector subscriber data.

In the region there is another regulation for data protection, which is not enforced at country level by within the Abu Dhabi Global Market, international financial centre located in the UAE and established to provide companies a place to operate under an international regulatory framework, with its own judicial and legislative infrastructure based on Common Law. Basically, the Abu Dhabi Global Market Data Protection Regulation passed in 2015 (ADGM Data Protection Regulation of 4th October 2015) applies only to the companies incorporated and operating within the ADGM as opposed to the broader UAE. In December 2017 an *ad hoc* Office of Data Protection was established in order to oversee the implementation of the law by the companies which collect and process personal data in this financial centre. Similar rules are in place in the Dubai International Financial Centre, which passed its Data Protection Law in 2007 (DIFC Law No. 1/2007), and its Data Protection Regulations in 2012 (DIFC Law No. 5/2012). However, Dubai is expected to update their legal framework in the near future through the adoption of a new data protection law.

The Bahraini Personal Data Privacy Law (PDPL)

On 12 July 2018 the Kingdom of Bahrain has issued the Law No. 30 of 2018 on Personal Data Protection (PDPL), which came into effect on 1 August 2019 (Wade, 2019). Before the enactment of the PDPL, personal data were not protected as such, but instead the right to privacy was protected in the Constitution of Bahrain of 2002, where Article 26 establishes that individuals have the right to privacy in regards to postal, telegraphic, telephonic and electronic communications nor will such communication's confidentiality will be desecrated except in those situations prescribed by the law (Bahrain.bh, 2002). Other laws that standardise data protection and confidentiality of information in Bahrain are the Electronic Transactions Law and the Telecommunications Law.

Taking a closer look into the Personal Data Protection Law of Bahrain, it can be noticed that the Kingdom espoused and embraced an analogous regulation to one of the GDPR (Christie, 2019), even though the Bahraini Law has a broader scope of application, describing the legal protection of personal privacy as -amongst others- the main constitutional rights of an individual, which should be protected considering the increasing use of electronic/digital means for processing information in the country. When drafting the data protection law, the Kingdom of Bahrain followed quite closely the GDPR since it is the most up-to-date and enforced regulations dealing with the subject matter, as this is Bahrain's first time issuing an explicit law on data protection. However, there are still some differences between the two set of laws.

The Structure of the PDPL

The PDPL comprises of 60 articles which laid down rules for the security of individual's confidentiality, definite consensus necessities for data processing, and the formation of a Personal Data Protection Authority.

The law is divided into three broad 'titles', which are:

Title 1: Processing Provisions – Including definitions and general rules for the legality of processing, controls of data processing and transfer, as well as the rights of the data holder.
Title 2: Data Protection Authority – Including provisions relating to the establishment of an ad hoc regulator, and its rights and responsibilities.
Title 3: Accountability of the data manager (data controller) and data processor - Including provisions relating to accountability to the regulator, investigation procedures, civil and criminal liability, and penalties for violation.

Personal data, like for other laws, is defined as any information of any form related to an identifiable individual, or an individual who can be identified, directly or indirectly, particularly through their personal identification number, or one or more of their physical, physiological, intellectual, cultural or economic characteristics or social identity.

Core Provisions

The scope of application is pertinent to the citizens, residents and firms processing the data, in addition to it applying to individuals not living or employed in the territory of Bahrain, as well as businesses not positioned in the Kingdom, yet that process personal data by tools existing in Bahrain. Therefore, the Personal Data Protection Law will have an extraterritorial effect, as per Article 2 of the Law. The law also stipulates that it is illegal for the Data Manager or any individual to process any confidential data or information nor are they permitted to use the concerned data for subjective profit or advantage or the profit of a third entity. Moreover, these impermissible acts shall stay prohibited even after the Data Manager finishes his/her professional service.

Furthermore, the security of processing provisions, and the confidentiality provisions, appear to be fairly standard. Data controllers are required to apply technical and organizational measures capable of protecting personal data against unintentional or unauthorized destruction, accidental loss, unauthorized alteration, disclosure or access, or any other form of processing. The measures adopted need to be appropriate, bearing in mind the nature of the data in question and the risks associated with processing it. Bahrain has also announced that there will be a new authority organised to withhold the infringements against individual's personal information, such as sensitive information, i.e. bank details. The "Authority", as per the Data Protection Law, is the Personal Data Protection Authority, which will be in charge of the whole spectrum of violations that occur within the radius of this law, either on its own powers, at the appeal of the competent Minister, or in acknowledgement to a complaint. Mr. Srikat Ranganathan, hosting a seminar on the Bahraini PDPL further emphasized stating, " Data owners, you and me, have rights to inquire; the right to object; the right to rectify, block or erase the right to withdraw consent; and the right to complain about how our data is being processed." (Gulf Daily News, 2019) As of October 2019, there was no one coherent body that was responsible for the competencies of the law at hand, even though the law officially enacted in August 2019. Regardless, on the 9th of October 2019, it was announced that the Bahraini Ministry of Justice is the authorised representative authority body to handle all tasks related to the Personal Data Protection Law (Al Tamimi & Co., 2019). As of now, the Ministry is the only governmental authority overseeing the implementation of the PDPL.

Data controllers are required to engage only data processors who provide sufficient guarantees regarding the application of technical and organisational measures. Importantly, there is an obligation on data controllers to take steps to verify compliance with such measures, and to enter into a written contract with the data processor requiring that the data processor shall only process data in accordance with the instructions of the data controller, and in accordance with the data controller's requirements regarding security and confidentiality.

Since the Bahraini Personal Data Protection Law is now in effect, data controllers will have to notify the authority prior to conducting any data processing unless they appoint a Data Protection Supervisor or the processing is limited to certain activities set out in Article 14 of the Law. Some types of data processing (including automated processing of sensitive personal data, biometric data for identification purposes, genetic information and video monitoring) will require the express prior approval of the authority.

The adoption of this law counts as a huge leap forward taken by the Kingdom in reforming the State and developing it, as it is the State's striving strategy to grow into a midpoint for data centre; just in time for the launch of data centres opening in Bahrain that are endorsed by Amazon Web Services. An additional motive to why the Kingdom of Bahrain has just recently passed the data protection law is so that it could be in line with its 2030 vision, which encompasses on sculpting and shaping the economic vision of the Kingdom from every single aspect, starting with the government, society and ending with economy (DLA Piper, 2018). The 2030 vision was launched in 2008 by His Majesty King Hamad bin Isa Al Khalifa, to guarantee an enhanced life for every Bahraini, and that is by altering the laws in the

Kingdom and concocting strategic interchanges that would conceal the gaps that are found, for it to renovate into a better state economically (Bahrain.bh, 2008).

The law will also be incredibly beneficial to the Kingdom as it enables the country to:

- Move forward in its plan to become a Data-Driven economy.
- Create opportunities for Cloud Computing, a key sector with the potential to create jobs.
- Facilitate secure and effective data processing for commercial use.
- Promotes effective data flows and cross-border data transfer.
- Ensure data confidentiality, availability, and integrity.
- Increase transparency in data processing and management.

In addition, according to Information Telecommunication Union 2017 Information Society Report, Bahrain's digital economy has received international recognition as the highest in ICT Development in the MENA region, 31st globally amongst 188 countries in ICT Development, and most dynamic in improving ICT Access. The report also demonstrated Bahrain's high broadband penetration, with 98% of the population being Internet users and 98% of households having Internet (ITU, 2017). Therefore, the Personal Data Protection Law comes as a natural step for Bahrain, who is considered as a regional leader in ICT.

GDPR VIS-À-VIS PDPL: A COMPARISON

While it is true that Bahrain shadowed the GDPR when ratifying their own law, the PDPL is not a fully verbatim adoption of the European regulation as there are prominent differentiations between the two laws.

Firstly, the mechanism for providing the consent is different in the two jurisdictions, because the EU, in its attempt to provide a high degree of protection, prescribes an opt-in mechanism whereby the data owner is required to explicitly consent to the treatment of personal data; on the other hand, the Bahraini law provides for an opt-out mechanism, requiring the data owner to consent by default to the treatment, unless stated otherwise.

The penalties regulated under the GDPR vary depending on the violation or the infringement occurred, and the highest penalty or consequence might be a fine up to four percent of annual global turnover or €20 million, whichever is greater. This type of penalty could be executed for a rather severe infringement, such as in cases where no adequate consent was provided by the data subject to process data. On the other hand, it is to be noted that not all GDPR infringements result to fines, since the GDPR contemplates a variety of sanction for not compliance, namely issuing warnings and reprimands, imposing a temporary or permanent ban on data processing, 0rdering the rectification, restriction or erasure of data, and suspending data transfers to third countries.

The consequences for non-compliance to the Bahraini Personal Data Protection Law have a criminal law nuance, since penalties generally comprise up to one year in prison and/or a fine of between BHD 1,000 and BHD 20,000 (between about EUR 2,300 to about EUR 45,000). The fact that the Law creates criminal offences means that compliance is all the more important and should be treated as a high priority. Moreover, the Data Protection Authority can issue orders to stop violations, including emergency orders and fines. Civil compensation is also allowed for any individual who has incurred damage arising from the processing of their personal data by the data manager or arising from the data protection supervisor's violation of the PDPL. Appeals can be made against decisions of the Authority.

Bahraini businesses that have already implemented a data protection compliance program under the GDPR may have developed some of the infrastructure that will apply under the PDPL but abiding by the GDPR does not guarantee compliance with the PDPL as such. For example, companies which operate as data managers will need to:

- Recognise the right of Bahraini data owners to object to the processing of personal data that causes harm or distress to the data owner or another person (this is not a data subject right found in the GDPR).
- Notify the Authority of their processing.
- Obtain prior written approval of the Authority to process certain types of personal data (this requirement is not established under the GDPR).

Another element of difference between the GDPR and the PDLP is the risk of criminal penalties not included in the GDPR, even though the latter imposes upon the regulated entities potentially staggering fines up to 4% of the global revenue.

The similarities found in the GDPR that is reflected in the PDPL are the requirements that both legislations oblige, which states that personal data:

- Is processed fairly and legitimately.
- Is collected for a legitimate, specific and clear purpose.
- Is sufficient, relevant and excessive for the purpose of the data's collection, or for the purpose for which subsequent processing is carried out.
- Is correct and accurate, and subject to updates whenever necessary.
- Shall not remain in a form allowing identification of the data owner after meeting the purpose of its collection or for the purpose for which subsequent processing is carried out. The PDPL does allow the storage of anonymised data for a longer time for historical statistical or scientific research purposes.

Another similarity between the Bahraini Law and the GDPR relates to the consent prior to the treatment. Likely to the GDPR the PDPL has specific requirements about how consent must be given. For consent to be valid it must be:

- Issued by an individual of full eligibility.
- Written, explicit and clear.
- Issued based upon the data owner's free will and consent, after being fully informed about the purposes of the processing of their personal data.
- The data owner has a right to withdraw consent at any time.

The Ministry of Justice, as it is the competent body and the designated authority for the implementation of the PDPL, must issue a resolution outlining these procedures for withdrawing consent and the data manager's decision on request for withdrawal of consent (Bahrain News Agency, 2019).

DISCUSSION

The advancement of technology and disruptive devices has made even harder to keep under control the proliferation of data shared and stored worldwide, in both analogue and digital environments. Therefore, legislators across the globe have taken immediate actions to mitigate the damages stemming from illegitimate usage of personal data. This, in the European Union, generated in the adoption of the European Union General Data Protection Regulation and in the GCC Region resulted in the Bahraini Personal Data Protection Law.

Since several states are heading towards a more cohesive and wide-ranging application of their data protection legislations, it is crucial that the rest of the states and regions update and amend their own domestic legislations and regulations, in order to avoid any possible sovereignty clashes. Moreover, it is recommended that the European Union, and the Kingdom of Bahrain -- considering that they have the most contemporary laws regulating data protection -- all adopt a comprehensive security system to govern the lacks that keep on resurfacing, and to aim for treatment of data in the digital system, such as online backups, firewalls, virus and malware.

Even though the GCC Member States have shown a slow beginning in the field of privacy, yet they are improving with the rest of the developing regions, and the fact that some Member States do not have a law exclusively regulating the right to privacy does not indicate that an individual's right to privacy is not respected or protected thereto, as this right granted of under the constitution, first and foremost, amongst other laws. Lastly, in the near future, it would deem as a benefit and crucial matter that the GCC States harmonise their laws regarding data protection, to reach its fullest capabilities and potential, paralleling the approach adopted by the European Union, especially in the light of the consistent commercial relationships between undertakings established in this two regional blocks.

CONCLUSION AND FUTURE RESEARCH DIRECTIONS

The chapter examines the extra-territorial impact of the GDPR in jurisdictions other than the European Union, with a focus on the experience of the Kingdom of Bahrain, a country located on the shores of the Arabian Gulf, which has very recently enacted a domestic privacy law resembling the EU Regulation.

The fact that a country so different in terms of cultural, historical, religious, and legal heritage from the EU Member States has decided to follow very closely the steps of the European Union in the adoption of their first ever legislation protecting privacy is an attestation that, despite some criticisms regarding the gaps in the GDPR, especially with reference to the ineffective rules for privacy protection in the digital environment and the vague approach to the enterprise accountability for cases of data breach, the GDPR is affecting the way in which legislators worldwide approach issues related to privacy. This also confirms that the GDPR might be seen as the most fascinating, yet complex regulation ever composed on the legal issues related to privacy, data protection and information security and, as such, will lead the next round of changes in Europe and abroad.

Once Bahrain will implement more effectively the PDPL, the EU effect might become even more evident and, if rumours about the possible implementation of similar laws in two of the wealthiest countries in the GCC, i.e. Saudi Arabia and United Arab Emirates, were confirmed, it would be interesting to scrutinise the domino effect that the EU legislator is having in the GCC at domestic level and, futuristically, also at regional level.

Since the Bahraini Personal Data Protection Law is relatively new many areas will require further research as soon as the Data Privacy Authority, currently the Ministry of Justice, will pass implementing regulations and the companies will start abiding by the law. Future research activities might focus also on decisions about cases of non-compliance. Moreover, the recent establishment of Amazon Web Service (AWS) Middle East in the Kingdom of Bahrain (AWS, 2019), which will further boost digitalisation and innovativeness, will most probably require legislative updates through amending the PDPL or enforcing new laws for the sector of information security. Lastly, because other countries in the region are moving towards the implementation of more updated privacy laws, another area to explore will be a comparative analysis among the privacy laws in the GCC countries also in the attempt to suggest a regional harmonisation in this field.

REFERENCES

Al Tamimi & Co. (2015). *Abu Dhabi Global Market: Public consultation on data protection*. Retrieved from https://www.tamimi.com/law-update-articles/abu-dhabi-global-market-public-consultation-on-data-protection/

Al Tamimi & Co. (2019). Retrieved, from https://www.tamimi.com/news/ministry-of-justice-islamic-affairs-and-awqaf-entrusted-with-the-tasks-and-competences-of-personal-data-protection-authority/

Al Tamimi & Co. (2012). *Data Protection and Privacy Issues in the Middle East*. Retrieved from https://www.tamimi.com/law-update-articles/data-protection-and-privacy-issues-in-the-middle-east/

Allen, D. W. E., Berg, A., Berg, C., Markey-Towler, B., & Potts, J. (2019). Some Economic Consequences of the GDPR. *Economics Bulletin*. Retrieved from https://ssrn.com/abstract=3160404

Amazon Web Services (AWS) The New AWS Region in the Middle East. (2019). Retrieved from https://aws.amazon.com/local/middle_east/bahrain/

Bahrain News. (2019). *Organisations to obtain customers' approval before storing their personal data from next month*. Retrieved from http://beta.gdnonline.com/Details/567248/New-body-on-way-to-guard-personal-data

Bahrain News Agency. (2019). *HM King designates entity to assume duties of the authority for protection of personal data*. Retrieved from https://www.bna.bh/en/HMKingdesignatesentitytoassumeduties-oftheauthorityforprotectionofpersonaldata.aspx?cms=q8FmFJgiscL2fwIzON1%2BDl9zQ5EMjiqZCB Nc6yqcKAE%3D

Borea, P. (2019). *The Gulf Cooperation Council: Institutions, Laws, Policies, External Relations*. Lexis Nexis.

Brazilian General Data Protection Law. (2018). Retrieved from https://iapp.org/media/pdf/resource_center/Brazilian_General_Data_Protection_Law.pdf

Chivot, E., Castro, D., Chivot, E., & Castro, D. (2019). *What the Evidence Shows About the Impact of the GDPR After One Year*. Retrieved from https://www.datainnovation.org/2019/06/what-the-evidence-shows-about-the-impact-of-the-gdpr-after-one-year

Christie, R. (2019). *General Data Protection Rules*. Lexis Middle East.

Council Post. (2018). *Is Your Business GDPR-Compliant?* Retrieved from https://www.forbes.com/sites/forbesagencycouncil/2018/06/11/is-your-business-in-compliance-with-the-eus-general-data-protection-regulation/#6761ec6d379c

Data Protection. 2019 | Laws and Regulations | Norway | ICLG. (2019). Retrieved, from https://iclg.com/practice-areas/data-protection-laws-and-regulations/norway

Ernst & Young. (2018). Retrieved, from https://www.ey.com/Publication/vwLUAssets/ey-iapp-ey-annual-privacy-gov-report-2018/$File/ey-iapp-ey-annual-privacy-gov-report-2018.pdf

Fines / Penalties | General Data Protection Regulation (GDPR). (2018). Retrieved, from https://gdpr-info.eu/issues/fines-penalties/

Francis, L., & Francis, J. (2017). *Privacy: What Everyone Needs to Know*. Oxford University Press.

GDPR Compliance Top Data Protection Priority for 92% of US Organizations in 2017, According to PwC Survey. (2017). Retrieved, from https://www.pwc.com/us/en/press-releases/2017/pwc-gdpr-compliance-press-release.html

GDPR - What happened? (2018). Retrieved, from https://whotracks.me/blog/gdpr-what-happened.html

How GDPR is shaping global data protection - PrivSec Report. (2018). Retrieved, from https://gdpr.report/news/2018/08/24/how-gdpr-is-shaping-global-data-protection/

Implementing the GDPR in Norway. (2018). Retrieved, from https://www.wr.no/en/news/news/implementing-the-gdpr-in-norway/

ITU Measuring the Information Society Report 2017. (2017) Retrieved, from https://www.itu.int/en/ITU-D/Statistics/Pages/publications/mis2017.aspx

Jia, J., Jin, G., & Wagman, L. (2019). *The Short-Run Effects of GDPR on Technology Venture Investment*. Retrieved, from https://ssrn.com/abstract=3278912

Kingdom of Bahrain - eGovernment Portal. (2008). Retrieved, from https://www.bahrain.bh/wps/portal/!ut/p/a1/jdDfE4FAEAfwv8VDr-3qqHg7TSlTwyByLybmHKY6k8ifLzz5Efbtdj7f2d0DBhGwL-D7vRFzsZBYntzfTl-4Q9aZmagOchg7S4aTl-rZLcGxUYPEECLEroBsjY9bRdBP_y6MWWE2v-VYEgQKRmb-xPHQuxT_7M1xT9OX_CM5gDe2HvV9zBtzUfoH6PATCRyNX9Txc0WxFTAM-v5huc8V0951d4WxeHYVVDBsixVIaVIuLqWqYKfllt5LCB6lnBIwzC6ePt2cvYpbTSuTGJy6Q!!/dl5/d5/L2dBISEvZ0FBIS9nQSEh/

Law in Brazil - DLA Piper Global Data Protection Laws of the World. (2019). Retrieved, from https://www.dlapiperdataprotection.com/index.html?t=law&c=BR

Mims, C. (2018). *Who Has More of Your Personal Data Than Facebook? Try Google*. Retrieved, from https://www.wsj.com/articles/who-has-more-of-your-personal-data-than-facebook-try-google-1524398401

Norway - The impact of the GDPR outside the EU | Lexology. (2019). Retrieved, from https://www.lexology.com/library/detail.aspx?g=34dfb199-c9ab-463c-8c5c-57404e1a3248

Panama Data Protection Law: much lower fines than GDPR. (2019). Retrieved, from https://www.interact. law/news/panama-data-protection-law-much-lower-fines-than-gdpr/

Panama: New Law on Protection of Personal Data. (2019). Retrieved, from https://sites.morimor.com/ newmorimor/panama-new-law-on-protection-of-personal-data/

Panama - The impact of the GDPR outside the EU | Lexology. (2019). Retrieved, from https://www. lexology.com/library/detail.aspx?g=e138a075-95e2-4959-8498-696967e63d18

Press corner. (2019). Retrieved, from https://ec.europa.eu/commission/presscorner/detail/en/IP_19_4449

Solove, D. J. (2006). A Taxonomy of Privacy. *University of Pennsylvania Law Review*, *154*(3), 477. doi:10.2307/40041279

The Constitution of Bahrain. (2002) Retrieved, from https://www.bahrain.bh/wps/wcm/connect/d749d20a-7545-4900-b64c-5443e6c20cd6/CA9SS7XP.pdf?MOD=AJPERES

UNCTAD | Data Protection and Privacy Legislation Worldwide. (2019). Retrieved, from https://unctad. org/en/Pages/DTL/STI_and_ICTs/ICT4D-Legislation/eCom-Data-Protection-Laws.aspx

Wade, G. (2019). *Privacy and Protection of Personal Data*. Lexis Middle East.

What the evidence shows about the impact of the GDPR after one year. (2019). Retrieved, from https:// growrevenue.io/2019/gdpr-impact/

Section 4
Studying Data Privacy Under Different Lenses

This section focuses on studying data protection beyond the boundaries of a traditional legal analysis.

Chapter 12

A Comprehensive Perspective on Data Protection Practices in Organizations:
Beyond Legal Considerations

Ine van Zeeland

imec-SMIT, Vrije Universiteit Brussel, Belgium

Jo Pierson

imec-SMIT, Vrije Universiteit Brussel, Belgium

ABSTRACT

The aim of this chapter is to take readers beyond the prescriptions of the law to present them with a practical perspective on what happens when organizations try to protect personal data. This is based on the acknowledgement that different sectors of society will have different concerns when it comes to the protection of personal data and privacy. The various conceptions of privacy connect a wide variety of academic disciplines, from anthropology to urban planning. We need to understand that there are many different perspectives on what privacy signifies, and hence, that there are many different considerations regarding what to do to protect it.

INTRODUCTION

Several articles of the General Data Protection Regulation (GDPR) suggest a need for insights beyond the traditional legal skill set. For example, data protection officers and supervisory authorities are required to raise data protection awareness within organizations and the general public (articles 39(1) and 57(1)), and stakeholder consultations are advised for both data protection impact assessments and codes of conduct (article 35(9) and recital 99). In these and other instances, the GDPR calls for an interdisciplinary effort to support personal data protection in the practical reality of organizations.

DOI: 10.4018/978-1-5225-9489-5.ch012

Interdisciplinarity is attended to in other ways in the GDPR, when it comes to acknowledging that different sectors of society will have specific concerns when it comes to the protection of personal data and privacy (e.g. in article 40(1)). Banks, for instance, have a centuries-long history in protecting secrecy and ensuring the security of personal information, while medical practitioners have been attentive to the intricacies of confidentiality and informed consent for millennia. Not only can this lead to sector-specific codes of conduct or collaboration, it can also promote inter-sectoral knowledge-sharing.

As Kagan et al (2003) point out, "regulation might be viewed less as a system of hierarchically imposed, uniformly enforced rules than as a coordinative mechanism, routinely interacting with other sources of pressure [...] such as markets, local and national environmental activists, and the culture of corporate management." In the same way, the GDPR can be viewed as a coordinative mechanism that interacts with other factors to constitute the protection of personal data in practice. Insight into this 'bigger picture', a comprehensive view of factors influencing practical data protection, can be indispensable to lawmakers, policy makers, supervisory authorities, data protection officers and other stakeholders. Obtaining such insight is the third reason interdisciplinarity matters to data protection practices, as we will argue below: many academic disciplines have in fact paid attention to what happens in practice to protect personal data and we cannot overlook such findings.

The aim of this chapter is to take readers beyond the prescriptions of the GDPR to present an initial attempt at a framework that can provide a holistic perspective on what happens when organizations try to protect personal data. The question that is addressed is: How to go about constructing an interdisciplinary framework for the study of factors that influence personal data protection in practice?

The GDPR may be the 'most sweeping' trans-national legislation protecting personal data (Roberts, 2018), but it is certainly not the only influence on the way commercial, public, and civil society organizations handle informational privacy. As the 'information society' evolved to the 'platform society' (Van Dijck et al., 2018) and societal interest in the protection of personal data increased, researchers from various academic disciplines investigated what happens when different kinds of organizations are confronted with new data governance demands. To give a few examples:

- Privacy economists have studied how internet users' perceptions of online data protection influence their behavior and how organizations can manipulate those perceptions (Acquisti & Grossklags, 2015).
- Psychologists have studied how employee training influences compliance with information security policies (Parsons et al, 2014).
- Scholars in media and communication studies and in management have studied how massive personal data-gathering gave rise to business models in which the audience and predictions of their behavior became the product (Van Dijck, 2013; Zuboff, 2019).

Several related terms have come up above: secrecy, confidentiality, informational privacy, personal data protection, information security. Some disambiguation therefore seems to be in order. We will briefly go into distinguishing the concepts of privacy protection and personal data protection, because within the European legal context the right to privacy is set apart from the right to the protection of personal data.

Protection for the right to privacy (respect for private life, family life, home, and correspondence) is provided in article 8 of the European Convention for Human Rights and in article 7 of the European Union's Charter of Fundamental Rights. In the rulings of the European Court of Human Rights, a wide range of issues are covered by this right: bodily integrity, wiretapping, gender identification, and protection against environmental nuisances, to name but a few. On the other hand, the right to personal data protection is established in article 16 of the Treaty on the Functioning of the European Union, while article 8 of the Charter of Fundamental Rights reinforces it and the GDPR specifies it.

Article 1(1) of the GDPR states that it regulates the processing of personal data and the free movement of personal data. This assumes that personal data will be processed, and as long as this processing remains within the bounds set by the GDPR, it may not affect the right to privacy (nor, presumably, other fundamental rights).

The protection of personal data is therefore not simply a subset of the protection of privacy. On the one hand, whereas personal data protection may be considered to cover a narrower domain than privacy protection, it may also be considered to cover a wider domain than privacy protection, because it also applies to situations in which personal data are processed but privacy is not at play (though perhaps other fundamental rights and freedoms are affected, e.g. non-discrimination). On the other hand, privacy protection applies in cases in which the processing of non-personal data affects an individual's privacy (Gellert & Gutwirth, 2013). Additionally, privacy protection applies to legal persons, while under the GDPR only natural persons' data are protected (Kokott & Sobotta, 2013).

In short, privacy protection and personal data protection overlap in some instances, but both also cover wider issues within the legal space of the EU. Furthermore, it is important to note that in non-EU jurisdictions, the protection of personal data is often subsumed under 'privacy protection'.

Defining or delimiting the concept of privacy has become somewhat of a holy grail to scholars of privacy in various academic disciplines (Koops et al, 2017; Solove, 2008), with distinctions being made between such aspects as 'decisional privacy' (Solove, 2008) and 'contextual integrity' (Nissenbaum, 2009), and with adjacent concepts like 'reserve', 'secrecy' and 'anonymity' (Westin, 1967). The various conceptions of privacy connect a wide variety of disciplines: psychology, anthropology, media and communication studies, law, sociology, political science, architecture and design, information technology, healthcare, business economics, urban studies, among others (Van der Sloot & De Groot, 2018). While this chapter focuses on the protection of personal data, the distinction with privacy protection is often less clear-cut in non-legal literature or in practice.

If we wish to learn more about what happens in organizations to protect personal data, we should start by integrating what we already know, by collecting research results from the various disciplines in which this subject has been studied, as well as from different jurisdictions than the EU. Doing so, we need to consider that it may be labelled as 'data protection' in one study and 'privacy protection' in another. This is not to blur the lines between the legal concepts, but to advance the comprehensiveness of our understanding.

Few have crossed the boundaries of their academic disciplines to integrate findings about organizations' data protection practices into a comprehensive view on what influences those practices. Yet, there is a clear need for an all-round perspective on data protection 'on the ground'. For different stakeholders in the digital economy – policy makers, watchdogs, privacy and consumer advocates, industries, technology developers – having a model of what actually influences practices means a better understanding of how to reconfigure personal data protection as well as meet privacy needs.

Which are the dominant theories in various academic disciplines that explain actual practices of personal data protection in organizations? A systematic literature review by the authors shows that researchers from over 100 different academic disciplines have studied practices of personal data protection, from nursing to robotics and penology. Those studies vary from small-scale ethnographic studies to substantial cross-cultural and cross-sectoral comparisons, such as the extensive qualitative research conducted by

Bamberger and Mulligan (2015) into the activities of Chief Privacy Officers, and subsequent work by Waldman (2017) on the role of designers and engineers.

This chapter presents the first steps towards a framework that incorporates insights from this large variety of disciplines, with a view to eventually offering a more holistic perspective on the practice of personal data protection, to inform policies and hands-on approaches at the macro (societal), meso (sectoral), and micro levels (organizational). The very first step will be to overcome disciplinary boundaries by finding different terms for 'personal data protection' as used in other academic disciplines, for which §2 will set out a structured approach. The next step will be to infer corroborated theories concerning practical data protection from a structured literature search using keywords that are not discipline-specific. In §3, a number of the theories found through the approach of the previous paragraph are discussed. A first outline of a more comprehensive perspective on practical data protection is then presented in §4, followed by discussion and recommendations in §5.

SEEKING DIFFERENT PERSPECTIVES

According to Kostoff et al (2006), "Efficient research requires awareness of all prior research and technology that could impact the research topic of interest and builds upon these past advances to create discovery and new advances". A structured review allows for systematic identification of key literature that can lay the groundwork for the creation of a comprehensive framework.

Different Disciplines Use Different Terminologies

The researcher who seeks to take account of findings from other academic disciplines than his or her own, faces the challenge of differences in terminology and variations in definitions. For example, the connotations for the concept of 'consent' differ between the context of website cookie policies and the context of clinical trials, even while certain core aspects of the term's references will overlap. Developing a specific terminology is part of the 'boundary work' that delimits and actualizes an academic discipline (Krishnan, 2009); hence, terminology will necessarily differ between disciplines. However, one should not exaggerate this notion: it is of course possible to communicate about data protection across disciplines, as long as we keep in mind that connotations and associations have a discipline-specific flavor and that concepts such as 'consent', 'anonymity', and 'confidentiality' have received varying amounts of attention.

Delimiting disciplines themselves in a very precise manner is not entirely necessary to take the perspectives from different disciplines into account. Disciplines are contingent abstractions, subject to constant change, and definitions of the 'discipline' concept are themselves discipline-dependent (Sugimoto & Weingart, 2015). While delineating academic disciplines is beyond the scope of this chapter, it is certainly feasible to cluster transdisciplinary perspectives on data protection practices in organizations.

A first step towards incorporating findings from different academic disciplines is therefore to find alternative terminology prevalent in those disciplines. In this pursuit, 'researcher bias' caused by researchers choosing their most familiar vocabulary must be reduced. A comparative analysis of search strategies by Huang et al (2011) found that a simple lexical query will inevitably be biased by the limited terminology used by the researchers, and that this bias can be reduced by adopting a strategy of 'evolutionary lexical query' or 'expanded lexical query' (Huang et al, 2015): iteratively obtaining search keywords for subsequent rounds of searches. By following a coherent set of rules in the search and selection phases, the reliability of results from structured search strategies is higher than in traditional reviews, offering more transparency and less researcher bias (Massaro et al, 2016).

Hence, the search strategy presented here comprises two rounds: an initial search round with 'simple' terminology ('personal data protection practices') and a second search round with keywords found on the basis of clusters of similar terminology. This two-step search strategy supports finding studies on data protection practices across academic disciplines.

Finding Alternative Terms

As argued in the introduction, while what we are looking for within the context of the GDPR would be empirical studies on practices of personal data protection, if those studies are conducted within non-legal disciplines or jurisdictions outside the EU, they will quite likely use the term 'privacy protection' instead of 'personal data protection'. Should this fact be overlooked, the search results may very well be severely skewed from the beginning.

Therefore, starting with two simple search queries – 'personal data protection practices' and 'privacy protection practices' – the authors conducted a first round of article search in the Web of Science and Google Scholar databases of academic literature. The combination of Web of Science with Google Scholar was intended to reduce another bias, known as 'indexing bias': because the two use different indexation mechanisms, they cover different shares of scientific literature (De Winter et al, 2014). The Scopus database could have been used as well, but an analysis by Harzing & Alakangas (2016) shows that coverage for the Web of Science and Scopus are similar.

The first search round led to results from 124 different academic categories as defined by Web of Science, for the term 'personal data protection practices' alone. Google Scholar does not provide similar statistics on disciplines. It is important to note here that publication classifications as the one offered by Web of Science cannot decisively function as a proxy for the designation of academic disciplines, as some journals are interdisciplinary or multidisciplinary, and besides, "if a physics paper is published in an interdisciplinary journal or a multidisciplinary journal such as *Science* or *Nature*, it does not necessarily mean that the paper itself is an interdisciplinary or multidisciplinary study" (Huang et al, 2011). The overview presented in Figure 1 therefore only serves as an indication of the large number and variety of different academic disciplines that have an interest in studying practices of personal data protection.

As the exact strings of 'personal data protection practices' and 'privacy protection practices' will be quite uncommon, Boolean operators were also used in the initial search round, meaning that a search query could also look like: 'personal data' AND 'protection practices'.

Subsequently, a quality assessment of the results was using the following criteria:

- Articles presented empirical research.
- The research focused on organizational practices rather than the practices of consumers, citizens, or individual users.
- Articles presented research into actual practices rather than models, guidelines or prescriptions.
- Articles presented research related to privacy protection or personal data protection.
- Articles were written in English (to allow for automatic term mapping).

Though the search queries eventually incorporated most of these criteria, manual selection of the 220 articles completed this selection stage.

Figure 1. Visualization provided by Web of Science of the top 25 academic categories (out of 124) for articles found with a simple search on 'personal data protection practices'

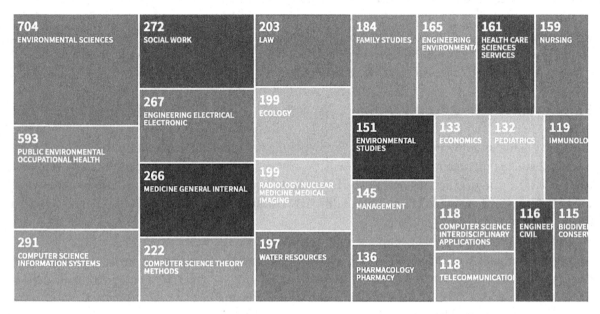

Table 1. Overview of simple lexical queries in first round of search

Source	Date	Query	Nr of Results	Comments
Google Scholar scholar.google.com	27 December 2018	"personal data protection practices"	15 (13) *	Searched from IP address in Amsterdam (NL)
Google Scholar scholar.google.com	27 December 2018	"privacy protection practices"	231 (225) *	Searched from IP address in Amsterdam (NL)
Web of Knowledge apps.webofknowledge.com (all databases, all years)	3 January 2019	"TS=("personal data" AND "protection practices")"	4	Searched from IP address in Brussels (B)
Web of Knowledge apps.webofknowledge.com (all databases, all years)	3 January 2019	"TS=(personal AND "data protection practices")"	12	Searched from IP address in Brussels (B)
Google Scholar scholar.google.com	4 January 2019	"privacy practices" -users -individuals -consumers +empirical	46 (45) *	Searched from IP address in Amsterdam (NL)
Web of Knowledge apps.webofknowledge.com (core collection, all years)	7 January 2019	"TS=(privacy practices AND empirical) NOT TI=(users OR individuals OR consumers)"	204 (203) *	Searched from IP address in Brussels (B)
Web of Knowledge apps.webofknowledge.com (all databases, all years)	28 January 2019	"TS=(privacy practices AND empirical) NOT TI=(users OR individuals OR consumers)"	346 (340) *	Searched from IP address in Brussels (B)

* Between brackets the number of results after deduplication of the results for that query.

After this selection round, the collection consisted of 220 articles. Terminology was extracted from these articles in two ways:

1. Collecting author keywords and tags allocated by databases, and
2. Mining keywords from titles and abstracts.

Several tools were used to conduct automatic analysis and keyword extraction. Author keywords were collected using output from bibliography software Zotero into an Excel sheet.

This output also offered an overview of 'automatic tags' provided by the databases from which the articles were retrieved. The Web of Science database additionally provided 'KeyWords Plus', index terms automatically generated from the titles of cited articles. This yielded a total of 770 unique keywords.

These 770 keywords were clustered through automated association rule learning, using the Apriori algorithm (Agrawal & Srikant, 1994). This procedure starts with counting the number of occurrences of keywords. The most frequent keywords in the set were: privacy, security, confidentiality, and informed consent. However, knowing the frequency of keywords alone will not suffice to create new search queries. For one thing, the most frequent words will also be the most general terms. Using 'privacy' as a keyword, for instance, will not yield very efficient results to further our understanding of personal data protection practices, though it will yield a lot of search results. More specific results will be obtained by using combined sets of keywords as search queries.

The Apriori algorithm creates so-called association rules based on co-occurrences of keywords in publications. The association rules resulting from application of the Apriori algorithm to the 770 keywords showed that the most popular and frequent combinations for the selected publications were 'informed consent + confidentiality' and 'security + privacy', whereas other popular combinations occured too infrequently. Upon closer evaluation, the keyword 'privacy' is too general, as it is not specific to any discipline and because all documents are related to privacy. For these reasons, 'privacy' should be excluded as a keyword. This leaves only 'informed consent + confidentiality' as a useful combination for subsequent search.

This disappointing result is a consequence of the small collection of 220 articles, but also indicates a limitation of the quantitative approach of Apriori: the algorithm yields frequencies of co-occurrences but does not reveal meaningful connections. Van Eck et al (2010) pointed out that "selection of terms based on their frequency of occurrence in a corpus of documents typically yields many words and phrases with little or no domain-specific meaning".

Furthermore, a search for terminology should not be focused on single words. A term selection strategy must recognize that terms often consist of more than one word: in many cases it would not make sense to count occurrences of e.g. 'European' and 'Union' or 'United' and 'States' separately. Noun phrases like 'general data protection regulation' or 'health insurance portability and accountability act' should be recognized and unified as one term. Moreover, certain terms should not be counted, similar to 'privacy', because they occur to frequently within a domain: think of the high occurrence of the term 'study' in a collection of academic articles. In other words, finding terminology needs to account for relevance.

A software tool developed in the field of bibliometrics, VOSviewer (Van Eck and Waltman, 2010), facilitates the clustering of terminology found in titles and abstracts of articles. In VOSviewer, 'relevance' of a term is constructed by an algorithm that includes:

- Identification and unification of noun phrases,

- Calculation of term frequencies,
- Exclusion of common academic terminology, and
- Calculating co-occurrence scores for terms.

Using VOSviewer, terms found in titles and abstracts of the 220 articles that resulted from the first search round were analysed. Additionally, a thesaurus file was created to merge different spellings (e.g. 'health-care' and 'health care'). In this way 94 additional terms were found, connected to each other in seven clusters. A first analysis showed that for the three biggest clusters, the fifth term in a relevance ranking would occur no more than twice. Therefore, the cut-off point for the number of keywords per cluster was chosen to be at the fifth position in the relevance ranking. In addition, the seventh cluster only contained one term, 'higher education', that occurred only twice and was not linked to other terms. The seventh cluster was therefore abandoned. Table 2 presents the five most-connected terms per cluster.

Table 2. Clusters of terms found through a search on 'personal data protection practices' and 'privacy protection practices'

Cluster 1	Cluster 2	Cluster 3	Cluster 4	Cluster 5	Cluster 6
model	confidentiality	privacy	ethics	care	technology
systems	attitudes	data privacy	health care	impact	future
user acceptance	information	facebook	perceptions	health information	online
privacy concerns	communication	guidelines	patients	quality	social networks
electronic medical records	informed consent	security of data	nurses	implementation	design

Again, not all of these keywords are specific. For instance, a search query using only the keyword 'model' will yield many results that have little to do with data protection practices. Terms were therefore scored independently by four researchers specialized in privacy and the selection of keywords for queries was based on a cumulative score. For example, a query could consist of a combination of 'privacy concerns', 'electronic medical records' and 'systems'.

Using these new queries, a second round of searches was conducted in Google Scholar and Web of Science. The eventual aim of this round was to find dominant theories in different disciplines in the resulting articles. Relevance and representativity of the results were therefore more important criteria than completeness. To reflect this focus on relevance, the results were filtered for scholarly impact. The filter consisted of two criteria:

- A citation count threshold of 10,
- An average annual citation threshold of 10.

As Google Scholar does not support a filter based on the number of citations the Publish or Perish tool (Harzing, 2007) was used to filter results from both databases. Publish or Perish computes annual citations as an average, i.e. total number of cites divided by years of publication. The second filter thus translates into an average of 10 (or more) citations per year. Using the average annual threshold reduces the age effect of older publications that have been cited more often, though it may exclude very recent publications.

This second round of queries resulted in 3707 unique articles. The next step is to deduce influential theories from these clusters of articles. To give a few examples, using the results from the second round of search, underlying theories found in this set were: the technology acceptance model for cluster 1, communication privacy management theory for cluster 3 and the theory of planned behavior for cluster 4. The next section will briefly discuss these theories to illustrate their utility in understanding what happens in practice to protect personal data.

THEORIES ON PRACTICES OF PERSONAL DATA PROTECTION

A full account of all theories mentioned in the 3707 articles found through the two-step search strategy outlined in the previous section is beyond the scope of this one chapter. By way of illustration, three theories are highlighted that were repeatedly represented in three clusters with clearly different perspectives:

- The technology acceptance model for cluster 1 (centered around electronic systems and their users),
- Communication privacy management theory for cluster 3 (centered around data privacy and security),
- The theory of planned behavior for cluster 4 (centered around health care).

These theories were selected for more extensive discussion (3.1) based on their prevalence and the range of clusters they represent. The emphasis in the discussion will be on what these theories tell us about the practical protection of personal data in organizations.

Studying organizational practices implies studying organizations. In §3.2, organizational theory perspectives are discussed that offer insights into how (compliance) practices are embedded in organizations. Zooming out from the specific views on the protection of personal data to what influences organization practices in general will support the more holistic framework needed to investigate influences on practical data protection.

Theoretical Perspectives on Personal Data Protection

A seminal theory in the field of information systems research, the technology acceptance model (TAM), first introduced by Davis (1989), describes factors that influence individuals' acceptance and use of new technologies. TAM is itself based on a psychological theory, the theory of reasoned action, that seeks to explain behavior by studying behavioral intention (Fishbein and Ajzen, 1975). In the original approach to TAM modeling, two beliefs predict behavioral intentions of potential users: perceived ease of use and perceived usefulness. It is assumed within TAM that intentions lead to actual behavior.

TAM has been adapted to model how individuals' concerns about data privacy influence their intentions to use new technologies, especially in studies on the adoption of electronic banking and electronic commerce. Specifically with relation to data protection practices, TAM has been used to model staff compliance with data protection regulations (e.g. Foth et al, 2012), finding, among others, gender differences in intentions to comply.

Table 3. Overview of queries in second round of search (July-August 2019; from IP address in Brussels)

Source Database	Query	Nr of Results	Filtered
Queries Based on Provided Keywords			
Google Scholar	+"informed consent" +confidentiality	208,000	384
Web of Knowledge	"TS=("informed consent" AND confidentiality)"	2,878	129
Queries Based on Cluster 1 of Keywords From Titles and Abstracts			
Google Scholar	+model +systems +"user acceptance" +"privacy concerns"	6,900	504
Google Scholar	+model +systems +"user acceptance" +"electronic medical records"	2,870	336
Google Scholar	+systems +"privacy concerns" +"electronic medical records"	4,140	345
Google Scholar	+"user acceptance" +"privacy concerns" +"electronic medical records"	402	76
Web of Knowledge	"TS=(model AND systems AND "user acceptance" AND ("privacy concerns" OR "electronic medical records"))"	74	15
Web of Knowledge	"TS=((systems OR "user acceptance") AND "privacy concerns" AND "electronic medical records")"	24	5
Queries Based on Cluster 2 of Keywords From Titles and Abstracts			
Google Scholar	+confidentiality +attitudes +disclosure	118,000	304
Google Scholar	+confidentiality +information +communication +disclosure	203,000	283
Google Scholar	+attitudes +information +communication +disclosure	521,000	560
Web of Knowledge	"TS=(confidentiality AND attitudes AND disclosure)"	505	23
Web of Knowledge	"TS=((confidentiality OR attitudes) AND information AND disclosure)"	3,995	279
Queries Based on Cluster 3 of Keywords From Titles and Abstracts			
Google Scholar	+privacy +"data privacy" +guidelines	32,100	412
Google Scholar	+privacy +"data privacy" +surveillance	22,000	459
Google Scholar	+privacy +"data privacy" +"security of data"	7,050	375
Google Scholar	+privacy +guidelines +surveillance	2,260,000	349
Google Scholar	+privacy +guidelines +"security of data"	7,650	351
Google Scholar	+privacy +surveillance +"security of data"	3,920	269
Google Scholar	+"data privacy" +guidelines +surveillance	11,000	279
Google Scholar	+"data privacy" +guidelines +"security of data"	1,960	229
Google Scholar	+"data privacy" +surveillance +"security of data"	1,170	150
Google Scholar	+guidelines +surveillance +"security of data"	2,090	140
Web of Knowledge	"TS=(privacy AND "data privacy" AND (guidelines OR surveillance OR "security of data"))"	9,161	229
Web of Knowledge	"TS=(privacy AND guidelines AND (surveillance OR "security of data"))"	344	9
Web of Knowledge	"TS=(privacy AND surveillance AND "security of data")"	234	2
Web of Knowledge	"TS=("data privacy" AND guidelines AND (surveillance OR "security of data"))"	179	4
Web of Knowledge	"TS=("data privacy" AND surveillance AND "security of data")"	139	2
Web of Knowledge	"TS=(guidelines AND surveillance AND "security of data")"	11	1
Queries Based on Cluster 4 of Keywords From Titles and Abstracts			
Google Scholar	+ethics +perceptions +patients +nurses	240,000	536
Google Scholar	+ethics +perceptions +patients +health-care	390,000	686
Google Scholar	+ethics +patients +nurses +health-care	659,000	608
Google Scholar	+perceptions +patients +nurses +health-care	859,000	565
Google Scholar	+ethics +perceptions +nurses +health-care	299,000	638
Web of Knowledge	"TS=(ethics AND perceptions AND patients AND (nurses OR health-care))"	1,232	71
Web of Knowledge	"TS=(ethics AND perceptions AND nurses AND health-care)"	355	18
Web of Knowledge	"TS=((ethics OR perceptions) AND patients AND nurses AND health-care)"	7,101	407
Queries Based on Cluster 5 of Keywords From Titles and Abstracts			
Google Scholar	+technology +facebook +online +"social networks"	255,000	866
Google Scholar	+technology +facebook +future +"social networks"	229,000	890
Google Scholar	+facebook +online +future +"social networks"	305,000	886
Web of Knowledge	"TS=(technology AND facebook AND "social networks" AND (online OR future))"	545	30
Web of Knowledge	"TS=(facebook AND "social networks" AND online AND future)"	287	20
Queries Based on Cluster 6 of Keywords From Titles and Abstracts			
Google Scholar	+care +impact +"health information" +implementation	222,000	747
Web of Knowledge	"TS=(care AND impact AND "health information" AND implementation)"	621	47

Communication privacy management (CPM) theory is an influential theory from the field of communication studies. First developed as 'communication boundary management theory' by Petronio (1991), it presents a theoretical approach to understanding how individuals disclose personal information to others. The later name change to CPM was intended to underscore its focus on disclosing private information. CPM sees the individual as an 'owner' of information who can choose to share that information (expanding boundaries) or not (setting a personal boundary). Privacy boundary management is a rule-based process, with rules for disclosure of information that may depend on culture, gender, context, motivation, and an assessment of risks and benefits of disclosure.

In the context of organizational practices, CPM theory has been applied to studying the reactions of employees to workfloor surveillance (e.g. Watkins Allen et al, 2007), finding that organizations set the privacy boundaries in surveillance while employees are socialized to accept the justifications given by employers. CPM theory has also been applied to studying how teachers develop privacy rules in their relationships with students (e.g. Hosek & Thompson, 2009), finding that teachers disclose private information when it is relevant to course content or to build relationships with students, and that teachers consciously weigh risks to their credibility, among other findings.

The third theory selected for discussion is the theory of planned behavior (TPB). Like TAM, TPB is based on the psychological theory of reasoned action. Unlike TAM, TPB recognizes that intentions do not directly lead to actual behavior, as individuals do not always have full control over circumstances. Ajzen (1985) therefore added another predictor to the theory of reasoned action: 'perceived behavioral control', which consists of the internal factor 'self-efficacy' (belief in one's abilities to succeed in attaining a desired outcome) and the external factor 'controllability' (outside influences that limit behavior).

When it comes to data protection practices, TPB has been used to study intentions to comply, as well as actual compliance, of employees with privacy and security policies (Kim & Kim, 2017). This study found (among other findings) that compliance support systems were not equally effective in different departments of the same company as an effect of characteristics of different roles and departments.

By reason of the close relation between TAM and TPB, attempts have been made to integrate these theories to provide a more integrated understanding of intentions and behavior. Among the integrated theories, the Unified Theory of Acceptance and Use of Technology (UTAUT, Venkatesh et al. 2003), which also synthesizes other models of acceptance, has found wide academic support. Most UTAUT-based studies naturally investigate the adoption of new technologies, in some cases with data protection concerns being one of the factors influencing attitudes and intentions of (organizational) users.

Organizational Theory

If we wish to study how personal data are protected in practice, more than formal data protection requirements, employee behavior and individual decision-making must be taken into account. According to Murray (1976), "corporate policies, organizational structure, measurement and control systems, long-range planning, incentive systems, and organizational culture" are important factors that influence the rate and degree of compliance. His results suggest that involvement of top executives makes a crucial difference in the success of social change programmes. Kagan et al (2003) found that while 'external drivers' – such as legal requirements, a firm's economic circumstances and social pressure – are important influences, what matters most is the interaction of an organization's management with those external factors. They also point to economic pressures, for instance in highly competitive markets, as a factor that can either limit compliance efforts or promote 'beyond compliance' performance.

Within the subfield of strategy research, the strategy-as-practice approach studies who does what in organizations, and how they do it. In the strategy-as-practice approach, strategy practitioners can be individuals or aggregate actors, inside or outside the organization: managers, consultants, engineers, regulators, professional associations, educational institutions, the media, activist groups, and so on (Jarzabkowski and Spee, 2009). In a sense, data protection strategies are co-developed in interaction with different partners within an organization, as well as with parties outside the organization, such as legislators and regulators, peers, data subjects, civil society actors, and with society at large.

Beyond merely human influences, it has been argued that techno-economic networks, such as a data-processing organization, have their own type of agency (e.g. Callon, 1991), a notion that in the age of machine learning and automated decision-making takes on a whole new meaning. Callon distinguishes three 'intermediaries' that give shape to such networks, next to human beings: texts (records, books, articles), technical artefacts (instriments, machines, robots), and money.

Institutional theory adds that practices of organizations in the same environment will grow to resemble each other ('isomorphism'). DiMaggio and Powell (1983) identify three mechanisms through Which this happens:

1. coercive isomorphism,
2. Mimetic isomorphism, and
3. Normative isomorphism.

The mandates of the GDPR and data protection authorities are examples of coercive isomorphism: organizations subject to the GDPR will all have to comply with the same requirements. While these may lead to some variation in practices depending on the sector and context, regulatory rules serve as benchmarks that stimulate convergent behavior (Kagan et al, 2003). Another form of coercive isomorphism are contractual agreements between data processors and data controllers. Mimetic isomorphism results from standard responses to uncertainty: when solutions or outcomes are unclear, organizations model themselves on other organizations that are perceived to be more successful, leading to a search for 'best practices'. This type of isomorphism may also be effected by advice from (legal) consultancy firms or industry trade associations, especially when there is a limited number of such advisors available. The third type of isomorphism stems from normative pressures on professionals, mostly produced by education and training, and discussions within professional networks and conferences, and trade associations. These pressures differ from coercion in the sense that they do not point to external obligations backed up by enforcement, but they arise from converging mindsets and (sectoral) consensus.

The strategy-as-practice perspective emphasizes that organizations do not exist in a vacuum; their practices are affected by their environment in a variety of ways, among which isomorphic pressures. Influences on data protection practices from outside of the organization can be distinguished at two levels: the meso level of actors and institutions directly surrounding the organization (partner organizations, suppliers, distributors, clients, competitors, industry associations, et cetera) and the macro level of influences, at which we find laws, societal interventions and activism.

INTEGRATING DIFFERENT PERSPECTIVES

Based on the discussion above, a more comprehensive approach to studying what happens 'on the ground' comes into sight. A research strategy that can support investigations of organizational practices of data protection should integrate the perspectives discussed 3.1 and 3.2 at the three levels mentioned: micro, meso, macro. A preliminary version of such an integrated view on influences is presented in table 4.

Table 4. Preliminary outline of a comprehensive research strategy to investigate organizational practices of personal data protection

Levels of Study	Objects of Study	Factors Influencing Data Protection Practices	
micro	employee behavior	individual intentions (3.1)
		privacy boundary management (3.1)
		perceived behavioral control (3.1)
	techno-economic networks	texts (3.1)
		technical artefacts (3.1)
		money (3.1)
	organizational policies (3.2)	
	organizational structure (3.2)	
	measurement and control systems (3.2)	
	long-range planning (3.2)	
	incentive systems (3.2)	
	organizational culture (3.2)	
	internal strategy practitioners (3.2)	
meso	external strategy practitioners (3.2)	
	mimetic influences (3.2)	
	normative influences (3.2)	
macro	economic pressures (3.2)	
	coercive influences (3.2)	

A few provisions should be mentioned about this preliminary outline. It is important to note that the factors mentioned cannot be teased out to be studied in isolation; rather, it is the interaction between these factors that shapes personal data protection practices. Moreover, the outline is by no means exhaustive. It does provide an indication of the extent of the framework that will be needed to provide effective insights into what actually happens to protect personal data in organizations.

One other aspect of note is that the element of 'sector' may have a considerable impact on practices. Various factors contain a sectoral element: individual intentions are influenced by (often) sector-specific education and training, technical artefacts will be sector-specific, as are normative influences. As a consequence, research into organizational data protection practices should take sectoral characteristics into account.

DISCUSSION AND RECOMMENDATIONS

This chapter included a fairly extensive description of a method for a structured, interdisciplinary literature review. While this method has its limitations (see §5.2 below), the type of comprehensiveness that is aimed for here cannot be reasonably be achieved in a non-automated manner. Recent advances in automatic search and analysis should not be overlooked, as automated tools improve the efficiency of the process and reduce bias caused by manual selection. Even so, the authors believe the final stage of the review process requires qualitative interpretation and in-depth analysis of a delineated body of literature to evaluate and integrate knowledge.

Creating a Framework to Study Influences on Personal Data Protection in Practice

As was indicated at the end of section 4, studying influences on practical data protection in isolation would overlook pertinent elements of interaction. For example, new technologies can intentionally or unintentionally create new market pressures on practices, and sectoral realities may differ immensely, leading to singular peculiarities for data protection on the ground. Studying organizational practices and policies as co-developed between internal and external actors provides for explanations that go beyond legalistic requirements or individual inclinations to comply.

Getting to a comprehensive view of influences on data protection practices will require the integration of research perspectives from many different academic disciplines, starting from an extensive literature review that will have to overcome terminology challenges. The space of one chapter does not permit the voluminous analysis of all results of such a review, which is why a judicious selection was made in the discussion of theories found through the review process. The authors acknowledge a certain degree of researcher bias in this selection. This can only be resolved by a more expanded review.

The framework presented was an initial attempt, a first step with more to follow to create a truly comprehensive perspective on what influences personal data protection in practice. Literature review will have to be followed by empirical studies to validate the set of factors and study interactions (see §5.3 below).

Strengths and Weaknesses of the Methodology

Deploying a search strategy that relied on automated search and analysis in the first steps offered a wide overview of the literature and a lower measure of researcher subjectivity. This approach also helped us attain the goal of finding relevant publications that surpassed our own specializations.

Excluding literature in other languages than English in the selection step of the structured part of the review, while for sound methodological reasons, meant that studies of practices under previous European legislation (the DPD) were not included. Especially studies in the German language might have contributed greatly to the corpus.

RECOMMENDATIONS

Aside from gains to theory, having a more comprehensive view of influences on organizational practices of data protection can inspire alternative regulatory interventions. For example, guidance on training of data protection officers from the part of regulatory authorities can influence compliance support systems within organizations, potentially inducing significant changes in practical protection without the need of legal adaptations or enforcement actions.

REFERENCES

Acquisti, A., Brandimarte, L., & Loewenstein, G. (2015). Privacy and human behavior in the age of information. *Science*, *347*(6221), 509–514. doi:10.1126cience.aaa1465 PMID:25635091

Agrawal, R., & Srikant, R. (1994). Fast algorithms for mining association rules. *Proc. 20th int. conf. very large data bases*, *VLDB*(1215), 487-499.

Ajzen, I. (1985). *From intentions to actions: A theory of planned behavior. In Action control* (pp. 11–39). Berlin: Springer.

Bamberger, K. A., & Mulligan, D. K. (2015). *Privacy on the Ground: Driving Corporate Behavior in the United States and Europe*. Rochester, NY: Social Science Research Network. doi:10.7551/mitpress/9905.001.0001

Callon, M. (1991). Techno-economic networks and irreversibility. In J. Law (Ed.), *A sociology of monsters: essays on power, technology and domination* (pp. 132–164). London: Routledge.

Davis, F. D. (1989). Perceived usefulness, perceived ease of use, and user acceptance of information technology. *Management Information Systems Quarterly*, *13*(3), 319–340. doi:10.2307/249008

De Winter, J. C. F., Zadpoor, A. A., & Dodou, D. (2014). The expansion of Google Scholar versus Web of Science: A longitudinal study. *Scientometrics*, *98*(2), 1547–1565. doi:10.100711192-013-1089-2

DiMaggio, P., & Powell, W. W. (1983). The iron cage revisited: Collective rationality and institutional isomorphism in organizational fields. *American Sociological Review*, *48*(2), 147–160. doi:10.2307/2095101

Fishbein, M., & Ajzen, I. (1975). *Belief, attitude, intention, and behavior: An introduction to theory and research*. Reading: Addison-Wesley Publication Company.

Foth, M., Schusterschitz, C., & Flatscher-Thöni, M. (2012). Technology acceptance as an influencing factor of hospital employees' compliance with data-protection standards in Germany. *Journal of Public Health*, *20*(3), 253–268. doi:10.100710389-011-0456-9

Gellert, R. & Gutwirth, S. (2013). The legal construction of privacy and data protection. *Computer Law & Security Review*, *29*, 522-530.

HarzingA. W. (2007). *Publish or Perish*. https://harzing.com/resources/publish-or-perish

Harzing, A. W., & Alakangas, S. (2016). Google Scholar, Scopus and the Web of Science: A longitudinal and cross-disciplinary comparison. *Scientometrics, 106*(2), 787–804. doi:10.100711192-015-1798-9

Hosek, A. M., & Thompson, J. (2009). Communication privacy management and college instruction: Exploring the rules and boundaries that frame instructor private disclosures. *Communication Education, 58*(3), 327–349. doi:10.1080/03634520902777585

Huang, C., Notten, A., & Rasters, N. (2011). Nanoscience and technology publications and patents: A review of social science studies and search strategies. *The Journal of Technology Transfer, 36*(2), 145–172. doi:10.100710961-009-9149-8

Huang, Y., Schuehle, J., Porter, A. L., & Youtie, J. (2015). A systematic method to create search strategies for emerging technologies based on the Web of Science: Illustrated for 'Big Data.'. *Scientometrics, 105*(3), 2005–2022. doi:10.100711192-015-1638-y

Jarzabkowski, P., & Spee, P. A. (2009). Strategy-as-practice: A review and future directions for the field. *International Journal of Management Reviews, 11*(1), 69–95. doi:10.1111/j.1468-2370.2008.00250.x

Kagan, R. A., Gunningham, N., & Thornton, D. (2003). Explaining Corporate Environmental Performance: How Does Regulation Matter? *Law & Society Review, 37*(1), 51–90. doi:10.1111/1540-5893.3701002

Kim, S. S., & Kim, Y. J. (2017). The effect of compliance knowledge and compliance support systems on information security compliance behavior. *Journal of Knowledge Management, 21*(4), 986–1010. doi:10.1108/JKM-08-2016-0353

Kokott, J., & Sobotta, C. (2013). The distinction between privacy and data protection in the jurisprudence of the CJEU and the ECtHR. *International Data Privacy Law, 3*(4), 222–228. doi:10.1093/idpl/ipt017

Koops, B.-J., Newell, B., Timan, T., Škorvánek, I., Chokrevski, T., & Maša, G. (2017). A Typology of Privacy. *U. Pa. J. Int'l L., 38*, 483.

Kostoff, R. N., Murday, J. S., Lau, C. G. Y., & Tolles, W. M. (2006). The seminal literature of nanotechnology research. *Journal of Nanoparticle Research, 8*(2), 193–213. doi:10.100711051-005-9034-9

Krishnan, A. (2009), *What are academic disciplines? Some observations on the disciplinarity vs interdisciplinarity debate.* National Centre for Research Methods, NCRM Working Paper Series.

Massaro, M., Dumay, J., & Guthrie, J. (2016). On the shoulders of giants: Undertaking a structured literature review in accounting. *Accounting, Auditing & Accountability Journal, 29*(5), 767–801. doi:10.1108/AAAJ-01-2015-1939

Murray, E. A. Jr. (1976). The social response process in commercial banks: An empirical investigation. *Academy of Management Review, 1*(3), 5–15. doi:10.5465/amr.1976.4400575

Nissenbaum, H. (2009). Privacy in context: Technology, policy, and the integrity of social life. Stanford University Press.

Parsons, K., McCormac, A., Butavicius, M., Pattinson, M., & Jerram, C. (2014). Determining employee awareness using the Human Aspects of Information Security Questionnaire (HAIS-Q). *Computers & Security, 42*, 165–176. doi:10.1016/j.cose.2013.12.003

Petronio, S. (1991). Communication boundary management: A theoretical model of managing disclosure of private information between marital couples. *Communication Theory*, *1*(4), 311–335. doi:10.1111/j.1468-2885.1991.tb00023.x

Roberts, J. J. (2018). The GDPR Is in Effect: Should U.S. Companies Be Afraid? *Fortune.com*. https://fortune.com/2018/05/24/the-gdpr-is-in-effect-should-u-s-companies-be-afraid/

Sobhani, M., & Saxon, L. (2019). All our data is health data. *Medium*. https://medium.com/@usccbc/all-our-data-is-health-data-57d3cf0f336d

Solove, D. J. (2008). *Understanding privacy*. Harvard University Press.

Sugimoto, C. R., & Weingart, S. (2015). The kaleidoscope of disciplinarity. *The Journal of Documentation*, *71*(4), 775–794. doi:10.1108/JD-06-2014-0082

Van der Sloot, B., & de Groot, A. (Eds.). (2019). *The Handbook of Privacy Studies: An Interdisciplinary Introduction*. Amsterdam University Press.

Van Dijck, J. (2013). *The culture of connectivity: A critical history of social media*. Oxford University Press. doi:10.1093/acprof:oso/9780199970773.001.0001

Van Dijck, J., Poell, T., & de Waal, M. (2018). *The platform society: Public values in a connective world*. Oxford: Oxford University Press. doi:10.1093/oso/9780190889760.001.0001

Van Eck, N. J., Waltman, L., Noyons, E. C. M., & Buter, R. K. (2010). Automatic term identification for bibliometric mapping. *Scientometrics*, *82*(3), 581–596. doi:10.100711192-010-0173-0 PMID:20234767

Venkatesh, V., Morris, M. G., Davis, G. B., & Davis, F. D. (2003). User acceptance of information technology: Toward a unified view. *Management Information Systems Quarterly*, *27*(3), 425–478. doi:10.2307/30036540

Waldman, A. E. (2017). Designing Without Privacy. *Houston Law Review*, *55*, 659.

Watkins Allen, M., Coopman, S. J., Hart, J. L., & Walker, K. L. (2007). Workplace surveillance and managing privacy boundaries. *Management Communication Quarterly*, *21*(2), 172–200. doi:10.1177/0893318907306033

Westin, A. F. (1967). *Privacy and freedom*. New York. *Atheneum*, *7*, 431–453.

Zuboff, S. (2019). *The age of surveillance capitalism: the fight for the future at the new frontier of power*. Profile Books.

Chapter 13
GDPR:
The Battle for European Consumer Data

Tomáš Pikulík
https://orcid.org/0000-0001-6802-0831
Faculty of Management, Comenius University in Bratislava, Slovakia

Peter Štarchoň
https://orcid.org/0000-0002-8806-4150
Faculty of Management, Comenius University in Bratislava, Slovakia

ABSTRACT

Implementation of the GDPR changed the way how personal data of EU customers are processed. The purpose of this chapter is to explore the links between the rights of customers as a data subject and related aspects of customer satisfaction. Entities in modern economy (encompassing not only goods and services but also intellectual property) generate and process huge quantities of customer data. Information and communication technology (ICT) infrastructure became a basis for the digital economy and society in the EU (settled by Eurostat as ISOC) that definitely replaced the previous era of the information economy that was based on the effective acquisition, dissemination, and use of information. Data-driven marketing puts data at the center of additional value creation and brings new insights and perspectives, included in the results of this research. The impact of GDPR on customer-centric ICT, stronger consumer awareness of data protection rights, creates new pathways to customer centricity and the legal and technical aspects of data processing within the digital economy ecosystem.

INTRODUCTION

In 2017, The Economist published an article titled "The world's most valuable resource is no longer oil, but data" (The Economist, 2017), reflecting the transformation of our modern economies, in which massive data collection and analysis have become a key competitive advantage. This transformation of market features kicked off the major reform of data protection framework in the EU which resulted in the adoption of the *General Data Protection Regulation ("GDPR")* in 2016. Since its enforcement in May

DOI: 10.4018/978-1-5225-9489-5.ch013

2018, EU-GDPR has been widely accepted as a paradigm of new rules in the field of data protection - towards a greater choice and sovereignty for individuals, and more accountability for organizations. A Study of Companies in the United States & Europe (*The Race to GDPR: A Study of Companies in the United States & Europe. Ponemon Institute* Ponemon Institute, 2018) conducted in April 2018 among more than 1,000 European and US companies reported that 40% of respondent organizations would not comply on May 25th, 2018. And even if companies have started to address GDPR, only 23% of US-based companies and 31% of EU-based companies stated that they were confident with their ability to comply. Data protection has become a truly global phenomenon as people around the world increasingly cherish and value the protection and security of their data.

Many countries have adopted or are in the process of adopting comprehensive data protection rules based on principles similar to those of the regulation, resulting in a global convergence of data protection rules. This offers new opportunities to facilitate data flows, between commercial operators or public authorities, while improving the level of protection for the personal data in the EU and across the globe. A new framework for data privacy affected everyday lives of 500 million customers in the European market by strengthening and unifying the aspect of data privacy rights of individuals as a data subject. No matter if they are in early position as suspect, prospect or act as a consumer, re-buyers in Customer Lifecycle Management ("CLM") - GDPR has a big effect on how businesses collect, store and secure customers' personal data. Consumers compare the value proposition with data privacy in every stages of this lifecycle. Many definitions of value proposition concept have been made, and the concept is widely used. Value proposition is an explicit promise made by a company to its customers that delivers a particular bundle of value creating benefits (Buttle, 2009). In other words, "value proposition is a written statement focusing all the organization's market activities onto customer critical elements. That creates a significant differential within the customer's decision process, to prefer and/or purchase the organization's offering over a competitor's" (Fifield, 2007). The value proposition was defined (Lanning, 2000) as an entire set of experiences, including value for money that an organization brings to customers. Customers may perceive this set or combination of experiences to be "superior, equal or inferior to alternatives". In early stage of applying CLM to customers and users (Medha Gore, 2013) customers were just a 'suspect' for marketers as someone who potentially may benefit from acquiring a physical product, non-physical product and/or service offering but may not be aware of it 'prospects' who may be ready, willing and able to acquire an offering and need to decide on a purchase – e.g. (1) actual customers who were prospects who 'signed up' (2) repeat customers who made more purchases and use more than one product or service. Even though customer satisfaction ("CS") has long been regarded as the key determinant of behavioral intentions (Xu et al., 2007; Ladhari et al., 2008; Jen et al., 2011; Chiabai et al., 2014; Sohn et al., 2016; Azizi et al., 2017) academic researchers and managers firmly believe that CS is an essential predictor of lasting customer behavior (Vera & Trujillo, 2017; Wieseke, Geigenmüller, & Kraus, 2012). This conventional belief has been challenged by recent empirical studies due to this evolution of today's competitive service sector, companies are striving hard to retain and hold their customers (Aksoy, 2013; Giovanis & Athanasopoulou, 2018; Tsoukatos & Rand, 2006). Although EU-GDPR was finalized in 2016 and presents a major paradigm shift in data protection, it has attracted relatively little attention in IS literature so far (see Table 1).

Table 1. Summary of EU-GDPR-related studies in IS literature

Source of Study	Study Type	EU-GDPR Aspects	Topic Area Based on	Level of Analysis	Research Focus
Petkov, P., Helfert, M. (2017)	Empirical	Data breach notification	Information privacy practices	Organization	Applying data breach notification to past infringements
Karyda, M., Mitrou, L. (2016)	Conceptual	Data breach notification	Information privacy practices	Organization	Information security / incident management
Engels, B. (2016)	Conceptual	Data portability	Information privacy impact	Market	Impacts of data portability right on competition dynamics
Alboaie, L. (2017)	Conceptual	Privacy-by design	Technologies and tools	Individual	Privacy label for GDPR
Fox, G., Tonge, C., Lynn, T., Mooney, J. (2018)	Conceptual	Transparency	Technologies and tools	Organization	Guidelines for compliant privacy notices
Kurtz, C., Semmann, M., Böhmann, T. (2018)	Conceptual	Entire regulation	Impact / Information privacy practices	Organization	Transformation framework for digital privacy
Russell, K.D., O'Raghallaigh, P., O'Reilly, P., Hayes, J. (2018)	Empirical	Accountability	Information privacy practices	Market	Review of third-party data processors

* scope beyond (Bélanger, F., Crossler, R.E., 2011), covering organizational and individual readiness and transformation

IMPACT OF GDPR ON CUSTOMER-CENTRIC ICT

The empowerment of data-driven business models ("DDBM") sets new methods and pathways in processing customer and location data. Results of the survey realized in 2018 by Global Alliance of Data-Driven Marketing Associations ("GDMA") and the Winterberry Group shows that 92% of companies use databases to store information on a customer or a prospect. This means that if GDPR impacts marketing, it changes also sales prospecting and it subsequently requires change in customer service departments because of fact that all personal data needs to be handled in a more professional manner. GDPR encompasses 3 main areas that every business needs to consider (see Figure 1):

1. The **GDPR** regulation itself
2. The **systems** that controller use to store all of customer data
3. The **legal aspects** of the regulation and correctness of processing of personal data

Marketing, CRM and other data-driven models and platforms and its approaches have thus to be reviewed and designed to ensure that all aspects as data, processes and activities are in compliance or close enough to GDPR rules and not to be at risk from complaints and fines. Processing of personal data should accept and provide transparent implementation and acceptance of main 8 rights and a data subject rights of customer could be defined in path of CLV (see Figure 2).

These rights are given to individuals to protect their private lives and control the digital footprints they leave behind when using internet-based applications and services. It is also a challenge for organi-

Figure 1. GDPR encompasses 3 main areas that every business needs to consider
Source: SuperOffice (European CRM provider and GDPR-Compliance White Paper)

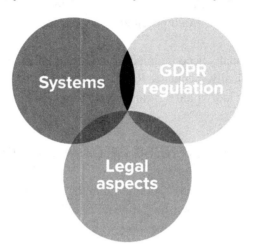

Figure 2. Main data privacy rights of subject on life cycle management path of customer
Source: SuperOffice (European CRM provider and GDPR-Compliance White Paper)

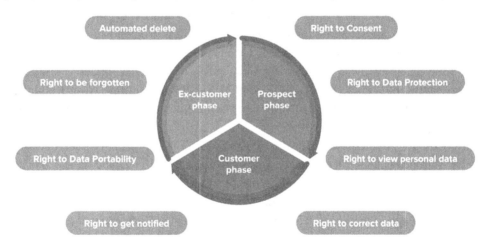

zations as providers because most companies use CRM systems in their distribution networks allowing them to collect, elaborate and share the data between all the worldwide web visitors and there are two possibilities for data processing:

- Where two or more controllers jointly determine the purposes and means of processing, they shall be joint controllers, determining in a transparent manner their respective responsibilities for compliance with the obligations under GDPR (Art. 26). This opportunity is encouraged for common marketing activities.
- When data processing agreement ("DPA") as a legal contract between the controller and the processor in writing or in electronic form need to be confirmed and signed. It regulates the particularities of data processing – such as its scope and purpose – as well as the relationship between

the controller and the processor. If the controller wishes to transfer customer data as outsourcing service to a third-party, then controller needs to sign a DPA with processor – e.g. an ICT provider and especially in case of using a cloud provider as a separate contract.

Every collection of data is usually accompanied by extensive information on the manner of the subsequent data processing. Specifically, Bennet & Raab underlined (2006), that data protection norms do not protect data itself, but rather individual's rights whose data is being processed.

STRONGER CONSUMER AWARENESS OF DATA PROTECTION RIGHTS

The work of the data protection authorities, cooperating in the context of the European Data Protection Board ("EDPB"), is a key driver to a consistent application of the new rules. The Commission would like to see further cooperation among the supervisory authorities, including alignment with the work of the European Data Protection Board, enhancing the means for stakeholders to inform the work of the EDPB, and greater efforts to support parties who may lack data protection knowledge or resources (e.g., small and medium-sized businesses). However, a number of stakeholders still consider that they have not received enough support and information, in particular small and medium size enterprises in some Member States (Register of Commission Expert Groups and Other Similar Entities, 2019). To help remedy this situation, the Commission provides grants to data protection authorities to reach out to stakeholders, in particular individuals and SMEs. Grants are eligible via Funding & tender opportunities through Single Electronic Data Interchange Area ("SEDIA"). SEDIA funded 2 million EUR up to 9 data protection authorities in 2018 for activities in 2018-2019 for authorities in: Belgium, Bulgaria, Denmark, Hungary, Lithuania, Latvia, the Netherlands, Slovenia and Iceland and 1 million EUR were allocated in 2019.

Individuals in the EU are increasingly aware of data protection rules and of their rights: Based on the views of 27,000 Europeans, the Eurobarometer results from May 2019 showed that 67% of respondents are aware of the Regulation (see Figure 3 and Figure 4) and 57% know that there is a national data protection authority to which they can turn for information or to lodge complaints.

Much more interesting is the impact of awareness of individual's rights - overall almost three quarters (73%) have heard of at least one right guaranteed by GDPR (see Figure 5).

The aspect of strengthening the awareness of data privacy is also visible in the case of UK consumers who will stay a part of the European economy after 'Brexit' (implemented in 2020, January 31st) with the common European ambition of building up a modern digital economy. According to the report 'Data privacy: what the consumer really thinks' published in 2018 (DMA (UK) Ltd, 2018), more than a half of consumers in the UK (51%) now understand that data is essential to the smooth running of modern economy – up sharply from 38% in 2012. This highlights the increased understanding that consumers have around data, although 88% said they also wanted organizations to be more transparent about how they use consumer data.

Figure 3. GDPR - prompted awareness of GDPR (general results)

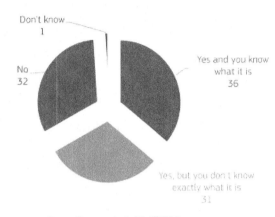

QB17 Have you heard of the General Data Protection Regulation (GDPR), which came into force in 2018? **(% - EU)**

Don't know
1

No
32

Yes and you know what it is
36

Yes, but you don't know exactly what it is
31

Base: all respondents (N=27,524)

Figure 4. Prompted awareness of GDPR (split by countries)

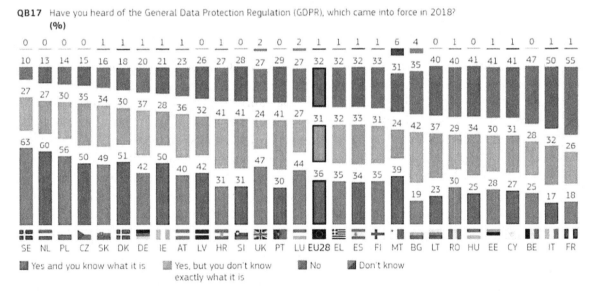

QB17 Have you heard of the General Data Protection Regulation (GDPR), which came into force in 2018? (%)

Base: all respondents (N=27,524)

Focus on Digital Economy in EU Brings Open Battleground

The real power of DDBM and CRM platforms as a main indicator of CLM in Digital economy is reflected in the fact that seven of the world's top eight companies by market capitalization use platform-based

Figure 5. Prompted awareness of GDPR (split by countries)

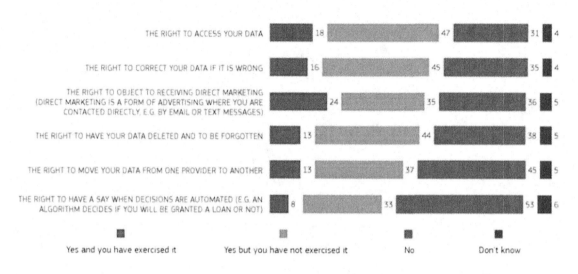

QB18 The General Data Protection Regulation (GDPR) guarantees a number of rights. Have you heard of each of the following rights? **(% - EU)**

Base: all respondents (N=27,524)

business models (Digital Economy Report - UN, 2019) based on analytical work on the development implications of information, ICTs and e-commerce. The ICT industry undoubtedly stands at the center of the digital economy, serving as a reliable yardstick of its performance. According Join Research Center technical report (Sörvik, Kleibrink, 2016) ICTs are major drivers of social and economic change. ICTs are also one of the key Thematic Objectives ("TOs") in the European Structural and Investment Fund ("ESIF"). When exploring the activity areas (groupings of keywords) and keywords are examined, a somewhat contrasting image appears. In the actions to be supported under ESIF, the most frequently mentioned keywords related to ICT innovation: e-Inclusion; broadband and digital networks; digital content; e-Government; and components. For single keywords, the most common examples are related to the following: digital products, services and applications; R&I; start-ups and venture capital; e-Infrastructure

Table 2. Examples of fines that are connected with individual's rights – break of GDPR rules

12th September 2018	5 000 €	on a sport betting café for unlawful video surveillance	Austria
26th March 2019	220 000 €	data broker company for failure to inform individuals that their data was being processed	Poland
12th June 2019	250 000 €	football league LaLiga, for lack of transparency in the design of its smartphone app	Spain
21st January 2019	50 mil. €	Google in France because of the conditions for obtaining consent from users	France
21st November 2019	500 000 €	midsized company, for serious infringements in connection with cold calling campaigns	France

and information systems; digital skills and literacy; training and education; and innovation clusters, hubs and incubators. The greatest investments by ESIF will be in:

- Broadband and ICT infrastructures (EUR 6.9 billion),
- E-Inclusion and digital skills (EUR 3.9 billion),
- Egovernment (EUR 3.4 billion),
- And smart cities and smart grids (EUR 3.1 billion).

Wide private usage of digital internet services for goods and services is visible through Eurostat (see Figure 6).

Figure 6. Individuals with ordered goods and services via ICT for private use in EU

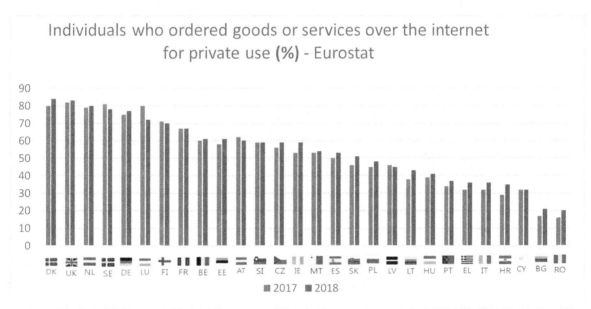

Digital economy and social patterns of European consumers are precisely clarified by The Digital Economy and Society Index (DESI). As a composite index it summarizes relevant indicators on Europe's digital performance and tracks the evolution of EU member states in digital competitiveness (see Figure 7). It consists of five dimensions:

1. **Connectivity**: Measures the deployment of broadband infrastructure and its quality. Access to fast and ultrafast broadband-enabled services is a necessary condition for competitiveness.
2. **Human Capital/Digital Skills**: Measures the skills needed to take advantage of the possibilities offered by digital.
3. **Use of Internet Services by Citizens**: Accounts for a variety of online activities, such as the consumption of online content (videos, music, games, etc.) video calls as well as online shopping and banking.

Figure 7. Digital economy and society index (DESI) 2019 ranking

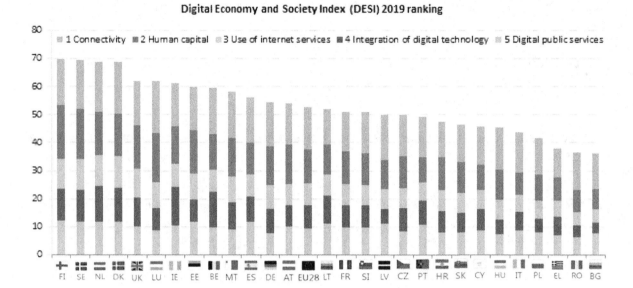

4. **Integration of Digital Technology by Businesses**: Measures the digitization of businesses and e-commerce. By adopting digital technologies, businesses can enhance efficiency, reduce costs and better engage customers and business partners. Furthermore, the Internet as a sales outlet offers access to wider markets and potential for growth.

5. **Digital Public Services:** Measures the digitization of public services, focusing on eGovernment and eHealth. Modernization and digitization of public services can lead to efficiency gains for the public administration, citizens and businesses alike.

Research and Development ICT presents analysis on the trends of ICT Sector and Research and Development provided by the European Commission as well as external studies conducted at the request of the European Commission.

THE NEW PATH TO CUSTOMER CENTRICITY

Further explained customer-centric structure's and its benefit of increased CS are diminished in market situation where (1) competitors have already adopted customer-centric structures, (2) competitors leave few unique customers' needs unaddressed in fragmented markets, and (3) appliance in less profitable industries. Ultimately, we show that aligning corporate structure around customers pays off only in specific competitive environments. To point out the industry typical for competitors - we can focus on retailers and their point-ot-view - all retailers are talking about transformation of their business models, but their approaches are alarmingly inconsistent: multichannel, omnichannel, data-driven, mobile-first, digitally-led, customer-centric, and more. In many cases it it just a veneer – transformation on the outside – but scratch beneath the surface and not much has changed.

Changes in Customer Satisfaction Due Digital era Phenomenon

In the past, retail decisions were aligned to stores and products. Customers were obviously important, but stores were a proxy – an aggregation of local customers. Store like-for-likes were a good measure of overall performance and customer relevancy. Customer actions were left to the CRM team, if one existed, and mostly consisted of broadcasting promotions.

Today, digitally-enabled consumers have changed the fundamental economics and dynamics of retail – consumers have been unshackled from the location of stores. As the share of online penetration and its influence has increased, online cannot be regarded as 'just another store.' The new reality becomes clear when retailers reach the tipping point of having negative like-for-likes but increasing overall revenue: the traditional "four walls" view of retail performance no longer works. Retailers need to pivot their focus from stores to customers.

Almost everything is different in the customer-centric, data-rich, digitally-driven retail world: New revenue drivers (customer acquisition and retention); New variable marketing costs (cost per click, visit, transaction); New variable per-order costs (picking, packing, packaging, delivery, returns); New digital levers that allow retailers to take surgical actions (at customer, stock keeping unit, session level). The four pillars represent the combination of these dynamics that requires retailers to change their approach to insight, planning, trading and reporting (see Figure 8). Digital principles of communication definitely settled the new perspective on tradition perspective aligned with storage, packaging and delivery of products and service providing.

Figure 8. Four pillar of change
Source: InternetRetailing

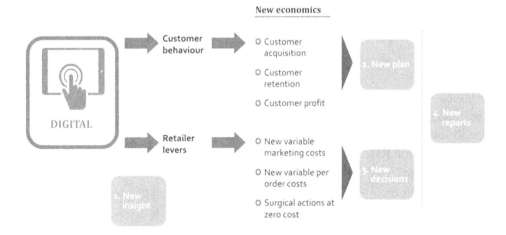

The Path to Digital Transformation: Digital Indicators for Performance

Today each and every company, even big or small, even startup or an industry cult are strongly believing in Digitalization or Digital Transformation and it very much scares about Disruptive Innovation. In terms of customer centric settlement in strategy all the companies measure their success by bunch of

KPIs. In order to increase CS, all companies are trying to measure bunch of mostly common and well known KPIs like (see Figure 9):

Figure 9. How we measure customer satisfaction today
Source: LearnTips

How we measure today

- Active Issues
- Resolved Issues
- Average Resolution Time
- Complaint Escalation Rate
- Net Promotor Score
- Customer Retention

We may add many other KPIs due to your Industry or capability.

Beside KPIs it is time to settle Key Digital Indicators that measures this indicator in digital era (see Figure 10):

CS has two Key Digital Indicators which makes the score "Net Profit" related: Customer Complaints and Cash. Obviously, it seems like a shortcut of management point of view to measure the business results from perspective of Marketing spends enhanced by CRM activities and Retail and Selling activities supported by spends on promotional activities. If the Digital Transformation project or roadmap focuses

Figure 10. Key digital indicators
Source: LearnTips

Finding Key Digital Indicators

on listening to new and live areas like social media with tools of mega trends (IoT, ML, AI), with digital data traps, organization (or start-ups) may immediately catch issues with smart applications and answer them personally by bots. It is not easy to react properly, actively by bots – but let us imagine it on an example: In Facebook somebody shared a picture of your product or service saying/posting: "I hate this because it made something again." This person has 10,000+ connections. Your smart trap should immediately catch this and a bot should answer it by saying: Hi Brian/Paula, we are very sorry hearing this, one of our agents will reach you immediately and your issue has been recorded. At the same time another bot will reach the person on duty and share the information including connection information. Once the case is closed smart bot will enter a comment after under the post will saying that we have reached Brian/Paula, the item that is being used is changed with a brand new one. It is not easy, but this is the path to digital innovation directly impacting Cash (see Figure 11).

The application landscape should store the data of 10000+ of this person and should measure Promotor score. Digitalization plays an important role on creating good words of mouth. Digital customer experience has significant effect on CS (Joshi, 2018) by providing better customer value (Bolton et al., 2018; Klaus, 2014). It provides better experience for customers through digitalization (Betzinget al., 2018) which has influence on brand image, significantly.

Figure 11. Digital innovation and impact on cash
Source: LearnTips

LEGAL AND TECHNICAL ASPECTS OF DATA PROCESSING WITHIN THE DIGITAL ECONOMY ECOSYSTEM

European consumer rights enhanced by GDPR and the DPA that will come into force after Brexit - both many of the same principles apply for data privacy protection. DPA does not contain the GDPR principle of data minimization in data processing. ICO, as the U.K. data protection authority, will act if the rights of the data subject are affected. They will assess processing aspects of offline and online communication in common with the collection of wide range of data by GDPR principle for data minimization in data processing. The case of Lloyd v. Google LLC [2019] EWCA Civ 1599 settled principles of data privacy in relation to customer - business interaction according to GDPR and DPA. The background of this law case was that between August 2011 and February 2012, Google took advantage of the exception for cookie blockers in Apple devices, the "Safari Workaround", which allowed Google to harvest browser generated information ("BGI") of Apple iPhone users by placing tracking cookies without the consumers' knowledge. This BGI, which constituted personal data for the purposes of DPA, gave Google unprecedented insight into the habits and preferences of Apple iPhone users (data subjects), which it sold to advertisers. The starting point in Lloyd is that Article 23 of the Directive and section 13 of the DPA 1998 fall to be construed on the basis that they were giving effect to one aspect of the article 8 of the Convention and article 8 (taken with Article 47) of the Charter of Fundamental Rights (the "Charter") (paragraph 42).

Sir Geoffrey Vos C considered that "the key" to this case is "the characterization of the class members' loss as the loss of control or loss of autonomy over their personal data" (paragraph 45). Notwithstanding the fact that data is not recognized as property in English law, it is clear that BGI has economic value and a person's loss of control over such data has a value (paragraphs 46-47):

"Even if data is not technically regarded as property in English law, its protection under EU law is clear. It is also clear that a person's BGI has economic value: for example, it can be sold. . . The underlying reality of this case is that Google was able to sell BGI collected from numerous individuals to advertisers who wished to target them with their advertising. That confirms that such data, and consent to its use, has an economic value. Accordingly, in my judgment, a person's control over data or over their BGI does have a value, so that the loss of that control must also have a value.".

Data subjects have the right to revoke their consent at any time. In contrast to the previous data privacy laws, the GDPR brings a new perspective: it introduces the responsibility on the controller to the compliance and show 'privacy by design'. This means that data-driven business models, platforms, organizational structures and technological solution (even if they use new aspects of Industry 4.0. – like ICT, IoT, AI, ML) must be built with data privacy as a key tenet.

To point out practical impact of new threats for applications it is worth to name the practical case from Google environment that affect Android Environment. In 6th of November 2019 Google by its representatives (Dave Kleidermacher, VP, Android Security & Privacy) announced launch of partnership called "The App Defense Alliance" with aim to reduce the risk of app-based malware by identifying and remediating new threats. The App Defense Alliance is collaboration between Google, ESET, Lookout, and Zimperium:

- ESET is a Slovak internet security company that offers anti-virus and firewall products,
- Lookout is a US IT security company (San Francisco, California) that develops and markets cloud-based security software for mobile devices,
- Zimperium is a US privately owned mobile security company based in the United States, with offices in Dallas, Texas and San Francisco, California. The company is known for developing several mobile threat defense software solutions.

The Android ecosystem is thriving with over 2.5 billion devices, but this popularity also makes it an attractive target for abuse. This collaboration between security business providers and its initiative that is designed to identify Potentially Harmful Apps ("PHAs") before they go live on the Google Play Store. The tech giant has proposed a fix to help protect its 2.5 billion mobile OS users worldwide. Malicious apps are nothing new to the Google Play Store – hundreds of them are found and reported by cybersecurity firms on a regular basis. What changed in case of user's protection point of view is the perspective change – from reaction to protection mode. "What was previously a reactive effort to catch security vulnerabilities is now a full-fledged and proactive campaign to protect billions of consumers and businesses at the source," said Tony Anscombe (ESET, 2019), global security evangelist and industry ambassador, ESET. iOS has developed Security White Paper that provides in-depth technical details as to how Apple has designed its products and services to protect user's security including on iOS, iMessage, FaceTime, ApplePay, and iCloud.

The effectiveness of the settled PDP methods is reflected by users and its initiatives (e.g. that is designed to identify PHA or Personal Data Apps) however Data Subject, Researchers and Organizations then should consider other alternatives. This is a question also for Google and corporations that have been begging since the birth of the internet and it seems, whilst this change would have been welcome a little sooner. It is still comforting to be able to look into the future of Personally identifiable information ("PII") in usage of Personal Data Apps and the future of the Android OS with such positivity. Cooperation that lead the alliance for cybersecurity started in 2014 during the debates in creation of Clean Software Alliance to support secure creation of applications. The example of Google is pointed out thanks to its special status (like other operation system providers like Microsoft) represented by its market position as:

- Owner of operation system
- Provider of various content – e.g. advertisements
- GSM alliance ("GSMA") member
- Browser provider – Chrome
- Application provider – Google Play
- Cloud provider - Google Cloud PlatformThat kind of various services and impact of security policy up to users brought solutions also in the past like:
- Chrome Cleanup (2017)
- Google's Authenticator app (2014)

According to various solutions Google learned by blocking 100 million phishing attacks on Gmail users daily. Phishing undoubtedly is interconnected with personal data of user and Google needs to defend its Chrome users before phishing – elicitation of personal information or passwords through fake messages or forms. In 2017 Google identified as victims of phishing kits, a total of 2,335,289 Google users, of which 578,434 had valid passwords—a match rate of 24.8% (for further details see Table 2 and Figure 12). Huge evolution confirms the statistics that 68% of the phishing emails blocked by Gmail are different from day to day.

Table 2. Risk associated with passwords stolen through leaks, phishing kits, or keyloggers

Password Source	Password Match Rate	Hijacking Odd Ratio	Failed Odd Ratio
Credential leak	6,9%	11,6x	1,4x
Phishing kit	24,8%	463,4x	1,7x
Keylogger	11,9%	38,5x	1,5x

ASSESMENT AND RECOMMENDATION

To build-up successful and long-term business model based on data-driven platforms should bring satisfied customers. If the organization would transparently communicate in every stage of attraction and interaction not only benefits of products and services (as a push selling/marketing strategy) but also deliver/fairly reveal their rights, terms and conditions and other information in easy to find manners, the steps of purchasing process would be without doubts and worries (perceived in dropped/cancelled orders) and success rate should be delivered. Build engaging and winning customer experiences across all lifecycle stages is the way of optimizing user experience. The way how to improve the lifetime value

Figure 12. Likelihood to have Google account compromised
Source: Google, University of California, Berkeley, International Computer Science Institute

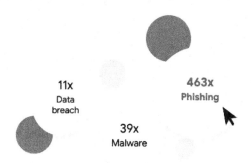

is not only issue for management of organizations but also for a potential lifecycle analytics. Plenty of orders could be clarified, processed with best manners to deliver goods or service, bill the customer and support his purchase in later stage but the further steps to keep the potential to build up the customer loyalty is still considered as more expensive way how to keep the customer. Two factors are in the scene on behind (1) the satisfied customer brings not only potential for further purchases as re-buyer but also worth-of-mouth potential to affect and persuade his environment – e.g. in family, neighborhoods, colleagues etc. (2) customer manager tools for CLM could bring increase of retention and improve lifetime value of customer.

CONCLUSION

Impact of the data privacy field that changed the environment and empowered individuals are visible through these principles: (1) higher standards on consent: consent needs to be active; (2) an affirmed action should be transformed into marketing and electronic communication, with respect of consumer rights; (3) genuine choice and (4) time limitation. All platforms, data-driven or digitally-driven business models will not succeed in correct data processing if they do not respect the fact that consent will not be valid unless separate consents are obtained for different activities, promotions or purposes. The use of pre-ticked opt-in boxes is invalid under GDPR. Silence or inactivity on the side of the data subject, as well as merely proceeding with a service cannot be regarded as an active indication of choice.

Consumer empowerment also lies behind the proposed ePrivacy Directive. If enacted, this regulation will align the rules for electronic communication in line with GDPR. The latter imposed new rules on businesses that process and store customer data, and will stimulate them to receive unambiguous consent before sharing or processing their data. The ePrivacy Directive extends the consent of processing customers' electronic metadata based on the GDPR principles.

The EU data protection rules guarantees the protection of personal data of users whenever they are collected. These rules apply to both companies and organizations (public and private) in the EU and those based outside the EU which offer goods or services in the EU, such as Facebook, Google or Amazon. It does not matter what format the data takes – online on a computer system or on paper in a structured file – whenever information directly or indirectly identifying an individual and his PII is stored or processed, data protection rights of users/consumers need to be respected.

Challenges of data protection rules are not only relevant for the IT, software/application and cyber-security providers but also evoked by the market needs to bring new online applications – especially with a high EU market impact like:

- loyalty retail programs – e.g. Lidl Plus (iOS and Android applications and pipeline payments solutions),
- applications for a specific purpose – e.g. Android Auto,
- special solutions for a user in specific role – e.g. a driver – Shell App, Shell Motorist App (Progressive Web App where the user can combine various data or share data - also localization data, telemetric data).

Current changes of the environment combine (1) retail and loyalty programs and market needs that follow the path of the CLV of the customer; (2) security manners for profiling and tracking consumer behavior on data-driven platforms; (3) combination of offline and online marketing activities. Global digital growth shows no sign of slowing down, with a million new people around the world connecting to the Internet for the first time every day. Encouraging companies and countries (e.g. Denmark has its own Digital Growth Strategy up to 2025) to unlock the digital growth potential is underlined by the actual EU thematic objectives. Actual Thematic Objective 3: Digital Growth with current investment period (2014-2020) followed the previous Thematical Objective 2: ICT. Digital Growth and Investment Priorities for enhancing access to and the use and quality of ICT through (a) developing ICT products and services, e-commerce and enhancing demand for ICT and (b) strengthening ICT applications for e-government, e-learning, e-inclusion, e-culture and e-health and related investment priorities by the European Social Fund (ESF). Yet, the world is only in the early days of the data-driven economy; by 2022 the global IP traffic is projected to reach 150,700 GB per second (UNCTAD, 2019), fueled by more and more people using the Internet for the first time and by the expansion of the Internet of Things (IoT). These aspects represent potential research opportunities for other researchers and studies.

ACKNOWLEDGMENT

This chapter represents a partial result of the research project VEGA 1/0737/20 Consumer Literacy and Intergenerational Changes in Consumer Preferences when Purchasing Slovak Products and was inspired by the GDPR Capability Model developed by the Legner, Labadie (2019) provided by Competence Center Corporate Data Quality ("CC CDQ"). Special thanks to the team of researchers, EU project team-members that prepared special issues of GDPR Handbooks and Reports, WP29 guidelines and EDPB reports and to Juraj Malcho, CTO at ESET for the idea that "using the Internet should always be a smooth and safe experience for everyone."

REFERENCES

Aksoy, L., Buoye, A., Aksoy, P., Larivière, B., & Keiningham, T. L. (2013). A cross-national investigation of the satisfaction and loyalty linkage for mobile telecommunications services across eight countries. *Journal of Interactive Marketing*, *27*(1), 74–82. doi:10.1016/j.intmar.2012.09.003

Alboaie, L. (2017). Towards a Smart Society through Personal Assistants Employing Executable Choreographies. ISD 2017 Proceedings.

Almoatazbillah, H. (2012). *The Value Proposition Concept in Marketing: How Customers Perceive the Value Delivered by Firms.* A Study of Customer Perspectives on Supermarkets in Southampton in the United Kingdom.

Azizi, M., Dehghan, S., Ziaie, M., & Mohebi, N. (2017). Identifying the customer satisfaction factors in furniture market. Economics. *Management and Sustainability*, *2*(1), 6–18. doi:10.14254/jems.2017.2-1.1

Barberis, J., Arner, D. W., & Buckley, R. P. (2019). *The REGTECH Book: The Financial Technology Handbook for Investors, Entrepreneurs and Visionaries in Regulation.* John Wiley & Sons Inc. doi:10.1002/9781119362197

Bélanger, F., Clossler, R.E. (2011). Privacy in the Digital Age: A Review of Information Privacy Research in Information Systems. *MIS Quarterly, 35*(4), 1017-1041. Doi:10.2307/41409971

Benini, F. (2019). Digital Single Market. Policy: The Digital Economy and Society Index (DESI). *European Commission Policies.* Retrieved September 17, 2019, from https://ec.europa.eu/digital-single-market/en/desi

Bennett, C. J., & Raab, D. Ch. (2006). *The governance of privacy: Policy Instruments in Global perspective.* Cambridge, MA: MIT Press.

Betzing, J. H., Beverungen, D., & Becker, J. (2018). Design principles for co-creating digital customer experience in high street retail. *Proceedings of the Multikonferenz Wirtschaftsinformatik*, 2083-2094.

Bolton, R. N., McColl-Kennedy, J. R., Cheung, L., Gallan, A., Orsingher, C., Witell, L., & Zaki, M. (2018). Customer experience challenges: Bringing together digital, physical and social realms. *Journal of Service Management*, *29*(5), 776–808. doi:10.1108/JOSM-04-2018-0113

Carey, P. (Ed.). (2019). Data Protection: A Practical Guide to U.K. and E.U. Law. Oxford University Press.

Chiabai, A., Platt, S., & Strielkowski, W. (2014). Eliciting users' preferences for cultural heritage and tourism-related e-services: A tale of three European cities. *Tourism Economics*, *20*(2), 263–277. doi:10.5367/te.2013.0290

De Hert, P., & Papakonstantinou, V. (2012). The Proposed Data Protection Regulation Replacing Directive 95/46/EC: A Sound System for the Protection of Individuals. *Computer Law & Security Review*, *28*(2), 130–142. doi:10.1016/j.clsr.2012.01.011

Deac, A. (2018). Regulation (EU) 2016/679 Of the European Parliament and Of The Council On The Protection Of Individuals With Regard To The Processing Of Personal Data And The Free Movement Of These Data. *Perspectives of Law and Public Administration, Societatea de Stiinte Juridice si Administrative, 7*(2), 151–156.

Engels, B. (2016). Data Portability and Online Platforms The Effects on Competition. BLED 2016 Proceedings, 19–22

ESET. (2019). *ESET Becomes Founding Member of Google's App Defense Alliance; ESET to Proactively Protect Mobile Applications on the Google Play Store.* Press Release Bratislava, Slovakia. Retrieved March 28, 2020 from: https://www.eset.com/in/about/newsroom/press-releases/announcements/eset-becomes-founding-member-of-googles-app-defense-alliance-eset-to-proactively-protect-mobile-ap-3/

EU Council. (2019). *Council position and findings on the application of the General Data Protection Regulation (GDPR).* https://data.consilium.europa.eu/doc/document/ST-14994-2019-REV-1/en/pdf

EU Fundamental Rights Agency (FRA), The General Data Protection Regulation – one year on: Civil society: awareness, opportunities and challenges, June 2019.

European Commission. Stronger Protection, New Opportunities: Commission Guidance on the Direct Application of the General Data Protection Regulation as of 25 May 2018, COM/2018/043 final, Brussels, 24.1.2018.

European Commission. Data protection as a trust-enabler in the EU and beyond - taking stock, COM(2019) 374 final, Brussels, 24.7.2019.

European Commission's info on Member States notifications under the GDPR.

Fifield, P. (2007). Marketing Strategy Masterclass: Making Marketing Strategy Happen. Elsevier Ltd. Butterworth-Heinemann.

Fox, G., Tonge, C., Lynn, T., & Mooney, J. (2018). Communicating Compliance: Developing a GDPR Privacy Label. AMCIS 2018 Proceedings.

Giovanis, A., Athanasopoulou, P., & Tsoukatos, E. (2016). The role of corporate image and switching barriers in the service evaluation process: Evidence from the mobile telecommunications industry. *EuroMed Journal of Business, 11*(1), 132–158. doi:10.1108/EMJB-01-2015-0002

GDPR Implementation: Updated State of play in the Member States (11/04/2019), by the Commission Expert Group on the Regulation (EU) 2016/679 and Directive (EU) 2016/680.

Jen, W., Tu, R., & Lu, T. (2011). Managing passenger behavioral intention: An integrated framework for service quality, satisfaction, perceived value, and switching barriers. *Transportation, 38*(2), 321–342. doi:10.100711116-010-9306-9

Joshi, A. (2018). Digital technologies for enhancing customer experience. *Sansmaran Research Journal,* 1-8.

Karyda, M., & Mitrou, L. (2016). Data Breach Notification: Issues and Challenges for Security Management. *MCIS 2016 Proceedings*.

Klaus, P. (2014). Towards practical relevance—Delivering superior firm performance through digital customer experience strategies. *Journal of Direct, Data and Digital Marketing Practice, 15*(4), 306–316. doi:10.1057/dddmp.2014.20

Kurtz, C., Semmann, M., & Böhmann, T. (2018). Privacy by Design to Comply with GDPR: A Review on Third-Party Data Processors. AMCIS 2018 Proceedings.

Ladhari, R., Brun, I., & Morales, M. (2008). Determinants of dining satisfaction and postdining behavioral intentions. *International Journal of Hospitality Management, 27*(4), 563–573. doi:10.1016/j.ijhm.2007.07.025

Lanning, M. (2000). *Delivering Profitable Value: A Revolutionary Framework to Accelerate Growth, Generate Wealth, and Rediscover the Heart of Business*. Basic Books.

Lee, J. Y., Sridhar, S., Henderson, C. M., & Palmatier, R. W. (2014). *Effect of Customer-Centric Structure on Long-Term Financial Performance*. Marketing Science Articles in Advance.

Max Clyde. (n.d.). *The App Defence Alliance. Android's new security initiative*. InsightPortal. Retrieved November 19, 2019, from https://www.insightportal.io/news/all-news/the-app-defence-alliance

McDermott Will & Emery LLP and Ponemon Institute LLC. (2018). The Race to GDPR: A Study of Companies in the United States & Europe. Ponemon Institute.

Medha Gore, J. (2018). Customer Life Cycle Management- Time and Beyond…-Expertise recognized by clients, Analysts like. *IOSR Journal of Business and Management, 12*(6). Retrieved from www.iosrjournals.org

Multistakeholder expert group to support the application of Regulation (EU) 2016/679, Contribution to the stock-taking exercise of June 2019 on one year of GDPR application, 13.06.2019.

Petkov, P., & Helfert, M. (2017). Identifying Emerging Challenges for ICT industry in Ireland: Multiple Case Study Analysis of Data Privacy Breaches. AMCIS 2017 Proceedings.

Polatateş, S. (n.d.). *Path to Digital Transformation: Key Digital Indicators*. LearnTips is Portal for SAP Information Services and the Expert Articles, SAP Tips and Tricks. Retrieved February, 20, from: http://www.learntips.net/path-to-digital-transformation-key-digital-indicators/

Register of Commission Expert Groups and Other Similar Entities. (2019). *Publication manual of the American Psychological Association*. Brussel: Multistakeholder expert group to support the application of Regulation (EU) 2016/679 (main group). Retrieved February 25, 2020 from: https://ec.europa.eu/transparency/regexpert/index.cfm?do=groupDetail.groupMeeting&meetingId=15670

Regulation (EU) 2016/679 of the European Parliament and of the Council of 27 April 2016 on the protection of natural persons with regard to the processing of personal data and on the free movement of such data, and repealing Directive 95/46/EC (General Data Protection Regulation). Corrigendum. Latest consolidated version.

Ross M. (2018, August 1). *The path to customer centricity*. Internet retailing. Retrieved March 26, 2020 from: https://internetretailing.net/magazine-articles/magazine-articles/the-path-to-customer-centricity

Russell, K. D., O'Raghallaigh, P., O'Reilly, P., & Hayes, J. (2018). Digital Privacy GDPR: A Proposed Digital Transformation Framework. AMCIS 2018 Proceedings.

Sohn, H. K., Lee, T. J., & Yoon, Y. S. (2016). Relationship between perceived risk, evaluation, satisfaction, and behavioral intention: A case of local-festival visitors. *Journal of Travel & Tourism Marketing, 33*(1), 28–45. doi:10.1080/10548408.2015.1024912

Sörvik, J., & Kleibrink, A. (2016). *Mapping EU investments in ICT - description of an online tool and initial observations*. Report number: JRC102233Affiliation: European Commission, Joint Research Centre, Institute for Prospective Technological Studies. Project: Smart Specialisation Platform.

SuperOffice AS. (2017). *GDPR Compliance in SuperOffice CRM*. Vismagic Software Solutions, The Boatshed, Steamer Quay Road, Totnes. Retrieved March 26, 2020 from: https://static1.squarespace.com/static/571649f9f85082a0a4edbbda/t/59fb13e5f9619ac07aac2823/1509626863243/superoffice-gdpr-compliance-whitepaper.pdf

Tamò-Larrieux, A. (2018). *Designing for Privacy and its Legal Framework: Data Protection by Design and Default for the Internet of Things (Law, Governance and Technology Series)*. Cham, Switzerland: Springer International Publishing AG. doi:10.1007/978-3-319-98624-1

The Direct Marketing Association (UK) Ltd. (2018). *Data privacy: What the consumer really thinks, 2018-February*. DMA (UK) Ltd.

The Economist. (2017, May 6). The World's Most Valuable Resource Is No Longer Oil, But Data. *The Economist*.

The EU General Data Protection Regulation (GDPR): a practical guide. (n.d.). Cham, Switzerland: Springer International Publishing AG.

Thomas, K., Li, F., Zand, A., Barrett, J., Ranieri, J., Invernizzi, L., … Bursztein, E. (2017). Data breaches, phishing, or malware? Understanding the risks of stolen credentials. CCS'17 Proceedings.

Tsoukatos, E., & Rand, G. K. (2006). Path analysis of perceived service quality, satisfaction and loyalty in Greek insurance. *Managing Service Quality, 16*(5), 501–519. doi:10.1108/09604520610686746

UNCTAD. (in press). *Digital economy report 2019. Value creation and capture: Implications for developing countries*. UNCTAD.

Veccini, C. (2018, June). *GDPR and CRM: How to Manage Customer Data in 2018*. Paper presented at the meeting of IDI CONFERENCE 2018, Florence, Italy.

Vera, J., & Trujillo, A. (2017). Searching most influential variables to brand loyalty measurements: *An exploratory study. Contaduría y Administración, 62*(2), 600–624. doi:10.1016/j.cya.2016.04.007

Voigt, P. (Ed.). (2016). *Maximize business profits through e-partnerships*. Hershey, PA: IRM Press.

Wieseke, J., Geigenmüller, A., & Kraus, F. (2012). On the role of empathy in customer-employee interactions. *Journal of Service Research, 15*(3), 316–331. doi:10.1177/1094670512439743

Xu, Y., Goedegebuure, R., & Van der Heijden, B. (2007). Customer Perception, Customer Satisfaction, and Customer Loyalty Within Chinese Securities Business. *Journal of Relationship Marketing*, 5(4), 79–104. doi:10.1300/J366v05n04_06

Section 5
Jurisprudential Developments on the Right to Be Forgotten

This section focuses on case law developments regarding the right to be forgotten by taking a closer look both at the EU and the Member States' levels.

Chapter 14

The Unexpected Consequences of the EU Right to Be Forgotten:
Internet Search Engines as Fundamental Rights Adjudicators

Maria Tzanou
https://orcid.org/0000-0001-5360-2038
Keele University, UK

ABSTRACT

The right to be forgotten as established in the CJEU's decision in Google Spain is the first online data privacy right recognized in the EU legal order. This contribution explores two currently underdeveloped in the literature aspects of the right to be forgotten: its unexpected consequences on search engines and the difficulties of its implementation in practice by the latter. It argues that the horizontal application of EU privacy rights on private parties, such as internet search engines—as undertaken by the CJEU—is fraught with conceptual gaps, dilemmas, and uncertainties that create confusions about the enforceability of the right to be forgotten and the role of search engines. In this respect, it puts forward a comprehensive legal framework for the implementation of this right, which aims to ensure a legally certain and proportionate balance of the competing interests online in the light of the EU's General Data Protection Regulation (GDPR).

INTRODUCTION

In its landmark judgment in *Google Spain*, the Court of Justice of the European Union (the Court or CJEU) held that data subjects have a 'right to be forgotten'[1] under EU data protection law, which requires the de-listing of links to web pages containing information relating to them from the list of results displayed following a search made on the basis of the person's name. The right to be forgotten is an important online right of the data subject recognized at the EU legal order. It is enforced against internet search engines who are considered data 'controllers' for the purposes of EU data protection law (*Google Spain*, para 38).

DOI: 10.4018/978-1-5225-9489-5.ch014

The right to be forgotten was not expressly spelled out in the Data Protection Directive (DPD), but the CJEU found that this could be derived from a combination of Arts 12 and 14 thereof that grant the data subject the rights of rectification, erasure or blocking of their personal data and the right to object to the processing of this respectively. The right to be forgotten is, nevertheless explicitly recognized in the General Data Protection Regulation (GDPR) that repeals and replaces the Data Protection Directive. More specifically, Art. 17 GDPR entitled 'Right to erasure ("right to be forgotten")' contains a much broader right than the one established in *Google Spain* allowing the data subject to obtain the erasure of personal data concerning him or her and creating the concomitant obligation of the controller to erase personal data without undue delay.

Much ink has been spilled in the academic literature on the right to be forgotten both regarding its recognition by the CJEU in *Google Spain* (Frantziou, 2014; Kulk &Frederik Zuiderveen Borgesius, 2014; Rees & Heywood 2014; Lynskey, 2015; Spiecker genannt Döhmann, 2015; Kranenborg, 2015; Post, 2017) and its legal entrenchment in Article 17 GDPR (Leta Ambrose, 2012; Leta Ambrose & Ausloos, 2013; McGoldrick, 2013; Sartor, 2013; Sartor, 2015; Keller, 2017). The academic debate has examined different aspects of this right, such as its content, its territorial application and its implications on freedom of information and internet governance. Taking into account the existing debate, this specific chapter focuses on the narrower online right to be forgotten that arose from *Google Spain* and explores two aspects of this, currently underdeveloped in the literature: its unexpected consequences on search engines and the difficulties of its implementation in practice by the latter.

More particularly, it addresses two crucial elements regarding the fundamental question of the implementation of the right to be forgotten by private parties that were left to a large extent unanswered after *Google Spain*: First, the horizontal application of the fundamental rights to privacy (Article 7 EUCFR) and data protection (Article 8 EUCFR) on private parties –as undertaken by the CJEU- is fraught with conceptual gaps, dilemmas and uncertainties that create confusions about the enforceability of the right to be forgotten. Secondly –and closely linked to this- the horizontality of EU privacy rights involves balancing between competing rights that has to be carried out in practice by search engines. Essentially, search engines are made adjudicators of fundamental rights online. This raises serious concerns about the role and responsibilities of internet search engines and ultimately –and more importantly- it questions the purpose of fundamental rights themselves.

This chapter explores the main issues that arise from the horizontality of EU privacy rights in the context of the right to be forgotten and puts forward a comprehensive legal framework for the implementation of this right, which aims to ensure a legally certain and balanced reconciliation of the competing interests online. The discussion provided, albeit focusing on the right to be forgotten as it emerged from *Google Spain*, is relevant for the implementation of the broader right to erasure and the right to be forgotten guaranteed in Article 17 GDPR; also by controllers that are not necessarily internet search engines operators.

NO CLEAR LEGAL FRAMEWORK FOR THE IMPLEMENTATION OF THE RIGHT TO BE FORGOTTEN

Before turning to the shortcomings concerning the right to be forgotten of the CJEU's analysis in *Google Spain*, it would be useful to briefly recall the factual and legal background of the case. The Spanish newspaper *La Vanguardia* published, in 1998, in its printed issues a real-estate auction connected with insolvency proceedings for social security debts taken against Mr Costeja González, a Spanish national. These reports were later made available online. In 2010, Mr Costeja González lodged a complaint with the Spanish Data Protection Agency (the AEPD) against *La Vanguardia* and against Google Spain and Google Inc. requesting the removal of both the publication from the newspaper's pages and his personal data from Google's search results. The AEPD rejected the complaint against *La Vanguardia* on the basis that the publication was legally justified as it took place upon order of the Spanish Ministry of Labour and Social Affairs, but upheld the complaint against Google, taking the view that search engines are subject to EU data protection legislation. Google challenged the AEPD's decision before the *Audiencia Nacional* (National High Court), which stayed the proceedings and referred three main sets of questions to the CJEU: the first group of questions concerned the territorial scope of EU data protection rules; the second referred to its material scope and in particular to the legal position of internet search engines under the Data Protection Directive; finally, the third set inquired about the scope and reach of the right to be forgotten.

The CJEU held that the Data Protection Directive indeed applied territorially to a search engine, such as Google, when this sets up in a Member State a branch or subsidiary, such as Google Spain, which is intended 'to promote and sell advertising space offered by that engine and which orientates its activity towards the inhabitants of that Member State.' Regarding the second set of questions, the Court found that the operators of search engines should be considered 'controllers' of personal data, because they determine 'the purposes and means of the processing of personal data'.

In order to answer the third set of questions regarding the scope of the right to be forgotten, the CJEU had to consider two issues: 1) Could a right to be forgotten be read in the provisions of the DPD and 2) and if so, when does it apply, or to put it differently how is it to be balanced with the opposing interests at stake? Regarding the first issue, the CJEU concluded that a right to be forgotten could be derived from a combination of Art. 12, which guaranteed the right of rectification, erasure and blocking of data the processing of which does not comply with the provisions of the Directive, in particular because of their incomplete or inaccurate nature and Article 14 (a) that granted data subjects the right to object 'at any time on compelling legitimate grounds relating to his particular situation' to the processing of data relating to him carried out under Article 7 (f).

To answer the second question, the Court turned its attention to the opposing interests at stake. According to the CJEU, these were, on the one hand, the economic interest of a search engine in the processing and 'the legitimate interest of internet users in having access to information' (para 81) and, on the other hand, interestingly, not the right to be forgotten found in secondary EU law, but the data subject's fundamental rights to privacy and data protection under Arts 7 and 8 of the Charter. The Court explained that the fundamental rights to privacy and data protection had to be brought into the analysis because the processing of personal data carried out by a search engine interferes significantly with these rights. In fact, such interference is so significant that 'it cannot be justified by merely the economic interest which the operator of such an engine has in that processing' (para 81).The CJEU, however, accepted that a fair balance should be struck between the interest of internet users in having access to information and the data subject's fundamental rights to privacy and data protection. In this respect, the Court held that 'as a general rule' (para 81), the data subject's rights to privacy and data protection override the interest of internet users in having access to information. It noted, however, that such a balance may 'depend, in specific cases, on the nature of the information in question and its sensitivity for the data subject's private life and on the interest of the public in having that information, an interest which may vary, in particular, according to the role played by the data subject in public life' (para 81).

Regarding the scope of the right to be forgotten, the Court noted that if the information appears to be inadequate, irrelevant or no longer relevant, or excessive in relation to the purposes of the processing at issue, the links concerned in the list of search results must be erased. However, such a right can be found without it being necessary that the inclusion of the information in the search results causes prejudice to the data subject. In this respect, the CJEU emphasized once again that the rights to privacy and data protection override, as a rule, the opposing interests. However, the Court accepted that this could be rebutted if it appeared that the general public has a 'preponderant interest' in accessing the information in question.

The first part of the Court's analysis dealing with the legal basis of the right to be forgotten on the DPD seems well reasoned. Following a well-established pattern, the CJEU employed a broad teleological interpretation of the Directive, but its conclusions are well founded on its Arts. However, the pronouncements of the Court in the second part of its reasoning are problematic for several reasons. Firstly, by bringing in the discussion the fundamental rights to privacy and data protection, the Court's judgment raises questions about the horizontal application of EU fundamental rights to private entities, such as search engines with all the complexities that surround this. Secondly, the forum of the Court's analysis of the right to be forgotten is confusing: on the one hand, this right is discovered in secondary legislation, on the other hand, it is balanced at the level of fundamental rights. Thirdly, the CJEU did not get the competing rights or interests right. It balanced, on the one hand, two fundamental rights that are expressly mentioned –privacy (Article 7 EUCFR) and data protection (Article 8 EUCFR); and, on the other hand, mere 'interests'. Instead of referring to freedom of expression and information which is a fundamental right enshrined in Article 11 EUCFR,[2] the Court chose to speak about 'the interest of internet users in having access to information.'

By completely failing to recognize that fundamental right and put it at equal footing with privacy and data protection, the Court established a framework of balancing that is *a priori* unbalanced. In fact, the CJEU replaced altogether the balancing mechanism with a general privacy- prevalence rule under which data privacy rights are favored with regard to opposing rights as a general, *a priori* rule. Admittedly, the Court has in general been quite favorable to data privacy rights in its case-law in the past (Bagger Tranberg, 2011) but at least until now it has not failed to balance data protection with the opposing rights. This new data protection activism –as I call it- that it displayed in *Google Spain* opens up its judgment to criticisms, especially from the other side of the Atlantic given the importance of the First Amendment right to free speech (Rosen, 2012). Taking into account that this has been one of the main issues raised against the right to be forgotten since its inception, it is regrettable that the Court missed the chance to develop a solid framework of reconciliation of the competing interests and rights at stake by clearly indicating the criteria that should be employed in order to achieve a fair balancing (Koutrakos, 2014; Kuner, 2014).

Moreover, the scope of the right to be forgotten itself is uncertain as it is not established independently but on the basis of some unclear balancing with other interests and the privacy presumption rule. What types of personal information can benefit from erasure? What are the criteria to be employed in order to determine this? Instead of providing a clear analysis to these questions, the Court found recourse to its already established privacy presumption: privacy and data protection override as a rule the opposing interests. This presumption can be rebutted only when balancing reveals that there is a 'preponderant' interest of the general public in having access to that information. Again, specific guidelines on how to determine this are missing. The Court merely noted, in this respect, that the role played by the data subject in public life should be taken into account.

The fundamental question of the implementation of the right to be forgotten by private parties has, thus, been left to a large extent unanswered after *Google Spain*. Two crucial aspects relate to this: First, the problematic issues that arise from the horizontal application of EU privacy rights raise questions about the role of search engines as adjudicators of fundamental rights. Secondly –and closely linked to this- the implementation of the right to be forgotten requires a balancing between competing interests that must be carried out in practice by search engines. The following sections aim to discuss these two interconnected aspects and provide a comprehensive legal framework for the implementation of the right to be forgotten.

THE HORIZONTAL APPLICATION OF EU PRIVACY RIGHTS

Horizontality of EU Privacy Rights: Underlying Values

Art 51 EUCFR states that the provisions of the Charter are binding on the EU institutions and the Member States when they implement EU law, but remains silent as to their effect on private parties. The horizontal effect of the EU Charter of Fundamental Rights has been a contested issue (Leczykiewicz, 2013; Frantziou, 2015; Fornasier, 2015). In *AMS*, the CJEU considered whether Article 27 EUCFR, which guarantees 'workers' right to information and consultation within the undertaking' could be invoked in a dispute between individuals. The Court held that the fundamental rights guaranteed in the EU legal order 'are applicable in all situations governed by European Union law' (*AMS*, para 42) and, therefore, since the national legislation at issue in the main proceedings was adopted to implement an EU Directive, Art 27 EUCFR was' applicable to the case in the main proceedings' (*AMS*, para 43). However, the Court concluded that this Article could not be invoked in the proceedings at issue because it had to be given 'more specific expression in European Union or national law' (*AMS*, para 45). *AMS* can be read as a recognition that Charter rights can apply to private parties in certain cases. Nevertheless, there is still no coherent approach as to the horizontality of different provisions of the Charter (Ladenburger, 2012) and the CJEU has been accused of not adopting a 'common stance vis-à-vis the justifications of horizontal effect' (Frantziou, 2015, p. 673).

Google Spain has confirmed that Arts 7 and 8 EUCFR apply to private parties. What is more, it can be argued that this is one of the first cases where the Court provided a normative basis justifying the horizontality of fundamental rights, albeit one limited to privacy rights. In particular, the CJEU based its decision on the recognition of a right to be forgotten and the concomitant imposition of obligations to search engines on five elements that characterise *what* information can be accessed, *who* can access this and from *where*, *how* this can be obtained and the *effects* of finding information online through search engines. All these elements were read in the light of the CJEU's well-known privacy-enhancing teleological interpretation that aims to ensure the 'effective and complete protection of data users'. As to *what* information can be accessed through an internet search, this concerns a vast number of aspects of an individual's private life. As to *who* can access this information, the CJEU emphasised that it was any internet user from everywhere in the world as information is ubiquitous in the era of the internet and search engines. The *how* this information can be accessed online is particularly important: it is appreciably easy to search on the basis of an individual's name using a search engine that will produce a 'structured overview' of all the information relating to that individual that can be found on the internet with the possibility of further interconnecting and aggregating this with further information. The *effects* of such a search are significant as it can establish a 'detailed profile of the individual' (*Google Spain*, para 80) and, thus, interfere with fundamental rights such as human dignity.

It seems that the underlying normative foundations of the horizontality of the fundamental rights to privacy and data protection evolve around two interconnected themes: the power imbalance between individuals (the data subjects) and technological corporations that operate on a global scale, such as internet search engines as 'controllers' of personal data, and the concomitant need to preserve informational self-determination, individual autonomy and ultimately human dignity.

The processing of personal data indeed bears inherent imbalances, which are manifest in the asymmetries between the two main actors involved in the processing: the data subject, on the one hand, and data controllers on the other hand (Nissenbaum, 1998, p. 576; Tzanou, 2013, p. 91; Tzanou, 2017, p. 26).It should be recognised that internet search engines play a crucial role in ensuring the 'universal accessibility' of information on the internet, whose searching would otherwise be too complicated and difficult and would produce limited results. However, this universal accessibility to the personal data made possible through search engines decreases the claims of data subjects to transparency and foreseeability in data processing, and to their own participation in this -to the extent that it is possible. Personal data may remain forever on the internet and can become easily accessible through a simple search using a search engine allowing for further processing without any virtual time limit. Individuals can, thus, find themselves powerless vis-à-vis search engines over the processing of their data online and the 'digital persona' (Clarke, 1994) that is constructed through the aggregation of this following a simple internet search. The 'digital persona' that emerges out of data processing presents such a powerful image of the individual, that it can be used as a 'proxy for the real person' (Clarke, 1994). Information on the internet leaves available in perpetuity both 'digital footprints' (Koops, 2011, p. 236); namely data created by users themselves and 'digital shadows' (Burkell, 2016, p.18), i.e data produced about users from others. Since internet search engines have commercial interests in the way they index the data in their search results this lack of power and participation of the data subjects can lead to inequalities between 'haves' and 'have-nots' (Cohen, 2000, p. 1378). The former can afford to hire online companies[3] or pay search engines to construct a favorable 'digital persona' while the latter are left with no means or power to control information that negatively affects them.

The horizontality of EU privacy rights enforced against search engine providers through the recognition of the right to be forgotten reflects, therefore, concerns regarding the exercise of informational self-determination, individual autonomy, and ultimately human dignity online. Informational autonomy prohibits that individuals are treated 'as mere conglomerations of transactional data' (Cohen, 2000, p. 1408) or simple 'algorithms' (Gstrein, 2015, p. 47) that rank people based on resources or desirable characteristics. The final value is to preserve human dignity that ensures -broadly understood in (simplified) Kantian terms- that individuals should not be treated as a means to an end (Dupré, 2013, p. 329) in their online lives.

Horizontality of EU Privacy Rights: The Conceptual Ambiguities

It should be accepted that the imposition of obligations to search engines advances several important values. However, there are certain conceptual gaps and uncertainties regarding the horizontal obligations of search engines that create confusions about the enforceability of the right to be forgotten. A first conceptual dilemma that often arises regarding the horizontality of fundamental rights in general concerns the *private - public law* divide. This is based on the premise that fundamental rights aim to address abuse of powers by governments, rather than impose obligations on individual autonomy by regulating the relationships between private parties.

Different arguments against the horizontality of fundamental rights have been advanced from both a public law and private law perspective. From a public law point of view, it has been argued that 'an application of human rights obligations to non-state actors trivialises, dilutes and distracts from the great concept of human rights [and that] such an application bestows inappropriate power and legitimacy on such actors' (Clapham, 2006, p. 58; Tushnet, 2003). From a private law perspective, the horizontality of fundamental rights has been criticised for posing 'a threat to private law's libertarian core of private autonomy (by placing private actors, ...under the same duties as public bodies acting in the common interest)', thus undermining 'the boundaries of spheres of private autonomy' (Gerstenberg, 2004, p. 769).

While the Court recognised the horizontal application of Articles 7 and 8 EUCFR to search engines in *Google Spain*, it did not discuss the *public-private* law conceptual dilemma. On the surface such a discussion could be seen as superfluous since the DPD-and the GDPR- apply to both public authorities and private parties.

It should be recalled that the Court balanced the opposing private interests at stake at the level of fundamental rights. However, there is a 'significant difference in the way in which fundamental rights function' (Collins, 2012, p. 3) on the one hand, in public law disputes and, on the other hand, in private law disputes between private parties involving private interests. Unlike public law, where fundamental rights are granted to individuals, but not to the state, private law disputes must take into account the fundamental rights of all private parties involved in the dispute (Collins, 2012, p. 3). To put it simply, private conflicts are characterised by the fact that all sides to the dispute can invoke rights (Oliver & Fedtke, 2007, p. 5).

This means that the fundamental rights that needed balancing in the case should have been considered more carefully since all the parties in the dispute have such claims that *in abstracto* are of equal value. The issue is relevant not only to the balancing that took place at the level of the CJEU's own decision in *Google Spain*, but most importantly to the balancing of the fundamental rights of private parties that Google and other search engines are required to undertake in order to enforce the right to be forgotten. The discussion will return to this point below.

At this stage, the analysis should focus on a further distinction of the horizontality of fundamental rights, namely this between *direct* and *indirect* effect. There is not a uniform definition of direct and indirect effect in the case-law and the academic literature, but three approaches can be broadly found (Leczykiewicz, 2013, p. 490). The first focuses on the outcome of the relationship between the fundamental right and the legal provision applicable at the particular instance: direct effect would mean that the conflicting lower-ranking legal provision must be disapplied; indirect effect would require that this provision is interpreted in accordance with the fundamental right. A second approach considers the material scope of application of a fundamental right: if this binds individuals directly, then we would be speaking of direct effect; if this binds only the organs of the State, indirect effect would arise where courts, as State bodies, impose obligations on individuals or create new causes of action in order to protect fundamental rights when they adjudicate disputes between private parties. A third approach focuses on the legal effects of the fundamental right in the legal system: in this case, a private party could be held liable for acting in contravention with a fundamental right; while indirect effect would mean 'any other effect of fundamental rights, where these are used as supplementary arguments, for example to strengthen the traditional meaning of a provision on which the claimant relies directly' (Leczykiewicz, 2013, p. 491) or as an interpretative mechanism used by courts. The three approaches overlap to an extent and scholars have cautioned against the use of the doctrines of direct and indirect effect 'as a way of delineating the horizontal effect of the Charter' (Leczykiewicz, 2013, p. 491).

Interestingly, in the *Google Spain* case the Court transferred the data privacy interests of Mr Costeja Gonzalez to a fundamental rights framework where the fundamental rights to privacy and data protection were applied indirectly and –remarkably- to an extent also directly. The Charter privacy rights were used to strengthen the arguments of the claimant and to interpret the provisions of the DPD (*Google Spain*, paras 68-69) (*indirect effect*) as well as to impose fundamental rights obligations on Google (*Google Spain*, paras 80 and 87) and balance these with conflicting interests (*direct effect*).

It has been argued that the practical difference between indirect and direct effect is 'negligeable' (Kumm, 2006, p. 352), but the approach of the Court besides increasing the conceptual confusions also has practical and doctrinal implications. At the practical level, as will be seen below, the judgment had unexpected consequences on search engines, such as Google, which are not only bestowed obligations, but also given significant 'gate keeper' powers that include the enforcement of fundamental rights. At a more doctrinal level, viewing every type of personal data processing as a question of fundamental rights protection might prove unduly prescriptive, rigid and cumbersome for private parties and might lead to circumstances where the actual outcome is dictated without paying due respect to other rights or interests as the Court's own decision in *Google Spain* demonstrated. It should be noted here that Google also has its own economic interests as the operator of the search engine and if the debate regarding balancing is elevated at the level of fundamental rights, there are questions whether this or other companies should be allowed to invoke fundamental rights in the way individuals do. Finally, at a theoretical level, the CJEU should be very careful when deciding whether the purpose of fundamental rights is to be treated as instruments for the realisation of the particular rights and interests of aggravated individuals (Van der Sloot, 2016, p. 456).

Leaving aside the horizontality of fundamental rights for a moment, it could be argued that the right to be forgotten was considered an obligation based on the DPD itself rather than the fundamental rights to privacy and data protection enshrined in the Charter. If that is the case, one can conclude that Google is required to enforce that Directive –and currently the GDPR- rather than adjudicate fundamental rights.

This brings me to the third conceptual confusion regarding the obligations imposed to search engines: are these a matter of *constitutional/primary* EU law or of *secondary* EU law? The conceptual dilemma as to which level the right to be forgotten should be placed at played out in two different phases in *Google Spain*: on the one hand, in the *recognition* of the right and, on the other hand, in its *balancing* with opposing interests. The recognition of the right to be forgotten was a matter of secondary law, as the CJEU read this in the provisions of the Data Protection Directive. Its balancing with opposing interests, however, was considered a fundamental rights issue and, thus, Arts 7 and 8 EUCFR came into play. Essentially, the CJEU decided without any clear reason to treat the conflicting interests at stake as a problematic case of a conflict of a 'constitutional nature' (Azoulai, 2008, p. 1336) which required the direct application of the Charter privacy rights- albeit not this of the right to freedom of expression.

It is unclear what purpose the dichotomy between *recognition*- at *secondary law* level- and *balancing*- at *primary law/fundamental rights* level- serves. This dichotomy is based on Article 7(f) DPD, which constitutes, according to the CJEU's analysis, the legal basis for the processing of personal data carried out by search engines (*Google Spain*, para 73). This provision permits the processing of personal data where it is necessary for the purposes of the 'legitimate interests' pursued by the controller or by the third party or parties to whom the data are disclosed, 'except where such interests are overridden by the interests or fundamental rights and freedoms of the data subject' (Balboni et al., 2013, p. 247; Ferretti,

2014).Yet, it is not clear why the competing interests at stake could not have been balanced at the level of secondary law. One could assume that the CJEU wanted to make clear that the right to be forgotten derives from secondary legislation (the Data Protection Directive) but is rooted in constitutionally protected fundamental rights (Articles 7 and 8 EUCFR). While this is acceptable, secondary law should remain the framework for balancing these interests.

Secondary law does not pose the problems of horizontality of fundamental rights since the DPD and the GDPR apply to both public and private parties. Furthermore, the GDPR expressly provides several principles as to how controllers should process personal data and dedicates specific provisions to the processing of personal data and freedom of expression. In particular, Article 85(1) GDPR requires Member States to reconcile by law the right to the protection of personal data with the right to freedom of expression and information, including processing for journalistic purposes and the purposes of academic, artistic or literary expression and Article 17(3)(a) GDPR states that paragraphs 1 and 2 of the same Article, guaranteeing the right to be forgotten do not apply to the extent that processing is necessary 'for exercising the right of freedom of expression and information'.

This chapter posits that the CJEU in *Google Spain* should have reconciled the opposing interests at stake by interpreting the DPD. Certainly, such an interpretation of secondary law that involves balancing of opposing interests should be 'guided by fundamental rights' that would form the 'background' against which secondary legislation should be read, as Advocate General Kokott succinctly put it in *Satamedia*.

What does this mean for the question of the horizontality of fundamental privacy rights? It is submitted that while there are good reasons for the horizontal application of the fundamental rights to privacy and data protection on search engines (imbalance of power between Google and individuals as data subjects, protection of further values and rights such as non-discrimination and human dignity), this should be limited only to *indirect effect*, namely, the reading of secondary law in the light of fundamental rights. This is because there is a significant amount of detailed legislation on data protection that already applies to private parties and can be flexibly interpreted in the light of the Charter rights, without necessitating their direct application which can create ambiguities and have unexpected consequences.

There are two important reasons that justify this approach. First, the balancing of the opposing interests at stake within the context of DPD in the light of the Charter rights could have prevented the conceptual confusions between *secondary* and *primary* law regarding the *recognition* of the right to be forgotten and its *balancing* by establishing secondary law as the forum for the discussion of both these aspects.

This approach is consistent with the CJEU case law in previous cases where the Court had to reconcile the fundamental rights to privacy and data protection with either intellectual property rights protected under Article 17 (2) EUCFR or freedom of expression. In *Österreichischer Rundfunk*, the Court held that 'the provisions of Directive 95/46, in so far as they govern the processing of personal data liable to infringe fundamental freedoms, in particular the right to privacy, must necessarily be interpreted '*in the light of fundamental rights*' (para 68). In *Promusicae*, the Court had to consider whether an internet service provider (ISP) had the obligation to disclose to a non-profit-making organization of producers and publishers of musical and audiovisual recordings acting on behalf of its members who were holders of intellectual property rights, the personal data of certain persons who were allegedly used peer-to-peer exchange of files. The CJEU first took a look at all the relevant Directives at stake and then went on to establish whether these required 'a different reading' 'in the light of the Charter' and the fundamental rights involved (para 65). It noted that Directives seek to respect the fundamental rights and principles recognized in the Charter (para 64) and held that 'the mechanisms allowing those different rights and interests to be balanced' are contained, first, in the rules of the relevant Directives themselves, and 'second, they result from the adoption by the Member States of national provisions transposing those directives and their application by the national authorities' (paras 66 and 68). In *Satamedia,* a case that involved the balancing of privacy rights with freedom of expression in order to ascertain whether the publication in a newspaper of the tax data of Finnish citizens as well as the making of such data available through a text-messaging service was compatible with the Data Protection Directive, the CJEU followed a similar approach. Having recalled its established case-law per which the provisions of a directive must be interpreted in the light of the aims it pursues and the system it establishes (para 68), it held that the aims pursued by Article 9 and Recital 37 DPD refer to a reconciliation between the fundamental rights to privacy and freedom of expression (para 54).

This line of cases demonstrates that CJEU has indeed applied fundamental rights in the balancing of rights of private parties, but has done so only *indirectly*: secondary EU law governing the relationship between private parties has been interpreted in the light of fundamental rights. It should be noted here that cases such as *Schecke, Digital Rights Ireland* and *Schrems* should be distinguished from *Google Spain* because the Court in these cases had to review the legality of secondary EU law against fundamental rights and, therefore, apply vertically –rather than horizontally- the Charter.

The Problems of the Horizontality of EU Privacy Rights

The second reason that justifies the positioning of the right to be forgotten at the level of the interpretation of secondary legislation relates to the problems that the horizontality of the fundamental rights to privacy and data protection as emerged in *Google Spain* creates. The horizontal application of these fundamental rights to Google demonstrated the CJEU's intention to make the internet 'subject to EU data protection law' (Kuner, 2013, p. 12) by imposing data privacy obligations to search engines. Yet, the obligation to delist links imposed on Google, bestows it at the same time with the significant power to balance fundamental rights against each other and to decide on the outcome of particular cases (Kuner, 2015, p. 18). In essence, it makes internet search engines adjudicators of fundamental rights online.[4] This can be seen as the paradox arising from *Google Spain*: as observed eloquently, instead of reining in Google, the CJEU's judgment had the effects of putting it 'at the forefront of Europe's enforcement of Internet privacy' (Scott, 2016).

This paradox has been criticised as 'upending conventional wisdom about the company' and raising several concerns about Google's role in protecting people's privacy (Scott, 2016). Firstly, it has been argued that private corporations such as search engines are not well-equipped to act as arbiters of fundamental rights online, a role that traditionally belongs to Data Protection Authorities (DPAs) and courts (Kuner, 2015, p, 19; Erdos, 2015, p. 537). Can Google be treated as a 'constitutional body' that is expected to assume adjudicatory powers in order to carry out public policy objectives? To an extent, this issue is not confined to data protection. Indeed, a similar discussion has arisen in the context of defamation law, copyright and hate speech, where intermediaries, normally tech giants, such as Google and Facebook are often required to remove material posted online by third parties (Horten, 2016; Brunner, 2016; Angelopoulos & Smet, 2016; Kosseff, 2017. For relevant cases, see for instance *Delfi v Estonia*).

It is outside the scope of this chapter to discuss in detail these cases, but it is worth pointing out that under the current construction of the right to be forgotten by the CJEU there are differences between these cases and data protection. The E-Commerce Directive exempts intermediate service providers from liability for material they store if they do not have 'actual knowledge of illegal activity or information', are 'not aware of facts or circumstances from which the illegal activity or information is apparent' or 'upon obtaining such knowledge or awareness act expeditiously to remove' the information. In the case of the right to be forgotten, however, search engines are considered 'controllers' of personal data that must comply with all the relevant obligations under EU data protection law. But, does the status of controller require an 'active role' (Keller, 2016, p. 70) rather than the more passive one under the E-Commerce Safe Harbors? It will be explained below that in the context of the right to be forgotten as constructed by the CJEU in *Google Spain*, there are comparisons to be drawn with the E-Commerce Safe Harbors. Nevertheless, the right to be forgotten is not merely about assessing 'illegality' in order to remove the relevant information -indeed, many times the personal information may have been posted for legitimate purposes under a clear legal basis (as in the case of Mr Costeja Gonzalez).

The second problem that arises concerns the impartiality of search engines as these have strong commercial interests themselves that might affect the balancing process. As Spiecker (2015, p. 1053) has astutely observed, it is like 'set[ting] a fox to keep the geese.' Admittedly, this problem does not seem insurmountable as search engines are subject to the oversight of DPAs and courts when they implement the right to be forgotten.

But ultimately, the paradox that arose in *Google Spain* goes beyond Google: it concerns fundamental rights themselves. By elevating a dispute between private parties –to which data protection legislation is perfectly applicable- to a fundamental rights discourse, the Court did not increase the importance of fundamental privacy rights, instead it reduced their value to a utilitarian understanding that requires their application at any instance and by anyone –even a private party- when a claim for the protection of the greater good can be made (Van der Sloot, 2016, p. 459).

The application of secondary law based on the interpretation of fundamental rights would have downplayed the symbolism of the horizontality of data privacy rights on search enginesand rendered their task more mundane: these would be mere 'controllers' of personal data that must enforce the various data subjects' rights with respect to the data they process often under the control and checks and balances of DPAs and courts. In addition, such an approach avoids the conceptual confusions and complexities identified above.

A LEGAL FRAMEWORK FOR THE IMPLEMENTATION OF THE RIGHT TO BE FORGOTTEN

Privacy, Data Protection and Competing Rights: A fair Balance

The right to be forgotten as it emerged in *Google Spain* is the right of the data subject to obtain the delisting of links to web pages published by third parties containing information relating to him from the list of results displayed following a search made on the basis of the person's name. The exact legal nature of the right to be forgotten has been the subject of debate. Is it a philosophical concept/value originating from Mayer-Schönberger's seminal work (2009) is it a legal entitlement/interest (Gstrein, 2015, p. 41) or is it a right? After the CJEU's judgment in *Google Spain* there is little doubt left that we are not talking only about a philosophical concept. Indeed, the delisting of links from a search engine's belongs to the so-called 'micro-rights' (Lazaro & Le Métayer, 2015,15) of the data subject, much like the rights found in the DPD and the GDPR, such as for instance, the data subject's rights to access, rectification, erasure and blocking and the data subject's right to object.

The basic premise, therefore, is that in line with Recital 4 of the GDPR, the right to be forgotten as -privacy and data protection- is not an absolute right but must be *balanced proportionately* with competing interests and rights. A proper balancing exercise requires, from the outset, the recognition that the competing interests or rights have an 'equal status in the abstract' (Alexy, 2009, p. 51). Equal footing is required so that the contrasting values are properly reflected. Thus, the fundamental right to freedom of expression and information enshrined in Article 11 EUCFR should have been put at equal footing with the rights to privacy and data protection recognized in Arts 7 and 8 EUCFR respectively and not mentioned solely as an 'interest', as the CJEU did in its *Google Spain* judgment.

A real, substantive, case by case balancing exercise of the opposing interests or rights at stake should then take place. This means that no automatic priority should be conferred to privacy rights and no *a priori* presumptions of the outcome of the balancing should be made. In order to avoid the problems of horizontality that arise when private parties, such as internet search engines are required to balance competing fundamental rights, this article has argued that the balancing exercise should take place between competing *interests* operating at the level of *secondary law* rather than fundamental rights themselves, as the CJEU did in a confusing and erroneous way in its judgment. This does not, however, negate the possibility of balancing competing interests in the light of fundamental rights.

Before the analysis turns to the question of balancing of the right to be forgotten with conflicting interests, it is worth noting that this right is not limitless, but prescribed by a number of limitations. These are briefly examined below.

The Limits of the Right to Be Forgotten

The enforcement of the right to be forgotten is prescribed by different types of limits. A first type of *inherent* limitations concerns the *content* of this right. This entails an obligation on search engines to remove from the list of results displayed following a search made on the basis of a person's name links to web pages, published by third parties and containing information relating to that person. This obligation is both limited in *scope* and *temporally*. *Rationae materiae* the right to be forgotten requires only the delisting of links, following a search made on the person's name – but not other indicators and it does not entail the removal of the publication from the web pages where it originally appeared.

Rationae temporis, the search engines' obligation to delist links comes *after* a relevant request of the data subject was submitted and considered well-founded. The right to be forgotten, thus, does not entail the active monitoring and surveillance of internet publications by search engines to remove links that fall within its remit. It, thus, resembles to an extent the notice-and-take down approach adopted by the E-Commerce Directive.

Further to these inherent limitations to the content of the right to be forgotten, this is also prescribed by *institutional* limits. As mentioned above, search engines do not operate in a vacuum when they enforce the right to be forgotten; on the contrary, their assessment is subject to oversight by DPAs and courts. DPAs can assess complaints by data subjects whose delisting requests were refused by the search engines and national courts can play an important role in overseeing the legality of search engines' decisions. These institutional safeguards guarantee that Google's power to adjudicate fundamental rights online is not boundless but subject to administrative and judicial control.

The Forgotten by the CJEU Proportionality Principle

Balancing the right to be forgotten with competing interests is not an easy task (Tzanou, 2010, p. 63; De Vries, 2013) and the balance between data privacy and the interest of the public in accessing the information at issue is 'by no means a precise science' (Bignami, 2008, p. 234). A proper balancing is required, however, when the two interests clash. It is submitted that such balancing can only be carried out by taking into account the principle of *proportionality*.

Proportionality is crucial for the determination of the outcome of the balancing exercise between two competing interests or rights. Proportionality is enshrined in article 5 TEU and has since long been recognized by the Court as a general principle of EU law and has been used by the Court as a criterion for deciding whether an interference with fundamental rights is legitimate according to Article 52 (1) EUCFR.

Proportionality 'applies on several levels' (Bagger Tranberg, 2011, p. 239) of EU data protection law. On the one hand, proportionality concerns run through the EU data protection legislation and underpin the operation of most of the fair information principles (Tzanou, 2017, p. 91). Direct references to the principle of proportionality can be found in the rules that require that personal data should be 'adequate, relevant' and 'not excessive' in relation to the purposes for which they are collected and further processed; that they are 'necessary'; and, that they are kept for no longer than is necessary for the purposes for which the data were collected or further processed. On the other hand, proportionality is used by the Court to determine whether an interference with the rights to privacy and data protection is justified.

It is not difficult to notice the Court's failure to mention proportionality in *Google Spain*. In fact, the principle of proportionality was mentioned only once in the whole judgment and this because it was raised by Google Spain and Google Inc. in one of their submissions (para 63). Even when the CJEU speaks about the need to strike a 'fair balance' between the fundamental rights to privacy and data protection and the other competing interests, proportionality is nowhere to be found.

The lack of a clear proportionality analysis in its right to be forgotten balancing test makes the decision of the Court in *Google Spain* extremely problematic. As was discussed in the previous section, the balancing of the conflicting interests was elevated by the Court at the level of fundamental rights and the burden of such adjudication was put on search engines. Yet, a proper balancing on the basis of the principle of proportionality that would have provided some guidance and clarification to search engines on how to perform their task was never provided by the Court. Instead, the Court contained itself in the privacy-prevalence rule. As already mentioned, such an approach did not do any favors to data privacy rights. Rather than clearly defining the scope of the right to be forgotten, the CJEU left this open to elevate the question to a meaningless fundamental rights discourse. This led to a further error: by not employing a proportionality analysis the Court failed to recognize that the fundamental right to freedom of speech at the correct level and put it at equal footing with the privacy rights. At the same time, it should also be noted that not all the questions regarding the balancing of the right to be forgotten revolve around fundamental rights. For instance, a valid question might be: is there a lawful interest in processing such information (Tjin Tai, 2016, p. 79)?

The Court only briefly mentioned in its judgment some factors that could be taken into account in the balancing, such as the 'preponderant' interest of the general public in having access to the information or the role played by the data subject in public life. Besides not further clarifying and explaining these, it is also very problematic from the point of view of legal clarity and consistency that these factors were not placed in the specific context of proportionality balancing, but were mentioned *in abstracto* as relevant arguments to be taken into consideration.

It is, thus, imperative that the principle of proportionality is taken duly into account when search engines, DPAs and courts are required to implement the right to be forgotten by balancing it with competing interests or rights, such as freedom of speech.

Since this article has argued in favor of undertaking the balancing exercise at the level of interests, rather than fundamental rights themselves, the function of proportionality within this context should be further qualified. When search engines and courts balance data privacy interests with the interest of the public in accessing the personal information at issue in order to enforce the right to be forgotten, they must try to minimize interference with both of these interests. The scheme of 'double proportionality', as this is understood in English law, could be helpful in this respect. Double proportionality was proposed by Lord Steyn in *Re S (FC)* as an appropriate mechanism to deal with the clash between the privacy interests of a child and the right of the press to publish information of court proceedings including the child's pictures and it requires that 'the proportionality test must be applied to each [interest or right]'.

With the necessary caveat that the present discussion focuses on the application of EU secondary data protection law between two private parties (the data subject and the search engine as data controller), double proportionality could provide a useful framework when it comes to the implementation of the right to be forgotten. This requires that strict scrutiny standards should apply to assess the proportionality of the interferences with both the privacy interests of the data subject and the freedom of expression and information interests of the public. Such an approach appears to be in line with Article 17 (3) (a) of the GDPR.

This contribution argues that different weighting factors can guide search engines in their double proportionality assessment. On the one hand, the proportionality assessment of the privacy rights and interests of the data subject must take into account the following factors: i) the *nature* and the *content of the personal data*, ii) the *particular circumstances of the data subject* and, iii) the *context and the particular circumstances of the publication*. On the other hand, the proportionality assessment of the competing freedom of expression and information rights must consider i) the *interest of the public in accessing the information* and ii) the *role that the data subject plays in public life*. None of these factors is meant to be decisive; they are indicative of how to consider the proportionality of a delisting request and should be weighted and balanced against each. Each of these factors are considered in detail below.

Data Privacy Interests and the Proportionality Test

The Nature of the Personal Data

In assessing a delisting request under the right to be forgotten, the application of the proportionality principle can provide specific guidance, first, with respect to the *type* and the *content* of the relevant personal data. The nature of the data can be relevant in cases where the personal information available through an internet search result i) does not comply with the fair information principles; ii) includes 'sensitive' data; and iii) may put the data subject at risk or cause him a disproportionately negative impact. I now turn to each of these conditions.

First, it should be examined whether the personal information for which delisting is requested is accurate, relevant, not excessive and not kept longer than necessary for the purposes for which it was collected.

Furthermore, proportionality should play a role when 'sensitive' personal information is at stake. 'Sensitive' personal data that can reveal racial or ethnic origin, political opinions, religious beliefs, an individual's sexuality, and health condition are subject to enhanced protection and their processing is, in principle, prohibited as a default rule in the European data protection context (Article 9 GDPR). If sensitive data are, therefore, at issue, delisting might be required, taking into account all the circumstances of the particular case.

Moreover, a case for delisting can be made when the personal information available through an internet search result, albeit not sensitive, can expose the data subject to risks, such as stalking or identity fraud. Finally, delisting might have to take place when the content of the data is causing a disproportionate negative impact on the data subject and, therefore, she objects to the indexing of her personal information in a search engine's results.

The Particular Circumstances of the Data Subject

The principle of proportionality should play a role when the *particular circumstances of the data subject* are considered. These include, questions such as, for instance, whether the data subject is a minor or belongs to a 'more vulnerable segment' (Article 29 Working Party, 2014, p. 41) of the population requiring special protection, such as, asylum seekers or the elderly. There are strong reasons advocating the delisting of search results linking to information that was published when the data subject was -and is- under 16 years old. The concept of 'the best interests of the child' enshrined in Article 24 (2) EUCFR should be also taken into account in this regard.

The Context and the Particular Circumstances of the Publication

A third factor that could be taken into account when assessing the proportionality of a delisting request concerns the *context* and the *particular circumstances of the publication*. A first issue to be considered in this respect is whether there is a valid legal basis for the publication of the information available on the internet. The consent of the data subject as well as the grounds for lawful processing provided in Article 6 (1) GDPR constitute valid legal bases. For instance, a valid legal basis for the publication of the information exists where the publisher was under a legal obligation to make the data available. In such instances, delisting might be more difficult to obtain, although a case-by-case proportionality assessment should be made. It should be recalled that Mr Costeja Gonzalez was successful in his delisting request, because the information concerning him was outdated, even if the initial publication was in fact required by the national law. The consent of the data subject poses slightly more complicated issues in certain instances, where the data subject has initially granted his concern or published, but subsequently revoked it- in these cases, the publishing of the personal data will normally lack legal basis and delisting might be required.

Freedom of Expression and Information Interests and the Proportionality Test

The Interest of the Public in Accessing the Information

From the point of view of freedom of information rights and interests, when assessing the proportionality of a delisting request it should be considered, first, whether *the public has an interest in accessing the information*. In fact, the CJEU spoke of a 'preponderant' interest of the public in accessing the information (*Google Spain*, para 97).The use of the term 'preponderant' shows that the interest of the public has to be 'significant', 'dominant', or 'superior'. This could be interpreted as meaning that delisting can be denied only when the public has an interest in accessing the information that is 'superior' to the data subject's rights. Such an interpretation, though, seems to be unduly favoring the right to data protection. The case-law of the ECtHR could provide some guidance here. The relevant criterion employed by the Strasbourg Court as established in *Von Hannover (No. 2)*is the 'contribution [of the publication] to a debate of general interest'. This criterion is closely related to whether the individual concerned is a 'public figure' or plays a role in public life, analyzed below.

For the moment, however, let us focus on the meaning of 'contribution to a debate of general interest'. An explicit definition of what constitutes a debate of general interest does not exist (Shackelford, 2012, p. 196), the ECtHR has only noted that such definition depends on the circumstances of each case. Nevertheless, the ECtHR has emphasized that 'a fundamental distinction needs to be made between reporting facts capable of contributing to a debate in a democratic society … and reporting details of the private life of an individual' (*Von Hannover No. 2*, para 109).

The Court has held that a debate of general interest exists where the publication concerns, for example, political issues, crimes, sporting issues and performing artists. The above case-law of the ECtHR can be particularly relevant when assessing the proportionality of delisting requests under the right to be forgotten. In this respect, it is submitted that the rather unclear criterion of the 'preponderant' interest of the public should be interpreted in line with the ECtHR case-law and the 'contribution to a debate of general interest' requirement. In addition, it should be investigated whether the information was published for journalistic, academic, artistic or literary purposes pursuant to Article 85 GDPR or for archiving in the public interest, scientific or historical research or statistical purposes according to Article 17 (3) (d) GDPR.

The Role That the Data Subject Plays in Public Life

A further factor that could play out in the proportionality assessment of freedom of information interests concerns *the role that the data subject plays in public life*. It was held in *Google Spain* that the prevalence of the rights to privacy and data protection could be rebutted if it appears, for particular reasons, that the data subject plays a role in public life. The Court, however, failed to provide further guidance on when that would be the case.

A closer look at the European Convention on Human Rights system and the relevant jurisprudence of the ECtHR may be helpful here as well. The relevant term used in the Convention system is 'public figure'. Resolution 1165 (1998) of the Parliamentary Assembly of the Council of Europe on the right to privacy that was adopted as a response to the debate held after the tragic accident which cost the Princess of Wales her life, defines 'public figures' as 'persons holding public office and/or using public resources and, more broadly speaking, all those who play a role in public life, whether in politics, the economy, the arts, the social sphere, sport or in any other domain.' The Resolution goes on to note that 'certain facts relating to the private lives of public figures, particularly politicians, may indeed be of interest to citizens, and it may therefore be legitimate for readers, who are also voters, to be informed of those facts'. Nevertheless, Resolution 1165 (1998) calls for a fair balancing between the rights to privacy and freedom of expression, since these rights are 'neither absolute', 'nor in any hierarchical order', but 'of equal value'.

The case-law of the ECtHR regarding 'public figures' is also particularly relevant here. In *von Hannover v. Germany (No. 2)*, the Strasbourg Court held that the role or function of the person concerned and the nature of the activities that are the subject of the report constitute an important criterion to establish a balance between the Article 10 ECHR right to freedom of expression and the Article 8 ECHR right to respect for private life. The ECtHR explained that private individuals unknown to the public are to be distinguished from 'persons acting in a public context, as political figures or public figures' that have a much weaker privacy claim. An important factor to be taken into account, in this respect, is whether the publication 'contributes to a debate of general interest' that was seen above.

For the purposes of the present discussion, it should be noted that the 'role in the public life' criterion employed by the CJEU is broader and even more protective of freedom of speech than the 'public figures' concept used by the ECtHR. According to the Article 29 Working Party, it seems that 'politicians, senior public officials, business-people and members of the (regulated) professions' can be considered as fulfilling a role in public life, and, therefore, the public should in general be able to search for information relevant to their public roles and activities. A criterion that could be used in this respect is whether the information would protect the public against 'improper public or professional conduct' of the individual in question (Article 29 Working Party, 2014, p. 41).

CONCLUSION

The right to be forgotten as established in the CJEU's decision in *Google Spain* is a significant online data privacy right recognized in the EU legal order. It empowers individuals to request the removal of links to web pages containing their personal information from the list of results displayed following a search made on the basis of their name.

While the Court is to be praised for giving birth to the right to be forgotten, its parental skills are not equally commendable. The right, albeit strongly favored with respect to other rights and interests, was left without clear guidelines on how it should be implemented in practice by internet search engines, NDPAs and courts. The Court's decision to elevate the debate surrounding the right at the level of fundamental rights raised unnecessary conceptual confusions regarding the horizontal application of fundamental rights to private parties, the public-private law divide, direct and indirect effect and the primary-secondary law dilemma. It put search engines, such as Google at the 'forefront' of the EU's enforcement of internet privacy.

This chapter argues that these issues should provide cautionary lessons regarding the Charter's function: this should not be made generally horizontally applicable just because we would like every dispute to be 'engulfed in the glow of fundamental rights' (Leczykiewicz, 2013, p. 496). Such an approach might have unexpected consequences both for private parties and the understanding of fundamental rights.

Even if there are indeed good reasons to apply fundamental rights to private parties, such as the power inequalities evident in the Google case, this article suggested that such an approach should still be avoided if the same outcome could be reached through the interpretation of the available secondary law –for instance Article 17 GDPR- 'in the light of fundamental rights' or 'guided by fundamental rights.' This approach downplays search engines powers as adjudicators of fundamental rights online. Search engines are controllers of personal data when asked to implement the right to be forgotten and, therefore, bound by the relevant obligations under EU data protection law.

The chapter pointed out that the powers granted to search engines under the right to be forgotten are prescribed by limitations inherent to the content and the temporal effects of this and by institutional limits that place its enforcement under the supervision of NDPAs and courts.

Insofar as the balancing of the right to be forgotten is concerned, it was submitted that this should take place at the level of interests – rather than fundamental rights- and should be carried out by paying due respect to the principle of proportionality that the CJEU failed to mention in *Google Spain*. Proportionality is fundamental because it provides the correct framework within which a fair balancing can be achieved. In this respect, the article put forward a comprehensive legal framework for the implementation of the right to be forgotten on the basis of a double proportionality test that aims to minimize interferences with both data privacy and freedom of information interests. This legal framework developed above can be extremely helpful when search engines, DPAs and courts are asked to implement the right to be forgotten and balance the competing interests at issue as controllers of personal data under EU data protection law.

The CJEU's insistence on a fundamental rights' discourse may have left unanswered many questions about its scope and its actual implementation in practice. Nevertheless, after the adoption of the GDPR, this right is not only judge-made anymore. The Data Protection Regulation will be particularly helpful in shaping the understanding and the enforcement of the right to erasure and ('the right to be forgotten') not the least because Article 17 provides a list of grounds where this right might be applicable and a list of overriding reasons against its application. However, given the broader scope of application of Article 17 GDPR -this does not apply only to search engines, but to controllers in general and is not only about de-listing but deleting- a cautionary note is needed here. When DPAs and courts implement Article 17 GDPR, they should, on the one hand, be very careful to avoid the misconceptions of the CJEU in *Google Spain*, and on the other hand, follow a fair balance framework based on proportionality -as the one suggested in this chapter- that prevents opening even more the scope of this right.

REFERENCES

Alexy, A. (2009). *A theory of Constitutional Rights*. Oxford University Press.

Angelopoulos, C. J., & Smet, S. (2016). Notice-and-fair-balance: how to reach a compromise between fundamental rights in European intermediary liability. *Journal of Media Law*, 266.

Article 29 Working Party (2014). Guidelines on the implementation of the Court of Justice of the European Union judgment on 'Google Spain SL, Google Inc v Agencia Española de Protección de Datos and Mario Costeja González' C-131/12', WP 225, 26 November 2014.

Azoulai, L. (2008). The Court of Justice and the social market economy: The emergence of an ideal and the conditions for its realization. *Common Market Law Review*, 1335.

Bagger Tranberg, C. (2011). Proportionality and data protection in the case law of the European Court of Justice. *International Data Privacy Law*, 239.

Balboni. (2013). Legitimate interest of the data controller. New data protection paradigm: legitimacy grounded on appropriate protection. *International Data Privacy Law*, 244.

Bignami, F. (2008). The Case for Tolerant Constitutional Patriotism: The Right to Privacy Before the European Courts. *Cornell International Law Journal*, 211.

Brunner, L. (2016). The Liability of an Online Intermediary for Third Party Content The Watchdog Becomes the Monitor: Intermediary Liability after *Delfi v Estonia*. *Human Rights Law Review, 16*(1), 163–174. doi:10.1093/hrlr/ngv048

Burkell, J. A. (2016). Remembering me: Big data, individual identity, and the psychological necessity of forgetting. *Ethics and Information Technology, 18*(1), 17–23. doi:10.100710676-016-9393-1

Clapham, A. (2006). *Human Rights Obligations of Non-state Actors*. Oxford University Press. doi:10.1093/acprof:oso/9780199288465.001.0001

Clarke, R. (1994). The Digital Persona and Its Application to Surveillance. *The Information Society, 10*(2), 77–92. doi:10.1080/01972243.1994.9960160

Cohen, J. (2000). Examined Lives: Informational Privacy and the Subject as Object. *Stanford Law Review, 52*(5), 1373. doi:10.2307/1229517

Collins, H. (2012). *On the (In)compatibility of Human Rights Discourse and Private Law. LSE Law*. Society and Economy Working Papers 7/2012. London School of Economics and Political Science- Law Department.

De Búrca, G. (2013). After the EU Charter of Fundamental Rights: The Court of Justice as a human rights adjudicator? *MJ, 168*.

De Vries, S. (2013). Balancing Fundamental Rights with Economic Freedoms According to the European Court of Justice. *Utrecht Law Review, 9*(1), 169. doi:10.18352/ulr.220

Dupré, C. (2013). Human Dignity in Europe: A Foundational Constitutional Principle. *European Public Law*, 319.

Erdos, D. (2015). Data protection confronts freedom of expression on the 'new media' internet: The stance of European regulatory authorities. *European Law Review*, 531.

Ferretti, F. (2014). Data Protection and the Legitimate Interest of Data Controllers: Much Ado about nothing or the Winter of rights? *Common Market Law Review*, 1.

Fornasier, M. (2015). The Impact of EU Fundamental Rights on Private Relationships: Direct or Indirect Effect? *European Review of Private Law*, 29.

Frantziou, E. (2014). Further Developments in the Right to be Forgotten: The European Court of Justice's Judgment in Case C-131/12, Google Spain, SL, Google Inc v Agencia Espanola de Proteccion de Datos. *Human Rights Law Review, 14*(4), 761–777. doi:10.1093/hrlr/ngu033

Frantziou, E. (2015). The Horizontal Effect of the Charter of Fundamental Rights of the EU: Rediscovering the Reasons for Horizontality. *European Law Journal, 21*(5), 657–679. doi:10.1111/eulj.12137

Gerstenberg, O. (2004). Private Law and the New European Constitutional Settlement. *European Law Journal, 10*(6), 766–786. doi:10.1111/j.1468-0386.2004.00243.x

Gstrein, O. (2015). The cascade of decaying information: putting the 'right to be forgotten' in perspective. *Computer and Telecommunications Law Review*, 40.

Horten, M. (2016). Content 'responsibility': The looking cloud of uncertainty for internet intermediaries. Center for Democracy & Technology.

Iglesias Sánchez, S. (2012). The Court and the Charter: The impact of the entry into force of the Lisbon Treaty on the ECJ's approach to fundamental rights. *Common Market Law Review*, 1565.

Keller, D. (2017). *The Right Tools: Europe's Intermediary Liability Laws and the 2016 General Data Protection Regulation.* Available at SSRN: https://ssrn.com/abstract=2914684

Koops, B-J. (2011). Forgetting footprints, shunning shadows: A critical analysis of the 'right to be forgotten' in big data practice. *Scripted*, 229.

Kosseff, J. (2017). Twenty Years of Intermediary Immunity: The US Experience. *Scripted*, 5.

Koutrakos, P. (2014). Editorial: To strive, to seek, to Google, to forget. *European Law Review*, 293.

Kranenborg, H. (2015). Case note: Google and the Right to be Forgotten. *European Data Protect Law*, 70.

Kulk, S., & Zuiderveen Borgesius, F. (2014). Google Spain v. González: Did the Court Forget about Freedom of Expression? *European Journal of Risk Regulation*, 5(3), 389–398. doi:10.1017/S1867299X00003949

Kumm, M. (2006). Who Is Afraid of the Total Constitution? Constitutional Rights as Principles and Constitutionalization of Private Law. *German Law Journal*, 341.

Kuner, C. (2013). *Transborder Data Flows and Data Privacy Law*. Oxford University Press. doi:10.1093/acprof:oso/9780199674619.001.0001

Kuner, C. (2014). *The Court of Justice of EU's Judgment on the 'Right to be Forgotten': An International Perspective.* https://www.ejiltalk.org/the-court-of-justice-of-eus-judgment-on-the-right-to-be-forgotten-an-international-perspective/

Ladenburger, C. (2012). *FIDE Conference 2012 Institutional Report, Brussels 2012.* https://www.fide2012.eu/ index.php?doc_id=88

Lazaro, C., & Le Métayer, D. (2015). Control over Personal Data: True Remedy or Fairy Tale? *Scripted*, 3.

Leczykiewicz, D. (2013). Horizontal application of the Charter of Fundamental Rights. *European Law Review*, 479.

Leta Ambrose, M. (2012). It's about time: Privacy, Information Lifecycles, and the Right to be Forgotten. *Stanford Technology Law Review: STLR: An Online High-Technology Law Journal from Stanford Law School*, 369.

Leta Ambrose, M., & Ausloos, J. (2013). The right to be forgotten across the pond. *Journal of Information Policy*, 1.

Mayer-Schönberger, V. (2009). *Delete: The Virtue of Forgetting in the Digital Age*. Princeton University Press.

McGoldrick, D. (2013). Developments in the Right to be Forgotten. *Human Rights Law Review*, 13(4), 761–776. doi:10.1093/hrlr/ngt035

Nissenbaum, H. (1998). Protecting Privacy in an Information Age: The Problem of Privacy in Public. *Law and Philosophy*, 559.

Oliver, D., & Fedtke, J. Human rights in the private sphere: The scope of the project. In Oliver & Fedtke (Eds.), Human rights and the private sphere: A comparative study. Routledge.

Post, R. (2017). Data Privacy and Dignitary Privacy: Google Spain, the Right to Be Forgotten, and the Construction of the Public Sphere. *Duke Law Journal*. Available at SSRN: https://papers.ssrn.com/sol3/papers.cfm?abstract_id=2953468

Rees, C., & Heywood, D. (2014) The 'right to be forgotten' or the 'principle that has been remembered'. *CLSR*, 574.

Rosen, J. (2012). The right to be forgotten. *Stanford Law Review Online*, 88.

Sartor, G. (2013). Providers' Liabilities in the new EU Data Protection Regulation: A threat to Internet Freedoms? *International Data Privacy Law*, 3.

Sartor, G. (2015). The right to be forgotten in the Draft Data Protection Regulation. *International Data Privacy Law*, 64.

Scott, M. (2016). Europe Tried to Rein In Google. It Backfired. *The New York Times*. https://www.nytimes.com/2016/04/19/technology/google-europe-privacy-watchdog.html

Shackelford, S. (2012). Fragile Merchandise: A Comparative Analysis of the Privacy Rights for Public Figures. *American Business Law Journal*, *49*(1), 125–208. doi:10.1111/j.1744-1714.2011.01129.x

Shima, B. (2015). EU Fundamental Rights and Member State Action after Lisbon: Putting the ECJ's Case Law in its Context. *Fordham International Law Journal*, 1095.

Sloot van der, B. (2016). The practical and theoretical problems with 'balancing': Delfi, Coty and the Redundancy of the Human Rights Framework. *MJ,* 439.

Spiecker genannt Döhmann, I. (2015). A new framework for information markets: Google Spain Case C-131/12, Google Spain SL, Google Inc. v. Agencia Española de Protectión de Datos (AEPD), Mario Costeja Gonzáles, Judgment of the Court of Justice (Grand Chamber) of 13 May 2014, EU:C:2014:317CMLR,1053. *Common Market Law Review*, 1033.

Tjin Tai, T. (2016). The right to be forgotten – private law enforcement. *International Review of Law Computers & Technology*, *30*(1-2), 76–83. doi:10.1080/13600869.2016.1138628

Tushnet, M. (2003). The Issue of State Action/Horizontal Effect in Comparative Constitutional Law. *International Journal of Constitutional Law*, *1*(1), 79–98. doi:10.1093/icon/1.1.79

Tzanou, M. (2010). Balancing Fundamental Rights: United in Diversity? Some Reflections on the Recent Case Law of the European Court of Justice on Data Protection. *CYELP*, 53.

Tzanou, M. (2013). Data protection as a fundamental right next to privacy? 'Reconstructing' a not so new right. *International Data Privacy Law,* 88.

Tzanou, M. (2017). *The Fundamental Right to Data Protection: Normative Value in the Context of Counter-Terrorism Surveillance*. Hart Publishing.

ENDNOTES

[1]   To be accurate, the CJEU did not itself use the term 'right to be forgotten' even though this was used by the applicant.

[2]   Article 11 EUCFR (Freedom of expression and information) provides: 'Everyone has the right to freedom of expression. This right shall include freedom to hold opinions and to receive and impart information and ideas without interference by public authority and regardless of frontiers.'

[3]   For instance, Reputation.com is a company offering such services.

[4]   Ironically enough, the CJEU itself has been criticized for having 'little experience of adjudicating human rights issues in any depth, despite now being tasked with applying the EU Charter of Rights across the whole range of EU powers' (De Búrca, 2013, 170; Shima, 2015; Iglesias Sánchez, 2012).

APPENDIX: TABLE OF CASES

Court of Justice of the EU

Joined Cases C-465/00, C-138/01 & C-139/01, *Österreichischer Rundfunk*, Judgment of 20 May 2003, Full Court, [2003] ECR I-4989.

Case C-275/06 *Productores de Música de España (Promusicae) v Telefónica de España SAU*, Judgment of 29 January 2008.

Case C-73/07 *Satakunnan Markkinapörssi and Satamedia*, Judgment of 16 December 2008.

Joined Cases C-92/09 and C-93/09 *Volker und Markus Schecke GbR, Hartmut Eifertv Land Hessen*, Judgment of the Court (Grand Chamber) of 9 November 2010.

Case C-70/10 *Scarlet Extended SA v Société belge des auteurs, compositeurs et éditeurs SCRL (SABAM) [2011] I-11959.*

Joined Cases C-293/12 and C-594/12 *Digital Rights Ireland and Seitlinger and others,* Judgment of 8 April 2014.

C-131/12 *Google Spain v. Agencia Española de Protección de Datos (AEPD) and Mario Costeja González*, Judgment of 13 May 2014.

Case C-176/12 *Association de Médiation Sociale v Hichem Laboubi* [2014] OJ C85/3.

Case C-362/14 *Maximillian Schrems v Data Protection Commissioner*, Judgment of 6 October 2015.

Case C-360/10 *Société belge des auteurs compositeurs et éditeurs (SABAM)* v *Netlog NV* [2012] I-0000.

European Court of Human Rights

Von Hannover v. *Germany (No. 2)*, Judgment of 7 February 2012, Appl. Nos. 40660/08 and 60641/08.
Delfi AS v Estonia, Judgment of 16 June 2015, Appl. No 64569/09

UK House of Lords

Re: S (Identity: Restrictions on Publication) [2004] UKHL 47.

Chapter 15
New Boundaries for the Right to Be Forgotten?
An Analysis of Italian Jurisprudence

Federica Casarosa
(iD) https://orcid.org/0000-0002-5256-3505
European University Institute, Italy

Dianora Poletti
University of Pisa, Italy

ABSTRACT

The right to be forgotten has come to the forefront of the academic debate as a reaction to Court of Justice's decision in case C-507/17 Google LLC c. CNIL concerning the issue of geographical extension of the delisting obligation. Along with the development of CJEU jurisprudence, national courts have developed their own caselaw interpreting and adapting the right to be forgotten, now included in art 17 of the General Data Protection Regulation, to the pre-existing legal framework. Italian courts, and in particular the Italian Supreme Court, have addressed in several occasions the features and facets of the right to be forgotten, and the recent decision of the Grand Chamber (n. 19681, 22 July 2019) is the last though not the least. Starting form this decision, the chapter will analyse how the Supreme Court has attempted to systematise the right to be forgotten distinguishing what is called the traditional application of the right from the ones emerging in the digital context.

INTRODUCTION

The right to be forgotten has come again in the spotlight after the recent intervention of the Court of Justice of EU (hereinafter CJEU), triggering a new wave of academic debates addressing its content and boundaries. The trigger was, obviously, the decision in C-507/17 *Google LLC v. Commission nationale de l'informatique et des libertés* (French Data Protection authority, hereinafter CNIL case) addressing the scope of application of the obligation of de-indexing for Internet service providers, and (re)propos-

DOI: 10.4018/978-1-5225-9489-5.ch015

ing the dilemma regarding the geographical boundaries applicable to the protection of data subjects' rights in the global dimension and the effective enforcement of such rights. The CNIL case stems from the landmark decision of the CJEU in case C-131/12 Costeja v. Google Spain in 2014, which for the first time qualified the right to be forgotten in EU law.[1] The decision in Google Spain case, addressed the requests of a Spanish individual against the search engine with specific regard to the search results provided when the name and surname of Mr Mario Costeja were typed as keywords (Kranenborg, 2015; Martinez, 2015; Haga, 2017; Finocchiaro, 2015; Pollicino, 2014, 2949; Resta and Zeno Zencovich, 2015).

The CNIL case is one of the few cases that reached the CJEU, though it is not the only case addressing the implementation of the right to be forgotten, as a large number of cases were decided by national courts since 2014. As a matter of fact, in the aftermath of the CJEU decision in Google Spain case, many courts had the difficult task of interpreting the national legal provisions implementing EU data protection legislation in the light of the CJEU decision (Kulk and Zuiderveen Borgesius, 2015; Friedl, 2019).[2]

This was not as easy as it may seem, because in some countries, such as Italy, the jurisprudence addressing the interplay between the persistence of personal data in press articles and in online archives and the protection of individual privacy was already well-established, both at First instance and at Supreme court level.[3] As a matter of fact, since 2014, many decisions of the Italian Supreme court addressed cases falling into the application of the right to be forgotten trying to identify a set of reasonable criteria, that lower courts may be able to adopt in order to provide a coherent approach.[4] Although the (then) Art 29 Working party provided for guidelines concerning the implementation of the Google Spain judgment, national courts were asked to adapt these general criteria to the real cases, ensuring consistency and coherence, as well as compliance with EU law.

In Italy, in particular, the Supreme court provided for several decisions addressing the right to be forgotten where it tried as much as possible to identify additional criteria applicable to the different factual circumstances. The latest decision of the Grand Chamber of the Italian Supreme Court n. 19681, 22 July 2019, was supposed to provide such criteria in a clearer manner. It must be underlined that the request for a decision of the Grand Chamber is a specific procedure aimed at granting the coherence of jurisprudence: any Chamber of the Supreme Court, when deciding a dispute, can raise a question to the Grand Chamber in order to receive a clarification on a certain point of law or, in case of a potential conflict of interpretation between different Chambers of the Supreme Court, to solve such conflict. Then, the decision of the Grand Chamber acts as an authoritative precedent to be followed not only by the recurring court, but by all courts (De Amicis, 2017).

As a matter of fact, the case decided by the Grand Chamber was interesting as it addressed the application of the right to be forgotten to printed press, and would have allowed to clarify how far the criteria identified by the CJUE in Google Spain case would be applicable to such factual circumstances. However, the court did not evaluate the right to be forgotten as a single concept, but rather it provided for a set of distinctions which resulted in different *rights* to be forgotten. As a result, this classification may barely fit with the EU approach and potentially hinder the harmonisation objective aimed at by the GDPR.

In order to verify the interplay between European and national jurisprudence, the contribution first assess how the right to be forgotten has been defined by the European jurisprudence and legislation (par. 2), then highlights the jurisprudence of Italian courts before and after the CJEU decision in Google Spain (par. 3). In par. 4, the recent decision of the Grand Chamber of the Italian Supreme Court is analysed presenting the issues that were still left open by the decision. Concluding remarks will follow.

THE RIGHT TO BE FORGOTTEN WITHIN THE EUROPEAN FRAMEWORK

New technologies have changed the world of information and in particular have impacted deeply on the relationships among information, facts and people: on the one hand, it is no longer possible distinguishing between the 'producer' and the 'recipient' of information, since online anyone can upload data (and obviously also personal data). On the other hand, the simple online presence ensures for most of internet users the continuous reception of information of any kind (Eskens, Helberger & Moeller, 2017). As a result, nowadays, it is common for any user to search online for information without any geographical boundary limiting such information gathering (Di Ciommo, 2018). Therefore, it is very difficult to speak about confidentiality, privacy and forgetfulness in this *mare magnum* of information.

The conflict between right to be forgotten and the persistence of information over Internet was at the heart of the already mentioned CJEU decision in Google Spain case. The landmark decision addressed the possibility for a data subject to exercise his right to be forgotten against search engines, in order to remove the link towards certain resource containing a piece of news (i.e. de-listing the link towards certain internet pages). The CJEU, after having qualified Google as a data controller according to the Data protection legislation (which at the time of the violation was the Directive 95/46), affirmed that the exercise of the right to erasure entails the obligation to delete the data that are "inadequate, irrelevant or excessive in relation to the purposes of the processing" (par. 92). In particular, the CJEU specified that Articles 12, letter b), and 14, paragraph 1, letter a), of Directive 95/46 have to be interpreted as meaning that the right to be forgotten prevails not only over the economic interest of the search engine operator but also over the interest of the public in having access to that information, unless it appears, for particular reasons - such as the role played by that person in public life - that interference with his fundamental rights is justified by the overriding interest of the public in having access to that information training itself. The consequence of such interpretation is that the search engine is require to de-index the search result and erase the personal data.

Such interpretation of the right to erasure was then translated into legislation, through the inclusion of Article 17 within the General Data Protection Regulation n. 2016/679 (hereinafter GDPR) (Soro, 2017). As a matter of fact, Article 17 is qualified as right to erasure, and it defines the prevalence of the data subject's right to the protection of personal data in all situations in which the data may be outdated, irrelevant or inaccurate, as well as when the processing is deemed unlawful. However, in par. 3 of the same article, the European legislator recognises that the primacy of the protection of personal data does not apply where the processing of the data is necessary "*for the exercise of the right to freedom of expression and information*" (Peron, 2010).[5]

In the case of conflict between the right to data protection and freedom of expression, Article 85(2) GDPR, preceded by recital 153, provides that it is the national legislator - and the courts by way of interpretation - to define the exceptions and exemptions provided for the processing of personal data, although this may pave the way to dissimilar national legislation as highlighted by Di Ciommo (2019).

This regulatory framework could lead to two interpretative solutions: the first which configures the right to be forgotten as outlined in Article 17 GDPR as a mere repetition, with a different label, of the right to erasure, which the data subject could already exercise in the light of the previous discipline in case of a processing which is unlawful since its beginning or whose conditions of lawfulness had ceased over time (Stradella, 2017). A second interpretation could exclude from the definition of the right to be forgotten the case of contrast between the right to information and the processing of personal data. In this sense, therefore, the right to be forgotten would be limited only to the case of processing carried out by search engines or online databases, with the possible remedy of delisting, anonymisation, or exact contextualisation of the personal data processed (Di Ciommo, 2019a, 14).

National jurisprudence then adapted to this legal framework struggling to identify a system based on fundamental rights and freedoms and the dignity of the individual in line with the demands for harmonisation expressed at European level.

THE JURISPRUDENCE OF ITALIAN SUPREME COURT

Italian jurisprudence had addressed the balancing between protection of personal data and publication by press (whether traditional or online) of personal data for journalistic purposes in several occasions before the CJEU decided the Google case. One of the landmark decisions, addressing the developments brought by technology and in particular the persistence of information on Internet, was the Supreme Court decision n. 5525/2012 where the court pointed out how the "right to be forgotten" essentially protected personal identity and data in social perspective,[6] so that the data subject must be protected against diffusion of information which may potentially harmful for his/her social life and reputation (Mantelero, 2012). In light of the passing of time, the information available online were not useful anymore nor of public interest. According to the court, the balancing exercise involving press freedom and the right to be forgotten should take into account the following indicators:

1. The time passed since the publication of the information;
2. The truthfulness of the information – according to the knowledge available at the moment of the decision;
3. The presence of a public interest in the knowledge of such information.

The Supreme Court ruled that the outcome of such balancing was obviously to be assessed on a case-by-case basis; however, judges had to consider that the right to the protection of personal data had reached the status of "fundamental right", thus protected both by Article 8 of the Charter of Fundamental Rights of EU and Articles 21 and 2 of the Italian Constitution.

On the other hand, the Italian case-law before *Google Spain* appeared to be fairly strict when assessing the obligations owed by search engine providers. Such providers were indeed regarded as mere "intermediaries" which could not be held responsible for the processing and publishing of personal data by the "source websites". Thus, the obligation to ensure that the data processing happened in accordance with the relevant legal provisions rested only on the shoulders of the first publishers of the information, such as the websites of the newspapers.

After 2014, Italian jurisprudence internalized the guidelines of the Court of Justice in Google Spain decision, under two major perspectives: i) the role attributed, from a legal point of view, to search engine as well as to hosting providers; ii) the criteria applicable in the balancing between data protection and respect of private life and press freedom.

Under the first perspective, the Italian case-law started to qualify search engines as "data controllers" under Article 2 (d) Directive n. 95/46 (Riccio, 2017). [7] It worth mentioning, nonetheless, that the Italian decisions based their reasoning also on the circumstance that the Data Protection Authority decision of 10th July 2014, referring to an official 2010 determination from Google Inc., ruled that Google Italy

S.r.l. should be considered as the Italian representative of Google Inc. for the scope of the legislation concerning data protection.

Under the second perspective, national courts took into account the guidelines on the implementation of the Google Spain decision issued by the Article 29 Working Party (2014), particularly with regard to the assessment of the public interest pursued by an information in relation with the role assumed by the data subject in the public life (Rizzuti, 2016).[8] Though, in principle, the role in public life must be assessed on the basis of the factual circumstances of the case, the guidelines state that "politicians, senior public officials, business-people and members of the (regulated) professions can usually be considered to fulfil a role in public life. There is an argument in favour of the public being able to search for information relevant to their public roles and activities" (Art 29 Working Party, 2014, 13).[9] On such grounds, intended as a further development of the balancing of interests already upheld by the CJEU, Italian courts regarded as "roles in public life" those played by officers and employers of a municipality-owned company, by a lawyer, by a member of a National Authority. [10]

Passing of time, therefore, becomes only one of the several criteria to be considered when carrying out the balancing of interests, even if, probably due to the relevance of the aforementioned decision n. 5525/2012, Italian courts still appear, in some cases, to retain such criterion in much more consideration than others.[11] This is the case also in decision n. 13161/2016 of the Supreme Court. Here, the Supreme Court dealt with a piece of news published on an online newspaper about a criminal event that triggered the claim from the persons involved in the case, complaining about their reputation and asking for the removal of content and compensation for damages. Although during the trial, the content was removed from the archive of the newspaper, the publisher and the editor in charge of the newspaper were ordered to pay damages and expenses. The Supreme Court affirmed that the period of time (of two years) between the moment of the notification of the request for removal and the time of the actual deletion, together with "sensitive" data, would be sufficient to qualify the data processing as unlawful. As a matter of fact, the Supreme court affirmed that press freedom should be limited by the right to reputation and image for two reasons: on the one hand, the exhaustion, due to weakening of the public interest, of the time necessary to achieve the purpose for which the data were collected according to Article 11 of the Italian Privacy Code on data processing requirements, on the other hand, the impossibility of mere news reports to benefit from the protection established by Article 99 of the Italian Privacy Code regarding data collected for historical purposes.

A different evaluation of time criteria is to be found in the subsequent decision n. 38747/2017, where the Supreme Court addressed the case of a crime involving a descendent of the former King of Italy, namely Vittorio Emanuele of Savoy. The Supreme Court affirmed that, even if the fact occurred more than thirty years ago, it is quite possible that there is still a public interest in the re-enactment of such piece of news, therefore the processing of personal data is legitimate. [12]

The more recent intervention is then the one provided by Supreme court in decision n. 6919/2018, where the court provided for a set of criteria according to which the right to be forgotten can be limited by the equally protected press freedom, if specific conditions are met, namely:

1.   The contribution made by the dissemination of the image or news to a public interest debate;
2.   The actual interest in the dissemination of the image or news (for reasons of justice, police or protection of the rights and freedoms of others, or for scientific, educational or cultural purposes);
3.   The high degree of notoriety of the subject, due to the peculiar position held in public life and, in particular, in the economic or political reality of the country;

4. The methods used to obtain and give the information, which must be truthful, disseminated in ways that do not exceed the purpose of information, in the interest of the public, and free from insinuations or personal considerations, so as to highlight an exclusive objective interest in the new dissemination;

5. Prior information about the publication or transmission of the news or image at a later date, so as to allow the person concerned the right of reply before its disclosure to the general public.

In the absence of such prerequisites, according to the Supreme Court, the publication of personal data, can only be qualified as a violation of the fundamental right to be forgotten. Although this decision seemed to provide well defined criteria, the jurisprudence of the national courts was not concluded and the new decision of the Grand Chamber of the Supreme Court sets a new step in this internal judicial dialogue.

THE DECISION OF THE GRAND CHAMBER OF THE ITALIAN SUPREME COURT N. 19681/2019

The Facts

A local newspaper published a crime story that had involved an individual, Mr S., twenty-seven years before. The publication had the effect of bringing to the fore the murder – such was the event mentioned – for which Mr S. was convicted and already served his sentence. The editorial choice was neither gratuitous nor persecutory toward Mr S., since the article was published as part of a weekly column aimed at presenting facts and events that took place in the city over the last thirty to forty years. The press article, moreover, did not indulge in criticism or criminalisation, but operated an objective and precise presentation of the factual circumstances in a consistent and unbiased form.

Although the article did not contain false information nor appear to be offensive to Mr S.'s dignity, he claimed before the court of first instance, complaining that his right to be forgotten had been violated and consequently seeking compensation for the damage suffered both morally and financially.[13] The Court of First Instance, and then the Court of Appeal, dismissed the claim on the basis of the following reasoning: Mr S.'s right to be forgotten, protected in the light of the rules on the protection of personal data, was in conflict with press freedom enjoyed by the local newspaper and by the journalist who wrote the article. Both rights are protected at constitutional level respectively by Article 2 and Article 10 of the Italian Constitution, therefore they must be balanced in the light of the criteria identified in Supreme Court's jurisprudence, taking into account the limits that can be placed on the exercise of press freedom.[14] In particular, the Court of First Instance, and in greater detail the Court of Appeal, considered the editorial choice of the newspaper to be compliant with press freedom as it aimed at offering *"a platform of reflection for readers on sensitive issues such as marginalization, jealousy, depression, prostitution, with all the implications and impact that these can have in daily life"* (translated by authors).

The subsequent appeal before the Supreme Court raised a doubt in the Third Civil Section in charge of solving the case. The Supreme court chamber perceived the jurisprudence from different Chambers still not consistent (*rectius* convincing), presented a question to the Grand Chamber of the Supreme Court. The question aimed at receiving uniform guidelines regarding the criteria to be applied in order to strike a balance between press freedom and the right to be forgotten - protecting the privacy of the individual – taking into account both the national and European legal and jurisprudential framework.

As a matter of fact, the Third Chamber did not agree with the list of criteria listed in the decision n. 6919/2018, previously mentioned, provided by the First Chamber. In particular, the Third Chamber highlighted that that the simultaneous presence of all such criteria would be very unlikely, thus leading to extremely restrictive effects on freedom of expression (Pardolesi and Bonavita, 2018; Giannone Codiglione, 2018; Di Ciommo, 2019a). Rather, the Third Chamber compiled a different list of elements based on the circumstances of the case, namely: the existence of public interest, the topicality, the seriousness and criminal relevance of the facts, the complete presentation of the facts, the purpose of data processing, the notoriety of the person concerned, the clear formal exposition. As a result, in order to avoid a possible jurisprudential conflict, the Third Section addresses the Grand Chamber in order to receive uniform guidelines on the matter.

The Decision of the Court

Unfortunately, the expectations of the Third Chamber were not met by the decision of the Grand Chamber, since the latter expressly stated the need to shift from the general perspective to the specific circumstances of the case. However, it must be acknowledged that the Grand Chamber examined in detail the various forms of conflict between freedom of expression (and then press freedom) and the protection of personal data (and then the right to be forgotten), and distinguished two different ways in which journalistic activity should be carried out when it addresses the so called right to historical re-enactment, as it will be described below.

The Grand Chamber, at first, affirmed that the right to be forgotten cannot be subject to a *reductio ad unum*, rather the right to be forgotten acts as a limit to the exercise of the freedom of expression and proves to be functional to the exercise of other personality rights, such as the right to digital identity (Giannone Codiglione, 2018). In fact, the decision distinguishes three types of conflict that may concern the individual's right to be forgotten vis-à-vis press freedom:

1. The ex novo publication of news related to events legitimately disseminated in the past;
2. The availability of online information (mainly on archives of newspapers and newspapers) not updated compared to the initial publication;
3. The possibility to access through search engines to information available online about events and facts no longer updated or relevant.

The Grand Chamber dwell only on the first type of conflict, in accordance with the case submitted.[15]

The decision underlines the fact that data processing for the first press publication was absolutely lawful, only the subsequent publication twenty-seven years later raises doubts regarding the compliance with the legislative framework. The reasoning of the Grand Chamber is therefore aimed at distinguishing the original press publication and the current publication (or subsequent republication), qualified as historical re-enactment. In this sense, the Grand Chamber reserves the classification of 'news' to the publication by press or other means of distribution of 'something' that concerns current event; in the absence of topicality element, the description of the events becomes an historical re-enactment. The Grand Chamber does not rule out the possibility that the topicality of the event may also emerge at a later date, due to new elements occurring, but only in that case is it still possible to protect the press freedom as such. This distinction should not be underestimated, since the Grand Chamber associates the right to historical re-enactment with a lower protection vis-à-vis the one endowed to press freedom, excluding that the former enjoys the same constitutional guarantee as the latter.

As a result of this analysis, the Grand Chamber recognise that the article was aimed at triggering readers' reflections on sensitive issues, due to a precise (and unquestionable) editorial choice, but given the pure re-enactment of the event without any additional topical element, the publication of the personal data of the individual could have been avoided.

Open Questions Emerging From the Decision

The distinction between press freedom and right to historical re-enactment which seems to be so clear in the arguments of the Grand Chamber, it is in practice very difficult to grasp as few are the criteria provided by the Grand Chamber to set the boundaries between the two. Moreover, when shifting from the traditional press dimension to online press, the distinction between the three categories of rights to be forgotten becomes tricky.

First of all, the time factor mentioned by the Grand Chamber as an element that contributes to the distinction between news and historiography, can be interpreted differently by the courts in the light of the factual circumstances in which the press publication takes place. Therefore, the problem arises when the time lapse since the first publication can be said to be "significant". In the case decided by the court, twenty-seven years may well justify the disappearance of the aspect linked to the topicality of the event. A different assessment has been made in previous decisions, where the right to be forgotten was defeated by the public interest in the re-enactment of the piece of news. The reference is in particular to decision n. 38747/2017 mentioned above in which the article dealt with an event occurred more than thirty years earlier and still apt to offer to the public "*a fact certainly suitable for the formation of public opinion*" (Sirotti Gaudenzi, 2018). A much shorter period of time led to the opposite result in the already mentioned decision n. 13161/2016. In this case, the publication via Internet was deemed by the Supreme Court as no longer supported by the criterion of topicality, not even in the short period of two and a half years from the first publication. On the contrary, the Court affirmed that the persistence online of such piece of news as exorbitant due to its "*objective and prevalent dissemination component, from the mere scope of the lawful processing of archiving and storage online of journalistic data for historical or editorial purposes*" (Pardolesi, 2016).

The Grand Chamber, therefore, delegates to lower courts the difficult task of verifying whether the time factor in a concrete case can lead to defining publication within the realm of press freedom or historical re-enactment. This could also lead to limitations to press freedom, as the passage of very little time could shift the news into a re-enactment: the current rapidity of news consumption and the very large number of news – which are information society's features - could lead the interpreter to qualify even the presentation of the news in a later edition of the periodical as a historical re-enactment. This is obviously an extreme case, but the doubt could well arise when the press article addresses an unresolved case, reminding the public exactly the lack of subsequent developments.[16] In this case, the topicality of the news is to be assessed in negative, due to the absence of additional elements, an opposite interpretation could compromise the function of the press as "public watchdog",[17] which can be seen precisely in drawing the attention of public opinion to the past event.

Additional doubts emerge when we move from the traditional press publication to online publications, where it is even more difficult to reconcile two events that are assumed to be distinct and separate - the first and second publication of the news - with the permanence online of a given piece of information

(Mazzanti, 2018). Except for the case of publication of the article in the online version of the newspaper, to which the Court's reasoning can be applied easily, a different situation may emerge: an article published consciously with historical purposes includes, through hypertext links, referring to one or more articles published in the previous publications of the same newspaper or periodical. In this case, if the same balancing exercise is applied, the historical purpose could be extended also to the linked article, triggering the deletion of personal data also from that document. Alternatively, the older article - being included in the newspaper online - could be subject to an update, contextualization and integration of data relating to the historical event occurred as a result of the different balancing exercise between press freedom and protection of personal data, as provided by Supreme Court decision n. 5525/2012.

CONCLUDING REMARKS

Oblivion or forgetting is far from being interpreted as a synonym for complete deletion, but it translates into an act of selecting data in order to identify those that appear relevant to public opinion or public interest and those that can be left out. In this sense a fitting figurative representation can be that of a digital image with a different level of resolution: the high resolution image includes a larger number of data, and vice versa the low resolution image includes a smaller number of data. However, the human eye may not have any difficulty in correctly reading and interpreting the image with a lower resolution, as the data included therein are necessary and yet sufficient for that purpose. It is therefore the data selection criterion that allows the objective of safeguarding the ability, to remain in the metaphor, to understand the image.

Precisely these criteria were considered necessary by the Third Section in order to strike a balance in the event of a conflict between the right to information and the protection of personal data. In most recent cases decided by the Italian Supreme court in Grand Chamber, the latter recognizes that the purpose of the published article was triggering the reflection of readers on sensitive issues, but the press article would have achieved the objective pursued also without providing the personal data of the individual involved in the events described.

The (not always punctual) applications of the right to be forgotten made by judges lead to its (sometimes) hypertrophic application (Abbt, 2018). However, it is important to consider the efforts courts make in the complex remodulation of personality rights (in particular, the right to privacy and personal identity) in today's reality, along with the safeguard of pluralism of information and critical knowledge. There is no doubt that the caselaw of courts have defined the new boundaries of the right to be forgotten and accordingly the limits to press freedom in processing personal data. The Grand Chamber decision add a further piece to this picture at national level, striking a balance between the opportunity to keep facts of the past confidential and the right to historical re-enactment. The reconstruction appears to be in line with the concrete case and correct in the conclusions, but it does not solve all the application problems that may arise in similar cases when addressed in the digital context. The ancient problems that the digital age proposes with greater urgency and in renewed terms still need meditated guidelines.

REFERENCES

Abbt, C. (2018). Forgetting in a Digital Glasshouse. In F. Thouvenin, P. Hettich, H. Burkert, & U. Gasser (Eds.), *Remembering and Forgetting in the Digital Age* (pp. 124–134). Cham: Springer. doi:10.1007/978-3-319-90230-2_9

Art 29 Working Party. (2014). *Guidelines on the implementation of the Court of Justice of the European Union judgment on Google Spain and Inc v. Agencia española de protección de datos (AEPD) and Mario Costeja González C-131/12, 14/EN, WP 225*. Retrieved from https://www.dataprotection.ro/servlet/ViewDocument?id=1080

De Amicis, G. (2018). *La formulazione del principio di diritto e i rapporti tra Sezioni semplici e Sezioni Unite penali della Corte di Cassazione*. Retrieved from http://www.cortedicassazione.it/cassazione-resources/resources/cms/documents/Rel.__Cons._DE_AMICIS-Il_principio_di_diritto_ed_i_rapporti_tra_Sez._simplici_e_Sez._Unite.pdf

Di Ciommo. (2019b). Diritto alla cancellazione, diritto di limitazione del trattamento e diritto all'oblio. I dati personali nel diritto europeo, 351-393.

Di Ciommo, F. (2018). Il diritto all'oblio nel Regolamento (UE) 2016/679. Ovvero, di un "tratto di penna del legislatore" che non manda al macero alcunché. *Quotidiano giuridico*, 16-31.

Di Ciommo, F. (2019a). Oblio e cronaca: rimessa alle Sezioni Unite la definizione dei criteri di bilanciamento. *Il corriere giuridico*, 5-15.

Eskens, S., Helberger, N., & Moeller, J. (2017). Challenged by news personalisation: Five perspectives on the right to receive information. *Journal of Medicine and Law*, 9(2), 259–284. doi:10.1080/17577632.2017.1387353

Finocchiaro, G. (2015). La giurisprudenza della Corte di Giustizia in materia di dati personali da Google Spain a Schrems. *Diritto dell'Informazione e dell'Informatica*, 779-799.

Franzoni, M. (2018). La compensatio lucri cum damno secondo la Cassazione. Responsabilità Civile e previdenza, 1092 – 1104.

Friedl, P. (2019). *New laws of forgetting – The German Constitutional Court on the right to be forgotten*. Retrieved from https://europeanlawblog.eu/2019/12/12/new-laws-of-forgetting-the-german-constitutional-court-on-the-right-to-be-forgotten/

Giannone Codiglione, G. (2018). I limiti al diritto di satira e la reputazione del cantante celebre ''caduta'' nell'oblio. Nuova Giurisprudenza Civile Commentata, 1317-1329.

Haga, Y. (2017). Right to be Forgotten: A New Privacy Right in the Era of Internet. In *New Technology, Big Data and the Law* (pp. 97–126). Singapore: Springer. doi:10.1007/978-981-10-5038-1_5

Kranenborg. (2015). *Google and the right to be forgotten. European Data Protection Law Review*, 1(1), 70 – 79.

Kulk, S., & Zuiderveen Borgesius, F. (2015). Freedom of Expression and 'Right to Be Forgotten' Cases in the Netherlands after Google Spain. European Data Protection Law Review, 2, 113-125.

Mantelero, A. (2012). Right to be forgotten ed archivi storici dei giornali. La Cassazione travisa il diritto all'oblio. Nuova giurisprudenza civile commentata, 836-849.

Martinez, C. O. (2015). The CJEU judgment in Google Spain: notes on its causes and perspectives on its consequences. In Protecting privacy in private international and procedural law and by data protection (pp. 45-56). Abingdon: Routledge.

Mazzanti, E. (2018). Processo mediatico e diritto all'oblio. Il possibile gioco di sponda tra UE e CEDU. In A. Mantelero & D. Poletti (Eds.), *Regolare la tecnologia: il Reg. UE 2016/679 e la protezione dei dati personali. Un dialogo fra Italia e Spagna* (pp. 379–394). Pisa: Pisa University Press.

Nivarra, L. (2018). Le Sezioni Unite restituiscono un ordine auspicabilmente definitivo al discorso sulla compensatio lucri cum damno. Responsabilità Civile e Previdenza, 1160-1167.

Palazzolo, N. (2019). L'hosting provider tra libertà di impresa, diritto di critica e tutela della reputazione professionale. Diritto dell'Internet, 520-529.

Pardolesi, R. (2016) Diritto all'oblio, cronaca in libertà vigilata e memoria storica a rischio. Foro it., 1, 2734-2737.

Pardolesi, R., & Bonavita, S. (2018). Diritto all'oblio e buio a mezzogiorno. Foro it., 1, 1151-1190

Peron, S. (n.d.). Il giornalismo d'inchiesta. Giurisprudenza Civile e Previdenza, 2257-2267.

Pollicino, O. (2014). Diritto all'oblio e conservazione di dati. La Corte di giustizia a piedi uniti: verso un digital right to privacy. Giurisprudenza Costituzionale, 59, 2949-2958.

Pollicino, O. (2019). L'autunno caldo della Corte di giustizia in tema di tutela dei diritti fondamentali in rete e le sfide del costituzionalismo alle prese con i nuovi poteri privati in ambito digitale. *Federalismi*. Retrieved at https://federalismi.it/ApplOpenFilePDF.cfm?eid=533&dpath=editoriale&dfile=EDITO RIALE%5F16102019201440%2Epdf&content=L%27%2B%27%27autunno%2Bcaldo%27%27%2Bde lla%2BCorte%2Bdi%2Bgiustizia%2Bin%2Btema%2Bdi%2Btutela%2Bdei%2Bdiritti%2Bfondamenta li%2Bin%2Brete%2Be%2Ble%2Bsfide%2Bdel%2Bcostituzionalismo%2Balle%2Bprese%2Bcon%2Bi %2Bnuovi%2Bpoteri%2Bprivati%2Bin%2Bambito%2Bdigitale&content_auth=%3Cb%3EOreste%2B Pollicino%3C%2Fb%3E

Resta, G., & Zeno Zencovich, V. (Eds.). (2015). *Il diritto all'oblio su Internet dopo la sentenza Google Spain*. Roma: Romatrepress.

Riccio, G. M. (2017). Il difficile equilibrio tra diritto all'oblio e diritto di cronaca. Nuova Giurisprudenza civile Commentata, 4, 549-559.

Rizzuti, M. (2016). Il diritto e l'oblio. Corriere Giuridico, 8-9, 1072-1082.

Senigaglia, R. (2017). Reg. UE 2016/679 e diritto all'oblio nella comunicazione telematica. Identità, informazione e trasparenza nell'ordine della dignità personale. Nuove Leggi Civili Commentate, 5, 1023-1061.

Sirotti Gaudenzi, A. (2018). Diritto all'oblio e diritto all'informazione: un difficile equilibrio. Corriere Giuridico, 8-9, 1107-1114.

Soro, A. (2019). Oblio, identità e memoria. Diritto dell'Internet, 1, 3-6.

Stradella, E. (2017). Brevi note su memoria e oblio in rete, a partire dal regolamento UE 2016/679. In P. Passaglia & D. Poletti (Eds.), *Nodi virtuali, legami informali: Internet alla ricerca di regole* (pp. 87–100). Pisa: Pisa University Press.

ENDNOTES

[1]   See also CJEU decision in Case C-18/18, Glawischnig-Piesczek v Facebook Ireland International, 3 October 2019, where the Court of Justice affirmed that the injuction imposing social platforms to remove defamatory content can have a global scope. Note that Pollicino (2019) affirms that, the rulings would in any case be less distant than at first sight might seem.

[2]   See for instance the recent cases of the German Constitutional court, BVerfG, Beschluss des Ersten Senats, 6 November 2019 - 1 BvR 16/13 -, Rn. (1-157) (available at http://www.bverfg.de/e/rs20191106_1bvr001613.html) and BVerfG, Beschluss des Ersten Senats, 6 November 2019 - 1 BvR 276/17 -, Rn. (1-142), (available at http://www.bverfg.de/e/rs20191106_1bvr027617.html).

[3]   See Italian Supreme Court, decision n. 3679/1998 and Milan Tribunal, decision 26 April 2013, n. 5820

[4]   Note that the Italian legal system is not based on the stare decisis doctrine, though the decisions of Supreme Court have a strong persuasive effect on the interpretation of the rules.

[5]   See the same results in the decision Supreme Court, 9 July 2010, n.16236, in *Resp. civ. e prev.*, 2010, 2262, in which the Supreme Court pointed out that both press freedom and privacy are constitutional rights, but the press freedom may prevail over the latter. As a matter of fact, privacy is an "exception" with respect to "the irrepressible and fundamental right of freedom of information and criticism", a right which guarantees democracy. The Court expressly states that "the activity of providing information clearly takes precedence over personal rights to reputation and confidentiality, in the sense that the latter, only where certain conditions are met, constitute a limitation thereof".

[6]   The decision recognized that the data subject can claim for the contextualization and updating of the news, in relation to the purpose of data processing, because *"the news, originally complete and true, becomes out of date, therefore partial and not exact, and therefore substantially untrue"* and as a result suitable to harm the personal identity, such as to require *"the contextualization, updating or integration of the data contained in the article, by means of a link to other information subsequently published concerning the evolution of the subject matter"*.

[7]   See, in particular, Milan Tribunal, decision of 5th October 2016 and the decision n. 618 of 2014 of the Italian National Data Protection Authority. Both decisions upheld that Google Italy S.r.l. could indeed be considered as representative of Google Inc. in Italy.

[8]   See Milan Tribunal, decision of 5th October 2016; Rome Tribunal, decision 3th December 2015; Milan Tribunal, decision 28th February 2017.

[9]   The same concept is reassessed by the Resolution 1165 (1998) of the Parlamentary Assembly of the Council of Europe on the right to privacy provides a possible definition of "public figures". It states that *"Public figures are persons holding public office and/or using public resources and, more broadly speaking, all those who play a role in public life, whether in politics, the economy, the arts, the social sphere, sport or in any other domain."*

[10]   See respectively, Milan Tribunal, decision 28 February 2017; Rome Tribunal, decision 3 December 2015; Milan Tribunal, decision 5 October 2016. It is worth mentioning that in last case, though the public role was in principle recognized, the Court eventually upheld the data subject's claim on account of the circumstance that the information indexed by the search engine provider were incomplete and not up-to-date, thus not relevant for the public.

[11]   See Court of Cassation, decision n. 13161/2016; Mantova Tribunal, decision 28 October 2016.

[12]   The Court in particular affirmed that "the right to be forgotten over one's own personal affairs, which belongs to each person, must be compared, indeed, with the right of the community to be informed and updated on the facts on which the formation of its own convictions depends, even when the person who is the holder of that right is discredited by it." (translation by Authors).

[13]   The judicial claim was presented after a complaint before the Italian Data Protection Authority, who did not find any violation of data protection legislation. See the reference in the Third Chamber, Ordonnance to Grand Chamber n. 28084, 5 November 2018, cit.

[14]   It is necessary to distinguish press freedom from right to criticise, since the former requires the compliance with the criterion of truth in the presentation of factual circumstances, whereas such element has not the same importance in case of criticism: see in this regard Trib. Roma, decision 1 February 2019 (Palazzolo, 2019)

[15]   This was justified on the jurisprudence of the same court, and in particular on the set of decisions addressing the subject of compensatio lucri cum damno, where the Supreme Court affirmed that each judicial decision finds its limit in the connection with a concrete case, given that the Grand Chamber is not entrusted with "the enunciation of general and abstract principles or dogmatic truths on law, but the solution of questions with nomophilactic value always referable to a specific individual case". See Cass. Sez. Un., 22 May 2018, n. 12564, n. 12565, n. 12566 e n. 12567 (Franzoni, 2018; Nivarra, 2018).

[16]   For instance, in case of a crime where there were no results from the investigations carried out and the news reports only about the persons questioned and suspected by the authorities.

[17]   The definition of democracy watchdog flows from the ECtHR jurisprudence in the landmark decision *Handyside v United Kingdom*, Application no. 5493/72, 7 December 1976, available at https://hudoc.echr.coe.int/eng?i=001-57499.

Chapter 16
Where Now for the Right to Be Forgotten?
A Review of the Issues in Post–Google Spain With Particular Regard to the Decision Reached in the UK

Evelyn (Patsy) Kirkwood
University of Reading, UK

ABSTRACT

Increased recognition of the pervasiveness of information collected and accessed has led to concern as to its impact on privacy. The ability to impact people's lives with the easy availability of information that in other eras would have remained hidden or "forgotten" is highlighted by the use of the internet for instant recall. Such information, which organizations often hold for commercial benefit, is increasingly made available through search results or from online archives. This chapter will focus on the impact of the Google Spain case, which was believed to have created a new right to be forgotten, leading to the finalization of Article 17 of the General Data Protection Regulation. The author will then examine more recent cases where the new right has been applied and their impact on defining its scope. In particular, the author will focus on the UK joined cases of NT1 and NT2.

INTRODUCTION

Despite early discussions taking place in 2009 within the European Commission, it was only in 2012 that there was the first formal announcement of the desire to see recognition of a right to be forgotten by the then Commission Vice-President in charge of Justice, Fundamental Rights, and Citizenship, Viviane Reding. Attempts to update the existing data protection laws which were often applied inconsistently throughout the EU, to create a regulation with direct effect were then met with considerable debate within the member states. Discussions polarized over the extent of the right to be forgotten or the right of erasure into which it would soon develop.

DOI: 10.4018/978-1-5225-9489-5.ch016

What would be called the "Google Spain" case brought sharp focus to this debate initially within Spain concentrating on the reluctance of Google both as Google.sp and, more contentiously, as Google. com to accept restrictions of their very profitable use of personal data or, indeed, to acknowledge any liability for removal of information under the ambit of data protection. This ultimately led in 2014 to the Court of Justice of the European Union (CJEU) considering the key elements of a claim by Mr. Gonzalez in respect of his desire to have links to certain information 'delinked'. Despite the existing view of the European Commission with regard to the liability of search engines on certain legal aspects of information society services, in particular electronic commerce, in the internal market, (European Parliament, 2000) and against the considered opinion of Advocate General Jääskinen in June 2013, given in respect of the referral to the CJEU, in the case of Google Spain SL Google Inc. v Agencia Española de Protección de Datos (AEPD) Mario Costeja González (Google Spain), the CJEU determined issues in three key areas, creating what the media then claimed as a new human right, namely the right to be forgotten.

In this chapter, the author examines the position resulting from the decision in Google Spain and the subsequent application of the right in specific cases, including the recent cases in Europe, particularly in the UK and France, where claims have been made against Google. The author aims to show how, notwithstanding the implementation of further regulation that in certain cases the decisions are shaping the way the right will be interpreted. The issues raised also engage with the idea of how society determines the relevance of an individual's past and the impact of past events particularly criminal convictions on not only reputation and private life, but also on the ability to make amends to his/her community as a whole. A link to rehabilitation takes the value of the right to be forgotten to a different perspective, increasing the importance of the right to apply its principles by potentially evoking aspects of human dignity. The focus of the chapter is a more detailed consideration of the impact of the Google Spain decision, with focus on the liability of search engines through the concept of "forgetting" the past and creating new opportunities within society.

BACKGROUND

A right to be forgotten has always existed in one form or another within Europe, for example in the French *droit d'oubli*. Here, the French Data Processing, Data Files and Individual Liberties Act of 6 January 1978, Law No. 78-17, specifically established that individuals are entitled to access, alter, correct or delete personal information in recognition of this old right. However, modern claims for the right could be said to be the result of privacy campaigners' mounting pressure. This was largely due to the recognition of the pervasiveness of information collected and accessed through the Internet. Such information is now not only held by organizations, often for pure commercial benefit, but increasingly made available through instant access or online archives largely due to the output of search engines. The particular nature of the Internet and specifically the availability of links to information through search engine activities has created a digital memory which conflicts with the human ability to allow memories to fade over time.

Deeply entwined within ideas around autonomy and the preservation of privacy and human dignity, the roots of the right to be forgotten began to emerge in line with the development of ever increasingly invasive technology. Initially the focus of this new right began to appear along with the building of the first accessible computers, in the 1960s. Thus, as early as 1977, the German Federal Data Protection Act made reference to the removal of incorrect personal data (*Bundesdatenschutzgesetz* [BDSG] 1977, Section 35 – *lonitle Gesetz zum Schutz vor Mißbrauch personenbezogener Daten bei der Datenverar-*

beitung). This was considered to be one of the first laws providing initial protection against misuse of personal data in data processing, covering the whole of Germany.

In early recognition as to the consequences of holding data, this law contained provision for every data subject to have the right of erasure in defined and specific circumstances. BDSG section. 1 (1) was intended to protect personal data against misuse during the retention, transmission, modification or deletion (i.e., safeguarding of "interests worthy of protection"). This could be considered to be the beginning of real awareness that holding such personal information and permitting its access indefinitely could present privacy as well as data control concerns. In addition, in Lynskey's (2015) view, another human right, that of dignity, might be argued to have provided a "conceptual foundation" to enable rights to data protection to be developed as was shown in the German case 1983 Population Census Decision (1983 Population Census Decision, 15 Dec 1983, BvR 209/83, BVerf G 65 1). In this decision, the German Constitutional Court determined that individuals should have the right to decide how their data are disclosed and how used. This represented an ability to withdraw consent for the use of specific personal data and also to remove such personal information, so as to limit accessibility in an attempt to preserve an individual's dignity. In this case, the German Court called such a right "informational self-determination," linking it to the German Basic Law (Basic Law for the Federal Republic of Germany 1949 as amended), which guarantees the general right of personality under Article 2.1. Article 2.1 (1) therefore provides "every person shall have the right to free development of his/her personality insofar, as he/she does not violate the rights of others or offend against the constitutional order or the moral law."

Following the early proposals of 2009 by the European Commission with regard to additional protection for individuals in the light of increasing technology balancing data subjects rights with the need for a free flow of information for economic purposes, in 2012 the Commission confirmed its desire to see formal recognition of the right to be forgotten. Viviane Reding then stated that, under the proposed reform, there would be a right to have online personal data deleted, "if there are no legitimate grounds for retaining it" (Press release; Viviane Redding, Vice President European Commission, EU, The EU Data Protection Reform 2012 'Making Europe the Standard Setter for Modern Data Protection Rules in the Digital Age 2; eu europa eu rapid press-release). This reflected the levels of concerns being expressed by the various member states and the beginnings of debate as to the ability to control not only the processing of data but the retention and accessibility of it.

THE DEVELOPMENT OF THE RIGHT TO BE FORGOTTEN

The Early Stages of the Recognition of the Right

The case of Google Spain brought sharp focus to this debate, initially within Spain concentrating on the reluctance of Google–both as Google.sp and, more contentiously, as Google.inc. to accept any restrictions on their very profitable use of personal data or, indeed, acknowledge any obligation to effect the removal of information under the ambit of data protection. In 2014, this ultimately led the Spanish Court to address the CJEU, which determined the key elements of Mr. Gonzalez's claim.

The outcome of the referral was not without controversy. In line with the procedural requirements of the court where unless there is no new point of law (see www.statewatch.org/news/2019/oct/ep-briuefing-a-g-cjeu.pdf) an opinion from one of the appointed Advocate Generals (AG/AGs) is required prior to the court hearing, the CJEU requested an opinion from an AG on the issues of the referred case whilst the national court decision was put on hold . This opinion was provided by the learned Advocate General Jääskinen in June 2013 (Opinion of Advocate General Jääskinen 25 June 2013- Case C-131/12 Google Spain SL Google Inc. v Agencia Española de Protección de Datos [AEPD] Mario Costeja González), and subsequently approved, particularly by Google itself, when he set out his well-considered reasons as to why a search engine was only carrying out an intermediary role and therefore could not, and indeed should not, be considered to exercise a level of control as would be required from a data controller with regard to personal data. In his conclusion, Jääskinen noted that Google's activities must be considered merely an ancillary function to the production of search results, rather than those of a data controller. This was very much in line with the thinking at that time, as it was considered essential that Internet service providers were able to facilitate the free flow of data and enable the growth of access to information.

Despite this valuable opinion and the existing policies of the European Commission with regard to the restriction of liability with regard to search engines, in order to promote the ease of flow of information required to benefit the digital single market (European Parliament, 2000), the CJEU determined otherwise in the case of Google Spain. The decision by the CJEU in the case of Google Spain resulted in recognition of the right to be forgotten in respect of the removal of links to information. Thus, the decision largely focused on balancing rights of privacy and family life with the impact on freedom of expression, if an individual was then able to erase past events potentially in the public interest.

Here it made decisions in three key areas, ultimately creating what the media then claimed as a new fundamental right, namely the right to be forgotten. Initially, the CJEU considered the activities carried out by a search engine specifically with regard to the holding and processing data and whether a search engine could be construed a data controller and therefore bound by the existing Data Protection Directive (DPD) (1995 95.46/EC). In addition, the CJEU debated whether a search engine was carrying out processing, within the relevant territories. Notwithstanding its previous approach to Internet service providers, the court found relatively simply that Google would be construed as a data controller, with the activities the company carried out within the jurisdiction, and that the provisions of the DPD would therefore apply to them. With these arguments settled despite being in opposition to the Advocate General's opinion, the next challenge of the CJEU was to consider finally if a search engine should be made to remove results (i.e. links to information) that caused prejudice to the person involved and potentially violated his/her fundamental rights under Articles 7 and 8 of the Charter of Fundamental Rights of the European Union (2012). Article 7 provided "everyone has the right to respect for his or her private and family life, home, and communications". In addition, Article 8, headed *Protection of Personal Data*, stated:

1. Everyone has the right to the protection of personal data concerning him or her.
2. Such data must be processed fairly for specified purposes and on the basis of the consent of the person concerned or some other legitimate basis laid down by law. Everyone has the right of access to data which have been collected concerning him or her, and the right to have them rectified.

Article 8, subsection 3, clearly stated that this decision was one that would not be made initially by courts: "Compliance with these rules shall be subject to control by an independent authority".

The insight the CJEU provided in determining the application of existing data protection provisions was of great importance to the case. In particular, paragraph 74 indicated a data controller, as defined under the DPD, should take every reasonable step to ensure data that do not comply with data protection requirements are erased or rectified. This was recognition of the need for the proper application of

Article 12 of the DPD, which evoked the right for the data subject (i.e., the individual whose data was being processed) to obtain:

(b) as appropriate, the rectification, erasure or blocking of data the processing of which does not comply with the provisions of this Directive, in particular because of the incomplete or inaccurate nature of the data.

(c) notification to third parties to whom the data have been disclosed of any rectification, erasure or blocking carried out in compliance with (b), unless this proves impossible or involves a disproportionate effort had to be carried out taking such other factors into account and not in isolation.

In paragraph 20, the CJEU also laid out the question that needed to be determined:

Must it be considered that the rights to erasure and blocking of data, provided for in Article 12(b), and the right to object, provided for by subparagraph (a) of the first paragraph of Article 14 of Directive 95/46, extend to enabling the data subject to address himself to search engines, in order to prevent indexing of the information relating to him personally, published on third parties' Web pages, invoking his wish that such information should not be known to Internet users, when he considers that it might be prejudicial to him or he wishes it to be consigned to oblivion, even though the information in question has been lawfully published by third parties?(para 20 (3))

Key to this discussion was the concern around the information being consigned to "oblivion" and where, in such circumstances, the new right to be forgotten would be applied. The decision in the case was therefore focused not purely on the liability of an intermediary such as a search engine, which had been a key issue, but on the ultimate balancing exercise between rights of privacy and family life and freedom of expression. This exercise needed to take place in order to determine if an individual should be able to erase past events or alternatively whether the public's right to receive information would prevail.

Despite expressing reservations of the decision, Google put in place an online process to provide for applications to delist links in search results. At the end of a page of search results it stated that some information had been removed under European data protection laws and provided a link to utilizing the new right to be forgotten. Other search engines were caught by the decision and were required to do the same. With Google ultimately holding a significant position with regard to search engine results (with approximately 90% of searches at least in Europe being made through its activities), it was essential that it initiated such a process, because some smaller search engines would then follow. To date, Google has produced around 850,785 applications for removing URLs (Google, Requests to delist content under European privacy law, Transparency report: available at https://transparencyreport.google.com/eu-privacy/overview). It seems as if many wished to adopt this right with the intention to delete access to any information no longer relevant or past events, in the attempt to bring about increased privacy and, potentially, a sense of self. However, the decision in the Google Spain case appears not detailed enough to provide the required clarity on the balancing of rights of privacy and freedom of expression and the ultimate scope of the right.

Many also considered freedom of expression to be paramount particularly with the use of the Internet (Byrum, 2017). As a result, there was criticism of the need to introduce any further rights that might restrict it, particularly from the U.S, where freedom of expression was considered to be violated by the

Google Spain decision (Byrum, 2016). Many other commentators questioned if such a right really did exist (Markou, 2015) or whether it was not a new right but a continuation of existing remedies (Zanfir, 2013).

However, in 2016, the European Union (EU) moved significantly towards concluding its new data protection regime in the form of the General Data Protection Regulation (GDPR) and confirmed the inclusion of the right of erasure under Article 17, also referred to as the right to be forgotten. Although this provided for removal of personal information, the provisions could be regarded as being more limited by virtue of the drafting of the specific circumstances where the right could be applied. As this new regulation then took until 2018 to be implemented, the right to be forgotten continued to be shaped by judicial interpretation of the principles established in the Google Spain case.

Post Google Spain

At the end of 2014, following the Google Spain decision with uncertainty as to how the principles would apply and in response to the reaction to it, the Article 29 Working Party issued guidelines on the application of the right to be forgotten (Guidelines on the implementation of the Court of Justice of the European Union judgment on "Google Spain and inc v. Agencia Española de Protección de Datos (AEPD) and Mario Costeja González" c-131/12).

In addition besides initiating the process to make applications to request delisting, Google, through its Transparency Report (Google, Requests to delist content under European privacy law, Transparency report: available at https://transparencyreport.google.com/eu-privacy/overview) gave limited examples of how they were dealing with applications under Google's autonomous decision-making process and under the Google Advisory Council Guidelines (available at https://archive.google.com/advisorycouncil).

Often, the person applying a delinking process does not need to show that the information is prejudicial or incorrect information potentially giving them more control over the information. However, this can potentially add to the lack of clarity as to what links to information will be removed and which will not. Certainly, it can be argued that no definitive standards were available on how decisions to apply the right would be determined, at that stage. As part of the new process, made available at the bottom of the page listing search results, Google has had to respond to many applications by concerned individuals. Certain criteria have been set out to consider the way Google deals with such applications and to provide some guidance as to where removal is permitted. However, with control remaining very much in the hands of Google, it seemed as if the control of policy for delinking had been handed to a nonstate regulator with commercially biased interests. Without clear guidelines imposed by relevant statutory authorities, Google remains the ultimate decision maker as to whether the data are "inadequate, irrelevant or no longer relevant or excessive" under the provisions of the DPD (Google Spain, para. 94).

The practise is also likely to continue under the provisions of Article 17 of the GDPR, as, although a data subject has the right to request removal of links, the first application must be made to the search engine with a right to refer onwards to the national data protection authority. This process appears to be a virtual conflict of interest, where such an organization that collects and processes personal data also decrees what is published. This potentially creates censorship, which is an unforeseen result of this new right. The right was originally intended to create new safeguards for individuals. Potentially, this can mean that the ability to shape an individual's identity through the management of no longer relevant information lies in the machinations of an unregulated third party commercial organization. From the outcome Google appears to have the additional responsibility of determining what information should remain available as being in the "public interest." This leads to the possibility of an individual still not having the ability to exercise his/her rights under Article 12, to decide what information can be accessed, and to hold any expectations as to what is retained or removed and whether his/her privacy can be protected.

The CJEU in Google Spain was relatively clear as to what needed to be determined, but not on what factors should be applied, setting out the following:

As the data subject may, in the light of his fundamental rights under Articles 7 and 8 of the Charter, request that the information in question no longer be made available to the general public on account of its inclusion in such a list of results, those rights override, as a rule, not only the economic interest of the operator of the search engine but also the interest of the general public in having access to that information upon a search relating to the data subject's name. (para.97)

The second part of the summing up expanded the criteria of a public image and explained:

However, that would not be the case if it appeared, for particular reasons, such as the role played by the data subject in public life, that the interference with his fundamental rights is justified by the preponderant interest of the general public in having, on account of its inclusion in the list of results, access to the information in question. (para.97)

This reference to a different standard which would apply when the individual concerned is a public figure has increased the ability to challenge such determinations where it would appear there is precedence to do so. With claims under the scope of Article 17 of the GDPR still to be made, the importance of these views post Google Spain, particularly on the balancing exercise within the decision, remains of real significance in establishing the scope of the right to be forgotten and any subsequent developments in its use.

In addition, the more limited scope of Article 17 may prove to be a more restrictive version of the right to be forgotten. The provisions of this provide for a right of erasure exercisable on specific grounds namely if the data are no longer necessary, that consent to the processing of the data is withdrawn and there are no legal grounds permitting such processing, the data subject objects and there are no legitimate grounds to continue processing or the data is in relation to a child (GDPR- Article 8). In such situations there is a legal obligation to erase the data. Here a controller who has made the data public takes on the responsibility of ensuring links to the data are removed or copies of the data deleted.

Application of the Google Spain Decision

Gradually further cases within Europe, including those that had been in the pipeline before Google Spain, following refusal of applications to remove links as requested by concerned individuals have been heard. It would appear that such cases tended to involve activities which would not generally be acceptable in society, such as acts of a sexual nature, convictions for murder and manslaughter, and other serious crimes, but regrettably the decisions were not always influential in creating clear precedents for the application of the right. There was also recognition that the DPD and the Charter of Fundamental Rights of the European Union (2012) were subject to interpretation within member states, and each would therefore cast its own view on the outcome. Additional cases outside of Spain have taken place within the EU especially in certain jurisdictions such as Ireland, Germany, Holland, and, more recently,

Finland, as well as in the UK. Some of these cases are examined below to see how the decisions were reached and whether there was any consistency in the approach to delinking by search engines.

In Ireland which was taking a particular interest in actions in respect of Google's activities due to it being the location of many of the tech giants, the first case occurred in 2016. A former local politician rejected the decision of the Irish Data Protection Commissioner in favour of Google's refusal to remove links referring to the politician as "Dublin's homophobic candidate." Google had argued that, as a public figure, the applicant had become involved in popular debates and that therefore there would be interest in his subsequent activities and discussions. However, on appeal to the court, it was considered that there was a breach of the applicant's fundamental rights, therefore the delinking would be allowed. The High Court however then reversed the decision ultimately ruling that Google was entitled to refuse the delinking of opinions on a public figure commenting on the impracticality of identifying such opinions online. The issues had developed around what was a question of *"opinion"* being expressed and what would be regarded as *"fact"* by the viewing public. The principles of Google Spain were considered in these actions, with emphasis on the balancing act required between privacy and freedom of expression, and the difficulty that would and had arisen in respect of the privacy of persons in the public arena.

The question of how a decision to remove or not to remove information concerning a publicly abhorrent crime can be reconciled under the right to be forgotten was also explored in a recent case in Finland (*Korkein Hallinto- Oikeus Högsta Förvaltningstomstolen*) The decision to permit removal of information which would have continued to be made available through search results (i.e. to "forget" details of the individual's past) was allowed, due to the individual's mental capacity at the time of the offence. Google had complained to the Administrative Court of Helsinki, arguing against the Data Protection Ombudsman, Reijo Aarnio's ruling, that Google should remove the information revealing the identity of convicted murderer on the grounds that the individual had been found to be mentally ill at the time of the offence (i.e., this extended his privacy protection in favour of removing links to his offence). The court however also considered that the mental health of the claimant was such, at the time of the offence, to be considered 'sensitive data', which therefore should be removed, or at least the relevant links to it. This concept would also be reflected in later cases and would also be relevant to any future applications under the GDPR with the need to consider 'special category' data.

The NT1 and NT2 Cases

In the UK, despite a flurry of initial applications, the first clear opportunity for a judicial examination and to apply the principles of Google Spain decision finally occurred in 2018. Here the High Court was able to potentially re-establish the principles of the Google Spain, in the joined cases of NT1 and NT2 (NT1 and NT2 v Google LLC, 2018).

These cases concerned applications to apply the right to be forgotten to links to events, revealed in search results, that the claimants wished to have "forgotten." It could be argued that the facts of these joined cases brought together some of the difficulties in not only looking at whether links to criminal convictions should be removed but did the convictions in themselves had the effect of making those so convicted 'public' individuals? The events revealed in search results involved criminal convictions "spent" under the UK's Rehabilitation of Offenders Act 1974 (c-53) (ROA). Accordingly under this law it had been determined that such convictions did not need to be disclosed, under the provision for the rehabilitation of offenders. This was in contrast to the references revealed in searches against Mr. Gonzalez which revealed only civil proceedings. The link to such criminal convictions was then considered together with the claimants' right to "rewrite" their past under ideas of rehabilitation and therefore to protect their reputation. The claim was based on the linking of the convictions to the claimants' names, being potentially in breach of both data protection and the claimants' right of privacy. This also raised more questions specifically not just on freedom of expression, but also on the public's right to receive information.

Although the claimants were unknown to each other, the facts relating to each of them were very similar, which had provided the opportunity for the cases to be heard together. The joined cases covered specific aspects of claims that the claimants had made, under the principles of Google Spain and the right to be forgotten, initially looking at whether the claimants should be granted anonymity in an earlier pretrial review. The court examined each individual's claims in full and also considered arguments Google had raised again, in effect repeating some of the issues raised in Google Spain such as journalistic purposes provided under the UK's Data Protection Act 1998 Section.32. In the quest for precedents and clarity on the application and scope of the right, the court offered some reinforcement of key principles, but it also introduced new concepts which appear to be based on a moral approach to privacy and protection.

The first step in the development of the NT cases was the initial application to the court to obtain anonymity for the claimants. The judge consented to the identity of the two individuals being withheld, recognizing that the ultimate aim of the right to be forgotten was indeed to prevent continuing access to historic events which the naming of the specific individuals would prejudice. This action had followed the earlier unsuccessful case of ABC v Google Inc. (2018), where a request for an interim injunction had been made. This request was to require Google to block all access to a specific site where blogs had referred to the claimant and his criminal conviction, despite the fact the sentence had been duly spent under the ROA. The claimants had argued that Google had breached Articles 3, 6, and 8 of the European Convention on Human Rights (European Convention for the Protection of Human Rights and Fundamental Freedoms, as amended by Protocols Nos. 11 and 14, 4 November 1950, ETS 5), and the Data Protection Act 1998 (c-29) which had implemented the DPD in the UK. In the hearing where Google was not represented and did not attend, Mr. Justice Knowles determined that there had not been any proper service on the correct Google entity with regard to ABC's claim. Therefore, although the Human Rights Act 1998 (c-42) permitted a derogation from such service, where there were compelling reasons to do so, in this instance he was not satisfied that such circumstances existed, particularly where the outcome might be a limitation on freedom of expression. He summed up: "There are no such compelling reasons, and so, in the absence of proper service on Google LLC in California, I cannot grant the injunction, even if it were otherwise appropriate to do so, about which I say nothing" (ABC v Google Inc., 2018). Although the ability to remain anonymous would be key to the success of upholding a right to be forgotten action, it was clear that such anonymity could only be allowed to the extent that it was equitable for a claim to be made by an unknown person.

Shortly thereafter, with applicants now granted anonymity in an earlier pretrial review, the joined cases of NT1 and NT2 (NT1 and NT2 v Google LLC, 2018) were heard. These cases were based on specific claims made under the principles of the right to be forgotten as established in Google Spain. These principles considered the impact of personal information concerning past activities relating to the claimants being revealed constantly in search results. What was critical in this case was the impact on the claimants' privacy and their right to a family life. The High Court examined each individual's claims in full and together with the points Google had raised again, cross referencing their arguments from the Google Spain case. In addition, the case drew on the issue of the spent convictions which formed part of the claim for protection of the claimants' privacy. Judge Warby referred back to the case of R (Pearson) v

DVLA (2002), where Sir Anthony Clarke M. R. had held that the ROA had put in place a rehabilitation regime which "protects an individual from being prejudiced by the existence of such convictions" (para.4). In addition, in paragraph 48, Warby drew attention to the cases that had accepted that convictions, with "the passage of time," had receded into the past, so as to become part of an individual's private life and capable of protection. The question of such information no longer being readily available as permitted by the law was central to the arguments for a right to be forgotten, along with careful consideration of the impact of data protection law. In addition the judge also considered various aspects in connection with details of crimes being made public and commented that following the Axel Springer case that a person could not complain of actions which are a 'foreseeable consequence of one's own actions such as, for example the commission of a criminal offence' (Axel v Springer AG v Germany (2012)).

In the quest for precedents and clarity on the application and scope of the right, the UK court not only offered reinforcement of some of the key principles of the Google Spain decision, but also introduced new concepts, which appear to be based on a more moral approach towards privacy and its protection. Based on the facts provided and arguments made, the court refused NT1's application, with the judge commenting on the claimant's negative character. However, the second individual's application was successful as he was seemingly of "good" character, and the court permitted him to have the links removed. The court was not able to confirm that the concept of a spent conviction could be considered to ensure that more privacy would be attributed to references to the conviction nor to the fact that the criminal conviction itself made the individuals 'public' figures. Judge Warby did however consider the behaviour of NT1 who had referred constantly in public to the conviction making it a more publicly debated issue and therefore being less capable of protection. Regrettably it could be considered that despite a detailed and well thought out decision, the case may have raised more issues on the application of the Google Spain principles with its emphasis on the moral nature of the claimants, rather than providing further clarification.

Accordingly, the future of the right remains unclear, partially due to the appeal by NT1 no longer proceeding, and the pending application of Article 17 of the GDPR now implemented with any insight this might provide. Judge Warby summing up in the case drew attention to the level of impact of the case, once the GDPR would be fully implemented in UK law under the Data Protection Act 2018, and whether the case would still have any relevance in any subsequent claims under the right of erasure in Article 17.

The approach of the European Court of Human Rights

At a similar time as these cases, the idea of a right to be forgotten in respect of access to information was also being considered in a different forum, with an action reaching the European Court of Human Rights. The case of M. L. and W. W. v Germany 2018 (European Court of Human Rights; application numbers 60798/10 and 65599/10), reviewed a judgment by the German Federal Court not to issue an injunction to stop Internet access to documentation concerning the applicants' convictions for the murder of a well-known actor (this was partially relevant in considering the public interest in the matter, as the actor was widely known). The applicants had started proceedings as early as 2004, before any formal recognition of any right to be forgotten, to try to obtain at least anonymity of their personal data as they approached their new lives, after being released on probation. However, earlier courts had determined that public interest in the information overrode the applicants' interest in no longer being confronted with their own very serious actions. Despite the claimants being successful in previous actions in the lower courts, the German Federal Court on appeal was clear that freedom of expression prevailed together with the public's right to be informed, a line very much followed in the declaration as to intent made by Google in how it would approach determining the right to be forgotten. In this case, the court considered the role of the media in determining what items should be made available, specifically if not current news or preserved in archives.

The Court of Human Rights was clear in its view that, despite the applicants having considerable interest in not being confronted by their crimes, and having spent time in prison for their actions, the public interest was significant. It was also important that there should be journalistic freedom (i.e. the ability of the media to determine what should be revealed under freedom of expression) and attempts to fetter this would be detrimental to healthy debate within a society. The continued media interest revealed that such debate had not faded away and there remained considerable interest in the applicants. In addition, though, the Court drew attention to the fact that the applicants were not private individuals who were unknown to the public and had in fact been exposed to the media by voluntarily granting interviews and similar activities. This approach was similar to that contained in the decision in the NT1 and NT2 cases despite the complete variance in the severity of the crimes committed. The claimants' activities in not only taking various legal proceedings, entering appeals and generally not letting the matter drift away had, in effect, been seeking publicity for their cause. This seemed very much at odds with their claims for anonymity and an application of a right to be forgotten (an action under Google's procedure to apply the right to be forgotten seemed to be one avenue that the applicants had not pursued, despite it being introduced just before the Court of Human Rights' decision). In brief, the decision was that there had not been any violation of Article 8 in the German Federal Court's decision. In this case, the judges had once again looked at the actions of the two men involved and had found that they had not acted in a manner which was remorseful or in any form apologetic. In fact, the active pursuit of media coverage and lack of any form of repentance seemed to be a key factor that the court considered in the final decision. Although this was not considered as one of the main themes of the case, it involved aspects of the morality of the crime being clearly taken into account, as was the behavior of the claimants in courting publicity in a similar stance to that taken by NT1.

The Territorial Scope to the Right to Be Forgotten

Another aspect that has also been the subject of various cases relates to the impact of links to personal information being removed, but still accessible by changing the VPN thereby limiting the protection offered to an individual by reducing the scope of the ability for the information to be forgotten. France in particular has been active in trying to clarify the situation, taking a robust stance that the delinking under the principles of Google Spain apply globally. The French Data Protection Authority, the Commission Nationale de l'Informatique et des Libertés (CNIL), took action by initially ordering Google to delist search results from all domains worldwide, in order to respect subjects' rights to effective protection of data. Google denied liability to do so and refused to comply, arguing that this would raise other issues, particularly in the U.S., with the focus on freedom of expression. Consequently, the CNIL took action by fining Google €100,000, as the right could not be properly applied if it remained simple to access the "forgotten" link to information no longer accessible in the country in which the application had been made. This was followed by Google filing an appeal. Ultimately, with such appeal reaching the European Court of Justice in the case Google Inc. v Commission Nationale de l'Informatique et des Libertés (CNIL), the matter was heard in late 2018, focusing on the need to determine the global extent of the right to delist. The CNIL had made it very clear that its priority was to ensure that Google.com would remove links on a global level. Its argument was that the right to be forgotten would be drastically reduced by search engine results being so easily accessed by changing the VPN. Advocate-General Szpunar's opinion, issued prior to the case, stated that search engines, here Google, would not be obliged to delist search results on a global basis, confirming that, in his opinion, de-referencing posed a grave risk to freedom of expression if carried out worldwide (Opinion of Advocate General Szpunar;10 January 2019).

The final phase of this challenge by CNIL was determined in September 2019, several years after Google Spain. To little surprise, but much consternation in France, the CJEU decided that the right to be forgotten should be limited to being exercised only within the relevant member state of the EU. In this regard, the CJEU expressed concern that the exercise of the right and "the balance between the right to privacy and the protection of personal data, on the one hand, and the freedom of information of *I*nternet users, on the other, is likely to vary significantly around the world" (para. 60). The court determined that EU law would not be able to provide sufficient authority for the balancing of such interests outside its own territory. However, the CJEU summing up stated that the search engine should at the least exercise the right by;

Using, where necessary, measures which, while meeting the legal requirements, effectively prevent or, at the very least, seriously discourage an Internet user conducting a search from one of the Member States on the basis of a data subject's name from gaining access, via the list of results displayed following that search, to the links which are the subject of that request. (para.74)

Although this decision presents a real threat to the use of the right as there is still a simple ability to view full search results through alternative access to the Internet. Despite this conclusion, some statements reconfirmed that there would still be provision for a member state to carry out the balancing exercise according to its own jurisdiction and views. As a result, commentators have argued that this decision is not as clear cut as would first appear with the door being left open under Para 72 of the judgement for national courts to still order global delisting when considering the balancing of the rights of privacy and freedom of expression. (Mary Samonte, 2019). It remains to be seen how the right to be forgotten will work within the global reach of the Internet and how, under this decision, the level of protection can be provided.

The Current Position

One of the most anticipated outcomes also came in September 2019, when a series of applicants under the right to be forgotten had their cases reviewed by the CJEU providing an opportunity for some additional clarity on the application of the right in particular circumstances. These involved claims that could be considered to be typical of the type of complaints being made in respect of delinking, initiated by the CNIL's refusal to order Google to remove the links. In Case C-136/17,where there was a request for a preliminary ruling under the proceedings taken by claimants GC, AF, BH, ED against decisions of CNIL it was explained that:

The request has been made in proceedings between GC, AF, BH and ED and the Commission nationale de l'informatique et des libertés (French Data Protection Authority, France) ('the CNIL') concerning four decisions of the CNIL refusing to serve formal notice on Google Inc., now Google LLC, to de-reference various links appearing in the lists of results displayed following searches of their names and leading to web pages published by third parties. (Key Facts no. 2)

It was determined that the claims of various individuals would be joined to be heard together in the case before the CJEU. Although the situations were different there was also some merit in joining the cases to obtain consistency of approach. In the case of GC, she had been a public figure as a local politician, and concern had been raised with regard to links to references about her sexual relationship with the mayor. Similarly, in a political field, in the case of BH, allegations of political corruption by him and references to actual charges in connection with this had been made. Two further applicants in the proceedings had similar requests to delink: one where delinking to a newspaper report of his activities as PR Officer of the Church of Scientology had been requested, and, for the final applicant, a request for delinking to references to a sentencing for two crimes of sexual assault on minors. Such instances showed clear overtones of morality in considering the acceptability of what should continue to be made available to the public even to the detriment of the person concerned and their private life. The applicable law was the law in force at the time of the original dereferencing requests. Accordingly, the case was determined on the basis of the DPD and the relevant French implementing legislation, rather than the GDPR. One of the main questions was the application of Article 8(1) of the DPD and how to determine whether a search engine operator is obliged to grant a request for delinking request where the data is incomplete, inaccurate or no longer up to date. Also, whether the reporting of a trial or a conviction amounts to data relating to offences and criminal convictions, processing which under Article 8(5) of the DPD may only be carried out under the control of the public authority, or subject to specific safeguards in national law, was considered. The wording of subsection 5 of the DPD specifically provided for;

Processing of data relating to offences, criminal convictions or security measures may be carried out only under the control of official authority, or, if suitable, specific safeguards are provided under national law, subject to derogations which may be granted by the Member State under national provisions providing suitable specific safeguards. However, a complete register of criminal convictions may be kept only under the control of official authority. (para.)

Google had refused each of the requests, resulting in the complaints to the CNIL. As the CNIL had rejected the complaints, the individuals then brought proceedings against the European Commission.

In AG Szpunar's Opinion, CJEU Case C-136/17/ Opinion GC, AF, BH, ED v Commission nationale de l'informatique et des libertés (CNIL) the right to request delinking or for information to be "forgotten" had to be balanced against other fundamental rights. These would include not only the fundamental right to data protection as contained in the Charter of Fundamental Rights of the European Union (2012), but that of privacy and freedom of expression for both the publisher and the public. However, AG Szpunar also found that in the balancing exercise there needed to be taken into account where the information relates to journalism purposes or constitutes artistic or literary expression. In addition, there was provision to determine that data meeting the requirements of "special data" would be removed upon request, even where this was potentially theoretical rather than practical due to the often-automated activities of a search engine. Despite concerns as to spent criminal convictions being treated differently, it is clear that the this is not defined as special data but caught under the provisions of Article 10 which relates to the processing of criminal convictions by appropriate authorities within the rules of the member states.

Links to such information will often be considered to be imperative to public interest and therefore this would override the individual's own interests.

CONCLUSION

Following the beginning of the right to be forgotten, European cases have sometimes lacked clarity. However, there seem to be some alignment with decisions on the removal of links, not only with regard to criminal convictions, but also with regard to behaviours which are generally not considered acceptable within the restraints of society. It seems varying approaches are emerging towards questioning whether past events or no longer relevant information about the past can be allowed to hamper the development of a reformed character. The issues raised within these cases on the right to be forgotten, and in particular highlighted by the differing decisions for the two individuals in the cases of claimants NT1 and NT2, also engage with the idea of how society determines the relevance of an individual's past and the impact of past events, on not only reputation and private life, but also on the ability to make amends to his/her community as a whole and for society to accept a "rehabilitated" and remorseful citizen. With the ever-increasing exposure provided by the Internet, the environment has been considerably changed from that in existence when the UK's Rehabilitation of Offenders Act (c-53) was introduced in 1974. A link to rehabilitation takes the value of the right to be forgotten to a different perspective, potentially increasing the importance of the right in the application of its principles to the balancing of human rights, namely privacy and freedom of expression, but also arguably evoking other rights, such as human dignity.

A more detailed consideration of the Google Spain decision, whilst not focusing on the liability of search engines or the specifics of data protection as such, but on the concept of "forgetting the past and creating new opportunities within society" has opened the door to further debate on how society needs to enable individuals to not only use the right to be forgotten as a form of self-determination, but also as a catalyst for the next stage of rehabilitation. This could be considered as introducing those who have in effect paid their debt to society to put them on a new path of self-reinvention, without the restraints provided by past events. Undoubtedly, removal of some activities as has been seen in relation or more serious crimes such as murder will always be unacceptable, but society's views on mental health rehabilitation and spent convictions must be reflected in the ongoing application of the right. The path to the right to be forgotten is one that is littered with process and procedure as well as cost, and for the average person not one easily taken. The impact of the right and its application have perhaps not developed in the same way as originally anticipated, with some believing that the right was inherently misplaced. It might be considered to place a burden of responsibility on a search engine, a form of Internet service provider, potentially creating a nonstate regulator which would have a dramatic impact on the public's right to know, potentially creating an erasure of the past. Whether the finely drawn lines between balancing the right of privacy with such freedom of expression has created the outcome so envisaged is debatable. Under a freedom of information request (Case Reference Number IRQ0856742 Aug 2019), the UK's Information Commissioner's office revealed that in the period from May to July 2018 102 requests were lodged, with none known to be proceeding to court. Despite an increased awareness of the potential loss of privacy, it does not appear that many are seeking to take advantage of an exercise in obtaining erasure of access to material they consider detrimental. It remains to be seen as to whether the application of Article 17 of the GDPR will prove a more feasible remedy, albeit in a potentially more limited scope.

REFERENCES

ABC v Google Inc. (2018) EWHC 137 (QB)

Abstract of the German Federal Constitutional Court's Judgment, 15 December 1983, 1 BvR 209, 269, 362, 420, 440, 484/83

Article 29 Data Protection Working Party Guidelines on the implementation of the Court of Justice of the European Union judgment on "Google Spain and Inc. v. Agencia Española de Protección de Datos (AEPD) and Mario Costeja González" c-131/12 Nov 2014

Axel v Springer AG v Germany (2012) 32 BHRC [83]

Byrum, K. (2017). The European right to be forgotten: A challenge to the United States Constitution's First Amendment and to professional public relations ethics. *Public Relations Review*, *43*(1), 102–111. doi:10.1016/j.pubrev.2016.10.010

Case C-136/17 Court of Justice of the European Union. (2019, January 10). *Advocate General's opinion in case C-136/17G.C. and Others v CNIL* [Press release N. 1/19Luxembourg].

Case C-136/17, Request for a preliminary ruling under Article 267 TFEU from the Conseil d'État (Council of State, France), made by decision of 24 February 2017, received at the Court on 15 March 2017, in the proceedings GC, AF, BH, ED. v Commission nationale de l'informatique et des libertés (CNIL), Google LLC (2019) ECLI:EU:C:2019:773

Case C-507/17, Request for a preliminary ruling under Article 267 TFEU from the Conseil d'État (Council of State, France), made by decision of 19 July 2017, received at the Court on 21 August 2017, in the proceedings Google LLC, successor in law to Google Inc. v Commission nationale de l'informatique et des libertés (CNIL), ECLI:EU:C:2019:772

Charter of Fundamental Rights of the European Union 2012/C 326/02

Data Protection Act. 1998, UK, C-29

Data Protection Act 2018 UK C-12

E-Commerce Directive, (Directive 2000/31/EC of the European Parliament and of the Council of 8 June 2000 on certain legal aspects of information society services, in particular electronic commerce, in the internal market, European Parliament. (2000).

EU General Data Protection Regulation, (EU) 2016/679 of the European Parliament and of the Council of 27 April 2016 on the protection of natural persons with regard to the processing of personal data and on the free movement of such data, and repealing Directive 95/46/EC (General Data Protection Regulation), OJ 2016 L 119/1.

European Convention for the Protection of Human Rights and Fundamental Freedoms, as amended by Protocols Nos. 11 and 14, 4 November 1950, Council of Europe, ETS 5

Freedom of Information Request, UK ICO (Case Reference Number IRQ0856742 Aug 2019),

German Federal Data Protection Act (*Bundesdatenschutzgesetz* [BDSG] 1977, Section 35 – *lonitle Gesetz zum Schutz vor Mißbrauch personenbezogener Daten bei der Datenverarbeitung*

Google. Requests to delist content under European privacy law, Transparency report: available at https://transparencyreport.google.com/eu-privacy/overview)

Google Spain SL and Inc. v Agencia Española de Protección de Datos (AEPD) and Mario Costeja González (2014) C-2012:131

Korkein Hallinto- Oikeus Högsta Förvaltningstomstolen(The Supreme Administrative Court of Finland) 2018: ECLI:FI:KHO:2018:112

Lynskey, O. (2015). *The foundations of EU data protection law*. Oxford, UK: Oxford University Press.

M. L. and W. W. v Germany, European Court of Human Rights; application numbers 60798/10 and 65599/10

Markou, C. (2015). The "right to be forgotten": Ten reasons why it should be forgotten. In S. Gutwirth, R. Leenes, & P. de Hert (Eds.), *Reforming European Data Protection Law* (pp. 203–226). Springer. doi:10.1007/978-94-017-9385-8_8

NT1 and NT2 v Google LLC (2018) EWHC 799 (QB)

Opinion of Advocate General Jääskinen in June 2013, the court in the case of Google Spain SL Google Inc. v Agencia Española de Protección de Datos (AEPD) and Mario Costeja González

Opinion of Advocate General Szpunar in 10 January 2019 in the case of Google Inc. v Commission nationale de l'Informatique et des Libertés C-2017; ECLI:EU:C:2019:15).

1983.   Population Census Decision, Germany, 15 Dec 1983 BvR 209/83, BVerf G 65 1 (unreported in full in English)

Press release; Viviane Redding, Vice President European Commission, EU, The EU Data Protection Reform 2012 'Making Europe the Standard Setter for Modern Data Protection Rules in the Digital Age 2; eu eupropa eu rapid press-release)

R (Pearson) v DVLA (2002) UK EWHC 2482

Rehabilitation of Offenders Act 1974 c-53

SamonteM. (n.d.). europeanlawblog.eu/2019/10/29/google-v-cnil-case-c-507-17-the-territorial-scope-of-the-right-to-be-forgotten-under-eu-law/

Zanfir, G. (2013). *Tracing the Right to be Forgotten in the Short History of Data Protection Law: The 'New Clothes' of an Old Right*. Available at SSRN: https://ssrn.com/abstract=2501312

KEY TERMS AND DEFINITIONS

Advocate General: Appointed for a period of 6 years to work with the CJEU. The most important work performed by the Advocates General is to deliver a written Opinion, named "reasoned submission". The role of the Advocate General is to propose an independent legal solution on cases referred to the court. It is important to note that the Court is not compelled to follow an opinion delivered by the Advocate General.

CJEU: The Court of Justice of the European Union interprets EU law to make sure it is applied in the same way in all EU countries, and settles legal disputes between national governments and EU institutions.

Directive: A "directive" is a legislative act that sets out a goal that all EU countries must achieve. However, it is up to the individual countries to devise their own laws on how to reach these goals.

EU: The European Union is an economic and political union between 27 EU countries that together cover much of the continent of Europe. The EU is governed by the principle of representative democracy, with citizens directly represented at Union level in the European Parliament and Member States represented in the European Council and the Council of the EU.

Regulation: A "regulation" is a binding legislative act by the EU. It must be applied in its entirety across the EU. For example, when the EU wanted to make sure that there are common safeguards on goods imported from outside the EU, the Council adopted a regulation.

Compilation of References

1983.   Population Census Decision, Germany, 15 Dec 1983 BvR 209/83, BVerf G 65 1 (unreported in full in English)

Abbt, C. (2018). Forgetting in a Digital Glasshouse. In F. Thouvenin, P. Hettich, H. Burkert, & U. Gasser (Eds.), *Remembering and Forgetting in the Digital Age* (pp. 124–134). Cham: Springer. doi:10.1007/978-3-319-90230-2_9

ABC v Google Inc. (2018) EWHC 137 (QB)

Abreu, J. C. (2017). Digital Single Market under EU political and constitutional calling: European electronic agenda's impact on interoperability solutions. *UNIO - EU Law Journal*, *3*(1), 123-140. Retrieved January 30, 2020 from https://revistas.uminho.pt/index.php/unio/issue/view/25

Abstract of the German Federal Constitutional Court's Judgment, 15 December 1983, 1 BvR 209, 269, 362, 420, 440, 484/83

Acquisti, A., Brandimarte, L., & Loewenstein, G. (2015). Privacy and human behavior in the age of information. *Science*, *347*(6221), 509–514. doi:10.1126cience.aaa1465 PMID:25635091

Additional Protocol to the Convention for the Protection of Individuals with regard to Automatic Processing of Personal Data, regarding supervisory authorities and transborder data flows, ETS 181.

Aghion, P. (2005). Competition and Innovation: An Inverted-U Relationship. *The Quarterly Journal of Economics*, 701.

Agrawal, R., & Srikant, R. (1994). Fast algorithms for mining association rules. *Proc. 20th int. conf. very large data bases*, *VLDB*(1215), 487-499.

Ajzen, I. (1985). *From intentions to actions: A theory of planned behavior. In Action control* (pp. 11–39). Berlin: Springer.

Akrivopoulou, X. M. (2011). The right to data protection via the lens of the right to privacy. *Theory and Practice of Administrative Law*, *7*, 679–691.

Akrivopoulou, X. M. (2012). *The right to privacy: From its genesis to its current development and protection*. Athens, Greece: Sakkoulas Publications.

Aksoy, L., Buoye, A., Aksoy, P., Larivière, B., & Keiningham, T. L. (2013). A cross-national investigation of the satisfaction and loyalty linkage for mobile telecommunications services across eight countries. *Journal of Interactive Marketing*, *27*(1), 74–82. doi:10.1016/j.intmar.2012.09.003

Al Tamimi & Co. (2012). *Data Protection and Privacy Issues in the Middle East*. Retrieved from https://www.tamimi.com/law-update-articles/data-protection-and-privacy-issues-in-the-middle-east/

Al Tamimi & Co. (2015). *Abu Dhabi Global Market: Public consultation on data protection*. Retrieved from https://www.tamimi.com/law-update-articles/abu-dhabi-global-market-public-consultation-on-data-protection/

Al Tamimi & Co. (2019). Retrieved, from https://www.tamimi.com/news/ministry-of-justice-islamic-affairs-and-awqaf-entrusted-with-the-tasks-and-competences-of-personal-data-protection-authority/

Alboaie, L. (2017). Towards a Smart Society through Personal Assistants Employing Executable Choreographies. ISD 2017 Proceedings.

Albrecht, J. P., & Jotzo, F. (2017). Das neue Datenschutzrecht der EU. Grundlagen, Gesetzgebungsverfahren, Synopse.

Albrecht, J. P. (2016). How the GDPR will change the world. *European Data Protection Law Review*, *2*(3), 287–289. doi:10.21552/EDPL/2016/3/4

Alexy, A. (2009). *A theory of Constitutional Rights*. Oxford University Press.

Allen, D. W. E., Berg, A., Berg, C., Markey-Towler, B., & Potts, J. (2019). Some Economic Consequences of the GDPR. *Economics Bulletin*. Retrieved from https://ssrn.com/abstract=3160404

Allen, J. P. (2014). Rules- or Principles-Based Regulation—Factors for Choosing the Best Language Strategy. *Canadian Business Law Journal*, *56*(3), 375–394.

Almoatazbillah, H. (2012). *The Value Proposition Concept in Marketing: How Customers Perceive the Value Delivered by Firms*. A Study of Customer Perspectives on Supermarkets in Southampton in the United Kingdom.

Alsenoy, B. (2016). Liability under EU data protection law: from Directive 95/46 to the General Data Protection Regulation. *JIPITEC, 7*(271).

Amazon Web Services (AWS) The New AWS Region in the Middle East. (2019). Retrieved from https://aws.amazon.com/local/middle_east/bahrain/

Angelopoulos, C. J., & Smet, S. (2016). Notice-and-fair-balance: how to reach a compromise between fundamental rights in European intermediary liability. *Journal of Media Law*, 266.

Anthimos, A., Avgitides, D., Valtoudis, A., Varela, M., Vervesos, N., & Georgiades, A. (Eds.). (2010). A brief interpretation of the Greek Civil Code, 2. Athens, Greece: Law & Economy- P.N. Sakkoulas.

Arrow, K. J. (2016) Welfare and the Allocation of Resources for Invention. In R. Nelson (Ed.), The Rate and Direction of Economic Activities: Economic and Social Factors. NBER Books.

Art 29 Working Party. (2014). *Guidelines on the implementation of the Court of Justice of the European Union judgment on Google Spain and Inc v. Agencia española de protección de datos (AEPD) and Mario Costeja González C-131/12, 14/EN, WP 225*. Retrieved from https://www.dataprotection.ro/servlet/ViewDocument?id=1080

Article 29 Data Protection Working Party Guidelines on the implementation of the Court of Justice of the European Union judgment on "Google Spain and Inc. v. Agencia Española de Protección de Datos (AEPD) and Mario Costeja González" c-131/12 Nov 2014

Article 29 Working Party (2014). Guidelines on the implementation of the Court of Justice of the European Union judgment on 'Google Spain SL, Google Inc v Agencia Española de Protección de Datos and Mario Costeja González' C-131/12', WP 225, 26 November 2014.

Article 29 Working Party. (2003). *Working document on biometrics*. Retrieved from https://ec.europa.eu/justice/article-29/documentation/opinion-recommendation/files/2003/wp80_en.pdf

Article 29 Working Party. (2006). Opinion 10/2006 on the processing of personal data by the Society for Worldwide Interbank Financial Telecommunication (SWIFT), WP 128.

Article 29 Working Party. (2007). *Opinion No 4/2007 on the concept of personal data*. Retrieved from https://ec.europa.eu/justice/article-29/documentation/opinion-recommendation/files/2007/wp136_en.pdf

Article 29 Working Party. (2009). *Joint contribution to the Consultation of the European Commission on the legal framework for the fundamental right to protection of personal data*. https://ec.europa.eu/justice/article-29/documentation/opinion-recommendation/files/2009/wp168_en.pdf

Article 29 Working Party. (2009). Opinion 5/2009 on online social networking, WP 163.

Article 29 Working Party. (2010). Opinion 1/2010 on the concepts of "controller" and "processor", 00264/10/EN WP 169.

Article 29 Working Party. (2010a). Opinion 2/2010 on online behavioural advertising, 00909/10/EN WP 171.

Article 29 Working Party. (2010b). Opinion 3/2010 on the principle of accountability, 00062/10/EN WP 173.

Article 29 Working Party. (2013). *Statement of the Working Party on current discussions regarding the data protection reform package*. https://ec.europa.eu/justice/article-29/documentation/other-document/files/2013/20130227_statement_dp_reform_package_en.pdf

Article 29 Working Party. (2014). Statement on the role of a risk-based approach in data protection legal framework, 14/EN WP 218.

Article 29 Working Party. (2014). *Statement on the role of a risk-based approach in data protection legal frameworks, 14/EN WP 218*.

Article 29 Working Party. (2017). *Guidelines on Data Protection Impact Assessment (DPIA) and determining whether processing is "likely to result in a high risk" for the purposes of Regulation 2016/679—17/EN WP 248 rev.01*.

Aus, J. P. (2006). Eurodac: A Solution Looking for a Problem? European Integration online Papers, 10(6).

Autorité de la Concurrence, Avis no 18-A-03 portant sur l'exploitation des donnees dans le secteur de la publicite sur internet, 6 March 2018

Averitt, N., & Lande, R. (2007). Using the 'consumer choice' approach to antitrust law. *Antitrust Law Journal*, 74.

Axel v Springer AG v Germany (2012) 32 BHRC [83]

Aziewicz, A. (2015). Due Process Rights in Polish Antitrust Proceedings. Case comment to the Judgment of the Polish Supreme Court of 3 October 2013 – PKP Cargo S.A. v. President of the Office of Competition and Consumers Protection (Ref. No. III SK 67/12, *YASS* 261. Bergkamp, L. (2002). The Privacy Fallacy: Adverse Effects of Europe's Data Protection Policy in an Information-Driven Economy. *Computer Law & Security Report*, 31.

Azizi, M., Dehghan, S., Ziaie, M., & Mohebi, N. (2017). Identifying the customer satisfaction factors in furniture market. Economics. *Management and Sustainability*, 2(1), 6–18. doi:10.14254/jems.2017.2-1.1

Azoulai, L. (2008). The Court of Justice and the social market economy: The emergence of an ideal and the conditions for its realization. *Common Market Law Review*, 1335.

Bagger Tranberg, C. (2011). Proportionality and data protection in the case law of the European Court of Justice. *International Data Privacy Law*, 239.

Bahrain News Agency. (2019). *HM King designates entity to assume duties of the authority for protection of personal data*. Retrieved from https://www.bna.bh/en/HMKingdesignatesentitytoassumedutiesoftheauthorityforprotectionofpersonaldata.aspx?cms=q8FmFJgiscL2fwIzON1%2BDl9zQ5EMjiqZCBNc6yqcKAE%3D

Bahrain News. (2019). *Organisations to obtain customers' approval before storing their personal data from next month.* Retrieved from http://beta.gdnonline.com/Details/567248/New-body-on-way-to-guard-personal-data

Balboni. (2013). Legitimate interest of the data controller. New data protection paradigm: legitimacy grounded on appropriate protection. *International Data Privacy Law,* 244.

Bamberger, K. A., & Mulligan, D. K. (2015). *Privacy on the Ground: Driving Corporate Behavior in the United States and Europe.* Rochester, NY: Social Science Research Network. doi:10.7551/mitpress/9905.001.0001

Barberis, J., Arner, D. W., & Buckley, R. P. (2019). *The REGTECH Book: The Financial Technology Handbook for Investors, Entrepreneurs and Visionaries in Regulation.* John Wiley & Sons Inc. doi:10.1002/9781119362197

Bauer, C., Korunovska, J., & Spiekermann, S. (2012). On the Value of Information –What Facebook Users are Willing to Pay. *ECIS 2012, Proceedings,* 197. Available at: https://aisel.aisnet.org/ecis2012/197

Bélanger, F., Clossler, R.E. (2011). Privacy in the Digital Age: A Review of Information Privacy Research in Information Systems. *MIS Quarterly, 35*(4), 1017-1041. Doi:10.2307/41409971

Benini, F. (2019). Digital Single Market. Policy: The Digital Economy and Society Index (DESI). *European Commission Policies.* Retrieved September 17, 2019, from https://ec.europa.eu/digital-single-market/en/desi

Bennett, C. J., & Raab, D. Ch. (2006). *The governance of privacy: Policy Instruments in Global perspective.* Cambridge, MA: MIT Press.

Ben-Shahar, O., & Strahilevitz, L. J. (2016, June). Contracting over Privacy: Introduction. *The Journal of Legal Studies, 45*(S2), S1–S11. doi:10.1086/690281

Betzing, J. H., Beverungen, D., & Becker, J. (2018). Design principles for co-creating digital customer experience in high street retail. *Proceedings of the Multikonferenz Wirtschaftsinformatik,* 2083-2094.

Bignami, F. (2008). The Case for Tolerant Constitutional Patriotism: The Right to Privacy Before the European Courts. *Cornell International Law Journal,* 211.

Bix, B. H. (2010). Contracts. In The Ethics of Consent: Theory and Practice, (pp. 251-279). Oxford University Press. doi:10.1093/acprof:oso/9780195335149.001.0001

BKA & Autorite de la concurrence. (2016). *Competition Law and Data.* Retrieved September 30, 2019 https://www.bundeskartellamt.de/SharedDocs/Publikation/DE/Berichte/Big%20Data%20Papier.pdf?__blob=publicationFile&v=2

BKA. (2019). *Case B6-22/16 Facebook, Exploitative business terms pursuant to Section 19(1) GWB for inadequate data processing.* Retrieved August 28, 2019 <https://www.bundeskartellamt.de/SharedDocs/Entscheidung/EN/Fallberichte/Missbrauchsaufsicht/2019/B6-22-16.html?nn=3600108>

Black, J. (2001). Managing Discretion. *ARLC Conference Papers.* www.lse.ac.uk/collections/law/staff%20publications%20full%20text/black/alrc%20managing%20discretion.pdf

Bolton, R. N., McColl-Kennedy, J. R., Cheung, L., Gallan, A., Orsingher, C., Witell, L., & Zaki, M. (2018). Customer experience challenges: Bringing together digital, physical and social realms. *Journal of Service Management, 29*(5), 776–808. doi:10.1108/JOSM-04-2018-0113

Bombois, T. (2009). L'administration ''juge'' de la légalité communautaire – Réflexions autor des arrêts *Fratelli Costanzo* et *Abna* de la Cour de Justice de Luxembourg. *Journal des tribunaux, 128,* 169-174.

Borea, P. (2019). *The Gulf Cooperation Council: Institutions, Laws, Policies, External Relations.* Lexis Nexis.

Brazilian General Data Protection Law. (2018). Retrieved from https://iapp.org/media/pdf/resource_center/Brazilian_General_Data_Protection_Law.pdf

Brotman, S. N. (2016). *The European Union's Digital Single Market Strategy: A conflict between government's desire for certainty and rapid marketplace innovation?* Retrieved November 12, 2019 https://www.brookings.edu/wp-content/uploads/2016/07/digital-single-market.pdf

Brouwer, E. (2008b). Digital Borders and Real Rights: Effective Remedies for Third-Country Nationals in the Schengen Information System. Academic Press.

Brouwer, E. (2019). *Interoperability and Interstate Trust: a Perilous Combination for Fundamental Rights*. https://eumigrationlawblog.eu/interoperability-and-interstate-trust-a-perilous-combination-for-fundamental-rights/

Brouwer, E. (2008a). *The other side of the Moon*. Center for European Policy Studies.

BRT v SABAM; ECLI:EU:C:1974:25, 27/03/1974

Brunner, L. (2016). The Liability of an Online Intermediary for Third Party Content The Watchdog Becomes the Monitor: Intermediary Liability after *Delfi v Estonia. Human Rights Law Review, 16*(1), 163–174. doi:10.1093/hrlr/ngv048

Bulgarian Commission for Personal Data Protection. (2016). *Guidelines on the GDPR*. Retrieved https://www.cpdp.bg/index.php?p=element&aid=1163

Burkell, J. A. (2016). Remembering me: Big data, individual identity, and the psychological necessity of forgetting. *Ethics and Information Technology, 18*(1), 17–23. doi:10.100710676-016-9393-1

Butler, O. (2015). *The expanding scope of the Data Protection Directive: The exception for a purely personal or household activity*. University of Cambridge Legal Studies Research Papers, no. 54.

Bygrave, L. (2002). Data protection law: approaching its rationale, logic and limits. The Hague: Kluwer Law International.

Bygrave, L. (2001). Automated profiling: Minding the machine: Article 15 of the EC Data Protection Directive and automated profiling. *Computer Law & Security Report, 17*(1), 17–24. doi:10.1016/S0267-3649(01)00104-2

Bygrave, L. A. (2017). Data Protection by Design and by Default: Deciphering the EU's Legislative Requirements. *Oslo Law Review, 4*(2), 2017. doi:10.18261/issn.2387-3299-2017-02-03

Byrum, K. (2017). The European right to be forgotten: A challenge to the United States Constitution's First Amendment and to professional public relations ethics. *Public Relations Review, 43*(1), 102–111. doi:10.1016/j.pubrev.2016.10.010

C-49/07 Motosykletistiki Omospondia Ellados NPID (MOTOE) v Elliniko Dimosio, [2008] ECR I-4863

Callon, M. (1991). Techno-economic networks and irreversibility. In J. Law (Ed.), *A sociology of monsters: essays on power, technology and domination* (pp. 132–164). London: Routledge.

Carey, P. (Ed.). (2019). Data Protection: A Practical Guide to U.K. and E.U. Law. Oxford University Press.

Carloni, E., & Falcone, M. (2017). L'equilibrio necessario. Principi e modelli di bilanciamento tra trasparenza e privacy. *Diritto Pubblico, 23*(3), 723-777.

Case 27/76 United Brands Company and United Brands Continentaal BV v. Commission, [1978], ECR 207

Case 395/87 Ministère public v. Jean-Louis Tournier, [1989] ECR 2521

Case C-136/17 Court of Justice of the European Union. (2019, January 10). *Advocate General's opinion in case C-136/17G.C. and Others v CNIL* [Press release N. 1/19Luxembourg].

Case C-136/17, Request for a preliminary ruling under Article 267 TFEU from the Conseil d'État (Council of State, France), made by decision of 24 February 2017, received at the Court on 15 March 2017, in the proceedings GC, AF, BH, ED v Commission nationale de l'informatique et des libertés (CNIL), Google LLC (2019) ECLI:EU:C:2019:773

Case C-209/10 Post Danmark A/S v Konkurrencerådet ECLI:EU:C:2012:172

Case C-235/08 Asnef-Equifax v Asociación de Usuarios de Servicios Bancarios ECR I-11125. [2006].

Case C-333/94P Tetra Pak International SA v. Commission (Tetra Pak II), [1996] ECR I-5951

Case C-468/06 Sot. Lélos Kai Sia v. GlaxoSmithKline [2008] ECR I-7139

Case C-507/17, Request for a preliminary ruling under Article 267 TFEU from the Conseil d'État (Council of State, France), made by decision of 19 July 2017, received at the Court on 21 August 2017, in the proceedings Google LLC, successor in law to Google Inc. v Commission nationale de l'informatique et des libertés (CNIL), ECLI:EU:C:2019:772

Case C-67/96 Albany EU:C:1999:430

Case M.8124 Microsoft/LinkedIn, 14 October 2016

Cases C-501/06 P etc GlaxoSmithKline Services Unlimited v Commission and Others [2009] ECR I-9291

Castro-Edwards, C. (2017). *EU General Data Protection Regulation: A guide to the new law*. London: The law. *Society*.

Cathryn Costello. (2006). *The European Asylum Procedures Directive in Legal Context*. UNHCR Research Paper No. 134. https://www.refworld.org/docid/4ff14e932.html

Charter of Fundamental Rights of the European Union 2010 OJ C 83/02

Charter of Fundamental Rights of the European Union 2012/C 326/02

Charter of Fundamental Rights of the European Union, 2016/C 202/02, Official Journal of the European Union C 202/389, 7.6.2016.

Charter of Fundamental Rights of the European Union, OJ C 83/391, 30.3.2010.

Chiabai, A., Platt, S., & Strielkowski, W. (2014). Eliciting users' preferences for cultural heritage and tourism-related e-services: A tale of three European cities. *Tourism Economics*, *20*(2), 263–277. doi:10.5367/te.2013.0290

Chivot, E., Castro, D., Chivot, E., & Castro, D. (2019). *What the Evidence Shows About the Impact of the GDPR After One Year*. Retrieved from https://www.datainnovation.org/2019/06/what-the-evidence-shows-about-the-impact-of-the-gdpr-after-one-year

Christie, R. (2019). *General Data Protection Rules*. Lexis Middle East.

Christodoulou, K. N. (2013). *Personal data protection Law*. Athens, Greece: Nomiki Bibliothiki Group.

Claes, M. (2015). The Primacy of EU Law in European and National Law. In A. Arnull & D. Chalmers (Eds.), *The Oxford Handbook of European Union Law* (pp. 178–211). Oxford, UK: Oxford University Press.

Clapham, A. (2006). *Human Rights Obligations of Non-state Actors*. Oxford University Press. doi:10.1093/acprof:oso/9780199288465.001.0001

Clarke, R. (2017). *The distinction between a PIA and a Data Protection Impact Assessment (DPIA) under the EU GDPR*. Paper presented at the Computers Privacy and Data Protection Conference (CPDP), Brussels, Belgium.

Clarke, R. (1994). The Digital Persona and Its Application to Surveillance. *The Information Society*, *10*(2), 77–92. doi:10.1080/01972243.1994.9960160

Clifford, D. (2019). The legal limits to the monetisation of online emotions. KU Leuven, Faculty of Law.

Clifford, D., & Ausloos, J. (2018). Data Protection and the Role of Fairness. *Yearbook of European Law*, *37*, 130–187. doi:10.1093/yel/yey004

Cobbaut, E. (2019). Article 11 - Freedom of Expression and Information. In F. Dorssemont, K. Lörcher, S. Clauwaert, & M. Schmitt (Eds.), *The Charter of Fundamental Rights of the European Union and the employment relation* (pp. 295–313). Oxford: Hart Publishing. doi:10.5040/9781509922680.ch-014

Cohen, J. (2000). Examined Lives: Informational Privacy and the Subject as Object. *Stanford Law Review*, *52*(5), 1373. doi:10.2307/1229517

Collingridge, D. (1981). *The Social Control of Technology*. Palgrave Macmillan.

Collins, H. (2012). *On the (In)compatibility of Human Rights Discourse and Private Law. LSE Law*. Society and Economy Working Papers 7/2012. London School of Economics and Political Science- Law Department.

Commission Delegated Regulation (EU) 2019/946 of 12.3.2019 supplementing Regulation (EU) No 515/2014 of the European Parliament and of the Council as regards the allocation of funds from the general budget of the Union to cover the costs of developing the European Travel Information and Authorisation System, OJ L 152, 11.6.2019, p. 41-44.

Communication of the Commission to the European Parliament, the Council, the European Economic and Social Committee and the Committee of Regions (2016). Online Platforms and the Digital Single Market – opportunities and challenges for Europe, Brussels, COM(2016) 288 final.

Consiglio di Stato, Judgment of 13 of December 2019, N. 02936/2019 REG.RIC.

Consolidated Version of the Treaty on European Union, 2010 OJ C 83/01

Consolidated Version of the Treaty on the Functioning of the European Union, 2008 OJ C 115/47

Convention for the Protection of Human Rights and Fundamental Freedoms of 4 November 1950, ETS 006.

Convention for the Protection of Individuals with regard to Automatic Processing of Personal Data, adopted on 28 January 1981, ETS No 108;

Convention for the Protection of Individuals with regard to Automatic Processing of Personal Data, ETS No.108.

Convention implementing the Schengen Agreement of 14 June 1985 between the Governments of the States of the Benelux Economic Union, the Federal Republic of Germany and the French Republic on the gradual abolition of checks at their common borders, OJ L 239, 22.09.2000, pp. 19-62.

Cordeiro, A. (2019). Portugal: A Brief Overview of the GDPR Implementation. *European Data Protection Law Review*, *5*(4), 533–536. doi:10.21552/edpl/2019/4/12

Council Decision 2008/633/JHA of 23.6.2008 concerning access for consultation of the Visa Information System (VIS) by designated authorities of Member States and by Europol for the purposes of the prevention, detection and investigation of terrorist offences and of other serious criminal offences, OJ L 218, 13.8.2008.

Council Decision 2009/316/JHA of 6.4.2009 on the establishment of the European Criminal Records Information System (ECRIS) in application of Article 11 of Framework Decision 2009/315/JHA, OJ L 93, 7.4.2009, p. 33-48.

Council of Europe. (1981). *Convention for the Protection of Individuals with regard to Automatic Processing of Personal Data.* https://www.coe.int/en/web/conventions/full-list/-/conventions/treaty/108/signatures

Council of Europe. (2017). Consultative Committee of the Convention for the Protection of Individuals with Regard to Automatic Processing of Personal Data (T-PD). *Guidelines on the Protection of Individuals with regard to the Processing of Personal Data in a World of Big Data.* Retrieved December 15, 2019, from https://www.coe.int/en/web/data-protection/-/new-guidelines-on-artificial-intelligence-and-personal-data-protection

Council of Europe. (2017). *Guidelines on the protection of individuals with regard to the processing of personal data in a world of Big Data, 2017, No. 9.* Retrieved December 16, 2019, from https://rm.coe.int/16806ebe7a

Council of Europe. (2018). *Study on the human rights dimensions of automated data processing techniques (in particular algorithms) and possible regulatory implications.* Retrieved December 16, 2019 from https://edoc.coe.int/en/internet/7589-algorithms-and-human-rights-study-on-the-human-rights-dimensions-of-automated-data-processing-techniques-and-possible-regulatory-implications.html

Council of the European Union (2008);

Council Post. (2018). *Is Your Business GDPR-Compliant?* Retrieved from https://www.forbes.com/sites/forbesagency-council/2018/06/11/is-your-business-in-compliance-with-the-eus-general-data-protection-regulation/#6761ec6d379c

Council Regulation (EC) No 1/2003 of 16 December 2002 on the implementation of the rules on competition laid down in Articles 81 and 82 of the Treaty

Council Regulation (EC) No 139/2004 of 20 January 2004 on the control of concentrations between undertakings

Council Regulation (EC) No 2725/2000 of 11.12.2000 concerning the establishment of "Eurodac" for the comparison of fingerprints for the effective application of the Dublin Convention, OJ L 316, 15.12.2000, p. 1-10.

Crofts, L., & Newman, M. (2016). Data abuses could be targeted by antitrust regulators as Vestager weights new law. *MLex.* Retrieved October 23, 2018 <www.mlex.com/GlobalAntitrust/DatailView.aspx?cid=831793&siteid=190&rdir=1>

Custers, B. H. M. (2004). The power of knowledge: Ethical, legal and technological aspects of data mining and group profiling in epidemiology. Nijmegen: Wolf Legal Publishers (WLP).

Cuthbertson, A. (2016, August 16). *Is your sex toy spying on you?* Retrieved January 15, 2017, from https://www.news-week.com/your-sex-toy-spying-you-489328

Dagtoglou, P. D. (2012). *Constitutional Law: Civil Rights* (4th ed.). Athens, Greece: Sakkoulas Publications.

Data Protection Act 2018 UK C-12

Data Protection Act. 1998, UK, C-29

Data Protection Working Party, Guidelines on consent under Regulation 2016/679, adopted on 28 November 2017, as last revised and Adopted on 10 April 2018, 17/EN, WP259 rev.01

Data Protection. 2019 | Laws and Regulations | Norway | ICLG. (2019). Retrieved, from https://iclg.com/practice-areas/data-protection-laws-and-regulations/norway

Davilla, M. (2017). Is Big Data a Different Kind of Animal? The Treatment of Big Data Under the EU Competition Rules. *JECL & Pract*, (8), 370.

Davis, F. D. (1989). Perceived usefulness, perceived ease of use, and user acceptance of information technology. *Management Information Systems Quarterly*, *13*(3), 319–340. doi:10.2307/249008

De Amicis, G. (2018). *La formulazione del principio di diritto e i rapporti tra Sezioni semplici e Sezioni Unite penali della Corte di Cassazione*. Retrieved from http://www.cortedicassazione.it/cassazione-resources/resources/cms/documents/Rel.__Cons._DE_AMICIS-Il_principio_di_diritto_ed_i_rapporti_tra_Sez._simplici_e_Sez._Unite.pdf

de Andrade, N. N. G. (2011). Data protection, privacy and identity: Distinguishing concepts and articulating rights. In *Privacy and identity management for life 6th Ifip Wg 9.2, 9.6/11.7, 11.4, 11.6/PrimeLife International Summer School, Helsingborg, Sweden, August 2-6, 2010, revised selected papers* (Vol. 352). Berlin: Springer.

De Búrca, G. (2013). After the EU Charter of Fundamental Rights: The Court of Justice as a human rights adjudicator? *MJ, 168.*

De Hert, P., & Gutwirth, S. (2006). Interoperability of police databases within the EU: An accountable political choice? *International Review of Law Computers & Technology, 20*(1-2), 21–35. doi:10.1080/13600860600818227

De Hert, P., & Papakonstantinou, V. (2012). The Proposed Data Protection Regulation Replacing Directive 95/46/EC: A Sound System for the Protection of Individuals. *Computer Law & Security Review, 28*(2), 130–142. doi:10.1016/j.clsr.2012.01.011

De Hert, P., & Papakonstantinou, V. (2016). The new General Data Protection Regulation: Still a sound system for the protection of individuals? *Computer Law & Security Review, 32*(2), 179–194. doi:10.1016/j.clsr.2016.02.006

De Vries, S. (2013). Balancing Fundamental Rights with Economic Freedoms According to the European Court of Justice. *Utrecht Law Review, 9*(1), 169. doi:10.18352/ulr.220

De Winter, J. C. F., Zadpoor, A. A., & Dodou, D. (2014). The expansion of Google Scholar versus Web of Science: A longitudinal study. *Scientometrics, 98*(2), 1547–1565. doi:10.100711192-013-1089-2

Deac, A. (2018). Regulation (EU) 2016/679 Of the European Parliament and Of The Council On The Protection Of Individuals With Regard To The Processing Of Personal Data And The Free Movement Of These Data. *Perspectives of Law and Public Administration, Societatea de Stiinte Juridice si Administrative, 7*(2), 151–156.

Debet, A. (2016). La protection des données personnelles, point de vue du droit privé. *Revue du Droit Public, 1,* 17–34.

Decision (EU) 2015/2240, of the European Parliament and of the Council, 25th November 2015, establishing a programme on interoperability solutions and common frameworks for European public administrations, businesses and citizens (ISA2 programme) as a means for modernizing the public sector.

Decker, C. (2018). *Goals-based and rules-based approaches to regulation.* BEIS Research Paper Number 8, 67.

Demirbolat, A. O. (2018). *The Relationship Between Democracy and Education.* Bentham Science Publishers.

Deutsche Telekom AG v Commission (2010) C-280/08

Di Ciommo, F. (2018). Il diritto all'oblio nel Regolamento (UE) 2016/679. Ovvero, di un "tratto di penna del legislatore" che non manda al macero alcunché. *Quotidiano giuridico,* 16-31.

Di Ciommo, F. (2019a). Oblio e cronaca: rimessa alle Sezioni Unite la definizione dei criteri di bilanciamento. *Il corriere giuridico,* 5-15.

Di Ciommo. (2019b). Diritto alla cancellazione, diritto di limitazione del trattamento e diritto all'oblio. I dati personali nel diritto europeo, 351-393.

Dictionary.com. (n.d.a). *Statistical.* Retrieved November 27, 2016, from https://www.dictionary.com/browse/statistical

Dictionary.com. (n.d.b). *Statistics.* Retrieved November 27, 2016, from https://www.dictionary.com/browse/statistics

DIGITALEUROPE. (2019). *Response to public consultation on draft EDPB Guidelines on codes of conduct and monitoring bodies*. https://www.digitaleurope.org/resources/response-to-public-consultation-on-draft-edpb-guidelines-on-codes-of-conduct-and-monitoring-bodies/

DiMaggio, P., & Powell, W. W. (1983). The iron cage revisited: Collective rationality and institutional isomorphism in organizational fields. *American Sociological Review*, *48*(2), 147–160. doi:10.2307/2095101

Directive (EU) 2016/680 of the European Parliament and of the Council of 27.4.2016 on the protection of individuals with regard to the processing of personal data by the competent authorities for the purpose of the prevention, investigation, detection or prosecution of criminal offences or the execution of criminal penalties and on the free movement of such data and repealing Council Framework Decision 2008/977/JHA, OJ L 119, 4.5.2016, p. 89-131.

Directive (EU) 2019/1024 of the European Parliament and of the Council of 20 June 2019 on open data and the re-use of public sector information.

Directive (EU) 2019/1937 of the European Parliament and of the Council of 23 October 2019 on the protection of persons who report breaches of Union law.

Directive 2002/58/EC of the European Parliament and of the Council of 12 July 2002 concerning the processing of personal data and the protection of privacy in the electronic communications sector (Directive on privacy and electronic communications), OJ L 201, 31/07/2002 P. 0037-0047

Directive 2003/4/EC of the European Parliament and of the Council of 28 January 2003 on public access to environmental information and repealing Council Directive 90/313/EEC.

Directive 2008/115/EC of the European Parliament and of the Council of 16.12.2008 on common standards and procedures in Member States for returning third-country nationals residing in the Community, OJ L 348, 24.12.2008, p. 98-107.

Directive 2009/136/EC of the European Parliament and of the Council of 25 November 2009 amending Directive 2002/22/EC on universal service and users' rights relating to electronic communications networks and services, Directive 2002/58/EC concerning the processing of personal data and the protection of privacy in the electronic communications sector and Regulation (EC) No 2006/2004 on cooperation between national authorities responsible for the enforcement of consumer protection laws. (Directive on privacy and electronic communications), OJ L 337/11, 18/12/2009 P. 0011–0036.

Directive 95/46/EC of the European Parliament and of the Council of 24 October 1995 on the protection of individuals with regard to the processing of personal data and on the free movement of such data.

Directive 95/46/EC of the European Parliament and of the Council of 24.10.1995 on the protection of individuals with regard to the processing of personal data and on the free movement of such data, OJ L 281, 23.11.1995, p. 31-50.

Directive 95/46/EU of the European Parliament and of the Council of October 1995 on the protection of individuals with regard to the processing of personal data and on the free movement of such data, OJ L 281, 23/11/1995 P. 0031-0050

Downes, L. (2009). *The Laws of Disruption: Harnessing the New Forces That Govern Life and Business in the Digital Age*. Basic Books.

Dublin Convention of 15.6.1990 determining the State responsible for examining applications for asylum lodged in one of the Member States of the European Communities, OJ C 254, 19.8.1997, p. 1.

Ducato, R. (2019). I dati biometrici. In R. D. Vincenzo Cuffaro (Ed.), *I dati personali nel diritto europeo* (pp. 1285–1321). Torino: Giappichelli.

Duhigg, C. (2012, February 16). *How companies learn your secrets*. Retrieved October 10, 2016, from https://www.nytimes.com/2012/02/19/magazine/shopping-habits.html

Dupré, C. (2013). Human Dignity in Europe: A Foundational Constitutional Principle. *European Public Law*, 319.

ECJ Judgment of the Court (Grand Chamber), 8 April 2014, Digital Rights Ireland, Joined Cases C-293/12 and C-594/12.

ECJ, Judgment (Ninth Chamber) of 22 March 2017, C-665/15, Commission v Portugal (failure of the Member State to use of and connect to the EU network within the EU driving licence network).

ECJ, Judgment (Tenth Chamber) of 5 October 2016, Commission v Portugal, C-583/15.

ECJ, Judgment of the Court (Grand Chamber) of 4 April 2017, European Ombudsman v Claire Staelen, Case C-337/15 P.

ECJ, Judgment of the Court (Grand Chamber) of 4 of April 2014, Digital Rights Ireland Ltd (C-293/12) and Kärntner Landesregierung (C-594/12).

ECJ, Judgment of the Court (Grand Chamber) of 9 November 2010, Volker und Markus Schecke GbR (C-92/09) and Hartmut Eifert (C-93/09) v Land Hessen.

ECJ, Judgment of the Court (Grand Chamber), 13 May 2014, Google Spain SL and Google Inc. v Agencia Española de Protección de Datos (AEPD) and Mario Costeja González, C-131/12.

E-Commerce Directive, (Directive 2000/31/EC of the European Parliament and of the Council of 8 June 2000 on certain legal aspects of information society services, in particular electronic commerce, in the internal market, European Parliament. (2000).

ECtHR, Antović and Mirković v. Montenegro, Judgment of 28 of November 2017, Application no 70838/13.

ECtHR, I v. Finland, Judgment of judgment of 17 of July 2008 (Fourth Section) Application 20511/03.

ECtHR, Leander v. Sweden, No. 9248/1981, judgment of 26.3.1987.

ECtHR, Magyar Helsinki Bizottság *versus* Hungary, Judgment of 8 November 2016 (Grand Chamber) Application no. 18030/11.

ECtHR, S. and Marper v. the United Kingdom, Judgment (Grand Chamber) of 4 December 2008.

ECtHR, S. and Marper v. United Kingdom, nos. 30562/04 and 30566/04, judgment of 4.12.2008.

ECtHR, Sérvulo & Associados – Sociedade de Advogados, RL and others c. Portugal, Judgment of 3 September 2015 (First Section), Application 27013/10.

EDPB. (2019a). *Guidelines 1/2018 on certification and identifying certification criteria in accordance with Articles 42 and 43 of the Regulation Version 3.0.* https://edpb.europa.eu/our-work-tools/public-consultations/2019/guidelines-12018-certification-and-identifying_en

EDPB. (2019b). Guidelines 1/2019 on Codes of Conduct and Monitoring Bodies under. *Regulation, 2016*(67). https://edpb.europa.eu/our-work-tools/our-documents/guidelines/guidelines-12019-codes-conduct-and-monitoring-bodies-under_en

EDPS. (2016). *On the coherent enforcement of fundamental rights in the age of big data* (Opinion 8/2016). Retrieved July 22, 2019 https://www.huntonprivacyblog.com/wp-content/uploads/sites/28/2016/10/14-03-26_competitition_law_big_data_EN.pdf

EDPS. (2017). *Assessing the necessity of measures that limit the fundamental right to the protection of personal data: A Toolkit.* https://edps.europa.eu/sites/edp/files/publication/17-06-01_necessity_toolkit_final_en.pdf

EDPS. (2019). *Assessing the proportionality of measures that limit the fundamental rights to privacy and to the protection of personal data.* https://edps.europa.eu/sites/edp/files/publication/19-12-19_edps_proportionality_guidelines2_en.pdf

Edwards, L., & Veale, M. (2018). Enslaving the algorithm: From a 'right to an explanation' to a 'right to better decisions'? *IEEE Security and Privacy, 16*(3), 46–54. Retrieved December152019. doi:10.1109/MSP.2018.2701152

Emmons, A. (2016, August 4). *Microsoft pitches technology that can read facial expressions at political rallies.* Retrieved August 18, 2016, from https://theintercept.com/2016/08/04/microsoft-pitches-technology-that-can-read-facial-expressions-at-political-rallies/

Engels, B. (2016). Data Portability and Online Platforms The Effects on Competition. BLED 2016 Proceedings, 19–22

Engström, V., & Heikkilä, M. (2014) *Fundamental rights in the institutions and instruments of the Area of Freedom, Security and Justice.* Frame Deliverable 11.1. Retrieved from http://www.fp7-frame.eu/wp-content/uploads/2016/08/09-Deliverable-11.1.pdf

Epiney, A., & Kern, M. (2016). Zu den Neuerungen im Datenschutzrecht der Europäischen Union. Datenschutzgrundverordnung, Richtlinie zum Datenschutz in der Strafverfolgung und Implikationen für die Schweiz. In Die Revision des Datenschutzes in Europa und die Schweiz / La révision de la protection des données en Europa et la Suisse, Zürich et al., 39 et seq.

Erdos, D. (2015). Data protection confronts freedom of expression on the 'new media' internet: The stance of European regulatory authorities. *European Law Review*, 531.

Erdos, D. (2015). From the Scylla of restriction to the Charybdis of license? Exploring the scope of the 'special purposes' freedom of expression shield in European data protection. *Common Market Law Review, 52*(1), 119–154.

Ernst & Young. (2018). Retrieved, from https://www.ey.com/Publication/vwLUAssets/ey-iapp-ey-annual-privacy-gov-report-2018/$File/ey-iapp-ey-annual-privacy-gov-report-2018.pdf

ESET. (2019). *ESET Becomes Founding Member of Google's App Defense Alliance; ESET to Proactively Protect Mobile Applications on the Google Play Store.* Press Release Bratislava, Slovakia. Retrieved March 28, 2020 from: https://www.eset.com/in/about/newsroom/press-releases/announcements/eset-becomes-founding-member-of-googles-app-defense-alliance-eset-to-proactively-protect-mobile-ap-3/

Eskens, S., Helberger, N., & Moeller, J. (2017). Challenged by news personalisation: Five perspectives on the right to receive information. *Journal of Medicine and Law, 9*(2), 259–284. doi:10.1080/17577632.2017.1387353

EU Council. (2019). *Council position and findings on the application of the General Data Protection Regulation (GDPR).* https://data.consilium.europa.eu/doc/document/ST-14994-2019-REV-1/en/pdf

EU Fundamental Rights Agency (FRA), The General Data Protection Regulation – one year on: Civil society: awareness, opportunities and challenges, June 2019.

EU General Data Protection Regulation (GDPR). *Regulation, 2016*(679).

EU General Data Protection Regulation, (EU) 2016/679 of the European Parliament and of the Council of 27 April 2016 on the protection of natural persons with regard to the processing of personal data and on the free movement of such data, and repealing Directive 95/46/EC (General Data Protection Regulation), OJ 2016 L 119/1.

European Commission (1992) XXIInd Report on Competition Policy

European Commission (2009). Guidelines on the Commission's enforcement priorities in applying Article 82 of the EC Treaty to abusive exclusionary conduct by dominant undertakings, (OJ C45/02)

European Commission (2012). COM(2012) 11 final, 2012/0011, (COD) C7-0025/12, Proposal for a Regulation of the European Parliament and of the Council on the protection of individuals with regard to the processing of personal data and on the free movement of such data.

European Commission, (2004) Guidelines on the assessment of horizontal mergers under the Council Regulation on the control of concentrations between undertakings. OJ C 31/5.

European Commission, (2004). Commission Notice Guidelines on the effect on trade concept contained in Articles 81 and 82 of the Treaty, 2004/C 101/07.

European Commission, (2004). Guidelines on the Application of Article 81(3) of the Treaty. OJ C101/97

European Commission, (2011). Guidelines on the applicability of Article 101 of the Treaty on the Functioning of the European Union to horizontal cooperation agreements. OJ C 11/1

European Commission, Amended proposal for a proposal for a European Parliament and Council Regulation establishing a framework for interoperability between EU information systems (police and judicial cooperation, Asylum and Migration) and amending [Regulation (EU) 2018/XX [Eurodac Regulation], Regulation (EU) 2018/XX [Regulation on the SIS in the field of law enforcement], Regulation (EU) 2018/XX [ECRIS-TCN Regulation] and Regulation (EU) 2018/XX [eu-LISA Regulation], COM(2018) 480 final.

European Commission, Amended proposal for a Regulation of the European Parliament and of the Council establishing a framework for interoperability between EU information systems (borders and visas) and amending Council Decision 2004/512/EC, Regulation (EC) No 767/2008, Council Decision 2008/633/JHA, Regulation (EU) 2016/399, Regulation (EU) 2017/2226, Regulation (EU) 2018/XX [ETIAS Regulation], Regulation (EU) 2018/XX [Regulation on the SIS in the field of border checks] and Regulation (EU) 2018/XX [eu-LISA Regulation], COM(2018) 478 final.

European Commission, Proposal for a Directive of the European Parliament and of the Council on common standards and procedures in Member States for returning illegally staying third-country nationals (recast), COM(2018) 634 final.

European Commission, Proposal for a Regulation of the European Parliament and of the Council amending Regulation (EC) No 767/2008, Regulation (EC) No 810/2009, Regulation (EU) 2017/2226, Regulation (EU) 2016/399, Regulation (EU) 2018/XX [Interoperability Regulation] and Decision 2004/512/EC and repealing Council Decision 2008/633/JHA, COM(2018) 302 final.

European Commission, Proposal for a Regulation of the European Parliament and of the Council concerning the establishment of Eurodac for the comparison of fingerprints for the effective application of [Regulation (EU) No Regulation (EU) No 604/2013 establishing the criteria and mechanisms for determining the Member State responsible for examining an application for international protection lodged in one of the Member States by a third-country national or a stateless person], for establishing the identity of illegally staying third-country nationals or stateless persons and for determining the identity of applicants for comparison with Eurodac data by the security and law enforcement authorities of the Member States and Europol for the purposes of security and law enforcement (recast), COM(2016) 272 final.

European Commission, Proposal for a Regulation of the European Parliament and of the Council concerning the Visa Information System (VIS) and the exchange of data between Member States on short-stay visas, COM(2005) 0835 final.

European Commission, Proposal for a Regulation of the European Parliament and of the Council establishing a framework for interoperability between EU information systems (borders and visas) and amending Council Decision 2004/512/EC, Regulation (EC) No 767/2008, Council Decision 2008/633/JHA, Regulation (EU) 2016/399 and Regulation (EU) 2017/2226, COM(2017) 793 final.

European Commission, Proposal for a Regulation of the European Parliament and of the Council establishing a framework for interoperability between EU information systems (police and judicial cooperation, asylum and migration), COM(2017) 794 final.

European Commission. (2016). Proposal for a regulation of the European parliament and of the council on the establishment of 'Eurodac' for the comparison of fingerprints for the effective application of [Regulation (EU) No 604/2013 establishing the criteria and mechanisms for determining the Member State responsible for examining an application for international protection lodged in one of the Member States by a third-country national or a stateless person], for identifying an illegally staying third-country national or stateless person and on requests for the comparison with Eurodac data by Member States' law enforcement authorities and Europol for law enforcement purposes. Retrieved from https://ec.europa.eu/transparency/regdoc/rep/1/2016/EN/1-2016-272-EN-F1-1.PDF

European Commission. (n.d.). *Digital4EU 2016 – Stakeholder Forum Report*. Retrieved December 16, 2019, from https://ec.europa.eu/digital-single-market/en/news/digital4eu-2016-report

European Commission. Amended proposal for a Regulation of the European Parliament and of the Council concerning the establishment of 'EURODAC' for the comparison of fingerprints for the effective application of Regulation (EU) No (establishing the criteria and mechanisms for determining the Member State responsible for examining an application for international protection lodged in one of the Member States by a third-country national or a stateless person) and requests for comparison with EURODAC data made by law enforcement authorities of the Member States and Europol for the purpose of prosecution and amending Regulation (EU) No 1077/2011 establishing a European Agency for the operational management of large-scale IT systems in the area of freedom, security and justice, COM (2012)254 final, p. 3.

European Commission. Data protection as a trust-enabler in the EU and beyond - taking stock, COM(2019) 374 final, Brussels, 24.7.2019.

European Commission. Stronger Protection, New Opportunities: Commission Guidance on the Direct Application of the General Data Protection Regulation as of 25 May 2018, COM/2018/043 final, Brussels, 24.1.2018.

European Commission's info on Member States notifications under the GDPR.

European Convention for the Protection of Human Rights and Fundamental Freedoms, as amended by Protocols Nos. 11 and 14, 4 November 1950, Council of Europe, ETS 5

European Court of Human Rights. (2019). *Guide on Article 8 of the European Convention on Human Rights*. https://www.echr.coe.int/Documents/Guide_Art_8_ENG.pdf

European Data Protection Board. (2019). *Guidelines 2/2019, On the Processing of Personal Data under Article 6 (1)(b) in the Context of the Provision of Online Services to Data Subjects, version 2.0*. Retrieved from https://edpb.europa.eu/our-work-tools/our-documents/smernice/guidelines-22019-processing-personal-data-under-article-61b_en

European Data Protection Board. (2019). Guidelines 4/2019 on Article 25 Data Protection by Design and by Default.

European Data Protection Supervisor (2018). Opinion 5/2018 Preliminary Opinion on privacy by design

European Data Protection Supervisor (2019). Guidelines on the concepts of controller, processor and joint controllership under Regulation (EU) 2018/1725.

European Data Protection Supervisor. (2017). *Opinion 4/2017, On the Proposal for a Directive on certain aspects concerning contracts for the supply of digital content*. Retrieved from https://edps.europa.eu/sites/edp/files/publication/17-03-14_opinion_digital_content_en.pdf

European Data Protection Supervisor. (2018). *EDPS Opinion 4/2018 on the Proposals for two Regulations establishing a framework for interoperability between EU large-scale information systems*. Retrieved from https://edps.europa.eu/sites/edp/files/publication/2018-04-16_interoperability_opinion_en.pdf

European Group on Tort Law. (2005). *Principles of European Tort Law*. Retrieved from http://www.egtl.org/petl.html

European Parliament. (2019). *Understanding algorithmic decision-making: Opportunities and challenges*. Study elaborated by Claude Castelluccia and Daniel Le Métayer at the request of the Panel for the Future of Science and Technology and managed by the Scientific Foresight Unit within the Directorate-General for Parliamentary Research Services of the Secretariat of the European Parliament. Retrieved December 15, 2019, from https://www.europarl.europa.eu/thinktank/en/document.html?reference=EPRS_STU(2019)624261

European Union Agency for Fundamental Rights. (2019). *Fundamental Rights Report 2019*. Retrieved January 30, 2020 from https://fra.europa.eu/en/publication/2019/fundamental-rights-report-2019

Europe, I. (2019). Response to the EDPB's draft-guidelines on Codes of Conduct & Monitoring Bodies, Position Paper referring to Guidelines 1/2009 on Codes of Conduct & Monitoring Bodies under. *Regulation, 20116*(679). https://www.insuranceeurope.eu/sites/default/files/attachments/Response%20to%20EDPB%20draft-guidelines%20on%20codes%20of%20conduct%20%26%20monitoring%20bodies.pdf

Ezrachi, A. (2018). The Goals of EU Competition Law and the Digital Economy. *BEUC*. Retrieved October 13, 2019 https://www.beuc.eu/publications/beuc-x-2018-071_goals_of_eu_competition_law_and_digital_economy.pdf

Ezrachi, A., & Stucke, M. (2014). *The Curious Case of Competition and Quality' The curious case of competition and quality*. Oxford Legal Studies Research Paper 64/2014.

Ezratchi, A. (2017). Sponge. *Journal of Antitrust Enforcement, 5*, 49.

Federal Constitutional Court, Order of 6 November 2019, 1 BvR 276/17 -Right to be forgotten II and Order of 6 November 2019, 1 BvR 16/13 - Right to be forgotten I.

Feiler, L., Forgó, N., & Weigl, M. (2018). *The EU General Data Protection Regulation (GDPR): A Commentary*. New York, NY: Globe Law and Business.

Felzmann, H., Villaronga, E. F., Lutz, C., & Tamò-Larrieux, A. (2019). Transparency you can trust: Transparency requirements for artificial intelligence between legal norms and contextual concerns. *Data & Society*, 1-14. Retrieved January 30, 2020, from journals.sagepub.com/home/bds

Fenwick, M., Kaal, W. A., & Vermeulen, E. P. M. (2016). Regulation Tomorrow: What Happens When Technology Is Faster Than the Law? *American University Business Law Review, 6*(3). doi:10.2139srn.2834531

Ferraris, V., Bosco, F., Cafiero, G., D'Angelo, E., & Suloyeva, Y. (2013a). *The impact of profiling on fundamental rights* (Working Paper 3 of the EU Profiling Project). Retrieved May 13, 2014, from http://www.unicri.it/special_topics/citizen_profiling/PROFILINGproject_WS1_Fundamental_1110.pdf

Ferraris, V., Bosco, F., Cafiero, G., D'Angelo, E., & Suloyeva, Y. (2013b). *Defining profiling* (Working Paper 1 of the EU Profiling Project). Retrieved May 13, 2014, from: http://profiling-project.eu/wp-content/uploads/2013/07/PROFILINGproject_WS1_definition_2607.pdf

Ferretti, F. (2014). Data Protection and the Legitimate Interest of Data Controllers: Much Ado about nothing or the Winter of rights? *Common Market Law Review*, 1.

Fifield, P. (2007). Marketing Strategy Masterclass: Making Marketing Strategy Happen. Elsevier Ltd. Butterworth-Heinemann.

Fines / Penalties I General Data Protection Regulation (GDPR). (2018). Retrieved, from https://gdpr-info.eu/issues/fines-penalties/

Finocchiaro, G. (2015). La giurisprudenza della Corte di Giustizia in materia di dati personali da Google Spain a Schrems. *Diritto dell'Informazione e dell'Informatica, 779-799.*

Fishbein, M., & Ajzen, I. (1975). *Belief, attitude, intention, and behavior: An introduction to theory and research.* Reading: Addison-Wesley Publication Company.

Fornasier, M. (2015). The Impact of EU Fundamental Rights on Private Relationships: Direct or Indirect Effect? *European Review of Private Law, 29.*

Foth, M., Schusterschitz, C., & Flatscher-Thöni, M. (2012). Technology acceptance as an influencing factor of hospital employees' compliance with data-protection standards in Germany. *Journal of Public Health, 20*(3), 253–268. doi:10.100710389-011-0456-9

Fox, G., Tonge, C., Lynn, T., & Mooney, J. (2018). Communicating Compliance: Developing a GDPR Privacy Label. AMCIS 2018 Proceedings.

FRA. (2019). *Handbook on European Data Protection Law.* Luxembourg: FRA.

Francis, L., & Francis, J. (2017). *Privacy: What Everyone Needs to Know.* Oxford University Press.

Frantziou, E. (2014). Further Developments in the Right to be Forgotten: The European Court of Justice's Judgment in Case C-131/12, Google Spain, SL, Google Inc v Agencia Espanola de Proteccion de Datos. *Human Rights Law Review, 14*(4), 761–777. doi:10.1093/hrlr/ngu033

Frantziou, E. (2015). The Horizontal Effect of the Charter of Fundamental Rights of the EU: Rediscovering the Reasons for Horizontality. *European Law Journal, 21*(5), 657–679. doi:10.1111/eulj.12137

Franzoni, M. (2018). La compensatio lucri cum damno secondo la Cassazione. Responsabilità Civile e previdenza, 1092 – 1104.

Freedom of Information Request, UK ICO (Case Reference Number IRQ0856742 Aug 2019),

Friedl, P. (2019). *New laws of forgetting – The German Constitutional Court on the right to be forgotten.* Retrieved from https://europeanlawblog.eu/2019/12/12/new-laws-of-forgetting-the-german-constitutional-court-on-the-right-to-be-forgotten/

Fundamental Rights Agency. (2018). *Under watchful eyes – biometrics, EU IT-systems and fundamental rights.* Luxembourg: Publications Office of the European Union.

Fundamental Rights Agency. (2019). *Facial recognition technology: fundamental rights considerations in the context of law enforcement.* Luxembourg: Publications Office of the European Union.

Fussey, P., & Murray, D. (2019). *Independent Report on the London Metropolitan Police Service's Trial of Live Facial Recognition Technology.* Academic Press.

Gal, M. S., Elkin-Koren, N. (2016). Algorithmic consumers. *Harv JL & Tech, 44.*

Gauer, C. (2001). Does the Effectiveness of the EU Network of Competition Authorities Require a Certain Degree of Harmonisation of National Procedures and Sanctions? In C. D. Ehlemann & I. Atanasiu (Eds.), *European Competition Law Annual: The Modernisation of EC Antitrust Policy* (pp. 187–201). Hart.

GDPR - What happened? (2018). Retrieved, from https://whotracks.me/blog/gdpr-what-happened.html

GDPR Compliance Top Data Protection Priority for 92% of US Organizations in 2017, According to PwC Survey. (2017). Retrieved, from https://www.pwc.com/us/en/press-releases/2017/pwc-gdpr-compliance-press-release.html

GDPR Implementation: Updated State of play in the Member States (11/04/2019), by the Commission Expert Group on the Regulation (EU) 2016/679 and Directive (EU) 2016/680.

Gellert, R. & Gutwirth, S. (2013). The legal construction of privacy and data protection. *Computer Law & Security Review, 29,* 522-530.

Gellert, R. (2016). We have always managed risks in data protection law. Understanding the similarities and differences between the rights-based and the risk-based approaches to data protection. *European Data Protection Law Review, 2*(4), 481–492. doi:10.21552/EDPL/2016/4/7

Genç, Ö. (2019, February 5). Notes on Artificial Intelligence (AI), Machine Learning (ML) and Deep Learning (DL).... *Medium.* https://towardsdatascience.com/notes-on-artificial-intelligence-ai-machine-learning-ml-and-deep-learning-dl-for-56e51a2071c2

Georgiades, A. S. (2010). *Corporeal property law* (2nd ed.). Athens, Greece: Sakkoulas Publications.

Georgiou, E. (2018). *The law of commercial profiling* (Unpublished doctoral thesis). Brunel University, London, UK.

German Federal Data Protection Act (*Bundesdatenschutzgesetz* [BDSG] 1977, Section 35 – *lonitle Gesetz zum Schutz vor Mißbrauch personenbezogener Daten bei der Datenverarbeitung*

Gerstenberg, O. (2004). Private Law and the New European Constitutional Settlement. *European Law Journal, 10*(6), 766–786. doi:10.1111/j.1468-0386.2004.00243.x

Giannone Codiglione, G. (2018). I limiti al diritto di satira e la reputazione del cantante celebre ''caduta'' nell'oblio. Nuova Giurisprudenza Civile Commentata, 1317-1329.

Giovanis, A., Athanasopoulou, P., & Tsoukatos, E. (2016). The role of corporate image and switching barriers in the service evaluation process: Evidence from the mobile telecommunications industry. *EuroMed Journal of Business, 11*(1), 132–158. doi:10.1108/EMJB-01-2015-0002

Gömann, M. (2017). The new territorial scope of EU data protection law: Deconstructing a revolutionary achievement. *Common Market Law Review, 54*(2), 567–590.

Google Spain SL and Inc. v Agencia Española de Protección de Datos (AEPD) and Mario Costeja González (2014) C-2012:131

Google. Requests to delist content under European privacy law, Transparency report: available at https://transparencyreport.google.com/eu-privacy/overview)

Google/DoubleClick, COMP/M.4731, OJ 2008 C184/10

Granger, M.-P., & Irion, K. (2018). The right to protection of personal data: the new posterchild of European Union citizenship? In Civil Rights and EU Citizenship. Cheltenham: Edward Elgar Pub. doi:10.4337/9781788113441.00019

Gstrein, O. (2015). The cascade of decaying information: putting the 'right to be forgotten' in perspective. *Computer and Telecommunications Law Review, 40.*

Guild, E. (2009). Security and Migration in the 21st Century. Cambridge.

Gürses, S., & Hoboken, J. (2017). Privacy after the Agile Turn. In J. Polonetsky, O. Tene, & E. Selinger (Eds.), *Cambridge Handbook of Consumer Privacy. Cambridge University Press.*

Gutwirth, S. (2016). Le droit n'est pas une science mais la science juridique existe bel et bien. In G. Azzaria (Ed.), *Les nouveaux chantiers de la doctrine juridique* (pp. 1–39). Montreal: Yvon Blais /Thomson Reuters Canada.

Gutwirth, S., & Hildebrandt, M. (2010). Some caveats on profiling. In S. Gutwirth, Y. Poullet, & P. De Hert (Eds.), *Data protection in a profiled world*. Dordrecht: Springer. doi:10.1007/978-90-481-8865-9_2

Hacker, P. (2019), Regulating the Economic Impact of Data as Counter-Performance: From the Illegality Doctrine to the Unfair Contract Terms Directive, In: Sebastian Lohsse, Reiner Schulze and Dirk Staudenmayer (eds.), Data as Counter-Performance: Contract Law 2.0? (Hart/Nomos, forthcoming). Available at: Regulating the Economic Impact of Data as Counter-Performance: From the Illegality Doctrine to the Unfair Contract Terms Directive by Philipp Hacker:: SSRN

Haga, Y. (2017). Right to be Forgotten: A New Privacy Right in the Era of Internet. In *New Technology, Big Data and the Law* (pp. 97–126). Singapore: Springer. doi:10.1007/978-981-10-5038-1_5

HarzingA. W. (2007). *Publish or Perish*. https://harzing.com/resources/publish-or-perish

Harzing, A. W., & Alakangas, S. (2016). Google Scholar, Scopus and the Web of Science: A longitudinal and cross-disciplinary comparison. *Scientometrics*, *106*(2), 787–804. doi:10.100711192-015-1798-9

Hendrickx, F. (2019). Article 8 – Protection of Personal Data Frank. In F. Dorssemont, K. Lörcher, S. Clauwaert, & M. Schmitt (Eds.), *The Charter of Fundamental Rights of the European Union and the employment relation* (pp. 249–271). Oxford: Hart Publishing.

Higgins, W., & Hallström, K. T. (2007). Standardization, Globalization and Rationalities of Government. *Organization*, *14*(5), 685–704. doi:10.1177/1350508407080309

High-level Expert Group on Artificial Intelligence (AI HLEG). (2019). Ethics Guidelines for Trustworthy AI.

Hildebrandt, M., & Backhouse, J. (2005). D7.2: Descriptive analysis and inventory of profiling practices. *FIDIS consortium*. Retrieved July 14, 2014, from http://www.fidis.net/resources/deliverables/profiling/

Hildebrandt, M., Gutwirth, S., & De Hert, P. (2005, September 5). D7.4: Implications of profiling practices in democracy. *FIDIS consortium*. Retrieved July 15, 2015, from http://www.fidis.net/resources/deliverables/profiling/

Hildebrandt, M. (2006). Profiling: From data to knowledge. *Datenschutz und Datensicherheit*, *30*(9), 548–552. doi:10.100711623-006-0140-3

Hildebrandt, M. (2008). Defining profiling: A new type of knowledge? In M. Hildebrandt & S. Gutwirth (Eds.), *Profiling the European citizen: Cross-disciplinary perspectives*. Dordrecht: Springer. doi:10.1007/978-1-4020-6914-7_2

Hildebrandt, M. (2009). Who is profiling who? Invisible visibility. In S. Gutwirth, Y. Poullet, P. de Hert, C. de Terwangne, & S. Nouwt (Eds.), *Reinventing data protection?* Dordrecht: Springer Netherlands. doi:10.1007/978-1-4020-9498-9_14

Holles de Peyer, B. (2017). EU Merger Control and Big Data. *JCL& E, 767*, 769.

Hoofnagle, C. J., & Sloot, B. (2019). The European Union general data protection regulation: What it is and what it means. *Information & Communications Technology Law*, *8*(1), 65–98. doi:10.1080/13600834.2019.1573501

Horten, M. (2016). Content 'responsibility': The looking cloud of uncertainty for internet intermediaries. Center for Democracy & Technology.

Hosek, A. M., & Thompson, J. (2009). Communication privacy management and college instruction: Exploring the rules and boundaries that frame instructor private disclosures. *Communication Education*, *58*(3), 327–349. doi:10.1080/03634520902777585

How GDPR is shaping global data protection - PrivSec Report. (2018). Retrieved, from https://gdpr.report/news/2018/08/24/how-gdpr-is-shaping-global-data-protection/

Huang, C., Notten, A., & Rasters, N. (2011). Nanoscience and technology publications and patents: A review of social science studies and search strategies. *The Journal of Technology Transfer, 36*(2), 145–172. doi:10.100710961-009-9149-8

Huang, Y., Schuehle, J., Porter, A. L., & Youtie, J. (2015). A systematic method to create search strategies for emerging technologies based on the Web of Science: Illustrated for 'Big Data.'. *Scientometrics, 105*(3), 2005–2022. doi:10.100711192-015-1638-y

Hubert, P., & Combet, L. (2011). Exploitative abuse: The end of the Paradox? *Doctrines l Concurrences, 1*, 44-51.

Igglezakis, I. D. (2004). *Sensitive personal data*. Athens, Greece: Sakkoulas Publications.

Iglesias Sánchez, S. (2012). The Court and the Charter: The impact of the entry into force of the Lisbon Treaty on the ECJ's approach to fundamental rights. *Common Market Law Review*, 1565.

Implementing the GDPR in Norway. (2018). Retrieved, from https://www.wr.no/en/news/news/implementing-the-gdpr-in-norway/

Information Commissioner's Office (ICO). (2014). *Big Data and Data Protection 20140728 version: 1.0*. Retrieved July 1, 2018 from https://www.huntonprivacyblog.com/wp-content/uploads/sites/28/2016/11/big-data-and-data-protection.pdf

Information Commissioner's Office. (2016). *Guide to the General Data Protection Regulation (GDPR)*. Retrieved from https://ico.org.uk/for-organisations/guide-to-data-protection/guide-to-the-general-data-protection-regulation-gdpr/accountability-and-governance/

ISO/IEC 27701 Security techniques—Extension to ISO/IEC 27001 and ISO/IEC 27002 for privacy information management—Requirements and guidelines, (2019). https://www.iso.org/standard/71670.html

ISO/IEC 29134 Information technology—Security techniques—Guidelines for privacy impact assessment, (2017). https://www.iso.org/standard/62289.html

ITU Measuring the Information Society Report 2017. (2017) Retrieved, from https://www.itu.int/en/ITU-D/Statistics/Pages/publications/mis2017.aspx

Jarzabkowski, P., & Spee, P. A. (2009). Strategy-as-practice: A review and future directions for the field. *International Journal of Management Reviews, 11*(1), 69–95. doi:10.1111/j.1468-2370.2008.00250.x

Jasserand, C. A. (2016a). Legal Nature of Biometric Data: From 'Generic' Personal Data to Sensitive Data. *European Data Protection Law Review, 3*(3), 297–311. doi:10.21552/EDPL/2016/3/6

Jasserand, C. A. (2016b). Avoiding terminological confusion between the notions of 'biometrics' and 'biometric data': An investigation into the meanings of the terms from a European data protection and a scientific perspective. *International Data Privacy Law, 6*(1), 63–76.

Jen, W., Tu, R., & Lu, T. (2011). Managing passenger behavioral intention: An integrated framework for service quality, satisfaction, perceived value, and switching barriers. *Transportation, 38*(2), 321–342. doi:10.100711116-010-9306-9

Jia, J., Jin, G., & Wagman, L. (2019). *The Short-Run Effects of GDPR on Technology Venture Investment*. Retrieved, from https://ssrn.com/abstract=3278912

Joined Cases T-213/01 and T-214/01 Österreichische Postsparkasse and Bankfür Arbeitund Wirtschaft v Commission [2006] ECRII-1601

Joshi, A. (2018). Digital technologies for enhancing customer experience. *Sansmaran Research Journal*, 1-8.

Kagan, R. A., Gunningham, N., & Thornton, D. (2003). Explaining Corporate Environmental Performance: How Does Regulation Matter? *Law & Society Review*, *37*(1), 51–90. doi:10.1111/1540-5893.3701002

Kaisis, A. G., & Paraskevopoulos, N. A. (2001). *Personal data protection*. Athens, Greece: Sakkoulas Publications.

Kamara, I., & De Hert, P. (2018). Data Protection Certification in the EU: Possibilities, Actors and Building Blocks in a Reformed Landscape. In R. Rodrigues & V. Papakonstantinou (Eds.), Privacy and Data Protection Seals (pp. 7–34). T.M.C. Asser Press. doi:10.1007/978-94-6265-228-6_2

Kamara, I. (2017). Co-regulation in EU personal data protection: The case of technical standards and the privacy by design standardisation "mandate.". *European Journal of Law and Technology*, *8*(1). http://ejlt.org/article/view/545

Kaminski, M. (2019). Binary governance: Lessons from the GDPR's approach to algorithmic accountability. *Southern California Law Review*, *92*(6), 1529. doi:10.2139srn.3351404

Kaminski, M. E. (2019). The Right to Explanation, Explained. *Berkeley Technology Law Journal*, *34*, 189–209.

Kang, J., & Buchner, B. (2004). Privacy in Atlantis. *Harvard Journal of Law & Technology*, *18*, 229–267. Available at: https://www.researchgate.net/publication/228189643_Privacy_in_Atlantis

Karyda, M., & Mitrou, L. (2016). Data Breach Notification: Issues and Challenges for Security Management. *MCIS 2016 Proceedings*.

Kelleher, D., & Murray, K. (2018). *EU data protection law*. Dublin: Bloomsburg Professional.

Keller, D. (2017). *The Right Tools: Europe's Intermediary Liability Laws and the 2016 General Data Protection Regulation*. Available at SSRN: https://ssrn.com/abstract=2914684

Kim, S. S., & Kim, Y. J. (2017). The effect of compliance knowledge and compliance support systems on information security compliance behavior. *Journal of Knowledge Management*, *21*(4), 986–1010. doi:10.1108/JKM-08-2016-0353

Kindt, E. J. (2013). *Privacy and Data Protection Issues of Biometric Applications*. Dordrecht: Springer. doi:10.1007/978-94-007-7522-0

Kingdom of Bahrain - eGovernment Portal. (2008). Retrieved, from https://www.bahrain.bh/wps/portal/!ut/p/a1/jdDfE4FAEAfwv8VDr-3qqHg7TSlTwyByLybmHKY6k8ifLzz5Efbtdj7f2d0DBhGwLD7vRFzsZBYntzfTl-4Q9aZmagOchg7S4aTl-rZLcGxUYPEECLEroBsjY9bRdBP_y6MWWE2vVYEgQKRmb-xPHQuxT_7M1xT9OX_CM5gDe-2HvV9zBtzUfoH6PATCRyNX9Txc0WxFTAMv5huc8V0951d4WxeHYVVDBsixVIaVIuLqWqYKfIlt5LCB6lnBI-wzC6ePt2cvYpbTSuTGJy6Q!!/dl5/d5/L2dBISEvZ0FBIS9nQSEh/

Klaus, P. (2014). Towards practical relevance—Delivering superior firm performance through digital customer experience strategies. *Journal of Direct, Data and Digital Marketing Practice*, *15*(4), 306–316. doi:10.1057/dddmp.2014.20

Klimas, T., & Vaičiukaité, J. (2008). The law of recitals in European Community legislation. *ILSA Journal of International & Comparative Law*, *15*(1), 61–93.

Kloza, D., Van Dijk, N., Casiraghi, S., Vazquez Maymir, S., Roda, S., Tanas, A., & Konstantinou, I. (2019). *Towards a method for data protection impact assessment: Making sense of GDPR requirements. d.pia.lab Policy Brief No. 1/2019*. Brussels: Vrije Universiteit Brussel.

Kloza, D., Van Dijk, N., Gellert, R. M., Borocz, I. M., Tanas, A., Mantovani, E., & Quinn, P. (2017). *Data protection impact assessments in the European Union: Complementing the new legal framework towards a more robust protection of individuals*. Brussels Laboratory for Data Protection & Privacy Impact Assessments Policy Brief.

Kohnstamm, J. (2014). Privacy by debate: The European Data Protection Supervisor's contribution to collaboration between National Data Protection Authorities. In H. Hijmans & H. Kranenborg (Eds.), *Data protection anno 2014: How to restore trust? Peter Hustinx, European Data Protection Supervisor (2004–2014).* Cambridge: Intersentia Publishing Ltd.

Kokott, J., & Sobotta, C. (2017). The distinction between privacy and data protection in the jurisprudence of the CJEU and the ECtHR. *International Data Privacy Law, 7*(4), 222–228. doi:10.1093/idpl/ipt017

Koops, B-J. (2011). Forgetting footprints, shunning shadows: A critical analysis of the 'right to be forgotten' in big data practice. *Scripted*, 229.

Koops, B.-J., Newell, B., Timan, T., Škorvánek, I., Chokrevski, T., & Maša, G. (2017). A Typology of Privacy. *U. Pa. J. Int'l L., 38*, 483.

Korkein Hallinto- Oikeus Högsta Förvaltningstomstolen(The Supreme Administrative Court of Finland) 2018: ECLI:FI:KHO:2018:112

Kosseff, J. (2017). Twenty Years of Intermediary Immunity: The US Experience. *Scripted, 5.*

Kostoff, R. N., Murday, J. S., Lau, C. G. Y., & Tolles, W. M. (2006). The seminal literature of nanotechnology research. *Journal of Nanoparticle Research, 8*(2), 193–213. doi:10.100711051-005-9034-9

Kotschy, W. (2014). The proposal for a new General Data Protection Regulation—Problem solved? *International Data Privacy Law, 4*(4), 274–281. doi:10.1093/idpl/ipu022

Koutrakos, P. (2014). Editorial: To strive, to seek, to Google, to forget. *European Law Review*, 293.

Kranenborg, H. (2015). Case note: Google and the Right to be Forgotten. *European Data Protect Law*, 70.

Kranenborg. (2015). *Google and the right to be forgotten. European Data Protection Law Review, 1*(1), 70 – 79.

Kranenborg, H. (2015). Google and the right to be forgotten. *European Data Protection Law Review, 1*(1), 70–79. doi:10.21552/EDPL/2015/1/13

Krishnan, A. (2009), *What are academic disciplines? Some observations on the disciplinarity vs interdisciplinarity debate.* National Centre for Research Methods, NCRM Working Paper Series.

Kühling, J., & Buchner, B. (2017). Datenschutz-Grundverordnung. Kommentar.

Kulk, S., & Zuiderveen Borgesius, F. (2015). Freedom of Expression and 'Right to Be Forgotten' Cases in the Netherlands after Google Spain. European Data Protection Law Review, 2, 113-125.

Kulk, S., & Zuiderveen Borgesius, F. (2014). Google Spain v. González: Did the Court Forget about Freedom of Expression? *European Journal of Risk Regulation, 5*(3), 389–398. doi:10.1017/S1867299X00003949

Kumm, M. (2006). Who Is Afraid of the Total Constitution? Constitutional Rights as Principles and Constitutionalization of Private Law. *German Law Journal*, 341.

Kuner, C. (2008). Proportionality in the European Data Protection Law and its importance for data processing companies. *Privacy and Security Law Report, 7*(1615).

Kuner, C. (2014). *The Court of Justice of EU's Judgment on the 'Right to be Forgotten': An International Perspective.* https://www.ejiltalk.org/the-court-of-justice-of-eus-judgment-on-the-right-to-be-forgotten-an-international-perspective/

Kuner, C. (2013). *Transborder Data Flows and Data Privacy Law.* Oxford University Press. doi:10.1093/acprof:oso/9780199674619.001.0001

Kurtz, C., Semmann, M., & Böhmann, T. (2018). Privacy by Design to Comply with GDPR: A Review on Third-Party Data Processors. AMCIS 2018 Proceedings.

Kwiecien, H. (2006). The Primacy of European Union Law Over National Law Under the Constitutional Treaty. In P. Dann & M. Rynkowski, (Eds.), The Unity of the European Constitution (pp. 67-86). Springer. doi:10.1007/978-3-540-37721-4_5

Kȩdzior, M. (2019). GDPR and beyond - a year of changes in the data protection landscape of the European Union. *ERA Forum, 19*(4), 505–509. Retrieved December 15, 2019, from https://link.springer.com/article/10.1007/s12027-019-00549-x

Lachaud, E. (2016). Why the certification process defined in the General Data Protection Regulation cannot be successful. *Computer Law & Security Review, 32*(6), 814–826. doi:10.1016/j.clsr.2016.07.001

Lachaud, E. (2018). The General Data Protection Regulation and the rise of certification as a regulatory instrument. *Computer Law & Security Review, 34*(2), 244–256. doi:10.1016/j.clsr.2017.09.002

Ladenburger, C. (2012). *FIDE Conference 2012 Institutional Report, Brussels 2012.* https://www.fide2012.eu/ index. php?doc_id=88

Ladhari, R., Brun, I., & Morales, M. (2008). Determinants of dining satisfaction and postdining behavioral intentions. *International Journal of Hospitality Management, 27*(4), 563–573. doi:10.1016/j.ijhm.2007.07.025

Lamadrid, A. (2019). *The Bundeskartellamt's Facebook Decision- What's not to like? Well....* Received October 30, 2019 https://chillingcompetition.com/2019/02/27/the-bundeskartellamts-facebook-decision-whats-not-to-like-well/

Lamadrid, A. (2017). Competition Law as Fairness. *JIPLP, 147*, 147–148.

Lambert, P. B. (2017). *Understanding the new European data protection rules.* Boca Raton, FL: CRC Press.

Lanning, M. (2000). *Delivering Profitable Value: A Revolutionary Framework to Accelerate Growth, Generate Wealth, and Rediscover the Heart of Business.* Basic Books.

Larouche, P., & Schinkel, M. P. (2013). *Continental Drift in the Treatment of Dominant Firms: Article 102 TFEU in Contrast to § 2 Sherman Act.* TILEC Discussion Paper No. 2013-020.

Law in Brazil - DLA Piper Global Data Protection Laws of the World. (2019). Retrieved, from https://www.dlapiper-dataprotection.com/index.html?t=law&c=BR

Lazaro, C., & Le Métayer, D. (2015). Control over Personal Data: True Remedy or Fairy Tale? *Scripted, 3.*

Leboeuf, L. (2016). *Le droit européen de l'asile au défi de la confiance mutuelle.* Limal.

Leczykiewicz, D. (2013). Horizontal application of the Charter of Fundamental Rights. *European Law Review, 479.*

Lee, J. Y., Sridhar, S., Henderson, C. M., & Palmatier, R. W. (2014). *Effect of Customer-Centric Structure on Long-Term Financial Performance.* Marketing Science Articles in Advance.

Leenes, R. (2008). Regulating profiling in a democratic constitutional state. Reply: Addressing the obscurity of data clouds. In M. Hildebrandt & S. Gutwirth (Eds.), *Profiling the European citizen: Cross-disciplinary perspectives.* Dordrecht: Springer.

Lepage, A. (2017). La protection contre le numérique: les données personnelles à l'aune de la loi pour une République numérique. In Le Droit Civil à L'Ère Numérique, Actes du colloque du Master 2 Droit privé général et du Laboratoire de droit civil - Paris II - 21 avril 2017 (pp. 35-39). La Semaine Juridique, LexisNexis SA.

Leta Ambrose, M., & Ausloos, J. (2013). The right to be forgotten across the pond. *Journal of Information Policy, 1.*

Leta Ambrose, M. (2012). It's about time: Privacy, Information Lifecycles, and the Right to be Forgotten. *Stanford Technology Law Review: STLR: An Online High-Technology Law Journal from Stanford Law School*, 369.

Lodge & Wegrich. (2012). *Managing Regulation: Regulatory Analysis, Politics and Policy* (1st ed.). Palgrave Macmillan.

Lynskey, O. (2020). Delivering Data Protection: The Next Chapter. German Law Journal, 21, Special Issue 1 (20 Challenges in the EU in 2020), 80-84. Retrieved February 24, 2020, from https://www.cambridge.org/core/journals/german-law-journal/issue/20-challenges-in-the-eu-in-2020/3F9E1FEE4C3CFAC8A84DE1431108C9CC

Lynskey, O. (2014). Deconstructing data protection: The 'added-value' of a right to data protection in the EU legal order. *The International and Comparative Law Quarterly*, *63*(3), 569–597. doi:10.1017/S0020589314000244

Lynskey, O. (2015). *The foundations of EU data protection law*. Oxford, UK: Oxford University Press.

Lynskey, O. (2015). *The Foundations of EU Data Protection Law*. Oxford, UK: Oxford University Press.

Lyon, D. (2003). Surveillance as Social Sorting: Computer Codes and Mobile Bodies. In D. Lyon (Ed.), *Surveillance as Social Sorting. Privacy, Risk and Digital Discrimination* (pp. 13–30). London: Routledge.

M. L. and W. W. v Germany, European Court of Human Rights; application numbers 60798/10 and 65599/10

Macenaite, M. (2017). The "Riskification" of European Data Protection Law through a two-fold Shift. *European Journal of Risk Regulation*, *8*(3), 506–540. doi:10.1017/err.2017.40

Macnish, K. (2012). The Unblinking Eye: The Ethics of Automated Surveillance. *Ethics and Information Technology*, *14*(2), 151–167. doi:10.100710676-012-9291-0

Mahieu, R., & Hoboken, J. (2019). *Fashion-ID: introducing a phase-oriented approach to data protection?* Retrieved from https://europeanlawblog.eu

Mahieu, R., Hoboken, J., & Asghari, H. (2019). Responsibility for data protection in a networked world: On the question of the controller, "effective and complete protection" and its application to data access rights in Europe. *JIPITEC*, *10*, 85.

Malgieri, G. (2019). Automated decision-making in the EU Member States: The right to explanation and other 'suitable safeguards' in the national legislations. *Computer Law & Security Review*, *39*, 1-26. Retrieved December 08, 2019, from http://creativecommons.org/licenses/by/4.0/

Mantelero, A. (2012). Right to be forgotten ed archivi storici dei giornali. La Cassazione travisa il diritto all'oblio. Nuova giurisprudenza civile commentata, 836-849.

Mantelero, A. (2019). Comment to Articles 35 and 36. In GDPR Commentary. Edward Elgar Publishing.

Mantelero, A. (2016). Personal data for decisional purposes in the age of analytics: From an individual to a collective dimension of data protection. *Computer Law & Security Review*, *32*(2), 238–255. doi:10.1016/j.clsr.2016.01.014

Mantelero, A. (2017). Regulating big data. The guidelines of the Council of Europe in the context of the European data protection framework. *Computer Law & Security Review*, *33*(5), 584–602. doi:10.1016/j.clsr.2017.05.011

Marchant, G. E. (2011). The Growing Gap Between Emerging Technologies and the Law. In G. E. Marchant, B. R. Allenby, & J. R. Herkert (Eds.), *The Growing Gap Between Emerging Technologies and Legal-Ethical Oversight* (Vol. 7, pp. 19–33). Springer Netherlands; doi:10.1007/978-94-007-1356-7_2

Markou, C. (2015). The "right to be forgotten": Ten reasons why it should be forgotten. In S. Gutwirth, R. Leenes, & P. de Hert (Eds.), *Reforming European Data Protection Law* (pp. 203–226). Springer. doi:10.1007/978-94-017-9385-8_8

Martinez, C. O. (2015). The CJEU judgment in Google Spain: notes on its causes and perspectives on its consequences. In Protecting privacy in private international and procedural law and by data protection (pp. 45-56). Abingdon: Routledge.

Martins, P. (2018). *National Public Administrations and European Union Law. Essential Questions and Case Law*. Lisbon, Portugal: Universidade Católica Editora. (in Portuguese)

Massaro, M., Dumay, J., & Guthrie, J. (2016). On the shoulders of giants: Undertaking a structured literature review in accounting. *Accounting, Auditing & Accountability Journal*, *29*(5), 767–801. doi:10.1108/AAAJ-01-2015-1939

Max Clyde. (n.d.). *The App Defence Alliance. Android's new security initiative.* InsightPortal. Retrieved November 19, 2019, from https://www.insightportal.io/news/all-news/the-app-defence-alliance

Mayer-Schönberger, V. (2009). *Delete: The Virtue of Forgetting in the Digital Age*. Princeton University Press.

Mayer-Schönberger, V., & Padova, Y. (2016). Regime change? Enabling big data through Europe's new data protection regulation. *The Columbia Science and Technology Law Review*, *XVII*, 319.

Mazzanti, E. (2018). Processo mediatico e diritto all'oblio. Il possibile gioco di sponda tra UE e CEDU. In A. Mantelero & D. Poletti (Eds.), *Regolare la tecnologia: il Reg. UE 2016/679 e la protezione dei dati personali. Un dialogo fra Italia e Spagna* (pp. 379–394). Pisa: Pisa University Press.

McDermott Will & Emery LLP and Ponemon Institute LLC. (2018). The Race to GDPR: A Study of Companies in the United States & Europe. Ponemon Institute.

McDerpott, Y. (2017). Conceptualizing the right to data protection in an era of Big Data. *Big Data &Society (BD&S)*, *4*(1). Available at https://journals.sagepub.com/doi/full/10.1177/2053951716686994

McGoldrick, D. (2013). Developments in the Right to be Forgotten. *Human Rights Law Review*, *13*(4), 761–776. doi:10.1093/hrlr/ngt035

Medha Gore, J. (2018). Customer Life Cycle Management- Time and Beyond…-Expertise recognized by clients, Analysts like. *IOSR Journal of Business and Management, 12*(6). Retrieved from www.iosrjournals.org

Meijers Committee (2007). Note on the proposal of the JHA Council to give law enforcement authorities access to Eurodac, CM0712-IV, 18.9.2007.

Meijers Committee (2012). Note on the coordination of the relationship between the Entry Ban and the SIS-alert. An urgent need for legislative measures. CM 1203.

Mexía, P. (2016). La singular naturaleza jurídica del reglamento general de protección de datos de la UE. Sus efectos en acervo nacional sobre protección de datos. In J. Mañas (Dir.), Reglamento General De Protección De Datos. Hacia un nuevo modelo europeo de privacidade. Madrid: Reus.

Mims, C. (2018). *Who Has More of Your Personal Data Than Facebook? Try Google.* Retrieved, from https://www.wsj.com/articles/who-has-more-of-your-personal-data-than-facebook-try-google-1524398401

Mordini, E., & Tzovaras, D. (2012). *Second Generation Biometrics: The Ethical, Legal and Social Context*. Dordrecht: Springer Netherlands. doi:10.1007/978-94-007-3892-8

Mortier, R., Haddadi, H., Henderson, T., McAuley, D., & Crowcroft, J. (2014). *Human-Data interaction: The human face of the data-driven society*. Available at SSRN: https://ssrn.com/abstract=2508051

Multistakeholder expert group to support the application of Regulation (EU) 2016/679, Contribution to the stock-taking exercise of June 2019 on one year of GDPR application, 13.06.2019.

Murray, E. A. Jr. (1976). The social response process in commercial banks: An empirical investigation. *Academy of Management Review, 1*(3), 5–15. doi:10.5465/amr.1976.4400575

Nazzini, R. (2019) Privacy and Antitrust: Searching for the (Hopefully Not Yet Lost) Soul of Competition Law in the EU after the German Facebook Decision. *CPI.* Retrieved October 23, 2019 <https://www.competitionpolicyinternational.com/wp-content/uploads/2019/03/EU-News-Column-March-2019-4-Full.pdf>

Netherlands's Constitution of 1815 (with amendments through 2008). (n.d.). Retrieved from https://www.constituteproject.org/

Nissenbaum, H. (2009). Privacy in context: Technology, policy, and the integrity of social life. Stanford University Press.

Nissenbaum, H. (1998). Protecting Privacy in an Information Age: The Problem of Privacy in Public. *Law and Philosophy*, 559.

Nivarra, L. (2018). Le Sezioni Unite restituiscono un ordine auspicabilmente definitivo al discorso sulla compensatio lucri cum damno. Responsabilità Civile e Previdenza, 1160-1167.

Norway - The impact of the GDPR outside the EU I Lexology. (2019). Retrieved, from https://www.lexology.com/library/detail.aspx?g=34dfb199-c9ab-463c-8c5c-57404e1a3248

NT1 and NT2 v Google LLC (2018) EWHC 799 (QB)

Obserdorff, H. (2016). L'espace numérique et la protection des données personnelles au regard des droits fondamentaux. *Revue du Droit Public, 1*, 41–54.

Oliver, D., & Fedtke, J. Human rights in the private sphere: The scope of the project. In Oliver & Fedtke (Eds.), Human rights and the private sphere: A comparative study. Routledge.

Ooijen, I., & Vrabec, H. U. (2019). Does the GDPR Enhance Consumers' Control over Personal Data? An Analysis from a Behavioural Perspective. *Journal of Consumer Policy, 42*(1), 91-107. Retrieved December 15, 2019, from https://link.springer.com/article/10.1007/s10603-018-9399-7

Opinion of Advocate General Jääskinen in June 2013, the court in the case of Google Spain SL Google Inc. v Agencia Española de Protección de Datos (AEPD) and Mario Costeja González

Opinion of Advocate General Szpunar in 10 January 2019 in the case of Google Inc. v Commission nationale de l'Informatique et des Libertés C-2017; ECLI:EU:C:2019:15).

Pajuste, T. (2019). The Protection of Personal Data in a Digital Society: The Role of the GDPR. In M. Susi (Ed.), *Human Rights, Digital Society and the Law: A Research Companion* (pp. 303–315). London: Routledge. doi:10.4324/9781351025386-21

Palazzolo, N. (2019). L'hosting provider tra libertà di impresa, diritto di critica e tutela della reputazione professionale. Diritto dell'Internet, 520-529.

Panama - The impact of the GDPR outside the EU I Lexology. (2019). Retrieved, from https://www.lexology.com/library/detail.aspx?g=e138a075-95e2-4959-8498-696967e63d18

Panama Data Protection Law: much lower fines than GDPR. (2019). Retrieved, from https://www.interact.law/news/panama-data-protection-law-much-lower-fines-than-gdpr/

Panama: New Law on Protection of Personal Data. (2019). Retrieved, from https://sites.morimor.com/newmorimor/panama-new-law-on-protection-of-personal-data/

Pardolesi, R. (2016) Diritto all'oblio, cronaca in libertà vigilata e memoria storica a rischio. Foro it., 1, 2734-2737.

Pardolesi, R., & Bonavita, S. (2018). Diritto all'oblio e buio a mezzogiorno. Foro it., 1, 1151-1190

Parsons, K., McCormac, A., Butavicius, M., Pattinson, M., & Jerram, C. (2014). Determining employee awareness using the Human Aspects of Information Security Questionnaire (HAIS-Q). *Computers & Security, 42,* 165–176. doi:10.1016/j. cose.2013.12.003

Peers, S., & Rogers, N. (2006). EU Immigration and Asylum Law: Text and Commentary. Academic Press.

Peers, S. (2016). *EU Justice and Home Affairs Law* (4th ed.). Oxford. doi:10.1093/acprof:oso/9780198776840.001.0001

Peron, S. (n.d.). Il giornalismo d'inchiesta. Giurisprudenza Civile e Previdenza, 2257-2267.

Petkov, P., & Helfert, M. (2017). Identifying Emerging Challenges for ICT industry in Ireland: Multiple Case Study Analysis of Data Privacy Breaches. AMCIS 2017 Proceedings.

Petronio, S. (1991). Communication boundary management: A theoretical model of managing disclosure of private information between marital couples. *Communication Theory, 1*(4), 311–335. doi:10.1111/j.1468-2885.1991.tb00023.x

Pfisterer, V. (2019). The Right to Privacy – A Fundamental Right in Search of Its Identity: Uncovering the CJEU's Flawed Concept of the Right to Privacy. *German Law Journal, 20*(5), 722–733. doi:10.1017/glj.2019.57

Polatateş, S. (n.d.). *Path to Digital Transformation: Key Digital Indicators.* LearnTips is Portal for SAP Information Services and the Expert Articles, SAP Tips and Tricks. Retrieved February, 20, from: http://www.learntips.net/path-to-digital-transformation-key-digital-indicators/

Pollicino, O. (2014). Diritto all'oblio e conservazione di dati. La Corte di giustizia a piedi uniti: verso un digital right to privacy. Giurisprudenza Costituzionale, 59, 2949-2958.

Pollicino, O. (2019). L'autunno caldo della Corte di giustizia in tema di tutela dei diritti fondamentali in rete e le sfide del costituzionalismo alle prese con i nuovi poteri privati in ambito digitale. *Federalismi.* Retrieved at https://federalismi. it/ApplOpenFilePDF.cfm?eid=533&dpath=editoriale&dfile=EDITORIALE%5F16102019201440%2Epdf&content= L%27%2B%27%27autunno%2Bcaldo%27%27%2Bdella%2BCorte%2Bdi%2Bgiustizia%2Bin%2Btema%2Bdi%2Btute la%2Bdei%2Bdiritti%2Bfondamentali%2Bin%2Brete%2Be%2Ble%2Bsfide%2Bdel%2Bcostituzionalismo%2Balle%2 Bprese%2Bcon%2Bi%2Bnuovi%2Bpoteri%2Bprivati%2Bin%2Bambito%2Bdigitale&content_auth=%3Cb%3EOreste %2BPollicino%3C%2Fb%3E

Post, R. (2017). Data Privacy and Dignitary Privacy: Google Spain, the Right to Be Forgotten, and the Construction of the Public Sphere. *Duke Law Journal.* Available at SSRN: https://papers.ssrn.com/sol3/papers.cfm?abstract_id=2953468

Poullet, Y. (2010). About the e-Privacy Directive: Towards a third generation of data protection legislation? In S. Gutwirth, Y. Poullet, & P. De Hert (Eds.), *Data protection in a profiled world.* Dordrecht: Springer. doi:10.1007/978-90-481-8865-9_1

Prechal, S. (2007). Direct Effect, Indirect Effect, Supremacy and the Evolving Constitution of the European Union. In C. Barnard (Ed.), *The Fundamentals of EU Law Revisited: Assessing the Impact of the Constitutional Debate* (pp. 35–71). Oxford, UK: Oxford University Press. doi:10.1093/acprof:oso/9780199226221.003.0003

Press corner. (2019). Retrieved, from https://ec.europa.eu/commission/presscorner/detail/en/IP_19_4449

Press release; Viviane Redding, Vice President European Commission, EU, The EU Data Protection Reform 2012 'Making Europe the Standard Setter for Modern Data Protection Rules in the Digital Age 2; eu europa eu rapid press-release)

Prins, C. (2006). Property and Privacy: European Perspectives and the Commodification of Our Identity. *Information Law Series, 16,* 223-257. Available at SSRN: https://ssrn.com/abstract=929668

Progin-Theuerkauf, S. (2019). The EU Return Directive - Retour à la "case depart"? *Sui-generis*, p. 32. https://sui-generis.ch/article/view/sg.91/1026

Protocol amending the Convention for the Protection of Individuals with regard to Automatic Processing of Personal Data, ETS No. 223.

Purtova, N. (2009). Property rights in personal data: Learning from the American discourse. *Computer Law & Security Review, 25*(6), 507–521. doi:10.1016/j.clsr.2009.09.004

Purtova, N. (2018). The law of everything. Broad concept of personal data and future of EU data protection law. *Law, Innovation and Technology, 10*(1), 40–81. doi:10.1080/17579961.2018.1452176

Quelle, C. (2017). The risk revolution in EU data protection law: We can't have our cake and eat it, too. In R. Leenes, R. van Brakel, S. Gutwirth, & P. De Hert (Eds.), *Data protection and privacy: The age of intelligent machines* (1st ed.). Hart Publishing.

Quelle, C. (2018). Enhancing Compliance under the General Data Protection Regulation: The Risky Upshot of the Accountability- and Risk-based Approach. *European Journal of Risk Regulation, 9*(3), 502–526. doi:10.1017/err.2018.47

R (Pearson) v DVLA (2002) UK EWHC 2482

Raab, C. D. (2013). *Privacy as a security value. Jon Bing: En Hyllest A Tribute.* Available at SSRN: https://ssrn.com/abstract=3057433

Recommendation Rec(89)2 of the Committee of Ministers to member States on the protection of personal data used for employment purposes.

Recommendation Rec(97)5 of the Committee of Ministers to member States on the protection of medical data.

Rees, C., & Heywood, D. (2014) The 'right to be forgotten' or the 'principle that has been remembered'. *CLSR*, 574.

Register of Commission Expert Groups and Other Similar Entities. (2019). *Publication manual of the American Psychological Association.* Brussel: Multistakeholder expert group to support the application of Regulation (EU) 2016/679 (main group). Retrieved February 25, 2020 from: https://ec.europa.eu/transparency/regexpert/index.cfm?do=groupDetail.groupMeeting&meetingId=15670

Regulation (EC) No 1987/2006 of the European Parliament and of the Council of 20.12.2006 on the establishment, operation and use of the second generation Schengen Information System (SIS II), OJ L 381, 28.12.2006, p. 4-23.

Regulation (EC) No 562/2006 of the European Parliament and of the Council of 15.3.2006 establishing a Community Code on the rules governing the movement of persons across borders (Schengen Borders Code), OJ L 105, 13.4.2006, p. 1.

Regulation (EC) No 767/2008 of the European Parliament and of the Council of 9.7.2008 concerning the Visa Information System (VIS) and the exchange of data between Member States on short-stay visas (VIS Regulation), OJ L 218, 13.8.2008, p. 60-81.

Regulation (EU) 2016/679 of the European Parliament and of the Council of 27 April 2016 on the Protection of Natural Persons with Regard to the Processing of Personal Data and on the Free Movement of Such Data, and Repealing Directive 95/46/EC (General Data Protection Regulation) Article 29 Working Party, 'Opinion No. 03/2013 on Purpose Limitation' adopted on 2nd April 2013 (00569/13/EN WP 203) Article 29 Working Party, 'Opinion No. 4/2007 on the Concept of Personal Data', adopted on 20th June 2007 (01248/07/EN, WP 136)

Regulation (EU) 2016/679 of the European Parliament and of the Council of 27 April 2016 on the protection of natural persons with regard to the processing of personal data and on the free movement of such data, and repealing Directive 95/46/EC (General Data Protection Regulation). Corrigendum. Latest consolidated version.

Regulation (EU) 2016/679 of the European Parliament and of the Council of 27 April 2016 on the protection of natural persons with regard to the processing of personal data and on the free movement of such data, and repealing Directive 95/46/EC, OJ L 119/1, European Parliament, Council (2016). https://eur-lex.europa.eu/eli/reg/2016/679/oj

Regulation (EU) 2016/679 of the European Parliament and of the Council of 27 April 2016 on the protection of natural persons with regard to the processing of personal data and on the free movement of such data, and repealing Directive 95/46/EC.

Regulation (EU) 2016/679 of the European Parliament and of the Council of 27.4.2016 on the protection of individuals with regard to the processing of personal data, on the free movement of such data and repealing Directive 95/46/EC (general data protection regulation), OJ L 119, 4.5.2016, p. 1-88.

Regulation (EU) 2017/2226 of the European Parliament and of the Council of 30.11.2017 on an entry/exit system (EES) for the collection of entry and exit data and data on refusal of entry of third-country nationals at the external borders of the Member States and laying down the conditions for access to the EES for security and law enforcement purposes and amending the Convention implementing the Schengen Agreement and Regulations (EC) No 767/2008 and (EU) No 1077/2011, OJ L 327, 9.12.2017, 20; Regulation (EU) 2017/2225 of the European Parliament and of the Council of 30.11.2017 amending Regulation (EU) 2016/399 as regards use of the entry/exit system, OJ L 327, 9.12.2017, 1.

Regulation (EU) 2018/1240 of the European Parliament and of the Council of 12.9.2018 concerning the establishment of the European Travel Information and Authorisation System (ETIAS) and amending Regulations (EU) No 1077/2011, (EU) No 515/2014, (EU) 2016/399, (EU) 2016/1624 and (EU) 2017/2226, OJ L 226, 30.9.2018, p. 1. OJ L 236, 19.9.2018, p. 1-71.

Regulation (EU) 2018/1241 of the European Parliament and of the Council of 12.9.2018 amending Regulation (EU) 2016/794 for the purpose of establishing a European Travel Information and Authorisation System (ETIAS), OJ L 236, 19.9.2018, p. 1-71.

Regulation (EU) 2018/1725 of the European Parliament and of the Council of 23.10.2018 on the protection of individuals with regard to the processing of personal data by the Union institutions, bodies, offices and agencies, on the free movement of such data and repealing Regulation (EC) No 45/2001 and Decision No 1247/2002/EC (Text with EEA relevance), OJ L 295, 21.11.2018, p. 39-98.

Regulation (EU) 2018/1860 of the European Parliament and of the Council of 28.11.2018 on the use of the Schengen Information System for the return of illegally staying third-country nationals, OJ L 312, 7.12.2018, p. 14-55. OJ L 312, 7.12.2018, p. 1-13.

Regulation (EU) 2018/1861 of the European Parliament and of the Council of 28.11.2018 on the establishment, operation and use of the Schengen Information System (SIS) as regards border controls, amending the Convention implementing the Schengen Agreement and amending and repealing Regulation (EC) No 1987/2006, OJ L 312, 7.12.2018, p. 14-55.

Regulation (EU) 2018/1862 of the European Parliament and of the Council of 28.11.2018 on the establishment, operation and use of the Schengen Information System (SIS) in the field of police cooperation and judicial cooperation in criminal matters, amending and repealing Council Decision 2007/533/JHA and repealing Regulation (EC) No 1986/2006 of the European Parliament and of the Council and Commission Decision 2010/261/EU, OJ L 312, 7.12.2018, p. 56-106.

Regulation (EU) 2019/816 of the European Parliament and of the Council of 17.4.2019 establishing a centralized system for the identification of Member States where information on convictions of third country nationals and stateless persons (ECRIS-TCN) is available, supplementing the European Criminal Records Information System and amending Regulation (EU) 2018/1726, OJ L 135, 22.5.2019, p. 1-26.

Regulation (EU) 2019/817 of the European Parliament and of the Council of 20 May 2019 establishing a framework for interoperability between EU information systems in the fields of borders and visas and amending Regulations (EC) No 767/2008, (EU) 2016/399, (EU) 2017/2226, (EU) 2018/1240, (EU) 2018/1726 and (EU) 2018/1861 of the European Parliament and of the Council, Council Decision 2004/512/EC and Council Decision 2008/633/JHA, OJ L 135/27.

Regulation (EU) 2019/818 of the European Parliament and of the Council of 20 May 2019 on establishing a framework for interoperability between EU information systems in the field of police and judicial cooperation, asylum and migration and amending Regulations (EU) 2018/1726, (EU) 2018/1862 and (EU) 2019/816, OJ L 135/85.

Regulation (EU) No 1077/2011 of the European Parliament and of the Council of 25.10.2011 establishing a European Agency for the operational management of large-scale IT systems in the area of freedom, security and justice, OJ L 286, 1.11.2011, p. 1-17. The Regulation has since been replaced by Regulation (EU) 2018/1726 of the European Parliament and of the Council of 14 November 2018, p. 39.11.2018 on the European Union Agency for the operational management of large-scale IT systems in the area of freedom, security and justice (eu-LISA), amending Council Regulation (EC) No 1987/2006 and Decision 2007/533/JHA and repealing Regulation (EU) No 1077/2011, OJ L 295, 21.11.2018, p. 99-137.

Regulation (EU) No 603/2013 of the European Parliament and of the Council of 26 June 2013 on the establishment of 'Eurodac' for the comparison of fingerprints for the effective application of Regulation (EU) No 604/2013 establishing the criteria and mechanisms for determining the Member State responsible for examining an application for international protection lodged in one of the Member States by a third-country national or a stateless person and on requests for the comparison with Eurodac data by Member States' law enforcement authorities and Europol for law enforcement purposes, and amending Regulation (EU) No 1077/2011 establishing a European Agency for the operational management of large-scale IT systems in the area of freedom, security and justice, OJ L 180, 29.6.2013, p. 1–30

Rehabilitation of Offenders Act 1974 c-53

Reid, D. A., Samangooei, S., Chen, C., Nixon, M. S., & Ross, A. (2013). Soft Biometrics for Surveillance: An Overview. In V. G. C. R. Rao (Ed.), *Handbook of Statistics* (pp. 327–352). Amsterdam, The Netherlands: Elsevier.

Renaud, K., Flowerday, S., Warkentin, M., Cockshott, P., & Orgeron, C. (2018). Is the responsibilization of the cyber security risk reasonable and judicious? - ScienceDirect. *Computers & Security*, 78, 198–211. doi:10.1016/j.cose.2018.06.006

ReNEUAL. (2014). *Model Rules on EU Administrative Procedures, Book VI – Administrative Information Management, Drafting Team: Diana-Urania Galetta and al.* Retrieved December 15, 2019, from http://www.reneual.eu/

Resta, G., & Zeno Zencovich, V. (Eds.). (2015). *Il diritto all'oblio su Internet dopo la sentenza Google Spain*. Roma: Romatrepress.

Riccio, G. M. (2017). Il difficile equilibrio tra diritto all'oblio e diritto di cronaca. Nuova Giurisprudenza civile Commentata, 4, 549-559.

Richard, J. (2016). Le numérique et les données personnelles: quels risques, quelles potentialités? *Revue du droit public, 1*, 87-100.

Rimbert, P. (2016). Socialize our digital labour: No such thing as free data. How do the world's suppliers of online data –anybody using a smartphone- get to share in the wealth they generate? (C. Goulden, Trans.). *Le Monde Diplomatique*. Retrieved from https://mondediplo.com/2016/09/09digitallabor

Rizzuti, M. (2016). Il diritto e l'oblio. Corriere Giuridico, 8-9, 1072-1082.

Roberts, J. J. (2018). The GDPR Is in Effect: Should U.S. Companies Be Afraid? *Fortune.com*. https://fortune.com/2018/05/24/the-gdpr-is-in-effect-should-u-s-companies-be-afraid/

Roosendaal, A. (2013). Digital personae and profiles in law: Protecting individuals' rights in online contexts. Nijmegen: Wolf Legal Publishers (WLP).

Rosen, J. (2012). The right to be forgotten. *Stanford Law Review Online*, 88.

Ross M. (2018, August 1). *The path to customer centricity*. Internet retailing. Retrieved March 26, 2020 from: https://internetretailing.net/magazine-articles/magazine-articles/the-path-to-customer-centricity

Rouvroy, A. (2008). Privacy, data protection, and the unprecedented challenges of ambient intelligence. *Studies in Ethics, Law, and Technology*, *2*(1). doi:10.2202/1941-6008.1001

Rubinfield, D., & Gal, M. (2017). Access Barriers to Big Data. *Arizona Law Review*, *340*, 350.

Russell, K. D., O'Raghallaigh, P., O'Reilly, P., & Hayes, J. (2018). Digital Privacy GDPR: A Proposed Digital Transformation Framework. AMCIS 2018 Proceedings.

SamonteM. (n.d.). europeanlawblog.eu/2019/10/29/google-v-cnil-case-c-507-17-the-territorial-scope-of-the-right-to-be-forgotten-under-eu-law/

Sartor, G. (2013). Providers' Liabilities in the new EU Data Protection Regulation: A threat to Internet Freedoms? *International Data Privacy Law*, 3.

Sartor, G. (2015). The right to be forgotten in the Draft Data Protection Regulation. *International Data Privacy Law*, 64.

Schermer, B. (2011). The limits of privacy in automated profiling and data mining. *Computer Law & Security Review*, *27*(1), 45–52. doi:10.1016/j.clsr.2010.11.009

Schermer, B. (2013). Risks of profiling and the limits of data protection law. In B. Custers, T. Calders, B. Schermer, & T. Zarsky (Eds.), *Discrimination and privacy in the information society: Data mining in large databases*. Dordrecht: Springer. doi:10.1007/978-3-642-30487-3_7

Schneider, G. (2018). Testing Art. 102 TFEU in the Digital Marketplace: Insights from the Bundeskartellamt's investigation against Facebook. *Journal of European Competition Law & Practice.*

Scholta, H., Mertens, W., Kowalkiewicz, M., & Becker, J. (2019). From one-stop shop to no-stop: An e-government stage model. *Government Information Quarterly*, *36*(1), 11–26. doi:10.1016/j.giq.2018.11.010

Schreurs, W., Hildebrandt, M., Gasson, M., & Warwick, K. (2005). D7.3: Report on actual and possible profiling techniques in the field of ambient intelligence. *FIDIS consortium*. Retrieved July 3, 2018, from http://www.fidis.net/resources/deliverables/profiling/

Schreurs, W., Hildebrandt, M., Kindt, E., & Vanfleteren, M. (2008). Cogitas, ergo sum: The role of data protection and non-discrimination law in group profiling in the private sector. In M. Hildebrandt & S. Gutwirth (Eds.), *Profiling the European citizen: Cross-disciplinary perspectives*. Dordrecht: Springer. doi:10.1007/978-1-4020-6914-7_13

Schumpeter, J. (1954). *Capitalism, Socialism, and Democracy*. George Allen & Unwin.

Schwartz, P. M. (2003). Property, Privacy and Personal Data, 117. *Harvard Law Review*, 2056–2128. Retrieved from https://pdfs.semanticscholAr.org/8d8d/e4cb107a627c7c7b0da9076248ed1e3b28b4.pdf

Scott, M. (2016). Europe Tried to Rein In Google. It Backfired. *The New York Times*. https://www.nytimes.com/2016/04/19/technology/google-europe-privacy-watchdog.html

Scott, J. (2014). Extraterritoriality and territorial extension in EU law. *The American Journal of Comparative Law, 62*(1), 87–125. doi:10.5131/AJCL.2013.0009

Senigaglia, R. (2017). Reg. UE 2016/679 e diritto all'oblio nella comunicazione telematica. Identità, informazione e trasparenza nell'ordine della dignità personale. Nuove Leggi Civili Commentate, 5, 1023-1061.

Shackelford, S. (2012). Fragile Merchandise: A Comparative Analysis of the Privacy Rights for Public Figures. *American Business Law Journal, 49*(1), 125–208. doi:10.1111/j.1744-1714.2011.01129.x

Shamir, R. (2008). The age of responsibilization: On market-embedded morality. *Economy and Society, 37*(1), 1–19. doi:10.1080/03085140701760833

Shima, B. (2015). EU Fundamental Rights and Member State Action after Lisbon: Putting the ECJ's Case Law in its Context. *Fordham International Law Journal*, 1095.

Singleton, S. (2015). Balancing a right to be forgotten with a right to freedom of expression in the wake of Google Spain v. AEPD. *Georgia Journal of International and Comparative Law, 44*(1), 165-193.

Sirene Manual, Commission Decision 2017/115/EU of 31.8.2017 replacing the Annex to Decision 2013/115/EU on the Sirene Manual and other implementing measures for the second generation Schengen Information System (SIS II), OJ L 231, 7.9.2017, p. 6-51.

Sirotti Gaudenzi, A. (2018). Diritto all'oblio e diritto all'informazione: un difficile equilibrio. Corriere Giuridico, 8-9, 1107-1114.

Sloot van der, B. (2016). The practical and theoretical problems with 'balancing': Delfi, Coty and the Redundancy of the Human Rights Framework. *MJ*, 439.

Sobhani, M., & Saxon, L. (2019). All our data is health data. *Medium*. https://medium.com/@usccbc/all-our-data-is-health-data-57d3cf0f336d

Sohn, H. K., Lee, T. J., & Yoon, Y. S. (2016). Relationship between perceived risk, evaluation, satisfaction, and behavioral intention: A case of local-festival visitors. *Journal of Travel & Tourism Marketing, 33*(1), 28–45. doi:10.1080/10548408.2015.1024912

Solove, D. (2015, November 13). *The Growing Problems with the Sectoral Approach to Privacy Law*. https://teachprivacy.com/problems-sectoral-approach-privacy-law/

Solove, D. (2013). Privacy self-management and the consent dilemma. *Harvard Law Review*, 126, 1880.

Solove, D. J. (2002). Conceptualizing Privacy. *California Law Review, 90*(4), 2. doi:10.2307/3481326

Solove, D. J. (2006). A Taxonomy of Privacy. *University of Pennsylvania Law Review, 154*(3), 477. doi:10.2307/40041279

Solove, D. J. (2008). *Understanding privacy*. Harvard University Press.

Soro, A. (2019). Oblio, identità e memoria. Diritto dell'Internet, 1, 3-6.

Sörvik, J., & Kleibrink, A. (2016). *Mapping EU investments in ICT - description of an online tool and initial observations*. Report number: JRC102233Affiliation: European Commission, Joint Research Centre, Institute for Prospective Technological Studies. Project: Smart Specialisation Platform.

Spanish Constitution of 1978 with Amendments through 2011. (n.d.). Retrieved from http://www.senado.es/web/conocersenado/normas/constitucion/index.html?lang=en

Spiecker genannt Döhmann, I. (2015). A new framework for information markets: Google Spain Case C-131/12, Google Spain SL, Google Inc. v. Agencia Española de Protección de Datos (AEPD), Mario Costeja Gonzáles, Judgment of the Courtof Justice (Grand Chamber) of 13 May 2014, EU:C:2014:317CMLR,1053. *Common Market Law Review*, 1033.

Spiekermann-Hoff, S., & Novotny, A. (2015). A vision for global bridges: Technical and legal measures for international data markets. *Computer Law and Security Review, 31*(2), *181-200*. Available at: https://epub.wu.ac.at/5485/

Spiropoulos, F., Kontiadis, X., Anthopoulos, X., & Gerapetritis, G. (Eds.). (2017). *The Constitution: Articles' Interpretation*. Athens, Greece: Sakkoulas Publications.

Stathopoulos, M. (2000). The usage of personal data and the combat in the field of liberties acknowledged both to controllers and to data subjects. *Legal Pontium, 48*, 1–19.

Stradella, E. (2017). Brevi note su memoria e oblio in rete, a partire dal regolamento UE 2016/679. In P. Passaglia & D. Poletti (Eds.), *Nodi virtuali, legami informali: Internet alla ricerca di regole* (pp. 87–100). Pisa: Pisa University Press.

Sugimoto, C. R., & Weingart, S. (2015). The kaleidoscope of disciplinarity. *The Journal of Documentation, 71*(4), 775–794. doi:10.1108/JD-06-2014-0082

SuperOffice AS. (2017). *GDPR Compliance in SuperOffice CRM*. Vismagic Software Solutions, The Boatshed, Steamer Quay Road, Totnes. Retrieved March 26, 2020 from: https://static1.squarespace.com/static/571649f9f85082a0a4edbbda/t/59fb13e5f9619ac07aac2823/1509626863243/superoffice-gdpr-compliance-whitepaper.pdf

Surblyte, G. (2016). *Data as a Digital Resource*. Max Planck Institute for Innovation & Competition Research Paper No. 16-12. Available at SSRN: https://ssrn.com/abstract=2849303

Svantesson, D. (2012). Extraterritoriality in the context of data privacy regulation. *Masaryk University Journal of Law and Technology, 7*(1), 87–96.

Switzerland's Constitution of 1999 (with amendments through 2014). (n.d.). Retrieved from https://www.constituteproject.org/

Tambou, O. (2018). National Adaptations of the GDPR. Opening Remarks. In *National Adaptations of the GDPR* (pp. 24-27). Blogdroiteuropéen. Retrieved December 15, 2019, from https://wp.me/p6OBGR-3dP

Tamò-Larrieux, A. (2018). *Designing for Privacy and its Legal Framework: Data Protection by Design and Default for the Internet of Things (Law, Governance and Technology Series)*. Cham, Switzerland: Springer International Publishing AG. doi:10.1007/978-3-319-98624-1

Tannert, C. (2016). *Could your personal data subsidize the cost of a new car?* Retrieved from http://www.thedrive.com/tech/4457/could-your-personal-data-subsidize-the-cost-of-a-new-car

Tassis, S. (2013). Privacy as a field of a commercial dispute between the EU and USA. *Media and Communication Law, 1*, 46–57.

Taylor, D. (2018). *GDPR – territorial scope and the need to avoid absurd and inconsistent results*. Retrieved from http://www.circleid.com/posts/20180214_gdpr_territorial_scope_need_to_avoid_absurd_inconsistent_results/

Taylor, M. (2017). The Misunderstood Implementation of a Landmark Decision and How Public International Law Could Offer Guidance. *European Data Protection Law Review, 3*(2), 196–208.

Telefónica UK/Vodafone UK/Everything Everywhere/JV, No COMP/M.6314, 4 September 2012

Tene, O., & Wolf, C. (2013). *Overextended: Jurisdiction and applicable law under the EU General Data Protection Regulation*. The Future of Privacy Forum White Papers, no. 1.

Tene, O. (2013). Privacy law's midlife crisis: A critical assessment of the second wave of global privacy laws. *Ohio State Law Journal*, 74, 1217.

The Constitution of Bahrain. (2002) Retrieved, from https://www.bahrain.bh/wps/wcm/connect/d749d20a-7545-4900-b64c-5443e6c20cd6/CA9SS7XP.pdf?MOD=AJPERES

The Direct Marketing Association (UK) Ltd. (2018). *Data privacy: What the consumer really thinks, 2018-February.* DMA (UK) Ltd.

The Economist. (2017, May 6). The World's Most Valuable Resource Is No Longer Oil, But Data. *The Economist.*

The EU General Data Protection Regulation (GDPR): a practical guide. (n.d.). Cham, Switzerland: Springer International Publishing AG.

Thibodeau, P. (2014). *The Internet of Things Could Encroach on Personal Privacy.* Retrieved October 2, 2019 https://www.computerworld.com/article/2488949/emerging-technology/the-internet-of-things-could-encroach-on-personal-privacy.htm

Thierer, A. (2018, August 16). The Pacing Problem, the Collingridge Dilemma & Technological Determinism. *Technology Liberation Front.* https://techliberation.com/2018/08/16/the-pacing-problem-the-collingridge-dilemma-technological-determinism/

Thomas, K., Li, F., Zand, A., Barrett, J., Ranieri, J., Invernizzi, L., … Bursztein, E. (2017). Data breaches, phishing, or malware? Understanding the risks of stolen credentials. CCS'17 Proceedings.

Tjin Tai, T. (2016). The right to be forgotten – private law enforcement. *International Review of Law Computers & Technology, 30*(1-2), 76–83. doi:10.1080/13600869.2016.1138628

TomTom/Tele Atlas, Case No COMP/M.4854, Decision of 14.5.2008

Torremans, P. (1996). Extraterritorial application of E.C. and U.S. competition law. *European Law Review, 21*(4), 280–293.

Townley, C. (2009). *Article 81 EC and Public Policy.* Oxford: Hart Publishing.

Treaty on the Functioning of the European Union (TFEU), consolidated version, OJ C 326/47.

Tsoukatos, E., & Rand, G. K. (2006). Path analysis of perceived service quality, satisfaction and loyalty in Greek insurance. *Managing Service Quality, 16*(5), 501–519. doi:10.1108/09604520610686746

Turner, J. (2018). *Robot rules.* Springer Berlin Heidelberg.

Tushnet, M. (2003). The Issue of State Action/Horizontal Effect in Comparative Constitutional Law. *International Journal of Constitutional Law, 1*(1), 79–98. doi:10.1093/icon/1.1.79

Tzanou, M. (2010). Balancing Fundamental Rights: United in Diversity? Some Reflections on the Recent Case Law of the European Court of Justice on Data Protection. *CYELP*, 53.

Tzanou, M. (2013). Data protection as a fundamental right next to privacy? 'Reconstructing' a not so new right. *International Data Privacy Law,* 88.

Tzanou, M. (2011). Data protection in EU law: An analysis of the EU legal framework and the ECJ jurisprudence. In C. Akrivopoulou & A. Psygkas (Eds.), *Personal data privacy and protection in a surveillance era: Technologies and practices* (pp. 273–297). Hershey, PA: Information Science Reference. doi:10.4018/978-1-60960-083-9.ch016

Tzanou, M. (2017). *The Fundamental Right to Data Protection: Normative Value in the Context of Counter-Terrorism Surveillance*. Oxford: Hart Publishing.

UNCTAD | Data Protection and Privacy Legislation Worldwide. (2019). Retrieved, from https://unctad.org/en/Pages/DTL/STI_and_ICTs/ICT4D-Legislation/eCom-Data-Protection-Laws.aspx

UNCTAD. (in press). *Digital economy report 2019. Value creation and capture: Implications for developing countries.* UNCTAD.

United States Supreme Court. (1976). United States v. *Miller, 425*, 437.

van Alsenoy, B. (2019). *Data Protection Law in the EU: Roles, Responsibilities and Liability.* Intersentia. doi:10.1017/9781780688459

Van Calster, G. (2015). *Regulating the Internet: Prescriptive and jurisdictional boundaries to the EU's right to be forgotten.* Retrieved from https://papers.ssrn.com/sol3/papers.cfm?abstract_id=2686111

Van der Sloot, B., & de Groot, A. (Eds.). (2019). *The Handbook of Privacy Studies: An Interdisciplinary Introduction.* Amsterdam University Press.

Van Dijck, J. (2013). *The culture of connectivity: A critical history of social media.* Oxford University Press. doi:10.1093/acprof:oso/9780199970773.001.0001

Van Dijck, J., Poell, T., & de Waal, M. (2018). *The platform society: Public values in a connective world.* Oxford: Oxford University Press. doi:10.1093/oso/9780190889760.001.0001

van Dijk, N., Gellert, R., & Rommetveit, K. (2016). A risk to a right? Beyond data protection risk assessments. *Computer Law & Security Review, 32*(2), 286–306. doi:10.1016/j.clsr.2015.12.017

Van Eck, N. J., Waltman, L., Noyons, E. C. M., & Buter, R. K. (2010). Automatic term identification for bibliometric mapping. *Scientometrics, 82*(3), 581–596. doi:10.100711192-010-0173-0 PMID:20234767

Vanclay, F. (2015). *Social Impact Assessment: Guidance for assessing and managing the social impacts of projects.* Fargo, ND: International Association for Impact Assessment.

Veccini, C. (2018, June). *GDPR and CRM: How to Manage Customer Data in 2018.* Paper presented at the meeting of IDI CONFERENCE 2018, Florence, Italy.

Venkatesh, V., Morris, M. G., Davis, G. B., & Davis, F. D. (2003). User acceptance of information technology: Toward a unified view. *Management Information Systems Quarterly, 27*(3), 425–478. doi:10.2307/30036540

Vera, J., & Trujillo, A. (2017). Searching most influential variables to brand loyalty measurements: *An exploratory study.* *Contaduría y Administración, 62*(2), 600–624. doi:10.1016/j.cya.2016.04.007

Verhoeven, M. (2009). The 'Costanzo Obligation' of National Administrative Authorities in the Light of the Principle of Legality: Prodigy or Problem Child? *Croatian Yearbook of European Law and Policy, 5*(5), 65–92. doi:10.3935/cyelp.05.2009.81

Vermeulen, M. (2013, September 1). Regulating profiling in the European Data Protection Regulation: An interim insight into the drafting of Article 20. EMSOC Working Paper. *SSRN Electronic Journal.* Available from SSRN: https://ssrn.com/abstract=2382787

Vestager, M. (2016). Competition in a big data world. *DLD 16.* Retrieved September 23, 2019 https://ec.europa.eu/commission/2014-2019/vestager/announcements/competition-big-data-world_en

Vestager, M. (2018). *Fair markets in a digital world*. Retrieved September 26, 2019 https://ec.europa.eu/commission/commissioners/2014-2019/vestager/announcements/ fair-markets-digital-world_en

Vestager, M. (2016). Competition for a Fairer Societ. *10th Annual Global Antitrust Enforcement Symposium*.

Vestager, M. (2019). *Defending Competition in a Digitised World*. Bucharest: In the European Consumer and Competition Day.

Victor, J. M. (2013). The EU General Data Protection Regulation: Toward a Property Regime for Protecting Data Privacy. *The Yale Law Journal, 23*, 513–528. Available at: https://digitalcommons.law.yale.edu/ylj/vol123/iss2/5

Voigt, P. (Ed.). (2016). *Maximize business profits through e-partnerships*. Hershey, PA: IRM Press.

Voigt, P., & von dem Bussche, A. (2017). *The EU General Data Protection Regulation (GDPR): A practical guide*. Cham: Springer International Publishing. doi:10.1007/978-3-319-57959-7

Wachter, S., Mittelstadt, B., & Floridi, L. (2017). Why a Right to Explanation of Automated Decision-Making Does Not Exist in the General Data Protection Regulation. *International Data Privacy Law, 7*, 76-99. Retrieved December 15, 2019, from https://academic.oup.com/idpl/article/7/2/76/3860948

Wade, G. (2019). *Privacy and Protection of Personal Data*. Lexis Middle East.

Waldman, A. E. (2017). Designing Without Privacy. *Houston Law Review, 55*, 659.

Watkins Allen, M., Coopman, S. J., Hart, J. L., & Walker, K. L. (2007). Workplace surveillance and managing privacy boundaries. *Management Communication Quarterly, 21*(2), 172–200. doi:10.1177/0893318907306033

Wayman, J. L. (2007). The Scientific Development of Biometrics Over the Last 40 Years. In K. de Leuw & J. Bergstra (Eds.), *The History of Information Security: A Comprehensive Handbook* (pp. 263–274). Amsterdam, The Netherlands: Elsevier. doi:10.1016/B978-044451608-4/50011-0

Westin, A. F. (1967). *Privacy and freedom*. New York. *Atheneum, 7*, 431–453.

What the evidence shows about the impact of the GDPR after one year. (2019). Retrieved, from https://growrevenue.io/2019/gdpr-impact/

Wieseke, J., Geigenmüller, A., & Kraus, F. (2012). On the role of empathy in customer-employee interactions. *Journal of Service Research, 15*(3), 316–331. doi:10.1177/1094670512439743

Wiles, P. (2018). *Annual Report 2018*. Office of the Biometrics Commissioner.

Wirth, D. (2009). The International Organization for Standardization: Private Voluntary Standards as Swords and Shields. *Boston College Environmental Affairs Law Review. Boston College. Law School, 36*(1), 79.

Witte, B. (2011). Direct Effect, Primacy and the Nature of Legal Order. In *P. Craig & G. de Búrca (Eds.), The Evolution of EU Law* (pp. 323–362). Oxford, UK: Oxford University Press.

World Economic Forum (Ed.). (2011). *Personal data: The emergence of a new asset class*. Retrieved from: https://www.weforum.org/reports/personal-data-emergence-new-asset-class

World Economic Forum. (2011). *Personal Data: The Emergence of a New Asset Class*. Retrieved August 29, 2014 http://www3.weforum.org/docs/WEF_ITTC_PersonalDataNewAsset_Report_2011.pdf

Xu, Y., Goedegebuure, R., & Van der Heijden, B. (2007). Customer Perception, Customer Satisfaction, and Customer Loyalty Within Chinese Securities Business. *Journal of Relationship Marketing, 5*(4), 79–104. doi:10.1300/J366v05n04_06

Zanfir, G. (2013). *Tracing the Right to be Forgotten in the Short History of Data Protection Law: The 'New Clothes' of an Old Right*. Available at SSRN: https://ssrn.com/abstract=2501312

Zapatero Gómez, V. (2019). A Soft Law. In V. Zapatero Gómez (Ed.), *The Art of Legislating* (pp. 83–100). Springer International Publishing. doi:10.1007/978-3-030-23388-4_6

Zech, H. (2017). Data as a tradeable commodity – Implications for contract law. In *Proceedings of the 18th EIPIN Congress: The New Data Economy between Data Ownership, Privacy and Safeguarding Competition*. Edward Elgar Publishing. Available at SSRN: https://ssrn.com/abstract=3063153

Zuboff, S. (2019). *The age of surveillance capitalism: the fight for the future at the new frontier of power*. Profile Books.

About the Contributors

Maria Tzanou is a Senior Lecturer in Law at Keele University. She holds a PhD from the European University Institute (EUI), and LLM degrees from Cambridge University, the University of Athens and Bordeaux IV and the EUI. Her research focuses on European constitutional and human rights law, privacy, data protection, big data and the Internet of things, counter-terrorism surveillance and transatlantic data privacy cooperation. She has published her work in journals such as International Data Privacy Law, Human Rights Law Review, Common Market Law Review, Yearbook of European Law and German Law Journal. Her book The Fundamental Right to Data Protection: Normative Value in the Context of Counter-Terrorism Surveillance was published by Hart in 2017.

* * *

Eman Mahmood AlSarraf received her LLB from the Royal University for Women, Kingdom of Bahrain, in May 2019 with a research project on the protection of privacy in a comparative perspective. After graduation, she has been employed as a trainee Research Assistant at the College of Law of the Royal University for Women and she has just been hired as a Legal Coordinator at Zayani Investment in Bahrain.

Alessandra Calvi holds an LLM in International and European law with a specialisation in Data law awarded by the Vrije Universiteit Brussel-Institute of European Studies (VUB-IES). She is currently a researcher at the Law, Science, Technology and Society (LSTS) group and at the Brussels Laboratory for Data Protection & Privacy Impact Assessments (d.pia.lab) at VUB. Her research interests include the interrelationships between law and technology, in particular between data protection and the circular economy. Before joining academia, she worked as IT Policy Trainee at the European Data Protection Supervisor.

Graça Canto Moniz wrote her Ph.D thesis about the extraterritorial scope of data protection law. She is currently Assistant Professor at Lusófona University, Guest Lecture at Nova School of Law, and Chief Privacy Officer at FUTURA - Law & Tech. She is also co-coordinator of the Observatory for Data Protection, a research group at CEDIS/Nova School of Law.

Federica Casarosa is Part-time professor at the Centre for Judicial Cooperation, European University Institute. Her research interests focus on the intersection between private law and fundamental rights, in consumer protection, data protection and media law. She has developed a rich experience in training for legal professionals through her role as scientific coordinator in several Training projects leaded by the Centre for Judicial Cooperation. Federica holds a bachelor's degree in Private Law (University of Pisa, 2001), a PhD in Law (European University Institute, 2008).

Maria Casoria is General Counsel at Royal University for Women, Kingdom of Bahrain, where she also serves as an Assistant Professor of Commercial Law at the College of Law and faculty mentor for the university team participating in the Willem C. Vis International Commercial Arbitration Moot Court Competition. She holds a PhD in Markets Law and is a key staff member of the European Union Research Grant Jean Monnet Activities 2018-2020 led by the University of Siena - Department of Law, Italy, awarded for the project: 'Boosting European Security Law and Policy: Focus on Flows of Migrants, Data Security and Movement of Capitals'. Apart for the security of data, her research activity mainly focuses on competition dynamics in the digital environment and comparative company law.

Athena Christofi is a doctoral researcher at the KU Leuven Centre for IT & IP Law. Her research investigates privacy and data protection challenges in smart cities, in particular the roles and obligations of public authorities and private entities in ensuring protection of fundamental rights in the multi-actor smart city environment where a complex privacy-utility challenge is at stake. Previously, she worked as an academic assistant at the law faculty of the College of Europe and subsequently as legal consultant at a law and policy consulting firm in Brussels. She has an LLB from the University of Cyprus and a Master of European Law (LLM) from the College of Europe.

Pierre Dewitte (1993, Brussels) obtained his Bachelor and Master degree of Laws with a specialization in Corporate and Intellectual Property law from the Université Catholique de Louvain in 2016 (magna cum laude). As part of his Master program, he spent six month in the University of Helsinki where he strengthened his knowledge in European law. In 2017, he completed the advanced Master of Intellectual Property and ICT law at the KU Leuven with a special focus on privacy, data protection and electronic communications law (magna cum laude). Pierre joined the KU Leuven Centre for IT & IP in October 2017 where he conducts interdisciplinary research on privacy engineering, smart cities and algorithmic transparency. Among other initiatives, his main research track seeks to bridge the gap between software engineering practices and data protection regulations by creating a common conceptual framework for both disciplines and providing decision and trade-off support for technical and organizational mitigation strategies in the software development life-cycle.

Charlotte Ducuing is a PhD fellow researcher at the Centre for IT and IP law (CITIP) of KU Leuven. Before joining CiTiP, she worked as in-house lawyer in the Belgian Railways for 6 years (Thalys International and Infrabel) and as teaching assistant at the University of ULB (Belgium) for four years. She holds a Master's degree in law from the University of Lille (France) with specialization in European law, a Master's degree in political sciences from the University Lille (Institut d'Etudes Politiques de Lille) and a LLM Intellectual Property and ICT Law from KU Leuven (2018). Within CiTiP, she conducts her doctoral research on the economic regulation and governance of data, particularly in transport and network industries. She is currently involved in research projects dealing with digitisation of transport (the use of blockchain and machine learning techniques in the railways with IN2DREAMS, connected and automated driving with CONCORDA) as well as the commodification of data with data marketplaces (with TRUSTS). Her research interests mainly extend to the regulation of data, data markets and data exchange, cybersecurity regulation and technical norms as a means to regulate (inter alia with the legal use of standardization and certification).

Arletta Gorecka is currently a PhD candidate at the University of Strathclyde. Arletta's current research explores the competition law and digital economy. Her thesis looks into competition law and privacy.

Yordanka Ivanova is a joint PhD candidate in the Law Faculty of Sofia University "St. Kliment Ohridski" (Bulgaria) and Vrije Universiteit Brussels (Belgium). The topic of her phd thesis is on the new EU legal framework for data protection (GDPR) and its interaction with Big Data and Artificial Intelligence. In addition to the research work, she is currently an acting attorney-at-law in Bulgaria, working in the field of EU regulations, in particular data protection and other fundamental rights, digital single market, e-commerce, intellectual property and financial services, money laundering etc. She has worked for four years as a policy officer in the European Commission (DG ECHO) and has done an LLM in EU Law in Leiden University (the Netherlands).

Dimosthenis Lentzis, PhD, is an Assistant Professor at the Aristotle University of Thessaloniki School of Law. In the past, he worked for the Greek Ministry of Justice (2002-2005) and as an administrator at the Directorate General "Library, Research and Documentation" of the Court of Justice of the European Union in Luxembourg (2005-2012). His research interests include a) the institutional law of the European Union, b) certain areas of the substantive law of the European Union (free movement of persons, goods and services, asylum and immigration policies, air transport regulation), as well as c) the protection of fundamental human rights under the European Convention on Human Rights and the European Social Charter.

Ana Neves is an assistant professor at University of Lisbon, School of Law. She holds a PhD from the Lisbon University, and an LLM degree from the University of Coimbra. Her research focus on European Administrative Law, Human Rights Law, Employment and Penitentiary Law. She is also a researcher at the Lisbon Centre for Research in Public Law and Member of the Institute of Legal-Political Sciences of School of law Lisbon University

Jo Pierson, Ph.D., is Full Professor in the Department of Media and Communication Studies at the Vrije Universiteit Brussel (VUB) in Belgium (Faculty of Social Sciences & Solvay Business School) and Principal Investigator at the research centre SMIT (Studies on Media, Innovation and Technology). In this position, he is in charge of the research unit 'Data, Privacy & Empowerment', in close cooperation with imec (R&D and innovation hub in nanoelectronics and digital technology).

Tomáš Pikulík is a Ph.D. student and "guest lectures on topics – "GDPR, Direct Marketing" in the Marketing Departments at the Faculty of Management at the University of Comenius in Bratislava. His research interests focus on the data privacy and GDPR, with specific emphasis on the interrelationships between GDPR-compliant methods of data protection, and processing of data with empirical experiences with processing data of subject for various consumer competitions, loyalty programs. He currently works in the biggest direct marketing agency in Slovakia - Direct Marketing, a.s.

Dianora Poletti is Full Professor at the University of Pisa. She is the director of the Interdepartmental Centre "Law and Frontier Technologies" (DETECT), belonging to the Department of Law of the University of Pisa. She is also the director of the II level Master's Degree Course at the University of Pisa in "Internet Ecosystem: Governance and Rights" (carried out in partnership with the Institute for Informatics and Telematics of the CNR and under the patronage of the Agency for Digital Italy, "AgID"). In addition, Professor Poletti has made several contributions on the subject of civil liability applied to new technologies, as well as issues relating to the protection of personal data.

Sarah Progin-Theuerkauf is Professor for EU Law and Migration Law at the University of Fribourg (since 2009).

Konstantina V. Samara holds the interdisciplinary MSc in "Law and Informatics" of University of Macedonia (Department of Applied Informatics) in partnership with Democritus University of Thrace (Department of Law). Her scientific interests focus on the convergence of new technologies and civil or penal law dogma. She has also been a lawyer since 2005.

Peter Štarchoň is a Professor and a Head of Department of Marketing at Faculty of Management at University of Comenius in Bratislava. As a marketing lecturer has acquired both theoretical knowledge and practical experience in special fields of marketing study such as marketing communication, international marketing, bank marketing, advertising or direct marketing. He presents new marketing trends in a various research projects with special emphasis on brands. In 2006 he established international scientific journal Marketing Science and Inspirations where he still works as editor-in-chief. In addition, he is a member of editorial board of scientific magazines Holistic Marketing Management and Auspicia, an author or co-author of several monographs and textbooks on marketing, direct marketing, marketing communications, and branding and more than seven dozen scientific works, studies and conference contributions.

Ozan Turhan is Assistant Professor for Public Law at MEF University, Istanbul.

Peggy Valcke is research professor law & technology at KU Leuven, member of the management board of the Leuven Centre for IT & IP Law (CiTiP), and principal investigator in the Security & Privacy Department of imec (previously iMinds). She has taken up positions as visiting and part-time professor at Tilburg University; Bocconi University Milan; the European University Institute in Florence; and Central European University in Budapest. Prof. Valcke has a broad experience with international and interdisciplinary research dealing with legal aspects of IT and media innovation. At KU Leuven, she teaches courses on ICT law, electronic communications law, media law, technology and law, and interdisciplinary study of law. She is also the academic coordinator of IusStart, KU Leuven's Law Incubator linking law students with tech start-ups and law firms.

Ine van Zeeland is a PhD researcher within the research chair on Data Protection On The Ground at the Vrije Universiteit Brussel (VUB). She has been working as a privacy researcher at the VUB research center SMIT (Studies on Media, Innovation and Technology) since 2017. Her PhD research is focuses on organizational practices of personal data protection, specifically for the media sector, the health sector, the financial sector, and smart cities.

Margarite Zoeteweij is a lawyer at the Swiss Refugee Council (OSAR), guest lecturer at the Chair for EU Law and Migration Law at the University of Fribourg (2020).

Index

A

Academic discipline 242

Accountability 61-62, 68-75, 79, 82, 87, 92, 98-99, 125, 141, 144-145, 156, 234, 245, 257

Advocate General 25, 119, 287, 316, 318, 326, 331

Anonymity 118, 241-242, 323-325

Article 5 GDPR 85, 87-88, 91, 99-100, 144, 171

asylum 170, 172, 175-179, 184, 186, 203, 208-210, 215, 293

Attribution of Responsibilities 76, 78-79

Automated Processing 21, 31, 87, 183, 231

B

Big Data 5, 41, 94, 114, 116-117, 119, 124, 149

Biometric Data 173, 181, 186, 202-215, 217-218, 221-222, 227, 231

Border Management 179, 202-204, 208-211, 214, 217-218

C

Competitive Process 107, 109, 112-113, 119-120, 124

consistent interpretation 74, 128, 145

Consumer Welfare 106-108, 115-120, 124

Contextual integrity 241

Court of Justice 19-20, 32, 62, 112, 127, 153, 279, 301-302, 305, 316, 320, 325, 331

Customer satisfaction 256-257, 265-266

D

Data Controller 20, 24-27, 31, 34, 46, 61, 63-64, 71, 82, 108, 112, 129-130, 132-133, 135-136, 138, 208, 215, 231, 292, 304, 318

Data Mining 95

Data privacy 29, 117, 230, 235, 247, 257, 259-260, 268-269, 271, 279, 282, 286, 288-289, 291-292, 295-296

Data Processing 6-7, 24-25, 27, 29, 51-52, 54-55, 61-67, 69-72, 74-76, 78-79, 82, 112, 117, 135, 141-143, 145-146, 148, 151, 153-154, 158-159, 177, 213, 215, 218, 230-232, 256, 259-260, 268, 271, 284, 286, 305-306, 308, 316-317

Data Processor 20-21, 24-27, 31, 61, 67, 73, 82, 130, 133, 138, 215, 231

Data Protection 2-8, 20-29, 36, 44-45, 47-49, 51, 53-55, 61-64, 68-72, 74-79, 85-88, 91, 96, 98-99, 106-110, 112-114, 116-120, 125-127, 131-132, 135-136, 139-146, 149-151, 153, 155-160, 169-172, 174, 177, 179, 181, 183-185, 187-188, 202-209, 211-215, 217-218, 221-222, 224-235, 239-247, 249-253, 256-257, 260, 268, 271-272, 279-282, 284, 286-296, 302-306, 315-320, 322-328

Data Protection By Design 156, 208, 213, 215

Data Protection Impact Assessment (DPIA) 141, 208, 217, 221

Data protection law 4, 19, 48, 54, 63, 67, 76, 107-109, 112, 114, 116-117, 119-120, 143, 146, 156, 217-218, 224, 227, 229-232, 234-235, 279, 288-289, 291-292, 295-296, 324

data retention 127, 136

Data Subject 4-6, 26-28, 31, 34-35, 43-46, 48, 50-53, 65, 71, 76-77, 82, 89, 108, 130, 134, 136, 138, 150, 154, 171, 174, 185, 206-207, 213, 232, 256-258, 268-269, 271, 279-282, 284, 286, 289-294, 304-306, 317, 319-321, 326

databases 85, 95, 109, 124, 169-170, 172, 176, 180-181, 186-187, 208, 210-211, 214-215, 243, 245-246, 258, 305

Data-driven marketing 256, 258

De Facto Personal Data Marketplaces 35, 40-41, 43, 58

Decisional privacy 241

Digital Economy 2, 19, 41, 50, 116-120, 124, 224, 232, 241, 256, 260-264, 268

Digital Market 117-120, 124

Directive 2-3, 5-6, 19-29, 40-41, 44, 46-48, 51-53, 61-62, 75, 86, 108, 136, 139, 144, 146, 151, 171, 175, 177, 203-204, 210, 268, 271, 280-283, 286-

R

S

T

V

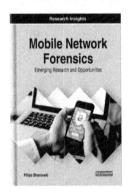

Ensure Quality Research is Introduced to the Academic Community

Become an IGI Global Reviewer for Authored Book Projects

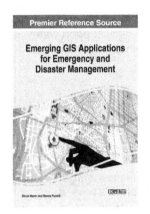

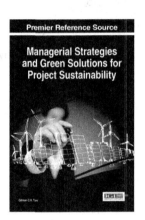

The overall success of an authored book project is dependent on quality and timely reviews.

In this competitive age of scholarly publishing, constructive and timely feedback significantly expedites the turnaround time of manuscripts from submission to acceptance, allowing the publication and discovery of forward-thinking research at a much more expeditious rate. Several IGI Global authored book projects are currently seeking highly-qualified experts in the field to fill vacancies on their respective editorial review boards:

Applications and Inquiries may be sent to:
development@igi-global.com

Applicants must have a doctorate (or an equivalent degree) as well as publishing and reviewing experience. Reviewers are asked to complete the open-ended evaluation questions with as much detail as possible in a timely, collegial, and constructive manner. All reviewers' tenures run for one-year terms on the editorial review boards and are expected to complete at least three reviews per term. Upon successful completion of this term, reviewers can be considered for an additional term.

If you have a colleague that may be interested in this opportunity, we encourage you to share this information with them.

IGI Global Proudly Partners With eContent Pro International

Receive a 25% Discount on all Editorial Services

Editorial Services

IGI Global expects all final manuscripts submitted for publication to be in their final form. This means they must be reviewed, revised, and professionally copy edited prior to their final submission. Not only does this support with accelerating the publication process, but it also ensures that the highest quality scholarly work can be disseminated.

English Language Copy Editing

Let eContent Pro International's expert copy editors perform edits on your manuscript to resolve spelling, punctuaion, grammar, syntax, flow, formatting issues and more.

Scientific and Scholarly Editing

Allow colleagues in your research area to examine the content of your manuscript and provide you with valuable feedback and suggestions before submission.

Figure, Table, Chart & Equation Conversions

Do you have poor quality figures? Do you need visual elements in your manuscript created or converted? A design expert can help!

Translation

Need your documjent translated into English? eContent Pro International's expert translators are fluent in English and more than 40 different languages.

Hear What Your Colleagues are Saying About Editorial Services Supported by IGI Global

"The service was very fast, very thorough, and very helpful in ensuring our chapter meets the criteria and requirements of the book's editors. I was quite impressed and happy with your service."

– Prof. Tom Brinthaupt,
Middle Tennessee State University, USA

"I found the work actually spectacular. The editing, formatting, and other checks were very thorough. The turnaround time was great as well. I will definitely use eContent Pro in the future."

– Nickanor Amwata, Lecturer,
University of Kurdistan Hawler, Iraq

"I was impressed that it was done timely, and wherever the content was not clear for the reader, the paper was improved with better readability for the audience."

– Prof. James Chilembwe,
Mzuzu University, Malawi

Email: customerservice@econtentpro.com   **www.igi-global.com/editorial-service-partners**

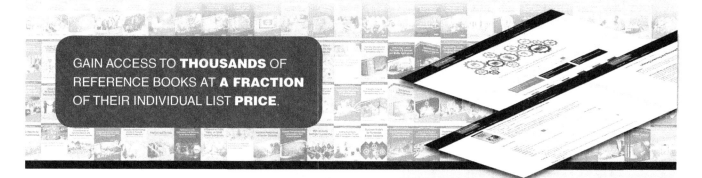

Printed in the United States
By Bookmasters